MONARCH NOTES

QUICK COURSE

William Shakespeare

EIGHT PLAYS

Macmillan General Reference
A Prentice Hall Macmillan Company
15 Columbus Circle
New York, NY 10023

An Arco Book

ISBN: 0-02-860015-0
Manufactured in the United States of America

10 9 8 7 6 5 4 3 2 1

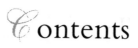ontents

Contributing Authors

ANTONY AND CLEOPATRA
William Walsh
Department of English
State University of New York

HAMLET
Leonora Broadwin
Associate Professor of English
St. John's University

JULIUS CAESAR
Robert Littman
Columbia University
and
Frances Barasch
Assistant Professor of English
State University of New York

KING LEAR
Robert Schuettinger
Earhart Fellow
Oxford University

MACBETH
David Shelley Berkeley
Professor of English
Oklahoma State University

THE MERCHANT OF VENICE
Laura Lippman
Department of English
Harvard University

OTHELLO
William J. Grace
Professor of English
Fordham University

ROMEO AND JULIET
Leonard Jenkin
Department of English
Columbia University

ᴀ ntony and ᴄ leopatra

Scene-by-Scene Summary and Comment

Act I: Scene i

The play opens upon the following political situation: Rome has extended its empire over most of the known world, from the British Isles to Parthia and Mesopotamia in the east, and from the African shore of the Mediterranean to Germany in the north. Much of its eastern empire has been conquered by Mark Antony who, together with Octavius Caesar and Lepidus, makes up the Triumvirate or ruling body of the empire. Octavius Caesar rules over Rome and the northern provinces, Lepidus over Africa, and Mark Antony over the east. Supposedly to govern his conquered territories, Antony has set up headquarters and remained in Egypt. Actually he has fallen in love with Cleopatra, queen of Egypt, which is one of his conquered kingdoms. Their love is the story of the play. It begins in Cleopatra's palace in Alexandria, the Egyptian capital. Two of Antony's lieutenants, Demetrius and Philo, are complaining in one of the rooms of the palace.

COMMENT: Since the theatres in Shakespeare's day did not use elaborate scenery but a rather bare stage for their productions, the descriptions of locale or scene are usually very general. While this meant that the author had to depend a great deal on the audience's imagination, it also enabled him to change scenes rapidly with a mere stroke of the pen. We shall see throughout the play how Shakespeare takes advantage of this freedom.

Philo condemn's Antony's infatuation with Cleopatra outright. Their general, he tells Demetrius, has lost his manliness and given over his pursuit of war and conquest to pursue his lust instead. He "is become the bellows and the fan/ To cool a gipsy's lust."

COMMENT: This opening speech sets up the central conflict of the play. But it presents only one side or view of the question that will be resolved. The whole play revolves around the question of whether or not Antony is justified in loving Cleopatra and abandoning all else for her. Philo here presents the Roman point of view, that he is not. According to him, Antony merely dotes on Cleopatra. He conceives of her as "tawny" or dark in color, and so not a fit match for

Antony, especially since she is a "gipsy," a person of little worth. And this "dotage" has caused Antony to neglect his duties to Rome and to become weak and effeminate in allowing himself to be dominated by the wily and capricious Cleopatra, especially since he has previously been famous for his bravery and military prowess. The Roman "ethic," that is, the code of conduct favored by Rome, is a martial one, emphasizing the virtues of manliness, discipline, and self-reliance.

Almost as if to give proof of Philo's speech, Antony, Cleopatra, and her servants enter, in a procession marked by oriental luxury and splendor. Philo, in an aside, promises Demetrius he shall see Antony, "the triple pillar of the world" (i.e., one of the three rulers of the world), become the plaything of a whore. And, indeed, Antony at once begins to exchange extravagant vows of love with Cleopatra. "There's beggary in the love that can be reckoned," cries Antony, expressing not only his love for Cleopatra but his contempt for the sound commercial account-keeping that has made Rome a great power. He is obviously annoyed when an attendant interrupts to announce a messenger from Rome. Antony refuses to see him. The business "grates" him, he says, and he demands "the sum" of it, quickly, so that he can turn back to Cleopatra. She, however, now begins to taunt him for being under the thumbs of Fulvia, his wife, and the boyish Caesar. (Octavius Caesar is in his early twenties. His youth, as compared to the other Triumvirs, is alluded to throughout. Despite his age, he is the leader of the Triumvirate.) Antony's reply is a ringing speech in which he renounces Rome's claims upon him, and determines to stay in Egypt with Cleopatra.

COMMENT: The Egyptian view is emerging, a direct contrast to the Roman one. The Egyptians love extravagant display, luxury, and pleasure, which the Romans scorn; and they in turn scorn the coldness, prudence, and calculating self-interest of Rome. Antony is a man in the middle, accused by Philo of being Cleopatra's fool, and by Cleopatra of being Fulvia's and Caesar's. He does indeed love Cleopatra; whether, as Philo complains, this love has made him womanish and a traitor to himself, remains to be seen. "The nobleness of life is to do thus," Antony exclaims, and the conflict of ideas is clear: Is it nobler to love passionately and magnificently, sacrificing in the process the worldly greatness which would otherwise be his due; or, by the exercise of reason and self-control, to sacrifice that love on the altar of fame and military glory? Antony, at this point, is of a mind to follow the former course: "Let Rome in Tiber melt . . . We stand up peerless." In other words, for all he cares, Rome may be washed away for a love like theirs justifies itself, and they cannot be blamed for renouncing everything for it.

Cleopatra, however, ignores Antony's grand rhetoric and continues to tease him. She wonders why Antony married Fulvia, since he does not love her, and whether, perhaps, the same fate will someday be hers. She urges him to see the messengers, although of course it is to her interest for Antony not to be in contact with Rome. Antony, who feels that he merits her praise for refusing to see them, talks only of love and pleasure; when Cleopatra interrupts with "Hear the ambassadors," he chides her for being so difficult: "Fie, wrangling queen." He is determined to fill every minute of their lives with pleasure, "for the love of Love"; there is no time to waste. They exit without hearing Caesar's messenger, and Demetrius, realizing that this is a grave insult, tells Philo that he is convinced that the rumors which have reached Rome of Antony's debasement are true.

SUMMARY: The opening scene has set the general mood of the play in the following ways:

1. It has introduced the lovers, Antony and Cleopatra.

2. It has given us a glimpse of their love and of the conflict surrounding it.

3. It has shown us the "Roman view" of this love, which condemns it, and the "Egyptian view," which praises it.

4. It has presented Antony's dilemma: Whether to choose Rome and Caesar's friendship or to reject both for Cleopatra and her Egyptian way of life.

Act I: Scene ii

In another room of the palace an Egyptian soothsayer (a kind of fortune teller) is revealing what life holds in store for Cleopatra's various attendants: Alexas, her male servant; Mardian, her eunuch; Charmian and Iras, her maids. Silently looking on and listening to the revelry and lewd joking are a group of Roman soldiers: Enobarbus, Antony's trusted lieutenant and close friend; Lamprius, Rannius, and Lucillius. Occasionally Enobarbus adds his rude voice to the coarse exchange.

But for the most part their silence represents a sober Roman reprimand to the loose conversation.

COMMENT: Some critics have taken Lamprius to be the soothsayer. But this does not seem probable because the name is too Roman-sounding for the obviously Egyptian character, and because this same soothsayer appears later with Antony in Rome and there is *not* called Lamprius (Act 2, Scene 3).

Alexas seems to have been teasing Charmian by predicting for her a husband whom she will cuckold. Charmian hopes he is right: "O that I knew this husband, which, you say, must charge his horns with garlands!" (A cuckold is a man whose wife has committed adultery. As a sign of her infidelity he is jokingly said to grow horns.) She asks the soothsayer to confirm the good fortune Alexas has promised. He replies that he cannot change her fate, only foresee it. She hopes for several husbands and many children; what he tells her, however, is that she will outlive Cleopatra, and that the part of her life which is to come will be less pleasant than that which she has already lived.

COMMENT: The atmosphere of the scene is curiously mixed or contradictory, like a summer sun-shower. Although the general tone is light and comic, the pronouncements of the soothsayer foreshadow the tragic events to come. His predictions deal with the deaths of Cleopatra and Charmian in language full of dramatic irony. The statement that Charmian will outlive Cleopatra sounds innocent enough at this point; it is only after we have witnessed the play in its entirety that we realize how sinister it is. Charmian will indeed outlive her mistress, but only by a minute or two. And she will not have the long life she loves better than figs. But the asp by whose bite she dies will be hidden in a basket of figs. It is not clear whether the soothsayer knows exactly what the outcome will be, but his statement that he is powerless to avert it, whatever it is, is significant.

Much sexual joking follows. The women wish for many children; because of the pleasure of begetting them, the soothsayer implies. Enobarbus knows what their fortunes will be at least that night: "drunk to bed." Iras, turning to palmistry, claims that hers is a palm which shows that she is nothing if not chaste; Charmian retorts ironically that if she is chaste, then the overflowing of the Nile is a portent of famine, when in fact it is just the opposite. The soothsayer claims simply that the fortunes of Iras and Charmian are alike, and refuses to give particulars. Charmian begs for news of a husband who is sexually well-endowed and, in mock-spite, wishes for Alexas a wife who is not, followed by one who will cuckold him. She begs the goddess Isis to grant her this wish, even if she denies her something more important later on.

COMMENT: Isis was an Egyptian goddess, patroness of fertility and of the sexual act which causes it. "A woman that cannot go" is a frigid woman who cannot perform the sexual act. This casual mention becomes very important to the imagery later on when Cleopatra dresses herself as an incarnation of Isis (Act 4, Scene 7). Isis was also associated with the changing moon, and this ties in with the moon imagery and the notion of fickleness, the waxing and waning of fortune, behind it. This scene is also rich in allusion and irony. The Egyptian court is seen as gay and fun-loving, in contrast to the unsmiling seriousness of the Roman soldiers uncomfortably watching it. The constant references to fertility and fruitfulness serve to identify the Egyptians with these qualities, which, like the sexual nature of man in this play, are both life-giving and destructive. It is significant that Enobarbus, who is a Roman, takes part in all this: he is not the prude that Philo is, but his good-humored cynicism about the validity of the soothsayer's prognostications will prove to be a mistake.

Enobarbus says, "Hush, here comes Antony," but it is Cleopatra who enters.

COMMENT: Enobarbus obviously does not want Antony to hear the jokes about cuckoldry, since he is being unfaithful to Fulvia with Cleopatra. The fact that it is Cleopatra who enters instead is explained later by the queen herself. The purpose of the surprise is to show us how swiftly changing is Antony's mood. One moment he is all gaiety, walking with his mistress; the next, he goes morosely off by himself.

Cleopatra asks for Antony; when last seen, she says, "He was disposed to mirth; but on the sudden/ A Roman thought hath struck him" (that is, either a thought of Rome, which sobered him, or a thought such as a Roman might have, implying that Romans are sour and incapable of mirth). Antony enters with a messenger from Rome, possibly the one he would not hear before. The messenger is afraid to tell Antony some bad news, and Antony magnanimously assures him that he, the messenger, will not be blamed for it.

COMMENT: This is in marked contrast to Cleopatra's treatment of the messenger who brings her news of Antony's marriage (Act 2, Scene 5), and shows the cooler judgment and sense of justice of the Roman.

Actually the messenger brings a military dispatch from the eastern frontier where Labienus and his Parthian armies have invaded Antony's territory. Antony

thinks he is withholding his real message out of deference and fear. He thinks it is that his reputation in Rome is suffering, and that Fulvia is angry. Before he can learn the truth, another messenger enters with news from Sicyon; Antony, caught up in this whirl of portentous activity and excited by all the comings and goings, muses: "These strong Egyptian fetters I must break/ Or lose myself in dotage." A third messenger enters and announces, without preamble, that Fulvia, Antony's wife, is dead.

COMMENT: It is to be noted that Antony, although he previously disavowed Rome and his responsibilities in favor of love, has now reversed his position completely. He now agrees, in effect, with Philo, that he is a prisoner of Cleopatra's charms, and he even uses the same word which Philo employed, "dotage," to characterize himself. It is in this excited and self-critical mood that he receives the news that Fulvia is dead from messengers whom he is now vitally interested in hearing.

Antony takes the news stoically and chides himself for desiring Fulvia's death, as he obviously did, because it would leave him free to marry or live with Cleopatra. The effect of the news is to strengthen his resolve to break off from Cleopatra, and resume his rightful place as leader of the world; his idleness, he thinks, is responsible for this and many other ills. All business, he summons Enobarbus and bids him make ready to leave without telling him why; Enobarbus retorts in a jocular tone, and makes what, under the circumstances, is an unfortunate joke about Cleopatra dying of grief if Antony leaves. He begins a mocking description of Cleopatra: "Alack . . . her passions are made of nothing but the finest part of pure love," but Antony cuts him short with the news that Fulvia is dead. Stunned at first, Enobarbus recovers and tells Antony that this is cause for rejoicing; now Antony can have Cleopatra. Antony, however, is resolved to leave, and sternly admonishes Enobarbus to stop joking. He will break with Cleopatra and return to Rome, despite Enobarbus' warning that Cleopatra will never survive it. Another reason for returning, Antony explains, is that Sextus Pompeius (usually referred to in the play as Pompey) is threatening to fight a sea-war against Rome; the Roman people are wavering in their allegiance to the Triumvirate, partly because of his, Antony's, refusal to meet his responsibilities.

COMMENT: Sextus Pompey was the son of Gnaeus Pompey, called Pompey the Great, who with Julius Caesar (adopted father of Octavius Caesar of this play) and Marcus Crassus formed the first Triumvirate. The earlier Pompey and Caesar fell out and made war on each other, and Caesar defeated his rival in the Battle of Pharsalia in 48 B. C. But the son inherited his father's hatred and resentment against Julius Caesar, and his claim to be ruler of the Empire. When Julius Caesar was assassinated, Sextus Pompey took out his grudge against Julius Caesar's heirs, especially his son Octavius.

If he does not act, says Antony, the situation may become dangerous, and he compares it in seriousness to the venom of a serpent.

COMMENT: Antony receives the news of his wife's death in a truly Roman fashion: unemotional, controlled, in full possession of his feelings. His generous nature is apparent when he praises her as "a great spirit," and the fact that he is an essentially good and moral man is shown by his self-accusation and feelings of guilt, and his wish that he might restore her to life. This is a grave moment, as Antony's Roman feelings assert themselves to dictate that he should make an act of atonement for his past sins. Egypt is beginning to appear to him as essentially the frivolous and wanton place that Philo claimed it to be. Enobarbus plays on the various senses of the word *dying*, which refers not only to Cleopatra's pretended loss of life but also to the weakness and lassitude which follows sexual intercourse, and, by extension, to the act of intercourse itself. Thus, when he says that Cleopatra "hath such a celerity in dying," he means both that she will make believe that the news of Antony's leaving will kill her, and also that she is a loose woman, quick to indulge in sex and quick to reach a sexual climax. The lines about "a serpent's poison" constitute the first of many references to snakes and venom, all leading up to Cleopatra's death by the bite of an asp (a poisonous snake). Another image which will be repeated is contained in Antony's use of the phrase "enchanting queen" to refer to Cleopatra. There will be more references to Cleopatra's power to enchant and bewitch; her powers are part of her connection with Egypt, a land of magic and prophecy (remember the soothsayer), in contrast to the rationalism of the Romans.

SUMMARY: This scene does the following:
1. Through its imagery, mainly sexual, it dramatizes the fertility and sexuality with which Egypt and Cleopatra are identified, and which are presided over by Isis, the moon goddess.
2. It shows us a new side of Antony's character: In addition to his weakness for pleasure, he is a moral man, and he is unable to renounce Rome as easily as he previously wished.
3. It identifies Egypt with the forces of mysticism and magic, in contrast to the Roman faith in reason and free will. It is suggested, by Antony himself, that he is literally under Cleopatra's spell.

4. It complicates the Roman and Egyptian views with which we started, suggesting that they are both inadequate, and that Antony must decide the problem on his own terms.

Act I: Scene iii

The place is the same, a room in Cleopatra's palace. We break in on a tactical discussion between Cleopatra and Charmian, who suspect that Antony is about to leave, but who do not know of Fulvia's death. Cleopatra reveals her feminine tricks and wiles; she sends Charmian to Antony with these instructions: "If you find him sad,/ Say that I am dancing; if in mirth, report/ That I am sudden sick." Charmian counsels her to give in to him, but Cleopatra's strategy is to battle him. Antony enters, and Cleopatra rails at him, simultaneously feigning illness. She postures heroically: "O, never was there a queen/ so mightily betrayed!" She is alternately eloquent—"Eternity was in our lips, and eyes,/ Bliss in our brows' bent," and waspish—"I would I had thy inches," (i.e., his great strength and size, so that she might beat him). Antony vows to go, giving Cleopatra all the reasons except the most important; he speaks of Pompey's rebellion and the civil unrest in Rome. Finally he tells her of Fulvia's death. This provokes from Cleopatra a perverse and unlooked-for reaction: Because Antony is not weeping for his wife, she calls him false, exclaiming, "Now I see, I see,/ In Fulvia's death, how mine received shall be." She then affects illness once more, but continues to rise from her fainting-spells to berate Antony energetically. She accuses him of lying pretense; of using Fulvia's death as a pretext to desert her; and of trying to make his action thus seem honorable. Antony grows angry, and begins to swear, "Now, by my sword—" but Cleopatra interrupts the oath to chide him further, scornfully calling him "this Herculean Roman."

COMMENT: This is the first, albeit ironical, reference to Antony's patron hero, Hercules, from whom he claimed to be descended. Hercules was a legendary hero or demigod of fabulous size and strength. His life, like Antony's, was checkered with good and bad, triumphing in his very faults and excesses. But above all he was larger than life, of gigantic proportions, and it is this quality which the play endows Antony with.

"O, my oblivion is a very Antony," she sighs, and then, sarcastically, bids him a conventional Roman farewell, to which he, missing the irony, replies in kind.

COMMENT: The tone of this scene is odd; the issues being argued are very serious, but because Cleopatra's language is witty, and because her posturings border on the absurd, the effect is half-comical. Cleopatra demonstrates here the full range of her emotions and powers of expression; she is by turns witty, serious, shrewish, noble, and wounded. It is this complexity in her character which has led to the disagreement on what kind of woman she really is. Our best course for the moment is to say that she is a woman capable of reconciling all of these disparate qualities; a creature of lightning shifts and a dozen moods. First she illustrates the essential woman in her, coolly mapping her campaign to get the better of Antony. But no sooner has she decided to pretend that she is sick, than she gives in to the temptation to snap at him: "What, says the married woman you may go?" she snarls, blaming him for not making an honest woman of her as he did of Fulvia. Next comes the heroic rhetoric; she is the conventional woman scorned, the innocent, betrayed damsel. But this in turn gives way to what many feel to be her genuinely felt love for Antony, expressed in language of surpassing beauty in the speech beginning "Nay, pray you, seek no colour for your going . . ." Here, she has at last attained a truly regal dignity.

Antony replies with all his reasons; the main one, Fulvia's death, comes last, for he fears her reaction to this news. He has reason to; she becomes acid again, and sides with Fulvia against him. He cannot win; had he wept at Fulvia's death, Cleopatra would doubtless have become furious. There is an unconscious irony in her lines about his reception of *her* death. In fact, later in the play, Cleopatra's death is reported to Antony, and far from treating it with indifference, he kills himself. But he is not indifferent to Fulvia's death either, as Cleopatra claims; he is merely trying to resolve a touchy situation with a woman who can always out-talk him and who has a positive genius for putting him in the wrong. "Cut my lace," she cries, when he lamely resorts to conventional rhetoric himself; she mockingly pretends to be sick and then instantly well, when he haltingly informs her that he loves her, by asking Charmian, in effect, to loosen her stays so that she can breathe as the fit comes over her. Constantly, she throws up to him the fact that the very protestations of love he makes to her are those that he once made to Fulvia. This scene contains the first of many references to Antony's sword, which is symbolic of his military accomplishments and also of his manhood; and it is significant that Cleopatra will not allow him to finish swearing by it, forcing him to leave the word sword ineffectually suspended in mid-air, until she lets it down with, "Upon your sword Sit laurel victory. . ." Also, for the first time in the play, Cleopatra uses Antony himself as a metaphor for sheer size, though she does it ironically: "O, my oblivion is a very Antony . . ." We shall encounter this image again.

SUMMARY: This scene:

1. Demonstrates the full range of Cleopatra's personality.

2. Shows dramatically how she casts her spells over Antony.

3. Establishes three new patterns of imagery: "the sword," "the world," and "the Herculean hero."

Act I: Scene iv

Now the scene shifts abruptly from Cleopatra's court in Alexandria to the house of Caesar in Rome (where Antony is going): the first of many such far-ranging movements in the action of the play. Caesar has received a letter from the attendant to whom Antony refused to listen in Scene 1. The agent writes that he was unable to deliver the message which Caesar had sent from Rome, and that Antony had shown no concern for his two partners in the Triumvirate. Besides this insult, the agent reports, Antony's idleness and luxury and his constant round of pleasures have taken away his manliness and made him as womanly as Cleopatra. Caesar quotes the letter as evidence to convince Lepidus that their partner in the east has grown soft and rotten. But Lepidus will not be convinced by Caesar's bad opinion. He thinks too highly of Antony to blame him. He says these faults are really only minor compared to his virtues; they are weaknesses which Antony has inherited, not evil habits that he actually chooses.

COMMENT: This speech by Lepidus does much to characterize him and Antony. It shows us that he wants to remain non-committal toward his partners so as to stay in their good graces. And by saying that Antony is not really responsible for his behavior, he is preparing us to accept Antony's downfall as the result equally of an evil destiny and a guilty will. (In this respect compare Caesar's speech at the end of this scene.)

Caesar will not be put off. Even if Antony's wantonness and carousals are not terrible in themselves, he argues, he has chosen a terrible time to indulge in them. It would be a small matter if Antony were only ruining himself by running around with Cleopatra, but the whole empire is at stake, and he knows it. He is putting his own sensual satisfactions before the welfare of the whole state.

COMMENT: The danger to which Caesar refers is the rebellion of Pompey; that is why Shakespeare chooses this moment to have the messenger bring news of the conspiracy.

Their conversation is here interrupted by a messenger, a kind of scout that Caesar has sent out to gather news. The information which he brings to the two Triumvirs picks up the subplot of Pompey's growing naval strength. Earlier, Antony had used Pompey's threat as an excuse to leave Cleopatra and return to Rome. We learn that Antony was correct when he estimated the loyalty of the common people. For, the messenger relates, those who never loved Caesar but merely followed him out of fear, are flocking to the seaports to join arms with Pompey when his ships attack. Caesar comments that the loyalty of the crowd is a fickle and a contrary one. They wish for something only until they have it; they do not value a great man until they've lost him.

COMMENT: Compare Antony's similar sentiment in Scene 2: "Our slippery people,/ Whose love is never link'd to the deserver/ Till his deserts are past . . ." Though at odds from the beginning, and enemies in deadly earnest at the last, these two men, Antony and Octavius, share the great man's contempt for the common masses and for the fickleness of fate. The waxing and waning of man's fortunate is a central theme in this play and in tragedy generally.

The messenger also brings information that Pompey has joined forces with two famous pirates of the Italian coasts, Menecrates and Menas. These two, trafficking in Pompey's name and fearful reputation, have been raiding the maritime provinces of Italy and plundering the coastal trade. This is too much for Caesar. Overcome with distress, he calls aloud on Antony to leave the base pleasure of the Egyptian court and come to Rome's aid. In doing this he tells how, in the old days, Antony was the strongest, manliest soldier of them all.

COMMENT: This description of Antony's withdrawal from Modena follows Plutarch's account pretty closely. Obviously its purpose here is to raise the audience's admiration for Antony by showing how great and how austere a soldier he had been in the past. Shakespeare must keep his balance in describing the tragic hero. He cannot make Antony too good or we will be angry at the injustice of his tragic fate; he cannot make him totally evil or we will not be able to admire him enough to feel sorry for him when he dies. Since we have last seen Antony resolved to do his duty as a Roman (Scene 3), and since this scene ends by praising him, we feel at this point that in our eyes he has returned to his former stature.

The scene ends as Caesar and Lepidus prepare a council of war to decide how best to defeat Pompey.

SUMMARY: This scene is important because:

1. It introduces Antony's fellow Triumvirs, Octavius Caesar and Lepidus.

2. It shows Caesar's anger at Antony's conduct in Egypt.

3. It brings us up to date on Sextus Pompeius's planned naval attack by showing that some famous pirates and the common people have gone to his support.

4. It describes the noble character of Antony before he fell in love with Cleopatra.

Act I: Scene v

Scene 5 returns to Cleopatra's palace in Alexandria. The Egyptian queen, surrounded by her attendants, complains of how much she misses her lover. She asks Charmian to give her a sedative, a kind of sleeping potion, so she can forget her loneliness in sleep. But she is not so sad that she cannot joke with her eunuch, Mardian, about his sexual impotence. She tells him to be glad he has no sexual desires which would make him long for some one as she does. He replies that while he might never perform the sexual act, he can dream about it. He has erotic thoughts about the adultery of Venus (goddess of love and wife of Vulcan) and Mars (god of war). Cleopatra tries to picture Antony in his absence, recalling his physical presence when he made love to her.

COMMENT: She calls him "the arm/ And burgonet of men." "Arm" here means sword, as "burgonet" means helmet. This supports the "sword" pattern of imagery of Scene 3. Mardian's mention of Venus and Mars may be a sly reference to Cleopatra and Antony.

Her thought of Antony's strength and manly prime leads her to contrast her own aging charms and she begins to doubt she can hold so great a man. She sees her Egyptian skin as burnt black from the sun and wrinkled with age. (Shakespeare obviously thought of Cleopatra as negroid, rather than the Greek she actually was.) She recalls, almost nostalgically, how her youthful beauty had conquered the hearts of the great Roman conquerors Julius Caesar and Pompey the Great (the father of the Sextus Pompeius of this story).

COMMENT: This passage contains one of several references to Cleopatra's age. Shakespeare wants to characterize the great queen as past her prime, her beauty somewhat faded. She must rely more and more on artifice and feminine wiles to attract her lover. While age makes Cleopatra more wily, however, it makes her more tragic and sympathetic to the audience.

Here Alexas, another of Cleopatra's attendants, enters with a message from Antony. The joy of hearing from him reassures her, lifts the gloom which had begun to thicken about her. She is impatient to hear his greeting and to find out how he looked when he gave it. Alexas hands her a pearl which Antony had kissed before sending, as his token of the kingdoms he will conquer for her. She is not surprised to hear that his disposition and demeanor were temperate when he sent it.

COMMENT: In Cleopatra's eyes, Antony can do no wrong. When she discovers that he was neither sad nor merry, but between both, she praises him: not sad, for he must inspire his troops with optimism: not merry, because he missed her. But had he been either, she would praise him equally: "Be'st thou sad or merry,/ The violence of either thee becomes,/ So does it no man else."

Immediately the queen, like a young girl in love again, sits down to answer Antony's message. Her mind goes back to her former Roman lover for a second, and she asks her maid, Charmian, "Did I . . ./ Ever love Caesar so?" And the maid taunts her by mimicking her former praises of Caesar when she was in love with him: "O that brave Caesar!" and "The valiant Caesar!" At this Cleopatra threatens to bloody her teeth. For she praised Caesar in her "salad days," when she was young and ignorant, she says: "green in judgment: cold in blood."

SUMMARY: This slight scene is introduced to tell us more about Cleopatra's character. We have seen her before always relating to Antony; now we see her true self when he is away. The effect is to make Cleopatra seem erotic by nature and not simply as a means to seduce Antony. She is genuinely in love with him but not completely sure of being able to keep him in his absence. Her mention of "salad days" is another indirect reference to her age.

Act II: Scene i

From Cleopatra's court in Alexandria we move back to Messina, in Sicily, where Pompey has his headquarters. (Remember, there were originally no Act divisions in the play.) There, in Messina, Pompey with the pirates Menecrates and Menas (mentioned earlier in Act 1, Scene 4) plans his rebellion against the Triumvirate. Pompey is unhappy because of the delay in their plan. He feels that the longer they wait, the worse will

become the Roman State for which they are going to fight. Menecrates, however, calms him by saying that the delay may all be for the best; it is in the hands of the gods. Then Pompey analyzes their chances in the forthcoming battle and describes the characters and weaknesses of their foes. His chances are good, he estimates. His navy holds mastery of the sea, and the common people of Italy have swung to his side. Besides, Mark Antony is away in Egypt, too caught up in court pleasures and intrigues to care about larger affairs. Octavius Caesar controls the purses of the citizens, but cannot control their love. And Lepidus is a weak sister: he keeps in the others' good graces, and they in his, but there is no love lost among them. Pompey realizes that the success of their plan depends upon the great warrior, Antony, remaining in Egypt; so much so that he apostrophizes (as Caesar did to Antony in Scene 4 of Act 1) to Cleopatra to keep Antony with her by means of her witchcraft and beauty. Pompey hopes that Antony, with his sense of honor dulled by sensual indulgence, will not come to aid his friends.

COMMENT: Here again Cleopatra's age is referred to. "Soften thy waned lip!" Pompey exhorts her, implying that her lip is withered or faded with age.

So Varrius' entrance at this point is very dramatic. Just as Pompey finishes wishing that Antony would stay in Egypt to insure their success, Varrius brings news that he has already left Egypt and is expected at any moment in Rome.

COMMENT: Note how great a reputation Antony has as a warrior, even among his enemies.

At first Pompey cannot believe it; but immediately he tries to take courage by saying that their conspiracy must be a grave threat indeed if Antony will leave Cleopatra just to fight against them. Menas is also shaken up by the news. He tries to find some comfort in the hope that Caesar and Antony may fall out with one another, since both Antony's wife and brother had formerly warred with Caesar. Pompey agrees that all is not right among the Triumvirs, but fears they might be able to overlook their own petty squabbles long enough to unite against the conspirators. At any rate, he will not fall victim to wishful thinking. Laying the outcome in the hands of the gods, he nevertheless bluffly counsels his friends "to use our strongest hands."

SUMMARY: The main purposes of this scene have been:

1. To introduce the conspirators, and to further the subplot of their conspiracy.

2. To provide an objective analysis of the characters of the Triumvirs and their mutual relationships.

3. To show what fear Antony's arrival in Rome inspires in the conspirators.

Act II: Scene ii

In the house of the third and weakest of the Triumvirs, Lepidus, Antony and Caesar's arrival is expected. Lepidus opens the scene by trying to persuade Enobarbus to use his influence on his friend and captain to greet Caesar with "soft and gentle speech," so as not to offend him and stir up ill-feeling among the Triumvirs. For Lepidus realizes that the three leaders must suppress their own quarrels with each other in order to pursue their common quarrel against Pompey successfully: only in their unity is their strength. Enobarbus has just refused Lepidus' request absolutely, when the two disgruntled leaders enter with their parties. With Antony is his lieutenant, Ventidius; with Caesar, his shrewd and politic adviser, Agrippa, and the wealthy patron of the arts, Maecenas. Both parties are absorbed in conversation. Lepidus immediately tries to buffer and soften the collision between the two by admonishing them not to let passions or hard words turn their trivial differences into a bitter fight, lest "we do commit murder in healing wounds."

COMMENT: The role of peacemaker is characteristic of Lepidus not only in this scene but throughout the play. Remember, it was he who stood up for Antony against Caesar's condemnation in Act 1, Scene 4. In fact, it is his lack of passion which is responsible in part for his own downfall.

Antony is the first to agree; he embraces Caesar, who welcomes him to Rome. But their show of friendliness is only on the surface; beneath it the old resentments rankle. Antony opens the conversation by telling Caesar, in effect, to mind his own business. What he, Antony, does in his own province (the East and, therefore, Egypt) is his own affair and no concern of Caesar's. Caesar denies having meddled, says that he does not criticize Antony's conduct in Egypt, but his conspiracy in Rome. He accuses his partner of having an interest in, or at least being the excuse for, the wars which his late wife, Fulvia, and his brother, Lucius, had waged against the Roman state. Antony pleads innocent to the charge, and claims he has reports from among Caesar's own troops that Lucius, in challenging Caesar's authority, challenged his own brother's as well. He put himself on Caesar's side of the dispute and assured his partner of it by means of letters at the time.

To question his loyalty now, at this late date, is only to pick a fight: any old stick will do to beat a dog, as it were. Antony's accusation hurts Caesar—"You praise yourself,/ By laying defects of judgment to me," Caesar says—and when the dispute threatens to break down into a personal squabble, Antony tries to keep the atmosphere cool. He first flatters Caesar with a gentle compliment on his good judgment of men and events, and then turns Fulvia's indiscretion into a joke at his own expense. Caesar is too astute not to be confident of Antony's loyalty, he says. And even Caesar himself, master of a third of the world, would have had his hands full taming Antony's spirited wife. After this note of humor Caesar breaks off and tries a new line of argument. He accuses Antony of disregarding his official letters and insulting his messenger.

COMMENT: This refers to Antony's dismissal of the messenger in Act 1, Scene 1, which Caesar considered an insult to himself.

Antony admits the incident but claims innocence of any insult intended, for two reasons: (1) the messenger overstepped himself by entering his chamber uninvited; and (2) he had a hangover that morning that soured his disposition. Besides, the next day he as much as asked the fellow's pardon. Again he accuses Caesar of patching a quarrel out of trivial slights that do not really matter. Get to the point, he says. This time Caesar is hurt by the accusation into his sharpest attack so far. Before, he had questioned, first, Antony's loyalty, and then his manners; now he attacks his honor by accusing Antony of having broken his promise to lend arms and aid when Caesar needed them to fight Fulvia and Lucius. This is the heart of Caesar's grievance, and Lepidus is alarmed, for it is a most serious charge. But Antony answers it calmly. He had not denied Caesar's requests but only neglected them, because he was so caught up in the pleasures of Cleopatra's court. It was to lure him out of Egypt and away from Cleopatra that Fulvia instigated the war against Rome. He asks Caesar's pardon, not for having intended any injury, but for having been "the ignorant motive" of it. At this concession the entire company are relieved and relax a bit. Lepidus praises Antony's nobility; Maecenas begs them to break off their dispute; even Enobarbus (despite what he said to Lepidus at the beginning of the scene) oversteps his place and advises the two leaders to turn their quarrel toward Pompey. Antony promptly rebukes him for it. Now it is Caesar's turn for concession, and he backs out of the argument neatly by claiming that he does not so much dislike what Antony says, as the way in which he says it. He would adopt any means, he vows, to strengthen their friendship and insure the unity of their dominion over the entire world. This is the cue for Caesar's calculating adviser, Agrippa, to put forth his plan for bringing the two quarreling leaders back together again. Caesar has a sister, Octavia, he says, and Antony is now a widower.

COMMENT: Plutarch tells us that Octavia was the eldest sister of Caesar, really his half-sister, by the same father, and had been "left the widow of her first husband Caius Marcellus, who dyed not long before . . ."

Let their marriage, Agrippa urges, be the knot that ties the two Triumvirs perpetually together. The match would be perfect: She is beautiful and virtuous; he is "the best of men." Their marriage would cool all jealousies, squelch all fears, scotch all rumors that threatened to divide the Triumvirate, while, as Caesar's sister, she would be the intercessor and mediator between the two. They receive his suggestion cautiously at first. Caesar is unsure whether Antony considers Cleopatra his mistress or his wife. But after they are sure of each other's acceptance their enthusiasm grows. Antony grasps Caesar's hand in friendship and swears brotherhood and loyalty, which Caesar returns. Then the two immediately fall to talking about the conspiracy of Pompey. Antony is awkward about defying the rebel leader. He feels obliged to repay certain "strange courtesies" which Pompey has lately lavished on him before he can openly quarrel with the rebels.

COMMENT: We have seen—Act 1, Scene 1—how afraid the conspirators were of Antony's military power. No doubt they have been "buttering him up" to keep him friendly and out of their quarrel with Caesar and Lepidus.

But time is pressing, Lepidus urges. Pompey's naval strength is second to none, and his land forces grow stronger daily. The three Triumvirs decide to seek a meeting with Pompey at his camp near Mt. Misenum, but first proceed to Caesar's house to settle the business of Antony's marriage to Octavia.

COMMENT: This marks the end of the Roman atmosphere of the scene. Antony has argued straightforwardly and convincingly; he has shown himself more than a match for Octavius. He has, finally, in accepting the offer of Octavia in marriage, demonstrated his sobriety, his sense of responsibility and his loyalty to Rome.

When they depart, Enobarbus, Agrippa and Maecenas remain alone on stage. The two Roman statesmen welcome the soldier back from Egypt and pump him for information and descriptions of Cleopatra's fabulous court. He not only vouches for the truth of their most fantastic stories about its luxury, but goes them one better in his sumptuous description of Cleopatra's arrival in Cilicia to appear before Antony's tribunal.

COMMENT: This speech gives us a good example of one of the ways in which Shakespeare borrowed from his sources. He takes not only his story or plot and his characters from Plutarch, but even some of his speeches as well. Here he puts into blank verse this description which comes out of North's translation of Plutarch: ". . . she disdained to set forward otherwise, but to take her barge in the river of Cydnus, the poop whereof was of gold, the sails of purple, and the oars of silver, which kept stroke in rowing after the sound of music of flutes, howboys, citherns, viols, and such other instruments as they played upon in the barge. And now for the person of herself: she was laid under a pavilion of cloth of gold of tissue, apparelled and attired like the goddess Venus commonly drawn in picture: and hard by her, on either hand of her, pretty fair boys apparelled as painters do set forth god Cupid, with little fans in their hands, with the which they fanned wind upon her. Her ladies and gentlewomen also, the fairest of them were apparelled like the nymphs Nereids (which are the mermaids of the waters) and like the Graces, some steering the helm, others tending the tackle and ropes of the barge, out of the which there came a wonderful passing sweet savour of perfumes, that perfumed the wharf's side, pestered with innumerable multitudes of people. Some of them followed the barge all alongst the river-side: others also ran out of the city to see her coming in. So that in the end there ran such multitudes of people one after another to see her, that Antonius was left post alone in the market-place in his imperial seat to give audience: and there went a rumour in the people's mouths, that the goddess Venus was come to play with the god Bacchus, for the general good of all Asia. When Cleopatra landed, Antonius sent to invite her to supper to him. But she sent word again, he should do better rather to come and sup with her."

Called before Antony to answer charges that she had supported Cassius and Brutus against him in the battle of Phillipi, Cleopatra plans to escape his inquisition and reprisals by making him fall in love with her. That accounts for her spectacular arrival by boat on the River Cydnus. And what a boat! Its poop (a partial deck raised above the main deck in the rear) was fashioned of solid gold. The oars which propelled it were of silver, and they kept stroke to the music of flutes on board (as soldiers, for example, march to the sound of drums and martial music). The sails were purple and perfumed so that the very breeze languished and grew lovesick in breathing on them, and their scent assailed the spectators who lined the river banks to watch.

COMMENT: Purple dye, sometimes called Tyrian purple, was made from the shells of certain mollusks. Because of its richness and its rareness it was considered the color of kings and queens in ancient times. That Cleopatra should use this to color her sails is a sign, like the golden deck, silver oars, etc., of fabulous wealth and wasteful extravagance.

The rigging and tackle were of silk, as befitted the softness of the ship's "hands," Cleopatra's attendants, who resembled so many mermaids or nereids (mythical water nymphs, daughters of the sea–god Nereus) as they managed the ship and fawned over its cargo, Cleopatra. Cleopatra herself was stunning beyond description. She neither stood nor sat, but reclined (probably on the golden poop deck), shaded by a sumptuous silken canopy into whose tissue were woven threads of purest gold. She resembled a painting of the Goddess of Love herself (probably the lost Venus Anadyomene, or "Venus Rising out of the Sea," painted by the Greek, Apelles, in the 4th century B. C.), only more lovely, surrounded by pretty young boys, who stirred the perfumed air about her with many-colored fans, like so many little cupids (Cupid was the son of Venus by Mars, God of War).

COMMENT: Some critics have this speech inappropriate in the mouth of the Roman soldier, Enobarbus. Its lush and sensual descriptions, its lavish use of imagination, its classical and mythological references are out of place coming from the usually straightforward, prosaic, and even vulgar Enobarbus. On the other hand, that contrast between Rome and the mysterious East is just what Shakespeare wanted. Even Enobarbus is overcome by Cleopatra's charms.

Word of the spectacle soon emptied the city as the people flocked to the river banks to watch, leaving Antony by himself in the market place, enthroned for his tribunals, "whistling to the air." He sent word to invite the queen to dinner with him: she refused his offer but returned the invitation, which he accepted. And there at the banquet Antony lost his heart to her.

COMMENT: Shakespeare seems to be confused about when and where Antony first saw and fell in love with Cleopatra. In line 187 Enobarbus says that "she pursed up his heart upon the river of Cydnus," but later in Scene 2, 214-216 that "Antony/ Enthroned in a market-place, did sit alone," all the while. It was only later that night, at her feast, that he first saw her and fell in love.

Agrippa and Enobarbus then exchange stories of Cleopatra's fabulous beauty which could bewitch great (Julius) Caesar, and which is made even more perfect by every defect in it. So when Maecenas says that Antony, pledged to Octavia, must give up Cleopatra for good, Enobarbus answers: "Never; he will not."

COMMENT: With this answer, Enobarbus brings out into the open his suspicion that the proposed marriage may not succeed in its purpose of uniting the two Triumvirs, if Octavia cannot overcome Antony's love for Cleopatra. Note also Enobarbus's reference to Cleopatra's advancing years—"Age cannot wither her"—which he discounts as a possible reason why Antony might have grown tired or jaded with his queen.

The scene ends on Maecenas' earnest, but somewhat hollow, hope that Octavia's "beauty, wisdom, modesty, can settle the heart of Antony," and reform the notorious rogue.

SUMMARY: This scene contains several important developments which can be divided into two distinct groups. Part one of the scene has a noticeable "Roman" atmosphere, and is dominated by Antony. It is developed in three stages:

1. The encounter between Antony and Caesar, and their argument.

2. The resolution of the argument and the plan to marry Octavia to Antony.

3. The decision of the Triumvirs to unite their forces against Pompey. Part two takes on an "Egyptian" coloring from Enobarbus' detailed description of Cleopatra, who dominates his conversation with the Roman statesmen. Shakespeare puts the two parts side by side to heighten the contrast between Roman rationality and Egyptian sensuality, which are also the two warring sides of Antony's nature. The climax of the scene is reached when Enobarbus and Agrippa raise the question of which side Antony will finally choose: Octavia or Cleopatra.

Act II: Scene iii

The conversation among Enobarbus and Caesar's counselors provides the time needed between the departure of the Triumvirs from Lepidus' house and their arrival at Caesar's. (Although Antony insisted upon Lepidus' accompanying them to visit Octavia, Lepidus does not appear with them in this scene at Caesar's house.) The scene opens with Antony's saying good-bye to Caesar and Octavia. In parting, he forewarns his prospective wife that, after their marriage, he will be away from her often on military and political adventures. She accepts this and promises that she will be on her knees all the while he is gone, praying constantly for him.

COMMENT: Shakespeare contrasts the "beauty, wisdom, modesty" that Octavia reveals here with the "infinite variety" of Cleopatra described by Enobarbus in the scene just before. "Vilest things/ Become themselves," in the Egyptian queen, so that "the holy priests/ Bless her, when she's riggish" (wanton). (Act 2, Scene 2, ll. 238 ff.) The effect is to make Antony's betrayal of Octavia almost certain.

No sooner are the sister and brother gone, when the soothsayer, who comes from Cleopatra's court and who reminds us of the magic and the mystery of the East, appears to tell Antony's fortune and to prophesy how his new friendship and alliance will turn out. Badly, the wizard tells him, and urges Antony to return at once to Egypt. For Antony's guiding spirit or guardian angel is greater than Caesar's when he is alone, but when they are together, it is overpowered; he suffers always by comparison with the younger man. His luck always deserts him; in games with Caesar, he is sure to lose.

COMMENT: The fortune teller's prophecy is a true one. In this speech we get a forewarning of the final outcome of the play, when Caesar will defeat Antony once again. Then the game will be war; and the stakes they play for will be the entire world and even life itself.

Antony is so struck by the soothsayer's advice, that he makes him promise not to repeat his prophecy to anyone else. He sends the soothsayer off to tell Ventidius, his lieutenant, that he wants to see him. When the wiseman is gone, Antony confirms his prophecy as true in a short soliloquy (a speech in which a character, usually alone, speaks his thoughts aloud to the audience, no one else on stage overhearing him). In his gambling with Caesar, Antony admits, the dice have always betrayed him; in sports, luck has been with his rival. He then makes a startling decision: he will follow the soothsayer's advice, and even while tying the marriage knot with Octavia, he vows he will return to Egypt to continue his affair with Cleopatra. "I make this marriage for my peace," he says, "In the East my pleasure lies."

COMMENT: Antony is like the prize in a tug-of-war between Rome and Egypt. To show this, Shakespeare alternates scenes in which Antony's sense of honor and duty to Octavia pulls him toward Rome with others in which Egypt and Cleopatra draw him toward love—and doom. In this scene the question of who will win, raised by Enobarbus and Agrippa in Act 2, Scene 2, is answered. Cleopatra wins. Antony, after promising faithfulness to Octavia and begging her trust, turns around and violates that trust in favor

of his Egyptian mistress. He is only using Caesar's sister for political purposes.

Antony's business with Ventidius is short: he gives his lieutenant orders to report to Parthia to check the enemy invasion there.

COMMENT: The expedition to Parthia was to defeat the armies of Labienus, who had been conquering all of Asia and invading the territory over which Antony was supposed to rule. The invasion is spoken of earlier in Act 1, Scene 2, ll. 96 ff.

SUMMARY: This scene though short is decisive for Antony's fate. It contains the following developments:

1. Introduces Caesar's sister Octavia, whom Antony has promised to marry, and contrasts her with Cleopatra.

2. In the fortune teller's prophecy we get an inkling of Antony's future defeat at the hands of Caesar.

3. Right after he has promised Octavia that he will reform his conduct in the future so as to act "by the rule," Antony decides to return to Cleopatra. This shows him to be two-faced, a slave to his own weaknesses and baser appetites.

4. His commission to Ventidius picks up the story of Labienus's invasion in Parthia and ties his lieutenant more closely into the action of the play.

Act II: Scene iv

Scene 4 is very short, ten lines of dialogue between Lepidus, Maecenas, and Agrippa to show the Romans marshalling their forces for the confrontation, several days later, with Pompey at Mt. Misenum.

Act II: Scene v

This scene whisks us back to Cleopatra's palace in Alexandria. The queen is restless, love-sick, longing for her absent Antony. To pass the time she first calls for music, "the food of love," but when Mardian, her eunuch, enters to play for her, she dismisses him and challenges her maid, Charmian, to shoot a game of billiards with her instead. Charmian declines, but Mardian takes up the challenge, and Cleopatra, with an obvious sexual jest, says she may as well play games with a eunuch as with a woman. She never gets to the game, however, for already her quicksilver mood has shifted again, and she wishes to go fishing. With every fish she catches she will pretend she is drawing home her roving lover. Charmian reminds her of a trick she once played on Antony.

COMMENT: Plutarch tells the whole story. Out fishing once, with Cleopatra nearby, Antony wanted to show off but could catch no fish. So he ordered some fisherman, when he dropped in his line, to dive under, unnoticed, and attach a fish to his hook. In this way he pulled in two or three fish. Cleopatra saw through his ruse but did not let on, and next day when he was fishing again she had one of her own divers attach an old salted fish—i.e., one that has been aged and preserved in salt a long time—to his hook, which he then pulled in to the laughter of all.

And Cleopatra reminisces about the wonderful times she had with Antony, including one in which, both drunk, she dressed him in her woman's garments while she "wore his sword Phillipan."

COMMENT: Shakespeare mentions their exchange of clothes here as a sign of weakness and effeminacy which overcame Antony in Egypt. Her wearing his sword continues the "sword" pattern of imagery. As the sign or emblem of Antony's manliness, it shows that she had assumed the masculine role. The fact that it was the sword he used to defeat Brutus and Cassius in the battle of Phillipi (and, hence, named after it), when he was at the peak of his glory and strength, deepens the irony.

But her laughter is suddenly stilled by the appearance of a messenger from Italy. Immediately she jumps to conclusions: "Antonius dead!" she screams, and alternately threatens and cajoles the messenger to give her good news, as though by promising gold or threatening death she could make his message any different from what it is. Continually interrupted by her gifts and threats, the messenger can only give his news piecemeal. Antony is well, he says, and friends with Caesar, and adds darkly, "Caesar, and he, are greater friends than ever"—but does not yet reveal the reason and seal of this friendship. Cleopatra is overjoyed, and over generous—"Make thee a fortune from me"—until the messenger's "But yet, madam . . ." gives her her first real reason to suspect something is wrong. She snatches at it immediately, but still does not catch the messenger's drift when he says, "he's bound unto Octavia." Why? For what purposes, she asks, and only slowly does the shock of despair overcome her when he replies, "Madam, he's married to Octavia." Once the truth is clear and out in the open, she reacts immediately and violently. Suddenly she is upon him, knocks him to the ground, cursing him and, despite his protests, kicking and scratching. She threatens to put out his eyes, tear out his hair, have him whipped with wire and boiled in brine. Then in an instant she relents, all softness again, begging him only to say it is not so to make his fortune. When he sticks by his message, she is at his throat once more, this time with a knife, and would have his life but that he runs away. Charmian tries to calm her when he is gone, and succeeds enough to have Cleopatra call the boy back again.

COMMENT: She lives up to her name, "Serpent of old Nile." She is thinking of herself as a serpent when after uttering the curse, "kindly creatures/ Turn all to serpents!" she says of herself, "Though I am mad, I will not bite him."

But the boy is afraid to come before the "fury of a woman scorned," and his fear awakens a spark of nobility and self-respect in Cleopatra. She regrets having struck the messenger for two reasons: (1) he is socially inferior to her and therefore she demeans herself by hitting him; (2) it is not his fault, but rather her own that Antony's marriage upsets her. In a sort of half-apology, she advises the boy when he reappears, to tell good tidings but let bad tidings tell themselves, and asks him again if Antony is married. When he confirms the news once more, once more she flies into a rage, over and over demanding that he repeat the bitter news and then cursing him for it when he does. However, she will not lay hands on him again, but banishes him from her presence. Her panic recedes with her violence. She begins to recover her wits, and though her heart is breaking, she is already weaving the snares and trammels that will snatch her lover out of his new wife's arms and fetch him back to hers. But first she must size her rival up. She sends Alexas to speak to the messenger to find out what Antony's wife looks like: how old she is, her temperament or disposition, the color of her hair, how tall she is. Then she asks her waiting-woman Charmian to pity her in silence and lead her to bed.

COMMENT: Though Cleopatra is broken-hearted at Antony's seeming rejection of her, she is so because she still loves him. Hence she is torn between two courses of action: (1) to abandon him to Octavia as a Gorgon (a mythological demon, Medusa, whose scalp was covered with snakes instead of hair and whose sight turned men to stone); or, to try to win him back as a Mars (Roman God of War). The description of Antony as both Gorgon and Mars is a metaphor based on a kind of Elizabethan painting called a perspective, which showed two or three different pictures according to the angle from which one viewed it. She is saying that Antony is like such a picture; from one point of view he is hateful, from another lovable.

SUMMARY: As in most of the Egyptian scenes, Shakespeare has really nothing new—neither action, nor piece of information, nor plot development—to tell us. Yet he must switch back to Cleopatra's court every so often to keep her image fresh in our minds. Sometimes he does this merely by having a character describe the court life (Enobarbus in Act 2, Scene 2) or by having some representative of the East (the soothsayer, Act 2, Scene 3) appear on stage. Here, as in the last scene that took place in Egypt (Act 1, Scene 5), he shows us a messenger bringing news to Cleopatra from Antony, only this time the news is disturbing. But the purpose and construction of the scene is the same. There is the preliminary conversation between the queen and her attendant, the joking (always including some sexual jest), the memories, all of which reveal Cleopatra's love-sickness and longing. Then comes the messenger whom she impatiently duns for his news. And, finally, her reaction to the news. Therefore, the purpose of the scene is twofold:

1. To strengthen the image of the mysterious and sensual East and to maintain its balance over the moral and rational West.

2. To deepen the characterization of Cleopatra, in particular by revealing some of "her infinite variety," the impetuosity of her actions, her quicksilver moods, her cunning and scheming, and last but not least her devotion to Antony.

Act II: Scene vi

Now comes the long-expected confrontation between the Triumvirs and the conspirators near Mt. Misenum in Naples. The two sides have exchanged hostages as pledges of their good intent, and the Triumvirs have sent Pompey terms for an armistice before the armies start to fight. Now Caesar starts negotiations by asking Pompey if he will accept their terms for a truce. Pompey replies by stating the reasons for his rebellion. Just as the Triumvirs—Caesar's adopted son Octavius and close friends—avenged Julius Caesar's murder by defeating Brutus and Cassius, his murderers, at the battle of Phillipi: so he, Sextus Pompey, with his friends, will overthrow the Triumvirs in order to avenge his father, Pompey the Great, whom Julius Caesar had overthrown.

COMMENT: Julius Caesar defeated his fellow soldier and rival, Gnaeus Pompey, in the battle of Pharsalia in 48 B. C. Pompey was later murdered in Egypt.

That is his personal grudge against the Triumvirs; his public purpose is to do what Brutus did in killing Julius Caesar: to rid Rome of an oppressive tyranny and return the people to their freedom. His aggressive statement puts Antony's hackles up, who challenges him to a sea contest, since he will not face the Triumvirs' superior forces on land, Pompey replies with a sarcastic jibe that Antony had bought his father's house (Pompey the Great's) at auction and then refused to pay for it.

COMMENT: The connection between Antony's vaunting challenge and Pompey's jibing reply is the word "over-count." Antony says his land armies "over-count" or outnumber Pompey's. Pompey uses the same word to mean "cheat"—You have cheated me of my father's house.

As the exchange becomes heated, Lepidus, the peacemaker, steps in to cool the atmosphere. He asks Pompey to answer Caesar's question—does he accept the truce or not? Antony is quick to remark that they are not begging him, and Caesar adds that it will be for his own good. Then Pompey repeats the terms of the treaty: In return for rule over Sicily and Sardinia (another large island in the Mediterranean off the west coast of Italy), he must promise to rid all the Mediterranean Sea of pirates and to pay an annual tax to Rome in the form of wheat.

COMMENT: We have seen how Pompey has been using the support of the notorious pirates Menas and Menecrates to raid the Italian coastal towns and prey upon shipping (Act 1, Scene 4, ll. 48 ff; Act 2, Scene 1).

This agreed upon, the two armies will pull back without fighting. "Know, then," he says, "I came before you here a man prepared/ To take this offer. But Mark Anthony/ Put me to some impatience." He feels he deserved better from the Roman general because he had welcomed Antony's mother and given her protection in Sicily when she was forced to flee from Italy, after her son Lucius's rebellion was defeated. Antony acknowledges the debt of friendship, and Pompey, grasping his hand, says he is surprised to see Antony at all, this far from Egypt. "The beds in the East are soft," Antony acknowledges, but duty has called him away from pleasure, "thanks to you." Then Pompey concludes the business of their meeting by asking that the terms of the treaty be written up and sealed.

COMMENT: Pompey offers only a show of resistance to the truce, and is quick to avoid a fight because of the unexpected return of Antony and the seeming friendliness of the Triumvirs. Remember, the rebels had hoped that the three would squabble and break apart (Act 2, Scene 1).

The pact will be sealed with a celebration party thrown by each of the four signers. Pompey offers to choose lots to decide who will begin. Antony wants the honor of being first, but Pompey repeats that they must choose lots. But whether first or last, he taunts Antony, your "fine Egyptian cookery shall have/ The fame." Did not Julius Caesar get fat on it? Antony stiffens at the remark. But Pompey assures him, disarmingly, "I have fair meanings, sir."

COMMENT: We know Pompey's feelings about Julius Caesar; he hated him for having deposed his father. We also know that the Triumvirs were friends of the first Caesar and revenged his death. It is no wonder, then, that when Pompey mentions his name jokingly, Antony should resent it, and no doubt that Pompey intended this. The peace they have just agreed to will be an uneasy one.

Pompey continues to rib Antony. Now he includes Cleopatra in the joke by referring to a famous episode, in which one of her friends, Apollodorus, carried the queen to Caesar wrapped in a mattress.

COMMENT: Plutarch gives this account, Caesar had secretly sent for Cleopatra, but when she had come to his palace she could find no way to enter without being seen. So she had Apollodorus wrap her in a kind of quilt or blanket and smuggle her in on his back.

Enobarbus finishes the story that Pompey starts and draws from the rebel leader a handshake, an offer of friendship, and praise for his qualities as a fighter. The straightforward soldier returns the compliment, though not the love, he says, and this openness even further ingratiates him with Pompey. Then Pompey with a flourish invites everyone at the parley to celebrate their treaty aboard his flagship, and all leave but Enobarbus and Menas, the pirate. Menas first speaks an aside in which he shows his apprehension over the new treaty: "Thy father, Pompey, would never have made this treaty."

COMMENT: An aside, unlike a soliloquy, is spoken when other characters are on stage and may be heard by them also. So it is much shorter than a soliloquy, and its purpose is not to explore character or provide motivation, but to awaken the audience's fear or arouse its curiosity.

Then Menas addresses Enobarbus before he can leave with the rest and falls into conversation with him. There is no pretense between the two; each recognizes the other for what he is: a thief. Menas makes his living as a pirate; Enobarbus as a mercenary (a soldier of fortune, who sells his services to the highest bidder and fights for pay, not patriotism). They shake hands and exchange roguish pleasantries until the conversation gets around to the present situation. "We came hither to fight with you," Enobarbus says, and Menas answers that he is sorry the battle did not come off. He distrusts the truce, he confides to his erstwhile enemy, and feels that "Pompey doth this day laugh away his fortune." Then Menas, surprised at seeing Antony back in Italy, brings up the subject of Cleopatra. This is Enobarbus' cue to blurt out the marriage plans between Antony and Octavia. But he does not agree with Menas that this will insure the continued friendship of Caesar and Antony. Just the opposite, this nuptial band that was supposed to bind the two together will turn out to be the rope that strangles their friendship. "Octavia is of a holy, cold, and still conversation (behavior)"; Antony is not. And Enobarbus predicts that Antony "will to his Egyptian dish again: then shall the sighs of Octavia blow the fire up in Caesar," and the marriage which was intended to bind the Triumvirate together will break it apart. Menas then suggests they go on to the party to drink each other's health, and Enobarbus accepts, saying, "we have used our throats in Egypt."

COMMENT: The feeling of confidence between the two which Shakespeare establishes early in the scene is necessary later on. We could not otherwise expect these men, enemies until just a few moments before, to speak so frankly and openly about their feelings toward their leaders. But that is just what Menas is after. Recall that it was Menas, in Act 2, Scene 1, who hoped the alliance between Caesar and Antony would dissolve when Antony came home. Here he pumps Enobarbus for some clue that may prove his hope true. To win the soldier's confidence, the pirate confides his own distrust of the new treaty. And when he has the information he wants, he breaks off the conversation.

SUMMARY: This scene produces three important developments:

1. The treaty with Pompey avoids a showdown fight for the time being and allows Antony to turn his attention to his Eastern empire and Cleopatra.

2. Menas's distrust of the treaty and the hard feelings between its signers make us suspect that it will be short-lived.

3. Enobarbus puts into words the suspicion held by all that not only will Antony's marriage not close the rift between him and Caesar, but will actually widen it instead.

Act II: Scene vii

This scene takes place soon after the last. Everyone has gone aboard Pompey's galley for the feast; they have eaten and drunk, and now it is time for the "banquet" or dessert. Two or three servingmen bring it on stage and chat and joke for a minute to set the scene. Their joking reveals that the party has been a success; the revelers are in different stages of drunkenness, and Lepidus in particular is flushed with his drinks. As the peacemaker, he tried to relax the tension building up between the two groups at the party and did this by encouraging them to drown their enmity in wine. When they became quarrelsome he would break it up by offering them a drink—and having one himself. Since he cannot hold his liquor as well as the others he has succeeded only in losing all sense of discretion. One of the servants observes that Lepidus has a name only among his companions; he is not their equal or fellow as a man. As useless to be too small for a job as too great; a reed is as useless in battle as a sword that is too heavy to wield, he reflects. His friend agrees: to have a job that one cannot do is like having empty sockets where eyes should be.

COMMENT: The servant's lines contain two metaphors. "To be called into a huge sphere, and not to be seen to move in it, are the holes where eyes should be, which pitifully disaster the cheeks." The reference to eyes is obvious; however, hidden in the language is a less obvious metaphor based on the stars. The words "sphere," "move," and "disaster" point the reference. Besides meaning "place in life," or "ruling circle," "sphere" refers to the Ptolemaic system of astronomy, which from ancient times was used to describe the movements of heavenly bodies. Hence the second meaning of "move" refers to the observed movements of the stars. Ptolemy taught that the planets and stars were the visible parts of seven hollow spheres which surrounded the earth concentrically (i.e., one sphere or hollow ball inside the next), and by the revolving of these spheres (rather than of the earth itself) explained the movement of the heavenly bodies. Hence the servant indirectly compares a man called to high position, but inadequate in it, to a star which does not shine. In the same way, empty sockets "disaster" the cheeks. "Disaster" refers literally to the calamitous influence of the stars (astrum means star in Latin); here it compares the ruined "cheeks" to the sphere in which no star shines.

Suddenly a trumpet sounds a sennet. (A "sennet" was a group of notes or a tune which was used to identify a particular person, a kind of musical signature). The music introduces the great men and their advisers and captains, Caesar, Antony, Pompey, Lepidus,

Agrippa, Maecenas, Enobarbus, Menas, and others. Antony is describing some Egyptian farming customs to Caesar. The farmers can gauge their crops according to the height to which the River Nile rises in flood season. "The higher Nilus swells,/ the more it promises," because the farmers plant their crops in the rich "slime and ooze" left behind when the waters recede. Lepidus pipes up, "You have strange serpents there?" and when Antony answers yes, the tipsy Triumvir ventures a foolish explanation of how Egyptian serpents are bred. "Your serpent of Egypt is bred now of your mud by the operation of your sun: so is your crocodile."

COMMENT: The belief that living creatures could be generated out of nonliving things (called spontaneous generation) was widely held in Shakespeare's time. The use of the personal pronoun "your" instead of "the" was, then as now, a common colloquialism. Lepidus' use of it here, among his betters, is a sign of his drunkenness.

The other leaders take advantage of Lepidus' condition to bait him. Pompey calls for another round of drinks, and offers a toast to him, and though he is sick and would rather not, Lepidus drinks with the rest and goes on talking about Egypt. While Lepidus is running on about the pyramids, Menas catches Pompey's attention, unnoticed by the others. He wants to speak to his chief alone for a minute, but Pompey, too much enjoying his spoofing of Lepidus, puts him off and pours the groggy general another drink. When Lepidus asks "What manner of thing is your crocodile," Antony takes up the teasing with as nonsensical an explanation of the crocodile as Lepidus had given him of the serpent. "It is shaped, sir, like itself, and it is as broad as it hath breadth: it is just so high as it is, and moves with its own organs. It lives by that which nourisheth it." This seems to satisfy Lepidus, who only asks, "What color is it of?" and learns that it is "of its own color too." "'Tis a strange serpent," he reflects, apparently forgetting that he had asked about crocodiles.

COMMENT: Antony also says, "the tears of it are wet." This mention of "crocodile tears" alludes to a once-popular belief that after killing a man, and before eating him, the crocodile wept over his body.

Again, Pompey's fun is interrupted by Menas, but this time the pirate's persistence succeeds in separating the host from his guests. The two go apart and, after pledging his loyalty to his chief, Menas asks bluntly, "Wilt thou be lord of all the world?" Pompey thinks he must be mishearing him and has Menas repeat the question. "How should that be," he asks. Menas assures him, "though thou think me poor, I am the man/ Will give you all the world." Now Pompey doubts his friend's sobriety: "Hast thou drunk well?" But Menas denies it: "No, Pompey, I have kept me from the cup"; and assures him again that he can make his chief the master of the world. "Show me which way," Pompey demands, and Menas reveals his scheme. "These three world-sharers, these competitors,/ Are in thy vessel. Let me cut the cable,/ And when we are put off, fall to their throats." Pompey's reaction is surprising. "Ah, this thou shouldst have done" on your own, he says, "and not have spoke on it first." For Menas, his lieutenant, his henchman, it would have been good service to ambush his enemies and kill them; but it would be dishonorable for Pompey himself to allow it. "Being done unknown,/ I should have found it afterwards well done,/ But must condemn it now."

COMMENT: Pompey's attitude must seem strange. We would expect him either to put political expediency above all and fall in with Menas's murder scheme, or to put his honor and integrity above all and reject the suggestion outright. But Pompey does neither of these—or rather, both. He tries to preserve his personal honor by rejecting any part in the scheme, while at the same time he applauds the treachery behind it and wishes Menas had done it without his knowledge. Surely this is the speech of a moral coward. Pompey wants the profit from the evil deed but not the blame for it. And this lack of courage he labels his "honor."

Menas sees the weakness of Pompey's character through this speech and grows wary of him. He says aside, as if to himself, that he will pull out of his alliance with Pompey because Pompey's good fortune is on the wane; he has the world in his hand and will not take hold of it. "Who seeks and will not take, when once 'tis offer'd," Menas predicts, "Shall never find it more." Pompey turns back to his guests, the genial host once more, to raise another toast to Lepidus. But by this time the tipsy general is under the table.

COMMENT: Lepidus must have collapsed during the conversation aside between Menas and Pompey, probably when Antony's voice interrupts the scheming of the conspirators to say, "These quick sands, Lepidus,/ Keep off them, for you sink (ll. 59-60)."

So Antony drinks Lepidus' pledge for him and the wine jug goes round again. Pompey fills his cup; Enobarbus toasts Menas and jokes, of the servant who is carrying out the unconscious Lepidus, that he "bears the third part of the world." (Lepidus as a Triumvir rules Africa, approximately one-third of the then known

world.) Menas replies that "the third part, then, is drunk: would it were all/ That it might go on wheels!" Again the wine is poured around; again the cups are raised. Pompey complains that the party has not yet reached the frenzy and orgy of an Alexandrian feast at Cleopatra's court. But we're trying, Antony adds, and raises a toast to Caesar to draw him into the drunken revelry.

COMMENT: "Strike the vessels, ho!" may be Antony's call to the steward to tap the cask of wine, or to the revelers to clash drinking vessels together, as today we might toast by clinking glasses.

Caesar declines another drink at first, but Antony urges him to comply for the sake of the party, and Caesar reluctantly raises his cup to answer Antony's toast. Enobarbus has no such reserve. Already in his cups, he carouses familiarly with Antony, whom he calls "my brave emperor," and suggests they climax their celebration with "the Egyptian Bacchanals," a dance in honor of Bacchus, the god of wine in classical mythology. Pompey is enthusiastic, and Antony bids them all to drink "Till that the conquering wine hath steep'd our sense/ In soft and delicate Lethe." (Lethe was believed by the Greeks to be a river in Hades which caused forgetfulness to those who drank from it.) Enobarbus then officiously places everyone in a ring, joining their hands, and gives instructions for the chorus. The men will carry the burden or refrain of the song, while the boy sings the descant. Then the musicians strike up and the drunken leaders reel through their song and dance to an orgiastic climax of their "Alexandrian feast." Their song invokes Bacchus, who is both the god of wine and the wine itself they are drinking. They bid him come, with his "pink eyne" (eyes) and his vats of wine, with clusters of grapes to crown their heads and make them all drunk "till the world go round." Hardly have they finished their tipsy song and dance when Caesar breaks off impatiently, chiding his drunken fellows with "What would you more?" He bids a hasty goodnight to Pompey, the host, and begs out with a none too gentle reprimand: "our graver business/ Frowns at this levity." They have all drunk so much, "the wild disguise" (drunkenness) "has almost/ Antick'd us all" (made clowns of us all).

COMMENT: Caesar's disgust at the drunken cavorting of the others is characteristic of him. Though younger than the rest, he is more proper than they and colder in temperament. He has drunk very little while they have been quaffing freely. We saw earlier how he hesitated to match Antony's toast and only reluctantly drank with him. Now, as the party reels to its highest pitch he can no longer tolerate their drunken excess and decides to call a halt to it. Shakespeare models his character after the Elizabethan ideal of the Roman statesman shrewd, sober, business-like, but for all that somewhat stiff, intolerant, cold, pompous—a stuffed shirt. So Caesar comes to stand for all the qualities Antony as his opposite, or antagonist, lacks.

At Caesar's urging the party breaks up; the revellers prepare to go ashore. Pompey, however, has no intention of letting the party die, so he offers to "try" Antony once more "on the shore." "And shall, sir" Antony accepts, "give's your hand," and the two erstwhile enemies grow maudlin over their boozy friendship. The stage is empty now but for Menas and Enobarbus, who decline to go ashore to continue the party and stagger off to Menas's cabin instead.

SUMMARY: This famous scene of the drinking bout aboard Pompey's galley seems intended exclusively to develop character and create atmosphere. Four of the characters drink too much:

1. Lepidus, the weakest of the Triumvirs heretofore, shows himself again to be inconsequential, a fool, the butt of the others' jokes.

2. Enobarbus drinks and makes merry with the same openness and gusto that he shows at other times.

3. Pompey plays the genial host, but under the geniality he reveals a nature that is morally weak and altogether too trusting and optimistic.

4. Although it is Pompey's party, Antony winds up leading it and turning it into an "Egyptian Bacchanal," so that much of the excess in the scene must be associated with him.

Two are more temperate in their drinking:

5. Menas, the unscrupulous pirate, keeps his wits about him so as to take advantage of those who are drowning theirs. His scheme to subvert the Triumvirs is an exemplary piece of Machiavellian treachery which violates every sacred bond of trust and hospitality.

6. Caesar abstains for its own sake, because in excessive drinking he will lose the clarity and self-control which he feels proper to his position. He takes himself very seriously and fears to be made a fool or to make a fool of himself. The scene is a Roman imitation of an Alexandrian feast: the inebriety and excess of Egypt have infected sober Italy. Though we may be put off by his aloofness, we must be impressed by Caesar's sobriety and sense of responsibility. And we can foresee already that Caesar, though a lesser man and soldier than Antony, is destined to triumph over him.

Act III: Scene i

This scene takes us to Syria where Ventidius, Antony's lieutenant, has accomplished his mission and defeated the Parthian hordes who had swept across the frontiers of the eastern provinces of the Roman Empire.

COMMENT: When we recall that there were originally no act divisions in this play we see that it is not by chance that this scene comes next. In fact, Shakespeare achieves a striking dramatic effect by taking us immediately from the drunken debauchery of Pompey's galley to Ventidius's military triumph on the plain of Syria. For it is the underling, Ventidius, who alone maintains his nobility by fighting Rome's legitimate enemies, not his fellow Romans. And even he must be cautious, lest he antagonize Antony.

Ventidius enters in triumphal procession behind the slaughtered body of his enemy, Pacorus, the Parthian general. He claims that his victory over "darting Parthia" and the death of Pacorus revenge the defeat and death of Marcus Crassus.

COMMENT: Together with Pompey the Great and Julius Caesar, Marcus Crassus formed the first Triumvirate. He was defeated by the Parthians in 53 B.C. and was treacherously killed by Orodes (father of Pacorus and king of Parthia) during a council of truce. His unavenged murder was a cause of popular complaint in Rome.

When Silius urges Ventidius to follow up his victory by pursuing the routed Parthians through Media and Mesopotamia, Ventidius is cautious. "I have done enough," he says. Rather than praise and honor, he would win Antony's displeasure for his pains. "For learn this, Silius;/ Better to leave undone, than by our deed/ Acquire too high a fame, when him we serve's away." He is afraid that if he makes too good a showing, defeats the enemy too soundly, Antony will be jealous of his renown. He quotes the example of Sossius, like himself one of Antony's lieutenants, in Syria, whose victories gained him renown and lost his captain's favor. "Who does i' the wars more than his captain can,/ Becomes his captain's captain . . ." (There is no authority in Plutarch for the story of Sossius's dismissal.) Paradoxically, the soldier's ambition is better served by gaining less than he might, than by gaining more. "I could do more to do Antonius good,/ But 'twould offend him. And in his offence/ Should my performance perish." Silius acknowledges the wisdom of Ventidius' words; without such wisdom a soldier is no better than his sword. Then Ventidius' tells how he will inform Antony of his victory, making it seem Antony's victory, disclaiming any credit for himself. Silius asks where their captain is now, and we learn from Ventidius' reply that Antony is on his way to Athens and that they plan to meet him there. With that the victorious lieutenant disappears from the play.

SUMMARY: This scene accomplishes the following:

1. Concludes the subplot of the Parthian invasion.

2. Develops the character of Ventidius further in order to contrast him with the other generals.

Act III: Scene ii

Ventidius' mention of Antony's going to Athens is the cue for this shift back to Rome. Here we shall see the newly-married Antony and Octavia taking leave of Caesar and Lepidus. Shakespeare introduces their farewells with the farewell conversation between the out-spoken Enobarbus (leaving with Antony) and the politic Agrippa, which comments on the scene about to take place. We learn from their exchange that the "brothers"—an ironic description of the new accord between Pompey, Caesar, Antony, Lepidus—are part-ing. Pompey is already gone (back to Sicily) and Antony is preparing to leave for Athens. "Octavia weeps/ To part from Rome;" Enobarbus says, and "Caesar is sad." However, they direct most of their sarcasm at Lepidus, who "since Pompey's feast . . . is troubled with the green-sickness." (Green-sickness was a kind of anaemia believed to affect love-sick young girls. Here it may be used sarcastically to describe Lepidus who is "in love" with Caesar and Antony.) They mimic Lepidus' fawn-ing adulation of his two partners: "O, how he loves Caesar!" But how dearly he adores Mark Antony!" If Caesar is "the Jupiter of men," then Antony is "the god of Jupiter." (Jupiter was father of the gods; high praise indeed to be god of Jupiter.) If Caesar is "the nonpareil" or utterly incomparable, then Antony is the "Arabian bird!" (The phoenix bird, a fabled creature, only one of which existed at any time.) And so on. Lepidus plies "them both with excellent praises," yet can praise neither enough. "Hoo! hearts, tongues, figures, scribes, bards, poets, cannot/ Think, speak, cast, write, sing, number, hoo,/ His love to Antony," Enobarbus paro-dies the sonneteers.

COMMENT: This device—a compound subject paral-leled by a compound verb, each of the latter appropriate to one of the former—was characteristic of some Elizabethan sonneteers. Since sonnets were often love-poems of ex-travagant praise, Enobarbus indirectly compares the infatu-ated Lepidus with one of these love-sick sonneteers.

Their fun is interrupted by a signal for Enobarbus to mount, and they exchange farewells.

COMMENT: Although the cues are unmistakable, the two evidently do not part and leave the stage here because they are present during the rest of the scene and make comments upon it (see l. 51 ff.).

Perhaps they are about to leave but are detained by the entrance of Caesar, Antony, Lepidus, and Octavia. These four have come, like Enobarbus and Agrippa, to say goodbye. But the light note of wit and banter changes now to one of sadness as brother and sister take their leave. Caesar gives each a final admonition: to his sister to "prove such a wife as my thoughts make thee"; to Antony to "let not the piece of virtue which is set/ Betwixt us, as the cement of our love/ To keep it builded, be the ram to batter/ The fortress of it . . ."

COMMENT: Of course, this is just what Enobarbus pre-dicted earlier (Act 2, Scene 6), and what will actually occur later (Act 3, Scene 6).

Antony's back goes up at this advice, and he protests that Caesar has no grounds for such a fear. When Caesar turns to Octavia for a last goodbye, the tears start from his sister's eyes. She is so broken up emotionally, "her tongue will not obey her heart, nor can/ Her heart inform her tongue," and she must whisper her goodbyes in Caesar's ear.

COMMENT: Antony compares her to "the swan's down feather/ That stands upon the swell at the full tide,/ And neither way inclines." Torn between brother and husband, like a feather between tides, she can go neither way.

Here Enobarbus is so surprised by any show of tender emotion in Caesar that he questions Agrippa aside, "Will Caesar weep?" (Obviously they have not left the stage; furthermore, their presence is unknown to the others.) Agrippa believes he may, because "He has a cloud in his face." Enobarbus replies that a cloud in the face is a bad sign in a horse and in a man as well.

COMMENT: Agrippa uses the cloud as a metaphor: as a cloud brings rain, so the sadness in Caesar's face will bring tears. Enobarbus uses a different metaphor. A "cloud" in a horse's face refers to some marking (perhaps the absence of a white star) regarded as a blemish. So Enobarbus regards tears or any soft emotion as a blemish in a man, and particularly in Caesar.

ANTONY AND CLEOPATRA **19**

Agrippa disagrees and accuses Antony of similar softness. (Enobarbus is almost taunting Agrippa with Caesar's tender youth; Agrippa cites Antony because he is old and battle-hardened.) Did he not weep when he found Julius Caesar dead, and when he found Brutus slain after Phillipi? But Enobarbus cynically dismisses Antony's tears as hypocritical—so much water, "a rheum." He wept over sorrow that he himself had caused; he wept until even the cynical Enobarbus wept with him. The two interlopers retire again to the background; Antony and Caesar embrace; Octavia bestows a final parting kiss on her brother and, trumpets sounding, the newlyweds start on their journey.

SUMMARY: The main purpose of this scene is to dramatize the close bond of affection between Caesar and his sister, so that this love may motivate him later in the play. We also see in what contempt Lepidus is held for fawning over his betters to keep in their good graces.

Act III: Scene iii

Back in Alexandria we find Cleopatra where we left her in Act 2, Scene 5, although considerable time has elapsed. Recovered from her original shock and despair at Antony's marriage, she summons the messenger again before her to learn more about Antony's new wife. Naturally he is terrified and reluctant to appear, but the queen is in good humor and soon puts him sufficiently at his ease. When she is sure he has actually seen Octavia with his own eyes, she pumps him for information about her appearance. "Is she as tall as me?" she asks, and learns she is not. "Didst hear her speak?" she asks; "Is she shrill-tongu'd or low?" "She is low-voic'd," the boy replies, and Cleopatra reflects, "That's not so good: he cannot like her long."

COMMENT: There are two interpretations of this line. Cleopatra thinks:

1. A low voice is unpleasant: therefore Antony cannot like Octavia long.

2. That piece of news about Octavia is not so good (so far as Cleopatra is concerned): Nevertheless, Antony cannot like her long. The first is supported by what comes immediately after (l. 16) and by the absence of a conjunction after the colon: we would usually read it as "therefore."

The second is supported by the meanings of the words themselves. Octavia's low voice would certainly be more attractive to Antony than a shrill one (compare Act 1, Scene 1, Line 32). Hence this piece of news is discouraging to Cleopatra.

Charmian is quick to agree with her queen, and that little bit of encouragement is all she needs. Cleopatra wants desperately to believe the worst reports about her rival, so wishful thinking soon turns all Octavia's felicities to faults. Her soothing voice and petiteness become "dull of tongue, and dwarfish." Heartened by her "discovery," Cleopatra moves onto surer ground with "What majesty is in her gait?" and adds the naked threat, "Remember if e'er thou look'dst on majesty." The messenger takes the hint, falls in with Cleopatra's self-deception. "She creeps," he answers, and from now on his enthusiasm for the game will feed hers. "He's very knowing," she says, "The fellow has good judgment," because he has told her what she wants to hear. So when she asks him how old Octavia is, he starts by saying, "She was a widow," because that will soften the fact that she is considerably younger than the aging Cleopatra. When he admits that Octavia is thirty, Cleopatra does not even acknowledge it but rushes on to question him about Octavia's looks. Is her face long or round, she asks, and of course he replies, "Round, even to faultiness." Not only is she moon-faced, which signifies foolishness, but her forehead is extremely low as well.

COMMENT: In Shakespeare's time a low forehead was considered a mark of ugliness. Physiognomy (a pseudo-science which claimed to evaluate character from the facial features) taught that a round head and face denoted a foolish person. Compare the picture of Octavia which emerges from this interview with that drawn by Agrippa earlier, in Act 2, Scene 2, which is based on Plutarch, and with what Octavia shows of herself in the play. The noblewoman—sister and wife to emperors—whose virtue, graces, and beauty make her a match for "the best of men"; and who demonstrates her honesty and loyalty toward both husband and brother later in the play (Act 3, Scene 4 and Scene 6); is travestied in Cleopatra's jealous eyes as dwarfish, dull of tongue, creepy, lifeless, aging, with a round face that bespeaks a foolish wit, and with a treacherously low forehead. Love's self-delusions are made to appear very amusing in this scene.

Charmian, out of pity for her queen and happy to see her happy, continues to flatter Cleopatra's mood, after the messenger leaves with a handful of gold for having been so obliging. She agrees that Octavia is nothing to lose sleep over and that the messenger's report is to be trusted. "The man hath seen some majesty," Cleopatra vaunts of herself, "and should know." Charmian agrees, a little too effusively, and leads her mistress off to write letters to Antony.

SUMMARY: Still nothing new in Alexandria to further the story. Shakespeare fills out his portrait of Cleopatra in yet another of her moods.

Act III: Scenes iv & v

Antony and Octavia have arrived in Athens. Already the rift between the two Emperors has begun to widen, and Octavia finds herself left in the breach. The scene opens in the middle of their conversation. Evidently Octavia has been defending her brother against Antony's charges, but has been fighting a losing battle. Now he raises his bitterest complaint. Caesar (1) has waged new wars against Pompey in violation of their agreement; (2) has made his will and read it; (3) has attacked Antony's honor and reputation indirectly by speaking grudgingly of him.

COMMENT: The second complaint is pointless on the face of it. What offense would Caesar give Antony by publishing his own will? But Plutarch tells us that it was Antony's will that Caesar got hold of by force and read aloud to the Senators to discredit his partner. Since it is unlikely that Shakespeare would depart from his source on so crucial a point, we must assume a corruption in the text.

Octavia defends her brother by claiming that perhaps these reports are not all true, or if true, perhaps not as offensive as they sound. She laments her position in the quarrel, abandoned between the two, her love and prayers equally divided. Antony woos her to his side of the quarrel, telling her that if Caesar succeeds in destroying his reputation she would as well be not married at all as married to him. He will be like a great tree left branchless. But he urges her to mediate between them as she has requested, and informs her that in the meantime he is raising an army which will eclipse her brother's. Scene 5 also takes place in Antony's house in Athens. When these two leave, Enobarbus and Eros come on to gossip about the latest news. They disclose that Caesar, after joining with Lepidus to defeat Pompey, turned on his erstwhile partner and denied him an equal share of the victory. Besides this, under the pretext of some "treasonous" letters which Lepidus had formerly written to Pompey, and with no other proof than his own accusation, he threw his former partner into jail to await execution.

COMMENT: We see now what Shakespeare's characterization of Lepidus has been moving towards. Having made the Emperor of Africa weak, inconsequential, and unstable, Shakespeare has no trouble getting rid of him, almost, as it were, behind the scenes.

Enobarbus responds to Eros's news with a flippant metaphor that pictures the world as so much food, ground between "a pair of chaps," i.e., the upper and lower jaws (Antony and Caesar). Antony has heard the news also and is upset by it, Eros reports. He is also outraged that one of his own officers has murdered Pompey.

COMMENT: After Pompey was defeated in Sicily by Caesar and Lepidus, he fled to the East, plotting against Antony's provinces. When his designs failed he was killed by Titius, one of Antony's officers, and probably at Antony's command. Here Antony is shown to reject any responsibility for it.

The backstairs gossip continues. We are informed that a great fleet has been equipped, ready to sail against Caesar. Eros finally gets around to the point of his errand: Antony wishes to speak with Enobarbus. Enobarbus shrugs the message off: the meeting will be pointless. Then he asks Eros to lead him to Antony, and the two go off.

SUMMARY: These two scenes mainly serve to bring us up to date on what has been happening among the Triumvirate. We learn that:

1. Antony and Caesar have had a falling out and Octavia has gone back to Rome to try to patch it up.

2. Caesar and Lepidus have attacked and defeated Pompey, despite their treaty of peace.

3. Pompey is dead, murdered in the East by one of Antony's lieutenants.

4. Caesar has jailed Lepidus on trumped-up charges and plans to execute him.

5. Antony has readied a great fleet to sail against Caesar at any moment.

Act III: Scene vi

As Scene 4 opened in the middle of Antony's denunciation of Caesar, this scene, back in Rome, finds Caesar denouncing Antony before his two advisers, Agrippa and Maecenas. He immediately reveals a new development in the story: Antony has left Athens a while before and has gone to Alexandria—to his mistress there.

COMMENT: Antony must have left Athens shortly after Octavia did. His compliance in her journey to Rome can now be seen in its proper light.

In Alexandria Antony has resumed his former life in the Egyptian court and has cast further insults on Rome. Caesar enumerates them: (1) He has had, or allowed, himself and his mistress to be publicly enthroned amidst extravagant display in the market-place. (2) He has given public recognition and a place of honor to Caesarius, Cleopatra's son by Julius Caesar, and all of their own "unlawful" offspring. (3) He has conferred independence on Egypt and made Cleopatra absolute queen over it and several other conquered territories: Lower Syria, Cyprus, and Lydia (Shakespeare follows North's confusion here, giving Lydia for Plutarch's Lybia, but corrects himself later, when North does, in line 69, "Bocchus, the king of Libya"). (4) He has proclaimed his sons kings of kings. (5) He has given outright the conquered territories of Media, Parthia and Armenia to his son Alexander. (6) To his son Ptolemy he has assigned Syria, Cilicia and Phoenicia. (7) His mistress, Cleopatra, appeared that day, and often in audiences, dressed as the goddess Isis (chief Egyptian goddess; patroness of motherhood and fertility).

COMMENT: This condemnation of Antony is, of course, from the viewpoint of Imperial Rome. It is taken with few substantive changes from Plutarch and reflects his sympathy for the Roman position which strongly opposed the creation of independent kingdoms within territories conquered by the Empire. He calls Antony's division of lands "arrogant and insolent… and done in derision and contempt of the Romanes."

Caesar's advisers urge him to make these complaints public, so as to turn popular opinion, which is already "queasy," completely against Antony.

COMMENT: The people are disgusted with Antony, North says, because of his treatment of Octavia. "For her honest love and regard to her husband made every man hate him, when they saw he did so unkindly use so noble a lady…"

"The people know it" already, Caesar replies, and have even heard Antony's accusations in turn. They are: (1) That Caesar took Sicily from Pompey but did not cut him in on the spoils. (2) That he loaned Caesar some ships and never got them back. (3) That Caesar despised Lepidus, then never split his confiscated property with Antony. And Caesar in turn has answered Antony's accusations. He has told him: (1) That Lepidus was put down because he had grown too cruel and abused his high position. (2) That he is perfectly willing to give Antony a share of all the spoils he has conquered, but in return demands a share of Armenia and all the other kingdoms Antony has conquered on his own.

COMMENT: Shakespeare repeats North's account that Lepidus "did overcruelly use his authoritie." But this does not at all agree with his characterization as mild and ineffectual, which Shakespeare has given Lepidus up till now.

They realize, of course, that Antony will never agree to the conditions. Suddenly, unexpectedly, Octavia walks in on the three conversing men. Caesar is first of all shocked to see her back in Rome, then pleased, then angry. He is shocked because he had no inkling she was not still in Athens, even though Antony had left for Egypt. He is pleased to see her because of the great affection he bears for his sister: "That ever I should call thee castaway!" he gently chides her. He is angry that she should arrive so quietly, so unannounced, almost so stealthily. She, Caesar's sister, wife of Antony, "should have an army for an usher," and their marching feet should have beaten a cloud of dust "to the roof of heaven" to tell of her approach. But she has come, he chides, like "a market-maid to Rome," and in coming so quietly has prevented a mammoth welcome and demonstration of love on their part. They would have given her the red-carpet treatment.

COMMENT: Naturally there is an implied criticism of Antony's niggardliness, if not an open suggestion of it in the mention of his name. Caesar is hurt on two accounts: (1) that Antony has neglected to provide properly for his wife's journey; (2) that he himself has not been allowed to provide properly for her welcome. Apart from its place in the story and characterization, this speech of Caesar's has another function in the play. There is an obvious contrast between Octavia's arrival in Rome and Cleopatra's arrival in Tarsus, as narrated by Enobarbus in Act 2, Scene 2.

But Octavia dismisses his objections and defends her husband. She was not forced to travel thus unaccompanied, but chose to do so for swiftness' sake. Antony agreed to her journey when he heard of Caesar's war preparations. Rather to get rid of you, Caesar answers, because you stood "'tween his lust and him."

COMMENT: There are two interpretations of the line, "Which soon he granted/ Being an abstract 'tween his lust and him." One reads this as "obstruct," meaning "you (Octavia) stood between Antony and Cleopatra"; the other holds the original "abstract" refers not to Octavia, but to her absence which allows Antony to have his desire.

"Where is he now?" he tests her. And when she replies "in Athens," he breaks the news ungently to her, "No, my most wronged sister, Cleopatra/ Hath nodded him to her." "He hath given his empire/ Up to a whore," he says, and then goes on to rehearse the list of kings and kingdoms that Antony has marshalled for his war against Rome (Shakespeare's list follows closely that of North). Octavia's heart is broken by this threatened break between the emperors, for she loves both men. Caesar tries to win her to his side. He has held back from openly attacking Antony thus far, he says, until he could be sure of two things: (1) that Antony in any way abused or mistreated Octavia; (2) that his own empire was in danger of attack. Now that he has evidence of both, the break must come. But, he says, think of this war as justice, who "makes his ministers of us, and those that love you." Again he welcomes her warmly to Rome; Agrippa and Maecena join him in extending their welcome, and the scene closes for the last time on a bewildered and broken-hearted Octavia.

SUMMARY: Much is accomplished in this scene. We learn:

1. Antony has enthroned himself and Cleopatra in the public market-place in Alexandria.

2. He has created an independent Egypt and made Cleopatra its absolute queen.

3. He has parceled out other conquered territories to Cleopatra's sons.

4. He has enlisted a number of eastern kingdoms in a war against Caesar.

5. Caesar, to avenge Octavia's honor and defend his own empire, is prepared to attack Egypt and Antony.

Act III: Scene vii

This scene is set in Antony's camp near Actium (on the west coast of Greece, across the Ionian Sea from the heel of the Italian boot). Enobarbus is arguing with Cleopatra that she should not take a personal part in the battle that is brewing. She claims that since the war was declared against her, she should be there in person. Enobarbus answers with a metaphor under his breath. If they were to use both stallions and mares in battle, the stallions would be so distracted by the mares that their services would be lost altogether: "the mares would bear/ A Soldier and his horse." Cleopatra does not hear what he says, so he explains his objection aloud. Her presence, he says, will only distract Antony's attention from the battle and prevent him from doing his best. They cannot afford that now. Already in Rome they are laughed at because it is joked "that Photinus, an eunuch [Mardian] and [Cleopatra's] maids/ Manage this war." But Cleopatra disdains Rome and its rumors. She has contributed heavily to Antony's forces and she *will* be present at the battle as head of her kingdom. Enobarbus breaks off the argument as Antony enters with Canidius, one of his captains. They are discussing Caesar's rapid maneuver, by which he has already transported his armies from the southwest coast of Italy across the Ionian Sea, to take Antony by surprise at Actium. Antony decides to meet his enemy by sea. Cleopatra agrees, "By sea, what else?" but Canidius asks him why. And Antony's only answer is because "he dares us to't." So you have dared him to single combat, Enobarbus objects, "Ay, and to wage this battle at Pharsalia . . ." Canidius seconds him; but Caesar has shrugged off both dares because neither is to his advantage. "And so should you," Canidius advises. Enobarbus argues against a naval encounter for several reasons: (1) Antony's fleet is less experienced than Caesar's. Caesar's navy fought against Pompey; Antony's ships are manned by land-lubbers—captured mule drivers and farmers—pressed into service quickly to fill the need. (2) Caesar's ships are light and maneuverable, built for warfare; Antony's, mainly borrowed, are heavy and built for display. (3) Antony holds the absolute advantage over Caesar's land army, in numbers and experience, and is himself the master strategist. He sacrifices his advantages and lays himself open to chance and hazard by choosing a sea battle. Still, Antony is firm: "I'll fight by sea." And we know the real reason for his firmness when Cleopatra joins in: "I have sixty sails, Caesar none better." So, committed to a sea encounter he is ill-prepared for, Antony draws up his strategy. He will burn all the ships he cannot fully man and meet Caesar's invasion head on as it approaches the headland of Actium from Toryne. "But if we fail," he second-guesses himself, "We then can do't at land," hoping to destroy the enemy forces on the beaches. When a messenger arrives to confirm the presence of Caesar's army at Toryne, the battle is joined. Antony is dumbfounded by Caesar's swiftness, but issues orders for Canidius to command his nineteen legions and twelve thousand cavalry on the beaches while he takes to his flagship to command the fleet. But before he can leave, an old soldier comes before him to raise his seasoned voice to beg Antony to avoid a naval engagement. "Trust not to rotten planks," he begs, but all he gets for his pains is Antony's brusque "Well, well, away!" He is eager for his doom. Now the stage is left to the old soldier, who spills out his anguish to the more receptive ears of Canidius. "So our leader's led," the latter agrees, "And we are women's men," referring to Cleopatra's power over Antony. But at least they have salvaged a sizable land contingent; all may not be lost. The two soldiers exchange news; Canidius learns that Caesar's lieutenant is an old acquaintance of his, Taurus. And then their gossip is interrupted by a messenger who summons Canidius to Antony.

SUMMARY: This scene is crucial to the outcome of the play. It explains these important developments:

1. The swiftness of Caesar's naval attack and Antony's lack of preparation to meet it successfully.

2. Cleopatra's presence in the heat of the forthcoming battle (very important) and her poor advice in urging a naval encounter.

3. The unanimous opposition of Antony's soldiers to the battle, and their advice to fight on land.

4. Caesar's arrival and capture of Toryne, from whence he attacks Actium.

Act III: Scenes viii-x

These three brief scenes keep us informed of the battle's progress. In Scene 8 Caesar gives orders to his lieutenant, Taurus, leading his troops. Caesar tells him not to attack Antony on land until after the naval battle is over, and hands him a scroll containing further orders and battle plans. Scene 9 shows the same thing happening on the other side. Antony gives Enobarbus instructions where to station his troops for the coming battle so they can watch the developments at sea (and, incidentally, so that Enobarbus and Scarus will have a good vantage from which to describe the battle in the next scene). Scene 10 is the actual battle scene, but of course we do not see it directly. First, Canidius marches across the stage with a group of Antony's soldiers, then Taurus does the same with some of Caesar's, and when they are gone, the noise of a sea fight is heard off-stage. Suddenly Enobarbus rushes on stage to spread the alarm. Cleopatra's flagship, *The Antoniad*, has turned and run from the battle! And behind her, following in full retreat, fly all sixty of the Egyptian ships. He cannot believe his eyes. But there is no mistake about it. On rushes Scarus to verify the defeat. "We have kiss'd away/ Kingdoms, and provinces," he cries in despair. How does the battle look now, Enobarbus asks, and Scarus answers, "On our side, like the token'd pestilence,/ Where death is sure."

COMMENT: "The token'd pestilence" refers to a symptom of the plague. When red spots appeared on the victim it was a sure sign he would soon be dead. These spots were called "God's tokens."

Antony's defeat is sure, because when his ships were beginning to get the upper hand, that worn-out jade, Cleopatra, like a cow stung by a gad-fly in the heat of summer, hoisted a full sail to the wind and scurried off in fright. This Enobarbus already knows; but there is

worse still to come. For, seeing his mistress' ships in flight, Antony hoisted his sails and took off after her, leaving the battle at its very height, and still undecided. "I never saw action of such shame," Scarus adds.

COMMENT: Both Romans take this as an evil sign of Cleopatra's magic power over Antony, who now has violated even his code as a soldier.

Canidius enters, full of the tragic news, and complains bitterly that the defeat is all Antony's fault. He echoes Scarus's opinion that Antony is not himself, hinting that Cleopatra holds some magic power over him. And Canidius adds, "O! he has given example for our flight . . ." He intends to surrender his legions of soldiers and cavalry to Caesar. Already six other kings have done the same and fled to the Peloponnesus. Scarus has half a mind to join him; but he decides to wait and see what will happen. Enobarbus decides against his better judgment to stick by Antony.

SUMMARY: These three scenes describing the battle produce three important developments:

1. Antony loses the naval encounter with Caesar because Cleopatra ups sail and runs, for no reason, and he follows behind her.

2. Antony's comrades no longer trust his leadership. They believe he is under Cleopatra's evil influence, and have begun to go over to the enemy side.

3. Canidius decides to turn against Antony; Scarus wants to, but decides to wait; Enobarbus, against his better judgment, still sticks by his foundering lord.

Act III: Scene xi

Some days have passed since the defeat at Actium. We find Antony back in Cleopatra's palace in Alexandria. He is off by himself, moody and crest-fallen over his cowardly performance. Only a few attendants are with him, and even them he urges to "fly,/ And make your peace with Caesar."

He is terribly ashamed and depressed over his recent defeat; he feels his cowardly example has instructed others to do likewise. "To run, and show their shoulders"—referring to those kings who have gone over to the enemy. Evidently contemplating suicide in his despair, he urges his friends to follow the others to Caesar's ranks. He offers them gold and letters of introduction to smooth their path and make their betrayal easier. Only, he prays, "look not sad,/ Nor make replies of loathness." He begs, not commands, them to leave him to himself, for he feels he has lost all right to command. Just as he slumps to his seat in utter dejection, Cleopatra is led on by her attendants Charmian and Iras, and Antony's lieutenant, Eros. Eros has evidently brought her to try to comfort his lord. The others second his urgings. But despite them, the two estranged lovers remain aloof at first. Antony reflects aloud how Caesar at Phillipi wore his sword merely for show, "like a dancer," while he did the actual fighting. "Yet now . . . ?" he adds wistfully. Moved by this speech and by the entreaties of her attendants, Cleopatra relents and goes to comfort him. "O, whither hast thou led me Egypt?" he addresses her, and confesses that he has been avoiding her out of shame. But she blames herself. "Forgive my fearful sails!" she begs, "I little thought/ You would have followed." You knew I would, he replies, for I was bound to you by my heart strings. You knew you had me completely in your power. Then he complains that he is reduced to grovelling before the youthful Caesar, begging favors—he who once ruled half the world. All because he loves her. "Pardon, pardon!" Cleopatra cries through her tears, overcome by sorrow. Instantly the scolding soldier is dissolved and goes to comfort his comforter. "Fall not a tear" he soothes her, for "one of them rates [is worth]/ All that is won and lost." When she is quiet again, he asks if "our schoolmaster" has come back.

COMMENT: North tells us that "our schoolmaster" is Euphronius, the tutor to Antony's children by Cleopatra. We will learn in the next scene that Antony has sent him as an ambassador to beg terms of surrender from Caesar. That he should entrust such important affairs to so lowly a messenger is a sign of how far his fortunes have fallen.

Then Antony calls for wine to lift their spirits and cries his defiance to fortune as the scene ends.

SUMMARY: This scene explains Antony's defeat at Actium and prepares us for his final defeat later. It shows:

1. That Antony, for the first time, realizes how completely he is overpowered by his love for Cleopatra and how this has caused him humiliation and defeat.

2. That Cleopatra recognizes her guilt in that defeat, but claims she intended no treachery by it.

3. How the lovers are reconciled because Antony is powerless to remove himself from Cleopatra's influence.

Act III: Scene xii

Antony mentioned "our schoolmaster" at the end of the last scene; now his reference is explained. At Caesar's camp in Egypt the schoolmaster (Euphronius)

comes before Caesar and his advisors—Agrippa, Dolabella, Thidias, and others—as Antony's ambassador to ask for terms of surrender. Dolabella takes it as a sign of Antony's weakness, who before could make his conquered kings errand boys, to send a lowly schoolteacher. The ambassador delivers his message. Antony surrenders and acknowledges Caesar as his lord in exchange for two requests: (1) That he may remain in Egypt, or if that is too much to ask, that he be allowed to live out his days as a private citizen in Athens. (2) That Cleopatra may keep the crown of Egypt for her heirs while recognizing Caesar's supremacy. Caesar turns down Antony's request outright. As for Cleopatra, he tells the messenger, she can have whatever favor she chooses on one condition: that she drive Antony out of Egypt or kill him there. The schoolmaster bows himself out to deliver his message. Then Caesar calls Thidias before him, to entrust him with an important mission.

COMMENT: Shakespeare follows North's account of Thidias' embassy to Cleopatra, but unaccountably changes the ambassador's name in doing so from Thyreus (North's version) to Thidias.

He dispatches this smooth diplomat to seduce Cleopatra away from Antony by eloquence and flattery and extravagant promises. He hopes that her marred fortunes with Antony will make her more receptive to a new lover. Caesar cautions Thidias also to observe how Antony's spirit is bearing up under his misfortunes and disgrace.

SUMMARY: A short scene, this nevertheless provides us with important information about the development of the plot:

1. Caesar denies Antony's request for asylum; he plans a fight to the finish, "give no quarter, take no quarter."

2. Caesar hopes to divide his enemy in order to conquer, by winning Cleopatra away from her disgraced lover.

Act III: Scene xiii

Gloom is thick in the halls of Cleopatra's palace. Through it Cleopatra, Enobarbus, Charmian and Iras try to see some brightness in the future. "What shall we do," the queen questions Enobarbus, and he answers bleakly, "Think, and die." But he reassures the queen that she is not to blame for the defeat at Actium; Antony is man enough and soldier enough, or should be, not to let "the itch of his affection" spoil his judgment in battle. He should have known better than to follow her ships in flight. It is the old conflict in Antony between reason and passion. Cleopatra silences him suddenly as

Antony enters, speaking loudly with his returned ambassador, Euphronius. He repeats Caesar's offer to Cleopatra: her kingdom for Antony's head. With four words she shows it is unthinkable: "That head, my lord?"

COMMENT: How much more love this simple and indirect question carries than any loud refusal or protestation!

So Antony sends the ambassador back with his refusal and a challenge to cap it. He accuses Caesar of cowardice and ineptitude: His captains win his battles for him. And he dares his brother-in-law to a duel, single combat, "sword against sword," as he leads the schoolteacher off to write it out in a letter.

COMMENT: Unlike the offer of surrender earlier, this message must bear the authority and seal of the sender because of the explosive nature of its contents.

Enobarbus shakes his head at this. Antony has lost his sense along with his sovereignty if he seriously believes Caesar will accept such a ridiculous challenge. Would ever the winner, riding high, give up his advantage and descend to fight on foot with the loser? "Caesar," he exclaims aside, "thou hast subdued/ His judgement too," A servant enters to announce a messenger from Caesar (the messenger is Thidias, dispatched by Caesar at the end of Scene 12). Cleopatra notices that he does not show any of the deference or forms of courtesy which servants are accustomed to use when they address their queen.

COMMENT: There are several such touches in this scene with which Shakespeare shows that Antony and Cleopatra, because of their disgrace, have lost prestige and authority among their own people, kings and menials alike. Notice the irony of her final words: "Admit him, sir." She addresses the servant as if he were better than he really is because he has pretended to be.

The servant's impertinence causes Enobarbus to consider again whether he should get out while there is still time. If we are loyal to a fool, he reflects, our loyalty is mere folly. But the man who can endure "To follow with allegiance a fall'n lord," conquers his conqueror "and earns a place i' the story."

COMMENT: There are two possible interpretations of these lines, depending upon the meaning of "To follow with allegiance a fall'n lord." (1) If it means merely to stick by him in defeat, then Enobarbus is saying that such selfless loyalty will win the admiration of the conqueror and secure a place of honor for the loyal soldier. (2) But it may mean to follow one's lord even to death, the normal course of suicide for the defeated in Roman times. So we speak of a soldier "fallen in battle." If the loyal soldier follows his lord even to death, he escapes the ignominy and disgrace of being captured, "and earns a place in the story." It is Antony's other lieutenant, Eros, who proves this loyalty unto death; and it is his name we remember affectionately at the end of this story.

Thidias enters on his errand of seduction. At first, Cleopatra is brusque with him. Naturally he wants to speak to her alone; but she will not dismiss her friends. So he starts by mentioning Caesar's generosity and leniency. Immediately he gives Cleopatra a ready-made excuse by saying that Caesar realizes she did not choose to consort with Antony out of love, but out of fear. Therefore, Caesar pities her frailties rather than blames them. Cleopatra falls in with the scheme. She accepts Caesar's out and denies she ever yielded her honor willingly. She was conquered by Antony. Enobarbus, overhearing their exchange is disgusted by her disloyalty, for he believes Cleopatra is turning against Antony and accepting Caesar's overtures of friendship. Outraged, he storms out to look for Antony and warn him of Cleopatra's treachery. He reflects again that Antony is like a sinking ship; even his dearest friends abandon him. With Enobarbus gone, Thidias presses his advantage. Caesar is generous as well as forgiving. If Cleopatra will quit Antony and put herself under Caesar's protection, she may have whatever she desires from him. To show her willingness, she grasps Thidias' hand and kisses it, in proxy for Caesar's feet to hear his judgment. Thidias commends her wisdom and nobility in choosing Caesar above Antony and bends to kiss her hand. As he does so, Enobarbus rushes back in with Antony just in time to witness what seems to both the emblem of her perfidy and the besmirching of her honor. Antony is furious: The storm breaks.

COMMENT: It is important that we are not taken in by Cleopatra's act as Thidias and Enobarbus and Antony are. We must never doubt Cleopatra's love and loyalty to Antony for an instant: we shall have ample proof of both at the end.

But Antony has seen just enough to convince him of the opposite. He berates Thidias severely as a "kite," but does not yell at Cleopatra in public, while any underlings are in the room. Then he sends Caesar's personal emissary out to be whipped like a common hoodlum because he dared to grow too familiar with Cleopatra's hand.

COMMENT: The term "Jack" was used contemptuously to mean a common rascal. It was such a common name in England that it came to be used in a number of epithets: "Jack the Journeyman"; "Jacks of all trades"; "Jack in office"; "Jack," or "knave," of "hearts" (playing cards), etc.

When the servants have dragged Thidias off, Antony turns on Cleopatra. He reflects bitterly on all that he has given up for her sake: his place in Rome; his wife Octavia, a "gem of women"; and the lawful children she would have borne him. And for what? To be made ridiculous by a queen who flirts with her servants! He shouts over her protests; he accuses her of always having been shifty and calculating, but says his better judgment has been so blinded by his passion that he has adored her for the very tricks and wiles by which she has deceived him. His anger rages like a fire: what he says, instead of damping it, feeds it. He dredges up old grievances against her: he picked her up after she had been dirtied and dropped by others. "I found you as a morsel, cold upon/ Dead Caesar's trencher: nay, you were a fragment/ Of Gnaeus Pompey's . . ." (Remember Cleopatra boasted of her youthful conquests in Act I, Scene 5). She does not know the meaning of chastity, he says. While she can only ask in bewilderment, "Wherefore is this?"—what have I done to deserve this? Antony does not mention what Enobarbus must have told him, only accuses her of what he has actually seen: letting a lackey, an errand boy, kiss her hand. But he feels like a cuckold.

COMMENT: We know there must be more to it than this: these are the actions of a desperate man. Thidias is no common "fellow"; he is Caesar's accomplished ambassador. But Antony finds himself deserted now by those he has trusted; he has lost his authority and prestige. The slightest hint of Cleopatra's infidelity can throw him into a rage of despair. Thus his reference to "the horned herd" on the "hill of Bason." Bason is a hill cited in the Old Testament (Psalms 22: 12; 68: 15) for its height and for the number of oxen on it. He thinks of himself as the greatest cuckold in the world, because he would "outroar the horned heads." This refers to a popular joke in which a man whose wife was unfaithful was said to grow cuckold's horns.

Feeling so wretched and betrayed, he cannot speak civily to her who caused it any more than a condemned man can thank the hangman for being handy with his noose. A servant interrupts the violent scene, bringing in Thidias who has been soundly whipped. Antony sends him back to Caesar to make his report and insultingly tells his rival to whip, or hang, or torture Hipparchusg one of Antony's freed slaves in exchange.

COMMENT: North tells us that in abandoning Hipparchus thus to Caesar's mercies, Antony was not condemning an innocent man but "the first of all his infranchised bondmen that revolted from him, and yielded unto Caesar...."

When they are gone, he turns back to Cleopatra, but the fire has died down now. He can reflect that, as our heavenly moon's eclipses portend disasters on earth, so the change in Cleopatra, his earthly moon, "portends alone/ The fall of Antony!" She is all patience, waiting for the fire of his anger to burn itself out. When it has died, she reassures him. If her heart is cold toward him, she swears, let it freeze into hailstones of poison and the first of these kill her slowly as it dissolves; and the second her cherished son Caesarion; and so on till all her children and the people of Egypt be dead and covered with flies. "I am satisfied," he says as she finishes. And with his restored faith comes back some of the old optimism and bounce: "There's hope in't yet," for him. But though his army is pretty much intact and his navy back in shape, he knows he will be battling against odds, so he will give no quarter on the battlefield. And since it may be his last night alive he determines to make it a gaudy, festive one. It is Cleopatra's birthday and they will celebrate it without stint, as in earlier, better times. Off they go, Antony bluffly boasting that next time he fights, he will deal death like the plague itself. Enobarbus remains behind; this scene has decided him. Hesitant before how to act, now he sees his path clear before him. Antony's optimism, he feels, is unwarranted; his courage, foolhardy, "In that mood/ The dove will pack at the estridge [hawk]." He can foresee only doom in Antony's action, for it is based on passion rather than reason. So Enobarbus follows the council of prudence and makes his decision: "I will seek/. Some way to leave him."

COMMENT: Enobarbus is a hard-headed realist and judges Antony from that point of view. "When valour preys on reason," he says proverbially, "it eats the sword it fights with." In other words, Antony is still torn between what his reason tells him is the wise thing to do and what his passions insist he must do regardless. Prudence or reason should tell him not to fight, at least until his forces are stronger; but his proud heart makes him foolhardy.

SUMMARY: This scene is eventful and rich in characterization. The important events that it chronicles are these:

1. Antony, in desperation, tries to salvage some of the old bravado by challenging Caesar to personal combat and by mistreating his ambassador.

2. Thidias attempts to seduce Cleopatra to Caesar's side, but fails.

3. Cleopatra's deception of Thidias arouses Antony's first suspicions of her disloyalty.

The atmosphere throughout Cleopatra's court is one of defeat and disillusion. Antony is desperate, strikes out wildly because he has lost control of the situation, flails like a groggy boxer. He sees his vast power melting away to a few friends, and even they are no longer to be trusted. Though he manages to hold on and even to come back at the end of this round, he will not survive the next. So Enobarbus, watching his master's dissolution, decides to join the traitors who have already gone over to Caesar. But though he sees clearly Antony being torn apart by the tug of war between reason and passion, he does not realize that a similar war is raging in himself.

Act IV: Scene i

Caesar, with Agrippa and Maecenas, receives Antony's letter of challenge in his camp and laughs it to scorn. Maecenas estimates Antony's anger to be desperation and urges Caesar to attack his enemy in the heat of it. Caesar concurs that the time is ripe; with so many deserters from Antony's ranks he feels he can win at the odds. He orders a huge celebration feast.

Act IV: Scene ii

Antony and his confidants receive Caesar's rebuke. Antony seems honestly perplexed by Caesar's refusal of a duel. Enobarbus explains that his advantage is in numbers, and Antony replies that he will beat him in open battle, too. Then he asks his most loyal lieutenant, "Woo't [Wilt] thou fight well," and Enobarbus says, "I'll strike and cry 'Take all."

COMMENT: Enobarbus means he will fight to the death, winner take all. The irony of his staunchness is that he plans to be fighting on Caesar's side against Antony.

Antony is pleased by his response and calls for the feast to celebrate Cleopatra's birthday. As his servants answer his summons, he takes each by the hand in what seems a farewell embrace. Cleopatra wonders at it; Enobarbus attributes it to his sorrow. Antony grows maudlin, asking his servants to tend him well at that night's feast for it may be the last time they serve him at all. He may be wounded or killed in tomorrow's battle. So he speaks to them as one who says goodbye,

and asks them to tend him in the same spirit. The servants are discomforted by these remarks; they grow uneasy and start to weep, and even Enobarbus says through his tears, "for shame,/ Transform us not to women." This jostles Antony out of his mood; bluff and confident again, he disclaims any sadness. "For I spake to you for your comfort," he says. He hopes well for tomorrow, he claims, for victory not death, and on that rising note bids them to supper and to drink.

Act IV: Scene iii

This is another short prelude to the battle that is brewing. A company of Antony's soldiers, standing guard before the palace, are frightened in the middle of their watch by strange music under the earth. At first, they do not know what it signifies, but one of them says it bodes no good. He interprets it to mean that Antony's patron god, Hercules, is leaving him.

COMMENT: Hercules is a mythological figure famous for his size, strength, and manliness. He is Antony's patron.

They are much agitated and disturbed by this explanation and confer with some other soldiers who also marvel at its strangeness. Then they all cautiously follow to investigate its source.

COMMENT: Indeed "'tis strange," as one of the soldiers observes. But men and particularly soldiers have at all times and in all places been superstitious and had the natural desire to know ahead of time the outcome of the next day's battle. Such prodigies and prophesies occur frequently in Shakespeare's plays, especially before battles. Compare, for instance, Richard III's visions before Bosworth Field and Brutus's before Phillipi. Here the unnatural music is an evil omen of eventual defeat for Antony's forces.

Act IV: Scene iv

The night is no more peaceful inside the palace. Antony, anxious for the dawn, cannot sleep. He rises early and calls for Eros to help him put on his armour. When Cleopatra cannot coax him back to bed, she goes to help him dress. But she does not understand the complicated contraption and fumbles with the buckles. Good-naturedly he puts her off; it is not for his body she provides the strength, but for his heart. But she insists on taking a hand, so he shows her the proper way to do it.

COMMENT: The elaborate armor plate is an anachronism. Shakespeare substitutes the Elizabethan full suit of iron for the simple breastplate and greaves of the Romans. What is most touching in the scene is Cleopatra's simplicity. She is no more the queen; she is an anxious wife, fearful for her soldier husband as he leaves for war. And Antony's jovial attempts to cheer her seem forced.

When she succeeds with the stubborn buckle, he half-seriously complains to Eros that his queen makes a defter squire than he. He tries to reassure her about the coming battle. A soldier enters, armed, to fetch the general; and Antony warms to his day's task. The men are ready; trumpets flourish. On come the captains and soldiers; they greet their general. He finishes donning his armour; it is time to go. He turns a moment to say goodbye to Cleopatra. No formal farewell; no "mechanic compliment." With a brief "soldier's kiss" he leaves her "like a man of steel." Then he bids her that gentlest of goodbyes: "Adieu." She turns to Charmian; "he goes forth gallantly," she says and is sure that were he to fight Caesar alone, he would win. "But now . . .?" she worries, as she leaves the scene.

Act IV: Scene v

Trumpets sound through Antony's busy camp. He greets the old soldier who advised him against a naval engagement at Actium (Act 3, Scene 7). Antony regrets not having taken that advice. The soldier reveals that one more has deserted from Antony's ranks: Enobarbus. The general is dumbfounded. Although Eros claims his property and gear are still in camp, the old soldier insists that he has fled. Antony's reaction is surprising. He does not blame his lieutenant, but himself: "O, my fortunes have/ Corrupted honest men." He asks Eros to write a letter to Enobarbus saying "that I wish he never find more cause/ To change a master." Then he sends it along with Enobarbus's abandoned treasure, after him.

Act IV: Scene vi

Caesar's camp is no less busy; no fewer trumpets flourish. Caesar enters with Agrippa and Dolabella and the deserter Enobarbus. Caesar gives orders to his troops to take Antony alive. He foresees victory that day and following it a period of universal peace.

COMMENT: In fact, after the civil wars the Roman Empire was united under Augustus Caesar for an unprecedented period of world peace called the Pax Romana, or Roman Peace.

A messenger announces the arrival of Antony in the field. Caesar gives his battle plan. He orders Agrippa to place all those who have come over from Antony's army in the front ranks so that he will be confused and seem to destroy his own men. They leave Enobarbus alone on stage. He ponders the fate of the others who have deserted to Caesar's side.

COMMENT: These second thoughts are no doubt natural enough but seem to be brought on by Caesar's battle plan. He is, in effect, using the deserters as so much cushion to absorb the shock of the attack.

Alexas, sent by Antony to confer with Herod, betrayed his master and persuaded the Jewish king to join him, in Caesar's service; and for this Caesar hanged him. Canidius and the rest of the deserters have been given tasks but no trust. "I have done ill," Enobarbus concludes of his betrayal; "I will joy no more." At this moment of moral crisis, he hears that a messenger has arrived with his abandoned treasure and equipment, bearing Antony's farewell note and a bounty besides. Enobarbus thinks he is being mocked at first, but then he is plunged even further into dejection. He contrasts the kindness and generosity with which Antony repays his own treachery, and his heart swells almost to bursting with the thought. "If swift thought break it not, a swifter mean/ Shall outstrike thought," Enobarbus vows, but feels sure that "thought will do't."

COMMENT: The depression into which Enobarbus sinks is suicidal. Here he vows that if he does not die naturally of a broken heart, his "swifter mean," his sword, will do it surely.

Act IV: Scene vii

The stage now represents the battlefield between the two camps, contended for by both armies. First a contingent of Caesar's troops, commanded by Agrippa, retreats across the stage. The battle is not going well for them. Then Antony helps the wounded Scarus to cover.

COMMENT: We are a little surprised to find Scarus still with Antony. It was he who, after the first defeat at Actium, had almost decided to quit his foundering lord, and along with Canidius go over to Caesar's side (Act 3, Scene 10). Here he has fought valiantly for Antony.

Though concerned over Scarus's wounds, the men are able to joke about their victory, Scarus says that his wound "was like a T,/ But now 'tis made an H."

COMMENT: Another cut has been added across the bottom of the T to make an H sideways (I). There also may be a pun on the pronunciation of "H", ("aitch"), which in Shakespeare's time was closer to "ache."

"We'll beat 'em into the bench-holes," Scarus boasts.

COMMENT: "Bench-holes" refers to the seat holes in privies or outhouses. "I have yet/ Room for six scotches more," does not refer to his drinking capacity, but to his ability to endure wounds.

Eros comes on to rally them after the retreating foe as the scene closes.

Act IV: Scene viii

The battle is over; Antony's formations return victorious to their camp under the walls of Alexandria. Antony congratulates them and gives them encouragement for the next day's battle, when they will annihilate the enemy. They have fought like Hectors, he compliments them.

COMMENT: Hector was the hero who defended Troy against the Greeks in Homer's *Iliad*.

Cleopatra rushes on to greet her victorious husband. He addresses her as "Thou day o' the world," and sweeps her into his embrace, harnessed in iron though he is. "Leap thou," he commands her, "to my heart ...." His high spirits spill over into jokes about his age and prowess, and he even offers to Scarus's lips the hand he was so jealous of the day before. He orders his men back into formation; calls to the trumpeters for a flourish, and a roll from the drums, and marches his army off in triumph through the city.

Act IV: Scene ix

The triumphal clamor of Antony's camp dies into the gloomy watchfulness of Caesar's. A group of sentries on the outskirts of the camp come upon Enobarbus spilling the last torment of despair from his soul. He calls upon the moon—"the sovereign mistress of true melancholy"—to witness his remorse for having betrayed his beloved lord. He wishes that the damp night air will poison him and be his death, a punishment for his infamous revolt against Antony.

COMMENT: Enobarbus calls the moon "mistress of true melancholy" because it was once generally thought to cause mental disorders or lunacy—from the Latin word for moon, luna. It was also believed that at night the moon, like a sponge, sucked up the dew from the earth, into a miasma or poisonous vapor which caused disease. In his guilt and despair Enobarbus begs the moon to "disponge" this poison on him.

Then begging Antony's forgiveness, he dies of a broken heart with his friend's name upon his lips. The watchmen of the guard, approaching to question him, are puzzled to find him dead. Suddenly they hear reveille mustering the troops; it is the signal that their tour of duty is over. They carry the dead man off to the guard-room.

COMMENT: It is ironical that Enobarbus, the hard-headed realist, should die so sentimentally, by moonlight from a broken heart. The irony points up a basic conflict in Enobarbus' character; he is a soft-hearted cynic.

Act IV: Scenes x-xii

Again we are on the battlefield between the two camps. A new day is breaking; the generals draw up their battleplans. First Antony and Scarus march across with their army. Antony says that Caesar, frightened to meet him again on land after yesterday's defeat, prepares for a naval engagement. Antony orders his foot-soldiers to take up positions on the hills commanding the city, from which they can follow the progress of the sea battle. His ships have already put to sea.

COMMENT: Line 7 is usually construed as incomplete; the passage does not seem to make complete sense. But if "order for sea is given,/ They have put forth the haven," is put in parentheses, then "where," line 8, can refer to "hills" and some sense be made of it. "On foot" in this case refers most probably to the foot-soldiers actually with them.

When they have gone to find their vantage point, Caesar leads his army on. He resolves that, unless he is attacked on land, he will depend that day on his seapower to win the advantage. With Antony already in command of the hills, he orders his soldiers into the valleys. When they have gone, the stage remains empty for a few moments, while an alarm, "as at a sea-fight," rises in the distance and then dies down again. When all is quiet once more, Antony comes on with Scarus.

COMMENT: The sea-battle has been joined, but Antony and Scarus are so far inland and so busy looking for a place from which to watch it, that they are unaware of the noise.

Antony spots a good vantage point further up by a tall pine tree and leaves Scarus alone on stage while he goes off to observe the battle. When he is alone, Scarus reveals that all is not well; he expects disaster that day, for "swallows have built/ In Cleopatra's sails their nests," and that is an evil omen. Although the augurers (soothsayers who could predict the future from signs and omens) say they do not know what this means, they show by their grim looks and their silence that it bodes no good. Antony too is moody, shifting unsteadily from hope to fear, from courage to dejection. Scarus's soliloquy is interrupted by a frantic Antony: "All is lost," he exclaims, and immediately accuses Cleopatra of betraying him. For his men, when they had sailed out of the harbor, instead of attacking the enemy fleet joined them, surrendered themselves, tossed their caps in the air and caroused together "like friends long lost." Antony's defeat is complete; he gives over utterly to thoughts of despair and death. But he promises to get even with the "triple-turn'd whore" who has sold him out "to this novice," as he contemptuously refers to Caesar.

COMMENT: Antony is accusing Cleopatra of being unfaithful three times: (1) She went from Julius Caesar to Gnaeus Pompey; (2) from Pompey to Antony; (3) and now from Antony to Octavius Caesar.

He cares for nothing now—loyalty, friends, nothing—but revenging himself on the enchantress who has cast her charm over him; and then his own death, for he no longer wants to live. The friends (or rather those he thought were friends, and Cleopatra chief among them) who were as slavishly devoted as spaniels to him when he was master, now abandon him: to "melt their sweets on blossoming Caesar." He is like a great pine tree that once towered over the forest and now is stripped of its bark and branches and left to decay.

COMMENT: Antony falls because his friends leave him. Their betrayal is both cause and characteristic of his downfall; the play's action and characters and imagery are based upon it. There are many betrayals, from those whose allegiance is prompted merely by political advantage to those whose loyalty and devotion are almost their only reason for existing. Conquered kings leave Antony after the first defeat; then closer supporters like Canidius; finally, the closest, most trusted of all: Enobarbus. This is at the very core of that soldier's character (he sees it plainly in Antony, but not in himself): the conflict between his head and his heart, between the counsels of prudence and the ties of affection. So the action of the play is finally decided by the mass surrender of Antony's mutinous navy, without a sword bared to fight. And finally, Antony's doubt of Cleopatra's loyalty and his fear that she has sold him out to Caesar bring on the tragic events which end the play: his suicide and hers shortly following. This idea of Antony's being stripped of his followers and friends as his fortunes decline is expressed in the imagery of the play also. Many times he refers to the treachery of those who have revolted. In the very first act, both he and Caesar speak of the fickleness of the common people's love for their leaders. Once Antony compared his lost honor to a great tree left branchless (Act 3, Scene 4). Here again, in his ultimate dishonor he speaks of himself as stripped of his bark and branches; the "friends" of his better days like spaniels have followed their fortunes to Caesar's camp. There is a kind of raw justice in his thus being abandoned; for his first and overriding fault was to abandon his own world—Rome and its values, his family and friends—for Cleopatra's sake. The wheel of fortune has come full turn.

Again he blames "this false soul of Egypt," this "right gipsy," who has cheated and beguiled him.

COMMENT: "Gipsy" is a play on the original meaning of the word. The name was derived from a corruption of the word "Egyptian," since gipsies were thought in medieval times to come from Egypt. A gipsy was also commonly thought of as a cheat. "Fast and loose" is the proverbial name for a cheating game, or trickery.

He calls for his faithful lieutenant; but Cleopatra answers his call. He is repulsed by the sight of her, but she does not understand his anger. In a torment of rage he sweeps over her, drowning her in abuse. Let Caesar take her back to Rome in his triumphal procession, a shameful mockery, a whore, to be displayed like a monster in a cage. Let Octavia have her for awhile to dull her nails on Cleopatra's face. The frightened queen runs before this wave of hatred which threatens to engulf her.

COMMENT: Antony seems uncertain as to what would be his best revenge on Cleopatra. He can kill her outright, as it almost seems at times he must do, swept to it by his rage. But in other, cooler moments he thinks the sharper pain would be to abandon her to Caesar and let her be degraded as his captive—which would be not one, but many deaths.

She is gone, but he cannot reconcile himself. The rage upon him is like Nessus' legendary shirt of fire which tortured Hercules to his destruction.

COMMENT: To revenge a wound, Nessus, the centaur, gave Dejanira, Hercules' wife, a shirt dyed with his own blood to be used as a love charm. The shirt caused Hercules' painful death. Lichas brought the deadly garment to Hercules, and for his pains was thrown into the sea. Alcides is another name for Hercules, after his ancestor Alcaeus. It is plain that Antony thinks of himself as Hercules here.

Hercules is Antony's patron among the gods, so in his misery the defeated general prays to him for strength. Then the accumulated anger and humiliation overcome him and he swears "the witch shall die." Thus sworn, he leaves to find Eros.

SUMMARY: Of course, this is Antony's fateful scene. The second naval defeat not only undoes his victory of the day before, but the surrender of his fleet without a fight convinces him of Cleopatra's betrayal. He sees his own death by suicide clearly before him, but wants first to inflict some punishment upon Cleopatra. He is not clear at first what form his revenge will take, but after meeting her and scaring her off by his fury, he decides she must die, and goes off to find her.

Act IV: Scene xiii

Meanwhile Cleopatra is frightened for her life by Antony's furious attack. She does not understand the reasons for it, and runs to her attendants for protection. "He's more mad/ Than Telamon for his shield," she laments.

COMMENT: When the Greek champion Achilles was killed before Troy his famous shield and armor were to be given to the bravest of the Greeks. Telamon Ajax went mad from disappointment when Odysseus was chosen instead of himself. "The boar of Thessaly/ Was never so emboss'd," refers to a legendary wild boar sent in revenge by Diana, goddess of the hunt, to ravage Thessaly. "Emboss'd" probably means foaming at the mouth from exertion.

Charmian devises a plan. Cleopatra will go to the mausoleum she has already prepared for her entombment and lock herself in. Meanwhile she will send Mardian, her eunuch, to tell Antony she is dead. She does so, saying she has killed herself.

COMMENT: Cleopatra is true to her character to the end. She adds to her instructions to Mardian: "And bring me how he takes my death to the monument."

Act IV: Scene xiv

Back in Cleopatra's palace, empty now but for Eros and himself, Antony's passion has subsided. His dejection is still profound—he will not come out of it again—but he is more reflective than furious now. He opens his conversation with a strange question: "Eros, thou yet behold'st me?" "Ay, noble lord," his bewildered friend replies. Antony is comparing himself and his fortunes to clouds that race across the evening sky. As we watch, the clouds assume various shapes, one looks like a dragon, another like a bear, a lion, a turreted castle, a cliff; a mountain, "a blue promontory with trees upon't."

The clouds no sooner take a shape—say, a horse—when they dissolve again back into nothing, "as water is in water." So, the defeated Antony reflects, am I "even such a body." He too will dissolve, like so much vapor. He went to war for Egypt's queen, because he loved her and thought she loved him. He thought he had a million loyal friends: all gone, dissolved. She has dealt from a stacked deck and played his cards into Caesar's hand. Now he is trumped. But, he comforts the weeping Eros, they still have a way out; "there is left us/ Ourselves to end ourselves." Upon this quiet scene comes Mardian with Cleopatra's false message to shock Antony back into anger. "O' thy vile lady!" he exclaims upon seeing him, "She has robb'd me of my sword."

COMMENT: Antony's "sword" here as elsewhere in the play stands for his manhood, power, all that he was before he fell in with Cleopatra.

Mardian denies it, protests his mistress's love and loyalty: he uses the past tense. Antony vows Cleopatra's death before Mardian lies that she is already dead. Not only dead, but by her own hand, and in despair for having lost Antony, with his name the last thought in her heart. When he hears this false message, all the life goes out of him. He has been living only to punish Cleopatra; now that he thinks she is dead, there is no more reason for him to go on. He starts to remove his armor, as if for sleep.

COMMENT: There is a double meaning in Antony's "Unarm, Eros, the long day's task is done and we must sleep," as he removes his armor. The sleep he refers to is not physical rest but the sleep of death. This parallel between the passage from light into dark, day into night, and the decline from life into death is repeated several times in the final scenes. It is repeated by Antony later "the torch is out"—and is picked up by Cleopatra and her maids: Act 4, Scene 15, Lines 9-10, 85; Act 5, Scene 2, Lines 80, 192-193.

Eros helps him; he cannot get it off fast enough. Finally, the uniform of his soldiery stripped, he sends Eros out with the "bruised pieces," while he prepares for death. Now he will be reconciled with his queen in that world beyond death "where souls do couch on flowers." Hand in hand they will walk like lovers so as to steal the show even from Dido and her Aeneas.

COMMENT: Dido and Aeneas are famous lovers from Book Four of Virgil's Aeneid. When Aeneas left her to sail for Italy, she killed herself. Later, visiting Avernus, the infernal regions, he saw her again with her husband, Sichaeus.

He calls Eros back into the room. Remember, he says, you have sworn, when the need should come, when death is the only alternative to disgrace and horror, you would kill me. "Do't, the time is come . . ." he commands. Eros turns pale at the thought; but Antony shows him the alternative: to see his master brought back to Rome disgraced, a captured slave behind Caesar's chariot. Again he exacts Eros's oath to kill him, and this time Eros complies. He draws his sword; he tells Antony to turn his face aside, and when he has done so Eros plunges the sword into—himself! "Thus I do escape the sorrow/ Of Antony's death," he exclaims. This is Antony's second example: Cleopatra and Eros have both shown him the way. Without more delay he draws his sword and falls on it, but the wound is not immediately fatal. A guard comes in followed by Decretas, and he begs them to finish the job. But they are all frightened to see their leader fallen, and refuse. Decretas, when the guard has fled, pulls the bloody sword from Antony's wound but not to answer his prayer. He intends instead to use it as his passport into Caesar's good graces. Diomedes enters looking for Antony. Decretas, hiding the bloody sword beneath his cloak, points to the dying man and leaves. And now, too late, Diomedes reveals that Cleopatra is not dead but locked in her monument and fearful that just this would happen as the result of her lies. With the last of his ebbing strength Antony summons his guard and as his last command bids them take him to Cleopatra. Weeping, they take him up and carry him off.

SUMMARY: In these final tragic scenes, Shakespeare's dramatic power is at its highest. This scene moves inexorably from event to event as Antony seeks his death.

1. Antony reflects on the vagaries of fortune, the dreamlike quality of a life which can change so suddenly and so drastically. He is stoically determined to end his own sufferings.

2. Mardian delivers the false message of Cleopatra's death, but does now try to persuade Antony of her innocence.

3. This knowledge frees Antony for his own death. Still thinking her guilty of betraying him, he seeks his mistress in the afterlife to beg her pardon. For he is sure of their immortality.

4. After Eros kills himself rather than bear that sword against his lord, Antony's suicide is unsuccessful. Nor will his soldiers finish it for him.

5. Decretas steals the bloody sword to show Caesar and win his friendship.

6. Dying, Antony learns from Diomedes that Cleopatra still lives and still loves him. But there is no tragic irony in this knowledge that comes too late; Antony would not have been saved. Unlike Romeo, whose suicide is similarly based on the mistaken belief that his lover is dead, Antony's doom is inevitable. All that keeps him alive is his passion to punish Cleopatra; once he believes she is beyond the reach of his revenge, he is reconciled with her again. His discovery that she still lives merely allows that reconciliation to take place on this side of the grave.

Act IV: Scene xv

Locked in her monument, Cleopatra complains to Charmian; she fears she will never leave her tomb. Charmian is attempting, unsuccessfully, to comfort her, when Diomedes returns with the dying Antony, borne by his guards. Cleopatra had feared he was dead, but how much more fearful is the reality of a dying Antony to the mere thought of a dead one. Surely the sun must burn up the heavens at this calamity and leave the world in darkness.

COMMENT: Her figure of speech is based on the Ptolemaic astronomy, which conceived of the sun as a planet whirling around a fixed earth in a hollow sphere (see above, Act 2, Scene 7). If the sphere were burnt up, the sun would fly off into space and the earth grow dark. Then the varying light and darkness of the heavens would sink into perpetual night.

Her lover's name breaks from her lips in anguish when she sees him wounded; she cries to those around her to help her lift him up into the monument. But he puts her fears at naught: it was not Caesar's hand produced this wound, but his own.

COMMENT: Cleopatra's urgency and Antony's reply seem to indicate that she is afraid Antony has been wounded by Caesar and pursued by him. He tells her he is in no danger of being captured. Later she will refuse to open the door of her mausoleum out of fear of being captured, and will insist on hauling her dying lover up to her.

"I am dying, Egypt, dying," he tells her, and begs one final kiss, but she is afraid to leave her sanctuary, lest she become Caesar's "brooch," or trophy. She has already decided to die there by knife, drugs, or, significantly, serpent. So with the help of her maids and his guards, she manages to lift Antony into the monument.

COMMENT: Cleopatra and her maids probably occupied the balcony over the Elizabethan inner stage. This was used to represent balconies, "the heavens," all high places, or to house the musicians. The women's efforts to raise Antony are extremely moving: remember that women's parts were played by young boys. Their difficulties were not pretense.

Again in his lover's arms, Antony repeats, "I am dying, Egypt, dying." "Die when thou hast lived" again, she says, brought back to life by her kisses. But he has not much strength left. He must use it to admonish her. He gives her three cautions. First, that she should not sacrifice her honor to Caesar in order to secure her safety. Second, that she should trust none of Caesar's advisers and lieutenants but Proculeius. She replies that she need not trust even him: her own hands and resolution will be enough. Third, that she ought not to mourn over his death, but glory in the nobility of his life who was "the greatest prince o' the world . . ." For he did not die basely, nor cowardly, but nobly by the hand of another Roman—"valiantly vanquished." That is all: three words of advice and he is dead in his mistress's arms: thus "the crown o' the earth doth melt." And in the almost superhuman eloquence of her grief she exclaims, "O, wither'd is the garland of the war,/ The soldier's pole is fall'n: young boys and girls/ Are level now with men: the odds is gone,/ And there is nothing left remarkable/ Beneath the visiting moon." With that she swoons.

COMMENT: "Soldier's pole" is variously interpreted according to what "pole" means. (1) If it refers to a flag or banner, it means the standard which leads them into battle. (2) If it refers to the northern pole star or lodestar, which is the constant in the compass, it means the norm by which a soldier is to be measured. This echoes the remark of the second guard in Scene 14, "The star is fall'n." "The odds is gone" means there is no standard left by which to separate the men from the boys, children from adults.

Iras is thrown into a violet agitation by her mistress's fainting spell. She calls upon her as "Royal Egypt: Empress!" until Charmian cries "Peace, peace, Iras!" Cleopatra revives saying, "No more but e'en a woman," like any, the simplest of her sex. What meaning is there left in titles or distinctions when Antony is dead? "All's but nought . . ." Patience or impatience to bear such suffering are equally meaningless. "Then is it sin," she asks herself, "To rush into the secret house of death/ Ere death come to us?"

COMMENT: The sudden and strange calmness that comes over Cleopatra in the midst of her anguish comes from her settled decision to kill herself. This will remove all of her sufferings, take her out of Caesar's hands as well, and reunite her with her love. Thus she repeats the image used earlier by Antony, "The torch is out," in Scene 14, line 46: "Our lamp is spent," she says to her waiting women, "it's out." They have but to bury Antony and die "after the high Roman fashion," i.e., by their own hands.

SUMMARY: This is recognized as one of the great death scenes in dramatic literature. Its greatness lies partly in the greatness of its characters, partly in the pathos of their love. We are not allowed to forget their greatness, though they are reduced by circumstance almost to absurdity. Analyzed coldly, the scene would be ludicrous. A man who has tried to kill himself, by mistake, and botched the job, is hauled up the side of his mistress's tomb by a bunch of her women because she is too frightened to open the door. But the characters are never allowed to become ridiculous; we do not laugh. We are reminded of who they are by Antony's calling her "Egypt" rather than Cleopatra, and by his concern that she should remember, not the miserable twilight of his career, but its blazing noon. He is jealous of honor even in death. And Cleopatra has never been more queenly than in mourning him. She is strengthened by his death much as he had been earlier by the report of hers. The calm that settles over her is accentuated by the panic of her waiting-women. She looks forward to death as he had; all else becomes meaningless. There is nothing more in life to interest her but leaving it.

Act V: Scene i

The scene shifts from the still depths of a doomed love to the efficient bustle of Caesar's camp, flushed with his recent triumph. A council of war is in progress. Caesar cockily dispatches Dolabella to demand Antony's surrender as Decretas enters, carrying the blood-stained sword of Antony. He passes himself off as Antony's loyal follower: "I wore my life/ To spend upon his haters." Now he offers his services—and his loyalty— to Caesar and promises to do the same for him: "As I was to him/ I'll be to Caesar." For, he explains, "Antony is dead." Caesar is surprised and genuinely moved. So great a catastrophe, he says, "should make a greater crack," should cause some similar catastrophe in "the round world."

COMMENT: The philosophical basis of ancient and medieval thought (and up to Shakespeare's time) about the natural world was that all objects and events, including man, were held together by bands of sympathetic magic and analogy. When some great moral evil was committed, it was thought to shake the foundations of nature, and its reverberations were felt in natural disasters. So, too, prodigies of nature were thought to presage or prophesy the fate of men. (See, for example, *Julius Caesar*, Act 1, Scene 3; or *Macbeth*, Act 2, Scene 4.)

For Antony's death is not just his personal tragedy; it alters that entire part of the world which he ruled. Caesar is saddened to hear it, and exchanges reminiscences of Antony's exploits with his advisors. "Say nothing of the dead but what is good," the Roman aphorism admonished, and their remarks are in keeping with its spirit. Agrippa reflects stoically that the gods who make men make them flawed so they will not challenge their supremacy. What makes the news specially poignant to Caesar is the knowledge that he has hounded Antony to this deed. He has cut Antony off as he would a diseased part of his body, not in despite or hatred, but to keep the sound part wholesome.

It was him or Antony; the world held not room enough for both. Then Caesar launches into a stirring eulogy of his defeated "brother," "competitor" (friendly rival), "mate in empire," "friend and companion in the front of war,/ Arm of mine own body and the heart where mine his thoughts did kindle." He blames their falling out, which has led them to this moment, on the influence of their guiding stars, doomed to opposition.

COMMENT: There is a natural bond among Shakespeare's great men, that does not hold them to men of lesser rank, the ordinary people. They can be better than most men; and when they are bad, they are always worse. But, good or bad, they remain alone, isolated by their stature like great trees. Caesar here feels this. He eulogizes Antony as once Antony eulogized the dead Brutus on the scarred field of Philippi, because he recognizes that a great man may fall from grace, but never from greatness.

Caesar abruptly breaks off his sorrowful praise of Antony to question an Egyptian messenger, sent by Cleopatra to learn of Caesar's intentions and accept his instructions. Caesar tells her not to worry: he will act honorably toward her and kindly. "For Caesar cannot live to be ungentle." Immediately he turns to Proculeius and orders him to reassure the Egyptian queen of his good intentions, "Lest, in her greatness, by some mortal stroke/ She do defeat us."

COMMENT: Caesar knows the caliber of his enemy. He reassures Cleopatra because her suicide will spoil his plans for a triumphal return to Rome. She is the trophy of this war; if he can bring her back alive his fame will be eternal.

Evidently concerned by this last thought he sends Gallus along to back up Proculeius and bids them a speedy return. Then he invites those closest to him who remain to hear the story of how and why this war came about.

SUMMARY: This scene contains two important events:
1. Caesar and his followers learn of Antony's death and lament it.
2. Caesar devises a stratagem to take Cleopatra alive. The first event puts Caesar in a favorable light; the audience has just been deeply moved by Antony's death and feels receptive to Caesar's eulogy. The tragic effect depends upon our admiration of the tragic hero. He cannot be thought of as completely evil or we will not be sorry for him. Caesar's eulogy helps make of Antony's tragic fall a truly cosmic catastrophe. But Cleopatra's sending a messenger to seek Caesar's instructions may seem puzzling. When last we saw her she was bent on death; now she seems bent on currying Caesar's favor. We will learn later that her purpose is to secure one promise from Caesar before she dies: that her son Caesarion (Octavius Caesar's half-brother) will wear the crown of Egypt after her. Caesar's reply to her puts him in a bad light. Nothing is further from the audience's sympathy at this point than his attempt to beguile her in her grief and add to her torment. It is typical of Caesar that he can move so easily and unselfconsciously from the noble sentiment to the base.

Act V: Scene ii

Just as Antony, before he commits suicide, reflects upon the insecurity of life that changes so quickly from prosperity to disaster, so Cleopatra opens the scene in which she will die. Since life is full of treacheries, hopes which are never fulfilled, misfortunes without meaning, changes for the worse—then suicide, which puts an end to all uncertainty, is a "better life." And so, she seeks "that thing that ends all other deeds": death.

COMMENT: She says that death "sleeps and never palates more the dung,/ The begger's nurse, and Caesar's." She confuses suicide with the state that it produces. In death the beggar and the emperor are equally free of the "dung" of mortal life. Compare Antony's speech in Act 1, Scene 1: "Our dungy earth alike/ Feeds beast as man . . ." in which he celebrates passionate love as that which separates men from beasts. Here, that love perished, Cleopatra seeks escape from "our dungy earth" through death. "Nurse" here means "wet-nurse," one who suckles an infant.

Proculeius breaks in upon her morbid reflections with Caesar's message. This is the man Antony told her to trust; but she has no use for him now. She asks her price: "Give me conquered Egypt for my son . . ." But her attitude toward her conqueror is hostile and aloof: she treats his messenger coldly with a "take–it–or–leave-it" tone. Though defeated, she will not give in. Proculeius tries to win her confidence. He tells her, in effect, she will catch more flies with honey than with vinegar. "Let me report to him/ Your sweet dependency," he says, and you'll find him begging you for suggestions how best to please you.

COMMENT: "Pray in aid" is a legal phrase meaning to ask for advice or assistance on some question.

She softens somewhat, shows her obedience to him, and asks to see him. Proculeius, gladdened by her change of tone, is about to deliver her request when a troop of soldiers, led by Gallus, surprises them from behind and surrounds the monument. He tells Proculeius and the soldiers to guard her till Caesar comes.

COMMENT: Now Caesar's purpose in backing Proculeius up is clear. He sends the trusted messenger to put Cleopatra off her guard and follows up with Gallus and his soldiers to catch her by surprise. He is determined to take her alive.

Immediately upon seeing the soldiers, Cleopatra's waiting women, Iras and Charmian, panic. Cleopatra is cooler-headed. She is determined not to be taken alive. She draws a concealed dagger and is about to kill herself when Proculeius lunges for her arm and manages to wrest the knife away before she can use it. He insists again that she mistakes Caesar's intentions: he means her no harm. Nor does death, she replies, that puts

injured dogs out of their misery. Proculeius's tone becomes firmer; he reprimands her for jealously trying to deny Caesar an opportunity to show his generosity. For if she is dead, to whom can he show it? But Cleopatra is distraught. Her accumulated misery breaks out in an anguished cry for death to comfort her. She will have death, she vows, if not from a dagger, then from hunger and thirst and lack of sleep. "This mortal house [her body] I'll ruin,/ Do Caesar what he can." She would prefer the vilest, most painful death to that which she could never tolerate: the mockery and censure of Rome's vulgar mobs. Dolabella, another of Caesar's diplomats, arrives to relieve Proculeius, whom Caesar wants to see. Proculeius, genuinely concerned for Cleopatra, asks if he may not deliver some message from her. "Say, I would die," she answers. When he is gone, Dolabella tries to break the ice by introducing himself as an old acquaintance. But Cleopatra could not be less inclined to social amenities. She treats him like any uncouth ruffian who will "laugh when boys and women tell their dreams . . ." For life seems like a sleep to her now, and the past all a dream, Antony a dream. "O such another sleep," she exclaims, longing for death, "that I might see/ But such another man!" This exclamation loosens a landslide of emotion; words of love and praise for her dead lord pour from her mouth around the bewildered Dolabella. He was like a constellation of stars in the heavens, she says; he was like the great Colossus bestriding the ocean; "his rear'd arm crested the world"; his voice was like the music of the heavenly spheres to those he loved, but those he hated, like "the rattling thunder." His generosity knew no barrenness of winter; he gave like an autumn harvest. Even his delights were so enormous they raised him out of the common sea of pleasure, as dolphins show their backs above the element they live in. He had kings for servants, and kingdoms and islands, were like small change "dropp'd from his pocket."

COMMENT: The picture Cleopatra imagines of Antony is of a huge giant, his head in the heavens, striding across the earth, spanning oceans, dropping islands like coins as he goes. This is what she was imagining when she complained at Antony's death: "Young boys and girls/ Are level now with men: the odds is gone. . ." Line 84, "the tuned spheres," refers to the Ptolemaic astronomy which taught that the seven spheres of the heavens were made to musical proportions like strings or reeds in an instrument, so that when they moved past each other they produced harmonious melody.

Dolabella is both perplexed and annoyed by her running on. He interrupts her several times but cannot stop her. Finally she asks him if he thinks such a dream could come true. When he says no, she protests loudly. If ever Antony lived, he was greater than her dream. Nature cannot produce men as great as we imagine them, she says, but Antony was nature's masterpiece, greater than any dream or imagination. Dolabella tries to quiet her. He tells her the greatness of her grief not only argues the greatness of her loss, but makes even him grieve deeply over Antony's death. This does quiet her; she trusts Dolabella. "Know you what Caesar means to do with me?" she asks. This puts him in an awkward position: He hates to have to tell her, but he thinks she should know. He starts by defending Caesar's honor; but she saves him embarrassment by saying it for him: "He'll lead me then in triumph." Dolabella admits she is right, as a flourish sounds announcing Caesar's arrival. With him are Proculeius, Gallus, Maecenas, and some other attendants. Caesar enters, asking, "Which is the Queen of Egypt?"

COMMENT: His question shows a certain insensibility that is part of Caesar's character. Perhaps it is due to his youth and lack of experience, perhaps to an innate lack of preception. But neither of his diplomatic errand boys, Proculeius or Dolabella, mistook Cleopatra for her maids, or doubted for an instant which of the women was the Queen of Egypt. On the other hand, Caesar is being very politic by using that title. He hopes to put her at her ease by showing her that he still considers her the Queen.

Cleopatra, playing along with his stratagem, falls to her knees in respect and obedience. He protests that she should not kneel; they are equals. He holds no grudges against her for the war, he says, though injured by it. She does not try to defend her actions or excuse them; she blames them on the frailities of her sex. Caesar reassures her of his kind intentions, if she cooperates. But if she tries to defeat him by taking Antony's course of suicide, he will destroy her children. He prepares to leave. Anxious to create a good impression, Cleopatra hands him an account of her wealth before he goes. In it are listed all the major items of her wealth: money, silver and gold plate, jewels. She summons Sileucus, her treasurer, to swear it is accurate. But he does not! He claims the account is fraudulent; she has kept back as much as she has made known. Cleopatra blushes— from shame or rage we cannot tell. But Caesar takes it in good spirit and even approves her business acumen. This does not subdue her anger. She lashes out at Seleucus as an ingrate, a slave she has raised to a position of trust, who now turns on her and curries favor with Caesar because she has been defeated by him. Seleucus recoils from her as she lunges for his eyes. Caesar comes between the two to restrain her. She turns to him, all apology and explanation. She has kept out a few trifles,

she admits, unimportant things of no value to give as presents to her common followers and servants, and a few more expensive things to win the friendship of Octavia and Livia, Caesar's wife.

COMMENT: By mentioning these women and their favor, Cleopatra cleverly deceives Caesar into believing that she desires to live and expects to see Rome. This has led some critics to believe that the whole episode with Seleucus was purposely staged for Caesar's benefit, perhaps even rehearsed. For if Cleopatra intends to commit suicide, why does she go to the trouble of giving Caesar an account of her assets and withholding some? The same question came up in the previous scene. If she is bent on death, why does Cleopatra try to curry favor with her conqueror? Perhaps the same reason holds here: for the sake of her children. But even so, her concern does not prevent her from throwing them upon Caesar's mercy when she kills herself.

But Seleucus exaggerates out of envy for her, she petulantly accuses him. He should rather have pity on me, she says, as she banishes him from her sight. For the leader is blamed for what his underlings do, and when he falls from grace he is punished for other's faults.

COMMENT: This statement is a concise theory of classical tragedy, which was supposed to inspire pity and fear in the audience by depicting the fall of a great man. It is the hero's greatness that makes him stand out as a scapegoat or sacrifice for the sins of others; and in his capacity to suffer greatly he is tragic.

Caesar tells her to put her account away; he wants none of her treasure. She continues to wrong him in estimation, he objects; he is no merchant: he will treat her as she herself dictates. "Feed and sleep," he counsels her, having in mind her threat to Proculeius earlier to starve herself. She goes to kneel once more in respect as he leaves, but he restrains her and bids her "adieu." As soon as Caesar is out of sight, Cleopatra drops the mask of meekness and subservience. She has seen through his kindness to the evil design behind it, and she rejects both in the only way left open to her.

COMMENT: Even the usually unstable Iras seems stolidly resigned to her death. "Finish, good lady," she says, "the bright day is done,/ And we are for the dark." Although this knots up one of the dominant threads of imagery in the play, it seems inconsistent for Iras to utter it. Light and dark, day and night, have been used often as emblems of life and death in the play. Antony's downfall and death is described as a passage from day into night. So this line describes a similar fate for Cleopatra and her maids. But it seems improbable that Iras understands all that when she says it. For later, after Dolabella leaves, Cleopatra goes out of her way to frighten Iras with the prospect of returning to Rome as Caesar's captives. Her reason for making the alternative so gruesome is to strengthen Iras's characteristically weak resolve to die. And Iras seems at that point to have no intention of dying. For rather than see her own dishonor she vows to put out, not her life, but her eyes.

Cleopatra whispers instructions to Charmian and sends her off on an errand.

COMMENT: She has already prepared the means of her death. Plutarch reports that she experimented with various poisons and drugs to discover the properties of each. She found that the bite of an asp brought on death with the greatest speed and least pain. It is evident in this scene that she sends Charmian past the Roman guard to fetch her the asp she already provided for her suicide.

Charmian passes Dolabella on the way out. He has come back secretly to tell her Caesar's plans. The conqueror intends to return to Rome by way of Syria. In three days he will send her and her children before him. Then this last man bows out of the life of a woman who has charmed many men.

COMMENT: The great charmer's power to win men has not diminished. When Dolabella first met her, earlier in this scene, he had to introduce himself to her. But he has been so moved by her grief and her grandeur that now he risks all to bring her Caesar's confidential plans.

Cleopatra rehearses again for Iras's sake the fate that awaits them in Rome. She reminds her servant of the vulgar rabble who will witness their disgrace, the foul breaths that will mock and jibe at them, the venal officers of the law who will snatch at them like strumpets, the dirty songs that will be sung about them. Comedians will make jokes about them, little scenes will be performed to mock them.

COMMENT: The reception she foresees in Rome is actually a description of what might happen in Shakespeare's London. The "Egyptian puppet" refers to popular Elizabethan puppet shows: the "mechanic slaves" are tradesmen with their dirty aprons and tools; the "lectors" were minor Roman officials here equated with the London "beadle," a law officer who dealt with prostitutes; hack writers composed ballads and sang them about the latest scandalous news: and the quick comedians extemporized farces in the London theatres and courtyards. The word which best betrays the scene Shakespeare is imagining is the word

"boy." Cleopatra is repelled that some boy will take part in the extempore farce. Boys took the women's parts on London stages because women were forbidden there until 1663. But this reference serves another, more important purpose, since it is a boy who, acting Cleopatra's part, squeaks this line out. Shakespeare is here purposely calling the audience's attention to this being only a play, the great queen only a boy actor. By puncturing any pretense, he makes his actors' limitations less noticeable: He strengthens his dramatic illusion by calling attention to its weakness.

With Iras now in a state of near-panic at the prospect of being taken alive to Rome, Charmian returns from her errand. She is no sooner back but Cleopatra sends her with Iras to fetch her royal robes, and her sign of office—the crown of Egypt. She wants to look as beautiful and seductive for this last meeting with Mark Antony as she had her first on the river Cydnus (Act 2, Scene 2). Now Shakespeare interrupts Cleopatra's morbid preparations with a humorous exchange, between the queen who is bent on death and a rustic clown who brings her a basket of figs in which are concealed the poisonous asps by whose bite she will die.

COMMENT: She has prepared the asps beforehand. She disguises her intent with the rural fellow and his figs in order to allay any suspicion on the part of the guards. We should read this scene after Caesar's departure as the inevitable working-out of Cleopatra's suicidal design. She is resolved to die: not even her conference with Caesar could sway her. "I am marble-constant," she says, "now the fleeting moon/ No planet is of mine." This evocation of the moon knots up the imagery of fickleness, changeability, in her character and throughout the play. She is no longer Isis, moongoddess, patronness of fertility and sex. She is now the very image of death and the tranquility it brings. Death puts an end to the vagaries and disappointments of life; after death there are no changes for the worse.

The clown gives up his burden reluctantly and with many warnings and cautions about the "worm of Nilus," the asp. He says that he heard all about how deadly and painful its bite is from a lady who had died from one. Cleopatra is rather impatient with his inane joking. She tries to get rid of him quickly. But he is either too stubborn or too stupid to take her none-too-gentle hints.

COMMENT: Shakespeare often introduces a scene of low comedy in the midst of serious, even tragic events. His reasons were probably these: (1) It relaxes the tension that might otherwise break into laughter at the wrong time. (2) It provides a sudden contrast which makes the serious events seem even more tragic.

The clown leaves, wishing the queen "joy of the worm." Charmian and Iras reenter, bearing Cleopatra's robes, royal crown, and jewels. She bids her maids attire her as for a state occasion; she is impatient at their slowness.

COMMENT: Compare the scene in which Antony commits suicide (Act 4, Scene 14). He hurries Eros to take his armor off, not put it on.

For she imagines Antony waiting for her, praising her courage, and laughing from the other side of death at the fickle "luck of Caesar." "Husband," she cries out, "I come," claiming for the first and last time in the play the sanction of that title for their guilty love. She is entitled to use it, she says, because she is willing to die for it.

COMMENT: "I am fire and air," she describes herself, "my other elements/ I give to baser life." This description of her singleminded resolve to die completes another pattern of imagery. She refers to the once popular physiology which thought of man as composed of four basic elements and their combinations, which produced the "humors." The four elements were air, fire, earth and water. The first two were light, hot, and dry; the latter were heavy, cold, and wet. Antony, in his first appearance (Act 1, Scene 1, Lines 35-36), swore his love for Cleopatra by contrasting "dungy earth" and its kingdoms with the nobility of his passion. And at the beginning of this scene (Line 7), Cleopatra spoke of death as that which frees man from dependence on "the dung" of earth. Here the two come together. Her devotion and self-sacrifice have purified her love for Antony of any dross or baseness. And so her death will free her spirit from any dependence on her body.

She gathers her faithful serving-women into a last farewell embrace. The moment is too charged with emotion for poor, fragile Iras: She dies on the spot of a broken heart. Almost playfully Cleopatra chides her; if she is the first to meet Antony beyond the grave, he will bestow on her "that kiss/ Which is my heaven to have." She takes one of the deadly snakes from the basket and pulling open her robe, applies it to her breast.

COMMENT: There are no grounds for this in North or Plutarch. There she applies the asp to her arm. But there are ample dramatic grounds for Shakespeare's alteration. Its full dramatic force is felt in her hushing Charmian: "Peace, peace!/ Dost thou not see my baby at my breast,/ that sucks the nurse asleep?"

Impatient still at the asp's slow work, she takes another and applies it to her arm. But none is needed; in the middle of a question that expects no answer, she dies. "What should I stay . . ." she begins, and Charmian finishes, "In this vile world?" Then the loyal maid closes her queen's eyes, straightens her royal crown, and applies an asp to her own arm. The guards come noisily in. When they see that "Caesar's beguiled," they call Dolabella. Just as he enters, Charmian dies. He precedes Caesar by only a moment. The conqueror and his train of followers march into a peaceful scene, not one of carnage. The queen, in full regalia, reclines on her couch, her maids dead at her feet, but nowhere a sign of blood. They seem asleep rather than dead. "She looks like sleep," the moved Caesar says, "As she would catch another Antony/ In her strong toil of grace." He wonders how death was caused; there are no usual signs of poisoning. Then Dolabella discovers the tell-tale swellings on her breast and arm, and a guard notices the trail of the asp on her skin and on the fig leaves in the basket. Caesar is resigned; "She shall be buried by her Antony." He is even moved by her death to some nobility of sentiment. "Their story is/ No less in pity than his glory which Brought them to be lamented."

COMMENT: Caesar is comparing the greatness of the compassion he feels for their tragic love with the glory of Antony, who brought its doom about.

And as his final act of the play, Caesar orders Dolabella to make arrangements for a state funeral and to observe "high order/ In this great solemnity."

SUMMARY: All the events in this scene should be seen in the light cast by Cleopatra's single-minded determination to die. Only in that way can we accurately judge her actions and motives. On the one side we have Cleopatra, who

1. determines to die;

2. deceives Proculeius that she wishes to live;

3. tries to kill herself with a dagger;

4. gains Dolabella's sympathy and confidence so as to discover Caesar's plans;

5. tages the scene with Seleuces so as to complete her deception of Caesar;

6. sends Charmian for the asps disguised as figs, as soon as Caesar is gone;

7. learns definitely that Caesar plans to take them alive to Rome;

8. bolsters up Iras's failing courage to die;

9. sends her maids for her royal costume while she brusquely gets rid of the clown;

10. bids goodbye to her ladies and dies.

Working against her determination to die we see Caesar's design to bring her back to Rome alive. It is executed:

1. by Proculeius, who is a trusted diplomat;

2. by Gallus and his soldiers who guard the tomb;

3. by Dolabella, who is sent to relieve Proculeius;

4. by Caesar himself, who does all he can to assure Cleopatra of his generosity and leniency.

This final scene also completes several patterns of imagery developed throughout the play:

1. the passage of life into death as day into night;

2. the contrast between the grossness of common life and the nobility of passionate love;

3. Cleopatra as Isis or moon-goddess, and the moon as an emblem of the waxing and waning of fortune;

4. the heroic size and grandeur of the protagonists.

CHARACTER ANALYSES

MARK ANTONY   The Antony we meet in this play is older than he was in *Julius Caesar*, hardened into middle age. He is still a great soldier, reputed the most successful general and statesman of his time: the "triple pillar of the world." But his reputation does not stop there. He is notorious also for his dissolute life, his sensuality and his vulgarity. We find him bedded in Alexandria, entangled in the charms of an infamous woman. He spends his nights in drinking and carousing and his days in feasting and making love. The business of state he neglects entirely. During the drinking bout in Pompey's galley we see more of this side of the man, when he conducts his Egyptian bacchanals. Meanwhile he leaves the soldiering to his lieutenants like Ventidius, but not without being jealous of their success. He is cruel and conscienceless in marrying the widowed sister of Caesar, Octavia, purely for political expediency, to gain a momentary advantage. He knows when he courts her that he will abandon her. For his reason and judgment, which brought him to the peak of fortune, have deserted him. After briefly struggling against his "dotage" on Cleopatra, he succumbs utterly to her witchcraft. Her insistence on a sea battle at Actium; his lack of preparation against the less skillful but more alert generalship of Caesar; his desertion from battle to follow his frightened mistress; all demonstrate his infatuation and his folly. His streak of cruelty flashes out in his whipping of Tidias, and his gigantic rage engulfs Cleopatra at the end.

But that is not the whole man; not even the greater part of him; certainly not the most enduring. He has the great Roman virtue of stoicism. He accepts Fulvia's death quietly, but with sadness, shame, and regret. His own death he goes to lovingly, like a bridegroom to his bed. He can endure hardship without complaining, as Caesar knows. And Caesar learns as well that Antony can out-talk him and out-think him in argument. He is the more seasoned statesman of the two, and the abler diplomat. His reputation for soldiership among his foes—Pompey is chary of him—is not less than among his followers. Above all he is kind. Despite all his callous cynicism he is soft and generous. He treats Lepidus as an equal after Caesar has snubbed him; he releases his lieutenants from their loyalty after he has led them to defeat. More, he offers them gold and letters of introduction. His supreme act of generosity is his forgiveness of Enobarbus when his friend and comrade-in-arms deserts him for Caesar's side.

He is jealous of this good opinion among his troops and his friends; he guards his reputation even at death. His last words to his mistress show his concern to be remembered at the height of his career and not in decline. So his downfall is tied in with his loss of reputation. He brings it on himself, certainly, but we have the feeling that his doom comes from without. He falls from strength to weakness, from prosperity to disaster, from triumph to defeat, almost without struggling against it.

His judgment leaves him; his soldiers leave him; his closest friends leave him; this guardian spirit, Hercules, leaves him; and at the end he runs out of luck. Misfortune does not fall like a mountain to crush him or strike him from afar like lightning. Rather, the flood of success which has borne him high ebbs from under him and sinks him in the mire.

CLEOPATRA   The chief note in Cleopatra's character is her "infinite variety." She is quicksilver in her moods; she moves from teasing to jealous, to imperious, to sulking. She is mischievous and complacent, flagrant and subtle by turns. She chides loudly and flatters softly; she is wantonly carefree and deeply thoughtful. There is no trick she will not use, no deceit she boggles at. But there is a pattern in all of her variety: Or is it two patterns? Readers do not seem to agree. Does she exercise all of her charms and wiles to keep her lover or to deceive him? At first she urges him to hear the news from Rome, then she tries to prevent him from acting upon it. She cannot bear the thought of his leaving and tries desperately to keep him. Rather than rejoice at Fulvia's death—an obstacle to her desire removed—she is stunned and sees her own in Fulvia's misfortune. Antony is hardly gone when she is love-lorn, and has twenty messengers pursue him with tokens and remembrances. No one may speak slightingly of her absent lover without risking bloody teeth. She attacks the messenger who brings her news of Antony's marriage to Octavia, and in the depths of despair allows herself to be deluded about her rival. She insists on taking part in her lover's war, and when she has caused his defeat she pleads repentance for it. When Antony accuses her of flirting with Thidias, she protests her love and fidelity convincingly enough. Or is it that he wants to be convinced? She is genuinely afraid for her soldier before the first day's battle, and she greets him enthusiastically when he returns triumphant. We hear the infinite relief in her voice. And we hear it again in the midst of her grief at the end: grief that his downfall is complete, and relief that her death is certain.

Or is it? Does she sincerely intend, her lover dead, to follow him in death? She says so, but we wonder. We remember that Antony knew she was "cunning past man's thought." We remember that her former conquerors wound up her lovers. May she not, as Antony accuses her, conquer the conqueror Caesar on her bed? After Actium, when defeat looks certain, does she "pack cards" with Caesar? She flatters his ambassador Thidias, gives him her hand to kiss, promises Caesar her compliance. Would she have followed all the others to his camp, had not Antony caught her in the act? He believes so in his rage after the final defeat. He suspects her complicity in the mass surrender of his army without a show of resistance. Had she arranged this with Caesar? She tries to arrange other things with him: a meeting, her son's future, a false account of her wealth. Does she in those final hours in the tomb hope to make some deal with Caesar, not to spare her life, but to spare her feelings? She is afraid to return as Caesar's captive to Rome. That is the prospect that stands uppermost in her dread. She practices her arts on Dolabella to learn Caesar's confidential plans. When she is sure of his intentions, she resigns herself to death. Or perhaps she knew all along what her end would be; perhaps she baited Caesar for the sport, or to win some concessions for her son. After all, she had already prepared the asps, disguised so as to deceive the guards. And when she first sees Roman soldiers she draws a concealed dagger, to remove herself from their power.

Of course, there are no answers. Perhaps Shakespeare has left us with the questions because he did not know the answers himself, because Plutarch does not give any. Except for the final answer of all, which Cleopatra writes, obliterating her own mystery in the mystery of death, "as water is in water."

ENOBARBUS   Our first impression of this cynical soldier is all edge. A confessed woman-hater, he shows a steadier judgment of and a profounder insight into Cleopatra at first than does his lord. And he always understands Antony better than Antony understands himself. Frank, straightforward, not disillusioned because he never entertained any illusions, he is a man's man. He is not awed by rank or reputation; he never fears the truth—but one. He can move from scathing appraisal to rhapsodic praise when he describes Cleopatra's arrival in Tarsus. He sees from the beginning through Antony's marriage to Octavia. But he does turn the broad flank of his affection to the view once before he dies. Although he rages against Antony's blundering incompetence, he never ceases to love the man. Perhaps it is because he is so much like Antony; in his tragic end we foresee his master's. Both men have the solid military virtues. Yet working against these in both is a certain softness of sentiment or self-deception. This is the one truth he cannot face—about himself. Such men fall because, being the kind of men they are, they cannot reconcile the two sides of their characters. Enobarbus sees this conflict in Antony; he does not even suspect it in himself. A mercenary soldier, he has every reason to abandon a losing cause and back a winner while the betting is still open. Yet what can prudence argue against Antony's lovely gesture of friendship and forgiveness? What can self-interest claim against compassion? It is as if the soft center of the man were strangled in his iron shell.

OCTAVIUS   A man without a center, Octavius reacts to the surfaces of men and events. He is not deeply committed to anything but his own success. His only passion is ambition; besides his rival he is passionless. He has the great politician's virtues: patience, caution, industry, a hard head. He has a realistic respect for things as they are and enough opportunism not to flinch from using people. He sells his sister to Antony, quite frankly for political reasons. Nor does he care about Antony's love affairs, except as they affect the state. He deals "in lieutenantry," but he is astute in his choice of lieutenants. He lulls Pompey with a bogus peace treaty in order to defeat him when he is off his guard. He wants to use Cleopatra to magnify his own fame; for the woman herself he cares nothing. He is one man she cannot wrap around her finger. Those he cannot use he has only contempt for: One thinks of Lepidus, Enobarbus, the others who went over to his winning side. He is self-righteous because it comes easily to him. He sets about to revenge Octavia's insult as if he were the instrument of heavenly justice. In truth she has been the tool of his ambition. He will do nothing to excess. He remains aloof and sober at the party aboard Pompey's galley because carousing is beneath his dignity. He husbands himself. But he can suffer from overconfidence, as when he loses the first day's battle and when Cleopatra finally defeats him. But setbacks also are only superficial for this able man. His kind is not great, but destined to be successful.

OCTAVIA   As Cleopatra's rival she is more important for what she is *not* than for what she is. Quite simply, she is *not* Cleopatra. Her "beauty, wisdom, modesty" are a foil to that queen's "infinite variety." She suffers quietly, bending all her weakness to the ends of helping her brother and remaining true to her husband. She speaks only some thirty lines in four scenes; she is the minor character in all of them. She is the victim: as much the victim of great policies as of Cleopatra's legendary power over men. So she must be got out of the way early. The structure of the play could not support a deeper, more sympathetic development of her personality. For she would become, in her injury, a rival to Cleopatra for the audience's affection if not admiration. And being a perfect example of Roman ethos, she might well tip the balance of sympathy away from Egypt and Antony.

SEXTUS POMPEIUS   The son of a great man, who reveals his own weakness in trying to claim his father's greatness. His weakness is not on the surface; he puts up a bluff and convincing show. But he lacks the fortitude to sustain it. He is as full of flourishes as of optimism. He foresees success for his conspiracy and even the news of Antony's return does not discourage him. He does not suspect though Menas does, and his father would have—the treachery behind Caesar's peace treaty. There is a moral flourish in his rejection of Menas's plan to ambush the Triumvirs and murder them aboard his flagship. But it is as empty as the rest. He is not above wanting the profits of evil, but will not pay the price—for his honor's sake. He is the type of his rival, Caesar, the ambitious politician; but with a little too much surface and too little center, and without the essential ingredient: success.

LEPIDUS   Lepidus is a weakling; he is out of place among strong men. Pompey is betrayed by his weakness, but he makes a show of strength. Lepidus always shows his weakness. The perennial peacemaker, he risks offending no one. When Caesar criticizes Antony, he tries to defend the one without offending the other. Yet he loves neither. At their confrontation he is the essence of politeness, as if mere good manners could

reconcile their differences. At the celebration of the peace treaty with Pompey he proves again that he has not the stuff of greatness; the others recognize it openly and make him the drunken butt of their jokes. He is no Caesar to recognize his limitations and respect them. He has an ostrich-like quality of ignoring unpleasantness in the hope it will disappear. And so he does; he disappears from the play, his absence hardly noticed, except in Caesar's sarcastic excuse for getting rid of him: that he had grown too cruel.

MINOR CHARACTERS   Shakespeare keeps a number of minor characters moving in and out of the play to liven our interest. But he does not develop any of them too much, lest they distract our interest from the main characters. Each of these main characters is surrounded by friends, courtiers, attendants, messengers, advisers, whose incidental figures contribute something of their color and character to their master. Co-conspirators and henchmen of Pompey are the pirates Menecrates and Menas. The first is the more philosophical of the two, less the maker of events than their minister. His is the voice of prudence. Menas is the opposite extreme, a headlong Machiavellian schemer. He has the politician's caginess and opportunism. He pumps Enobarbus for information about the Triumvirate because he suspects the peace treaty is a trap; he sees the advantage he might take of the Triumvirs in their drunken carousing. And when his master can grasp neither, he abandons him. Caesar leans heavily on his advisers, perhaps because of his comparative youth and inexperience. Entering Lepidus's house to meet Antony, he says, "I do not know,/ Maecenas; ask Agrippa." And it is the more politic of the two, Agrippa, who puts forth the plan to marry Octavia to Antony. He defends his lord against Enobarbus's sarcasm when they eavesdrop on the Triumvirs' farewells. Both are rather provincial, for all their worldliness. They are astonished and a little scandalized by Enobarbus's account of Cleopatra's court. Maecenas may even display a little sentimental optimism in believing Octavia can hold Antony from Cleopatra. We watch the courtiers' characteristic weakness harden on them like fat when with Caesar's success their deference ripens into flattery. Thidias and Dolabella are accomplished ambassadors, diplomats chosen for their ability to attract and influence Cleopatra. Notice how Dolabella addresses the defeated queen as if she, not Octavia, were Antony's lawful wife: "Empress," he calls her. Antony's relationship to his followers is a friendlier one. He does not lean so heavily on their judgment—perhaps he should—as on their love. Ventidius is aware of this, and so sacrifices his better judgment to keep in his jealous master's good graces. Canidius withdraws his loyalty when he finds Antony's judgment lost. Scarus' immediate wrath over Actium spends itself and though his better judgment tells him to desert, his love keeps him by his lord. But the image of love and loyalty is Eros—Eros who independently fetches Cleopatra to comfort Antony after Actium; Eros who spends his last hours weeping over Antony's disgrace. And it is Eros whose last act of love overcomes his judgment when he kills himself rather than kill his friend. Cleopatra's court is all women except for Mardian, who is all but a woman, and Alexas, who is "much unlike" Mark Antony. One epicene man in a hive of women, just as Octavia is one colorless woman in an army of men. And then Alexas deserts to Caesar, leaving only Charmian and Iras. Charmian is the more robust of the two, the outspoken "wild bedfellow." She keeps her head when Iras is near hysteria. As the soothsayer predicts, she outlives her mistress, but only by a minute. Iras is the quieter, more fragile girl. She panics easily; she

has to be reassured constantly; her courage is always on the point of breaking. Yet she knows what is finally expected of her, and precipitate as always, she does not wait for the asp. The very expectation of death, grief in anticipation, kills her. The soothsayer and clown are not characters at all, in the sense of developed personalities. They are stage conventions which Shakespeare uses to create mood and atmosphere. Around the wizard hovers the odor of incense, some mystery of the East. As usual in tragedy, he enigmatically sees the end of the play in its beginning. The clown is a low comedian, probably much beloved by the audience. He takes some of the tension out of Cleopatra's death scene, and by contrast he adds some. He gives the audience something to laugh at legitimately, yet when he takes his gallows humor with him, he leaves the stage darker than before.

Hamlet

Scene-by-Scene Summary and Comment

Act I: Scene i

The play opens at a sentry post before the castle of Elsinore, Denmark, during legendary times. It is midnight and Francisco, a sentry, is at his post awaiting his relief. Bernardo enters and asks, "Who's there?" But Francisco challenges him for the password, saying, "Nay, answer me; stand, and unfold yourself."

COMMENT: These opening two lines are significant, for they set a tone of watchful suspicion which is later to characterize the major characters and their supporters: Hamlet, with the aid of Horatio, spies on Claudius, while Claudius, with the aid of Rosencrantz, Guildenstern, Polonius, Ophelia and Gertrude, spies on Hamlet; on a minor level, Polonius also spies on his son Laertes.

Horatio and Marcellus, who are to share Bernado's sentry duty this evening, now enter. Horatio is not a regular sentry but has been especially asked by Marcellus to spend this watch with them because of something unusual which has occurred on the two previous nights for which they wish his opinion and help. When Bernardo greets Horatio with the question whether it really is he, Horatio replies, "A piece of him." Marcellus now tells Bernardo that Horatio has rejected their story as "fantasy" and will not allow himself to believe it.

COMMENT: These few remarks help to define the character of Horatio. We later learn that Horatio is a Stoic, a follower of an ancient Greek and Roman philosophy which held that the pain of life could be overcome by the suppression of all personal desire, by remaining equally unmoved by joy or grief, and by submitting without complaint to what was unavoidable. Since a person who has suppressed all of his emotional reactions might be said to be living on only a partial level, Horatio has well replied that all that is present is "a piece of him." The other aspect of Horatio's character which is here suggested is his skeptical turn of mind, his refusal to accept superstitious hearsay evidence and also, as we shall later learn, his avoidance of the deeper mysteries of life.

Marcellus proceeds to explain the "dreaded sight" that has appeared before them the last two nights, but, before he and Bernardo have half begun their tale, the Ghost enters. Horatio agrees with the two sentries that the Ghost, who is dressed in armor, has a form like that of the dead King Hamlet. Marcellus suggests that, since Horatio is a "scholar," he should be the one to know how to speak to the Ghost. Horatio does this, beginning by asking the Ghost, "What art thou?" and closing with the challenge, "by heaven I charge thee, speak!" But Marcellus notes that "It is offended," and Bernardo that "it stalks away." Now that his own eyes have seen the Ghost, Horatio admits that it is "something more than fantasy" and that it forbodes "some strange eruption to our state," some coming disaster.

Marcellus now asks Horatio whether he knows why there is such a strict watch and why the country is so busy building armaments. Horatio replies that, as they know, the late King Fortinbras of Norway, jealous of the martial conquests of the late Danish King Hamlet, challenged the Danish King to combat, staking all his possessions on the outcome, and that the late Hamlet killed Fortinbras and took over his forfeited lands as had been agreed. Recently, however, young Fortinbras, son of the slain King, had raised an unlawful army with the apparent aim to recover by force of arms the territories his father had lost to the Danes. It is against such a possibility, Horatio thinks, that the present Danish military preparations have been undertaken. Bernardo agrees with this and further suggests that it may be in connection with these wars, with which the late King Hamlet is still so involved, that his Ghost has now been aroused. Horatio is not so sure of this as he is troubled by the remembrance of similar supernatural occurrences before the murder of Julius Caesar: ghosts in the Roman streets, comets, bloody dews, ominous signs in the sun, and a lengthy eclipse of the moon. He suggests that "heaven and earth" are demonstrating a similar "omen" to "feared events" for their own country.

COMMENT: Shakespeare had placed much importance on these supernatural occurrences in his earlier tragedy, *Julius Caesar*, and is to use the supernatural prophetic figures of the witches in his later tragedy, *Macbeth*. This suggests that Shakespeare is using these supernatural appearances not only to thrill and amaze the "groundlings" (the poor, uneducated part of the audience that stood on the ground before the stage to watch the performance), although he is certainly using these figures with great dramatic effectiveness, but also to suggest something about reality, namely that the whole of the universe is involved in and disrupted by human evil and will work in mysterious ways to right the balance of nature.

At this point the Ghost re-enters and Horatio, recognizing the danger involved, vows to cross it even if it destroys him. He challenges the Ghost to speak to him, but only on certain conditions. He first proposes "If there be any good thing to be done/ That may to thee do ease and grace to me,/ Speak to me." The second condition under which Horatio will permit the Ghost to speak to him is if he has some secret knowledge of his country's fate which his country might avoid by being told of it; and the third condition is if the Ghost wishes to reveal the hiding place of any treasure he may have buried. Before the Ghost can answer, however, the cock crows and, as the three characters try vainly with their swords to force the Ghost to stand and answer the questions, the Ghost fades away. Horatio notes that he has often heard that at the cock's warning of the approach of day the "erring spirit" must return "to his confine" and that the present disappearance of the Ghost seems to confirm the truth of this saying. Marcellus agrees, but further notes that there are those who say that at the Christmas season,

> *Wherein our Saviour's birth is celebrated,*
> *The cock crows all night long.*
> *And then, they say, no spirit dare stir abroad,*
> *The nights are wholesome, then no planets strike,*
> *No fairy takes, nor witch hath power to charm.*
> *So hallowed and so gracious is that time.*

COMMENT: From the last speech there would seem to be some opposition between the religion of Christ and such supernatural manifestations as were earlier discussed, ghosts, fairies, witches and planetary disturbances. Furthermore, we have seen that Horatio was very careful, in confronting the ghost, to guard himself against any evil power it might possess. In his first confrontation, he charged the ghost to disclose its true nature and to speak to him "by heaven." In his second confrontation, he charges the ghost only to speak to him if he wishes him to do a good thing which will bring him grace. Horatio's behavior suggests the morally questionable nature of the ghost and serves as a Christian model against which Hamlet's later confrontation with the ghost may be judged.

As it is now morning, Horatio suggests that they break up their watch and go to Hamlet to tell him what they have seen, for he suspects that "This spirit, dumb to us, will speak to him." Marcellus agrees and they depart from the stage.

SUMMARY: This opening scene has the following important purposes:

1. It serves as an "exposition," a setting forth of the important occurrences which precede the beginning of the play: the war between Norway and Denmark which was won by the late King Hamlet, young Fortinbras' military preparations to regain Norway's lost territories, and Denmark's countermilitary preparations.

2. It provides an exciting and suspenseful beginning to the play through the introduction of the ominous and silent ghost who is, in fact, going to motivate the action of the entire play.

3. It raises some questions as to the nature and importance of supernatural manifestations in general and of this ghost in particular and also questions the relation of such manifestations to Christianity, questions which will be raised repeatedly throughout the play.

4. It introduces us to the character of Horatio, a skeptical Stoic, who is to become Hamlet's one close friend and in relation to whom we may better judge Hamlet.

Act I: Scene ii

The second scene opens on the following day with the entrance of King Claudius and the important members of his court into a room of state in the castle at Elsinore. Claudius begins the scene with a formal public address to his court which touches on the important matters of state before him.

The first item which Claudius takes up is his hasty marriage to his brother's widow, Queen Gertrude. He explains that, as she has an equal right to the throne and as his own desires also favored her, he has married her even though it is less than two months since the death of her husband and his brother, the late King Hamlet. He admits that it might have been more fitting for him and the whole kingdom to remain in mourning for the late King rather than to celebrate a marriage, but he states that he has only proceeded in this matter because his chief counselors of state had freely advised him to do so, for which he thanks them.

The second item of state, and the real reason for this meeting, is concerned with the activities of young Fortinbras, of which we have already learned something in the first scene. We are now told that Fortinbras, believing Denmark to be disorganized and weak as a result of the death of King Hamlet, had sent several messages to Claudius demanding the surrender of the lands lost by his father. Claudius' response is to send an envoy to the King of Norway, the uncle of young Fortinbras, who, old and bedridden, has scarcely heard of the unlawful activities of his nephew. In the letter he is sending to the King of Norway, Claudius demands that he suppress the unlawful activities of his nephew, further suggesting that the cost of rearming Norway is all coming out of the King of Norway's own revenues and that he had better look into this matter. Claudius now dispatches Cornelius and Voltemand to carry this letter to the King of Norway as quickly as possible.

The third item is the personal request of Laertes, son of the Lord Chamberlain, Polonius, to be permitted to return to Paris, from which he had come to attend Claudius' coronation. Before Claudius allows Laertes to make his request, he tells him how willing he is to grant him any request because of the great respect the throne of Denmark holds for his father. Upon learning the nature of the request, he refers the decision to Polonius, who gives his consent to his son's leaving, which is then seconded by Claudius.

COMMENT: The style of Claudius' opening speech is majestic, balanced and controlled, indicating similar qualities in his character. These qualities may help to explain why he was elected to the throne of Denmark over the pretensions of his nephew, Hamlet, son to the late King Hamlet (for the king of Denmark was elected to the throne by the nobility from among the members of the royal family). His imposing statesmanship is further indicated by his activities since gaining the throne, as shown in this speech. He has only fulfilled his personal desire to marry Gertrude after gaining the cooperation and support of his chief counselors, one of whom, Polonius, we here see him treating with exaggerated marks of deference. Claudius, then, appears to be an able politician with regards to members of his own court. But, more than this, he is also a statesman. Although preparing for war, as we have learned from Horatio in the first scene, he prefers to avoid war if it is possible to do so through diplomatic means, and, as we shall later learn, his letter to the King of Norway is successful in accomplishing this purpose. Fortinbras' conjectures as to the weak and disorganized state of Denmark are seen to be completely false as Claudius, in less than two months of rule, has ably taken the situation in hand.

Claudius now turns to the last item of business, the desire of his nephew, now stepson, Hamlet, to return to his studies in Wittenberg. But, as Claudius addresses him with the words "my cousin Hamlet, and my son," Hamlet says to himself, "A little more than kin, and less than kind!"

COMMENT: In this first silent speech (called an "aside" in the stage directions) of Hamlet, we learn something of the quality of his mind. For what Hamlet is doing is making a bitter little joke to himself. This joke is based upon a pun on the meanings of the word "kind." Originally, and still in the seventeenth century when *Hamlet* was written, the word "kind" meant that which naturally pertains to "kindred," especially those feelings of care and concern, "kindness," which blood relations should feel for each other. When Hamlet uses the word "kind," then, he is referring to both "kindness" in our sense of the term and "kinship." Claudius, then is "a little more than kin," than that second degree of relationship indicated generally by the term "cousin" since he is now also his stepfather, but he is also a little less than kin, in the older sense of the term "kind," an apparent paradox which is resolved by the other meaning of "kind," namely, the "kindness" associated with blood relations. This bitter joke, made for his own amusement, conveys Hamlet's suspicious regarding Claudius' integrity: first, that though Claudius may be acting with a show of kindred concern, his feelings for him are far from fatherly, and secondly and more vaguely, that his feelings for Hamlet's true father may have been far from brotherly, though how far Hamlet does not dare suggest even to himself. Since such suspicions would be serious, indeed, if valid, Hamlet is protecting himself from the full weight of his suspicions through the use of humor, though it is humor of a very biting variety.

Claudius now asks Hamlet how it is that he is still in such a downcast state of mourning, and Hamlet quickly retorts that his mourning is not sufficient. His mother begs him to put off his mourning attire and gloom and look with more friendliness upon Claudius, to seek in him rather than in the dust for his father, and, finally, to accept the fact of his natural father's death since he knows "'tis common. All that lives must die." Hamlet agrees: "Ay madam, it is common." Gertrude next asks why it then "seems" so special to him, not understanding that the very commonness of death may increase rather than diminish Hamlet's despair. Hamlet picks up her innocent use of the word "seems" to disclaim any such false appearance: "Seems, madam? Nay, it is. I know not 'seems'." His full mourning is not simply an outward show which a man might play since his inner feelings go beyond all such external appearances: "I have that within which passeth show." Claudius says that it is good for a son to give such mourning duties to his father as long as it is held to some prescribed term but that to continue beyond such a time is impious and unmanly; "It shows a will most incorrect to heaven" since it stubbornly refuses to accept the will of heaven. Claudius begs Hamlet to put aside his mourning, to think of him as his father for he does feel towards Hamlet as a father, and to make him happy by remaining beside him in Denmark rather than returning to Wittenberg. The Queen seconds this desire on her own account and Hamlet replies that he will obey her. Claudius is so delighted with this unforced reply that he vows to spend the evening toasting Hamlet's apparent reconciliation with him. With this, the formal audience is over and the King and court depart from the stage, leaving Hamlet alone.

We have now arrived at Hamlet's first "soliloquy," a term for the Elizabethan stage convention which permits a character to speak directly to the audience his inner, silent thoughts. Hamlet begins with the anguished wish that his "solid" (some scholars, following Kittredge, would substitute "sullied" here as the word Shakespeare originally intended) "flesh would melt" away by itself. Since this cannot be, he wishes that God had not given a direct law forbidding suicide. He continues with an anguished general cry against the will of heaven: "O God, God, / How weary, stale, flat, and unprofitable / Seem to me all the uses of this world!" He is led to this cry of despair by his recent recognition that justice does not rule the world, that "things rank and gross in nature possess it merely." The world appears to him in this light because his "excellent" father has died and Claudius, so far inferior to his father, has succeeded to his place, not only to his father's throne but also to his wife. But it is his mother's behavior which has most disillusioned him. His father had been "so loving" and gentle to his mother and she had seemed to return his affection, "would hang on him" as if the more she was with him the more her "appetite" for him would grow. (Note that Hamlet expresses his father's feelings for his mother as "love" but his mother's feelings for his father as "appetite," a sign of his new awareness of the "grossness" of nature in general and of his mother in particular.) Not only that, she had seemed genuinely overcome by grief at his father's funeral. "And yet within a month" she had married. The thought is so horrifying to him that he tries to close it out from his mind, "Let me not think on't," for as soon as he does think of it he must condemn his mother and, with her, all women: "frailty, thy name is woman." (The fact that the happy marriage of his parents, in which he had believed all of his life, now seems to have been a delusion—that his mother could not have loved his father as much as she appeared to since she now acts the same way with another man, and that man her brother-in-law—shows Hamlet that he did not know the true nature of the person closest to him, his mother, and that, if he cannot even trust his own mother, there is no one he may trust. In the past two months, then, two terrible facts of human existence have been brought personally home to him through his loved ones: the fact of death and the fact of human imperfection and falseness, and these have so disillusioned him with the value of life that he has sunk completely into a suicidal state of mind.) He is particularly heartbroken over the behavior of his mother and over the fact that there is nothing he can do about it: "It is not, nor it cannot come to good. / But break my heart, for I must hold my tongue."

At this point Horatio enters with Marcellus and Bernardo. Hamlet quickly rouses himself from his suicidal reflections and is delighted to see Horatio, a fellow student of his at the University of Wittenberg whom he holds in high respect. Asked what he is doing in Elsinore, Horatio, who for some unexplained reason has not previously greeted Hamlet, replies that "I came to see your father's funeral." Hamlet ironically returns: "do not mock me fellow student. / I think it was to see my mother's wedding." When Horatio agrees that it followed quickly upon the funeral, Hamlet replies with further satiric bite: "Thrift, thrift, Horatio. The funeral baked meats / Did coldly furnish forth the marriage tables." And then he more seriously expresses his displeasure.

COMMENT: In the past scene we have seen rapid shifts in Hamlet's moods. First he reflects satirically to himself on the nature of Claudius; then he expresses himself in a melancholy fashion to his mother on the subject of his continuing mourning; thirdly, he reflects in a melancholy fashion to himself on his desire for suicide as a result of his mother's remarriage; lastly, he expresses himself satirically to Horatio, also on the subject of his mother's remarriage. We see, first, that he does not express himself differently to himself from the way he does to others; he is both satiric and melancholy to himself and both satiric and melancholy to others, depending upon his particular mood at the moment. Secondly, we see that he alternates only between these two moods, moods that have a special relationship to one another.

Satire is a particularly destructive form of wit, as is indicated by such an expression as a "satiric thrust," but it achieves its destructive purpose through humiliating laughter. If satire directs a destructive mood outwards, even though only through laughter, melancholy is, in its extreme form, a suicidal, self-destructive mood. Both are responses to a similar vision of the tormenting imperfections of life; in the former case the desire is to destroy the imperfections of life; in the latter to destroy the self because it can no longer endure these imperfections. But whether directed with murderous or suicidal intent, this destructive impulse shows, in Claudius' words, "a will most incorrect to heaven," for both of these desires are equally forbidden by religious law, as Hamlet is aware in his first soliloquy; he is forbidden to commit suicide and he must hold his tongue. Since death is so common that it expresses the will of heaven, Claudius asks Hamlet: "Why should we in our peevish opposition/ Take it to heart?" But this is exactly Hamlet's condition; the evil in the universe has suddenly come home to him and he does "take it to heart." He cannot accept the will of heaven in this regard and yet, as he will not actively oppose God, his opposition is reduced to frustrated peevishness which expresses itself in alternating moods of satire and melancholy.

Horatio now tells Hamlet that a ghost with the appearance of his father has three times appeared before the midnight sentries at their guard post and that he had been present at the last visitation. Hamlet questions Horatio minutely as to the appearance of the spirit and, convinced of its similarity to his father, resolves to appear at the watch that night. He vows: "If it assume my noble father's person,/ I'll speak to it though hell itself should gape."

COMMENT: At the time when *Hamlet* was written, rather than in the legendary time in which it was set, the University of Wittenberg was a center of Protestant theology. With historical inconsistency, Shakespeare casts his legendary character, Hamlet, as a student at a contemporary university. As a student at Wittenberg, Hamlet would have been taught the orthodox Protestant position on ghosts which was that they were not the spirits of the deceased but either angels or, what was far more general, devils who "assumed" the appearance of a deceased person to tempt a surviving relative into spiritual damnation. Whereas Horatio had originally accepted the more extreme, skeptical position that ghosts do not exist, Hamlet approaches his coming meeting with the ghost with the belief that it is probably a devil who has "assumed" his father's form in order to damn him to hell. But he is willing to risk this danger to learn the ghost's message.

Hamlet asks the guards to tell no one of the appearance of the ghost, saying that he will reward them for their silence, and, appointing a meeting for that night, bids them farewell. They leave and, alone, Hamlet expresses his suspicion that there has been "some foul play," a reechoing of his earlier, half thought suspicion.

SUMMARY: This scene accomplishes the following purposes:

1. It serves as an introduction to the play's two leading characters, Claudius and Hamlet, whom Hamlet is later to call "mighty opposites." Claudius is presented as immensely capable of dealing with the problems of state and of life; he has established an ordered, efficient state and diplomatically avoids war, and he preaches to Hamlet the acceptance of life with all its evils. Hamlet is shown to be a brilliant, sensitive, highly erratic and moody person who refuses to accept the imperfections of life and has been driven into a suicidal frame of mind by the death of his father and infidelity of his mother.

2. By the end of the scene, Hamlet, despite his personal withdrawal, has become involved in the action. He has complied with the request of Claudius and his mother that he remain at the Danish court rather than return to Wittenberg as he had desired, and he has resolved to speak with the ghost and learn its bidding even though it damn him (further indication of the uncertain nature of the ghost).

Act I: Scene iii

The scene is set in Polonius' rooms within the castle at Elsinore later that day. Laertes is about to leave for Paris and is bidding his sister, Ophelia, farewell. In a long speech, he warns her not to trust Hamlet's intentions towards her and to protect her chastity, for even though Hamlet may say he loves her and perhaps now does, he cannot marry as he wishes since he is of royal birth and is thus far above her. She answers that she will follow his advice but that he should not simply preach strictness to her and then act like a libertine himself. At this point Polonius enters surprised that Laertes is still there since the wind is up and he is waited for at the boat. He hurries him to go, gives him his blessing, and then delays his departure with moral commonplaces: he should be discreet in words and action; devote himself to true friends rather than every new acquaintance; avoid quarrels but, once involved, bear himself strongly; listen to all but reserve his true thoughts only to a few; accept other men's criticism but refrain from criticizing others; dress with an elegance that is not gaudy, for appearance is often used as a guide to the nature of a man; neither borrow nor lend; "This above all, to thine own self be true,/ And it must follow as the night the day/ Thou canst not then be false to any man."

COMMENT: We see that Laertes takes after his father in long-winded, moral preaching. Polonius, in fact, appears foolish in this regard. He comes out, hurrying Laertes to leave, "Yet here, Laertes? Aboard, aboard, for shame!" And yet he delays him with standard moralizing. That this extremely well written speech does not reflect the wise fruits of a lifetime of reflection, as it is often held to do, is shown by the fact that, although he claims integrity to be the most important moral quality, he is himself the falsest of men, as we shall later see.

Laertes now leaves, bidding Ophelia to "remember well what I have said to you." Polonius questions Ophelia as to what this is and is told that it concerns Hamlet. This reminds Polonius that he has been told of the meetings between Hamlet and Ophelia and asks her what there is between them. To her reply that Hamlet has recently given her many signs of his "affection," Polonius expresses disgust: "Affection? Pooh!" He tells her that she is just an innocent girl if she believes Hamlet's intentions. When she says that he has spoken to her of "love in honorable fashion," Polonius says that this is just a trap to seduce her. To protect his daughter's honor and his own, he tells her first that she should not see Hamlet so often—in fact, should play harder to get. But as he continues to explain the ways of men to his innocent daughter, he becomes more and more convinced of her danger until he suddenly decides that she must not see him again and so commands her. She is an obedient daughter and agrees to obey him, at which they leave the stage.

COMMENT: Polonius' lack of true wisdom, earlier suggested, is here confirmed. He does not investigate the nature of Hamlet's intentions but assumes that they must be dishonorable and that a marriage between the prince and his daughter would be impossible. We later learn that he was wrong on both counts as, at Ophelia's funeral, Gertrude says that she had hoped Ophelia would be Hamlet's wife and Hamlet proclaims his love for her. Furthermore, his sudden decision not to permit his daughter to see Hamlet again, a decision arrived at without any considered judgment, is a serious error, as he later admits, since it serves to reinforce Hamlet's disillusionment with women which, in turn, helps to break Ophelia's heart and destroy her sanity. In his relations to his daughter, then, he shows an overbearing authority and apparent worldly wisdom without true discretion.

SUMMARY: This scene serves the following purposes:

1. It introduces us more fully to the important character of Polonius and shows him to be a foolish, authoritarian old man, verging on senility. His foolish self-importance, which is even more fully revealed later on, causes him to be treated in many instances as a comic character. But his effects and end are far from comic.

2. It also introduces us to Ophelia, an innocent, obedient young girl, and to the fact of Hamlet's love for her.

3. The action of the scene is important in so far as Polonius' decision to restrict his daughter from seeing Hamlet bars Hamlet's love from any normal development it might have had, and also seriously hurts Ophelia.

Act I: Scenes iv-v

Hamlet, Horatio and Marcellus enter the platform before the castle where the sentry post is situated. It is midnight, as they note, and some trumpets are heard to sound. Horatio asks Hamlet what it means and Hamlet replies that the King and court are spending the evening drinking and that every time Claudius makes a toast, the trumpets and drums sound. Horatio asks whether this is a Danish custom and Hamlet says that it is, but that though he is a native here "and to the manner born," he thinks it better not to keep this time-honored custom which has given Denmark a reputation for drunkenness among other nations.

COMMENT: In Scene 2, Claudius had referred to his habitual evening drinking when he said that once "again" he would make loud toasts with wine that evening in honor of his reconciliation with Hamlet. When Hamlet greeted Horatio he said to him: "We'll teach you to drink deep ere you depart." Here we see another difference between Claudius and Hamlet; Claudius indulges in sensual pleasure while Hamlet views such indulgence with puritanical disgust.

Hamlet continues that, just as Denmark's positive achievements are overshadowed by its reputation for drunkenness, so it can happen in the case of particular men. A personality defect with which they are born, and for which they cannot be held guilty, may so develop that it leads to irrational behavior, or a habit may similarly overcome the control of their reason. Then such men, carrying "the stamp of one defect," though they have all other virtues, will come under general condemnation for this one fault.

COMMENT: This has generally been taken to represent Shakespeare's discussion of the concept of the "tragic flaw." This concept holds that the proper tragic hero is one who is above average in virtue but is brought to tragedy as a result of one flaw in his character. The concept is generally thought to be derived from Aristotle's *Poetics* but is actually a Renaissance interpretation of Aristotle. In any case, critics are in greater agreement about the meaning of this passage than about the nature of Hamlet's supposed "tragic flaw."

At this point the ghost enters. Hamlet calls upon the angels to defend him and then addresses the ghost. He says that whether he is an angel come from heaven with charitable intent, or a damned spirit come from hell with wicked intent (the only two possibilities he considers), the question is so uncertain that he will speak to him as though he were the true spirit of his father. He asks him why he has returned from death, but the ghost, rather than answer him, silently beckons Hamlet to follow him. Horatio and Marcellus advise Hamlet not to follow the ghost, but Hamlet says he has nothing to fear since "I do not set my life at a pin's fee." Horatio says that the ghost might tempt him to the edge of the cliff, drive him mad, and then cause him to commit suicide (possibilities which might follow if the ghost were a devil). But Hamlet answers, "My fate cries out," and, breaking away from Horatio and Marcellus who are now physically holding him back, he follows the ghost to another part of the platform, leaving the stage. Though Marcellus now says, "Something is rotten in the state of Denmark," Horatio hopes the coming of the ghost may have a blessed effect. He says, "Heaven will direct it." In any case, they decide it is not fit to leave Hamlet alone and follow him.

The fifth scene begins with the entrance of the ghost on another part of the platform. Hamlet follows but then tells the ghost to stop and speak because he will follow him no further. The ghost turns and now finally reveals that he is the true spirit of Hamlet's father, doomed for a certain term to purgatory; he has returned to earth to tell Hamlet that if he ever loved his father he should "Revenge his foul and most unnatural murder."

COMMENT: Up to this point we have noted three different attitudes towards ghosts: Marcellus' superstitious belief in the existence of ghosts without too much certainty as to their nature; Horatio's initial disbelief in the existence of ghosts; and Hamlet's Protestant belief that ghosts are the appearance of either angels or devils in the assumed form of a deceased person. Now we see the fourth possible Renaissance attitude towards ghosts, the Catholic position that ghosts are the true spirits of deceased persons who are in purgatory. This is the position the ghost holds of himself, though this does not necessarily mean that he is telling Hamlet the truth.

Whatever be the truth of the matter (and the doubt is to continue to torment Hamlet), the ghost is acting in a way traditional for ghosts since pre-Christian, Classical times— he is calling for revenge. There is a whole tradition of revenge tragedy dating from ancient Greece and Rome and continuing in plays in the Elizabethan drama before *Hamlet*

in which a ghost appears calling for revenge and establishes the motive for the tragic action. The difference between Classical and Christian tragedy, however, is that in the latter the ghost's demand for revenge conflicts with the Christian commandment against murder. This fact serves to reinforce the possible identification of the ghost with the devil since his demand would lead to damnation in Christian terms. (For a fuller discussion of the subject of the ghost, see John Dover Wilson's *What Happens in Hamlet,* to which the present treatment is much indebted).

Upon learning of his father's murder, Hamlet is anxious to learn the name of his murderer that he may be "swift" in his revenge. But when the ghost reveals that the murderer is Claudius, Hamlet exclaims, "O my prophetic soul!" (This indicates that Hamlet had dimly suspected as much, as was earlier shown.) The ghost now reveals something else, that Claudius had seduced his "most seeming-virtuous queen" to "shameful lust" before his death. And the ghost agrees with Hamlet as to the relative merits of Claudius and himself when he says: "O Hamlet, what a falling-off was there." Though he considers Claudius "a wretch whose natural gifts were poor to those of mine," he also understands that lust will leave "a radiant angel" to "prey on garbage." He then explains how he was killed, that he was sleeping in his orchard in the afternoon when Claudius poured poison in his ear which quickly killed him. "Most horrible" of all, Claudius' murder deprived him of the opportunity of confession and of the Sacraments before death. He now tells Hamlet that if he has any natural feeling for his father he should not allow his murderer to live and, what is even worse, turn his royal bed into a couch for incestuous lust. Whatever he does, however, he should not "taint" his mind by even contemplating anything against his mother but "leave her to heaven" and to her own conscience. As morning is coming, he bids Hamlet a quick farewell with the words, "remember me."

COMMENT: It is interesting that apart from the actual story of the murder and adultery, the ghost did not tell Hamlet anything he did not already suspect and, what is more, the telling was done exactly in terms of Hamlet's own values, as shown in his first soliloquy. There also his father's attributes were held to be far superior to those of Claudius, his mother's lustful change was viewed with disgust, and greater emphasis was placed upon the horror of his mother's infidelity than upon his father's death. This suggests one of two possibilities: either Hamlet takes after his father, as Laertes does after his, or that the ghost is simply telling Hamlet what he wants to hear, justifying his most horrible imaginings so that he may have a reason to take direct action which may damn him. Even the true piece of information he gives him, the manner of the murder, which can be and later is tested, is something that a devil would know and might use to tempt Hamlet to his damnation.

Hamlet's immediate response is to call for help upon all the host of heaven and the earth, and then he has the terrible suspicion that perhaps he had better also call upon the help of hell in remembering his father. But he immediately rejects this suspicion that the ghost may come from hell; "And shall I couple hell? O fie!" Taking hold of himself, he vows to wipe everything from the tablet of his memory except his father's commandment to revenge his murder. But as he thinks of his evil mother and still more of Claudius, a "villain, villain, smiling, damned villain," he suddenly begins to lose control of his reason. He feels he has discovered a wonderful truth that he must write down in the notebook he carries with him to record memorable sayings, and he writes "that one may smile, and smile, and be a villain." Such a statement is, of course, neither a brilliant discovery nor an especially well-phrased observation and so would not normally be written down. But that Hamlet is not in a normal frame of mind is immediately shown when he responds to his friends' calling to him with a falconer's cry used for summoning his hawk: "Hillo, ho, ho, boy! Come, bird, come." They ask him for his news and, after pledging them to secrecy, reveals that any "villain dwelling in all Denmark" is a thorough "knave" or scoundrel. To this Horatio well responds: "There needs no ghost, my lord, come from the grave to tell us this." Hamlet agrees and somewhat hysterically says that they should part, the others to their business and he to pray. Horatio notes: "These are but wild and whirling words, my lord," again indicating that Hamlet is not in a rational state.

Hamlet collects himself for a moment and tells them that "it is an honest ghost," that is, the true spirit of his father rather than a devil who has assumed his form, but that he cannot tell them what they said to each other. He now asks them once again to swear that they will never reveal what they have seen tonight, but they feel insulted that Hamlet should ask them again what they have already promised him. Hamlet continues that he wants them now to formally swear to this upon his sword and, as they continue to hesitate, the ghost cries from under the stage, "swear." This once again unsettles Hamlet's reason and he becomes hysterical, saying to the ghost: "Ha, ha, boy, say'st thou so? Art thou there, true-penny." He tells them to swear as they "hear this fellow in the cellarage." They shift ground but the ghost continues to follow them under the stage, repeatedly telling them to "swear by his sword." At this point Hamlet exclaims to the ghost: "Well said, old mole! Canst work i' th' earth so fast? O worthy pioner!"

COMMENT: During his meeting with the ghost, Hamlet was convinced that this was the true spirit of his father. Immediately thereafter, as he is swearing by heaven that he will carry out his father's command, a slight suspicion rises that it may after all have been a devil from hell. He rejects this idea but, as he thinks of his revenge, his mind becomes unsettled, a possibility Horatio had stressed in the event the ghost proved to be an evil spirit. Hamlet gains control of his reason and tells Horatio that the ghost was "honest" rather than a devil, but, as the ghost cries out from the several places beneath the platform, Hamlet's reason again becomes unsettled and he treats him as though he were a familiar devil with whom he had made a pact. Devils were often compared to "pioners" (miners) or "moles" in that they worked underground and were even thought to mine for treasure. Furthermore, Hamlet's complete lack of respect would not be fitting to the true ghost of his father. However much Hamlet's reason may tell him that this is "an honest ghost," then, he has a lurking suspicion that it may, in fact, be a devil and this suspicion acts to unsettle his reason. In addition, the ghost not only acts like a devil in the last part of the scene, but his effect upon Hamlet has been devilish, which continues the audience's own uncertainty as to the true nature of the ghost.

Hamlet once more returns to rationality, but his unsettling experience with the supernatural causes him to tell Horatio: "There are more things in heaven and earth, Horatio, / Than are dreamt of in your philosophy." Though the supernatural appears mysterious to Hamlet, his experience with it causes him to grant it a validity which Horatio's earlier scepticism would have denied. He now tells them that they should be careful not to give any indication, whether by look or word, that they know anything about this night as he may later think it necessary "to put an antic disposition on," that is, to act as though he were insane.

COMMENT: As Hamlet does periodically act insanely for much of the remainder of the play and as he here says that he is going to consciously put on an act of madness for his own purposes, the question has long been argued as to the true nature of Hamlet's madness. Though this question can never be answered with any certainty, the fact that Hamlet's sanity had begun to totter before he got the idea of playing mad is significant. It suggests that Hamlet may have decided to play mad because he is afraid of actually going mad and can use the role of madness to mask and relieve his true psychological instability. It is true that in the original story the Hamlet character assumes the role of madness to further and conceal his investigation of the king, but Shakespeare's Hamlet makes little if any use of his assumed madness in this way, and so the psychological interpretation of Hamlet's assumed madness seems more justified.

Horatio and Marcellus now formally swear to keep Hamlet's two secrets, the meeting with the ghost and Hamlet's assumed madness, and they now prepare to part. Before leaving, however, Hamlet says, "The time is out of joint. O cursed spite / That ever I was born to set it right!"

COMMENT: Hamlet sees his mission of revenge as one of social reform. We have seen this impulse to change the world rather than to accept its evils in his earlier moments of satire, and the ghost has now given this impulse a positive direction and purpose. But, however much part of Hamlet may desire to cause a drastic change in the world, the other part of him desires only to withdraw from this evil world and may provide a constitutional hindrance to the easy accomplishment of his assigned task. When the ghost had first appeared, Hamlet had said: "My fate cries out." But now he considers it spiteful of fate to have assigned him a task so difficult for a person like himself to carry out—how difficult we shall see in the remainder of the play.

SUMMARY: These two scenes accomplish the following purposes in closing the first act:

1. Claudius, who impressed us favorably in the second scene, is now revealed to have been the murderer of his brother after having committed adultery with his wife. This places his Christian advice to Hamlet about accepting the evil of the world as the will of heaven in a new light.

2. Hamlet is given the task to revenge his father's murder and rid his court of evil. This task is given supernatural sanction, which may indicate that, as Horatio said, "Heaven will direct it." This is especially possible since Claudius has been shown to be an improper spokesman for the will of heaven. There are, however, strong counter suggestions that the ghost may be a devil and that Hamlet may be endangering his life and soul in following his commands.

3. Two reasons are given which may help to explain Hamlet's later delay in carrying out his assigned task:

　　a. The uncertain nature of the ghost, which is the main theme of the first act. Hamlet's own uncertainty, which carries with it an uncertainty as to whether the ghost's commands ought to be followed, has already troubled him to the point of mental instability.

　　b. Hamlet's melancholic and generally unstable state of mind, shown in the second scene. The former quality causes Hamlet to feel that he is personally unsuited to the active role of the revenger; the latter, already increased to near insanity by his confusing encounter with the ghost, may make it difficult for him to concentrate rationally upon the act of revenge.

4. The act had begun by showing us first an ominous ghost and then an apparently well-ordered state. It ends with Hamlet in the power of the ghost, sworn to overthrow the state, mentally unstable and considering further assuming the role of madness. The action of the play, the course of Hamlet's revenge, has now been determined. The introduction of situation, characters and theme now completed, the stage is set for action.

Act II: Scene i

We are once again in the rooms of Polonius, and Polonius is seen sending off his servant, Reynaldo, to Paris with money and letters for his son, Laertes. He tells Reynaldo that he should inquire about the behavior of Laertes before he visits him. Reynaldo, who seems to know his master's ways very well, tells Polonius that he had already intended to do this and is well praised for this in turn. Polonius now instructs him in some of the refinements of spying. He is to find some Danish acquaintances of Laertes and casually bring up the subject of Laertes. He is then to suggest that Laertes is a libertine, that he gambles, duels, swears and goes to brothels. Reynaldo objects that this would dishonor Laertes, but Polonius explains that this will draw out, either by agreement or denial, the truth about Laertes' behavior as it has been seen by these other Danes. In the middle of this explanation, Polonius forgets what he wants to say and has to be reminded of what he had just said by Reynaldo. Polonius then concludes with a generalization about his tactics, that it is wisdom to be devious in approaching one's target for one can best "by indirections find directions out." Satisfied that Reynaldo has learned his lesson, Polonius bids him goodbye but with a final order to make sure that Laertes is keeping up his musical studies.

COMMENT: In this scene we see the absent-minded old man give Reynaldo the true fruits of his life-long experience, not the high moralizing about integrity he gave to Laertes, but the knowledge of successful spying and falsehood which has become almost second nature to him. His conclusion is doubly significant to the play, for we shall see that all attempts at direct planning are doomed to failure.

Ophelia now enters in a very frightened condition. She explains that, as she was sewing alone in her room, Hamlet had entered in a very disordered state, his jacket unlaced, without a hat, his stockings dirty and hanging down ungartered to his ankles, his knees knocking together, "And with a look so piteous in purport / As if he had been loosed out of hell / To speak of horrors."

He had taken hold of her wrist and held her hard at arm's length with one hand while his other hand was held over his brow. Staying a long time in this position, he observed her face with the intense concentration of one who would draw it. At last, shaking her arm a little and nodding to himself three times in silent agreement with something, he made such a pitiful and deep sigh that it seemed capable of ending his life. He then let her go and went out of the room, but as he left his head was turned over his shoulder and he continued to stare at her until he was out of the door.

COMMENT: When last we saw Hamlet, his mind had been unsettled by his meeting with the ghost, which raised further questions about the nature of this ghost. Ophelia's comment that he now looked "as if he had been loosed out of hell to speak of horrors" strengthens the view even further that the ghost has been playing a devilish role towards Hamlet both in his disclosures and commands, for Hamlet's soul now appears to be in the power of hell.

As this scene comes right after the scene with the ghost and as nothing has yet been said about any passage of time, its dramatic effect upon the spectator is to reinforce the evidence of the ghost scene. In Act III: Scene ii, Ophelia reveals that two months have passed since the events in Act I. But, as we shall see, when Ophelia says that it is "twice two months" since his father died, Hamlet replies, "died two months ago, and not forgotten yet?" This indicates that, for Hamlet, time has stopped since his encounter with the ghost, for this occurred on the day when, in his first soliloquy, Hamlet had said that his father was "but two months dead, nay, not so much, not two."

In terms of Hamlet's psychology, then, as well as of dramatic effect, the scene with Ophelia seems to be a direct effect of his encounter with the ghost. In despair over the ghost's disclosures about his mother's incestuous adultery with his uncle, Hamlet comes to his beloved's room to search her face for some proof that she is not like his mother. But, as he searches her frightened face he seems to find only confirmation for what he feared, as his nodding head and anguished sigh reveal. Furthermore, he has some justification for his disillusionment with her. As we immediately learn, Ophelia, following her father's orders, has rejected Hamlet's advances after having first been most obliging. Her face may look innocent, as it most assuredly does, but this only proves her falseness, that like his mother to his father, she can appear loving and then immediately change her behavior. And as he looks so deeply into her eyes, he may perceive some potentiality for lust which nobody should suspect but which is later revealed by the sensual vulgarity she displays in her insanity. Finally, even in this scene she fails him, for she stands with mute terror at the sight of his anguish and does nothing to try to understand or calm him. The effect of this is to destroy whatever lingering love he may still have felt for her and to confirm his belief in the frailty of all women.

Polonius decides that Hamlet is suffering from frustrated love and, forgetful once more, asks Ophelia whether she has quarrelled with him. She replies: "No, my good lord; but as you did command / I did repel his letters and denied / His access to me." Polonius, having forgotten all about his hasty command, now concludes that this is the source of Hamlet's madness. He now makes an unusual admission about his own character; he admits that he showed poor judgement with regards to Hamlet's intentions but excuses this on the grounds of old age: "By heaven, it is as proper to our age / To cast beyond ourselves in our opinions / As it is common for the younger sort / To lack discretion." Old age, he says, is given to authoritarian presumption of its wisdom while having lost the power of true judgement. He now decides to take Ophelia to the King with this discovery as to the source of Hamlet's madness.

SUMMARY: This scene accomplishes the following purposes:

1. It confirms our opinion of Polonius from his own mouth, showing him to be a foolish, authoritarian old man who yet prides himself on his power of intrigue. The scene begins with Polonius' instructions to Reynaldo as to how he should spy upon his son and ends with his going to Claudius with, as we shall see, new plans for spying. In both of these instances he shows no more respect or regard for the true feelings of his children than he did for Hamlet's: he is sending his servant to spy upon his son and violating his daughter's modesty and feelings by bringing her before the King in order to advance his own position in the King's respect, to prove to him that, despite his advancing age, he is just as good a counselor-of-state as he ever was under the late King Hamlet.

2. The narrated scene in Ophelia's room (called "closet" in Elizabethan times) serves three purposes:

a. It continues the thematic questioning of the ghost's true identity, reinforcing the suspicion that it is actually a devil, since Hamlet's soul has been reduced to a state of hell.

b. It introduces through narration the change in Hamlet's behavior and attire before we actually see him. In Act I: Scene i, we were told that Hamlet was dressed in complete mourning but there was nothing said of any disarray. Now we are told that his clothing is completely disordered and dirty. John Dover Wilson suggests that this is the way he is to dress for much of the remainder of the play: it is the sign of his assumed madness, though his emotional disturbance over Ophelia seems genuine enough.

c. It shows that Hamlet's continuing disturbance over the infidelity of his mother has now affected his ability to love Ophelia, and it marks his last moment of genuine involvement with her while she lives.

Act II: Scene ii

The scene shifts to a room in the castle where Claudius and Gertrude are greeting Rosencrantz and Guildenstern. These gentlemen are boyhood friends of Hamlet whom Claudius has recalled to Denmark in the hope that they may be able to help him investigate the nature of Hamlet's increasing mental disorder. His "transformation," earlier described by Ophelia, seems to Claudius to have resulted from more than simply his father's death, and he hopes that by discovering the reason for this these friends may help him to restore Hamlet's health. The Queen seconds this with the promise of an ample reward, and they agree to help the King.

COMMENT: This scene indicates that there has been some passage of time during which Hamlet's behavior has become increasingly mad. Whether Hamlet has achieved anything by this means we do not yet know, but we do know that it has caused speculation in the court and sufficient worry on Claudius' part for him to have sent for two spies to investigate Hamlet. Whereas earlier he was anxious only to gain Hamlet's goodwill, Hamlet's "madness" has now placed Claudius on his guard against him. Polonius' delight to have discovered, as he thinks, the cause of Hamlet's "madness" and his immediate going to Claudius with the news show how concerned the court and particularly Claudius had become with the topic of Hamlet's "madness."

Polonius enters with the news of the return of the ambassadors to Norway. He then says: "And I do think—or else this brain of mine / Hunts not the trail of policy so sure / As it hath used to do—that I have found / The very cause of Hamlet's lunacy." (If Polonius was forced in the last scene to admit that his lack of judgment was a symptom of old age, he now hopes to dispel any similar doubt that Claudius may have about his continuing usefulness.) Claudius is more anxious to hear of this than of the results of his ambassadors: "O, speak of that! That do I long to hear." But Polonius asks that the ambassadors be attended to first and Claudius agrees. While Polonius goes to bring in the ambassadors, Claudius tells his "dear Gertrude" that Polonius thinks he has discovered the source of her son's disorder, but she is convinced that she already knows the reason: "I doubt it is no other but the main / His father's death and our o'er-hasty marriage."

COMMENT: This private conference reveals two things about Gertrude: good insight into her son's character (as these were the original reasons for Hamlet's despair), and lack of any possible knowledge of her former husband's murder. It is interesting that while Claudius had only mentioned his father's death as a possible reason for Hamlet's madness, Gertrude is also sensitive to the effect her hasty remarriage has had upon her son. Claudius' term of endearment towards her also indicates that his feelings for her far exceed lust, as will be shown more fully later on.

Voltemand now enters with the news of his successful mission to Norway; the King of Norway, upon investigating Fortinbras' activities, had found Claudius to be correct and, very grieved by this, had restrained his nephew from attacking Denmark. He has, however, decided to deploy Fortinbras and the force he has raised against Poland, and now asks Claudius' permission for the safe passage of these troops through Denmark on their way to Poland. Claudius' immediate reaction to this is positive but he is far too impatient to hear Polonius' theory about Hamlet to give him his full attention to this matter now. Telling the ambassadors that they will feast together at night, he bids them retire now and turns to Polonius.

Although saying that "brevity is the soul of wit," Polonius is so long-winded about getting to the point that the Queen finally interrupts him with the words, "more matter, with less art." But Polonius continues awhile with comically pretentious rhetoric until he finally gets to the point: his daughter has obediently given him a love letter to her from Hamlet. He now proceeds to read this letter which almost rivals his own comic speeches in its over-wrought, conventional love melancholy. Claudius, satisfied with Hamlet's love for Ophelia, asks Polonius how she has received his love, and he replies his duty towards the King led him to tell his daughter that, as the Prince was so far above her, "she should lock herself from his resort, / Admit no messengers, receive no tokens." She had done this and the result of this rejection of his love, Polonius concludes, has led to Hamlet's progressive madness. Claudius asks Gertrude whether she thinks this is the reason, and she replies, "It may be, very like." Polonius claims that his advice has always been correct and that they should behead him "if this be otherwise."

Claudius now asks him what they might do to further investigate his theory and Polonius suggests a plan with which he had evidently come prepared. He says that there is a spot near where they are standing where Hamlet often walks for four hours at a time. "At such a time I'll loose my daughter to him," he suggests, while the King and he observe from behind a hanging tapestry the nature of their encounter. If this does not prove his case, he concludes, "Let me be no assistant for a state / But keep a farm and carters." The King agrees to try Polonius' plan, whereupon Hamlet enters.

COMMENT: John Dover Wilson in *What Happens in Hamlet* has proposed the theory, which has recently gained widespread critical and theatrical acceptance, that Hamlet entered unobserved at the back of the stage before his announced entrance and thus overheard the plot. Such a theory seriously alters the usual reading of this later scene, as shall be discussed at that time. Although Mr. Wilson argues his case very persuasively, it is by no means proven. A second point about this last portion of the scene is the complete reduction of Polonius to a comic figure, posturing ridiculously about both his verbal style and his subtle reasoning, though we may note a touch of increasing insecurity about his value to the state.

The Queen notes how "sadly the poor wretch comes reading," and Polonius begs them to leave him alone with Hamlet. He tries to make conversation with Hamlet but Hamlet counters everything he says with apparently mad but actually quite satiric thrusts. He calls Polonius a "fishmonger," which also meant a pimp, and tells him that he had better not let his daughter walk in the sun as she may conceive spontaneously like maggots.

COMMENT: Wilson uses this to support his theory that Hamlet overheard Polonius' conference with the King, since Polonius' statement to "loose" his daughter to him is language which an Elizabethan procurer would use in reference to his whore. In any case, Hamlet is speaking very coarsely about Ophelia.

Polonius, further convinced by this that Hamlet's madness has resulted from his disappointed love, now asks him what he is reading. After bandying about with this for a while, Hamlet finally says that he is reading slanders against old age by a "satirical rogue" who says that "old men have grey beards, that their faces are wrinkled" and "that they have a plentiful lack of wit, together with most weak hams," all of which, though he agrees with it, he does not think it decent to write down since Polonius, himself, is old. At this Polonius silently comments, "Though this be madness, yet there is method in't." After a few more lines in which Hamlet shows a disconcerting wit, Polonius decides to leave and says, "I will most humbly take my leave of you." Hamlet begins to return this satirically but then his mood abruptly changes: "You cannot, sir, take from me anything that I will more willingly part withal—except my life, except my life, except my life." After Polonius starts to leave, Hamlet expresses his final disgust with Polonius: "These tedious old fools!"

COMMENT: This is the first glimpse we gain of Hamlet's supposed "madness" and we see it take the form of brilliant but savage satirical wit. Hamlet is using the post of madness here as a license to say anything he feels like saying. That he genuinely feels Polonius to be a tedious old fool and has no use for such people we know from his own statement, but his role of madman permits him to make unmerciful fun of Polonius. Indeed, Hamlet here exhibits an extreme hatred and bitterness towards Polonius. This might be explained by Hamlet's awareness of Polonius' interference with his love and, possibly, Polonius' plan to use Ophelia against him in the service of his enemy, Claudius. Our respect for Polonius has been so reduced by this time, however, that we can hardly blame Hamlet for his treatment of him. In his last lines to Polonius moreover, we see that Hamlet is still in the same psychological state in which we first saw him, the rapid alternation between destructive satire and self-destructive melancholy, between hysteria and depression.

Rosencrantz and Guildenstern now enter and are happily greeted by Hamlet as "My excellent good friends!" After some introductory kidding with them about the state of their fortune, he asks them what they have done to deserve being sent here to "prison." When they question Hamlet's reference to Denmark as a prison, he replies: "Why, then 'tis none to you, for there is nothing either good or bad but thinking makes it so. To me it is a prison." Seizing this opportunity to begin their investigation, they suggest, "Why, then your ambition makes it one." After arguing this point, he asks them again, in the "way of friendship," what they are doing at Elsinore. They reply that they have come simply to visit him. Hamlet thanks them for this but then immediately asks whether it is a free visit or whether they were sent for by the King and Queen. They hesitate to answer him; he asks them again; and, as they finally confer on an answer, Hamlet says to himself, "Nay then, I have an eye of you." They finally do admit, "My, lord, we were sent for," but it is too late—Hamlet's trust has been alienated. In one of the most beautiful speeches in the play, Hamlet now explains to them why they were sent for: "I have of late—but wherefore I know not—lost all my mirth." In his depressed state the good earth seems to him "a sterile promontory," the majestic heavens appear "nothing to him but a foul and pestilent congregation of vapors," man, himself, with his noble reason, infinite faculties and beauty, seems to him the "quintessence of dust."

COMMENT: Hamlet here explains the source of his statement that "there is nothing either good or bad but thinking makes it so," that our understanding of objective reality depends upon our perception of it which differs from individual to individual and from time to time. Although Hamlet's reason and memory tell him that the earth, heavens and man are beautiful and meaningful, something in his spirit has made him no longer able to perceive them that way. Life and the heavens seem sterile and meaningless because man can only come to dust. Why it is he should feel this so deeply that it has warped his whole perception of existence, however, he admits that he does not know. Although he is countering their earlier suggestion, which evidently came from Claudius, that it is disappointed ambition, there is also about his words the tone of true confession. Hamlet is to continue through most of the play to try to analyze what it is that has placed him in this psychological state of depressed inactivity and general irrationality; Claudius and his followers also try to analyze Hamlet's condition, as we have seen; finally, all critics of the play for three hundred years have tried to explain this central mystery at the heart of the play. Hamlet's statement here, then, is the starting point for the "problem of Hamlet."

Rosencrantz and Guildenstern now tell Hamlet of the coming of a company of actors and there is some discussion between them of acting companies which reflects the conditions in the Elizabethan theatre at the time. Before the players enter, however, Hamlet tells Rosencrantz and Guildenstern that they are welcome to Elsinore. More than this, he also tells them that Claudius and Gertrude are deceived about his madness, that he is only mad when he feels like it and can otherwise be perfectly sane, as indeed has been shown in this scene with them.

COMMENT: Since Hamlet has already concluded that they are spies, he is very careless in making this important admission to them. This can only be explained as forgetfulness on Hamlet's part due to his enjoyment of their company, to his ability to discuss with them such varied topics as the state of his soul and the condition of theatrical companies. This is one of the first signs of Hamlet's lack of precaution in his dealings with Claudius, as opposed to Claudius' many precautions throughout the play.

Polonius now enters with the players. He introduces them with comical pretentiousness which leads Hamlet once again to make fun of him in the role of madman. Hamlet now welcomes the players and asks them as a proof of their quality to recite a speech from one of their plays about the death of Priam, the old King of Troy, which he begins. Hamlet's delivery is praised by Polonius and then the player continues: Pyrrhus

drives at Priam but "in rage strikes wide." Nonetheless, Priam, the "unnerved father," falls from the wind of Pyrrhus' sword. Instead of killing him then, however, "his sword, / Which was declining on the milky head / Of reverend Priam, seemed i' the' air to stick" and, against his own will, "did nothing." Finally however, "aroused vengeance sets him new awork" and never did blows fall like those now on Priam. He now continues with an impassioned speech on Hecuba's grief over the death of her husband, Priam. Hamlet is delighted with the player's recitation and asks him whether the company could play "The Murder of Gonzago" that night with an insertion of a speech of "some dozen or sixteen lines" which he would write himself. The player agrees to do this and Hamlet tells Polonius to see that they are well looked after, upon which they all depart, leaving Hamlet alone.

COMMENT: The speech that Hamlet remembers and wants to hear recited is interesting as a reflection of Hamlet's own preoccupations. In the speech a revenger is at first unable to commit revenge, but can only act wildly. This, however, disarms his opponent and eventually he is able to accomplish his revenge with great vigor. The situation parallels Hamlet's own plight. Months have passed and instead of sweeping to his revenge as he had told the ghost he would do, he has only acted madly. That he is beginning to feel some guilt about his delay is shown by his remembrance of this speech with its similar mad delay in revenge. He hopes to quiet his conscience by remembering that a similar revenger finally did accomplish his purposes. But the guilt only further emerges when he is alone.

We now come to Hamlet's second soliloquy. Hamlet begins with the exclamation: "O, what a rogue and peasant slave am I!" It seems monstrous to him that the player could so work himself up "for nothing, / For Hecuba! / What's Hecuba to him, or he to Hecuba, / That he should weep for her?" He wonders "what would he do / Had he the motive and the cue for passion / That I have?" Though the player, with such real motivation would "make mad the guilty," he, "a dull and muddy-mettled rascal," moans about in a dream without any real feeling for his cause and "can say nothing," no, not even for a dear King who was cursedly murdered. He then asks himself whether he is a "coward." At first he is horrified by such a humiliating suggestion, but then he concedes that it must be so, that "I am pigeon-livered and lack gall / To make oppression bitter" since he has not yet fattened the vultures with Claudius' guts. He then tries to work up a passion against Claudius by yelling: "Bloody, bawdy villain! Remorseless, treacherous, lecherous, kindless villain! / O, vengeance!" But then he immediately realizes,

"Why, what an ass am I!" This is some bravery, that the son of a dear murdered father, "prompted to my revenge by heaven and hell," must release the feelings of his heart simply with words rather than with action.

He now finally puts his brains to work upon the revenge. He remembers having heard "that guilty creatures sitting at a play" which represented their own crime have been so struck by guilt that they have confessed their crime. He decides (apparently having already forgotten that he had just instructed the players to do the same thing) that he will "have these players / Play something like the murther of my father / Before mine uncle. I'll observe his looks" and if he but flinches "I know my course." This is the first time we have seen Hamlet express any doubt about his course, but the reason he gives is one that he may well have entertained:

> The spirit that I have seen
> May be a devil, and the devil hath power
> T'assume a pleasing shape, yea, and perhaps
> Out of my weakness and my melancholy,
> As he is very potent with such spirits,
> Abuses me to damn me.

He decides that he needs further objective proof of Claudius' guilt and that "The play's the thing / Wherein I'll catch the conscience of the king."

COMMENT: The second soliloquy shows us the following important things about Hamlet:

1. Hamlet has not been able to concentrate on the subject of his revenge for reasons that he cannot understand. When a chance circumstance does cause him to think about it, he feels guilt which, in turn, causes him to rationalize about his delay. Not that his suspicion about the ghost is not valid, but it is an afterthought to explain his delay rather than its actual cause.

2. We see, however, that when Hamlet does think about his revenge he is caught up in a conflict of values. This conflict, which has persisted throughout Western culture and was particularly strong during the Renaissance, is that between the honor code and the religious code. The honor code was the mark which distinguished the aristocrat from the "peasant slave." His "gall" was quickly raised by any sign of "oppression" or humiliation and he was always ready to bravely risk his life to vindicate his honor or the honor of his family. One of the obligations of a man of honor was to revenge the death of his father; not to do this was to be a "coward," the mark of the "peasant slave" who desired only to preserve his life whatever the cost. When, however, dishonor was inevitable, the honor code preached suicide as the only way of proving one's superiority to his fate. The man of honor aspired to greatness and was only afraid of shame. In contrast to this, the religious code preached that

goodness was superior to greatness. The signs of the "great soul" according to the honor code, its willingness to commit murderous revenge or suicide, were mortal sins according to religious interpretation. Goodness expresses itself not through a vaunting superiority to fate but a humble acceptance of whatever heaven may send. As Job says in the Bible, "The Lord giveth and the Lord taketh away. Blessed be the name of the Lord." As a Christian gentleman, Hamlet is pulled by both of these opposing codes of values. He cannot bear the thought of dishonor, though the vindication of his honor and nobility can only be accomplished through murder, and he is also anxious to secure the salvation of his soul which premeditated murder would place in danger of damnation. The "Christian gentleman" was a contradiction in terms since such a character desired to avoid both shame in this world and damnation in the next and he could not have it both ways.

3. If this conflict in values is not the primary cause of Hamlet's delay and mental disorder, which remains mysterious, it is of primary thematic importance for the play, for it is by means of these codes that we are asked to evaluate Hamlet. Thus it is the spectator as well as Hamlet who must decide which of these codes is to be preferred, and it is also in terms of this question that the ghost is to be judged. If the ghost is demanding of Hamlet that which will damn him, and if the question of salvation is more important than that of honor, then the spectator should seriously entertain with Hamlet the possibility that the ghost may be a devil who has been attracted by his melancholy to tempt him into a damnable murder. It may well be, then, that Hamlet is ethically right to delay his revenge even though the question of ethics is not the primary source of delay.

SUMMARY: This scene accomplishes the following purposes:

1. It exhibits Hamlet's assumed madness in both words and behavior and starts the theorizing as to its source: Polonius believes it comes from disappointed love; Rosencrantz and Guildenstern, probably from a cue by Claudius, believe it results from frustrated ambition for the throne; Gertrude believes it results simply from Hamlet's shock at the death of his father and her hasty remarriage; and Hamlet is at a loss to explain the drastic inner change that has come over him.

2. It begins the cross-plotting of the chief characters against each other. Hamlet's assumed madness, decided upon at the end of Act I, which was supposed to achieve some unspecified and probably unthought-of purpose, has now so raised Claudius' suspicions that he has sent to Rosencrantz and Guildenstern to spy upon Hamlet, which they begin to do in this scene. Polonius plans to test his theory by confronting Hamlet with his daughter while Claudius and he spy upon the meeting from behind a tapestry. Hamlet plans to test the ghost's truth and Claudius' guilt through the performance of a play upon a similar crime which he will revise for this purpose. These last two plots are to occupy much of the first two scenes of Act III.

3. It further exhibits the character of Hamlet, his savage wit towards Polonius (who has become little more than a pretentious fool), his profound reflective quality in conversation with Rosencrantz and Guildenstern, his delight to see them and also the players, his love of the theatre, and his savage attack upon himself, combined with his lack of personal understanding.

Act III: Scene i

The scene is set in the room in the castle where the planned encounter of Hamlet and Ophelia is to take place. The King and Queen are present surrounded by Polonius, Ophelia, Rosencrantz, Guildenstern and other lords. Claudius is in the midst of asking Rosencrantz and Guildenstern whether they have discovered anything concerning the cause of Hamlet's madness, but they answer that Hamlet "with a crafty madness" has kept from "confession of his true state." Gertrude asks them how he received them and whether they have been able to interest him in any pastime. They reply that he treated them like a gentleman and was overjoyed by their news of the arrival of a company of players whom he has already ordered to appear this night before him. Polonius says that Hamlet has also asked the King and Queen to attend the performance, and Claudius says that he is happy to hear of Hamlet's new interest and to support it by attendance.

Rosencrantz and Guildenstern now leave and Claudius suggests that Gertrude leave also as he has secretly sent for Hamlet that he may accidentally meet Ophelia. Claudius and Polonius mean to spy on the encounter to test whether Polonius' theory of the source of Hamlet's madness, disappointed love, is correct. Gertrude tells Ophelia that she hopes Ophelia is "the happy cause of Hamlet's madness" and that, if her virtues are able to cure him, there would be a hope for their marriage. As Ophelia seconds her hope, Gertrude leaves. Polonius now instructs Ophelia that, while the King and he hide themselves, she is to walk there by herself reading a pious book since this would serve to explain her lonely presence. He now reflects, as well he might, that people are often to blame for covering evil behavior with a show of "pious action." In an "aside" (a speech spoken to the audience and meant to indicate silent thought), Claudius reveals that Polonius' words have stung his conscience, for he too covers his deed with behavior as false as a harlot's

painted charms. The maintenance of this falsehood has become so difficult for him that he must cry out, "O heavy burden!"

COMMENT: This is the first objective proof we have had to substantiate the ghost's charges against Claudius, for he admits an unspecified evil "deed." In this admission, furthermore, we see that Claudius does have an essentially moral nature, for his conscience can become anguished by a chance remark. This also prepares us for Claudius' hysterical breakdown during the performance of the play in the next scene. All of this shows us that Claudius is not naturally evil and is oppressed both by the guilt of having committed evil and by the falseness he has to assume to cover the fact of his guilt.

As Hamlet is now heard approaching, Claudius and Polonius withdraw behind the painted tapestry to watch his encounter with Ophelia.

Hamlet enters so involved with his own thoughts that he does not at first see Ophelia. We now hear the famous "To be or not to be" soliloquy. He begins by questioning which is the "nobler" code of behavior, that which bids one "to be," to live even though this means "to suffer" from "outrageous fortune," or that which bids one "not to be," to commit suicide and thus "end" one's suffering through the act of "opposing" the outrage which fortune would do him. "To die," he reasons, is "to sleep—no more," and by such a sleep it is possible to "end the heartache, and the thousand natural shocks" that human beings inherit in the process of being born. Such an end to human troubles, he concludes, is "a consummation devoutly to be wished." "To die," he repeats, is "to sleep," but in sleep, he now remembers, there is also the possibility of dreams and this creates a new difficulty. For when we have cast off the difficulties of life "in that sleep of death," we do not know "what dreams may come," and this must cause us to hesitate before committing suicide. This is what causes people to endure the "calamity" of a "long life." For who would bear the injuries of existence, the wrongs and humiliations of oppression, "the pangs of despised love," the delay in both law and position which those with merit must patiently bear from the unworthy and insolent people who do receive high office, who would bear the general burdens of "a weary life,

> But that the dread of something after death,
> The undiscovered country, from whose bourn
>   [confinement]
> No traveller returns, puzzles the will,
> And makes us rather bear those ills we have
> Than fly to others that we know not of?

This consciousness of the religious problem involved with suicide, the dread of eternal punishment, "does make cowards of us all," and "the pale cast of thought" sickens the power of "resolution," and this not only with regards to suicide but to all great "enterprises," whose force is similarly turned away into inaction through overconsideration. He now sees Ophelia at her prayers and tells her to include in them "all my sins."

COMMENT: In our last view of Hamlet during the "rogue and peasant slave" soliloquy, we saw Hamlet in a state of guilt over his long inaction which was resolved by a new commitment to a course of positive action. Now, but a few hours later, we see him sunk once more in suicidal melancholy, forgetful of the whole question of this revenge. He is, however, still concerned by the conflict between the honor and religious codes, but it is now centered on the question of suicide rather than murder. As either course, however, would lead him into mortal sin, he does well to tell Ophelia to pray for "all my sins." Though prompted by honor first to revenge and now to suicide, his religious beliefs inhibit him from taking such action.

But the power of his religion over him is more negative than positive; it is fear of eternal punishment rather than the value of righteousness which motivates him. As fear, however, is an ignoble emotion, his sense of honor arises once more to accuse him of cowardice, just as it did in the previous soliloquy. He concludes that the reason for the cowardly inaction which he despises in himself is that he thinks too much and overintellectualizes his problems to the point of inertia. Hamlet's conclusion here has been accepted by the great nineteenth century English poet and critic, Samuel Taylor Coleridge, as the solution to the problem of Hamlet's inactivity, and it has remained one of the standard critical approaches to the play although it is less in favor at present. To return to our earlier discussion, we see that as long as the power of Hamlet's religion over him is a negative one, it cannot destroy the influence of the honor code upon his spirit, but simply inhibits its power to motivate sustained positive action. The result is that Hamlet remains a prey to the worst effects of both codes, guilt and shame, which has the additional result of driving him still further into suicidal melancholy. He has but to think of taking action, as he does in the second soliloquy, and he becomes so overwhelmed by internal conflicts, that he soon can desire nothing but suicide, as we see in the third soliloquy. But this in turn produces its own vicious cycle of guilt, followed by shame which proceeds to such a point that he feels shackled by his very consciousness of such thoughts, and blames them in turn for his inactivity.

It is, however, the nature of his conflicts, part of which he admits that he does not himself understand, which produces his inertia rather than any overintellectualizing he may do about them. The inertia is there; the intellectualizing comes afterwards as an attempt to understand the inactivity and then becomes useful to Hamlet as a means of rationalizing his unfathomed apathy and melancholy. As we have seen in the two past soliloquies, Hamlet thinks about his problems just to the point at which he can develop some rationalization for his inactivity (in the second soliloquy it is doubt about the ghost's nature, in the third soliloquy it is overintellectualization of his problems), and then he concludes his inner investigations, fully satisfied for the time.

One other interesting statement he makes here is that "no traveller returns" from "the undiscovered country" of death. Such a statement would deny that the ghost was the spirit of his father returned from death and would indicate that the doubt about the ghost had grown stronger in the interval between the two soliloquies. This in turn would free him from the sense of obligation to commit revenge, and so the necessity for life, and enable him more freely to contemplate suicide. But this statement also indicates a weakening of his religious convictions to a point of agnosticism, further showing the negative quality of his religion and perhaps even a result of the ever more deadening effect of religious commandments upon his impulses. This agnosticism, however, is important for tragedy which requires the spectator to feel that death is dreadful. If there were no question that Hamlet was going to heaven at the end of the play (as Horatio claims), his death would not really be tragic.

One final question concerns the form of this soliloquy. There are some modern critics who see it only as an exercise in rhetoric such as Hamlet might have studied at the University of Wittenberg. While it is true that the question form of the soliloquy, with the balancing of two alternatives, is similar to rhetorical exercises of the time and might indicate that Hamlet was using his logical training to attack his personal problems, to dismiss the whole soliloquy as an intellectual exercise or game is going too far, for the first soliloquy is also personally concerned with suicide and Hamlet is immediately to make some further suicidal statements in his scene with Ophelia.

The meeting between Hamlet and Ophelia begins politely as Ophelia asks Hamlet how he has been feeling these past days and he replies that he has been feeling well. She then tells him that she has with her some things he had given her which she has long desired to return to him and prays him now to receive them. He denies having given her anything and she, apparently hurt by this, says that she knows very well that he did and with his presents added such sweet words "as made the things more rich." Since this sweetness is now gone, she bids him take back his presents, for "rich gifts wax poor when givers prove unkind." He then laughs out hysterically and asks her whether she is "honest," and again whether she is "fair" (that is, "white" as is the color of purity and virtue). She does not understand what he is driving at and asks him what he means, to which he answers, "That if you be honest and fair, your honesty should admit no discourse to your beauty," that is, if she were truly virtuous, she would not admit anyone to approach her beauty. She takes his verbal quibble in another sense and asks him whether beauty could do better than to go with honesty. He becomes ever more hysterical and says that she is right, for beauty has such power that it can "transform honesty from what it is to a bawd." Though this seems a paradox, it has recently been proven. He then abruptly claims, "I did love you once." She, still hurt though now apparently vindicated, answers, "Indeed, my lord, you made me believe so." To this Hamlet lashes out at her that she should not have believed him since his stock is so sullied that it is incapable of virtue. He now as abruptly claims, "I loved you not," and she even more sadly replies, "I was the more sadly deceived." He then cries out to her in a long, bitter speech: "Get thee to a nunnery. Why wouldest thou be a breeder of sinners? I am myself indifferent honest, but yet I could accuse me of such things that it were better my mother had not borne me: I am very proud, revengeful, ambitious, with more offenses at my beck than I have thoughts to put them in, imagination to give them shape, or time to act them in. What should such fellows as I do crawling between earth and heaven? We are arrant knaves all; believe none of us. Go thy ways to a nunnery." He then abruptly asks her where her father is and, when she replies that he is at home, he says that Polonius should be locked in there "that he may play the fool nowhere but in's own house." He bids her "farewell," but, as she prays to heaven to help him, he continues that if she should marry she can take this curse with her that however chastely she may behave she will still gain a bad reputation. He tells her again to go to a nunnery, says farewell again, and then continues that if she must marry she should marry a fool, "for wise men know well enough what monsters you make of them." He sends her to a nunnery again, says farewell again, and, as she prays again to heaven to restore his sanity, he continues his outburst against her, this time directed against women's cosmetics, "paintings." He charges, "God hath given you one face, and you make yourselves another." As he continues against the seductive movements, tones and nicknaming habits of women, he finally cries out, "Go to, I'll no more on't; it hath made me mad." He demands that there be no more marriages, though, "all but one" of those who are married "shall live." He tells her to go to a nunnery a final time and leaves without another word. Ophelia is left in a state of shocked despair at the behavior of her former lover. In a return to poetry after the prose of the last section, she exclaims, "O, what a noble mind is here

o'erthrown!" He who was the ideal courtier, soldier and scholar, the hope of the state, the model of fashion and manners, and of a most noble intelligence, is now completely disordered by madness, while she who received the sweetness of his love is the most wretched of ladies.

COMMENT: This scene calls for much discussion. The first point is Ophelia's attitude towards Hamlet and his reaction to this. We see that curiously enough Ophelia acts as though she were the injured party though we know it was she who first rejected Hamlet. His amazed question as to whether she is being honest or hypocritical is, then, natural enough. Though her sense of injury may have come from their last, silent meeting (which she recounted to her father) in which he did, indeed, reject her, she seems to have little understanding then as now of her own responsibility for his present behavior towards her. Hamlet's suspicions towards her may have been aroused not only by her assumption of innocence but also by her presence, fully prepared with all the things he had given her, at a place to which he was summoned. His belief that she is playing a hypocritical part with him may be even further explained by the theory that he overheard the plan for this meeting and is now remembering this. In any case, he begins to play a part of his own with her, assuming once more his role of madman. But the savagery of his attack on her and the nature of his disclosures about himself indicate that it may be not all an act, that his mind has been truly unsettled behind its assumed madness by this new "proof" of the falseness of a woman he once loved.

This proof further supports the generalization he had made about his mother, "frailty, thy name is woman," and in his continuing attacks he identifies Ophelia more and more with his mother. As he thinks about his mother's lustful nature, however, he begins to doubt his own feelings, since he is her son and has inherited a debased nature from her which may be incapable of any higher feeling than lust. But if his own feelings for Ophelia could not be trusted, neither can any other man's and it were better for Ophelia to leave the world of dishonest men and get to a nunnery. And not only should she not continue the process of breeding sinners, but neither should anyone else; there should be no more marriages, no more sex. (Some critics, following John Dover Wilson, argue that since the term "nunnery" was used in Elizabethan slang to refer to brothels, Hamlet is actually suggesting the opposite of what he appears to be saying, namely, that since she is playing the false part of the harlot with him she may as well drop any pretense of virtue and become a professional whore. This view is further strengthened by Wilson's theory that Hamlet overheard Polonius' slang references to his daughter as a whore, now recognizes that she is being used by her father and is directing this to Polonius' ears as well.)

We have already touched on the second important item, Hamlet's attitude towards himself. We remember that just before the start of this scene, upon seeing "the fair Ophelia," he had asked her to remember his sins in her prayers. Now he says that he could accuse himself "of such things that it were better my mother had not borne me," not only the things which are present to his conscious mind but offenses which he cannot even put into thought, which defy the power of his imagination though he senses them so deeply and is so revolted by them that he cannot see why such a person as he should be allowed even to crawl upon the earth. He feels, however, that it is something for which his mother is ultimately responsible. As he thinks about the whore-like falseness of his mother and Ophelia and all women, with their "paintings" and seductive ways, he cries out for an end to sex, for "it hath made me mad."

Now what all of this means at the very least is a definite sexual nausea: his mother's sensuality has revolted him and the thought that he may have inherited her nature and may be capable of equally base sexual desires is more than he can bear. The famous psychoanalyst, Ernest Jones, who was a student and the biographer of Freud, has suggested a psychoanalytic explanation of these lines and, following Freud, of the whole "problem of Hamlet," namely that Hamlet had an "Oedipus Complex." Freudian theory states that all men at a certain stage of their development subconsciously desire to reenact the crimes of the mythical Greek King, Oedipus, who murdered his father and married his mother. Like all growing children, Hamlet had repressed these forbidden desires and grown up into a model young man. When, however, Hamlet learns that Claudius has murdered Hamlet's father and married his mother, has fulfilled his own repressed desires, his old "Oedipus Complex" is reactivated though still repressed, because it is too horrible to be accepted by his conscious mind. Therefore, he feels suicidally revolted with himself for reasons that he cannot fathom. Moreover, he is subconsciously unable to condemn Claudius for having committed the very crimes he himself desired subconsciously to commit. But since he is not consciously aware of his "Oedipus Complex," he is at a loss to understand the source of his inability to act or even to think in any sustained fashion of such action.

While this theory explains very neatly aspects of the play which are difficult to explain otherwise, particularly Hamlet's obsessed preoccupation with his mother's sexual life, the difficulty with it is that it could not have been Shakespeare's expressed intention since he could not have known of Freud's theories. Jones gets around this difficulty by suggesting that Shakespeare's knowledge of the nature of the "Oedipus Complex" was intuitive since it was also true of himself and since it is generally agreed that Hamlet was Shakespeare's most autobiographical creation. However

this may be, Shakespeare could not have been consciously aware of this explanation for Hamlet's behavior, no matter how well he portrayed its symptoms, and this behavior remained for him as for his character, Hamlet, an ultimate mystery.

A final explanation of this scene is based on the theory that Hamlet overheard the plot to test him with Ophelia and that he is here acting a mad role primarily for the benefit of Claudius and Polonius. What is more, he is playing a rather reckless game with them in telling Claudius that he is "revengeful" and "ambitious." Thus he justifies Claudius' theory while at the same time warning him that "all but one shall live," and justifies Polonius' theory that it is women's false love which "hath made me mad," while at the same time attacking him directly as a fool and father of a whore.

Finally, Ophelia's closing description of Hamlet, it is generally agreed, is meant to be viewed as an objective portrait of Hamlet as he was before the death of his father and remarriage of his mother, which had already affected his state of mind at the beginning of the play.

Claudius and Polonius now come out from their hiding place each convinced of the truth of his own theory as to Hamlet's condition. Claudius begins by rejecting outright Polonius' theory about love. He also notes that "what he spake, though it lacked form a little, was not like madness." He believes that there is something in Hamlet's soul which is causing him to brood and which will finally "hatch" into some "danger." To prevent this eventuality, Claudius immediately decides to send Hamlet "with speed to England" with the covering excuse that he is going to demand of England the tribute it owes to Denmark. He tells Polonius that he hopes the change of surroundings "shall expel this something-settled matter in his heart," and asks Polonius what he thinks of the plan. Polonius agrees to it though he still believes "the origin and commencement of his grief / Sprung from neglected love." He asks Ophelia how she is but immediately turns from her to continue his discussion with Claudius despite his daughter's grief. He now suggests a new spying plan to Claudius, that after the play Gertrude should send for Hamlet and ask him to come alone to her room. She should then ask Hamlet plainly to explain to her what is troubling him. Polonius will himself be hidden in the room to overhear their conference. If Gertrude does not discover the source of his melancholy, then Claudius should send Hamlet to England. Claudius agrees with Polonius' new plan, concluding "Madness in great ones must not unwatched go." They leave and the scene ends.

SUMMARY: This scene again contrasts the characters of Claudius and Hamlet as follows:

1. Claudius actively investigates Hamlet's disturbing behavior, first with Rosencrantz and Guildenstern and then with Ophelia. Though he discovers nothing definite, Hamlet's behavior with Ophelia is so threatening to him that he acts with immediate decision to send Hamlet to England and thus protect himself. Claudius is a man of practical action who does what is necessary to achieve his goals, whether these be the gaining of a throne through murder or simple self-preservation. But though Claudius will murder to gain a selfish end, he is not thoroughly evil but feels genuine remorse for what he has done. What he desires most of all is for things to remain as they were at the beginning of the play so that he will not be forced to commit further evil to preserve himself.

2. Hamlet, on the other hand, is still incapable of action. Though he had recently decided on a plan of attack, when we see him now he has returned to suicidal melancholy and to the unsuccessful attempt to explain his behavior and nature. His scene with Ophelia brings out the worst aspect of his character, the almost inhuman savagery he shows to anyone he feels has injured him, here the innocent and too obedient Ophelia. His savagery, however, is verbal, and no matter how he may threaten Claudius, its effect is to place him at a greater disadvantage with regard to its object.

Act III: Scene ii

Hamlet enters a hall of the castle explaining to the players how they are to perform. They are to pronounce the words easily rather than mouth them broadly; they are not to "saw the air too much" with their hands "but use all gently"; their passion should be controlled and smooth, for it is offensive to hear a "fellow tear a passion to tatters, to very rags, to split the ears of the groundlings, who for the most part are capable of nothing but inexplicable dumb shows and noise." But neither should they be too tame. He tells them to "suit the action to the word, the word to the action, with this special observance, that you o'erstep not the modesty of nature," for the purpose of drama from its origin to the present "was and is, to hold, as 'twere, the mirror up to nature." Though overacting may cause the uneducated to laugh, it "cannot but make the judicious grieve," and one of these outweighs a whole theatre of the others. He has seen actors who "have so strutted and bellowed that I have thought some of Nature's journeymen had made men, and not made them well, they imitated humanity so abominably." This should be completely reformed as well as the license for improvization given to clowns; these should

"speak no more than is set down for them" so that they do not obscure "some necessary question of the play" through the laughter of "barren spectators." The players agree and leave to prepare themselves for the performance.

COMMENT: These speeches seem to reflect Shakespeare's own ideas on acting and the drama. He seems to favor a more naturalistic form of acting than was then practiced. This is in line with the theory of drama he inherited from Aristotle which held that "tragedy is an imitation of an action and of life," that is, that it should be true to life. Shakespeare also feels that the play, itself, is more important than the performers, and that the few judicious observers who can understand the play are the playwright's real concern rather than a theatre full of "barren spectators" who simply come to be entertained.

Polonius, Rosencrantz and Guildenstern now enter to tell Hamlet that the King and Queen will attend the performance, and Hamlet sends them out again to hurry the royal couple.

He now calls Horatio over to him and tells him that he considers him the most just man he has ever met and that, ever since he has been able to distinguish between men, his soul has chosen Horatio to be his truest friend. It is Horatio's stoicism which most attracts him:

> . . . *for thou hast been*
> *As one in suff'ring all that suffers nothing,*
> *A man that Fortune's buffets and rewards*
> *Hast ta'en with equal thanks; and blest are those*
> *Whose blood and judgement are so well commeddled*
> *That they are not a pipe for Fortune's finger*
> *To sound what stop she please.*
> *Give me that man who is not passion's slave, and*
> *I will wear him*
> *In my heart's core, ay, in my heart of hearts,*
> *As I do thee.*

COMMENT: It is clear that Hamlet is attracted to Horatio because he represents opposite qualities from those he, himself, has. Hamlet is one who is "passion's slave," an instrument for "Fortune's finger" to play upon as "she please." He cannot help but admire one like Horatio, therefore, who can accept Fortune's blows without suffering anything. He considers this a blessed condition and hopes that Horatio's presence may help him to control his own nature.

Hamlet reveals that he had earlier confided in Horatio about the circumstances of his father's death. He now continues this by confiding in Horatio his plan about the play soon to be performed. He asks Horatio to help him observe the way Claudius reacts to the part of the play which reenacts his crime and then to compare these observations with his own. He concludes that if Claudius' guilt does not reveal itself under these circumstances then "It is a damned ghost that we have seen, / And my imaginations are as foul / As Vulcan's stithy [smithy]." Horatio agrees and, as the court is now approaching, he tells Horatio to part from him as he must now be "idle." This may refer to the resumption of a madman's role.

The King and court enter with a flourish of trumpets and drums. Claudius asks Hamlet how he is and Hamlet answers somewhat obscurely that he is not satisfied with eating promises (a suggestion of his disappointed ambition), but Claudius says he cannot make sense of what he is saying. Hamlet now turns to Polonius and asks him about his university acting. Polonius says that he once played Julius Caesar and was killed in the Capitol. (This remark serves as a dramatic foreshadowing of Polonius' fate in the next scene.) The players are now ready to appear and Gertrude asks Hamlet to sit by her. He rejects her, however, saying he prefers the more attractive Ophelia. This supports Polonius' theory as he is quick to point out to Claudius. Hamlet now lies at Ophelia's feet but he treats her with no respect, making several lewd sexual puns (particularly one on "country matters" in which a pun is intended on the first syllable of "country"). These, however, seem to escape Ophelia's understanding. She notes simply that he is "merry." Hamlet replies: "O god, your only jig-maker! What should a man do but be merry?" Since God's creation is a farce, man can do nothing better than to laugh. Both of these points are proven by his mother's behavior: "For look you how cheerfully my mother looks, and my father died within's two hours." When Ophelia objects that "'tis twice two months, my lord," Hamlet ironically returns, "O heavens! die two months ago, and not forgotten yet? Then there's hope a great man's memory may outlive his life half a year." (This is the reference to the time lapse between the first and second acts earlier referred to, at which place the significance of Hamlet's slip that it is two rather than four months since his father's death was explained as revealing that for Hamlet time has really stopped since his encounter with the ghost.)

At this point the players put on the kind of "dumb show" that Hamlet just recently disapproved of in his discussion with them. This "dumb show" silently enacts the plot of the play: a king and queen embrace lovingly; then he lies down in a garden and she leaves. Another man comes in, takes off his crown and kisses it, pours poison in the sleeper's ear and leaves him. The queen returns to discover that the king is dead, at which she displays passionate grief. The poisoner returns with some others and they try to comfort her. When the body is carried out, the poisoner woos the queen who, after some harshness, accepts his love.

COMMENT: The question arises as to why Claudius does not react to this clear demonstration of his crime. W. W. Greg first suggested that this proves Claudius innocent of the specific crime recounted to Hamlet by the ghost and that this also disproves the validity of the ghost. John Dover Wilson counters this conclusion with the suggestion, unsupported by any clear reference in the text, that Claudius was probably still arguing with Polonius about the significance of Hamlet's sitting with Ophelia and so did not notice the rapidly performed dumb show. Wilson also argues that the dumb show was not ordered by Hamlet and that he was angered by it, but that it fortunately did no harm. As with Wilson's other theory of the "overheard plot," this makes good dramatic sense though without any textual support. Grebanier suggests that Claudius did recognize the similarity but, with strength of mind, rejected it as a coincidence.

The Player King and Player Queen now enter to begin the play and we are surprised to learn that the major emphasis of the play is not to be on the murder of the king but the infidelity of the queen. The King begins by remembering how long they have been married and the Queen hopes they may continue married just as long, though she is very worried by his recent sickness. He replies that he shall not live long and hopes that she may find as kind a husband as he has been after he dies. She interrupts him, horrified by such a treasonous thought: "In second husband let me be accurst! / None wed the second but who killed the first." In a long reply, the king says that though she may feel that way now, such purposes "like fruit unripe sticks on the tree, / But fall unshaken when they mellow be." In time many things may change her present purposes, for, he concludes: "Our thoughts are ours, their ends none of our own." Nonetheless the queen now makes a powerful vow that she will never remarry, and Hamlet exclaims: "If she should break it now!" He then asks his mother how she likes the play and Gertrude, perhaps with fellow feeling for woman's frailty, replies: "The lady doth protest too much, methinks." To Hamlet's more serious charge against her in the play, complicity in the murder, she seems, however, quite innocent.

Claudius, apparently aroused by the connection Hamlet seems to be intimating between the Player Queen and Gertrude, now asks Hamlet whether he knows the plot of the play and whether there is any offense in it. Hamlet answers that there is "no offense i' th' world," and, when asked the play's name, that it is called "The Mousetrap." We remember that he had said, "The play's the thing / Wherein I'll catch the conscience of the King," and he now continues to play his little cat-and-mouse game with Claudius by saying that it is the story of a murder committed in Vienna. He then continues: "'Tis a knavish piece of work, but what o' that? Your majesty, and we have free souls, it touches us not." The Player Murderer now enters and Hamlet announces that it is "Lucianus, nephew to the king." When Ophelia comments that he is as good as a stage narrator of the action, Hamlet turns to her and continues his earlier sexual joking with her. He finally calls to the actor playing Lucianus and tells him to begin. The Player King, having in the meantime gone to sleep, Lucianus approaches him, notes the fitness of all things and carefully describes the properties of the poison he is to use. As he pours the poison in the Player King's ear, Hamlet once again starts to explain the story, but Claudius has already risen very upset, as indicated by Gertrude's concern for him, calls for more light, and quickly leaves the hall followed by all except Hamlet and Horatio.

Hamlet reacts to Claudius' breakdown with hysterical glee. He begins to sing and asks Horatio whether this play would not win him a share in a company of players. Horatio calmly answers that he would only earn "half a share" which Hamlet heartly disputes and then continues to sing. As he ends the verse poorly, Horatio again calmly notes, "You might have rhymed." This finally has the effect of dampening Hamlet's high spirits long enough to discuss Claudius' reaction with Horatio and to conclude, "I'll take the ghost's word for a thousand pound."

COMMENT: Although Hamlet had earlier said that he would only write one speech of twelve to sixteen lines, at the end of the performance he seems to claim authorship for the whole scene, and, indeed, there is much about the scene which points to Hamlet's authorship. First, it displays greater preoccupation with the infidelity of the queen than with the murder of the king and seems designed to catch the conscience of his mother as well as of Claudius. Despite the warning of the ghost, Hamlet, as we shall later see, suspects his mother of knowledge of the murder and wishes to test her, a test she passes very well. Secondly, the long speech by the king about "ripeness" and the contrary relationship of will to fate contains ideas which Hamlet is later to embrace as the explanation for his experiences. This speech may represent, then, Hamlet's early testing of these ideas before he is fully ready to affirm them. Thirdly, the relationship of murderer to victim, as Wilson noted, is significantly changed from that of brother to nephew. As this is Hamlet's relationship to Claudius, rather than Claudius' relationship to his brother, the effect of the play in practical terms is to warn Claudius of his intentions. This is, in fact, the

meaning which the rest of the court derives from the play, as we shall see in the next scene, and may even explain Claudius' disturbance and so still not prove the ghost's story.

Hamlet's reaction to the performance of the play is so triumphant, however, as to suggest something further. Jones pointed out that as a playwright Hamlet has already accomplished his revenge vicariously through an artistic creation which substituted for reality. We have seen that Hamlet characteristically releases his destructive impulses through verbal play. What more natural, then, that as Hamlet sat down to compose a single speech he should have become so excited by the various opportunities offered by the play that he proceeded to rewrite the whole of the first scene up to the point of the murder, and that when he came to the murder, itself, something he seemed unable to commit in real life, he should restructure the murder so that it symbolically represented the very deed he was supposed to perform and could stand as an artistic fulfillment of this deed. This is certainly an accepted phenomenon in the case of actual writers and Shakespeare is perhaps most autobiographical in turning his princely character into an amateur playwright with a deep love and knowledge of the theatre.

In continued high spirits, Hamlet calls for some music, asking the players to bring in the recorders, simple flute-like instruments. At this point Rosencrantz and Guildenstern enter and desire to talk with him. They tell him that the King is extremely upset and, as Hamlet jokes about this with great gaiety, Guildenstern urges him: "Good my lord, put your discourse into some frame, and start not so wildly from my affair." Hamlet becomes tamer and Guildenstern continues his message, that Hamlet's mother "in most great affliction of spirit" has asked him to come to her room to speak with her before he retires. Hamlet had interrupted this message several times in the telling until even he apologizes that he cannot make "a wholesome answer; my wit's deceased."

Rosencrantz now asks him, in virtue of the love Hamlet formerly had for him, to open his heart to him and tell him the cause of his diseased mind. Hamlet quickly returns the answer Rosencrantz has been fishing for in their earlier meeting: "Sir, I lack advancement." When Rosencrantz asks how that can be since he has "the voice of the King himself for your succession in Denmark," Hamlet replies with half a proverb which obscurely intimates dissatisfaction with a long delay. A player enters with the recorders and Hamlet takes one. He now asks his friends why they are trying to drive him into a snare. Guildenstern objects that it is just the result of excessive love. Hamlet then asks Guildenstern to play the recorder for him. Guildenstern says he is unable to play the instrument. After repeated entreaties, Hamlet finally says: "Why, look you now, how unworthy a thing you make of me! You would play upon me, you would seem to know my stops, you would pluck out the heart of my mystery, you would sound me from my lowest note to the top of my compass; and there is much music, excellent voice, in this little organ, yet cannot you make it speak." Polonius now enters to tell Hamlet again that his mother wishes to speak to him and immediately. Hamlet, however, proceeds to have fun at his expense. He asks Polonius whether he sees a cloud shaped like a camel. When Polonius agrees, Hamlet changes his mind and says he thinks it looks first like a weasel and then like a whale with Polonius agreeing each time. Finally, he tells Polonius that he will come to his mother soon. In an "aside" he says, "They fool me to the top of my bent," and then asks them all to leave him.

COMMENT: Hamlet's state of mind after the play has been genuinely unsettled, as Guildenstern points out and Hamlet agrees, but he then consciously puts on his mad pose for Polonius. He is, finally, thoroughly tired of all of them, of their hypocritical attempts to "fool" him and of his attempts to fool and befuddle them. But, though he despises them for their attempts to "pluck out the heart of my mystery," he is no closer to understanding the real cause of his diseased mind than they.

Worn out by all the "fooling" with Rosencrantz, Guildenstern and Polonius and committed to visit his mother, Hamlet's mood now changes. Left alone in depressed spirits after his recent hysteria, he notes:

'Tis now the very witching time of night,
When churchyards yawn, and hell itself breathes out
Contagion to this world. Now could I drink hot blood
And do such bitter business as the day
Would quake to look on.

As he is going in this murderous mood to visit his mother, he tells his heart not to lose its natural feelings for her however cruelly he may act: "I will speak daggers to her, but use none." He then exits.

COMMENT: It is interesting, first, that the call to visit his mother brings out murderous feelings in him despite her recently proven innocence, and, secondly, that he sees such murderous impulses in the context of "hell" and the contagious disease it spreads. It is also interesting that when Hamlet believes the ghost to have been vindicated by his play, his mind becomes diseased and that he now feels himself to be in power of hell. His primary concern at this

point is to keep himself from murdering his mother; he seems to have completely forgotten about Claudius.

SUMMARY: Hamlet dominates this scene and reveals the following things about himself:

1. His understanding, love and talent for the theatre are shown by his advice to the players, the play he writes, and his delight with the performance.

2. He seems to be enjoying the game of espionage that he and everyone else is playing: he tests his mother as well as Claudius, bringing Horatio in to help him with the latter; and he throws out clues to everyone interested in the cause of his own disorder—he suggests to Claudius, directly, through the play and through his agents Rosencrantz and Guildenstern, that the cause is frustrated ambition, and he arouses Polonius and perhaps his mother through his exhibitionistic attentions to Ophelia.

3. He makes a decisive choice with regards to all his associates. He chooses to accept Horatio as his bosom companion and he rejects all others. He treats Ophelia as though she were an indecent woman, and becomes thoroughly fed up with Rosencrantz, Guildenstern and Polonius.

4.   He undergoes various changes of mood from complete seriousness at the beginning with the players and with Horatio to growing hysterical high spirits throughout the performance of the play and especially after its close, to a final murderous seriousness as he leaves for his mother's chamber.

Act III: Scene iii

The King is seen talking to Rosencrantz and Guildenstern in a room of the castle about the danger which Hamlet's madness poses to him. He informs them that he is dispatching them to go with Hamlet to England. Guildenstern says that the danger of regicide represents a "most holy and religious fear" to the very many people who depend upon the King, who "live and feed upon your majesty." Rosencrantz continues that a king is more obligated to protect himself than a private person since the welfare of many lives depend upon him. He compares the death of a king to a whirlpool which draws "what's near it with it," then to a huge wheel fixed on the summit of the highest mountain "to whose huge spokes ten thousand lesser things" are joined which attend "the boist'rous ruin" when it falls. He concludes: "Never alone / Did the king sigh, but with a general groan." The King now tells them to hasten their preparations for the journey which will imprison the cause of "this fear" and they leave to attend to this.

COMMENT: The remarks of the courtiers reflect the general Renaissance belief in "the Divine Right of Kings," which James I, shortly after the writing of *Hamlet*, presented as a formal decree. This doctrine holds that kings are divinely established to ensure the welfare of their subjects and that regicide, the murder of a king, is therefore not only a political crime but a religious sin. Claudius again makes use of this doctrine in Act IV: Scene v, as we shall see, when he says that divinity protects a king from treasonous acts. The effect the presentation of this doctrine has upon the play is to place Hamlet's proposed revenge in a still more serious light, not merely as the sin of murder but of regicide. Though it is true that Claudius himself committed regicide, he is now the anointed king and the horror of regicide, which an Elizabethan audience would have felt most keenly, attends him as much as it formerly did Hamlet, Sr.

Polonius now enters to tell Claudius that Hamlet is going to his mother's room and that he is now also going there to hide himself in her room.

Left alone, Claudius gives way to the guilt which is beginning to torment him despite all his practical efforts to protect himself. We saw it earlier in his reaction to a chance remark by Polonius about hypocrisy and then in his reaction to the play. Now he cries out: "O, my offense is rank, it smells to heaven; / It hath the primal eldest curse upon't, / A brother's murther." The curse of Cain, who killed his brother Abel in the first biblical murder, was alienation from God. This is now the condition of Clauduis, for he says: "Pray can I not, / Though inclination be as sharp as will. / My stronger guilt defeats my strong intent." But then he asks himself what the purpose of divine mercy is if not to forgive the guilty. Feeling more hopeful, he now asks himself what form of prayer he can use. He realizes that he cannot simply ask God to "forgive me my foul murther," since he still possesses the results "for which I did the murther, / My crown, mine own ambition, and my queen." Though it may be possible in this "corrupted" world to be pardoned while still retaining the fruits of crime, he is fully aware that "'tis not so above. / There is no shuffling; there the action lies / In his true nature." Aware that he cannot be divinely pardoned and so be relieved of his guilt while he still enjoys the fulfillment of his royal ambition and the possession of his beloved Queen, he realizes that his only remaining possibility of pardon is to "try what repentance can," though such repentance would involve his giving up of the worldly happiness he has derived from his crown and Queen. He knows that such repentance could effect his pardon, yet is still in despair because he is too much in love with his crown and Queen to give them up: "Yet what can it when one cannot repent? / O wretched state! O bosom black as death / O limed soul, that struggling to

be free / Art more engaged!" And yet the despair of his guilt is so great that he finally does pray to receive the grace which would enable him to give up the beloved effects of his crime and achieve true repentance: "Help, angels! Make assay. / Bow stubborn knees, and, heart with strings of steel, / Be soft as sinews of the new-born babe. / All may be well." He kneels in such a deeply engrossed state of desperate prayer that he does not hear Hamlet's entrance.

When we last saw Hamlet, his mother's invitation to visit her had put him in a murderous rage against her which he was trying to control. Now on his way to his mother's room, as Polonius has recently informed us, he accidentally comes upon Claudius alone and in prayer. He realizes that this is a perfect opportunity to perform the revenge, especially as his conscience is now clear as to Claudius' guilt (based on Claudius' reaction to the play) and as he has already been informed (as he tells his mother in the next scene) that he must leave immediately for England. His threatening behavior to the King, both in the scenes with Ophelia and with the play, have thoroughly aroused Claudius to take precautions against him so that, if he does not perform the revenge now, he may never again have as good an opportunity. Seeing his opportunity, Hamlet says: "Now might I do it pat, now 'a is a-praying, / And now I'll do't." But his use of the word "might" already shows his lack of inclination to kill Claudius now, for his whole spirit is eagerly bent on his coming confrontation with his mother, and so he finds an immediate excuse to delay his revenge: "And so 'a goes to heaven / And so am I revenged. That would be scanned." It is not religious scruples which prevent him from killing a man in the pious act of prayer, but the thought that, as Claudius is purging his soul, he would go to heaven upon death whereas his father's soul was unprepared for death and so went to purgatory. Unsatisfied simply to perform earthly justice, Hamlet wants his revenge to have eternal effects and he therefore wants to ensure Claudius' damnation as well as death. It is with this thought that he puts away his drawn sword:

> Up, sword, and know thou a more horrid hent
> [occasion].
> When he is drunk asleep, or in his rage,
> Or in th' incestuous pleasure of his bed,
> At game a-swearing, or about some act
> That has no relish of salvation in't—
> Then trip him, that his heels may kick at heaven,
> And that his soul may be as damned and black
> As hell, whereto it goes.

Looking forward to this more horrid occasion and also to seeing his mother who has been waiting for him during this unfortunate delay ("My mother stays"), he leaves the room. Claudius now rises to reveal that his prayer has not been effective, that he has not been truly able to repent: "My words fly up, my thoughts remain below. / Words without thoughts never to heaven go."

COMMENT: In this scene the ethical stature of the two leading characters has been reversed. As Claudius kneels in desperate prayer for the religious strength to give up his crown and Queen in true repentance, there is little doubt that at that moment he is ethically superior to the dark figure standing above him with drawn sword whose only reason for not committing murder is that such murder would not be horrible enough to satisfy his vengeance. Hamlet's vengeance here goes beyond the requirements of even the honor code, which is only concerned with the overcoming of earthly sin through the execution of earthly justice. Nowhere else is Hamlet so fully infected by the power of hell which "breathes out contagion to this world." But as this power is fully directed at this moment against his mother, it simply provides a devilish excuse to end this unforeseen delay to its true purposes.

In following personal inclination rather than policy at this moment, however, Hamlet is placing himself at a fatal disadvantage with regards to Claudius, the master intriguer. All of Hamlet's mad behavior and intrigues have led him to this moment of necessary action. His misuse of this moment now allows Claudius' plan to send him away from Elsinore to take effect. No further opportunity will arise for Hamlet to take revenge without also losing his own life.

The final irony of the scene is that even Hamlet's expressed reason for the delay, the effectiveness of Claudius' prayer, proves to be invalid and that he could have achieved his evil wish to send Claudius' soul to hell. From the religious perspective of Hamlet's own soul, if not his life, it is well, however, that he did not perform his revenge at this time, for though he might have survived the murder, his spiritual state at the time he committed the murder would have damned his own soul to hell.

Act III: Scene iv

We are now in Gertrude's room in the castle. Polonius, alone with Gertrude, tells her that Hamlet will be there immediately and that she should be very forceful with him, should tell him that she has protected him as much as she could but that his behavior has been too unrestrained to be endured any longer. Polonius now withdraws behind a hanging tapestry as Hamlet is heard approaching.

He enters and immediately asks his mother "what's the matter?" She answers: "Hamlet, thou hast thy father much offended." Offended by this reference to Claudius

as his father, he sharply returns: "Mother, you have my father much offended." The conversation quickly proceeds with Gertrude objecting to Hamlet's "idle tongue" and Hamlet objecting to her "wicked tongue," until she finally asks, "Have you forgot me?" Though she is asking Hamlet whether he has forgotten the respect due to a mother, he answers with a bitter identification: "You are the queen, your husband's brother's wife, / And (would it were not so) you are my mother."

Seeing that she will not get anywhere with him, she proposes to end their meeting, but Hamlet is not going to let this longed-for opportunity to speak his mind to his mother get away from him so easily. Forcing her angrily to sit down, his expression must appear to her so murderous that she is forced to cry out in terror for help: "What wilt thou do? Thou wilt not murther me? Help, ho!" At this the startled Polonius also begins to cry for help and Hamlet, quickly drawing his sword, drives it through the tapestry killing the figure behind it with the words: "How now? a rat? Dead for a ducat, dead!" The Queen cries out to ask him what he has done and Hamlet replies, "Nay, I know not. Is it the King?"

COMMENT: In the next scene, Gertrude describes what happened in the following words, which are best discussed here: "Mad as the sea and wind when both contend / Which is the mightier. In his lawless fit, / Behind the arras [tapestry] hearing something stir, / Whips out his rapier, cries, 'A rat, a rat!' / And in this brainish apprehension kills / The unseen good old man." There is little doubt that this is a good description of what actually happened, that Hamlet, as he says, did not "know" what he was doing because he was temporarily insane.

That Hamlet truly felt murderous as he was coming to his mother's room is proven by the fact that within a few minutes in her room he does commit murder. That this murderous impulse was not directed at Claudius is proven by the fact that he does not take advantage of his opportunity to kill Claudius even though everything points to the necessity for doing so but quickly rationalizes away this chance to murder Claudius so as not to further delay his coming to his mother. That the murderous impulse is directed at his mother is proven, first by the need he feels to control himself against murdering her ("Let me be cruel, not unnatural; / I will speak daggers to her, but use none."), and secondly by his mother's terror for her life as she looks at his expression seconds before he murders.

What must have happened, then, is that the murderous impulse towards his mother so overpowered his reason as he physically forced her to sit, that he was on the point of murdering her when another sound distracted his attention from her long enough for his will to reassert itself and deflect the intended blow from his mother onto the nearest object. His temporary insanity at this moment is clearly shown by his incoherent cry which accompanies the murder: "How now? a rat? Dead for a ducat, dead!" At the moment when he murders he does not know what he is doing, only what he must not do, that he must not murder his mother. At this moment of murderous rage at his mother's infidelity, however, he hears the sound of an intruder in his mother's bedroom when she was supposed to be alone with him and, associating all such intruders as the lowest vermin, he vents his wrath upon it. It is only after the deed is done that he associates the intruding "rat" with Claudius and hopes that he may have actually accomplished his long-delayed revenge without having planned it. That this hope is only an afterthought rather than the motive of his deed is proven by the fact that he had just left Claudius kneeling in prayer as he was on his way to his mother's room and so he could not have expected Claudius to have gotten to his mother's room before him, as, indeed, would have been impossible.

The Queen well describes the act when she exclaims: "O, what a rash and bloody deed is this!" But Hamlet is still more concerned to attack his mother than to care about what he has done, and he immediately replies with his worst accusation against her: "A bloody deed—almost as bad, good mother, / As kill a king, and marry with his brother." The Queen is innocently shocked and confused by the meaning of such a suggestion—"As kill a King?"—and so Hamlet, simply repeating "Ay, lady, it was my word," drops the subject. He then lifts the tapestry and, seeing it is Polonius, reacts only with a casual coldness which becomes a bit mocking: "Thou wretched, rash, intruding fool, farewell! / I took thee for thy better. Take thy fortune. / Thou find'st to be too busy is some danger." Then, immediately dismissing the whole subject, he returns to his primary object of attacking his mother with verbal daggers and says to her: "Leave wringing of your hands. Peace, sit you down / And let me wring your heart."

When the Queen asks what she can have done to deserve such rudeness from him, Hamlet begins to describe in fierce terms the immodesty, hypocrisy and irreligiousness with which she has debased her "marriage vows." He then tells her to compare the pictures of her two husbands and asks: "Have you eyes? / Could you on this fair mountain leave to feed, / And batten on this moor?" Not only was his father far superior to Claudius but she cannot even excuse her change as resulting from love since she is too old, he claims, to be capable of such romantic feelings. Her behavior is so lacking in sense that it must be the work of a "devil" who has so blinded her that she has lost all sense of shame. And as he continues to cry out against her lack of shame, she finally begs him to "speak no more" for he is turning her eyes inward to look upon the guilt in her soul which she cannot erase. The admission of her

guilt only inspires Hamlet to make his most revolting description of her act: "Nay, but to live / In the rank sweat of an enseamed [greasy] bed, / Stewed in corruption, honeying and making love / Over the nasty sty—" Once more she interrupts him to beg him to stop tormenting her with "these words like daggers." But he continues until he forces a third anguished cry, "No more."

At this point the ghost reappears, this time dressed in his nightgown rather than his armor, and Hamlet is stopped from the relentless and increasing fury of his attack upon his already crying mother. Calling for angelic protection, he asks the "gracious figure" of the ghost if he has come to "chide" his "tardy son" for having let his "dread command" become "lapsed in time and passion." The ghost agrees that this is why he has had to return: "This visitation / Is but to whet thy blunted purpose." But, as Gertrude is looking upon Hamlet's conversation with "amazement," having already said, "Alas, he's mad," the ghost tells Hamlet to "speak to her." To his question as to how she feels, she responds with concern for him since he seems to be talking to nothing. Hamlet points to the ghost and describes for her his pitiful expression but she can neither see nor hear anything unusual. At this point the ghost "steals away" out of the door and, as Hamlet continues to describe the ghost's last motions, Gertrude concludes that what he has seen must have been a hallucination produced by his own brain, such hallucinations being a special effect of madness. Hamlet denies that he is mad and, as proof, says that he can repeat everything he has said. Then, fearing he is to lose the whole effect of his earlier tirade, he tells her that she should not flatter her soul that it is his madness which has magnified her sins for this will only increase her corruption.

COMMENT: The reappearance of the ghost at this point has been puzzling to most critics. Is this the same objective ghost as before or is Gertrude right that it is a hallucination? If this is a hallucination, does this cast doubt on the earlier ghost as perhaps a product of group hysteria? If this is an objective ghost and the same one as earlier, what is the meaning of Gertrude's inability to see it? Is it that her innocence protects her from seeing a diabolic agent, or is it her guilt which has alienated her from the sight of her abused husband's ghost or of an angel? As for the ghost being produced by Hamlet's madness, Hamlet had earlier suggested that his melancholy may have attracted diabolic interest to undertake the ghostly impersonation as a means of damning him and his mind has been nowhere as diseased as in his recent murder. Although Hamlet speaks sanely enough after the ghost's exit in his compelling need to prove his sanity to his mother, he was becoming quite agitated again before the ghost's entrance. Does the ghost reappear at this point to prevent a possible second murder attempt upon Gertrude? Does this prove that the ghost is the genuine spirit of Hamlet, Sr., that he returns out of love for his wife, tries to shield her from any disturbance and leaves brokenhearted at her failure to perceive him? Or is the ghost simply a figment produced by Hamlet's own growing guilt over his preoccupation with his mother's sins which, as he immediately explains as the ghost's reason for appearing, has caused his "passion" for revenge to lapse even at the most opportune moment and when he could no longer excuse his delay with doubt? Shakespeare does not provide us with sufficient means for answering all of these questions. Indeed, he seems more concerned to raise these final questions about the ghost than to answer them, to keep the nature of the ghost ambiguous. The effect of the ghost's appearance, however, is clear. It does serve to calm Hamlet's spirit at a point where he is becoming agitated once more and to make Hamlet consciously aware of his misdirected efforts. (This will be further discussed in the Summary to this scene.) The ghost had earlier told Hamlet that he should "leave her to heaven" rather than attempt to punish her. Now Hamlet does return to this more proper attitude.

Attempting to turn his mother's spirit back to her former purity, he advises her to do what Claudius had earlier himself attempted: "Confess yourself to heaven, / Repent what's past, avoid what is to come, / And do not spread the compost on the weeds / To make them ranker." Calmer now and feeling sorry for his former rudeness to her, he asks her to "forgive me this my virtue." But then, excusing himself by the needs of a corrupt time, he again shows a touch of self-righteous disrespect when he concludes that "Virtue itself of vice must pardon beg, / Yea, curb and woo for leave to do him good."

But Hamlet has achieved his wish; he has caused his mother to contritely admit her guilt to him as she now does in saying, "O Hamlet, thou hast cleft my heart in twain." Happy with his success, he tells her to "throw away the worser part of it" by never again going to his uncle's bed. By way of farewell, he says: "Once more, good night, / And when you are desirous to be blest, / I'll blessing beg of you."

COMMENT: For months Hamlet has felt himself wronged by his mother's remarriage. Now that Hamlet has returned the injury to her, has made her cringe in torment under his dagger words and admit her guilt to him, he is able to achieve an emotional reconciliation with her. As she begs him for forgiveness, he can do the same to her and they can both kneel down for blessing to each other. Shakespeare is to repeat this mode of parent-child

reconciliation in *King Lear* when King Lear says to Cordelia, the daughter he disinherited: "Come, let's away to prison. / We two alone will sing like birds i' th' cage. / When thou dost ask me blessing, I'll kneel down / And ask of thee forgiveness."

In this moment of harmonious reconciliation with his mother, Hamlet achieves a sense of general well-being and harmony with the universe which enables him to view his murder of Polonius in a new light. Noticing the dead body of Polonius for the first time since the murder, he says:

> For this same lord, I do repent; but heaven hath
>   pleased it so,
> To punish me with this, and this with me,
> That I must be their scourge and minister.

COMMENT: This is the first time that Hamlet has expressed his harmony with heaven's purpose. Earlier he believed his desires for suicide and revenge to be opposed by heaven, had viewed the whole of creation as a sterile "quintessence of dust" and God as a maker of farces. Now he accepts the murder of Polonius and its consequences for himself as being the will of heaven and sees himself in a new role as heaven's "scourge and minister." Although he had accepted his role of revenger from the first as a means of achieving the reformation of his society, the murder it involved had seemed religiously forbidden and had involved him in a conflict between the honor code and religious commandments. Now the two seem to have become joined for him. The question arises as to why he should have experienced this general reorientation at this time and in relation to the murder of Polonius and what its significance is for the play as a whole.

One immediate explanation is the one mentioned above, the spreading out of his harmonious reconciliation with his mother to embrace the whole of creation. Though this may explain his acceptance of the will of heaven, how is the act, itself, to be explained as the work of heaven? An answer to this may be provided by the Queen's statement that his deed was "rash." Not only was the deed unpremeditated, but Hamlet seemed not to "know" what he was doing. But if the murder he accomplished while beside himself was a good deed, then some other intelligence, which could only have been divine, must have directed it. The question now arises as to how Hamlet could view the accomplished fact of Polonius' death as good, in fact, as divinely desired. To this point we already have Hamlet's words to the dead Polonius: "Thou find'st to be too busy is some danger." And what was this "wretched, rash, intruding fool" busying himself about if not the evil business of the adulterous regicide who had thrown the time "out of joint" and whose evil he had already vowed himself to "scourge," to punish as with a whip. He now sees that he was divinely appointed not only to kill Claudius but also to destroy all those to whom his evil influence has extended and, as we shall see, this is soon to include Rosencrantz and Guildenstern. While Hamlet might just as well have construed the deed as the result of diabolic possession, indeed, he felt himself so possessed as he went to his mother's room, he never considers this possibility. He has, instead, that sense of inner conviction, which might also be termed "conversion," that he has received ordination as heaven's "scourge and minister." To ask why this should be takes us onto somewhat more shaky ground.

Certainly Hamlet detests Polonius both for his stupidity and his hypocritical conniving. He is soon to treat Polonius' body in a most contemptuous fashion and to call him "a foolish prating knave." He has never missed an opportunity to make contemptuous fun of him and his satire has often been directed at Polonius' relationship to his daughter. Here we may see a further motive for Hamlet's dislike of Polonius, his suspicion that Polonius may be responsible for Ophelia's rejection of him, that Polonius was as much an interloper in Hamlet's own love relationship with Ophelia as Polonius had just been in his mother's bedroom. The satiric daggers Hamlet had earlier thrust at Polonius have now found their emotional fulfillment in the accidental murder of the man Hamlet detests as fully if not more than he does Claudius, and this inner satisfaction supports the sense of cosmic harmony which his reconciliation with his mother had produced in him. Though consciously he repents the accident both because he cannot consider his grounds against Polonius sufficient to justify his planned destruction and because this killing will make his actual task of revenge more difficult to accomplish, he is so far from denying his satisfaction with the result that the death of this hated "counsellor" of his enemy seems to him part of a cosmic plan to scourge the evil of the Danish court.

This is perhaps sufficient explanation, certainly as far as the actual text can take us, but the psychoanalytic interpretation does provide us with an interesting further hypothesis here. We remember that Ernest Jones, following Freud's earlier suggestion, had elaborated the theory that Hamlet has an "Oedipus Complex." In line with this, Jones suggests that Hamlet subconsciously views Polonius as a father substitute and that his expressed hatred of Polonius is really the expression of his repressed hatred for his own father, also an interloper between his mother and himself. His satisfaction with the murder of Polonius, then, reflects his subconscious sense of fulfillment of the repressed Oedipal desire to murder his father.

There is much in the text to support Jones' suggestion that Hamlet subconsciously identifies Polonius with his father. In Act II: Scene ii, Hamlet had directed his most vicious satire against Polonius' old age: "Slanders, sir, for the satirical rogue says here that old men have grey beards."

In Act I: Scene ii, moreover, the first mark of identification of the ghost with his father that Hamlet asks of Horatio is the following: "His beard was grizzled [grey], no?" Hamlet's father also was an old man, and what further similarity he may have had with Polonius may be guessed from the fact that Polonius' present position in the court is so high because he was apparently the most intimate counselor of the former King, Hamlet, Sr. In fact, the possible similarity of Hamlet, Sr., to Polonius, which Hamlet has never admitted to his conscious mind, may help to explain Gertrude's adultery with her husband's younger brother. Certainly Hamlet's view of both his mother's love relationships has not been accurate; the relationship of his parents was not as ideal as he had imagined and, from what we know and are to learn of Claudius' devotion to Gertrude, this new relationship of his mother can hardly be considered simply as "stewed in corruption, honeying and making love over the nasty sty." As Jones and other commentators have pointed out, Hamlet's obsession with sexual corruption, both in this scene and elsewhere, is hardly normal.

Whatever Hamlet's subconscious feelings about the murder of Polonius may be, there is no doubt, however, that Hamlet's accidental murder of Polonius marks the turning point in the play, both in terms of Hamlet's external situation and of his spiritual orientation: this act places him in the power of Claudius but it also gives him his sense of ordination as heaven's "scourge and minister."

Hamlet excuses the fatal effects of his new role by saying, "I must be cruel only to be kind." He says that he will take the body from the room and "will answer well the death I gave him." Aware that "worse remains behind" for him as a result of this killing, he prepares to say goodnight again but then remembers to tell his mother that she should not "let the bloat king" for "a pair of reechy kisses" cause her to confess that Hamlet is not truly mad "but mad in craft." Gertrude promises this and then Hamlet reminds her that, as she knows, he must leave for England. He now confides in her that he neither trusts the sealed letters Claudius is sending nor his "two schoolfellows," Rosencrantz and Guildenstern, whom Claudius is also sending along with him: "They bear the mandate; they must sweep my way / And marshall me to knavery." With his new sense of divine mission, however, Hamlet is not worried for his own safety and success:

Let it work.
For 'tis the sport to have the enginer
Hoise with his own petar [mine], and't shall go hard
But I will delve one yard below their mines
And blow them at the moon. O, 'tis most sweet
When in one line two crafts directly meet.

So far from being worried, Hamlet is elated with the thought that he will somehow turn against his former friends the evil that they are now helping Claudius to work against himself. He feels no sympathy for any of Claudius' accomplices. Seeing Polonius only as a means of getting himself shipped off to England, he says most crudely: "This man shall set me packing. / I'll lug the guts into the neighbor room." Then, calling Polonius "a foolish prating knave" and saying a final goodnight to his mother, he leaves the room tugging the body of Polonius after him.

SUMMARY: This scene is the turning point in the play for the following reasons:

1. After having missed his opportunity to murder Claudius, Hamlet's "rash and bloody" accidental killing of Polonius makes it impossible for either Hamlet or his mother to delay Claudius' purpose to send him away to England. This makes his own task of revenge more difficult.

2. The effect of this deed, as we shall see in Act IV: Scene iii, is to make Claudius' purpose in sending him to England more deadly. Hamlet has not only made his revenge more difficult but placed his life in danger.

3. The accidental killing of Polonius works a drastic change in Hamlet's nature. This violent act, the result of two months of mounting tension, marks the end of his downward spiritual progress and the beginning of a more positive spiritual movement. If the first appearance of the ghost caused a hellish state of spiritual alienation from God which reached its most extreme form in Hamlet's diabolic reasons for not killing Claudius and his equally thoughtless killing of Polonius minutes later, the appearance of the "gracious figure" of the ghost in this scene begins to effect his reconciliation to divine purposes. This suggests that the ghost's nature may, itself, have changed and this for one of two reasons. Either this is his father's spirit come from purgatory, as it earlier claimed, and the effects of purgatory are beginning to be seen in the purging of his formerly evil desire for selfish revenge and its replacement by a new sense of divine justice; or these are two different ghostly impersonations, the former by a devil and the latter by an angel. In any case, Hamlet is now animated by a new sense of identification with divine justice just as earlier he had been moved by his alienation from it.

Act IV: Scenes i, ii, iii

The King and Queen, with Rosencrantz and Guildenstern, enter another room of the castle soon after the killing of Polonius. Claudius asks Gertrude why she is sighing so heavily and, after asking Rosencrantz lnd Guildenstern to leave them alone a while, she answers with a description of Hamlet's "mad" killing of Polonius. After a brief statement of sorrow, "O heavy deed!," Claudius immediately sees the danger Hamlet's action poses to him:

> It had been so with us, had we been there.
> His liberty is full of threats to all,
> To you yourself, to us, to every one.
> Alas, how shall this bloody deed be answered?
> It will be laid to us.

Not only might Hamlet have killed either himself or Gertrude in place of Polonius, but he might yet do so if he is not immediately restrained. Even as it is, he is afraid that he himself will be blamed for the murder and rightly so, for it was his "love" which prevented him from truly recognizing the danger earlier. Asking Gertrude where Hamlet is, she tells him that he has gone to draw away the body and, now sorry for his deed, "weeps for what is done." Claudius now tells Gertrude that he must ship Hamlet away by dawn and then must use his utmost skill to excuse the dead. He calls back Rosencrantz and Guildenstern, tells them of Hamlet's action and that they should find him, speak politely to him and bring the body into the chapel. After they leave, he tells Gertrude that they must also go and tell the council what has happened and what he means to do with Hamlet so as to offset any possible rumors that may arise. Very disturbed by this situation, he says as they leave, "My soul is full of discord and dismay."

In the second scene, Rosencrantz and Guildenstern come upon Hamlet just after he has hidden the body of Polonius. Hamlet's attitude throughout the next two scenes is viciously satirical, though his satire is primarily a reaction to his renewed awareness of death through contact with Polonius' body. To their question as to what he has done with the body, Hamlet replies that he has "compounded it with dust." As they insist upon knowing, Hamlet objects to being "demanded of a sponge," and he explains this reference by saying: "Ay, sir, that soaks up the king's countenance, his rewards, his authorities. But such officers do the king best service in the end. He keeps them, like an ape, in the corner of his jaw, first mouthed, to be last swallowed. When he needs what you have gleaned, it is but squeezing you and, sponge, you shall be dry again." Hamlet satirically tells them that they have lost all human identity by selling their services to the King and that the only reward they may expect for selling their souls is to be destroyed by the King who uses them, but they claim not to understand him. After continuing his contemptuous satire against both them and the body for a bit longer, he demands to be brought to the King and they all leave to go to Claudius.

The third scene begins with Claudius' explanations to some of his advisers. He tells them that he has sent for Hamlet since it is dangerous to let Hamlet continue to go about "loose" but that he must not "put the strong law on him" and "he's loved of the distracted multitude." All he can do, therefore, is to send Hamlet immediately away while giving the impression that this has been done with much deliberation. Rosencrantz now enters to say that they have been unable to find where Hamlet has put the body but that they have brought him guarded to the King and that he is waiting outside the room. Claudius orders Hamlet's appearance and, when he enters, immediately demands of Hamlet to be told where Polonius is. Hamlet satirically answers that Polonius is "at supper," and then, when questioned about this, explains that this supper is "Not where he eats, but where 'a is eaten. A certain convocation of politic worms are e'en at him. Your worm is your only emperor for diet. We fat all creatures else to fat us, and we fat ourselves for maggots. Your fat king and your lean beggar is but variable service—two dishes, but to one table. That's the end."

COMMENT: In Act III: Scene iii, Guildenstern had described the courtiers' dependence upon the King by using the image of eating; he had said that they "feed upon your majesty." In Act IV: Scene ii, Hamlet had said to Rosencrantz and Guildenstern that the King keeps courtiers like themselves "in the corner of his jaw, first mouthed, to be last swallowed." Such images conjure up a vision of a jungle in which the animals are engaged in eating each other. In other words, we are being told through images that the court is really a dog-eat-dog world. Not only is ambition described in this fashion but also such other "appetites" as sensual lust. Hamlet had asked his mother in Act III: Scene iv, "Could you on this fair mountain leave to feed,/ And batten on this moor?" And in Act IV: Scene i, Claudius had compared his "love," which kept him from imprisoning Hamlet, to a "foul disease" which he allowed to "feed / Even on the pith of life." Love then, is a diseased appetite which feeds either on oneself or on another. The ironic conclusion to this picture of humanity as the prey to animal appetites is now given in the speech by Hamlet in which he says that the result of all this feeding is simply to fatten ourselves for worms and that no position in this world can protect a man from the final appetite of death. Such a vision of the world is close to that of Hamlet's first soliloquy, in which he said: "How weary, stale, flat, and unprofitable / Seem to me all the uses of this world! / Fie on't, ah, fie, 'tis an unweeded garden / That grows to seed. Things rank and gross in nature / Possess it merely." The world is composed of "rank and gross" animals feeding upon one another for the "unprofitable" end of feeding worms.

From this study of the imagery, however, we can see that such a sentiment is not simply Hamlet's, although he is its best and most frequent spokesman, but also Shakespeare's, for the pattern of feeding imagery is contributed to by other characters besides Hamlet. This is to be considered, then, as the objective vision of reality in this play. Hamlet is more perceptive than others insofar as he sees something of the whole pattern, and his problem, as we shall see more fully in his next soliloquy, is to determine what action is demanded of him in the face of such a reality.

Hamlet continues to discuss the conversion of men to worms to fish to men again until Claudius finally demands of him "Where is Polonius?" To this Hamlet flippantly answers: "In heaven. Send thither to see. If your messenger find him not there, seek him i' th' other place yourself. But if indeed you find him not within this month, you shall nose him as you go up the stairs into the lobby."

After sending attendants to find the body of Polonius, Claudius informs Hamlet that "for thine especial safety," he is to leave immediately for England. To this Hamlet says "Good," and Claudius adds, "So is it, if thou knew'st our purposes." Hamlet does see through Claudius' false mask of goodwill, however, as he indicates by his ambiguous reply, "I see a cherub that sees them." Feeling heaven to be on his side, he is not overly worried, and, after another bit of verbal quibbling, he leaves to prepare himself for England.

Left alone, Claudius reveals that his letter to the King of England demands "the present death of Hamlet." This alone can cure the feverish anxiety which Hamlet's free raging produces in him and which prevents his enjoying his fortune. The scene now ends as Claudius leaves the stage.

COMMENT: We are not told whether Claudius' original purpose in sending Hamlet to England was to effect his death or whether this is a new purpose resulting from Hamlet's killing of Polonius. The evidence of the play would seem to argue, however, that Claudius wrote a new letter after he learned of Hamlet's killing. Had he already planned this in his earlier letter to England, there should have been some mention of this when Claudius was unburdening his guilt to heaven. Since at that time the only sin upon Claudius' conscience was his murder of his brother and since this single sin was so tormenting his conscience, it is difficult to believe that he would want to add a new sin to his conscience or that, if he did, his conscience would have been free of it.

Once Hamlet has killed, however, it is clear to Claudius that he can no longer allow his squeamish conscience to further endanger himself. What is more, Hamlet's behavior to him is so tormenting that, after having allowed him complete liberty for four months to say or do anything while himself exercising complete self-restraint in Hamlet's presence, Claudius is finally at the breaking point and can endure Hamlet's taunting existence no more. Hamlet, for his part, has done everything to antagonize Claudius and break his composure. He has, indeed, been more concerned to make Claudius squirm, than actually to murder him. But Hamlet's very success in making Claudius squirm in getting under his skin, has destroyed Claudius' original good intentions towards him with the final result that Claudius now means to cause Hamlet's death. Claudius had hoped that one murder would solve all his problems and he had delayed longer than he should have even considering the necessity of a new murder. When he does, however, he can no longer actually commit the murder himself and delegates this task to another.

While Hamlet has been throwing Claudius' soul into "discord and dismay" with his final murderous decision, Hamlet, himself, has shown nothing of the repentent reaction to his killing that Gertrude mentions. Instead, he continues to cavort in a most unseemly fashion, making a gay game out of hiding the body. Despite this new theological insight, he is in the same hysterical state as he was at the close of the play-within-the-play and little changed from the way he was at the first. His psychological distress has thus far only resulted in an unnecessary death and his own mortal danger.

Act IV: Scene iv

The scene opens the following morning on a road near the Danish border. Fortinbras enters with his army and stops to talk to his Captain. He tells the Captain to go to the Danish King with his greetings and to remind him of the permission he had earlier granted Fortinbras to transport a Norwegian army over Danish territory. The Captain agrees to do this and is left alone on stage after the departure of Fortinbras and the army. Hamlet now enters with Rosencrantz, Guildenstern and others on their way to the ship which is to bear them to England. He questions the Captain as to the nature and purpose of the army and is told that it is a Norwegian army commanded by Fortinbras on its way to conquer a small piece of Polish land "that hath in it no profit but the name." When Hamlet suggests that the Poles then "never will defend it," he is told that "it is already garrisoned." Hamlet now comments that the expenditure of "two thousand souls and twenty thousand ducats" over "the question of this straw" is the sick result of "much wealth and peace." He now tells the men with him to go on a little before him and is left alone on the stage.

We now come to Hamlet's last soliloquy, his fourth (unless his speech over the praying figure of Claudius be considered a soliloquy, in which case the present soliloquy would be numbered his fifth, or his speech about the "witching time of night" be so considered, in which case this would be his sixth). The sight of this army going out to fight a worthless war for a point of honor serves to stir Hamlet's shame once more at his own dishonor in having allowed revenge to be so long delayed: "How all occasions do inform against me / And spur my dull revenge!" He now asks himself "what is a man" if his chief value and occupation be "but to sleep and feed." In line with his recent contemptuous view of man as engaged solely in eating and being eaten, he answers himself that such a man is "a beast, no more." Referring now back to the subject of his earlier speech to Rosencrantz and Guildenstern about the wonderful qualities of man, he reasons that the Creator did not give man "that capability and godlike reason" so that it would grow mouldy with disuse.

Realizing that man was given his abilities to accomplish something more worthy than mere bestial feeding, he now asks himself whether it was "bestial oblivion" (the forgetfulness of an unaware animal) or some cowardly "scruple" produced by "thinking too precisely on th' event" which explains his lack of action on his revenge. But he finally must conclude: 'I do not know / Why yet I live to say, 'This thing's to do,' / Sith I have cause, and will, and strength, and means / To do't.'

In comparison with his own shameful lack of action, he now must witness the behavior of Fortinbras "whose spirit, with divine ambition puffed," exposes his own "mortal and unsure" existence "to all that fortune, death, and danger dare" for nothing more valuable than "an eggshell." He concludes from this that to be truly "great" one must not simply be ready to fight for a sufficient and worthy cause "But greatly to find quarrel in a straw / When Honor's at the stake." As he had said in the second soliloquy, the man of true honor is he who has sufficient "gall to make oppression bitter," who is willing to fight a duel at the slightest excuse. Once again he must compare himself with this model of honor, here represented by Fortinbras who is going out to battle to regain his father's lost territories and thus restore the family honor. With both his reason and his natural feelings excited by his father's murder and mother's dishonor, Hamlet can "let all sleep" while, to his "shame," he sees "the imminent death of twenty thousand men" for a merely imagined point of honor. Having shamed himself into renewed commitment to his revenge at a time when such a revenge is almost impossible, he concludes strongly: "O, from this time forth, / My thoughts be bloody, or be nothing worth!"

With this he leaves to rejoin his companions and the scene ends.

COMMENT: Just before the start of his soliloquy, Hamlet had judged Fortinbras' action as the "imposthume," the abscess or sickness, produced by "much wealth and peace." The claim of the honor code upon his spirit is still strong enough, however, to produce an inward shame at the comparison with his own inaction and to produce this final meditation on the nature of honor. But it is interesting that while he ostensibly convinces himself of the need to pursue honor, he is also undermining the validity of the honor code at its most vulnerable point. He shows that what makes a man of honor superior to a bestial man is simply his willingness to "dare" any danger, and that the reason for this almost suicidal exposing of his life to death is immaterial. Although Hamlet tries to identify the honor code here with religion, calling honor "divine ambition" and claiming that honorable action is a proper use of one's God-given talents, such an identification is highly questionable and is later dropped by Hamlet in favor of a more proper understanding of Divine Providence. Hamlet ends by mourning the unnecessary deaths of twenty thousand men for an imaginary point of honor while himself being convinced by their example to pursue the bloody path to honor. In other words, the very means by which Hamlet renews his commitment to honor serve to undermine his purpose. But this is only a new example of Hamlet's peculiar way of rationalizing himself into momentary self-acceptance. And he will only be left once more with the problem: "I do not know / Why yet I live to say, 'This thing's to do,' / Sith I have cause, and will, and strength, and means / To do't."

This last point refutes those critics who claim that the only reason Hamlet did not accomplish his revenge is that he had no opportunity to do so except in the one case when Claudius was praying, at which time specific scruples prevented him. Here Hamlet states that he has had the "means to do't" and "let all sleep." He also asks himself whether the reason for his delay was, as Coleridge later claimed, that he overintellectualized his problem, an excuse he earlier suggested in the "To be or not to be" soliloquy. But we have seen that, in fact, Hamlet does not think "too precisely on th' event" but uses his reason primarily to rationalize away "all occasions" of action or guilt, and he thus misuses his God-given reason even in the soliloquy in which he condemns such misuse. We are left with the reason that springs first to his mind, "bestial oblivion," the fact that he simply cannot concentrate on the subject of his revenge, but this seems to him so "bestial," something he has just condemned in man, that he immediately goes to the opposite extreme of suggesting that he thinks too much about it, which we have just disproven.

The fact seems to be that Hamlet is guilty of "bestial oblivion," that he then responds to his guilt by producing an intellectualized rationalization, but that this does not ultimately satisfy him and he is left with the mystery of his inaction. Though he had apparently had a change of orientation after the killing of Polonius, we see confirmed here our earlier suspicion at Hamlet's playful hiding of the body, that he is still essentially unchanged in his inability to consciously pursue his revenge against Claudius, and this despite his apparent commitment to this course in the present soliloquy.

Act IV: Scene v

This scene returns us to the castle of Elsinore after a lapse of perhaps a month in time. (This is the first lapse in time since the end of Act I, for all of Act II, Act III, and the first four scenes of Act IV took place in a very crowded twenty-four-hour period.) The Queen enters with Horatio and another gentleman. They have been trying to persuade her to see Ophelia, but Gertrude insists: "I will not speak with her." The Gentleman says that Ophelia is very desirous of seeing Gertrude and that her state should be pitied. When Gertrude asks what Ophelia wants with her, the Gentleman only describes her behavior, that "she speaks much of her father" and of the deceit of the world, that she acts and speaks in a disordered way which observers construe in a lascivious way, though Ophelia's "winks and nods and gestures" seem to support such an interpretation. Horatio urges that "'Twere good she were spoken with" for she is giving malicious minds unfortunate ideas. Gertrude now relents and tells them to admit Ophelia; the two gentlemen leave and, left alone, Gertrude admits that her "sick soul!" has dreaded to confront any new misfortune because of her already agitated sense of "guilt" (thus showing that Hamlet's efforts to arouse her conscience have had a permanent effect).

Ophelia now enters in a distracted state of insanity. She first asks, "Where is the beauteous majesty of Denmark?" (This is the only objective statement in the play that Gertrude is a beautiful woman and it helps to explain Claudius' love for her, the tender concern of the ghost and, perhaps, even Hamlet's oversensitivity to his mother's sexual activities. Clearly she is a woman fully in her prime.) Though Gertrude addresses her, Ophelia does not seem to know her but starts to sing two snatches of song: the first asks how one is to know her "true-love" from another, and the answer is by his clothes, which are those of a pilgrim; the second snatch of song announces, "He is dead and gone, lady," buried under grass with a stone at his heels. She continues to sing of a burial as Claudius comes in, and he concludes that her insanity was caused by thoughts of her father. Ophelia does not wish to hear of this and, by way of explaining the meaning of her state, sings another song. This is a rowdy ballad about a girl's loss of virginity on St. Valentine's day: her lover opens his chamber door to "Let in the maid, that out a maid / Never departed more"; when she later tells him, "Before you tumbled me, / You promised me to wed," he answers that he would have done so had she "not come to my bed." She now returns to weeping at the thought of her father's death and that "they would lay him i' th' cold ground," reminds them that her "brother shall know of it," and, calling for her coach, departs saying "Good night, ladies." Claudius sends Horatio to look after her and again concludes that her insanity "springs all from her father's death."

COMMENT: Although Claudius rejects the possibility of disappointed love as a cause of Ophelia's insanity, just as he had in the case of Hamlet, it is clear that this contributes as much to her state as the death of her father. Though there is no evidence in the play that Hamlet did seduce Ophelia (despite the opinion of some critics that her St. Valentine's day song does constitute evidence), Hamlet's change from offering honorable love to her to treating her as a discarded whore has evidently convinced her insane mind that she must have yielded to this most guarded against temptation if his rejection of her is to be at all understood. It is clear that she did not understand her responsibility for his change of heart, since she was simply following her father's orders which were designed to protect her from being discarded, and that Hamlet's treatment of her in the "nunnery" and "play" scenes affected her more deeply than was then apparent. Since her "true-love" has betrayed her trust, she no longer knows by what means to recognize him, only knows that there is deceit in the world. That she does not further connect Hamlet with the murder of her father indicates the secrecy with which Claudius has concealed this fact, as he will, himself, mention almost immediately. On the same day as she felt herself so brutally betrayed by her lover, however, she was also faced with the death of her father, a father on whose judgment she had been totally dependent for all her actions and opinions. The effect of this double tragic loss was so overwhelming that it completely destroyed her sanity.

The comparison of her circumstances with those of Hamlet at the beginning of the play should be obvious. Both were faced with the horrible fact of a parent's death at the same time as their trust in one in whose love they had

believed was betrayed. Both faced the twin evils of human existence, hypocrisy and death, at the same time and both of their minds were unsettled by this double confrontation with the evils of existence. The fact that Ophelia's reaction duplicates Hamlet's serves to universalize his experience, to give it greater validity as, indeed, the most tragic of human experiences.

But the differing extent of their reactions also serves to illuminate Hamlet's stature. The fact that in similar circumstances Ophelia's mind completely lost its grip on reality reveals Hamlet's greater heroic stature: Hamlet has faced up to a tragic reality which can destroy a lesser spirit and, however unsettled it made him, has maintained a final grip on his sanity. As such Ophelia serves as a "foil" to Hamlet. (A "foil" is the setting of a ring which displays the jewel more advantageously, allowing the light to shine through it and thus make it more brilliant. This image has been taken over by dramatic criticism to refer to a character who serves to illuminate the virtues of the more important central character. It is in this sense that Hamlet, himself, in Act V: Scene ii, says to Laertes as they are about to duel: "I'll be your foil, Laertes. In mine ignorance / Your skill shall, like a star i' th' darkest night, / Stick fiery off indeed.")

Claudius now tells Gertrude that Ophelia's insanity is not their only sorrow: first Ophelia's father was slain; next Gertrude's son was justly exiled; thirdly, the people are confused by Polonius' death since no explanations were given and he was hurriedly and secretly interred; lastly, Laertes has secretly returned from France and, since no true information has been provided, has been filled with rumors of Claudius' own responsibility for Polonius' death. This last fact makes him particularly fearful. At this a noise is heard and a messenger enters. Claudius is so unnerved by this that he calls for his "Switzers," his hired Swiss guards. The messenger tells him that he must act to save himself since Laertes at the head of a riotous rabble has overcome the King's officers. The rabble mob, having forgotten the ancient hierarchy and customs of society "cry, 'Choose we! Laertes shall be king!'" At this point another noise is heard; the King cries "The doors are broke;" and Laertes with some followers enters demanding the King. Laertes tells his followers to leave him alone but guard the door, and then he says to Claudius, "O thou vile king, / Give me my father." The Queen tries to calm Laertes but he replies: "That drop of blood that's calm proclaims me bastard." Claudius now asks Laertes the cause of his rebellion. Gertrude has tried to physically restrain Laertes, but Claudius tells her to let him go since "There's such divinity doth hedge a king / That treason can but peep to what it would, / Act little of his will." Laertes answers with the question, "Where is my father?" Claudius answers, "Dead," and Gertrude immediately interjects, "But not by him." Since Claudius now tells him to demand whatever he wants to know from him, Laertes answers:

> *How came he dead? I'll not be juggled with.*
> *To hell allegiance, vows to the blackest devil,*
> *Conscience and grace to the profoundest pit!*
> *I dare damnation. To this point I stand,*
> *That both worlds I give to negligence,*
> *Let come what comes, only I'll be revenged*
> *Most thoroughly for my father.*

COMMENT: Laertes' reaction to his father's death stands in marked contrast to that of Hamlet. Laertes has gathered a mob together, stormed the palace and is ready both to revenge himself upon the King and himself take over the kingdom. How easily Hamlet could have accomplished the same is shown by Claudius' earlier statement about Hamlet, "He's loved of the distracted multitude." Since Hamlet is one of the two royal Danes with a genuine right to the throne and since he is beloved by the mob, he could have aroused the mob as easily as Laertes and swiftly swept to this revenge, regaining the throne through force. But the very fact that Laertes, without any royal pretensions, could arouse this same mob to an anarchic overthrowing of ancient custom shows how illegitimate is such support, how far from justice and right.

Shakespeare had strongly condemned the mob in his earlier play, *Julius Caesar*, when he showed how easily it could be swayed, first by Brutus and then by Antony. In *Troilus and Cressida*, written a few years after *Hamlet*, he had as strongly urged the necessity for degree and hierarchy in society as in nature. In a long speech in Act I: Scene iii, Ulysses says: "O, when degree is shak'd, / Which is the ladder to all high designs, / Then enterprise is sick!... / Take but degree away, untune that string, / And hark what discord follows!" In the history plays written just before *Hamlet*, Shakespeare makes the same point. King Henry the Fourth was wrong to have deposed the rightful King Richard the Second even though Richard was not ruling the kingdom well, and it is Henry the Fifth who is the ideal king since he is both a legitimate and good ruler. It is clear, then, that Shakespeare does not approve of regicide and especially disapproves of mob support. Though Laertes has taken the shortest path to success, he has compromised his ends by the means used. That even Laertes is aware of this is indicated by the respect he accords Claudius when Claudius invokes the divine right of kings.

But Laertes further compromises the validity of his revenge by the terms in which he is willing to undertake it. He throws his former allegiance, vows, conscience and grace away, though this means vowing himself "to hell" and to "the blackest devil," and, aware of the religious implications of such revenge, proclaims, "I dare damnation." He is unconcerned about the question of his soul's salvation as long as he can be "revenged most thoroughly for my father."

Such an attitude places Hamlet's predicament in its clearest relief. For Hamlet has always been concerned about this problem. However tempted and even momentarily controlled by the power of hell he may have been, he has never finally been able to commit an act which he felt might damn his soul and has been continually concerned with this question. Though his questioning of the ghost's nature may not have been the primary reason for his delay, it is clearly a problem uppermost in his conscious mind. He is not willing to commit a revenge which would involve his conscious allegiance to hell. It is not only Ophelia, then, but also Laertes who serves as a foil to Hamlet. Laertes shows us that such direct revenge on Hamlet's part would have resulted in both a social crime and spiritual damnation and that Hamlet is the better man for having, unlike Laertes, delayed his revenge.

Claudius now tells Laertes that he will not hinder his revenge but asks whether Laertes means to include in his revenge "both friend and foe." When Laertes answers that he is only opposed to "his enemies" and is willing to learn the true circumstances of his father's death, Claudius says that he will prove to Laertes that he is guiltless of his father's death. At this point Ophelia reenters and Laertes is shocked and grieved to discover his sister's mental state. As Ophelia proceeds to sing of her father's funeral and offer flowers to the various people there, Laertes tells her, "Hadst thou thy wits, and didst persuade revenge, / It could not move thus." Continuing to sing of her father's death as she departs, she leaves a grief-stricken Laertes whom Claudius now turns to comfort. He tells Laertes that he should choose his wisest friends to judge between them as he explains the circumstances of Polonius' death. If they still find him guilty, Claudius is willing to give Laertes his crown and life, but if they find him innocent he says that he will be willing to help Laertes to accomplish his revenge against the truly guilty party. Laertes agrees to this and says that he wishes a full explanation of his father's "obscure funeral" with "no noble rite nor formal ostentation." Claudius says that he shall be satisfied and then "where th' offense is, let the great axe fall." They now all leave to attend to this inquiry.

SUMMARY: This scene accomplishes the following purposes:

1. It shows us further unfortunate effects of Hamlet's killing of Polonius—Ophelia's madness and Laertes' vowed revenge.

2. Both of these unfortunate effects of Hamlet's killing, however, serve ironically as foils to show Hamlet's greater virtue. This is one of the most important dramatic effects in the play. At a point where our respect for Hamlet is at its lowest, due to his inhuman reasons for not killing Claudius, his insane slaughter of Polonius and his contemptuous treatment of his body thereafter, Shakespeare takes him out of both Denmark and our view for a period and shows us situations parallelling Hamlet's. By showing us how similar situations completely destroy Ophelia's sanity and lead Laertes into behavior both criminal and damnable, we are able to more truly judge Hamlet's actions, to see in them not a lack of control but, on the contrary, an extraordinary grip on himself and a grasp of a most agonizing and spiritually dangerous situation. Having shown us Hamlet's flaws with the greatest of detail, Shakespeare is now beginning his rehabilitation as a tragic hero worthy of our admiration.

Act IV: Scenes vi and vii

The sixth scene takes place in another room of the castle immediately following the last. Horatio has been called to this room to meet some sailors who have asked for him. He is given a letter from Hamlet which describes Hamlet's adventures at sea as follows: after they were two days at sea, a pirate ship chased and then came alongside of his ship. Some fighting ensued during which Hamlet alone boarded the pirate ship. (This shows his customary quickness to undertake physical activity when not related to his revenge and refutes the idea of Hamlet as a simply intellectual man.) Immediately the pirate ship got clear of the Danish ship with the result that Hamlet became their prisoner. They have treated him well, however, and Hamlet now means to reward them for the freedom they have given him. He tells Horatio to see that they get to the King with the letters he has sent to Claudius and then that Horatio should come with these "good fellows" to where he is as he has "words to speak in thine ear will make thee dumb." Horatio now leaves with them immediately to go to the King.

The scene now shifts to another room in the castle where the King has been in conference with Laertes. The seventh scene begins with Claudius' conclusion to the inquiry: Laertes must now acquit him since he understands "That he which hath your noble father slain / Pursued my life." Laertes grants him the appearance but asks him why he did not proceed to take justice against the offender who so threatened his own life. Claudius responds that it was "for two special reasons" which might not seem as strong to Laertes as they do to him. The first reason he states as follows:

> The queen his mother
> Lives almost by his looks, and for myself
> My virtue or my plague, be it either which

> She is so conjunctive to my life and soul
> That, as the star moves not but in his sphere
> I could not but by her.

COMMENT: Here Claudius seems to be making a genuine confession of love for Gertrude. It may be that his love is "plague" since, as we have seen, it did not allow him to repent his murder and so save his soul and is now endangering his life. Or it may be that his love is his "virtue" since it provides the major value and meaning to his life. In any case, she is so necessary to his "life and soul" that even if his love for her destroys both his present life and eternal hope these would both be meaningless without her; he simply cannot live without her. Such a confession may even explain the dreadful murder of his brother. His need to wholly possess his mistress may have become so great that he could no longer live without making her his wife. Such a desperate love, leading as it does to murder, may not be sanctified, but it is certainly more than the simple lust for which Hamlet and his father's ghost condemn it. And we may even understand the appeal such a desperate love must have had upon Gertrude. That it is love rather than lust is further shown by Claudius' tender concern to protect Gertrude from any unpleasantness. In Gertrude's unwillingness to see the disturbed Ophelia, we may see a general characteristic of hers, an unwillingness to be disturbed by anything unpleasant. We can easily imagine, then, how much the unpleasant necessities of maintaining a secret adultery must have upset her. Possibly it was this which made it urgent for Claudius to murder his brother. Unable to face the possibility of losing her love, this deed would enable him to return her to the mental peace of a conventionally married woman. Certainly he took great pains to conceal the deed from her so that she was able to enter the marriage without too much moral difficulty. It was certainly for her sake that he tried to develop good relations with her son and even now, when her son has clearly indicated his murderous intentions against him, he cannot bear to alienate her affections by openly condemning her son to death.

The fact that all his plans for disposing of his vowed enemy must be done behind her back certainly handicaps him in dealing effectively with Hamlet. The fact that the death of Hamlet, even if not ascribed to him, would upset Gertrude is perhaps responsible for his long hesitation in even taking these steps. If Hamlet, for known and unknown reasons, has been hindered from taking effective action against Claudius, there are also factors which hinder Claudius as much from effectively protecting himself against Hamlet. The first, as indicated by his growing remorse over his murder of his brother, is his unwillingness to add another sin to his conscience. The second reason, already mentioned and now to be again repeated, is Hamlet's popularity with the people and his unwillingness to take action against Hamlet which might turn the people against him. A third unspoken reason may be his fear of bringing Hamlet before a court where Hamlet might be able to present his own charges against him. But certainly the greatest reason is his love for Gertrude.

Claudius now tells Laertes that the second reason he did not prosecute Hamlet was that he was afraid the "great love" the common people bear for Hamlet would cause his plans to backfire against himself "and not where I had aimed them." Laertes complains that this does not satisfy his need to revenge the death of his father and mental breakdown of his sister, but Claudius calms him with the assurance that he will help him accomplish his purposes.

At this point a messenger arrives with the letters from Hamlet. Claudius is shocked at this event but he then proceeds to read the following letter to Laertes: "High and mighty, you shall know I am set naked on your kingdom. Tomorrow shall I beg leave to see your kingly eyes; when I shall (first asking your pardon thereunto) recount the occasion of my sudden and more strange return. HAMLET."

COMMENT: Since, as we are soon to learn, Hamlet is well aware of Claudius' plan to have him murdered in England, it is surprising that he should continue to act with so little concern for his own safety. What he does is to warn Claudius of his "naked," that is unarmed and unaccompanied, return into Claudius' power, thus providing Claudius with a new means to plan his destruction. What is more, Hamlet indicates his continuing hatred of Claudius by addressing him rudely as "High and mighty." Hamlet's behavior is in marked contrast to Laertes' mode of re-entry into Denmark, but if it is lacking in treason it is also lacking in even the slightest degree of self-protection, not to speak of any apparent means of attack. Though this may seem foolish on the face of it, it is, as we shall soon see, the product of a new understanding he had gained while on shipboard.

While both Laertes and Claudius are confused by this turn of events, as well they might be, they are quick to see advantage for themselves in it. Laertes says "it warms the very sickness in my heart" that he will be able to return his injury back to Hamlet. Claudius immediately conceives a new plan which will so cleverly dispose of Hamlet that "for his death no wind of blame shall breathe, / But even his mother shall uncharge the practice / And call it accident." Laertes says that he will only be fully satisfied with the plan if he might be its instrument, and Claudius replies that this is in line with his thoughts.

He now tells Laertes about the visit of a Norman two months earlier who astonished the court with his horseback riding. This Norman had known and praised Laertes extravagantly, particularly for his skill in fencing. This had made Hamlet so envious that he had kept wishing for Laertes' sudden return so that he could have a sporting fencing match with him. It is from this fact that Claudius now means to work Hamlet's destruction. Before explaining his idea, however, Claudius asks Laertes how much he loved his father and then, very much like the Player King, reminds him that the passage of time can weaken any purpose and that one should quickly accomplish his will. To his final question as to what he would do to prove himself his father's true son, Laertes replies that he would "cut his throat i' the' church!" And Claudius agrees: "No place indeed should murther sanctuarize; / Revenge should know no bounds." (Here we see most clearly the damnable nature of revenge in its essential opposition with religion. It is ironic that Claudius seconds Laertes' willingness to do that which Hamlet refrained from doing, that is killing a man in prayer, though it is also to Hamlet's discredit that his reason for not then killing Claudius was not Hamlet's reverence for piety. In any case, Laertes' statement underscores his eagerness to "dare damnation" to effect his revenge, and in this he is in marked contrast to Hamlet. Claudius now explains that his plan is to propose a fencing match between Hamlet and Laertes. Since, as just markedly shown by his letter, Hamlet is "remiss, / Most generous, and free from all contriving," he will not examine the foils and Laertes should easily be able to choose a sharply pointed rather than practice foil with which, during the course of the match, he can kill Hamlet. Laertes agrees and, not to be outdone in villainy, adds that he will also dip the tip of his foil in poison so that a mere scratch will prove fatal. Claudius now suggests that if even this should fail there had better be a reserve plan so that their failure would not be apparent. He now suggests that he will prepare a poisoned chalice for Hamlet to drink when he becomes thirsty during the match so that "if he by chance escape your venomed stuck, / Our purpose may hold there."

COMMENT: There is surely something wrong with such a plan, for any death by a sword wound in a practice match in which the foils are supposed to have dull rounded tips could hardly be considered accidental. What is more, if Hamlet were to die after publicly drinking a drink offered by Claudius, this would also cast suspicion on Claudius. Since this plan is so inferior to the "perfect crime" of his first murder, it can only be taken as an indication of Claudius' increasing hysteria in the face of Hamlet's continued dangerous and mocking existence. Laertes is willing to go along with this plan since he feels that any kind of murder would serve to clean the stain off his "honor."

Gertrude now enters with the sorrowful news that Ophelia has drowned and beautifully describes the scene of her death. Ophelia had attempted to hang a wreath of wildflowers on the bough of a willow tree which had grown over a brook and the bough on which she was climbing broke, throwing her into the water below. There she lay for a time, buoyed up by her clothes while she sang snatches of old songs and was incapable of recognizing her danger. At last her drenched garments pulled her down to death.

COMMENT: It might be noted that anyone who could have observed this scene well enough to have reported it to Gertrude would have been criminally negligent in not saving Ophelia from death. Though this problem can be argued away by considering Gertrude's tale as a stage convention for reporting an event which could not be presented on stage, the fact remains that, in the next scene, it is common rumor that Ophelia's death was the result of suicide and this is reflected in the form of her funeral. We are then left with the possibility that Gertrude was told a story which would not upset her, or that she herself elaborated a story which placed Ophelia's death in its least unpleasant light, whether for her own benefit or for Laertes. These possibilities are in line with what we know of Gertrude's character. In view of the general uncertainty about Ophelia's death at the time of the funeral, we can only conclude that her death was unobserved and that Gertrude's version is simply one interpretation after the fact. But the fact that, whether consciously or not, Ophelia's mental condition resulted in her death again serves as a foil to Hamlet's rejection of the temptation of suicide.

Laertes tries to restrain his tears at the recounting of his sister's death but finally is forced to quickly leave the room. Claudius and Gertrude quickly follow to try to comfort him as the fourth act ends.

SUMMARY: These last two scenes mark the off-stage return of Hamlet and serve to sharply distinguish him from Claudius and Laertes. While Hamlet is, as Claudius notes, "Most generous, and free from all contriving," Claudius and Laertes busy themselves with treacherously planning his death. The rehabilitation of Hamlet begun in the previous scene is continued in these, even in the face of Ophelia's death.

Act V: Scene i

The scene takes place in a graveyard near the castle at Elsinore on the following day. Two gravediggers, who are to be played by clowns, are discussing the funeral rites of the lady for whom they are preparing a grave. It appears that she is to have a Christian burial though, to their way of thinking, she was clearly a suicide and they resentfully see this as a result of her high position: "And the more pity that great folk should have count'nance in this world to drown or hang themselves more than their even Christen. Come, my spade. There is no ancient gentlemen but gard'ners, ditchers, and gravemakers. They hold up Adam's profession." Here a more democratic Christian gentility is asserted in the face of the false aristocratic notion of honor, and the proof of this is in their profession, for their graves serve all and must "last till doomsday."

The chief gravedigger now sends the other for some liquor and, after he leaves, continues to dig while singing a song of youthful love: "In youth when I did love, did love, / Methought it was very sweet." At this point Hamlet and Horatio enter and Hamlet is surprised that the gravedigger is so lacking in "feeling of his business, that 'a sings at grave-making." Horatio explains this as a product of "custom" and Hamlet agrees. The gravedigger now throws up a skull and Hamlet reflects on the vanity of human wishes: "How the knave jowls it to the ground, as if 'twere Cain's jawbone, that did the first murther! This might be the pate of a politician, which this ass now o'erreaches; one that would circumvent God, might it not? . . . . Or of a courtier, which could say 'Good morrow, sweet lord!'" (Here Hamlet seems to be thinking of Claudius and such courtiers as Polonius, Rosencrantz and Guildenstern. Claudius has tried to "circumvent God" through a brother's murder like that of Cain and yet all he shall finally gain is a death like that which Hamlet has already awarded to Claudius' courtiers, as we shall soon see. Hamlet's readiness to identify the skull he sees being rudely thrown about with that of Claudius shows us that Hamlet has Claudius' coming death very firmly in mind.) As Hamlet continues to reflect on the generality of death, however, he becomes upset by it: "Did these bones cost no more the breeding but to play at loggets with 'em? Mine ache to think on't." After continuing to reflect on the losses of the grave's occupant, whether lawyer or great landowner, he finally asks the gravedigger whose grave it is. When the gravedigger answers that though "I do not lie in't, yet it is mine," Hamlet replies in as humorous a vein, "Thou dost lie in't, to be in't and say it is thine. 'Tis for the dead, not for the quick; therefore thou liest." (Here we see Hamlet once more moving quickly from melancholy to punning wit and still very upset by the fact of death as at the first. But his mood is more controlled, his melancholy brief, his wit more playful. He is not a different Hamlet, but he seems to have himself in better control.) After finally being told that the grave is being prepared for a woman, Hamlet asks him how long he has been a gravedigger, and the gravedigger replies that it has been thirty years, that he began on "that day that our last king Hamlet overcame Fortinbras" which was also "the very day that young Hamlet was born." (Here we have our first indication of Hamlet's exact age. Shakespeare has refrained from informing us that Hamlet was a man rather than a boy until Hamlet had matured to his full thirty years. As Hamlet is soon to reach his tragic end, it is important to fully establish his significance as a grown rather than young man whose actions are not motivated by youthful disillusionment but mature consideration.)

The gravedigger now comes upon the skull of one he knew, Yorick, the king's jester, who had died twenty-three years before. Hamlet takes the skull and says to Horatio: "Alas, poor Yorick! I knew him, Horatio, a fellow of infinite jest, of most excellent fancy. He hath borne me on his back a thousand times. And now how abhorred in my imagination it is! My gorge rises at it. Here hung those lips that I have kissed I know not how oft. Where be your gibes now?" (In his disturbance over Yorick's death, Hamlet may also begin to fear his own since he is also "a fellow of infinite jest, of most excellent fancy." Indeed, the gravedigger's mention of Hamlet's age reminds him that he has already lived a full generation, and he is soon to leap into this very grave dug by one who has been preparing graves since the day Hamlet was born. If death is waiting for Claudius, it may also be waiting for him.) When Hamlet now begins to wonder whether one's imagination can "trace the noble dust of Alexander till 'a find it stopping a bunghole," Horatio sanely advises him that "'Twere to consider too curiously, to consider so." Hamlet, however, continues to elaborate this subject, just as he had after Polonius' death, until he is interrupted by the approach of a funeral party led by the King. He notes that the "maimed rites" indicate the funeral of a suicide and he decides to withdraw with Horatio to observe the event unseen.

After the entrance of the King, Queen, Laertes, a Doctor of Divinity, and other lords following the corpse, Laertes suddenly cries out: "What ceremony else?" The Doctor of Divinity explains that since "her death was doubtful," they have enlarged her funeral rites as much as they could and are at least burying her with prayers in sanctified ground rather than throwing rocks on her unsanctified grave. The disgusted Laertes is forced to agree to the funeral but tells the Doctor, "A

minist'ring angel shall my sister be / When thou liest howling." At this the shocked Hamlet says, "What, the fair Ophelia?" Gertrude now scatters flowers on Ophelia's grave with the sad mother's reflection: "I hope thou shouldst have been my Hamlet's wife. / I thought thy bride-bed to have decked, sweet maid, / And not have strewed thy grave." But her mention of Hamlet enrages Laertes with the remembrance of Hamlet's guilt for all his family's woes, and he exclaims: "O, treble woe / Fall ten times treble on that cursed head / Whose wicked deed thy most ingenious sense / Deprived thee of!" At the thought of her fate he longs to embrace her once more and, leaping into the grave, calls upon the gravediggers to bury him with her under such a mountain that it "o'ertop old Pelion" or Olympus itself. (This refers to the mythical war in which the Titans attempted to pile the mountain Ossa upon the mountain Pelion in order to reach the heaven of the Olympian gods.)

At this point Hamlet (aroused, as he later says, "into a tow'ring passion" by the ostentatious display of Laertes' grief and also perhaps by his sense of guilt at Laertes' accusation of his responsibility for Ophelia's death) comes forward, questions Laertes' right to such grief when he, "Hamlet the Dane" is there, and leaps into the grave after Laertes. Laertes begins to fight with him, saying, "The devil take thy soul!" But Hamlet objects to this prayer and his reply further indicates his self-awareness of his dangerous tendency to rashness: "Thou pray'st not well. / I prithee take thy fingers from my throat, / For though I am not splenitive and rash, / Yet have I in me something dangerous, / Which let thy wisdom fear." Though he has leaped belligerently into the grave, he tries to control himself from fighting with Laertes and especially right there in Ophelia's grave. After they have parted and leave the grave, however, Hamlet says that he is willing to fight Laertes to the death on the subject of his love for Ophelia. Though Laertes holds him guilty of her death, he proclaims: "I loved Ophelia. Forty thousand brothers / Could not with all their quantity of love / Make up my sum." Hamlet is willing to match any attempt on Laertes' part to prove his love for Ophelia. If Laertes wishes "to outface me with leaping in her grave," so will he and will call down as much earth to cover them as will "make Ossa like a wart!" He concludes his unseemly harangue with the words "I'll rant as well as thou," at which point his mother explains to Laertes that "this is mere madness." She continues her explanation by saying that for "a while the fit will work on him" and then, "as patient as the female dove," he will silently "sit drooping." Upon hearing his mother's words, he does calm himself sufficiently to ask Laertes: "What is the reason that you use me thus? / I loved you ever." With no apparent awareness of his responsibility for the deaths of Laertes' father and sister and for his present disruption of Ophelia's funeral, he self-righteously concludes: "But it is no matter. / Let Hercules himself do what he may, / The cat will mew, and dog will have his day." Believing that no amount of heroic endeavor would keep a low animal like Laertes from making noises at him, he abruptly turns from them and leaves.

COMMENT: Hamlet's behavior at Ophelia's funeral calls for some discussion. Though his tender regard for her is momentarily revived at the moment he becomes aware of her death, the time when he could approach love simply is as far behind him now as it is for the gravedigger whom he had just heard singing, "In youth when I did love, did love, / Methought it was very sweet." This memory of former love immediately becomes mingled with a sense of guilt when Laertes accuses him unseen of responsibility for her death. Though Hamlet has not been told the reasons for Ophelia's death and so might not immediately guess his responsibility for her apparent suicide, he tries to suppress the sense of guilt occasioned by Laertes' words by clutching that memory of former feeling and so heightening it that he can prove his love superior to that anyone else can feel (just as, in his very first long speech in the play, he had tried to prove his integrity to be superior to that of all others at the court).

This seems to be the explanation of Hamlet's challenging leap into the grave and showy proclamation of love for Ophelia as the excuse for his behavior. Any true love for her would hardly express itself in such emotionally exaggerated terms, exaggeration which had angered him when similarly expressed by Laertes. But as he is angered by Laertes' loud show of grief even as it stings his conscience, he tries to evade his guilt by affirming the continuity of his deep love for Ophelia and the superiority of his love to that of Laertes. He challenges Laertes to this test of love quite blinded as to Laertes' just grounds for hating him. At the funeral, he had said to Horatio: "That is Laertes, a very noble youth." Aware only of his own feelings, first for Ophelia, now for Laertes, he cannot understand why Laertes should be treating him so rudely: "What is the reason that you use me thus? / I loved you ever." And when Laertes refuses to condone Hamlet's present and past behavior, Hamlet's self-righteous involvement with his own feelings reaches a dreadful climax in the contemptuous insults he hurls at Laertes in apparent requital for his own wrongs.

Hamlet still reveals a complete lack of sympathy for anyone whom he believes to be wronging him. As he acted this way with Polonius, Ophelia and, as we shall soon see, Rosencrantz and Guildenstern, so does he here with Laertes. This whole scene at the funeral marks, indeed, one of Hamlet's lowest moral points. We see him essentially unchanged from the man who belittled and then murdered Polonius and could then still mock his corpse. But there is

this slight development of self-awareness and control that he is now aware that there is something in him which can make him dangerously rash and, though he has acted rashly enough in leaping into the grave and making such an unseemly scene, he does exert his utmost power to control himself from rashly murdering Laertes.

Claudius tells Horatio to follow Hamlet and then tells Laertes to keep his patience in the memory of the previous night's conference and in the assurance that very soon "this grave shall have a living monument," that is, the life of Hamlet. Upon this note of discord between Hamlet and Laertes, the scene ends.

SUMMARY: This scene has the following important aspects:

1. The gravediggers' joking about death provides some comic relief just before the final scene of multiple death at the same time that it prepares us thematically for this outcome.

2. In Hamlet's easy familiarity with the gravediggers, as earlier with the players and pirates and with his less well-born college friends, we see the true gentility of one who, being "to the manner born," is able to forget his special aristocratic privileges and become "even - Christen" with all men of good will. In this he stands in immediate contrast with Laertes, who always stands upon "ceremony."

3. In addition to this democratic quality, we are shown a variety of Hamlet's moods by which we may gauge the extent of his development before the final tragic scene. We see Hamlet still considering "too curiously" the common horror of death and still reacting to such horror with his characteristic alternation of melancholy and wit. Though he seems to be in firmer control of himself, this control is still imperfect and almost completely breaks down at the sight of Ophelia's grave and Laertes' showy grief. And though he is so sensitive to the horrors of existence, he can still show himself as completely insensitive to the feelings and rights of others if he believes himself to be wronged by them. He is still highly unstable, able to go at any moment into an irrational state in which he is capable of rash cruelty, but he is more aware of this now and better able to control himself than formerly.

4. At the moment when Hamlet offers to duel with Laertes and then when he asks him his grievance, Laertes has the opportunity to explain himself honestly to Hamlet and then either accept their mutual love for Ophelia as reason for their reconciliation or attempt to revenge his father's death in an honorable duel to the death. Laertes, however, is so angered by the blind self-righteousness of this murderer of his family that he cannot be open with him and continues to nurse his secretive and ignoble revenge. Claudius is easily able to use Hamlet's irrational behavior as a means of strengthening Laertes' allegiance to himself and ensuring the speedy enactment of their plan.

Act V: Scene ii

The final scene takes place in a major hall of the castle at Elsinore soon after the funeral. Hamlet enters in the act of explaining his recent behavior to Horatio. He immediately comes to the important events on shipboard which, in his letter to Horatio, he had said would make Horatio "dumb." In all of his soliloquies, he precedes his discussion of events with generalizations he has drawn from them. What he did on shipboard was rash and, in what is probably the most significant speech in the play, he now explains the culminating insight of his experience:

> *And praised be rashness for it—let us know,*
> *Our indiscretion sometime serves us well*
> *When our deep plots do pall, and that should learn us*
> *There's a divinity that shapes our ends,*
> *Rough-hew them how we will—*

Shakespeare has Horatio underscore the significance of these statements by saying, "That is most certain."

COMMENT: What Hamlet has learned is that man cannot carve out his own destiny but that this is ultimately shaped by Providence. Such an idea is not new to him or to the play, for he had earlier expressed it in the following lines given to the Player King: "Our wills and fates do so contrary run / That our devices still are overthrown; / Our thoughts are ours, their ends none of our own." The "devices" and "deep plots" by which man attempts to shape his fate cannot achieve final success since man is and must recognize that he is dependent upon Divine Providence. Hamlet's experiences now cause him to accept this idea with full conviction. Human ends can only be realized when they express the will of heaven and this, in turn, requires man to make himself into an agent for the divine will, acting only when seized by divine inspiration.

Such a person moves from the simple religion based upon obedience to the written law of God to the more difficult and often tragic religion of prophet and saint which is based upon obedience to the personally received commandments of God, commandments which often involve violations of the written law. The best example of this, as the great nineteenth century Danish theologian Søren Kierkegaard pointed out in *Fear and Trembling*, is Abraham's willingness to obey the divine commandment to sacrifice his son Isaac to God, even though this involves the violation of the moral written commandment against murder. Such

obedience may lead to martyrdom but, as the prophet Isaiah has explained of the nature of divine election, the Lord says "I have chosen thee in the furnace of affliction." The tragic reality of religion is that God often sacrifices his best and most beloved servants to achieve His will for the good of the whole. This is, in fact, the essence of the Christian mystery. And this is also Shakespeare's great understanding of reality.

For Shakespeare the essential moral distinction between men is not simply between those who do good and those who do evil, but between those who recognize their dependence upon the divine will and are willing to follow it to whatever end it demands and those who reject the idea of their dependence upon God and, in a modern secular spirit, believe that they alone must bear the responsibility for shaping their destiny. Thus, in *Julius Caesar*, the villain Cassius says to Brutus: "The fault, dear Brutus, is not in our stars, / But in ourselves, that we are underlings." And in *King Lear* the villain Edmund says: "This is the excellent foppery of the world, that, when we are sick in fortune, often the surfeit of our own behavior, we make guilty of our disasters the sun, the moon, and the stars; as if we were villains on necessity; fools by heavenly compulsion; knaves, thieves, and treachers by spherical predominance; drunkards, liars, and adulterers by an enforc'd obedience of planetary influence; and all that we are evil in, by a divine thrusting on." Similarly the villain Macbeth, in the tragedy which bears his name, though saying "If chance will have me King, why, chance may crown me, / Without my stir," does not leave his foretold destiny to "chance" but tries to shape his ends directly.

Shakespeare's villains, then, begin their course with an attitude which sounds very sensible to modern ears, that if there is such a thing as divinity it is quite irrelevant to human actions and that if man is to achieve anything in this world he can only do so through his own efforts. But such an attitude places man alone in the universe and thereby causes man to see himself as its center. This cosmic loneliness joined to a necessary egocentricity then leads to man's sense of alienation from his own community. What he desires is alone important. There is nothing, therefore, which can hinder him from attempting to achieve his desires at whatever the cost to others. At this point he becomes capable of any villainy. This is the genesis of Shakespeare's villains and, though less articulated by Claudius, also explains his behavior.

Claudius has made himself the god of his universe. This he indicates throughout the play by his celebration of his own power with trumpets, drums and cannons: "But the great cannon to the clouds shall tell, / And the king's rouse the heaven shall bruit again, / Respeaking earthly thunder." If he desires his brother's crown and wife, he acts to take them; if he must preserve his gains through the murder of Hamlet, he is ever ready to use "deep plots" to shape events to his own ends.

In opposition to this, Hamlet has been ever engaged in trying to fathom the divine will, has come to recognize his dependence upon it, the futility of all humanly conceived plots, and the primary necessity of only acting, in Edmund's words, with "a divine thrusting on." It is this, as we shall soon see, which motivates all of Hamlet's actions after his return to Denmark and which, in spite of all the murders he accomplishes, far more than those of the villain Claudius, makes him fit to be Shakespeare's tragic hero.

Hamlet now explains that one night on shipboard he felt so extremely restless that he "rashly" left his cabin, found his way in the dark to the cabin of Rosencrantz and Guildenstern, discovered their package of letters, and returned to his own cabin. Once there, he was "so bold" as to "unseal / Their grand commission; where I found, Horatio— / Ah, royal knavery!—an exact command" that without any loss of time, "No, not to stay the grinding of the axe, / My head should be struck off." Hamlet gives this important piece of concrete evidence against Claudius into the care of a shocked Horatio. He then continues his story. Surrounded as he was "with villainies," he again acted upon impulse without any prior planning of this course of action: "Or I could make a prologue to my brains, / They had begun the play." Although he had earlier considered fine penmanship the mark of a lower mind and had tried to forget his early training in fine handwriting, this training now served him well for it enabled him to write a formal state document. He immediately "devised a new commission, wrote it fair," and demanded of the English King that without any debating of this order "He should the bearers put to sudden death, / Not shriving time allowed."

When Horatio asks him how he was able to seal this forged commission, Hamlet replies, "Why, even in that was heaven ordinant. / I had my father's signet in my purse." That he was able with this model of the Danish seal to make a perfect forgery Hamlet sees as a sign of the shaping hand of heaven in these events. And further, the whole exploit by which he discovered Claudius' villainous designs against himself, was able to convert this plan so that it would lead to the destruction of Claudius' accomplices, and then return the forged commission so that the change was never known, finally led him to his grand conclusion that "There's a divinity that shapes our ends, / Rough-hew them how we will."

Horatio now notes in what must be a faintly disapproving tone, "So Guildenstern and Rosencrantz go to't." But Hamlet strongly justifies his actions with words:

Why, man, they did make love to this employment.
They are not near my conscience; their defeat
Does by their own insinuation grow.

'Tis dangerous when the baser nature comes
Between the pass and fell incensed points
Of mighty opposites.

Horatio's next comment, "Why, what a king is this!" enables Hamlet to come to the real issue on his conscience, the question of regicide:

Does it not, think thee, stand me now upon—
He that hath killed my king, and whored my mother,
Popped in between th' election and my hopes,
Thrown out his angle for my proper life,
And with such coz'nage—is't not perfect conscience
To quit him with this arm? And is't not to be damned
To let this canker of our nature come
In further evil?

COMMENT: We see from this last speech that Hamlet's conscience had not earlier been perfectly convinced of the rightness of killing a king. By waiting until this time, however, and forcing Claudius to show his hand, he now has solid ground for proceeding to enact not simply a possibly damnable personal revenge, but clear justice. The initial strong reason for action, Claudius' regicide against Hamlet's father, followed by the supporting though less mortal indictments against Claudius of incestuous adultery with his mother and of winning the election to the throne which Hamlet had hoped would come to him, has been superceded by Claudius' attack upon his own life. He is not now going to revenge his father's murder on the basis of spectral evidence from an unknown supernatural source, a course of premeditated action which might be damnable. He is acting in self-protection to openly rid Denmark of a king who has gained and would keep his throne through recourse to repeated, secretive murders of which Hamlet has concrete evidence. Not to act in this clear case of justice would now be as damnable as personal revenge on behalf of family honor might earlier have been. In this new bid for personal justice, his father's murder is but the first item in a long list of Claudius' injuries to him which has culminated in Claudius' hidden attempt to have him murdered.

But while it is commendable for Hamlet's conscience to be so concerned to establish the justice of his actions against Claudius, it is all the more surprising that his own planned murders of Rosencrantz and Guildenstern "are not near my conscience." Though his present attitude towards them is less offensive than was his attitude towards Polonius immediately after his murder of him, his justification is the same: "Take thy fortune. / Thou find'st to be too busy is some danger." Once Rosencrantz and Guildenstern have forfeited his trust by hesitating a single moment before confessing that they were sent for, Hamlet has no further use for them. Though they were childhood and college friends of his, he immediately sets them down as no more than corrupt accomplices of a vile king, and that very evening, in his mother's room, is already anticipating his destruction of them.

If it is true that they were carrying sealed orders for his murder, there is no evidence that they had any knowledge of the contents of this commission. Nor does their compliance with Claudius' wishes constitute definite proof of their baseness. They were sent for by their King, a King who had proved himself a good ruler, concerned for his people's welfare, and who seemed to be showing a benevolent concern for Hamlet's health in thus sending for them in the expressed hope that they might help him to understand and thereby cure Hamlet's disorder. During their single day at court, Hamlet's wild behavior after the performance of the play, his murder of Polonius and subsequent display of irrational playfulness could only have convinced them that Hamlet was dangerously mad and that Claudius was taking the most lenient course open to a king forced to protect himself. Though they ally themselves so fully with the King's purposes after the murder of Polonius as to appear high-handed with Hamlet, there is no other way for them to act since Hamlet has grown increasingly belligerent toward them during the course of the day. Moreover, their horror at the possibility of regicide is no different from what Hamlet, himself, would have felt in their place. Indeed, even in his position of revenger, Hamlet's conscience was apparently so disturbed by the complication of regicide involved in his revenge that he did not feel perfectly free to proceed until his own life was placed in danger. Finally, the very extenuation of self-defense, which Hamlet provides for his own coming murder of Claudius, is equally applicable to Claudius' present designs against Hamlet. How much more, then, does Claudius seem to be justified in the simple exiling of Hamlet, which is all that Rosencrantz and Guildenstern would most probably have been told of Claudius' designs.

It would seem, then, that Hamlet is being unfair in condemning Rosencrantz and Guildenstern to death for their apparently innocent obedience to their King. But, as we have seen that Hamlet wishes his revenge to extend beyond Claudius' mortal life, so does he feel it should extend to all the accomplices of his illegitimate reign, and these too he feels should be withheld from going to heaven just as his father was by Claudius' refusal to allow him "shriving time." This explicit addition to Claudius' own order for hasty death shows us that Hamlet's moral condition is still not perfect. He has acted with excessive severity towards Rosencrantz and Guildenstern and still feels no guilt for his action.

Even as Hamlet reaches his most profound and objective justification for his coming murder of Claudius, we see that he already stands far more guilty of wanton death than Claudius. Where Claudius is guilty of regicide and of planning the murder of the heir apparent, Hamlet is guilty of the direct deaths of Polonius, Rosencrantz and Guildenstern and the indirect death of Ophelia. Though Claudius'

murders may make up in quality what they lack in quantity, Hamlet has certainly compromised the purity of his intentions by the murderous course he has travelled toward his end, a course for which universal justice will exact its punishment regardless of the fact that it is on the life of its own "scourge and minister."

Horatio now stresses the practical need of speedy action since Claudius will undoubtedly be soon informed of the result of his mission to England. Hamlet blandly agrees: "It will be short; the interim is mine. / And a man's life no more than to say 'one.'"

COMMENT: Hamlet feels quite confident, both of the ease with which he can murder Claudius now that his conscience is perfectly clear, and that he will accomplish this task in the interim before the arrival of the ambassador from England. From Hamlet's behavior during this interim, however, it is also clear that he has made no plan as to how or when he will kill Claudius. He has acted and continues to act in a way which is almost foolhardy in being so extremely "free from all contriving." First he sends word to Claudius that he is returning without any effort at self-protection. Next he virtually ignores Claudius at the funeral which he so angrily disrupts. Finally, he spends his remaining free time engaged, as we shall soon see, in a fencing match with Laertes. From this it should be evident that Hamlet, in accordance with his new understanding of the divine control over human events, has placed his entire reliance upon Providence, confident that the "divinity that shapes our ends" will arrange the circumstances necessary for his action and do this better than he could himself.

But now that his own revenge seems so close to accomplishment, he suddenly becomes aware of Laertes' just grievance against himself and feels "very sorry" that "to Laertes I forgot myself." Although he excuses his treatment of Laertes on the grounds that "the bravery [ostentation] of his grief did put me / Into a tow'ring passion," he hopes to be able to gain Laertes' forgiveness and vows, "I'll court his favors."

At this providential moment of Hamlet's concern to regain Laertes' goodwill, the courtier Osric enters with a message of welcome from Claudius. Turning aside to Horatio and finding that he does not know "this waterfly," Hamlet tells Horatio that he is the better for not knowing such an ostentatious, land wealthy fool, and it is characteristic of Claudius that, though "a beast be lord of beasts," he allows him to eat at his own "mess." Osric doffs his hat before Hamlet as he is about to deliver his message, but Hamlet democratically tells him to return his hat to his head. When Osric refuses on the grounds that "it is very hot," Hamlet begins to make fun of him as he earlier had with Polonius, insisting first that it is cold and then hot, Osric agreeing to everything Hamlet says, until Hamlet finally prevails on Osric to wear his hat. Osric now tries to get to the point of his coming, the "great wager" the King has placed on Hamlet's head. When he begins to extol Laertes' merits in the most ridiculously affected manner, however, Hamlet cannot restrain himself from imitating Osric's absurd manner of speech. But Osric is too foolishly vain of his own accomplishments to realize that Hamlet is making fun of him and replies: "Your lordship speaks most infallibly of him." Hamlet continues his marvelous caricature of Osric, to the delight of Horatio, until he finally gets the bewildered Osric to come to the point of the wager. Regaining his speech with all its affection, Osric now explains that Claudius has wagered six Barbary horses against six French rapiers and poniards that in a fencing match between Hamlet and Laertes, of a dozen passes, Laertes would not exceed Hamlet by three hits. The odds are laid twelve to nine in Hamlet's favor. He now wishes to know whether Hamlet is willing for this match to come "to immediate trial," and Hamlet answers that he is willing to have the foils brought immediately to this very hall and to begin the match, that Osric can deliver this message "after what flourish your nature will." After Osric leaves, Hamlet and Horatio continue to comment on the comic absurdity of courtiers like Osric until another lord enters from Claudius to know whether Hamlet still wishes to play immediately with Laertes or would "take longer time." As Hamlet says that he is ready if the King so wishes, the lord informs him that the King, Queen and court are coming to the match and that the Queen desires Hamlet to greet Laertes in a gentlemanly fashion before they start to play. Hamlet says that he will follow this instruction and the lord leaves.

When they are once more alone, Horatio suggests that Hamlet will "lose this wager," but Hamlet disagrees as he has been "in continual practice" since Laertes went to France and should be able to "win at the odds." Nonetheless, he feels a premonition of danger in his heart, though he rejects such "foolery." Horatio advises Hamlet to obey his intuitions and says that he will delay the match on the grounds that Hamlet is not well. But Hamlet replies:

Not a whit, we defy augury. There is special providence in the fall of a sparrow. If it be now, 'tis not to come; if it be not to come, it will be now; if it be not now, yet it will come. The readiness is all. Since no man of aught he leaves knows, what is't to leave betimes? Let be.

COMMENT: This speech is one of Hamlet's most important utterances. Here we see Hamlet's most complete statement of his belief in the providential nature of all events. As every event down to "the fall of a sparrow" has been determined by the special concern of Providence, one will die whenever and only whenever it has been appointed. Moreover, no man "knows" anything of what he has left behind once he is dead. (It is unclear here whether Hamlet

is denying the existence of an afterlife, the survival of personal consciousness or merely the survival of a spirit's earthly memory. Since even the last two would seem to contradict the evidence provided by the ghost, assuming him to be "honest," it is possible that Hamlet may be here defining the nature of spiritual salvation, and that the process of Purgatory is to purge the spirit of its disquieting personal memories and egocentricity so that it can achieve this final salvation.) The fact of death, therefore, need provide no concern for man.

The important thing is to achieve a state of "readiness." In Shakespeare's later development of this idea in *King Lear*, the virtuous Edgar says to his despairing father Gloucester: "What, in ill thoughts again? Men must endure / Their going hence, even as their coming hither; / Ripeness is all. Come on." What is important is not the length of life but its quality. Life is given to a man so that he may develop to his full "ripeness," a state which is reached when he has developed sufficient insight into his true position in the cosmic order to give him the proper "readiness" to endure both life and death. This is the highest moral development of which man is capable and it also serves to distinguish between Shakespeare's heroes and villains. Where Shakespeare's heroes achieve this "readiness," this "ripeness" which is "all," before death, his villains meet "untimely" deaths for which they are spiritually unprepared.

The proof that Hamlet has achieved this "readiness" is given in the last words of this speech, "Let be." This is the one attitude of which Hamlet was earlier incapable. When faced with the horror of death and infidelity, his spirit refused to let it be. Rather than accept the evils of existence, he felt impelled to either suicide or revenge, though these impulses showed "a will most incorrect to heaven." Though this consciousness of evil warped his sensitive nature to the point that he felt "I must be cruel only to be kind" and acted as such, his spirit also began to develop a new healing consciousness of the providential nature of reality. The "Everlasting" was no longer viewed as the harsh, damning lawgiver whose creation thus became a sterile farce, but as a sanctifying Providence, inspiring man with a new liberation of spirit to do and affirm the work of the "Divinity." This is very much the central Christian message preached by St. Paul in his epistles to the Galatians, Corinthians, Romans and Ephesians. Hamlet has now transcended his earlier despair through an affirmation of spirit which reveals his true spiritual heroism.

The King and court now arrive to the accompaniment of trumpets and drums. While the hall is being prepared for the fencing match, Claudius places Laertes' hand into Hamlet's in an apparent bid for their reconciliation. Hamlet begins in the most cordial terms by saying: "Give me your pardon, sir. I have done you wrong, / But pardon't, as you are a gentleman." As Gertrude had done twice before, he now attempts to excuse his behavior on the grounds of madness, a madness which, as he also said over the corpse of Polonius, punishes him as much as his victims: "His madness is poor Hamlet's enemy." If Hamlet "when he's not himself does wrong Laertes," he can at least offer in his own defense: "Let my disclaiming from a purposed evil / Free me so far in your most generous thoughts / That I have shot my arrow o'er the house / And hurt my brother."

COMMENT: Hamlet's defense of unpremeditated murder, caused by temporary insanity, for which his mother is witness, would stand up in our own courts and lead to his acquittal. What is more, it is also true that he has only hurt himself through this unpremeditated act by adversely affecting those he loved (Ophelia and Laertes), and by causing Claudius and Laertes to seek his own life. And what is objectively true in the case of his killing of Polonius also seems to him subjectively true in the case of Rosencrantz and Guildenstern. Here we may be less convinced by his argument, though he carefully stresses to Horatio the rash spontaneity with which he acted against them. He may be guilty of more killing than Claudius, but Claudius' past and future murders of father and son would legally be considered first-degree murders, while Hamlet's lack of "purposed evil" might reduce the charges against him to manslaughter or acquittal. In terms of our own legal structure, as well as Shakespeare's moral system, Hamlet's actions, while certainly not safe to society, do finally appear less criminal than Claudius' actions and so should free him in our "most generous thoughts."

Laertes admits that he is "satisfied in nature" though it is this which should stir him most to his revenge, but he is not willing to make a formal reconciliation with Hamlet until "some elder masters of known honor" can show him by precedents that his honor will not be stained by such a peace. Until that time, however, he says that he will "not wrong" Hamlet's offering of love. Hamlet embraces Laertes' reply and is ready to begin "this brother's wager." They call for the foils and, making a pun on the word "foil," Hamlet generously tells Laertes, "I'll be your foil," his own poor performance making Laertes' skill shine the more brightly. As they go to choose the foils, Hamlet seems to convince Laertes that he does not "mock" him. Hamlet is satisfied with the foil he chooses but Laertes is not and goes to choose another foil while Claudius explains to Hamlet once more the terms of the wager. As they prepare to play, Hamlet asks whether the foils are all alike, that is, have dulled ends, and Osric replies, "Ay, my good lord."

COMMENT: In Laertes' reply to Hamlet's apology, we see again his primary concern with "ceremony" and "terms of honor" rather than with the deeper emotional reality of a situation. Though Hamlet seems to have genuinely touched Laertes and perhaps confused his purposes, it does not prevent Laertes from choosing the fatally sharp and poisoned sword while Claudius connives to distract Hamlet's attention. In his concern for the outward appearances of honor, then, Laertes is really dishonoring himself as he goes against his sworn word not to "wrong" Hamlet's love. Osric's assurance to Hamlet about the similarity of the foils suggests that he is also in on the plot. But it is possible that the foils may have been grouped for him by Claudius or Laertes without his knowledge of the sharpened foil.

Claudius now calls for wine to be placed on a table and says that if Hamlet hits Laertes in the first three exchanges "the king shall drink to Hamlet's better breath." He will then drop a rich "union" or pearl into the cup for Hamlet while "the kettle to the trumpet speak, / The trumpet to the cannoneer without, / The cannons to the heaven, the heaven to earth." They begin to play and on the first exchange Hamlet scores, as Osric says, "A hit, a very palpable hit." The drum, trumpets and cannon sound and the King stops the play to drink to Hamlet, drop the pearl into the cup and offer the ceremonial cup to him.

COMMENT: The pearl which Claudius drops in the cup after he drinks from it is apparently the means by which the drink is poisoned. It is interesting that he accompanies this attempt to shape his destiny by the thunderous sounds of his self-deification which are to resound from "heaven to earth." But we may wonder at Claudius' haste to poison Hamlet. This can only be explained by his loss of faith in Laertes' willingness or ability to fulfill his part of their agreement. Perhaps Claudius believed Laertes' promise of fair play to Hamlet; perhaps he senses in Laertes' performance a hesitance to play up to his full ability. Certainly, Laertes' fencing is so poor that, by the third exchange, even Hamlet taunts him with this. At any rate, Claudius turns almost immediately to what was supposed to be left as a last resort.

Hamlet, however, unceremoniously refuses to join Claudius in a toast and asks that the cup be set by awhile until he finishes the next bout. He calls for the beginning of the second bout and immediately makes "another hit," as Laertes confesses.

Claudius now tells Gertrude "our son shall win." In apparent delight over his son's good performance, she goes to wipe Hamlet's brow with her handkerchief. As this brings her close to the table near the fencers on which the cup has been placed, she picks up the cup and tells Hamlet that she too is going to toast his fortune. To this action Hamlet exclaims "Good madam!" but Claudius calls out to her imperiously, "Gertrude, do not drink." She insists, however, "I will, my lord; I pray you pardon me." In silent agony, Claudius reflects: "It is the poisoned cup; it is too late." Hamlet still does not wish to interrupt his fencing and says to her, "I dare not drink yet, madam—by and by." She then goes to wipe his face once more before he starts to play again.

COMMENT: It has been suggested that Gertrude acts in a spirit of motherly self-sacrifice because she suspects the cup's poisoned contents and that Hamlet's exclamation reflects his own suspicions. But such suspicions would hardly account for their subsequent actions, Hamlet's insistence upon continuing his match with Laertes and Gertrude's coming forth to wipe his brow once more. It seems more likely, therefore, that Gertrude is acting with fatal consistency to her character. We have seen that Gertrude tends to withdraw from any unpleasant truth and to delude herself that all is or, at any rate, will be well. She knows that Laertes means to revenge his father's murder and probably suspects that Claudius has explained Hamlet's responsibility for Polonius' death to him. Her fears were then so aggravated by Hamlet's insulting behavior to Laertes at Ophelia's funeral that she sent special word to Hamlet to apologize to Laertes and try to be reconciled to him. In an unusually tense state, she was delighted by Hamlet's gentlemanly behavior towards Laertes and their apparent reconciliation. Not only that, but Hamlet has been willing to fight as Claudius' champion, which seems to promise their reconciliation as well. And Hamlet's reasonable and sportsmanlike behavior seems also to promise her that Hamlet has finally been cured of his dreadful madness. If all this were true, then her growing fears of a great catastrophe might all be forgotten and all might yet be well. Since this is what she most fervently wishes to believe, she accomplishes the miracle of self-delusion once more and comes to believe it so fully that she must actively join into this happy occasion and show her son how happy he has made her. Her inability to face any unpleasant truth is her tragic flaw and it now destroys her. At this fateful moment Claudius might yet have prevented her death by confessing the poison. But since he is unable to protect her without giving himself away, he chooses his own survival and his throne over his love and can only look on in shocked horror at the ironic twisting of destiny which brings the poison to her lips instead of to Hamlet's as he had designed it. With all this, he too deludes himself into thinking that he can still shape his ends.

As the third round is about to start, Laertes tells Claudius that he will hit Hamlet in this bout. Claudius replies that he doubts it and Laertes admits to himself, "And yet it is almost against my conscience." Hamlet now playfully taunts Laertes about his poor performance, "You but dally," to which Laertes responds, "Say you so? Come on." Playing now to his best ability, Laertes can only bring Hamlet to a draw by the end of the bout. Enraged, he lunges at Hamlet after the close of the round—"Have at you now!"—and manages to wound Hamlet. When Hamlet realizes by his wound that Laertes has been fencing with an illegally sharp sword, he returns the attack with such fury that he gains control of the poisoned weapon in exchange for his own with which he seriously wounds Laertes.

COMMENT: As Gertrude was destroyed by her tragic flaw, so is Laertes by his tragic flaw of false pride and honor. As Laertes' better instincts begin to disturb his conscience, there is a moment when he might have dropped his dishonorable vindictive design against Hamlet in that true spirit of reconciliation which he had pledged but violated. But at this crucial moment, Hamlet makes the fatal mistake of playfully taunting Laertes. This immediately touches Laertes' ever-sensitive pride about outward appearances. Playing now as best he can, he feels so dishonored by his inability to defeat Hamlet that he completely dishonors himself by attacking Hamlet after the close of the bout. Jealousy, pride and a false sense of honor have overridden the better promptings of his conscience with the result that he truly dishonors himself and is fatally wounded. The price of venging himself against Hamlet, as he soon realizes, is his own just destruction.

Though Hamlet is anxious to continue his fight with Laertes despite Claudius' attempts to have them parted, the fight is finally stopped by the fall of the Queen. Horatio also notes that "they bleed on both sides" and asks Hamlet how he is. Osric also asks Laertes how he is and Laertes replies: "Why, as a woodcock to mine own springe [trap], Osric. / I am justly killed with mine own treachery." Hamlet, not as seriously wounded as Laertes, is more concerned about his mother, but Claudius answers his query by saying that Gertrude is only swooning at the sight of their blood. When she hears Claudius' false words, the dying Gertrude cries out: "No, no, the drink, the drink! O my dear Hamlet / The drink, the drink! I am poisoned."

COMMENT: Though it must have been a terrible act of duplicity for Claudius to lie about his beloved wife's fatal condition, the lie does clear Gertrude's mind of her own delusions. She suddenly understands what has happened to her, that she has been poisoned by the drink prepared by her husband for her son and, what is even more important, that to protect himself Claudius allowed her to drink poison and is now lying to cover his guilt. In her final moments she fully faces the evil that she had tried to avoid seeing in Claudius and, allying herself completely with her son against this poisonous destroyer of her peace, her family and her life, she cries out his guilt for all to hear.

With the Queen's full confession of Claudius' villainy before the assembled court, the enraged Hamlet attempts to assume control of the state and begin an immediate inquiry into Claudius' guilt: "O villainy! Ho! let the door be locked. / Treachery! Seek it out." But Laertes now falls with the words, "Hamlet, thou art slain." He explains that the sword in Hamlet's hands is not only sharp but poisoned and that Hamlet has no more than "half an hour's life." Laertes is also doomed, for his "foul practice / Hath turned itself on me." For both their deaths and for the poisoning of the Queen, he cries out to all, "The king, the king's to blame." Hearing that his life is now forfeit, Hamlet turns his poisoned sword on the King with the words, "The point envenomed too? / Then, venom, to thy work." But though Claudius is apparently convicted by the reigning Queen and by Laertes of the "treacherous" murder of themselves and of the crown prince, so great is the court's horror of regicide and reverence for a King's life that they all cry out "Treason! treason!" against Hamlet's murderous act. At this cry of support from his court, the fatally poisoned Claudius speaks his last words. "O, yet defend me, friends, I am but hurt."

COMMENT: Hamlet was just about to present his own evidence against Claudius in an official court of justice which he hoped would lead to the judicial execution of Claudius and his own assumption of rule when Laertes informed him that he was poisoned. But if Hamlet was not expecting to die, how much more dreadful is Claudius' state of spiritual unpreparedness. Having just wronged his beloved wife by blatantly lying about her condition, he now descends to the more desperate lie of self-delusion, saying that he is "but hurt." Unprepared to die, Claudius desperately clings to the delusion of possible life as before he had clung to the hope of preserving his throne while helplessly watching his wife die. Trying to play god to the end, he has only succeeded in destroying both his wife and himself.

But Hamlet quickly dispatches him with the poisoned drink he had prepared. Forcing this down his throat, he cries: "Here, thou incestuous, murd'rous, damned Dane, / Drink off this potion. Is thy union here? / Follow my mother." As the King dies, Laertes says that "he is justly served" by the poison he had prepared for Hamlet. He now turns to Hamlet with his last words: "Exchange forgiveness with me, noble Hamlet. / Mine and my father's death come not upon thee, / Nor thine on me!" The dying Hamlet accepts the dead Laertes' wish as he says: "Heaven make thee free of it! I follow thee."

COMMENT: Hamlet had earlier referred to Laertes as "a very noble youth" and now Laertes fulfills that potential nobility which had been buried under the false honor of appearances he had learned from his father. He rises to the true reconciliation which Hamlet had earlier desired but which he had fatally delayed out of false pride and jealousy, and he, too, is won completely to Hamlet's side. This final movement of Gertrude and Laertes to Hamlet's side serves to redeem them from the guilt of their complicity with Claudius, if not to save their lives. But it also serves in the rehabilitation of Hamlet in our eyes. Gertrude's "dear Hamlet" and Laertes' "noble Hamlet" remain our final image of Shakespeare's transformed hero.

Hamlet wishes he could more fully explain his act to the horrified spectators but, "as this fell sergeant, Death, / Is strict in his arrest," he tells Horatio that he must "report me and my cause aright / To the unsatisfied."

COMMENT: The most important thing about the accomplishment of Hamlet's "revenge" is that revenge for his father's murder is no longer the motive for his action. What finally unleashes Hamlet's lethal thrust is his recognition that he, himself, has fallen a mortal victim to Claudius' plot against him: "The point envenomed too? / Then, venom to thy work." Though he had meant to take judicial action against Claudius for his responsibility in the death of his mother and the plot against his own life, he now uses the little time left him to avenge his own murder, witnessed to before the court by Laertes' dying evidence against Claudius. After taking action on his own behalf with the weapon which had cost him his life, Hamlet turns to avenge his mother's death with the same drink which had poisoned her. Condemning Claudius for only those actions of which the court has objective knowledge, his incestuous marriage to his brother's widow and final murder of her before their eyes, for both of which he ought now to be "damned," Hamlet's final words to Claudius are: "Follow my mother."

But if Hamlet has finally caught Claudius in an act "that has no relish of salvation in't," as is proven by Claudius' state of spiritual unpreparedness for death, he, himself, has now transcended the earlier spirit of revenge which might also have caused his own damnation. He has not committed the premeditated revenge commanded by the ghost. Though the ghost's command unsettled his reason and led him to other acts of cruel death, for which he is now paying with his life, he has not acted upon the ghost's direct and possibly diabolic order for his father's revenge and, however shamed his sense of honor may have been by this delay, he has as well transcended his former allegiance to the honor code, now so thoroughly discredited by Laertes' conformity to its dictates. Moreover, it is only through this transcendence of the ultimately unchristian honor code that Hamlet rises to the height of true nobility, as is indicated by first Laertes and then Horatio's appellation of him as "noble." This noble transcendence of the damnable dictates of honor was only accomplished, however, by his new understanding and final commitment to the "divinity that shapes our ends." He had had faith that, without any direct planning on his part, heaven would so dispose events that he would be able to fulfill its will and his own as long as they remained in harmony. And events did so dispose themselves to cause him once more to act "rashly," though his spontaneous act against Claudius was undertaken in the spirit of such "perfect conscience" that it could only appear to objective viewers as the purest justice. Though it was at the unfortunate cost of his own and his mother's lives, Hamlet was thus able to execute Claudius in the most "perfect conscience" for these public events alone.

That the events which led Hamlet to this just execution of Claudius also involved his own death and the deaths of his mother and Laertes only shows the more clearly the working of universal justice through them. Laertes judges that not only is Claudius "justly served" but he, himself, is "justly killed with mine own treachery." Though he excuses Hamlet's murder of Polonius on the grounds of madness which Hamlet had offered, cosmic justice is less generous and has used this same repentant Laertes to effect the final punishment of its "scourge and minister," but this only after it has also allowed him to achieve the highest development of man, that state of "readiness," of true nobility, which must earn our admiration. And what of the Queen, left to heavenly justice? Cannot the hand of heaven be traced in the "accidental" death she willfully purchased through the poison prepared by the one who had originally infected her? Though Ernest Jones may find confirmation of his Freudian theory in the fact that, because of his supposed subconscious identification with Claudius' crimes, Hamlet only kills Claudius when he himself is dying, it seems clear that in Shakespeare's mind, as in Hamlet's, the explanation reaches beyond any such personality defects or complexes into the very heart of a religious mystery.

For once, Horatio attempts to go against Hamlet's wishes. Objecting that he is "more an antique Roman than a Dane" (that is, a Stoic who believes in suicide rather than survival with shame), Horatio attempts to emulate Hamlet's nobility, as he understands it, by drinking the remaining poison and following his beloved friend to death. But with his last strength Hamlet forcibly wrests the poisoned cup from Horatio's hands: "Give me the cup. Let go. By heaven, I'll ha't." Death may provide final happiness, but if Horatio truly loves him he would better follow his example by continuing the painful process of living and justifying Hamlet's name: "If thou didst ever hold me in thy heart, / Absent thee from felicity awhile, / And in this harsh world draw thy breath in pain, / To tell my story."

Hamlet now hears a "warlike noise" and is informed by Osric that it is the greeting of Fortinbras, returned from his conquest in Poland, to the ambassadors from England whom he has met on his way to Elsinore. The poison has so overcome him, however, that Hamlet fears he will not live long enough to hear the result of his substituted commission to the English King. As his death will also mark the end of the Danish royal line, he now turns his last thoughts to the question of the Danish succession, for he is now *de facto* ruler of Denmark and must attend to the good of his state: "I do prophesy th' election lights / On Fortinbras. He has my dying voice." Horatio is to tell Fortinbras of this and of all that has happened because for Hamlet "the rest is silence." As Hamlet dies, Horatio bids farewell to his noble friend in the full confidence of his spiritual salvation: "Now cracks a noble heart. Good night, sweet prince, / And flights of angels sing thee to thy rest!" Immediately upon the death of Hamlet, Fortinbras enters with the ambassadors from England.

COMMENT: The entrance of the ambassadors from England immediately following the close of the short "interim" time in which Hamlet was confident that he would end Claudius' life can only be viewed as Shakespeare's structural support for the validity of Hamlet's theological conclusions. If there was any question that such conclusions were no more than new rationalizations on Hamlet's part for his behavior, Shakespeare's dramatic plotting must give this the lie. The fact that without any plan Hamlet was exactly able to accomplish his purpose in the allowed time and do this more justly than he could have thought possible is proof that, within the universe of Shakespeare's play, Hamlet's insight into the nature of reality is as valid as it is profound. The moral significance of this new understanding is given further validity by the spiritual change it has worked in Hamlet. Though Hamlet still views the world as "harsh," as how should he not with such proof of the harsh workings of universal justice, he now rejects any suggestion of suicide, using his last strength to insist upon the necessity for Horatio to live, however painful it may be to continue to draw breath. And his own last thoughts are his most life-affirming. He is concerned for the healthy continuance of the state whose evils he has scourged with such fatal consequences for himself. Though his life was tortured by the black vision of death, he dies with the dearly earned vision of the high value of life. Entirely purged of its evils, his spirit will not need to break its eternal "silence" as may have been the case with his father's spirit. Though dreadfully tempted by the powers of damnation, his spirit has most nobly won its salvation.

As Fortinbras views the royal deaths he can only ask, "O proud Death, / What feast is toward in thine eternal cell" (reminding us thereby of the equal validity of Hamlet's earlier if less graced vision of death's universal feeding upon man). To complete death's feast, the ambassador from England informs us "that Rosencrantz and Guildenstern are dead." Horatio now suggests that the bodies be arranged in state and placed on view after which he can tell them "Of carnal, bloody, and unnatural acts, / Of accidental judgments, casual slaughters, / Of deaths put on by cunning and forced cause, / And, in this upshot, purposes mistook / Fall'n on th' inventors' heads." Fortinbras is anxious to hear of this but also takes the opportunity to state his claim to the throne of Denmark. Horatio says that he has cause to speak of this as well but that first the funeral arrangement should be made to quiet "men's minds." Fortinbras now orders four captains to "bear Hamlet like a soldier" to a high platform accompanied by the rites of a military funeral, "For he was likely, had he been put on, / To have proved most royal." As the soldiers bear Hamlet upwards to the sounds of cannons, the tragedy comes to a fitting end.

CONCLUDING COMMENT: Horatio has spoken of two kinds of deaths, "of accidental judgments, casual slaughters," on the one hand, and, on the other, "of deaths put on by cunning and forced cause, / And, in this upshot, purposes mistook / Fall'n on th' inventors' heads." The first type characterizes the actions of Hamlet, whose killings have all been accidental or casual. The second type characterizes the "deep plots" of Claudius and Laertes, who have tried to shape their ends directly with the ironic result of punishing themselves and, in the case of Claudius, the one most dear to him. In either case we may equally see the hand of the "divinity that shapes our ends." Hamlet has allowed Providence to work itself out through him; Claudius and Laertes have tried to shape their own destinies and for this are punished. The distinction between them, however, raises Hamlet above Claudius and all his accomplices, whatever the extent of their complicity.

But if Hamlet deserves our admiration for his final "readiness" to accept and further the will of heaven, his life also stands forfeit for the bloody course he has traveled to this end. It is this tension between earthly defeat and spiritual redemption which makes Hamlet's death truly tragic. For at the very moment when he has finally achieved a full "readiness" for a noble life, when "he was likely, had he been put on, / To have proved most royal," his life is over. Though we mourn the tragic waste of his potential, hindered from its continuance by the fatal interaction of the tragic flaws in his personality and his world, we must also glory that he has won a victory in defeat, seeing with Hamlet that "the readiness is all."

CHARACTER ANALYSES

HAMLET Hamlet dares us, along with Rosencrantz and Guildenstern, to "pluck out the heart of my mystery." This mystery marks the essence of Hamlet's character as, in spite of our popular psychologies, it ultimately does for all human personalities. Granting this, we can attempt to chart its origin and outward manifestations. Ophelia tells us that before the events of the play Hamlet was a model courtier, soldier and scholar, "The glass of fashion and the mould of form, / Th' observed of all observers." With the death of his father and the hasty, incestuous remarriage of his mother to his uncle, however, Hamlet is thrown into a suicidal frame of mind in which "the uses of this world" seem to him "weary, stale, flat, and unprofitable." Though his faith in the value of life has been destroyed by this double confrontation with death and human infidelity, he feels impotent to effect any change in this new reality: "It is not, nor it cannot come to good. / But break my heart, for I must hold my

tongue." All he can do in this frustrated state is to lash out with bitter satire at the evils he sees and then relapse into suicidal melancholy.

It is in this state that he meets the equally mysterious figure of his father's ghost with its supernatural revelations of murder and adultery and its injunction upon Hamlet to revenge his father's murder. While this command gives purpose and direction to Hamlet's hitherto frustrated impulse towards scourging reform, it also serves to further unsettle his already disturbed reason. When two months later he forces his way into Ophelia's room, he looks "As if he had been loosed out of hell / To speak of horrors." Whether or not the ghost was actually a devil, its effect upon Hamlet has been diabolic.

In the two months after his meeting with the ghost, he puzzles the court with his assumed madness but does nothing concrete to effect or further his revenge. His inability to either accept the goodness of life or act to destroy its evils now begins to trouble him as much as his outward hysteria and depression does the court. He first condemns his apparent lack of concentration on his revenge as the sign of a base, cowardly nature. The advent of a company of players, however, gives him an idea for testing the truth of the ghost and the guilt of Claudius. Rationalizing his inactivity as an effect of his doubt about the ghost's nature, he plans to have the players perform a play which reproduces Claudius' crime and observe Claudius' reaction to it, thereby dispelling his own doubts as to the proper course of his action. Having momentarily silenced his shame at his inaction, however, he immediately relapses into his former state; he meditates upon suicide and then lashes out with satiric cruelty at Ophelia.

The performance of the play is successful in revealing Claudius' guilt to Hamlet, and Hamlet reacts to this proof with wild glee. His old friends Rosencrantz and Guildenstern, who had returned that day to Elsinore to help further Claudius' investigation into Hamlet's disorder and had thereby alienated Hamlet's affections, enter with a message from Hamlet's mother that she wishes to see him immediately. Hamlet treats them contemptuously before returning his answer that he will go to his mother. His coming visit with his mother inspires him with a murderous rage appropriate to the hellish time of night. Once more in the power of hell, he accidentally comes upon the praying figure of Claudius but does not take this opportunity for revenge because of the devilish rationalization that such revenge would not damn Claudius' soul. But the truth seems to be that Hamlet's murderous rage is misdirected at his mother rather than at Claudius, even though Hamlet is now fully convinced of his guilt. Coming to his mother's room with the intent to punish her with verbal daggers for her unfaithfulness, her unwillingness to listen to him releases his murderous impulse against her. In a moment of temporary insanity he manages to exercise enough control to deflect the blow designed for her to the direction of an unexpected sound, killing the hidden figure of Polonius. In the ensuing scene he all but forgets the body of Polonius in his urgency to arouse his mother's guilt for her treatment of his father and injury to his own trust.

This fact, together with his obsessed preoccupation with his mother's sexual life, may provide a clue to the "mystery" of Hamlet. Hamlet, himself, had admitted to Ophelia that women's sensual falseness "hath made me mad." Elaborating on this clue, Ernest Jones has provided a well-reasoned Freudian explanation of Hamlet's behavior, namely the reactivation of his repressed Oedipus Complex. But whatever the truth of the matter, Hamlet's intuition does not extend this far. All he knows is that his mother's behavior has contributed

to wrenching the time "out of joint" for him, and that he has been fated "to set it right."

Once he is reconciled to his mother, the whole of reality appears to him in a different light. Where before his will was "most incorrect to heaven," the "Everlasting" seeming to be the creator of sterile farces and imposer of harsh laws, he now can accept heaven's purposes and ally himself with them as heaven's "scourge and minister." If Hamlet's nausea with life as well as sex seems to the modern intelligence to have a hidden psychological basis, Hamlet raises the discussion of his nature to the ultimately more profound level of religious existential confrontation. Seeing the hand of heaven in his accidental slaying of Polonius as well as in the exile to England which will result from it, he is able to accept this turn of events with new confidence in his ultimate success.

Though Hamlet does not appear outwardly changed, as witnessed by his contemptuous treatment of Polonius' body, continued obsession with the horror of death and with the obligations of honor, the change in attitude begun in his mother's room continues to develop while on shipboard and is responsible for his actions there. Inspired by his restlessness, he rashly discovers the letter ordering his death, forges a new commission which substitutes for his death the deaths of Claudius' accomplices, Rosencrantz and Guildenstern, returns the commission unknown, and, in a sea fight with pirates, manages to free himself from the Danish ship. In all of this he sees "heaven ordinant" and this teaches him that "There's a divinity that shapes our ends, / Rough-hew them how we will." Recognizing by this that humanly conceived plots are doomed to fail, he places himself completely in the hands of Providence.

Nonetheless, his first actions upon his return do not seem to indicate any real change in his nature from our last view of him in Denmark. He is still overly sensitive to the decomposition of the body after death and, in his treatment of Laertes at the funeral he so rudely disrupts, he still shows a cruel insensitivity to the feelings of anyone he believes to have wronged him. This insensitivity also extends to his lack of any qualms about his murders of Rosencrantz and Guildenstern, as was also true of his earlier murder of Polonius. If Hamlet had once been a model human being disillusioned in life by the double blows of his father's death and mother's remarriage, his oversensitivity to these evils of existence has warped his nature into an equally extreme insensitivity to all those whom he suspects of impurity. He cruelly torments his mother and Ophelia, bitterly mocks Polonius, Rosencrantz and Guildenstern and then wantonly kills them without a qualm and with the attempt, in the last two cases, of ensuring their eternal damnation, and he refrains from killing Claudius for this same evil reason. In terms of vindictive cruelty and wanton slaughter, he stands far more condemned for evil than Claudius and in danger of his own eternal damnation.

This warping of a sensitive nature into one capable of inhuman evil is perhaps the clearest proof of the evils of existence, though Hamlet must now be numbered among the evils to be punished by cosmic justice. But if Hamlet's actions condemn him to death, his growing perception of reality finally redeems his soul in our eyes. Though Claudius has planned Hamlet's destruction and Hamlet has proof of this, he has returned to Denmark without any plan for his revenge, even warning Claudius rudely of his approach. In "perfect conscience" now about the sin of regicide, he is confident that, in the "interim" before the arrival of the English ambassadors, heaven will so dispose events that he will be able to execute Claudius without any prior planning.

And his belief in the providential control of all events is justified by the outcome. Claudius' responsibility for Hamlet's death and the death of his mother is established before the court by Laertes and he is able to execute Claudius for these crimes alone. Hamlet has transcended his earlier damnable intention of premeditated revenge in a spontaneous act of just repayment for the loss of his own life. Recognizing that "the readiness is all," Hamlet has finally achieved this readiness to endure both life and death. His final actions are his most life-affirming, his restraining of Horatio from committing suicide and his concern for the continuing welfare of Denmark. The tragedy of his death is that it comes at the moment when "he was likely, had he been put on, / To have proved most royal." Destroyed and redeemed by the same brilliance of perception, Hamlet's spirit has undergone a tragic development from the self-destructive negation of life and of heaven's purposes to a new affirmation of the providential sanctity of life, and it is this final "readiness" which redeems him.

CLAUDIUS   At the beginning of the play, Claudius is a man who has achieved his heart's desire and is fully confident of his ability to preserve his position. If it cost him any pain to commit adultery with his brother's wife and then kill him, this cost is now forgotten in the happy possession of his crown and beloved Queen. But this possession required more criminal daring than knowing what he wanted and taking it. If he was not an able politician, his murder would not have assured him election to the throne over the pretensions of his nephew, Hamlet. If he was not an attractive person, he could never have won the sentimentally conventional Gertrude to his adulterous love. Now that he has his throne and Queen he wants only peace to enjoy them.

In an admirable diplomatic move, he averts war with Norway. In his more personal diplomacy, he wins the support of the chief counselors of state for all of his plans and tries most earnestly to win the goodwill of Hamlet by requesting that he remain in Denmark to enjoy his royal favor. He believes in making the best of a difficult situation and preaches such acceptance to Hamlet.

But if Hamlet was still in conspicuous mourning two months after his father's death and appeared to grudge Claudius his throne and marriage, in four months time his behavior has become dangerously provocative. Anxious to overcome this single impediment to his security and the smooth functioning of his state, Claudius sets spies on Hamlet to try to understand what is troubling him. Rosencrantz and Guildenstern can tell him nothing, but the scene he witnesses between Hamlet and Ophelia, in which Hamlet seemed to threaten his life, convinces him that he must act immediately to protect himself, and he decides to do this by sending Hamlet off to England for a time.

Though he has controlled himself very well up until this time, his composure breaks down when, through the performance of the play ordered by Hamlet and Hamlet's accompanying remarks, he faces the incredible fact that Hamlet has exact knowledge of his crime against Hamlet's father and is dedicated to revenge it. But though a cool, criminal head would dictate Hamlet's destruction, Claudius is instead plunged into spiritual despair. All his hidden guilt now comes to the surface and, rather than add a new crime to his conscience, Claudius' only concern is to try to repent his former sins and so win the salvation of his soul. This is very difficult for him because he knows it would require him to confess his sins, give up his crown and Queen and face possible execution. Moreover, he loves Gertrude so profoundly that he cannot bear her loss. He is a man in love with life, pleasure and especially power and he only wishes to be able to enjoy them and to use them well. But Hamlet has so succeeded in arousing his guilt that all of this seems nothing beside the sin of brother murder by which he gained them. Despite even his own nature, then, he desperately prays for the grace which would enable him to give up his worldly pleasures and achieve spiritual peace. Though his ties to crown and Queen are too strong to permit this total renunciation, the extent of his guilt and hesitance to proceed further into crime reveal a nature not essentially evil.

Claudius is a man capable of deep love, hearty enjoyment and a beneficial use of power. He wants nothing more than to win the love and admiration of all and, even in the face of Hamlet's rudest provocations, manages to maintain a cordial politeness and concern. His only flaw is that he feels himself entitled to more than his given portion and there is no inner hindrance to prevent his taking it. Though he preaches the acceptance of his evil as the will of heaven, he was unable to accept the heavenly dispensation which gave his brother everything that he, himself, desired; and so he made himself the god of his own universe and celebrates his power with the earthly thunder of cannons. Hamlet's insane killing of Polonius, however, puts an end to Claudius' hesitation. He can no longer deny Hamlet's extreme danger to him and self preservation overrides the objections of his conscience and his loving concern for Gertrude's peace of mind. But as his conscience was strong enough to arouse his guilt but not sufficiently powerful to cause him to forego his life and happiness, so now it does not prevent him from planning Hamlet's murder but makes him too squeamish to perform it himself. He plots to convert Hamlet's exile into his death, though he does not stop to consider how he will later answer for this death. And when this plot fails, he immediately plans another, this time using Laertes instead of the King of England as his instrument. Again the plot is conceived in too desperate a state to really mark its consequences, and this time its failure is so awful that it involves the accidental death of his beloved wife and his own final end.

Relying upon his continuing ability to shape his destiny, Claudius piles misconceived plot upon plot in a desperate attempt to preserve his ill-gotten gains. Though he keeps his head when Laertes threatens his throne and, more fearfully, when Gertrude drinks the poison he had prepared for Hamlet, he is so concerned to preserve his life that he has forgotten his soul. He has missed the opportunity of repenting his former sins and when he dies nonetheless, it is in the act of piling more crimes and lies upon his unprepared soul. He had earlier explained that his reason for not taking direct action against Hamlet was "that my arrows, / Too slightly timbered for so loud a wind, / Would have reverted to my bow again, / And not where I had aimed them." And so has it also been of the puny plots by which he hoped to outwit the "divinity that shapes our ends."

GERTRUDE   The beloved wife and mother of the "mighty opposites" of the play, who is largely responsible for Hamlet's anguished inability to proceed with his revenge and Claudius' hesitation to preserve himself through the destruction of Hamlet, she who was "my virtue or my plague, be it either which," for both of her loves, is herself a most ordinary creature. Beautiful and warmhearted, she has no mind of her own and is pulled by whatever force is most powerfully directed at her at any moment. By temperament she turns to the sunny side of life and cannot bear to face any pain or conflict. What pain her adultery with Claudius may have cost

her we cannot know though we can guess it may have provided the most urgent motivation for his murder of her husband. That he so carefully concealed the knowledge of his crime from her is further indication of her lack of criminal daring and of his concern for her peace of mind. When circumstances so worked out that she was able to marry her lover, however, she was most happy and desired only that all the difficulties of the past be forgotten.

Hamlet's refusal to forget the death of his father or to forgive her hasty and incestuous remarriage is the only blot on her happiness; it continues to remind her of the continuing difficulties of her position which she had naively hoped would be ended by her restoration to the conventionally accepted state of marriage. If she could only get Hamlet to accept her new husband as his new father, she could completely bury the past in the happy present. She therefore begs him to remain at Elsinore so that this reconciliation can take place. But as she watches her beloved and remarkable son only become more and more mentally deranged with the passing months and sees his provocative behavior beginning to upset even the composure of Claudius, her happiness becomes increasingly blighted. She hopes that Rosencrantz and Guildenstern will be able to bring him out of his depression. Then she snatches at the possibility that Hamlet's disturbance might actually be caused by his love for Ophelia rather than her own behavior and hopes that Ophelia will be able to cure him. Her spirits rise for a moment when she sees Hamlet's excited involvement with the play and his attentions to Ophelia, but then they immediately drop as Claudius rises from the performance in anguish. Finally she is prevailed upon by Polonius to do that which she has avoided for all these months, to meet Hamlet privately to discuss his behavior and try to understand its source. And it is probably only as the last resort to the exiling of Hamlet that she permits this dreaded meeting at all.

Hamlet's immediate charge, "Mother, you have my father much offended," confirms her worst fears of her own responsibility for Hamlet's state, and she tries to put a quick end to the interview rather than have to face his further condemnation. But she is shocked into submission by the murderous rage he displays towards her and finally releases onto the hidden figure of Polonius. To Hamlet's continuing insults, she first answers in the pride of an innocent conscience: "What have I done that thou dar'st wag thy tongue / In noise so rude against me?" Her avoidance of self-scrutiny is so complete, that she really believes that she has nothing to answer for beyond the unfortunate effect her hasty remarriage has had upon her son. But as Hamlet continues to compel her attention to the horror of her remarriage, she gradually comes under his spell and begins to experience a new guilt for her actions. Though the entrance of the ghost, which she cannot see, convinces her that Hamlet is mad and his abuse the product of an overwrought moral sensibility, she cannot fully undo the sense of guilt he has aroused in her.

When Ophelia goes mad, Gertrude wishes to avoid the painful sight of her as much as she had earlier wished to avoid looking into her own soul. This is especially so since Gertrude sees Ophelia's mental breakdown as further proof of the continuing evil caused by her unthinking behavior, and this chain of evil effects seems, to her guilty conscience, to bode some great catastrophe. Though deeply grieved by Ophelia's death, she tries, nonetheless, to explain it to herself and to Laertes in the least damaging way. But her sorrow at Ophelia's funeral is accentuated by the madness her son displays there in his unexpected return. His insulting behavior to Laertes, who has already felt himself sufficiently wronged by Hamlet to demand revenge, now so worries her that she sends word to Hamlet that he should excuse himself to Laertes and try to regain his goodwill.

When Hamlet appears at the fencing match in such a reasonable frame of mind, she is delighted. Not only does Laertes appear to accept Hamlet's offer of love, but Hamlet's own willingness to fight as Claudius' champion seems to promise her their reconciliation as well. If Laertes were reconciled to Hamlet and Hamlet to Claudius, all the horror of her guilt and Ophelia's death might yet be forgotten and she might still be granted the happiness that she had thought Ophelia's marriage to Claudius would bring her. In this blind hope of future happiness, her son's gentlemanly behavior and excellence of fencing so intoxicate her that she joins fully into the event, coming forward to wipe her dear boy's brow and finally insisting upon toasting his coming victory. Against Claudius' objection, she drinks to her son to show him how happy he has made her.

As she has ever evaded the prospect of anything painful in the hope of achieving happiness, so it is fitting that this flaw should prove her destruction. Only as she feels the poison creeping over her and hears her husband lie about her condition to save himself does she truly face reality. Only then does she begin to understand Hamlet's objections to Claudius and recognize that Claudius has poisoned her whole life as now he has her body. Trying too late to protect her "dear Hamlet," she dies the miserable victim of her sentimental and deluded hope for happiness.

POLONIUS   The Lord Chamberlain and chief courtier at Elsinore, Polonius appears to have been flattered into giving his support to Claudius. At any rate, this flattery, which probably gained Claudius his election to the throne, is poured on him by Claudius when we first view him. But Claudius' flattery is nothing to Polonius' self-flattery. He detains his son Laertes' departure, which he had come to hurry, with a set of old saws about proper behavior which have nothing to do with his own behavior but which he rattles off as a mark of his elderly wisdom. Old he is and so proud of his apparent wisdom that, upon learning of his daughter Ophelia's involvement with Hamlet, he immediately decides that Hamlet's intentions must be dishonorable and forbids his too innocent daughter from seeing him again. Judging both Hamlet and Laretes by his own youthful indulgences, he not only prejudges Hamlet's interest in his daughter but sends his servant, Reynaldo, to spy upon Laertes in Paris. He is at his height as he explains the refinements of spying to Reynaldo and cares nothing that in his concern to find out the worst about his son he may actually be hurting Laertes' reputation. Though he seems almost to encourage his son to take some youthful liberties, he keeps his daughter on a tight leash, demanding her confidences, telling her what to think and how to act. Whatever spirit she might have had he has apparently broken, molding her into a model daughter of silent, mindless obedience. (One wonders if such an upbringing might also explain Gertrude's lack of moral independence.)

Like a dutiful daughter, Ophelia comes immediately to her father to report Hamlet's strange behavior upon forcing himself into her room. As quickly as he had assumed Hamlet's dishonorable intentions, so now he decides that it was true love and that Ophelia's rejection of him has driven him mad. He now admits that his earlier orders to Ophelia were lacking in sound judgment but sets his authoritarian presumption down to the natural effects of age. Seeing in Ophelia's relationship to Hamlet a way to further endear himself to the King and perhaps offset any other adverse effects his age may have had against him, he immediately takes his trembling daughter off to the King.

The ludicrous effects of his age soon make themselves apparent in the long-winded, pretentious way he takes to get to the point. With no concern for his daughter's feelings, he proceeds to read a love letter Hamlet had written to her, making literary comments on Hamlet's style all the while. Having interested the King and Queen in his theory of Hamlet's madness, he now further plans to prostitute his daughter's modesty to gain the King's favor by suggesting that a meeting be arranged between his daughter and Hamlet which the king and he would spy upon. In fact, so sure is he of his theory and, through it, of his continuing usefulness to the King that he arrogantly asserts that they can behead him or send him off to keep a farm if he is wrong. All of this does indicate, of course, a growing insecurity about his position in the state since his recent blunder with his daughter.

He now tries to investigate Hamlet himself, though Hamlet only makes fun of him in the most contemptuous way. Though he sets all of Hamlet's remarks about his old age down to madness, he is yet forced to admit, "Though this be madness, yet there is method in't." When the players come he again takes the opportunity to be with Hamlet and, as Hamlet and the players recite certain speeches, he is pleased once more to offer them his critical opinions on the verse and their acting. After conveying to Claudius Hamlet's invitation to a performance of a play that evening, he directs his daughter to her own performance for Hamlet's benefit as well as their own; she is to excuse her lonely presence at the arranged spot with a show of pious meditation. Though in the ensuing scene Hamlet treats Ophelia cruelly, Polonius is too concerned with the King to pay her much attention. All his concern is now to maintain his privileged position at court as Chief Counselor to the King. Since, despite his own opinion to the contrary, Claudius no longer will entertain his theory of Hamlet's madness and decides to send Hamlet off to England, Polonius now suggests a new spying plan to Claudius which might vindicate his own theory or reveal a new solution to their dilemmas: after the performance of the play, the Queen should send to Hamlet for a private conference in her room, and he will himself hide in her room the better to report the conclusion to Claudius. At the play performance he is quick to point out to Claudius Hamlet's attentions to Ophelia as further support to the wisdom of his theory. And after the play he cannot rely upon Rosencrantz and Guildenstern to get Hamlet to Gertrude's room but comes himself to hurry Hamlet. Then, quickly reporting his success to Claudius, he rushes to Gertrude's room, gives her final instructions on how to deal with Hamlet and hides himself.

But the overanxious, presumptuous and self-deluding fool has blundered again. Concerned only with his own self-importance and incapable of taking the measure of one like Hamlet, he precipitates a situation which ends with his own accidental death. Hamlet speaks the most fitting closing description of him when he says: "Thou wretched, rash, intruding fool, farewell!" But if Polonius' efforts on behalf of his children have been as damaging to them as they have been on his own behalf, their effects live on beyond him. Lost without the father upon whom she had obediently depended for her every thought and act, Ophelia loses her mind and meets her death. And the false and outward sense of honor Polonius has implanted in Laertes causes him to try to revenge his father's death in a most underhanded way and leads to his own death as well. As poor a counselor to himself as he was to others, we must finally agree with Hamlet: "Indeed, this counsellor / Is now most still, most secret, and most grave, / Who was in life a foolish prating knave."

OPHELIA   "Pretty Ophelia," as Claudius calls her, is the most innocent victim of Hamlet's revenge. Attracted by her sweet beauty after the depressing event of his father's death, Hamlet had fallen in love with her. She had "sucked the honey of his music vows" and returned his affection. But when her father had challenged the honor of Hamlet's intentions, Ophelia could only reply: "I do not know, my lord, what I should think." Used to relying upon her father's direction and brought up to be obedient, she can only accept her father's belief, seconded by that of her brother, that Hamlet's "holy vows" of love were simply designed for her seduction, and obey her father's orders not to permit Hamlet to see her again.

When his mother's hasty remarriage had led Hamlet to the disillusioned view that "frailty, thy name is woman," Ophelia's affection might yet have restored his spirit. But her unexplained refusal to see him soon after his mother's remarriage completes Hamlet's disillusionment with women. The ghost's revelation that his mother had not only dishonored his father's memory but also their marriage by her adultery with Claudius festers in his mind for two months until he finally forces his way into Ophelia's room to look upon her again. Searching her innocent face for some sign of loving truth that might restore his faith in her and, through her, in womankind and in love, he takes her mute terror for a further sign of her guilt and sees her as but another false Gertrude. And, indeed, there is much similarity between the two women in his life and in the play. Both are beautiful and rather simpleminded women, easily molded by the more powerful opinions and desires of others. Perhaps it was this similarity which first attracted Hamlet to Ophelia as now it disenchants him with her. They are the same type of woman at different stages of life. But Ophelia is still too much under the influence of her father to question his wisdom or authority, and she has no mind of her own to understand how she has made her lover suffer. As she could not believe that her father's orders were wrong, no matter how much it pained her not to see Hamlet, so all she can see in his present behavior is the madness of which the whole court is talking and which terrifies her. Though her father admits that he had made a mistake in questioning the depth of Hamlet's love, she still does not dare to question his authority as he takes her precious love letters to the King and then orders her to meet Hamlet at a place where he and the King can observe their meeting. Her hopes for this meeting are raised, however, by the Queen's kind statement to her that she hopes Ophelia will prove to be the cause of Hamlet's madness for then there would be the hope that Ophelia might cure him and that they might be married. Though her father's admission of error and the Queen's blessing for her marriage might have embittered a more independent Ophelia towards her father for having hindered her love and turned her lover against her, Ophelia still accepts his guidance in a hopeful spirit. Hamlet's actions in her room, though deranged, show that he still loves her. Now her father is permitting her to see Hamlet once more and she has the Queen's blessing for her possible cure of and marriage to Hamlet. Like Gertrude, she hopes that all might yet be well, and she has even taken it upon herself to bring all of Hamlet's presents to this meeting in the hope of reawakening his love.

But after a hopeful beginning, Ophelia ruins her chances by the foolish feminine strategy of accusing Hamlet of rejecting her. This only enrages him against her duplicity and he cruelly denies ever having loved or given her anything. He then launches an ever more savage attack against her, telling her to enter a nunnery or else marry with his curse upon her. As this savage attack proceeds, Ophelia is again convinced of his madness and her hopes sink to despairing prayers to heaven to restore him. As she sees what has happened to her noble lover and to her earlier hopes for their love, she is overcome by her woe. At the play that evening he comes to sit by her, but whatever joy this might have given her is blasted by the disrespectful and vulgar way that he jokes with her. No longer addressing her "with love / In honorable fashion," he treats her like his familiar whore. When that night her father is mysteriously killed and then obscurely buried in great haste it is too much for her. Abused by her lover, bereft of her father's protection, alone and overcome by the sense of her dishonor and that of her father, she loses control of her mind.

In her insane state she comes to believe that that which her family tried so hard to protect her from, her seduction, has come to pass and that this explains Hamlet's rejection of her. Feeling by this the hypocrisy of the world and tormented by the vision of death and burial, she reaches out to the remaining loveliness of flowers and, in her careless attempt to hang them upon a sorrowing willow tree, somehow drowns. In an almost ironic repayment for her failure to understand what he has suffered, Hamlet has unthinkingly created a situation for her which parallels his own, death of a father and betrayal by a loved one. But whereas he managed to maintain final control over his sanity and rise above the temptation of suicide, her weaker spirit, unable to bear up under the burden of sorrow and disillusionment, finds its release in insanity and final death. That weakness of mind and will which permitted her obedience to her father and thus destroyed her hope in Hamlet's love finally results in her insanity and death.

LAERTES Laertes is a young man whose good instincts have been somewhat obscured by the concern with superficial appearances which he has imbibed from his father, Polonius. After a brief appearance at court to beg Claudius' leave to return to Paris, we see him again pompously lecturing his sister Ophelia about men's hypocritical ways and warning her to protect her chastity against "Hamlet, and the trifling of his favor." With some apparent knowledge of her brother's ways, she replies that he should not preach strictness to her while himself acting like a "reckless libertine." This suspicion of his behavior is later strengthened by Polonius' interest in spying upon Laertes' libertine habits in Paris. Like his father, Laertes apparently preaches a morality he does not practice and fully believes in a double standard of behavior for the sexes. But if his father allows him these liberties, it is that he may better approximate the manner of a so-called gentleman. More concerned with the outward signs of gentility than with any inner refinement of spirit, Laertes has well observed his father's advice to be concerned with appearances since "the apparel oft proclaims the man."

When he learns of his father's unexplained death and obscure funeral, Laertes' superficial sense of honor is touched to the quick. Since honor demands that he revenge his father's death, he returns to Denmark, gathers a rabble mob together and storms the castle, demanding that the King answer for his father's death. As unconcerned for the order of society as he is for his own salvation, he would rather "dare damnation" than leave his father's honor and his own besmirched. Though the sight of his sister's madness brings him to a moment of true grief, he is still primarily enraged by his father's "obscure funeral— / No trophy, sword, nor hatchment o'er his bones, / No noble rite nor formal ostentation." When Claudius explains Hamlet's responsibility for Polonius' death and his own reasons for covering up this fact, Laertes is satisfied to work with Claudius to achieve his revenge against Hamlet. Since he would be willing "to cut his throat i' th' church" to prove his honor, he is willing to stoop to any underhanded plan of Claudius' by which he can have his revenge. In fact, he even improves upon Claudius' suggestion for an illegally sharpened sword to be used in a fencing contest with Hamlet; Laertes volunteers to anoint the sword's point with poison, "that, if I gall him slightly, / It may be death." To vindicate his honor, he stoops to a most dishonorable practice.

If there was any chance of his renouncing such a dishonorable plan, Hamlet's behavior at his sister's funeral puts a quick end to this. Though his grief may take an ostentatious form, Hamlet's challenge to his right to grieve, his fight with him in the very grave and then his insulting remarks upon leaving only re-enforce Laertes' resolution. Still, there was an opportunity during the scene for Laertes to achieve his revenge in the spirit of true honor. When Hamlet responds to Laertes' curses by offering him a duel to the death, Laertes might have accepted this offer and tried to achieve his revenge in a fair manner. But Hamlet's self-righteous behavior so outrages Laertes that his sense of honor becomes completely warped by his hatred for Hamlet and he cannot afford to take his chances with him.

One final opportunity is given to Laertes to act with true honor. When, at the start of the fencing match, Hamlet excuses his behavior at the funeral and his accidental slaying of Polonius on the grounds of his madness and asks for Laertes' pardon, Laertes has an opportunity to renounce his plan of revenge. Indeed, Hamlet's explanation and gentlemanly behavior towards him satisfies his natural feeling of vengeance. But Laertes is so concerned about his formal and outward "terms of honor" that he cannot permit his natural feelings to rule his will. In this concern for outward honor he further dishonors himself by the false statement that he will act honorably with Hamlet. Saying that "I do receive your offered love like love, / And will not wrong it," he goes and chooses the lethally sharp and poisoned weapon. Still, Hamlet's behavior towards him has been so gentlemanly that he cannot bring himself to dishonor his own word, and so fights poorly with Hamlet on the first two rounds, permitting Hamlet two easy hits against him. When the King chides him for his performance, he admits to himself that to kill Hamlet under these circumstances "is almost against my conscience." But when Hamlet begins to taunt him for his poor performance, it is too much for Laertes' pride. Playing as best he can, he is astonished to find that he can only bring Hamlet to a draw. His vengeance now enraged by jealousy at Hamlet's fine sportsmanship and true gentlemanly bearing, he lunges at Hamlet after the close of the formal bout and manages to wound him. When, by his wound, Hamlet realizes Laertes' false practice, he returns to the fight with such power that he captures Laertes' foil and wounds him fatally with it.

Had Laertes acted upon the honorable promptings of his conscience, he would have avoided his own death and, by allying himself with Hamlet, would have won the gratitude of the future King. Laertes' testimony of Claudius' responsibility for the poisoning of the Queen would have permitted Hamlet his just revenge against Claudius and would have left both Hamlet and Laertes alive. But Laertes' false sense of honor and pride override his better instincts to the fatal harm of both. Recognizing his dishonor too late and admitting that he is "justly killed with mine own treachery," Laertes finally rises to the true honor of admitting his fault to Hamlet, informing him of Claudius' designs, and then, in a tragically belated reconciliation with Hamlet, offering him an exchange of forgiveness. But if his rise to true honor finally redeems him in our eyes, his false honor has destroyed his life.

ROSENCRANTZ AND GUILDEN-STERN Shakespeare's doubling of the type of courtier represented by both Rosencrantz and Guildenstern shows that tragic lack of individuality which this type possesses. They so revere their King that they are willing "to lay our service freely at your feet, / To be commanded." But Claudius' employment of them seems perfectly consistent with their honor. They are to try to interest their old but much changed friend Hamlet in some pleasures which might dispel his depression and also try to understand its cause that Claudius might be able to remedy it. Hamlet's most friendly greeting to them gives them hope of early success and they immediately suggest that his depression is caused by ambition. Hamlet denies this but it causes him to wonder why they have come to Elsinore. When they reply that they have come "To visit you, my lord; no other occasion," Hamlet finally demands that they tell him directly whether or not they were sent for. Unused to lying though honoring their royal commission, they are unsure of how to answer. Finally their friendship for Hamlet prevails and they admit, "My lord, we were sent for." But it is too late. Hamlet already has "an eye of you" and will no further trust them. Their momentary hesitance to be honest with Hamlet has alienated his affection. And the passing of time only serves to increase his enmity. Though they are intelligent enough for Hamlet to share some general confession of his spiritual state with them and for him to engage in pleasant conversation with them about the latest theatrical news from Wittenburg, the open-hearted generosity with which he greeted them is now a thing of the past.

They immediately report the ill success of their interview and then are soon employed again to bring Hamlet to his mother's room after the performance of the play. The King's disturbance followed by Hamlet's wild behavior upon their return to him further convince them of Claudius' just concern over Hamlet's dangerous condition. They therefore intensify their investigation of Hamlet's admittedly "diseased" mind. This further antagonizes Hamlet so that he throws their own suspicions back at them, saying, "Sir, I lack advancement." Finally he becomes so annoyed by their attempts to "pluck out the heart of my mystery" that he uses the recorders to make fun of them in a most contemptuous manner. Hamlet's belligerence towards them further alienates them from him and draws them closer to the King. Fully convinced now of the danger his madness poses to the King, their concern for the King's safety becomes paramount. Accepting the common Renaissance belief that the King is divinely appointed to rule the state for its own good, they accept their dependence upon the King as the divinely sanctioned order of nature. When the King now orders them to accompany Hamlet on his voyage to England, a voyage which Claudius says he hopes will cure Hamlet's disturbance, they are only too willing to comply. By this means they may both help their friend and protect their King. But when they learn of Hamlet's insane killing of Polonius, they become fully committed to the welfare of the King. Sent to find the body and bring Hamlet to the King, they treat Hamlet in a high-handed manner. Hamlet reacts to their manner by condemning them as courtiers wholly without integrity who are willing to do anything commanded of them by the King in the hope of reward but who will finally be unrewarded because of their lack of character. He submits himself to their control with full enmity of spirit. When aboard ship Hamlet discovers that the commission they are carrying demands his death, he condemns them without a hearing as criminal accomplices of a criminal King and sentences them to death "not shriving time allowed." Though Rosencrantz and Guildenstern are not conscious criminals, since they are unaware of the criminal designs of the King they obey, the fact that "they did make love to this employment" without any scrutiny into the King's purposes does condemn them as unthinking accomplices. If as model courtiers they feel they have nothing on their consciences, their lack of individual integrity and total dependence upon the King dooms them to the fate of the King to whom they are thus "mortised and adjoined."

HORATIO   Unlike Laertes, who had returned for Claudius' coronation and then left Elsinore for Paris, and unlike Rosencrantz and Guildenstern, who had not come for the royal events but had been sent for to investigate Hamlet, Horatio returns to Elsinore from Wittenburg for the funeral of Hamlet's father and remains to become Hamlet's one true friend. When Marcellus brings this university scholar to witness the sight of the ghost, with which the sentinels do not

understand how to deal, he reports this event not to Claudius but to Hamlet. Although a courtier would have gone directly to the King, the blunt soldiers, Bernardo, Francisco and Marcellus, try to understand the matter for themselves and Horatio, whom they have sent for to this end, decides on his own judgment that this knowledge is for Hamlet's ears rather than the King's.

Horatio had come to see the ghost in a spirit of scepticism but, when he could not deny his own eyes, he carefully addressed the ghost in such a way as not to endanger his soul. When he comes to the same battlement the next night with Hamlet, he warns Hamlet not to follow the ghost as it might lead him into madness and suicide. After Hamlet's hysterical return from his conference with the ghost, Horatio tries to calm his spirit. He wins enough confidence from Hamlet for him to admit to Horatio that "it is an honest ghost," and later to generalize that "There are more things in heaven and earth, Horatio, / Than are dreamt of in your philosophy." He then swears Horatio and the soldiers to keep the knowledge of the ghost and of Hamlet's further purposes confidential, and they never break this confidence.

During the next two months Horatio's integrity and emotional reserve so win Hamlet's admiration that he fully takes him to his heart. Here is a friend whose integrity he can fully trust and whose Stoic reserve acts to calm his own passionate response to evil. He takes Horatio fully into his confidence about the disclosures of the ghost and about his further plan to test Claudius through the performance of a play. When Hamlet reacts to Claudius' breakdown with hysterical glee, he quietly calms him down with a touch of mockery so that they can discuss the implications of Claudius' reaction more sanely.

Hamlet had earlier praised Horatio as one "whose blood and judgment are so well commingled." Upon returning to Denmark, he immediately sends for Horatio as he longs to confide the new horrors of his trip to him and gain his judicial acceptance for his further plans. They meet near a graveyard and, as the sight of skulls being thrown about by the gravedigger leads Hamlet back into morbid reflections on death and decomposition, Horatio again tries to control his friend's excessive sensibility by saying, "'Twere to consider too curiously, to consider so."

When, after the funeral interruption, they are finally alone again, Hamlet proceeds to explain Claudius' treacherous design upon his life and his own order for the execution of Rosencrantz and Guildenstern. To this Horatio mildly comments, "So Guildenstern and Rosencrantz go to 't." Though Hamlet takes this as an objection and proceeds to excuse his behavior on the grounds of their dangerous complicity with Claudius, whatever objection Horatio might have felt is quickly silenced by Hamlet's aroused reply and he returns to the subject of Hamlet's just grievance against the King. Hamlet now lists his grounds against Claudius and asks for Horatio's judgment as to whether he is not proceeding in "perfect conscience." But Horatio declines to answer this question directly, noting instead the urgency for Hamlet to act immediately if he is to act at all. They are now interrupted by the foppish Osric with his invitation from Claudius for Hamlet's participation in a fencing match with Laertes. During this scene Horatio shows his appreciation for Hamlet's witty undercutting of Osric.

When they are alone again and waiting for the match to begin, Hamlet confides that he feels uneasy about the coming match and Horatio tells him that he should not discount this and should refrain from participating in the match. As he has earlier warned him against following the ghost, so now he does of the fencing match and to as little avail. Hamlet wishes for Horatio's support but he will not abide his restraint. But as Horatio tries to protect Hamlet when he is dying, Hamlet acts to protect his friend from his one passionate gesture, Horatio's desire to follow his friend through suicide. This shows how fully "mortised and adjoined" Horatio feels towards Hamlet. However much he may have questioned Hamlet's reactions and behavior, he has fully committed himself to Hamlet's fate and only permits himself to live so that he may justify Hamlet's life and death. When Hamlet dies he speaks the eulogy over him, commending his "noble heart" and his soul to heaven. With his death, Horatio takes control of events, arranges for the funerals and hands over the kingdom, in accordance with Hamlet's wishes, to Fortinbras.

Throughout the play, Shakespeare has presented Horatio as the norm or model of correct behavior. If there are more things in heaven and earth than are dreamt of in his philosophy, his passionless acceptance of the good and evil in life has resulted in his survival and, with it, the hope for his continuing influence in a healthier state. In Shakespeare's strategy for rehabilitating Hamlet as a proper tragic hero after his descent into evil, Horatio's acceptance of Hamlet's actions during his exile and after his return is most important. And here we come to an important problem in the play. For Horatio's acceptance of Hamlet's murders of Rosencrantz and Guildenstern turn him into as much of a "yes-man" for Hamlet as they were for Claudius, and suggests the cosmic logic for his destruction as well. This may, in fact, be Shakespeare's intention as Hamlet tells Horatio that he should only defer the happiness of death "awhile" until he has told his story.

But the significance of Horatio's acceptance of all of Hamlet's actions and his final eulogy upon him still serves as a vindication for the justice of Hamlet's actions; and here we may convict Shakespeare of "special pleading" for his hero. "Special pleading" occurs when an author so sets the terms of his work that a more positive evaluation for his hero is offered than the objective facts depicted in the work would seem to warrant. The charge of "special pleading" can, moreover, be levelled against the whole *genre* of revenge tragedy from Kyd and Marston to Tourneur. The revenger is a dramatic type of exquisite moral sensibility who is warped by the existence of evil into a being capable of committing with relish more depraved evil than that which he has set out to revenge, but whose character is redeemed at the end and treated heroically. Though Hamlet transcends the type he also represents it and Horatio plays an instrumental role in his perhaps overly favored rehabilitation.

FORTINBRAS　　Perhaps the greatest irony in this most ironic of plays is Fortinbras' inheritance of the Danish kingdom. For Fortinbras is the son of the Norwegian King whose defeat was Hamlet's father's greatest victory. If Hamlet's revenge was supposed to vindicate his father's honor, the suicidal way in which he proceeded with this revenge resulted in completely burying his father's glory with his empire. The fifth act began with the clownish gravedigger's commemoration of "that day that our last king Hamlet overcame Fortinbras," and it ends on the day that young Fortinbras inherits the kingdom which was to have come to young Hamlet.

Fortinbras' activities provide a largely unseen backdrop to the play. At the beginning of the first act we learn that Claudius has embarked on massive military preparations to defend Denmark against Fortinbras' martial intentions. Attempting to restore the honor that his father had lost, Fortinbras had levied an army to attack and conquer Denmark. Though son of the late King of Norway, the crown of Norway had gone to his uncle, just as the crown of Denmark had gone to Hamlet's uncle. This shows that in the world of the play it was not unusual for brothers to late kings to be elected to the throne over the pretentions of their younger nephews. But Fortinbras was not prepared to accept his constitutional dispossession so easily. If he had been deprived of the throne of his father, he would try to conquer a kingdom of his own in which, as he later tells Horatio, he has "some rights of memory." Claudius, however, defeats Fortinbras' hopes through diplomatic negotiations with the King of Norway. Informing the old and bedridden King of his nephew's activities and of his allegiance to Denmark, Claudius gets the

Norwegian King to curtail Fortinbras' military plans against Denmark.

But Fortinbras is not willing to put an end to his military adventures and so he substitutes for the rich Danish crown a worthless piece of Poland as the object of his plans for conquest. Desiring to win honor through the sword, he cares not that the prize of his glory is worthless or that he will sacrifice thousands of lives and much wealth for this hollow victory. On the passage of this army over Danish soil to Poland, as prearranged with Claudius, Hamlet meets the expedition and comes to admire Fortinbras' heroic resolution to seize honor at all costs. Comparing his own lack of honorable resolution after his father's death with that of Fortinbras, he finds himself deficient and hopes to emulate Fortinbras' endeavors with "bloody" thoughts. Hamlet might well see in Fortinbras a more fitting son to his own father than he has been. Like Hamlet, Sr., Fortinbras is an empire builder who desires only to fight for glory and so, in an ironic way which compounds the irony first mentioned, he is fitted by character to inherit the kingdom of Hamlet, Sr.

Having proven his honor in the successful exploit against Poland, Fortinbras picks the plum of Denmark without any effort. Polonius has earlier said that one can best "by indirections find directions out," and so it has proven to be in the case of Fortinbras. By not attacking Denmark, the Danish crown has fallen into his lap. Here we may again detect the ironic hand of Providence. But what has Providence finally accomplished by its holocaust, its wholesale destruction or sacrifice of the Danish ruling family and its many adjuncts, eight or nine in all? Though ironically defeating Hamlet, Sr.'s glory, it has restored his kingdom to the martial values he had exalted in it, bypassing the secular pacifism of Claudius and the inspired religious dependence of Hamlet. The "mighty opposites" both lie vanquished before the avenging spirit of the ghost whose values are resurrected in Fortinbras and who promises us a restoraration to the false values of military honor with its perpetuation of the tragic human condition, of round upon round of excessive glory being punished by the envy it inspires until all are punished by the scourge of heaven.

THE GHOST The mystery of the supernatural background to the action, of that something more within heaven and earth than is dreamt of in most of our secular philosophies, is concentrated in the mysterious figure of the ghost. Whether it be the "honest ghost" of Hamlet's father come from Purgatory or a diabolic or angelic agent of Providence is never made completely clear and this ambiguity reinforces the central mystery of the play. Though Providence accomplishes the destruction of Claudius which the ghost had demanded of Hamlet, his demands also unsettle Hamlet's reason, warp his character and lead to his death as well as the wholesale destruction of the chief members of the court. Such results indicate the morally questionable nature of the ghost's demands and therefore of its nature. Whether it is the true ghost of his father's spirit in Purgatory or a diabolic impersonation of this spirit, the ghost in either case represents an unhallowed spirit and the direct accomplishment of its demands would lead to the damnation of Hamlet. Hamlet's salvation is only assured because he has transcended the ghostly demands for revenge in his final killing of Claudius. But the ghost's influence upon Hamlet has been powerful enough to wrench Hamlet's spirit out of its normal frame so that he destroys himself in the destruction of his enemies.

The ghost appears twice to Hamlet, the first time dressed in the armor which Hamlet, Sr., wore when he won his great victory over Norway and in a setting of military preparations in which his spirit gloried, the second time dressed in his nightclothes in the setting of his wife's bedroom. Both scenes represent his most cherished joys and dearest defeats, for his wife betrayed his love through adultery with Claudius and now Claudius is about to negotiate away another glorious victory over Norway followed by the final loss of his empire to the son of the King he had defeated. For these reasons, as well as his murder, the ghost desires the death of Claudius. It wishes Hamlet to quickly dispatch Claudius, take over the kingdom and defeat Fortinbras in battle. Hamlet reveres his father's uncomplicated masculine resolve: "'He was a man, take him for all in all, / I shall not look upon his like again." But he is himself incapable of such simple heroics. The result is that he destroys himself with the corrupt court and leaves the throne to the inheritance of Fortinbras. Though the ghost's demands do not seem to change in their second interview, its effect upon Hamlet is more "gracious." Hamlet comes to recognize himself as heaven's "scourge and minister" and finally accepts his complete dependence upon the "divinity that shapes our ends." This suggests that the ghost who appears in Gertrude's bedroom is either the more purified spirit of his father or a providential angel who has come to turn Hamlet's spirit from its damnable course and into the way of heaven. Though these identifications can never be made with any certainty, the effect of the ghost's coming is to unleash death and evil onto the stage and to achieve a final scourging of all the past and present evils in the state. If all the victims of avenging Providence fall through flaws in their own characters, the need for such a thorough purgation and the questionable result of Fortinbras' inheritance of the vanquished kingdom remain part of the mysterious "secrets" of supernatural justice which the ghost is forbidden to reveal.

REMAINING SURVIVORS Of the remaining survivors to the holocaust, the first group may be roughly categorized as courtiers. The most important of these, *Osric,* arrives late on the scene after Claudius' more favored aides have been dispatched either to death or England. In addition to providing some final comic relief before the final scene of destruction, the introduction of Osric is primarily significant for the light it casts on Claudius' spiritual decline. That Claudius, after being freed from the necessity of courting the favors of a fool like Polonius and after gathering to himself such reverential and able courtiers as Rosencrantz and Guildenstern, should be reduced to using such an ostentatious fop as Osric is a sign of his own declining judgment and need for extravagant and uncritical flattery. As Hamlet says of him: "Let a beast be lord of beasts, and his crib shall stand at the king's mess. 'Tis a chough [chatterer], but, as I say, spacious in the possession of dirt." Though Osric may be guilty of criminal complicity in the final plot against Hamlet, he is such a contemptible fool that he is beneath the notice of tragedy. Unlike Polonius, who interfered in his romance with Ophelia, and Rosencrantz and Guildenstern, who betrayed his friendship, Osric has always been too far beneath Hamlet's contempt to betray any trust, and his active association with Hamlet's enemy comes too late to arouse any distracting hatred away from Claudius. Osric's survival, therefore, is partly the product of his complete shallowness and partly of his luck in arriving too late on the scene to capture any sustained attention from Hamlet.

Of the others, *Voltemand* and *Cornelius* serve only as Claudius' ambassadors of peace to Norway, and this solitary and good service frees them from any association with the guilt of Claudius. With Horatio, they represent the positive elements in the court with which Fortinbras may build a better society. There is also a Gentleman who appears twice in association with Horatio, once when they go to prevail upon Gertrude to see Ophelia and the other time when he brings Horatio the sailor with his letters from Hamlet. His compassion seems also to bode well for Denmark. Of the many other unnamed *Lords, Ladies, Messengers* and *Attendants* who people the stage, the most important are the *English Ambassadors,* for they serve to report the deaths of Rosencrantz and Guildenstern and their entrance serves as the knock of fate which closes the "interim" during which Hamlet's revenge must needs have been completed. The other Lords and Ladies serve as the background of any state. They believe, with

Rosencrantz and Guildenstern, in the divine right of kings, and all cry "Treason! treason!" when Claudius is wounded by Hamlet. If Fortinbras does not make use of such willing tools of villainy as Osric and *Reynaldo,* Polonius' well-instructed servant, Denmark's hopes are good; but such willing tools are, unfortunately, always available, and the remainder of the court will support even a corrupt king.

In addition to the courtiers, the state also makes use of a "churlish" *Priest.* As he is referred to in the stage directions as a Doctor of Divinity, the suggestion is that he is a Protestant. In any case, he represents the forces of established religion with its preference for the letter over the spirit of the law. Because Ophelia's death was "doubtful," he does not permit her the full pomp of a religious funeral. For this Laertes suggests that "A minist'ring angel shall my sister be / When thou liest howling."

To the representatives of court and church we must now add the army. Despite the bloody honor of its royal leaders, this group represents one of the most healthy elements in the state and stands in marked contrast to the courtiers. *Francisco* we just see for a fleeting moment before he is relieved at his sentry duty by *Bernardo,* who is soon after joined by his more important fellow officer, *Marcellus.* Both Bernardo and Marcellus are honest men with a healthy religious dread and a superstitious awe of ghosts. Marcellus has brought Horatio along for his opinion on the ghost and himself offers the belief that ghosts and other supernatural phenomena are opposed by the religion of Christ. He later offers the most pregnant remark on the significance of the ghost's coming, that "something is rotten in the state of Denmark." With a natural sense of honor combined with his religious dread, he does not wish to "swear" to confirm his already given word to his secrecy. It is perhaps the incorruptible integrity of the common Danish soldier which has led Claudius to surround himself with "Switzers," mercenary Swiss guards such as to this day protect the Vatican. But what is true of the Danish soldiers is also true of their Norwegian counterparts. On his trip to the sea, Hamlet meets a *Captain* of the Norwegian army who is just as blunt and honest a fellow as Bernardo and Marcellus. Completely unimpressed by Fortinbras' mission against Poland, he criticizes this futile pursuit of honor with the homely words: "We go to gain a little patch of ground / That hath in it no profit but the name. / To pay five ducats, five, I should not farm it." With as natural a religious feeling as the Danish soldiers, he bids farewell to Hamlet with the words, "God bye you, sir."

In addition to the various soldiers, Hamlet maintains an easy familiarity with other uncourtly members of society. For the *Players* he has a special affection and tells Polonius that they should "be well used, for they are the abstract and brief chronicles of the time." When Polonius replies that he will "use them according to their desert," Hamlet returns with natural Christian charity, "God's bodkin, man, much better! Use every man after his desert, and who shall 'scape whipping?" He joins in with them in dramatic recitation and works familiarly with them on the play they are to perform.

Of other rogues and peasant slaves, there are two groups with whom Hamlet enters into easy friendship. The first are the pirates who attack the Danish ship taking Hamlet to England and who capture Hamlet. Of them Hamlet says, "they have dealt with me like thieves of mercy," and he further refers to them as "good fellows." Of these *Sailors* who come to Horatio with Hamlet's letter, one of them greets Horatio with the words, "God bless you, sir." When Horatio replies, "Let him bless thee too," the sailor returns with easy confidence in the disposition of Providence, "'A shall, sir, an't please him." The second group are the clowns who play the part of *Gravediggers*. With a Christian sense of democracy, the chief Gravedigger says: "And the more pity that great folk should have count'nance in this world to drown or hang themselves more than their even-Christen. Come, my spade. There is no ancient gentlemen but gard'ners, ditchers, and grave-makers.

They hold up Adam's profession." Singing casually of the loss of youth and the sweetness of young love with the coming of age and final death, "custom," says Horatio, has made the fact of death "in him a property of easiness." As familiar with skulls as he is with Hamlet, he reflects with relish on the pleasure of life one of these grinning skulls once gave him when the man was alive: "A pestilence on him for a mad rogue! 'A poured a flagon of Rhenish on my head once. This same skull, sir, was—sir—Yorick's skull, the king's jester." Rogues and peasants these jesters and clowns, players, pirates, soldiers and gravediggers may be, but they are the salt of the earth. They are "even-Christen" with all men of goodwill, and their easy endurance in the face of death and easy familiarity with their Maker is the hope of their world. Hamlet may have transcended their religious understanding in a profound perception of divinity, but he can still be "even-Christen" with them. Though Fortinbras has inherited the world of the court and will perpetuate its false sense of honor, however purified of its grosser abuses, these nameless "good fellows" are Hamlet's legacy and they endure through all dynastic changes. It is ironically to Hamlet's final credit that he can claim: "O, what a rogue and peasant slave am I!"

Julius Caesar

Scene-by-Scene Summary and Comment

Act I: Scene i

The play opens in a street in Rome. Two tribunes, Flavius and Marullus, are dispersing the crowds that have gathered there. The tribunes have trouble extracting an explanation from a cobbler who appears to be leading the mob, for the cobbler gives equivocal answers to the direct questions of the officials. He claims to be a "mender of bad soles," "a surgeon to old shoes," and one who lives by the "awl." Finally, he admits that the workingmen have left their shops and have assembled "to see Caesar and to rejoice in his triumph."

COMMENT: Although the scene is Rome, the atmosphere is Elizabethan, and the workers here behave like pert Tudor craftsmen. In his portrayal of crowds and of working-men, Shakespeare frequently relied on humor to establish the unruly atmosphere and vulgar tone of the scene. The cobbler's humor is typical of his craft, and he puns on the words of his trade: "all" (awl), "cobbler" (shoemaker, bungler), "sole," (soul), "out" (out of shoes, out of temper), "recover" (save, mend).

Elizabethan trades were ranked according to the dignity of the craft, and although the shoemaker's trade was among the lowest, Shakespeare has the cobbler lead the mob, partly to show how vulgar the leadership is, and partly because of the popular legend of the shoemaker who became the leader of the people and the mayor of London.

Flavius and Marullus are Tribunes of the People, officers who were appointed to protect the interests of plebeians from injustices that might be perpetrated by patrician magistrates. They could reverse a magistrate's judgment or inflict punishment on a plebeian. In Caesar's time, however, their powers were nominal. In this scene, the tribunes are trying to protect the democracy of Rome by preventing their charges from installing a dictator in office.

Marullus is incensed by the reason he is given. He rebukes the commoners for gathering to honor Caesar. What territories has Caesar conquered for Rome, the tribune asks; what prisoners has he led home? He reproaches the people for their hard hearts and senseless cruelty in forgetting Pompey so soon after they had cheered him. He reminds the mob of how they had lined the streets and climbed the battlements of buildings, sitting there all day with babes in arms to get just a glimpse of Pompey when he returned after a victory. "And do you now strew flowers in his way/ That comes in triumph over Pompey's blood?" Marullus harangues. He warns the unfeeling mob that their ingratitude will be repaid by plague if they do not disperse immediately and pray mercy of the gods. Flavius enjoins the people to run to the Tiber and weep for Pompey until the river is filled with tears up to its highest bank.

COMMENT: The tribunes' harangues are spoken from the point of view of the Republican who is sickened by the conquest of a Roman over a Roman. Caesar's triumph was not over a foreign nation but over Pompey and his sons, all fellow Romans. Pompey had been a member of the first triumvirate, formed in 60 B.C. by Pompey, Caesar, and Crassus. They were a coalition group, holding supreme political authority over Rome, subject to the advice and veto of the Senate, a legislative body, comprised mainly of noblemen or patricians. Pompey was married to Caesar's daughter by a former wife, but after the daughter's death, disagreement flared out between Caesar and Pompey. As champion for the Senate, Pompey fought Caesar when he sought to overthrow the triumvirate, disobey the Senate, and establish himself as dictator of Rome. Pompey was assassinated in Egypt, but his sons continued his fight at Munda in Spain. The death of Pompey's sons, that is "Pompey's blood," meant the death of the Republic, for which the plebeians should have no cause to rejoice.

The commoners, however, are more concerned with personal favors than with abstract political principles and the interests of the mainly patrician Senate. They have been won over to Caesar's side by his previous gifts to the people. After his triumph of 46 B.C., for example, Caesar entertained the people with feasts and shows and gave one hundred denarii to each citizen. The capricious nature of the mob is established at this point when Marullus complains about their ingratitude and the fickle transfer of their affections from Pompey, whom they had formerly adored, to Caesar.

When the commoners leave, Flavius remarks, "They vanish tongue-tied in their guiltiness." Then he instructs Marullus to go through the city and "disrobe the images," that is, remove the decorations intended to honor Caesar. Marullus asks if it would not be sacrilege to remove the decorations for the Feast of Lupercal, which is being celebrated on this same day, but Flavius replies that it does not matter. He also orders Marullus to drive the vulgar from the streets so that the absence of the people (who grew like feathers on Caesar's wing and enable him to fly higher than he otherwise could) will keep Caesar's ambitions in check.

COMMENT: The idea of desecration is suggested at this point in connection with the removal of the decorations for Caesar's triumph and the Feast of Lupercal. The Lupercalia was an annual festival, celebrated in honor of the god Pan or Faunus and administered by the members of two ancient families of Rome. In 44 B.C., the Luperci Iulii was instituted in honor of Julius Caesar, which probably explains why Shakespeare condensed history so that Caesar's triumph and the Lupercalia would fall on the same day.

The purpose of the feast held in February was to secure expiation, purification, and fertility for the spring planting. The rites included a race around the Palatine by two youths carrying thongs made from a sacrificed he-goat. Women who stood in the path of the runners would receive blows from the thongs, which were believed to be a charm against barrenness.

Shakespeare achieved special effects by telescoping history. In this scene, he makes Caesar's return coincide with the Lupercalia, suggesting thereby that Caesar, the astute politician, had timed his arrival for a day on which the streets would be crowded with a cheerful public and the statues adorned for the feast as well as for his return. In this way, objections that the people were not at work or that the statues were adorned in his honor would be answered by the feast. At the same time, Caesar would be associating his return with a religious occasion and work on the superstitions of the people who would eventually proclaim him a god and accept him as their dictator. It was in this month, in fact, that Caesar was proclaimed *Dictator Perpetuus* (dictator for life) and that the Lupercalia was named in his honor.

The idea of Caesar's ambition is introduced in Flavius' metaphor of the bird, in which he states that the people's adulation allows Caesar to place himself above other citizens of the Republic and that there is danger he will become a king and keep "us all in servile fearfulness."

SUMMARY: This first scene works as a skillful introduction to the major action of the play. It represents the crowd as a vulgar and capricious mob, who will be important in the political action which ensues. It supplies the background of

events to come by representing the civil disorder which exists in Rome and the differences which exist between two main factions of the city; the commoners who favor Caesar and the tribunes who are Republicans. The case for the Republicans is stated by Marullus, who is angry at the "senseless" mob for celebrating Caesar's triumph over Pompey, another Roman. Flavius establishes the fact that Caesar is ambitious, that he flies too high, and that he is a danger to free men. It is suggested that Caesar is a shrewd politician for arranging his arrival to coincide with the Feast of Lupercal, when crowds would be available to cheer him and when images would be adorned to honor him as well as the god Faunus. The idea of desecration is suggested when Flavius orders the disrobing of the images.

Act I: Scene ii

Shortly after the crowds have been dispersed by the tribunes, a procession arrives. There is music and pageantry as Caesar, Antony, Calpurnia, Portia, Decius, Brutus, Cicero, Brutus, Cassius, and Casca, dressed in elegant attire, march through the street. A large crowd follows the procession which is on its way to the race traditionally held on the Lupercal.

Caesar calls to his wife, Calpurnia, and tells her to stand directly in Antony's way, as he runs through the streets. He orders Antony to strike her since "the barren touched in this holy chase, /Shake off their sterile curse." Antony replies to Caesar's command, "When Caesar says 'do this,' it is performed."

COMMENT: At the Feast of Lupercal, young noblemen ran naked through the streets, striking women, who deliberately stood in their way, believing that if they were pregnant, they should deliver well, and if they were barren, that they would become pregnant. Antony's comment shows that he is Caesar's devoted and obedient follower.

From the crowd a Soothsayer emerges and cries to Caesar, "Beware the ides of March!" Caesar asks the Soothsayer to come forward and repeat what he has just said. He peruses the man's face, hears the warning again, and decides, "He is a dreamer; let us leave him."

COMMENT: The Soothsayer's prophetic warning is heavy with dramatic irony, for the audience knows that Caesar will be killed on the ides (the fifteenth) of March, while Caesar, who studies the man and his words, exercises poor judgment in dismissing both.

In ancient Greek drama, the solution of an oracle or riddle brought about the tragic resolution of the play at the point when the hero learned the true meaning of the oracle.

The ambiguous prophecy of the Soothsayer works in a similar way. It creates dramatic suspense as the audience anticipates Caesar's discovery of the tragic import of the riddle.

As Caesar and his followers go off to the feast, Cassius and Brutus remain behind. Brutus tells Cassius that he will not follow the course of the young men (as they race around the city), for he is not "game-some" and has not Antony's "quick spirit." Cassius expresses his fear that his good friend Brutus disapproves of him, for his looks no longer show his former love. Brutus assures Cassius that he is not vexed with his friend but with himself. He is, in fact, "with himself at war" and "forgets the show of love to other men."

COMMENT: The friendship and love between Brutus and Cassius is established in this conversation, and indication is given for the first time that Brutus is in a state of inner conflict. The face as a reflection of the feelings and thoughts of men is a recurrent theme in this scene. Caesar has scanned the soothsayer's face and has misjudged him as a dreamer, and Cassius has misjudged Brutus' "ungentle" eyes as a sign of his own disfavor.

Next, Cassius will read Brutus' face to him as if he were holding up a mirror before him. The mirror as a reflection of the moral nature of man was a popular device in the literature of Tudor England. The book called *A Mirror for Magistrates*, consisting of a series of morally edifying biographies of famous princes, went through eight editions in the years between 1555 and 1587. Its theme, copied by such notable writers as George Gascoigne, Samuel Daniel, and Michael Drayton, had a powerful influence on the chronicle plays of the 1580s and 1590s, Shakespeare's included. The idea was to present stories or biographies of important men who, through some flaw of character, worked out their destinies in a tragic way. The retelling of these tragedies was expected to have a moral influence on the reader.

In addition, poems like Gascoigne's *Steel Glass* and Sir John Davies' *Nosce Teipsum* used the mirror device as a means of reflecting the abuses of the times and the horrors of man's own sinful nature. It was important for man to learn to "know thyself," these poems taught; man was to search his own nature for the causes of evil. Cassius' desire to show Brutus his reflection in other men's eyes has a Machiavellian cast to it. He wishes to influence him to join a conspiracy. Morally speaking, Brutus must discover his own nature by himself.

The various characters who participate in this scene are also described as reflections in other men's eyes, and it should be noted that Shakespeare unites dramatic exposition, characterization, and dialogue through the use of the mirror metaphor.

Relieved to learn that he is still in Brutus' favor, Cassius tells his friend that he had misunderstood his emotional state and had refrained from discussing important matters with him. He asks Brutus if he can read his own character, which shines in his own face, revealing that Brutus is a just man. Many men, "except immortal Caesar," are now enslaved by Caesar's rule and wish that Brutus had Caesar's eyes so that Brutus could see his own nobility as Caesar sees his own.

COMMENT: Cassius has uttered the first in a series of persuasive remarks designed to win Brutus to the anti-Caesarsist cause. His reference to "immortal Caesar" is a sarcastic and covert allusion to the dictator's wish to be declared a god and to his ambitious desire to rise above his fellow Romans, who consider themselves his equals. Brutus is self-effacing, apparently, and Cassius works on his natural humility by reporting the praise other men have given, him. At the same time, he is suggesting that many respected men of Rome compare Brutus to Caesar, wishing that Brutus had a higher opinion of himself so that he might take action against the self-esteeming dictator. Thus, the characters of Brutus and Caesar are juxtaposed from the conspirator's point of view; Brutus' humility is contrasted with Caesar's presumptuousness and arrogance.

Having thus complimented Brutus, Cassius prepares to tell Brutus the subject of his argument. But first, he testifies to his own honest character, his veracity, his sobriety, his loyalty to friends.

COMMENT: Cassius is following rhetorical procedure in the persuasive argument he is about to deliver. He fails to come straight to the point, but first greets and compliments his audience, then attempts to establish the authority of the speaker. (Brutus will use this device in his address to the mob after Caesar's death.) Cassius' oratory is cut short, however, when a fanfare is sounded from the market-place, but after the interruption, Cassius announces his subject and proceeds to develop it.

Shouts are heard and a sennet is sounded (a series of bars played on a trumpet, symbolizing sovereignty). Brutus blurts out his fear that the people have chosen Caesar for their king. Cassius latches on to Brutus' expression of fear: "Ay do you fear it/ Then must I think you would not have it so." Briefly, Brutus answers that he would not have Caesar king, and yet he loves him. Then he urges Cassius to go on with his message and promises that if it concerns the general good, even the fear of death will not permit him from doing what is honorable.

COMMENT: Caught unaware, Brutus states his inner conflict between his duty to the Republic and his personal love for Caesar. He admits, however, that he loves honor more than he fears death, and that he will act in the public good at any cost. Cassius' course is now clear to him. He must convince Brutus that the removal of Caesar is in the public interest.

Elizabethans associated the ancient Romans with the idea of noble friendship and dedicated statesmanship. Shakespeare expected his audience to realize the deep perturbation which would arise in a man when these two ideals came into conflict.

Returning to his speech and taking his cue from Brutus' remark about honor, Cassius announces his subject is honor. He cannot tell what other men think, but speaking for himself, Cassius states his preference for death to subjugation under a man who is no better than he. Caesar is just another such man, Cassius argues. He and Caesar were born equally free, were nurtured equally and endure the cold in the same way. In fact, Cassius claims, Caesar cannot swim as well as he, for once in a swimming contest, Cassius, like Aeneas (founder of Rome, who bore his father Anchises on his shoulders to save him from the flaming city of Troy), bore Caesar to safety on his shoulders. Another time, when Caesar was afflicted by fever in Spain, he cried for water as a sick girl might. Cassius is angered at the thought that a man of such "feeble temper" should now rule the majestic world alone, while Cassius, his equal, must bend to Caesar's slightest nod.

COMMENT: Cassius' reasons for hating Caesar are all personal ones and are, therefore, considered ignoble and envious. Cassius has indicated, however, that other noble Romans prefer death to slavery, although he does not pretend to be able to advance their motives. The portrait of Caesar is painted from a Republican's point of view, it should be remembered. Cassius emphasizes the physical deterioration, which Caesar actually displayed in the declining years of his life, but he ignores the heroic parts of the conquering hero. Cassius' amazement at Caesar's success reveals his own blindness to an important point. It is not Caesar's physical strength which has made him a dictator, but the spirit of Caesar, an intangible idea, which has raised him above his fellows.

The crowd roars and the trumpet flourishes a second time. Brutus surmises that some new honors are being heaped on Caesar. Cassius compares Caesar to a Colossus and calls Brutus and himself "petty men," who walk under the legs of this giant. "The fault, dear Brutus, is not in our stars,/ But in ourselves, that we are underlings," Cassius states. Then he asks: "Why should that name be sounded more than yours." Once more he alludes to Caesar's physical attributes and asks by what virtue he has become great: "Upon what meat doth this our Caesar feed/ That he is grown so great?" The reputation of Rome rests in the fact that it does not esteem "one only man." He ends his exhortation to Brutus by reminding him of his namesake, Lucius Junius Brutus (a Roman hero who had expelled Rome's last king, Tarquin, five hundred years earlier).

COMMENT: Cassius' reference to Brutus' namesake links Brutus with the ideal of liberty and the Republic. Cassius shows that he is concerned with the reputation of Rome and that he does not want Caesar's position for himself when he argues that "since the great flood" Rome "was famed with more than with one man." It has been argued, however, that Cassius is motivated solely by the desire for personal power and envy of Caesar. Antony says this too in the closing scene of the play. We should view Cassius, however, not as a black or white figure, but as a gray one, who is noble, although not the "noblest."

Brutus replies to Cassius' argument point for point. He assures Cassius that he is not suspicious of his love and that he is somewhat inclined toward Cassius' sentiments. But exactly what he thinks of conditions in Rome must be discussed at another time. Brutus promises to consider what Cassius has already said, to listen to him further and to answer him at a later time. For the present, Brutus tells Cassius, "chew upon this: "Brutus had rather be a villager/ Than to repute himself a son of Rome/ Under these hard conditions as this time/ Is like to lay upon us."

COMMENT: The "villager" to whom Brutus refers was neither a patrician nor a plebeian and did not have rights as a citizen of Rome, but Brutus rhetorically asserts that even the villager's position is preferable to a Roman's under a monarchy. Brutus is not easily persuaded or inflamed by Cassius' passions. He shares Cassius' sentiments but has not yet decided if action is called for. Cassius, we shall see, is aware of Brutus' reflective nature and will use means other than argument to win Brutus to his cause.

The conversation is concluded by Caesar's return from the race. Brutus detects anger on the face of the dictator; he notices the paleness of Calpurnia's cheeks and the fires that burn from Cicero's eyes as if he had been "crossed in conference by some senators." Caesar, on his part, spies Cassius standing by, and turning to Antony, he tells him that he trusts fat men above lean ones. "Yond Cassius has a lean and hungry look!/ He thinks too much, such men are dangerous." Antony urges Caesar not to fear Cassius, for he is a noble Roman of excellent disposition. Caesar asserts that he has no fear, "for always I am Caesar," but if he had, he would avoid Cassius more than any other man. He contrasts Cassius with Antony, who loves plays and music and laughter. Cassius, on the other hand, is never entertained; he reads a great deal, watches men, and penetrates the motives behind their deeds. He rarely smiles, except as if in self-mockery. Such men are dangerous, Caesar warns Antony, insisting that he says this by way of instructing Antony in the ways of men and not because he is expressing his own fear. As Caesar leaves with his train, he bids Antony come to his right side, because he is deaf in the left ear, and tell him what he really thinks of Cassius.

COMMENT: The reading of faces is continued in this episode, and the respective observers interpret character from the appearance and habits of the man in question. Brutus observes the spot of anger on Caesar's brow and remarks that the whole company looks like a "chidden train." He deduces that something has happened which they do not like. Caesar characterizes Cassius as dangerous because he is observant and perceptive, traits which are appropriate to Cassius' lean and hungry look. Antony is apparently fatter, loves pleasure more than Cassius and values the noble arts of poetry and music; as a follower, Caesar implies, he is a man to be trusted.

This is the second of Caesar's brief appearances onstage since the opening of the play. Much has been said about him from the Republican point of view. The tribunes and Cassius fear Caesar's ambition, and Brutus indicates that he has similar trepidations himself. Apart from Caesar's costume and the pomp and ceremony which accompany his appearance, Caesar so far displays none of the special virtues which have made him a conqueror and dictator and beloved by the common people of Rome. His physical condition is in a state of decay. In his first appearance we learned that his wife is sterile, which suggests Caesar's own aging impotence. Now we see that he is deaf in one ear. According to dramatic chronology and Cassius' report, Caesar has recently suffered from fever in Spain and that he has never been especially adept in physical feats. Disease and infirmity will continue to be associated with Caesar until his tragic death scene. These infirmities reflect the diseases of his times; factionalism, civil disorder, and sacrilege, which finally overcome Caesar, but not his spirit, which lives on in Octavius. (Compare Caesar's infirmities with those of the king in Shakespeare's *2 Henry IV*.)

Also worthy of notice is Caesar's protestation that he does not fear Cassius, "for always I am Caesar." This has been interpreted as a cover for Caesar's real fear of Cassius, as a sign of Caesar's arrogance for disdaining the emotions which other men have, and also as a mark of real fearlessness which is associated with the regal and courageous nature of the man.

When Caesar leaves, Brutus grasps Casca's cloak and asks the cause of Caesar's anger. Casca replies that Antony had offered him the crown three times and that three times Caesar refused it. Each time Antony held out the crown, Caesar fingered it, but discerning the mood of the mob which rejected monarchy, he put it aside. To Casca's thinking, however, he refused the crown more reluctantly each time. Then, Casca relates, Caesar fainted. Brutus remarks that Caesar has the falling-sickness (epilepsy). Cassius ironically replies that it is not Caesar, but they, who have the falling-sickness (that is, the Republic is falling). Having thrice refused the crown and thrice seen how glad the people were at his refusal, Casca continues, Caesar opened his doublet and offered them his throat to cut. Casca admits that if he had had a weapon, he would have taken up Caesar's offer. Casca goes on to say that when Caesar recovered from his fainting spell, he blamed his actions on his infirmity, and the mob forgave him. Casca ends his description with the words: "If Caesar had stabbed their mothers, they would have done no less."

COMMENT: We learn shortly that Casca is a "blunt fellow," who had a "quick mettle" (a good wit) at one time and which he still has when noble action calls for it. However, he has learned to put on "tardy form" (to act like a fool) and to appear to be rude in order to add "sauce" to "his good wit" so that men can better receive the truth he utters. Casca himself calls the business at the race "foolery," and so it was, according to Plutarch, who was Caesar's biographer. Like Plutarch, Casca suggests that Antony's offer of the crown and Caesar's refusal was a prearranged plan, designed to test the reactions of the crowd toward the elevation of Caesar from dictator to monarch. The crowd loves Caesar as dictator, but it is not ready to install him as monarch. The disappointment at having been cheered for refusing the crown explains Caesar's anger as he leaves the race.

Casca is a Republican, however, and he later joins the conspirators against Caesar. His interpretations of Caesar's refusal of the crown, as Casca repeatedly insists, is "to my thinking," "and for mine own part." Shakespeare emphasizes that the description of events is being given from Casca's point of view and suggests that Caesar is more noble than Casca (or Plutarch) believes.

Casca's report and opinion roughly follows that of Plutarch's in his treatment of the episode in which Caesar offers his throat to be cut. In Plutarch, there is no doubt that Caesar wanted the crown and that he used ruses to test the people's reactions to his ambition. But in Shakespeare, the description of events is put into the mouth of a fool (who may not be a fool), and the entire subject of Caesar's ambition is thus put open to question. Was he ambitious, as Brutus later states, or did he put by the crown sincerely, as Antony implies?

In reply to Brutus' question on Cicero's reaction to the events at the Lupercalia, Casca answers that Cicero spoke Greek to his friends, but "it was Greek to me." He states further that Marullus and Flavius have been "silenced" for pulling garlands off Caesar's statues.

COMMENT: We learn that the images disrobed by the tribunes were really statues of Caesar bedecked with scarves of honor. The suggestion is that Caesar has allowed the people to treat him as a diety and that he has punished the tribunes for attempting to prevent their action. There is no doubt from Casca's point of view that Caesar is ambitious and presumptuous.

Seeing that Casca feels the same way toward Caesar as he does, Cassius invites him to dinner. After Casca leaves, Brutus comments that Casca is unpolished, but Cassius explains that Casca's rudeness is a mask behind which he can speak the truth freely. Repeating his promise to talk more the next day, Brutus leaves.

Alone on the stage, Cassius states that Brutus is a noble man, but that he sees Brutus can be diverted from his natural inclinations. Reflecting that noble minds should always keep company with other noble minds lest they be seduced, Cassius also observes that no one is so firm that he cannot be persuaded to change his course. He acknowledges that he is in Caesar's disfavor and that Brutus is loved by Caesar, but if he were Brutus, Cassius asserts, he would not let Caesar's love prevent him from following his principles. Cassius then announces his plan to win over Brutus completely. He will forge letters from leading citizens in which he will praise Brutus' name and hint covertly at Caesar's dangerous ambition to overthrow the Republic. After the letters have been thrown into Brutus' window and he has read them, Caesar should beware, for "We will shake him or worse days endure."

COMMENT: Cassius speaks the play's first soliloquy, a monologue in which the speaker reveals his thoughts to the audience. Since no dramatic interaction takes place during the soliloquy, it is a traditional dramatic convention that the speaker always utters the truth.

We learn Cassius' real feelings, motives, and plans from this speech. Brutus is indeed noble, but he can be moved. Cassius' reflection on the company noble minds should keep may mean that Brutus has made a mistake in befriending him, but it is more likely that Cassius feels Brutus is lucky to have him as a friend, for Cassius will lead him to "noble enterprise" (of the sort Casca will also participate in).

Cassius reveals, however, that he is capable of using devious means to achieve his "noble" end, the suppression of tyranny, but he raises the question of the nobility of the enterprise. Cassius is being portrayed as a careful and deceitful conspirator. As a lean and hungry man, he has already been identified as a Machiavellian type, whose cold statesmanship knows expediency, not honor. This was the common Elizabethan view of Machiavelli, author of *The Prince*, a book in the tradition of mirror-of-princes literature, which was extremely popular in the latter decades of the Tudor dynasty. The intellectual spirit of Machiavelli's book, however, did not reflect the moral teachings of English works in the same tradition. Machiavelli rejected metaphysics, theology, and idealism, and emphasized the necessity of political realism if the prince were to achieve and maintain his power. Deception, lies, and forgeries were all part of the Elizabethan conception of Machiavelli's statesmanship, and this conception is precisely what Cassius is meant to convey at this point. His cause may be honorable, but since his methods are not, he dishonors his cause. Cassius, however, will not always be seen as the practical, shrewd opportunist who would betray his friend (Caesar) if he were loved by him, for his character changes as the play progresses, and he commits suicide at the end, partly because he believes "his best friend" has been captured.

SUMMARY: Scene ii develops the political conflict already introduced in the first scene between the commoners who love Caesar and the tribunes who fear for the safety of the Republic. The mob and tribunes manifest the state of conflict in Rome on the plebeian level. Cassius, Brutus, and Caesar, in Scene ii, display political factionalism on the patrician level.

The major characters of the play are introduced in this scene, and their dispositions are examined from varying points of view. Caesar is seen amid all his pomp as a man concerned with religious ritual, the sterility of his wife, and the envious looks of Cassius. He shows his failing powers of perception when he dismisses the Soothsayer; he insists that he knows no fear; and he shows his wisdom of men and manners when he correctly diagnoses Cassius as a dangerous man. However, he admits to infirmity when he tells Antony to avoid his deaf ear and speak into his good one, and he suggests a growing hesitation in his own judgment when he asks Antony to give him his opinions of Cassius.

Antony, a member of Caesar's train, is a "game-some" fellow who runs in the race of the Lupercal. He is unlike Brutus who has no inclination to participate in popular festivities, and he is opposite Cassius in that Antony is not lean and enjoys plays, music, and laughter. Caesar implies he is a loyal fellow, which he is indeed.

Cassius' character is opposed both to Antony's and Brutus'. He reads a great deal, fails to participate in entertainments, stands apart watching and thinking, and rarely laughs. He is a jealous man, uneasy at seeing another in power. He is a man to be feared. Cassius, moreover, is admittedly capable of betraying those who love him for the sake of his particular principles. He would use dishonorable means to achieve ends which he judges to be honorable.

Brutus' noble character is established by both Cassius and Caesar. Brutus is a reflective man, dedicated to the principles of the Republic, to love and friendship, to duty, and to honor. For the sake of honor, he will even face death (as, in fact, he does at the end of the play). But as strongly as he holds his ideals, he is just as strongly torn by conflicting loyalties to those ideals. Brutus makes decisions deliberately, and he is not quickly influenced by persuasive and passionate argument. He is torn between his love for Caesar and the anti-Caesar sentiments he admittedly shares with Cassius.

Casca has a rude manner and saucy wit, which he uses to disguise his satirical commentary on political events. He does not sympathize with Caesar and tends to interpret Caesar's behavior in the worst possible light. As a result of his denigrating interpretations of Caesar's ambition, he is invited to join the conspiratorial meeting which Cassius is planning.

Cicero is seen but not heard. He has a fiery look in his eye of the sort he has been known to show when arguing with senators. It is reported by Casca that he spoke Greek to the commoners who (since Casca cannot understand Greek) were not expected to understand Cicero. Those who did comprehend Cicero's Greek simply smiled at one another and shook their heads. Casca's implication is that Cicero is a pedant, who does not choose to speak in the language of the people.

Shakespeare foreshadows Caesar's assassination through the prophecy of the soothsayer and in the dialogue among Brutus, Cassius, and Casca. Thus, this scene lays the foundation for the conflicts, characterizations, and tragedy which will be developed throughout the play.

Act I: Scene iii

It is the eve of the ides of March. Lightning flashes through the sky and thunder roars. On a street in Rome, Casca is seen with drawn sword, frightened out of his wits by the storm. He meets Cicero on the street and tells him that either there is "civil strife in heaven" or else men have offended the gods. He then describes other prodigies he has seen that night. A common slave's left hand was burned with flame, yet remained unscorched; a lion roamed loose near the Capitol; a hundred women have sworn they saw men walk in fire up and down the streets, and the birds of the night hooted and shrieked at noonday. Cicero philosophically replies, "Indeed, it is a strange-disposed time," but men interpret things absolutely contrary to the meaning

of the events themselves. He asks Casca if Caesar is coming to the Capitol tomorrow, and Casca says he will be there. Declaring that "this disturbed sky/ Is not to walk in," Cicero departs.

COMMENT: Cicero is stoically calm in face of the storm and the fantastic events related by Casca. Casca's credibility is called into question by Cicero's refusal to discuss the meaning of these wonders and in his dispassionate statement that men often err in their interpretations of unnatural phenomena. Casca's report of the Lupercalia may be reexamined in the light of this conversation. Cicero questions Casca's interpretation of events, and so may we.

Casca hears someone coming and issues a challenge. It is Cassius, who recognizes Casca by his voice. Casca asks why the heavens are so menacing. Cassius replies that he has been walking through the storm, exposing himself to the lightning, and asserts that these unnatural events are heaven's instruments of fear and warning that something unnatural is happening on earth. Then he compares the storm to a man no mightier than himself or Casca, a man who roars like a lion in the Capitol. Casca replies, "'Tis Caesar that you mean."

COMMENT: Having just been advised by Cicero that men tend to interpret events in their own fashion, that is, according to some personal predisposition that they may have, Casca proceeds to ignore this piece of Stoic wisdom and demands an explanation of the wonders from Cassius, the next man he meets in the storm.

Unwittingly confirming Cicero's statement, Cassius explains the monstrous wonders produced during the storm as a warning from heaven that something monstrous is going on on earth. The monstrosity he has in mind, of course, is Caesar's ambitious bid for the crown. Cassius may not believe his own interpretation of the supernatural events because he is an epicurean (later in the play he says he has renounced his epicureanism) and does not believe that gods concern themselves with human affairs. He may only be pretending such concern in order to persuade Casca to join the conspiracy. But Cassius, apparently unsuperstitious, has walked "unbraced" (with doublet open), exposing himself to the storm as he intends to face Caesar.

Casca remarks that on the morrow the senators plan to establish Caesar as king over all lands of the empire except Italy. At this Cassius delivers a tirade against tyranny and hurls abuse at the servile Romans for following "so vile a thing as Caesar!" Cassius declares that he is armed and ready to fight Casca should he turn out to be one of Caesar's men. But Casca gives his hand as a pledge of his cooperation, telling Cassius he will join his cause. Cassius then tells Casca that he has already enlisted some of the "noblest-minded Romans" to join him in the deed, "most bloody, fiery and most terrible."

COMMENT: Although it has been seen that Cassius cannot stomach Caesar's power, that he personally cannot bow to a man who was formerly his equal, we learn from his speech on tyranny that Cassius' feelings are noble ones. It is his methods that are reprehensible, such as the seduction of Brutus from his natural inclinations and the forged letters which he hopes will do the trick.

As Cassius and Casca conclude their pact, Cinna, a member of the conspiracy, arrives. He begins to talk of the storm, but Cassius cuts him short, anxious to know if the conspirators are waiting for him. Cinna says they are and adds how beneficial it would be to their cause if Cassius could "but win the noble Brutus to our party." Cassius orders Cinna to put one of the forged letters on Brutus' seat of office, to throw another in his window, and to place a third on the statue of Lucius Junius Brutus (the ancient and heroic namesake of Marcus Brutus). Then Cinna is to meet him at Pompey's theater. Cassius then tells Casca that Brutus is three-parts won to his cause, and at their next encounter he will be entirely persuaded. Casca remarks that Brutus "sits high in all the people's hearts," and that what would appear to be evil if done by them, would appear virtuous if done by Brutus. Cassius agrees with Casca's judgment that Brutus is of great worth and is much needed for their cause, and he bids Casca join him in securing Brutus for their party.

SUMMARY: This scene advances the conspiracy against Caesar. Cassius has already enlisted many noble Romans to his cause, and the plotters are anxious to have Brutus as a "front." In the first scene, we saw the conflict between the people and the Republicans; in the second, the major characters began to take sides in the impending power struggle. In the third, it becomes obvious that the conspiracy against Caesar has grown, and the noblest of the Romans, Brutus, is being drawn into it. The development of Brutus' character continues. In Scene ii, he was a respected and honorable man, who was hardly aware of his own worth. In this scene, he is judged the most honored of men in Rome who, because of his virtue, can make black appear white. Cassius continues to be characterized as a schemer who is able to manipulate men, but also as one who has a passionate hatred of tyranny and the courage to prefer death to a life of servility.

Act II: Scene i

Brutus is seen in his orchard at three o'clock in the morning of the ides of March. He cannot sleep because he is troubled by the conflict between his love for Caesar and his love for freedom and Rome. He bids his servant, Lucius, to bring him a candle, and muses over what must be done. He resolves that the only way to stop Caesar is to kill him. Brutus has no personal motive for murdering him; he believes that Caesar must die for the general good. Since he can find nothing in Caesar's past conduct which would justify murder, Brutus projects his thoughts into the future. He considers the possibility of Caesar receiving the crown, changing his nature, and becoming a tyrant. It would be better not to give Caesar this opportunity, not to give the adder its chance to strike. Brutus resolves to "think him as a serpent's egg/ Which, hatch'd, would as his kind grow mischievous,/ And kill him in the shell."

COMMENT: Brutus' soliloquy reveals that he has no personal grievance against Caesar but that he fears Caesar may become a danger to the "general good," the public welfare. He has a strong sense of honor and deep feelings of responsibility to protect the freedom of his native city. Reason as he may, he can find no grounds in Caesar's past behavior for believing that he will abuse his power once he is crowned monarch. Yet, Brutus knows, it is the nature of tyrants to disjoin "remorse from power," that is, to rule without conscience or mercy. So, while he can find nothing in reason to argue against Caesar's coronation, he decides to base his reasoning on possibility. As a monarch, Caesar *may* run to "extremities" and become excessive in his despotic rule. On the basis of this possibility, which would ruin the Republic, he must be killed. Brutus is an idealist, but he confuses treachery with honor when he decides to kill Caesar for no existing reason.

Lucius reenters with a letter he has found while lighting the candle in Brutus' study. It is the forged note which Cinna has tossed into the window and bears the cryptic message, "Brutus, thou sleepst. Awake, and see thyself!/ Shall Rome, etc. Speak, strike, redress!" Brutus interprets "Shall Rome, etc." to mean "Shall Rome stand under one man's awe?" Lucius returns to report that tomorrow is the fifteenth of March. When the servant leaves to answer a knock at the gate, Brutus continues his thoughts. He says that since Cassius has "whet" him against Caesar, he has not slept a wink. His wakefulness has been a nightmare of conflict between "the genius and the mortal instruments" which work on the human condition as insurrection does on a kingdom.

COMMENT: The letter contains an ironic comment on Brutus' disturbed condition; it exhorts him to awaken when, in fact, Brutus has not slept since his conversation with Cassius. And like Cassius, he has become dangerous to Caesar, who, we recall, preferred "sleek-headed men, and such as sleep o' nights" (I.ii). Brutus' dangerous line of thinking is made even clearer when he interprets the incomplete but suggestive sentence, "Shall Rome, etc." as a complaint against the potential tyranny of Caesar. The seeds of insurrection, which Cassius had sowed, have taken root in the fertile soil of Brutus' rebellious mind. Brutus' description of the "hideous dream" he is experiencing, in which his mind ("genius") and his body ("mortal instruments") suffer an inner turmoil comparable to the effects of insurrection in a kingdom, reflects the moral philosophy of the Renaissance. In that philosophy the relationship between the body and the mind (or the body and the soul) and the correspondence between the human condition and the body politic were basic assumptions. Shakespeare carefully designed Brutus' personal emotional upheaval to reflect and foreshadow the political chaos which would follow Caesar's assassination.

The word "insurrection" still rings on the stage as Lucius enters to announce the arrival of "your brother Cassius" (Cassius is married to Brutus' sister). Others are with him, but their hats are pulled low over their ears and their faces are buried in cloaks so that they cannot be identified. Brutus comments on the shamefulness of conspiracy that fears to show its monstrous face even in a state full of evil. But he quickly overcomes his sense of shame by reasoning that even if the conspirators continued in their normal ways, the blackness of Erebus (the path to hell) could not hide them from Caesar's tyranny ("prevention").

Cassius, Casca, Decius Brutus, Cinna, Metellus Cimber, and Trebonius enter. Before introducing these men, Cassius tells Brutus that each one is acquainted with and honors him. Brutus and Cassius whisper to each other as the rest of the conspirators engage in small talk, disagreeing over the direction in which the sun is rising. The conclave finished, Brutus takes their hands one by one as fellow conspirators. Cassius proposes that they swear an oath, but Brutus says it is unnecessary, since "the sufferance of our souls, the time's abuse" are strong enough motive to assure their good faith. Honesty and the promise of a Roman is enough, Brutus patriotically asserts.

COMMENT: Brutus overcomes his natural sense of shame over the idea of conspiracy by using more of the fallacious reasoning which he has already demonstrated in his soliloquy. He allows himself to believe that the evils Caesar *may* inflict *if* he becomes monarch actually exist at the moment.

However, he shows his own integrity, although misguided, when he rejects Cassius' proposal of the oath. Brutus is convinced that the souls of free men suffer by the "time's abuse" (Caesar's potential coronation), and that the conspirators are all honest Romans nobly concerned with the good of the state.

The apparently insignificant talk about the direction of the rising sun is a humorous and meaningful incident in which Shakespeare characterizes the conspirators as a discordant group who cannot agree on a simple issue and suggests that they are ill-equipped to decide political issues as well.

The oath rejected, Cassius then proposes that Cicero be included in their group. Casca and Cinna agree, and Metellus Cimber reasons that Cicero's dignity and age will win them the good opinion of the masses. "It shall be said his judgment rul'd our hands," Cimber states. Brutus rejects Cassius' second proposal, arguing that Cicero "will never follow anything/ That other men begin." Cassius grudgingly agrees to leave Cicero out. Decius proposes to kill Antony as well as Caesar. Cassius readily agrees, on the grounds that Antony is a "shrewd contriver" and may well harm them later. For a third time, Brutus opposes Cassius on the grounds that "Antony is but a limb of Caesar. / Let us be sacrificers, but not butchers. As for Caesar, "Let's carve him as a dish fit for the gods,/ Not hew him as a carcass fit for hounds." Naively, Brutus adds, "We shall be call'd purgers, not murderers. And for Mark Antony, think not of him;/ For he can do no more than Caesar's arm/ When Caesar's head is off."

COMMENT: Brutus has taken Antony's love of pleasure and his loyalty to Caesar as a sign of political weakness. He conceives of the murder of Caesar as a religious sacrifice rather than a slaughter and is blind to the possibility that his sacrifice may, in fact, be sacrilege, because the gods have ordained that Caesar rule. Brutus also fails to realize that, although he personally may be fearful of Caesar's power, the people are not. He is acting out of a patrician and Stoic sense of duty to the state, which according to his philosophy is the highest motive from which men may act.

Unlike Brutus, Cassius observes and understands men. He perceives that Antony is a "shrewd contriver" and that he has a large force which, if increased, could endanger the conspirators' cause. Cassius errs against his own judgments by acceding to each of Brutus' three decisions.

The clock strikes three, and Trebonius says it is time to part. Cassius finds it doubtful that Caesar will come forth because of the "apparent prodigies" and unaccustomed terrors of the night, "for he is superstitious grown of late." But Decius promises to get Caesar to the Capitol by flattering him with praise of his hatred for flatterers. Cassius proposes that instead, all the conspirators go and fetch Caesar. Metellus Cimber bids them include Caius Ligarius in the plot, and Brutus assents, asking that, Caius Ligarius be sent to him. Their plans concluded, the conspirators adjourn. Brutus calls his servant, but finding him asleep, he tenderly wishes him sweet dreams and reflects on the sound slumber of those unburdened by care.

COMMENT: In Elizabethan philosophy, superstition was a sign of the diseased senses. Thus, by calling Caesar superstitious, Cassius adds to the portrait of Caesar as a decaying and declining man. Caesar's susceptibility to flattery suggests that his moral sense is decaying as well as his mental power.

Brutus' address to Lucius his servant expresses his affection for the boy and reveals his own gentle nature. Shakespeare frequently uses the unburdened sleep of humble people as a contrast to the restless state of the leaders of men, particularly insurgents.

When the conspirators have gone, Brutus' wife, Portia, comes to inquire why Brutus is up in the middle of the night. She wants to know what has been absorbing him so much of late. Brutus replies that he is not well. Portia retorts that Brutus is not acting like someone sick in body but like someone with a troubled spirit. She implores him on her knees to tell her what is wrong and asks about the visitors who had come in with their faces hidden. She declares that by failing to share his secret, Brutus excludes her from part of the marriage and makes her his harlot rather than his wife. Brutus insists she is his honorable wife, but Portia continues to protest her good repute, by virtue of her father, the noble Cato, and by her own act of courage, a self-inflicted thigh wound that was intended to prove her worth as Brutus' wife and the sharer of his secrets.

COMMENT: The theme of disease is continued in this dialogue in Brutus' feigned excuse for his behavior and in Portia's accurate and ironical diagnosis that there is "some sick offense within your mind." Physical and mental diseases repeatedly figure as symbols of the disease of civil rebellion, which Caesar's murder and its results represent.

The nobility and courage of Portia are expressed in this passage. She is the daughter of Marcus Porcius Cato, who killed himself at the battle of Utica in the civil war against Caesar rather than fall into Caesar's hands. Plutarch wrote that Portia cut her thigh with a razor to prove her courage, and this is undoubtedly the meaning of her "voluntary wound" in the thigh.

Brutus is touched by his wife's devotion and is about to tell her his plans when he is interrupted by the entrance of Ligarius. Ligarius has been ill but is ready to throw his bandages aside if Brutus proposes some exploit worthy of the name of honor. Brutus says such an exploit is planned, and at these words, Ligarius throws aside his bandages and presents himself ready for action. Brutus says that the plot is one which will make sick men whole and that he will tell Ligarius of it as they walk. Ligarius replies that even though he is ignorant of the plot, it is enough for him that Brutus leads it.

COMMENT: The theme of sickness or disease is continued in this interview. Ligarius, literally ill, says he will become well when a deed of honor is proposed. Caesar's later remark that Ligarius' illness has made him lean (like dangerous men) is a dramatically ironic reference to Ligarius' statement here. Equally ironic is the fact that the plot against Caesar which should make "sick men whole" has disturbed Brutus' quiet mind and turned it from health to sickness. The entire conspiracy is, thus, associated with the disease of insurrection, and Caesar's own rule is given a similar unhealthy cast through its association with the infirmities of Caesar.

SUMMARY: The main purpose of this scene is to show the change which takes place in Brutus after his first conversation with Cassius. The seeds of insurrection having been planted. Brutus is torn by inner conflict as he decides to join and head the conspiracy. His motives are honorable, but he mistakes treachery for honesty and murder for sacrifice. He finds oaths unnecessary among noble Romans; he vetoes an invitation to Cicero to join the conspiracy, and he objects to Antony's murder, underestimating the shrewdness and potential danger in the man. Each of these judgments is based on high civic and moral principles, and, in contrast with Cassius' suggestions, they are impractical and unrealistic, as we shall see.

The conspirators show their true colors when they disagree over a trifling matter such as the direction of the sun's rising and when they invite Ligarius to join the conspiracy because he hates Caesar, not because he loves Rome. Their desire to enlist Cicero for the dignity he will bring their "youths and wildness" is similar to the reason for choosing Brutus for the virtue with which he will coat their offenses (I. iii).

Cassius shows skill in judging men and opposes the naive decisions of Brutus. Nevertheless, he is influenced by Brutus' principled behavior and betrays his own judgment in yielding to Brutus' wishes. The noble and courageous Portia is introduced in this scene, and her reference to Cato her father (who fought for Pompey against Caesar) suggests that she will endorse her husband's plot.

Act II: Scene ii

The storm is still raging as the scene shifts to Caesar's house. It is three A. M. in the morning of the ides of March. Caesar, like Brutus, is spending a restless night. He exclaims that neither heaven nor earth is peaceful on this night; even Calpurnia, his wife, is having disturbed dreams and has cried out three times in her sleep, "Help, ho! They murder Caesar!" Caesar sends a servant to the priests and orders them to make a sacrifice and send him the results. Calpurnia enters and begs Caesar not to stir out of the house that day, but Caesar fatalistically replies, "What can be avoided Whose end is purposed by the mighty gods?"

Calpurnia says that she is not normally upset by prodigies, but that the unnatural occurrences of the proceding night have disturbed her: a lioness was seen giving birth in the streets; the dead rose from their graves; and fiery warriors fought in the clouds so fiercely that blood drizzled upon the Capitol. There were also reports that horses neighed, that dying men groaned, and that ghosts shrieked and squealed along the streets.

COMMENT: The appearance of the lioness, the warriors, and the dying men are foreshadowings of Caesar's death and the civil chaos which will follow his death. Caesar's resigned acceptance of the will of the gods is the position taken by the Stoic philosophers who purged their minds of all fear and passion to leave them free for virtuous thought and action.

Calpurnia interprets the comets in the air, also seen during the night, as a prophecy of the death of a prince, for comets are never seen when beggars die. Caesar firmly encourages his wife with the now famous lines, "Cowards die many times before their deaths;/ The valiant never taste of death but once." He finds it strange that men should have fears, since death is a necessity which "will come when it will come."

COMMENT: Calpurnia's superstitious interpretations of the wonders of the night express her fears for Caesar's life; they are projections of the thoughts which trouble her most just as Cassius' interpretation of the prodigies reflect his greatest fear, that Caesar will become king. Caesar's courage is asserted here; it is the characteristic courage of a man who has known war and conquest and is confident of his own bravery. But Caesar also shows that he has lost touch with ordinary men and no longer understands their passions.

Calpurnia's dream has already foreshadowed Caesar's murder, and the dramatic irony of the situation continues as she warns Caesar not to leave the house and Caesar replies that the only real threats that can be made to him are those made to his back, that is, through conspiracy, which is now being organized behind his back.

The sacrifice Caesar had ordered earlier has been done, and the servant returns to report that the priests advise Caesar to stay at home, for the beast, when opened, was found to have no heart. Caesar defies this answer of the gods sent by the priests, and like Cassius and Calpurnia, he gives his own interpretation of the sacrifice, which is colored by his personal predilections. The heartless beast, Caesar asserts, is a chatisement of the gods against cowardice. If he should stay at home this day, Caesar would be a beast without a heart. (The heart was regarded as the seat of courage in Renaissance physiology and philosophy.) He calls himself the brother of danger; metaphorically, he and danger are two lions born on the same day, and of the two, Caesar is the more terrible. (The lion, the king of the beasts, traditionally represented the king of men, the masculine spirit, and male courage.) "Caesar shall go forth," the intemperate ruler declares.

COMMENT: Caesar's defiance of the priests and of the gods themselves is immoderate and even blasphemous. His judgment fails when he sacrilegiously defies the advice of the priests and the "ceremonies" (religious superstitions) which frighten Calpurnia. He is, indeed, tempting the gods, and his fate awaits him.

The likeness of men and animals was the basis of the study of physiognomy during the Renaissance, and the lion metaphor repeatedly reflects this habit of comparison. Cassius, Calpurnia, and now Caesar himself interpret the appearance of the lion in the Capitol as the animal corresponding symbolically to Caesar.

When Caesar declares himself braver than danger itself, Calpurnia exclaims that Caesar is losing sight of his wisdom in his overconfidence. She implores him to send Mark Antony to the Senate to say Caesar is not well. According to her "humor," Caesar agrees to send the message and to remain at home.

COMMENT: The reason for Caesar's concession to Calpurnia's fears has been a point of critical contention. Either Caesar is hiding his real fears by seeming to consent to Calpurnia's "humor" or he means just what he says and grants his wife's wish out of tenderness for her. (Brutus in a parallel scene with his wife also grants her wish, although his granting of it does not become apparent immediately.) Calpurnia's accusation that Caesar has become overconfident is the first clear indication that Caesar has been afflicted with that state of mad arrogance which in ancient Greek theology was believed to arouse the wrath of Nemesis, the goddess of moderation who hated every transgression of the bounds of temperance and restored the proper and normal order of all things through chatisement and vengeance.

Decius Brutus enters to fetch Caesar to the Senate. Caesar asks Decius to bear his greeting to the senators and tell them that he will not come today. He adds that to say he cannot come is false, and to say he dares not come is even falser. Calpurnia tells Decius to say that Caesar is sick, but Caesar insists that he will not send a lie. He bids Decius again to say simply that he will not come. Craftily, Decius asks Caesar to give him some cause so that Decius will not be laughed at when he delivers the message. Arrogantly, Caesar answers that it is enough to tell the Senate that Caesar will not come, but because he loves Decius, for his personal satisfaction, he will give him the reason: Calpurnia keeps him at home because she dreamed she saw his statue like a fountain with a hundred spouts, pouring forth blood in which smiling Romans bathed their hands.

Decius protests that Calpurnia's dream has been misinterpreted, that it really means that Rome sucks reviving blood from Caesar and through him regains its vitality. Decius adds that the Senate has decided to give Caesar a crown this day. If he does not come, the Senate may change its mind. Decius argues that the dream as a reason for his absence "were a mock/ Apt to be rendered for someone to say/ 'Break up the Senate till another time,/ When Caesar's wife shall meet with better dreams.'" That is, Caesar's excuse might be interpreted as an insult by one of the senators. Furthermore, if Caesar does not appear, senators will say that Caesar is afraid. Caesar is persuaded to see that Calpurnia's fears are foolish ones and tells his wife to get his robes, for he will go.

COMMENT: Caesar is a man of personal tenderness as well as public ambition, courage, and virtue. Personally unafraid, he is nevertheless capable of conceding to the fears and wishes of those he loves. Such softness at this point in his life is a sign of his age and growing infirmity, for the conquering hero of Caesar's youth was more decisive and more firm in his convictions. It has been argued that Caesar's words are not to be trusted and that he is really a frightened man, covering his fears with a show of bravado, and using Calpurnia as an excuse to act out his own cowardly inclinations. Decius' argument may then be interpreted as the crafty manipulation of an arrogant, conceited, and fearful old man.

Publius, Brutus, Ligarius, Metellus, Casca, Trebonius, and Cinna enter to escort Caesar to the Senate, and Caesar graciously welcomes them. Alluding to their former enmity, Caesar also notes that Ligarius' illness

has made him lean. The clock strikes eight as Antony enters. Caesar remarks that despite the fact that Antony revels all night, he is able to get up in time for his duties in the morning. Caesar apologizes for keeping his escorts waiting and bids Cinna, Metellus, and Trebonius to sit near him in the Senate. Trebonius replies in an aside that he will be so near Caesar that Caesar's best friends will wish he had been further away. Caesar invites the men to drink wine with him and then "like friends," they shall be off together. In response to Caesar's show of trust, Brutus mourns, in an aside, that every "like" is not the "same."

COMMENT: Caesar is portrayed among his apparent friends as a gracious, polished and courteous host. (He is neither arrogant nor pompous as in his other appearances.) When Brutus sees Caesar behave in his usual generous and gracious manner, his personal love for Caesar comes to the fore, and he grieves ("earns") over Caesar's assumption that they are all "like friends." Punning on several meanings of the word "like" (love, the same as, apparent), Brutus regrets that all meanings of "like" are not "same," and that all loving friends are not what they appear to be, nor do they remain the "same" in their loyalty. Caesar's wish that the conspirators remains close to him in the Senate is another instance of dramatic irony, for as Trebonius implies in his aside (intended only for the audience's hearing), he will be close enough to murder Caesar.

SUMMARY: This crucial scene serves many purposes in advancing the plot and characterizations of the major figures. First, this scene is carefully balanced with the one immediately preceding in which Brutus meets with the conspirators and with his wife Portia. Here Caesar and his devoted wife Calpurnia are seen, then the conspirators arrive as guests. Like Portia, Calpurnia petitions her husband on her knees and at first wins her point that he remain at home. Like Portia, Calpurnia is fearful, restless, concerned for her husband. Both wives are well-suited to their husbands. Portia and Brutus are young, strong, and courageous; Calpurnia and Caesar are aging, infirm, and superstitious.

Both Brutus and Caesar entertain the same guests. Ironically, however, the guests arrive in friendship in Brutus' garden, concealed by hats and cloaks, to form a conspiratorial alliance, while the same men visit Caesar as enemies, wearing no disguise at all. They simply mask their monstrous visages under "smiles and affability" as Brutus had planned in the preceding scene (II. i. 85-6).

Both Brutus and Caesar are seen as tender and yielding husbands and gracious and courteous hosts. Both trust the honesty of the conspirators; both succumb to their flattery. Brutus, however misguided, relies on his reason and his sense of duty, and is firmly decisive in dealing with the plans for the assassination. Caesar's behavior has been vacillating in dealing with the omen of Calpurnia's dream and the advice of the priests whose augurs he had demanded. The assured rashness of Brutus' youth in the preceding scene is contrasted with the vacillation and overconfidence of the aging Caesar in the present scene.

The themes of prodigies, dreams, augurs, and their interpretations are carried on in this scene, establishing an atmosphere of unrest, insurrection, and foreboding which is so essential to the building of suspense for the crucial murder scene and the subsequent events.

Act II: Scene iii

In a street near the Capitol, Artemidorus appears reading a paper. Artemidorus places himself in a spot where Caesar must pass on his walk to the Capitol, and rereads the letter he plans to thrust into Caesar's hands. The letter warns Caesar to beware of Brutus, Cassius, Casca, Cinna, and other members of the conspiracy because they are plotting against his life. It warns Caesar that unless he is immortal, overconfidence opens the way for conspiracy. His letter ends, "If thou read this, O Caesar; thou mayst live;/ If not, the Fates with traitors do contrive."

COMMENT: Artemidorus was a "doctor of rhetoric in the Greek language, who, because of his profession, associated with certain of Brutus' confederates, knew most of their practices against Caesar," according to Plutarch. This explains how Artemidorus was in a position to learn of the plot. Suspense is created by establishing the fact that the plot against Caesar is in danger of failure. The letter suggests that Caesar's failure to recognize the conspiracy will be a result of hubris or overconfidence, of presuming to be immortal like the gods, who alone are secure in their immortality. Calpurnia has already warned Caesar against overconfidence, but he has chosen to ignore her. This presumptuous sense of security on Caesar's part will prevent him from reading the second warning.

Act II: Scene iv

On the morning of the ides of March, Portia stands before the house of Brutus, directing her servant Lucius to run to the Senate House. Having been informed of the assassination plot by Brutus, she is visibly distraught over the possible danger to her husband should his plans

miscarry. The boy asks what errand he is to perform at the Senate, and Portia realizes that she cannot tell. How hard it is for a woman to keep a secret, Portia reflects, for although she has a man's mind, she has only a woman's might. The bewildered servant asks if he must run to the Capitol and back again and do nothing else, but Portia, now composed, orders him to bring her word if Brutus looks well, for he seemed sick when he left.

Portia imagines she hears a "bustling rumor" (uproar, report) from the Capitol, but it is only the Soothsayer who arrives on his way to the Capitol. Hoping to get news of him, Portia asks the Soothsayer which way he has been, but when she learns that he has just come from home, she asks him the time and inquires whether or not Caesar has gone to the Capitol. The Soothsayer replies that Caesar has not gone yet; he adds that he himself is going to find a place to see Caesar pass on the way to the Senate. Portia wants to know if he has a suit with Caesar, to which, he replies that he is going to "beseech him to befriend himself." Fearfully, Portia asks if the Soothsayer knows of any harm intended toward Caesar, and she is told that the Soothsayer *knows* of no harm intended but *fears* there will be some. He excuses himself, saying that he must find a good spot before the crowds gather.

After he leaves, Portia complains about the weakness of the woman's heart, "O Brutus!/ The heavens speed thee in thine enterprise." Fearing that the boy has overheard her prayer, she adds that "Brutus hath a suit/ That Caesar will not grant." She grows faint and, forgetting her former errand, tells the boy to run to Brutus, inform him that she is well, and return with word of what he says.

COMMENT: This brief scene serves as another stage in the building of suspense for the crucial action of the assassination. The dramatization of Portia's anxiety creates a sympathetic emotional response to her own impatience and fears over the outcome of the plot, as she nearly gives the plans away several times during this brief interval. The arrival of the Soothsayer and the disclosure of his prophetic warning adds to the cumulative effect of the suspense which is being created. The prophet's warning to Caesar in the following scene is prepared for at this point, and it is seen that Caesar will have still another opportunity to "befriend himself," as mortals must. By the time that Caesar overconfidently rejects each of the warnings prepared for him, it will be clearly understood that Caesar has been chastised (warned by the gods) and that vengeance is in order. Caesar, as much as Brutus, is responsible for his own tragic fate.

Act III: Scene i

Brutus, Cassius, Casca, Decius Brutus, Metellus, Trebonius, Cinna, Antony, Lepidus, Popilius, Peblius, and others accompany Caesar through the streets to the Capitol. A crowd has gathered to watch the procession, among them Artemidorus and the Soothsayer. As Caesar and his train pass, Caesar sees the Soothsayer in the crowd and confidently reminds him that "the ides of March are come." "Ay, Caesar," replies the Sooth-sayer, "but not gone." Artemidorus then comes forward and begs Caesar to read his note, but Decius hastily intervenes with another note, asking Caesar to read Trebonius' suit at his leisure. Impetuously, Artemidorus demands that Caesar read his first, for it is of personal importance to Caesar. Magnanimously, Caesar replies, what concerns Caesar himself will be read last. When Artemidorus insists again, Caesar indignantly exclaims, "What! is this fellow mad?" Cassius steps in and chides Artemidorus for presenting petitions in the streets; the Capitol is the proper place for such things.

COMMENT: Caesar has just gone down for the third time. He has overruled Calpurnia's fears, confidently mocked the Soothsayer, and now indignantly rejects Artemidorus' plea that Caesar think of himself. His arrogance on these matters is his own contribution to the tragedy which must now ensue.

Caesar goes up to the Senate House, followed by the crowd. Popilius whispers good luck to Cassius on his enterprise, but when the startled Cassius asks, "What enterprise, Popilius?" the senator simply replies, "Fare you well" and advances toward Caesar. Cassius tells Brutus of Popilius' ambiguous remarks and expresses his fear that their conspiracy has been discovered. He vows that if the plot is unsuccessful, he will kill himself. Brutus tells Cassius to be calm, for Popilius is smiling as he talks to Caesar and Caesar's face shows no sign of change.

COMMENT: Popilius' ambiguous remark brings the play to its height of suspense, for Cassius' guilty conscience causes him to give the most fearful interpretation to the senator's good wishes. As Popilius walks to Caesar's side and speaks to him, attention is focused on Cassius who watches Caesar. The fear of disclosure makes Cassius vow his own death, but at the peak of excitement, Brutus reads Caesar and the senator's faces. Be calm, Brutus urges, and we learn that the plot is still on. (According to Plutarch, Popilius told Cassius that their enterprise had already been betrayed, but Shakespeare, who certainly knew this historical fact, artfully rephrases Popilius' words so that their ambiguity will create a most intense dramatic moment.)

Cassius notices that the plan is beginning to work, for Trebonius is drawing Antony out of the way. Antony and Trebonius leave as the senators take their seats. Cassius asks for Metellus Cimber so that he can present his suit to Caesar, while Brutus urges the conspirators to press near Caesar and aid Metellus. Cinna tells Casca that he is to be the first one to strike Caesar. As Caesar calls the Senate to order, Metellus kneels before Caesar and begins a flattering address. Caesar cuts him short with a lengthy reply in which he asserts that Caesar is not like ordinary men who succumb to flattery and make childish decisions. He cannot be melted by praise from the "true quality" of a suit. He says that if Metellus is pleading for his brother who has been banished, Caesar will "spurn thee like a cur out of my way." Metellus asks if anyone else will aid his suit for his banished brother. Brutus comes forward and kisses Caesar's hand, saying that he does this not in flattery, but out of desire for Caesar to repeal the banishment of Publius Cimber. Next, Cassius humbly entreats Caesar, falling "low as to thy foot." But Caesar remains adamant.

In a piece of over-extended self-eulogy Caesar asserts, "I am constant as the Northern Star,/ Of whose true-fixed and resting quality/ There is no fellow in the firmament." Among men on earth, Caesar continues, "men are flesh and blood, and apprehensive;/ Yet in the number I do know but one/ That unassailable holds on his rank,/ Unshaked of motion; and that I am he." Publius Cimber shall remain banished, for Caesar cannot be moved. Cinna and Decius implore Caesar, but he dismisses them, uttering the most arrogant statement of all, "Hence! Wilt thou lift up Olympus?" Casca signals the attack, "Speak, hands, for me!" He stabs Caesar, and one by one, the other conspirators add their blows. Seeing Brutus among their number, the stricken Caesar cries, *Et tu, Brute? Then fall, Caesar.*

COMMENT: The assassination is one of the most dramatic moments on the Shakespearean stage. Metellus begins the action by petitioning for his brother's repeal from banishment. One by one, the conspirators join in the plea, kneeling abject and humble before the merciless ruler who shuns their petitions with arrogant boasts of his own firmness of decision and constancy. As Caesar extravagantly compares himself to the brightest star of all, he is surrounded by kneeling figures who seem to inflate the already immoderate sense of his own worth. Caesar's self-praise grows stronger and more intemperate; he above all men is "unassailable." The assailants bide their time. Ignobly dismissed by Caesar, who now reaches the height of arrogance and blasphemy as he likens himself to an Olympian god, Casca signals the attack.

Caesar's merciless response to his petitioners, his abuse of power, his arrogant self-praise, have worked on the passions of the audience as well as the conspirators, and Casca's death blow comes as a welcome relief from the madness of self-inflation which Caesar has imparted. Once stricken, however, Caesar becomes the object of total sympathy. *"Et tu, Brute?"* Even you, Brutus, the pathetic query of the fallen leader, three words, counteracts all the injury Caesar has done by his outrageously hubristic boasts. His friend's betrayal ends his will to live. "Then fall, Caesar." From this point on, Caesar's sins will be forgotten and only his noblest attributes will be remembered, suggesting that the play may be pointing to a political lesson, that a tyrant, however intolerable, is a force against disorder, which is far worse than tyranny.

As Caesar dies, the senators and people retreat in confusion. Cinna cries out, "Liberty! Freedom! Tyranny is dead!/ Run hence, proclaim, cry it about the streets." Cassius bids the conspirators to run to the common pulpits and call out "Liberty, freedom, and enfranchisement!" Casca encourages Brutus to go to the pulpit, and Decius urges Cassius to go also. Brutus and Cassius advise the senator Publius to leave, lest the people attack the conspirators and harm the aged senator. Brutus adds that no man should bear the consequences of the deed, except the conspirators themselves. Trebonius returns and tells his fellows that Antony had fled to his house amazed and that "Men, wives, and children stare, cry out, and run,/ As it were doomsday."

Brutus asks the Fates what is in store for the assassins now. Agreeing with Cassius that life involves the fear of death, Brutus declares that they are Caesar's friends for having cut off his life from years of fearing death. Then Brutus exhorts the conspirators to bathe their hands and arms in Caesar's blood, and with their swords besmeared with the blood, to walk into the market place, shouting "Peace, freedom, liberty!" Cassius envisions that in ages to come this noble scene will be enacted by nations yet unborn and in languages yet unknown. Brutus wonders how many times plays will be held portraying the bleeding of Caesar, who now lies by Pompey's statue, "No worthier than the dust!" And Cassius adds that in these plays of the future, they will be remembered as the men who gave liberty to their country.

COMMENT: The chaos and disorder which reigns immediately after the assassination is narrated by the conspirators. The silently amazed Publius, venerable senator of the Republic, represents the astounded confusion of the general public. Brutus' noble concern for Publius' age and safety, even in the passionate aftermath of the slaughter,

reveals the truly noble nature of the man, as does his claiming responsibility for the assassination and his willingness to yield to the decision of the Fates. Brutus' exhortation to the blood-bath is not expressive of the blood lust of the man but of his desire to treat the assassination as a sacrifice by the ritualistic smearing of the victim's blood on the priests of liberty and by showing the public that an offering has been made in the name of "Peace, freedom, and liberty."

Infused by the lofty purpose of their deed, Cassius and Brutus envision themselves as heroes of liberty who will be immortalized on the stages of nations (like England), which are yet unformed. Thus, the effects of the murder are shown from two points of view. The senate and the public flee in confusion or are paralyzed by astonishment, while the conspirators are inspired by the lofty purpose of their deed, which they imagine has ennobled their names and will receive the acclaim of all posterity.

The structural unity imparted to the play by the device of the dream and the arrangement of events is embedded in this scene. The blood-bath fulfills and explains Calpurnia's dream of the statue pouring blood, and the death of Caesar at the foot of Pompey's statue complements the initial reference in the play to Caesar's triumph over Pompey's blood. Visually, the statue of Pompey can now be seen standing in triumph over Caesar's blood.

The conspirators have decided to leave the Senate House with Brutus at their head when a servant of Antony's arrives. The servant says that Antony instructed him to kneel before Brutus and deliver the message that Antony loves and honors Brutus, that he feared, honored, and loved Caesar, and if Brutus can show him why Caesar deserved to die, "Mark Antony shall not love Caesar dead/ So well as Brutus living; but will follow/ The fortunes and affairs of noble Brutus." Brutus at once replies that his master is a wise and valiant Roman. He instructs the slave to fetch Antony to the Capitol to learn the cause of Caesar's murder and to tell him that by Brutus' honor, he will depart unharmed. While the servant runs to get Antony, Cassius tells Brutus that he fears Antony and that his fears very often prove correct.

Antony arrives, and ignoring Brutus, he addresses Caesar's body, "O mighty Caesar! Dost thou lie so low?/ Are all thy conquests, glories, triumphs, spoils,/ Shrunk to this little measure?" Then Antony asks who else must die and says that if he is marked for death, he will never be more ready than now. If he lived a thousand years, he would find no place, nor hour, nor weapon more pleasing than those which have accompanied Caesar's death, nor would he find executioners more fitting than those who are now "the choice and master spirits of this age."

COMMENT: Antony's arrival on the scene of the crime is partly out of loyalty to his master Caesar and partly out of the desire to effect a reconciliation with the assassins until he can muster the force to oppose them successfully. Although he says he is prepared to die, he has first made certain through his servant that Brutus promises him safe conduct. His flattering address to the killers then may be interpreted as the first cautious step in a counter-rebellion, and Cassius' misgivings over Antony seem to be falling "shrewdly to the purpose," to be proving true. Antony from this point on begins to display the dangerous and shrewd political judgment which Cassius has perceived in him. He is more than the lover of plays and music and all-night revels; he will be seen to be as calculating as Cassius, as persuasive as Decius Brutus, as noble and far more loyal than Brutus.

Brutus tells Antony not to beg for death, for although the conspirators appear to be bloody and cruel, their hearts are actually filled with pity for the general wrong done to Rome by Caesar. Antony is welcome to join their ranks. Cassius adds that Antony will have as much power to dispense favors in the new state as the conspirators do. Brutus asks Antony to await an explanation patiently until the people, who are beside themselves with fear, have been appeased; then he will explain why he who loved Caesar struck him down.

COMMENT: Once again we see the sharp contrast between Brutus and Cassius. The idealistic Brutus has been explaining Caesar's murder and Antony's welcome in terms of "our hearts" and "all kind love, good thoughts, and reverence." On the other hand, the practical Cassius realizes these words mean little to Antony and offers him some of the powers the insurgents have won.

Pretending to be satisfied with the assassins' wisdom in overthrowing Caesar, Antony takes the bloody hand of each of the men. Antony realizes that to the conspirators he must appear to be either a coward or a flatterer, and turning to the dead body of Caesar, he begs its forgiveness for befriending Caesar's enemies. He declares how unbecoming it is to the love he bore Caesar to make peace with the assassins in the very sight of the corpse; it would be more fitting to weep at the fall of Caesar, whom Antony now compares to a noble deer, run down and killed by a pack of hounds.

Cassius interrupts Antony's apology to Caesar, at which Antony begs his pardon for praising the dead man before his slayers. Still, Antony points out, his praise is slight; Caesar's enemies will do him as much credit. In a friend, however, Antony's words are merely passionless understatement. But Cassius is not prepared to blame Antony for praising Caesar; what he wants to

know is can Antony be counted on as one of his allies, or shall the conspirators go along their way without depending on Antony's support. Antony explains that he shook their hands in order to indicate his alliance with their cause, but the sight of Caesar did indeed sway him from that resolution. Therefore, Antony qualifies his pledge of friendship; he will join their ranks if they are able to supply reasons why and in what way Caesar was dangerous. Brutus promises that the reasons he will give Antony would satisfy him even if he were the son of Caesar himself.

COMMENT: Antony's eulogy over the body of Caesar includes a simile in which Caesar is compared to a hart and his murderers to hounds. The figure, however covert to the conspirators, is that Antony has likened them to dogs. We shall see shortly that this is exactly how he feels about them.

There may be a touch of historical irony in Brutus' promise to give reasons so satisfactory that even a son of Caesar would be satisfied. Although in this play Shakespeare makes no use of the fact that Caesar and Brutus' mother were lovers during the time when Brutus was born, the phrasing of Brutus' promise may be a subtle allusion to the unconfirmed report that Brutus was Caesar's bastard son.

Antony asks if he can deliver the funeral oration over Caesar's body in the market-place. Without any hesitation, Brutus agrees to Antony's request. Cassius pulls Brutus aside and cautions him not to allow Antony to speak. "You know not what you do," Cassius warns. Antony easily may stir up the people. Convinced of the justice of his crime, Brutus answers that he will speak first and tell the people the reasons for the murder of Caesar, and that Antony speaks with their permission, since they want Caesar to have "true rites and lawful ceremonies." Brutus is sure "it shall advantage more than do us wrong." Cassius says he still doesn't like it. Brutus then orders Antony not to blame the conspirators during his oration, but to speak good of Caesar without condemning his killers. Furthermore, he is to say he speaks with the insurgents' permission, and he must agree to speak after Brutus. Antony assents, and Brutus bids him to prepare the body and follow them. The conspirators go off, leaving Antony alone with the body.

COMMENT: Brutus is not a subtle man; he cannot imagine that Antony may be lying about joining their cause. Besides, he has such confidence in his own powers of reasoning that he believes he can convince Antony, the people, and even Caesar's son, if he had one, of the justice of his deed. Cassius continues to be suspicious and finds it more and more difficult to concur with Brutus' decisions. His strongest arguments, however, are based on feelings not reasons, and his only course in view of Brutus' idealism is to submit to it entirely.

Alone with the body, Antony speaks his true feelings to the corpse. He begs pardon for being so meek and gentle with Caesar's butchers. "Thou art the ruins of the noblest man/ That ever lived in the tide of time," Antony declares. He swears an oath so strong that he calls it "prophecy" over the gaping wounds of Caesar which "like dumb mouths, do ope their ruby lips/ To beg the voice and utterance of my tongue." The limbs of men shall be cursed for Caesar's death, domestic fury and civil strife shall spread through Italy. Blood, destruction, and other monstrosities of war will become such a familiar sight in the land that mothers will merely smile when they see their infants cut up by the hands of war. Caesar's spirit, with Ate (the hellish god of discord) at his side, shall range through the land and "Cry 'Havoc.'" And "this foul deed shall smell above the earth/ With carrion men, groaning for burial."

COMMENT: The soliloquy reveals Antony's true purpose in seeming to befriend the conspirators. He is anxious to give his prince a ceremonial burial before he musters forces and ranges through the land carrying destruction to the farthest reaches until Caesar's death has been avenged. The imagery in this speech is, perhaps, the most revolting imagery to be found in Shakespeare. It is designed to show the full extent of Antony's hatred and rage against "this foul deed." The images of civil chaos are grotesque and grisly in the extreme; mother's smiling at their quartered babes and dead men rotting above the ground, crying out for burials, are the horrible conceptions of an impassioned brain. These are the feelings of Antony as he looks at the gaping wounds of Caesar, which seem to him like repulsive yet appealing ruby lips, begging Antony for revenge.

Once more Cassius' suspicions fall "shrewdly to the purpose"; Antony intends to betray his new-made friendship. Brutus' judgment has been wrong again. There can be no good reasons to satisfy the angry spirit Antony has just displayed. The remainder of the play is foreshadowed by Antony's "prophecy"; civil strife and destruction will follow; Caesar's spirit will seek revenge.

Antony's harangue is ended by the arrival of a messenger whom Antony recognizes as the servant of Octavius Caesar. The messenger begins to relay his message, but when he sees the body of Caesar, he cries out. Tears welling in his eyes, Antony asks the slave if his master is coming and learns that Octavius is only seven leagues from Rome. Antony orders the slave to tell his master what has happened and to warn him that Rome is not safe for entry. On second thought, Antony decides to have the servant wait until after the funeral oration.

After they see how the people react to the murder, the slave may report to Octavius on the state of things. Then Antony and the servant carry Caesar's body off.

COMMENT: A new character, Octavius Caesar, is introduced just at the point when Julius Caesar is carried off. Octavius was the grand-nephew of Caesar, his son by adoption, and his first heir. He actually arrived in Rome a month after Caesar's demise and took his name Caesar only after he heard the terms of his uncle's will. His arrival at this point, however, as another Caesar, has obvious dramatic significance; he is meant to convey the idea that "Caesar" is not dead. (The king is dead; long live the king.) Octavius is generally known as Augustus (the revered one) after the title given him later by the people of Rome. Shakespeare ignores the exact chronology of historical facts, although he knew them well, because adherence to them would clearly interfere with the development of the plot and destroy the dramatic effect and thematic significance of Octavius' timely arrival.

SUMMARY: This scene brings the play to its first climax. The first two acts dealt with the events leading up to Caesar's death; the remainder of the play deals with the events leading to the death of Cassius and Brutus. The stage is set here for the action which follows the assassination.

Once Caesar has been killed, the focus of the play shifts to Brutus, whereas it has previously been on Caesar as well as Brutus. Brutus has been shown as a noble, honorable, and virtuous man who, because of these very qualities, is blind to reality and practicality. Brutus' role now changes from conspirator to victim, hunter to fugitive, and Antony's role expands as he plans action against Brutus. Brutus' blindness becomes more and more evident after this point. Caesar's excessive courage had made him blind to the normal precautions taken by men, while Brutus' excessive idealism now obscures his view of the practical reality of politics. Brutus' stubborn naivete, his tragic flaw, leads to his destruction, for his quick acceptance of Antony's friendship, despite the warnings of Cassius, is neither the first nor the last mistake in judgment that Brutus makes.

In this scene, Antony emerges as a loyal friend, but he is also a wily, conniving, vengeful, and ambitious man. He declares that he will plunge all Italy into civil war in order to avenge Caesar and actually does this in the play, while Brutus has been anxious that only the conspirators suffer for the assassination.

The death of Caesar so early in the play raises a legitimate question—who is the main character of *Julius Caesar*? Some critics maintain that Caesar is the focus of the entire play, the man being replaced by the spirit or ghost of Caesar after the assassination. Others insist that Brutus is the real tragic hero, that the focus is on him throughout the play, that the assassination is the first climax of his career, and that the remainder of the play leads to a second climax in Brutus' downfall and death. Still others suggest that this is a play without a hero, that Shakespeare's point of view was ambigious, and that he was examining the many aspects of civil insurrection. The decision finally falls into the hands of each reader, for Shakespeare, above all else, was conscious of his audience, an extremely mixed breed of men comprised of members from all levels of social, economic, and intellectual life. His plays communicate with people on all levels because Shakespeare designed them to do just that and their durability may be directly attributed to the fact that Shakespeare had the genius of ambiguity, the power to suggest different meanings to different men of different times. Perhaps the problems of the climax, the play's hero, and its unity, should be confronted stoically with the thoughts Shakespeare put into the mouth of Cicero: "But men may construe things after their fashion, Clean from the purpose of the things themselves" (I. iii).

Act III: Scene ii

Later on the same day, the ides of March, throngs of citizens crowd the Forum of Rome. They are angry and fearful at Caesar's death. When Brutus and Cassius arrive, some among them cry, "We will be satisfied! Let us be satisfied." Brutus divides the crowd so that some stay to hear him speak, while others go off to listen to Cassius. Brutus begins to speak in a dry, emotionless prose. Logically and coldly, he appeals to the wisdom and judgment of the crowd, asking them to trust his honor so that they may believe his reasons. First he addresses "any in this assembly, any dear friend of Caesar's," to whom Brutus says that his own love for Caesar was no less than his. If then that friend demand why Brutus rose against Caesar, this is the answer: "Not that I loved Caesar less, but that I loved Rome more." He declares that Caesar would have enslaved them if he had lived, and asks them if they would rather be slaves and have Caesar alive or be free men and have Caesar dead. He tells the mob: "As Caesar loved me, I weep for him; as he was fortunate, I rejoice at it; as he was valiant, I honor him, but as he was ambitious, I slew him." He asks any so base as to be a slave to speak up, or any so rude as to be other than a Roman, or any "so vile as will not love his country?" Brutus then asserts that the reason for Caesar's death is a matter of official record in the books of the Senate.

As Antony appears with the body of Caesar, Brutus announces that Antony, although he had no part in the slaying, will receive all the benefits of Caesar's death, a place in the commonwealth, as shall all the crowd. Finally, he closes his speech with the words, "As I slew my best lover for the good of Rome, I have the same dagger for myself, when it shall please my country to need my death." Moved by Brutus' oratory, the crowd cries, "Live, Brutus! Live, live!" Some of the citizens suggest that they build a statue of Brutus. Another exclaims, "Let him be Caesar." Brutus silences the mob and asks them all to stay and hear Antony praise Caesar. Before he leaves, he orders that none depart before Antony finishes his speech, save himself.

COMMENT: Brutus' speech is typical of his own fallacious reasoning. He naively believes that by claiming honor for his name his deed will be accepted as honorable. He feels that by calling Caesar ambitious, he has given clear and cogent reasons for Caesar's death. He believes that the mob will be won over by the simple explanation of his motives, and, indeed, they are. But the mob is not won by any reasoning they have heard; Brutus has flattered them by addressing them as equals, by claiming his concern for their liberty, and by forcing them to deny that they are base, uncultivated, unpatriotic slaves. He has moved the passions of the crowd by his theatrical promise to kill himself if it should please the country, and he hopes to show the mob how noble and just he really is by demanding that Caesar's funeral oration gets a respectful hearing. As for the reasons for Caesar's murder, the mob learns only that Caesar was "ambitious." They are easily persuaded by the tricks of oratory, although Brutus has made a sincere speech which he thinks reasonable. The crowd, however, has missed Brutus point, for although he has intimated that he has freed them from the bondage of a monarch, shouts are raised that Brutus should be crowned, immortalized by a statue, or be made Caesar himself. They have no idea of the point of the murder and are only aware that Brutus is an honorable and agreeable man who likes Romans and hates ambition.

Antony, however, is not a man of the crowd. He listens carefully as Brutus speaks, finds no satisfaction in Brutus' "reasons," and prepares a shrewd and ironic rebuttal for his funeral speech.

Brutus' naive political judgment is nowhere more evident than at the moment when he turns the mob over to Antony, when he gives Antony the last word and leaves the scene entirely, foolishly trusting that all will go as he has ordered it without his personal supervision, and foolishly believing that his personal idealism and fallacious reasoning will prevail with Antony as well as with the crowd.

As Antony makes his way to the pulpit, one citizen exclaims, "'Twere best he speak no harm of Brutus here," while another cries out, "This Caesar was a tyrant," and another answers, "Nay, that's certain,/ We are blest that Rome is rid of him." Antony mounts the pulpit and begins his speech: "Friends, Romans, countrymen, lend me your ears;/ I come to bury Caesar, not to praise him." Antony declares that the evil which men do lives after them, not their good; "So let it be with Caesar." Pretending thus to agree with Brutus, Antony continues, "The noble Brutus/ Hath told you Caesar was ambitious: If it were so, it was a grievous fault." (He does not state it was so.) Antony repeats again and again that Brutus has called Caesar ambitious, "and Brutus is an honorable man." The speech continues to relate how Caesar wept when the poor cried out. "Ambition should be made of sterner stuff:/ Yet Brutus says he was ambitious;/ And Brutus is an honorable man." Antony reminds the crowd that Caesar had refused the crown three times at the Lupercal. "Yet Brutus says he was ambitious;/ And sure, he is an honorable man." Antony reminds his listeners that they all loved Caesar once and not without cause. What keeps them from mourning him now, Antony exclaims, crying, "O judgment, thou art fled to brutish beasts,/And men have lost their reason!" Bursting with emotion, Antony mourns, "My heart is in the coffin there with Caesar,/ And I must pause till it come back to me."

As Antony weeps, the plebeians comment on his remarks. There is reason in them, one plebeian observes. "He would not take the crown; / Therefore 'tis certain he was not ambitious." Another, totally converted to Antony's cause, asserts, "There's not a nobler man in Rome than Antony."

COMMENT: Antony's skill in verse and dramatic presentation displayed throughout the oration may be attributed to his love for plays and music. These arts were regarded as important aspects in the education of a Renaissance prince or statesman-orator, a value effectively displayed in Antony's verbal victory over the mob.

Antony does not present a direct line of reasoning at first but uses irony, implication, and constant repetition. Hoping to strike home his point that the only proof of Caesar's ambition which Brutus has offered is that Brutus, a man of honor, says that Caesar was ambitious, Antony works the idea of Caesar's ambition and Brutus' honor into every other line. He alternates ironical allusions to Brutus' honor with concrete instances of Caesar's generosity, public concern, and lack of ambition. The he applies reason to the emotional brew he is concocting. If Caesar was ambitious, why did he refuse the crown three times. The crowd is in no position to consider the question rationally for they had actually forced him to reject it by cheering his refusals. Instead, they draw the conclusions which Antony desires. To make the dam of public opinion burst, Antony theatrically weeps over Caesar's coffin. He appeals to the sympathy of the crowd, dropping real tears and growing red in the eyes. Many plebeians are moved; one is totally won over, but the speech goes on until every last man in the crowd is a frenzied avenger.

Having composed himself, Antony begins to speak again. He says that he means not to inflame them against the conspirators, for they are all honorable men. Then he produces Caesar's will from his cloak, and holds it up for the people to see. Antony says he cannot read the will, since if he does, "they would go and kiss dead Caesar's wounds,/ And dip their napkins in his sacred blood." A citizen shouts out for Antony to read the will. He refuses again, saying that if he reads the will, they would find out how much Caesar loved them, and the knowledge would inflame them and make them mad. The same citizen cries out again for the will to be read. Antony calls for patience and ironically says that he has gone too far: "I fear I wrong the honorable men/ Whose daggers have stabbed Caesar: I do fear it." Another citizen cries, "They are traitors. Honorable men!" Still another shouts, "They were villains, murderers. The will! Read the will!" Antony finally consents to read the will and tells the crowd to make a ring about Caesar's body so that he can show them him who made the will.

COMMENT: Part of the crowd had already been won over when Antony paused to weep. Recovering his composure and continuing in an ironic vein, Antony claims that he doesn't want a counter-rebellion, while this is actually his very desire. But Antony draws from a large bag of rhetorical tricks and next produces Caesar's will, which he refuses to read. Thus, he works on the curiosity of the crowd until they are eating out of his hand. When the citizens persist long enough, Antony promises to read but does not do so at once. The reading requires staging to be most effective, Antony knows. The plebeians must gather around the corpse, and they eagerly do so. Thus, the hostile crowd has been subdued and seduced. Brutus' argument for Caesar's killing has been successfully undermined by Antony's insinuations by the time the citizens, like children anxious to hear a story, form a circle around the coffin.

Antony descends from the pulpit and comes down to Caesar's body. He takes Caesar's cloak in his hand and begins to speak. He says that Caesar first put on this cloak on the day he conquered the Gallic tribe, the Nervii. He points to a tear in the cloak and says, "Look in this place ran Cassius' dagger through./ See what a rent the envious Casca made." Then he points to the wound that Brutus made and explains, "Brutus, as you know, was Caesar's angel:/ Judge, O you gods, how dearly Caesar loved him!/ This was the most unkindest cut of all;/ For, when the noble Caesar saw him stab,/ Ingratitude, more strong than traitors' arms,/ Quite vanquish'd him. Then burst his mighty heart,/ And, in his mantle muffling up his face,/ Even at the base of Pompey's statue/ (Which all the while ran blood), great

Caesar fell." Then Antony openly calls the bloody deed treason. The crowd is weeping now over Caesar's mutilated clothing, and Antony asks why they weep over mere clothing. "Look you here! Here is himself, marred as you see with traitors." Dramatically, Antony reveals Caesar's corpse to the horror-stricken view of the public.

COMMENT: Now that Antony knows the crowd is on his side, he proceeds to arouse their wrath against the conspirators. He uses visual aids to illustrate well-known anecdotes. He displays Caesar's cloak, torn by foul wounds and tells them it was worn against the Nervii to remind the crowd of Caesar's glories. Next Antony makes them visualize the slaughter by describing how the rents in the cloak were made and by naming a conspirator for each hole. The fact that Antony did not witness the murder has no bearing on his oratory. Antony's indictment of the conspirators becomes open at this point, and the plebeians who had warned him not to speak ill of Brutus are now ready to tear Brutus limb from limb. Effectively and completely, Antony has won over the mob, but he is not finished yet. He must direct them to action.

At the point when Antony drops his irony and openly calls the conspirators traitors, the crowd becomes angry and ugly. The citizens shout, "Revenge! About! Seek! Burn! Fire! Kill! Slay! Let not a traitor live!" But Antony cries halt and, resuming his irony, he says this murder was the deed of honorable men. He adds that he is not an orator like Brutus and that he speaks with the leave of the conspirators, who know very well that Antony has "neither wit, nor words, nor worth,/ Action, nor utterance, nor the power of speech to stir men's blood." He only tells the crowd what they already know and shows Caesar's wounds so they can speak for him. He adds, "But were I Brutus,/ And Brutus Antony, there were an Antony/ Would ruffle up your spirits, and put a tongue/ In every wound of Caesar, that should move/ The stones of Rome to rise and mutiny." The suggestion planted, the citizens shout out, "We'll mutiny." One citizen suggests, "We'll burn the house of Brutus." As the citizens are about to leave the Forum and begin the pillaging of the murderers' houses, Antony calls halt again, for they have forgotten the will which Antony was going to read. Antony then reads: "To every Roman citizen he gives/ To every several man, seventy-five drachmas" (about one hundred fifty dollars in modern purchasing power). A citizen calls out, "Most noble Caesar! We'll revenge his death." Antony continues, "Moreover, he hath left you all his walks,/ His private arbors, and new-planted orchards,/ On this side Tiber; he hath left them you,/ And to your heirs for ever-common pleasures,/ To

walk abroad, and recreate yourselves./ Here was a Caesar! When comes such another?"

The citizens are now wild with fury; they pile up benches, tables, and stalls from the Forum to use as fuel for Caesar's funeral pyre, which they plan to erect in a holy place. The crowd leaves with the body of Caesar to bring it to the holy place for cremation. Antony muses to himself over the results of his speech, "Now let it work. Mischief, thou art afoot,/ Take thou what course thou wilt."

COMMENT: Antony has played the crowd as he might a flute, sounding them and stopping them at will. He has used wit, words, worth, action, utterance, and "the power of speech to stir men's blood" (all the rhetorical tricks which, ironically, he claimed he did not have) to work the crowd into a frenzy of passion, to set mischief afoot, as he remarks in his Machiavellian aside.

A servant enters with a message that Octavius has already arrived in Rome. He and Lepidus are at Caesar's house. Antony replies that he will come at once, that Octavius' arrival is like the granting of a wish. "Fortune is merry," Antony remarks, and so is Antony. The servant reports that he has heard that Brutus and Cassius "are rid like madmen through the gates of Rome." To this, Antony remarks, "Belike they had some notice of the people,/ How I had moved them." Antony and the servant leave for the house of Caesar where Octavius awaits them.

SUMMARY: The first climax of the play having been reached and the action having been pointed in the direction of revenge and civil disorder, as Antony had prophesied, the second scene of Act III works as a transition between the two phases of the plot, the murder and the revenge.

The capriciousness of the mob had been prepared for in the first scene of the play. Thoughtlessly, the mob had turned out to celebrate Caesar's triumph over Pompey whom they had formerly loved. Now they are moved by Brutus, the betrayer of Caesar, not by reason but out of thoughtless respect for Brutus' honor. Just as rapidly as they turned to Brutus' views, so do they turn to Antony's. But Antony has the shrewd judgment of a practiced orator and public manipulator. He does not let his audience go until they are so enraged that they will not listen to the simplest reason or answer the simplest plea for mercy. Worked to a frenzy by Antony's "mischief," the mob goes off crying "havoc." Antony's prophesy over the body of Caesar has moved toward fulfillment, and the plebeians' irrational behavior in the next scene has been prepared for amply.

The two speeches given in this scene are designed to contrast their speakers and their oratorical styles. Brutus' speech, in prose, is terse, emotionless; it appeals to the cool judgment of men, although its reasoning is questionable. Antony's speech, in verse, is emotional, lengthy, dramatic; it makes use of wit, repetition, action, visual effects. Antony makes his listeners participate in the development of his argument by pausing frequently to give them time to react, by drawing them into a circle around Caesar's body, by making them recall a famous victory in which, as Romans, they had shared Caesar's glory.

A new powerful side of Antony's character is revealed in this scene. This is a far shrewder Antony than we have seen before, when he followed at the heels of Caesar, a fat, sleek-headed fellow, given to pleasures. Then he was simply a man to be trusted, but his taste for the arts suggested his nobler parts; now his loyalty in friendship, his skill in oratory, his ability to know men (perhaps, learned from Caesar) come to the fore.

Brutus is seen in the first stages of his decline. His faulty reasoning and his poor judgment of men combine with his overconfidence in the virtues of reason and lofty idealism and make him reject the minor vices which must be practiced in persuasive oratory. His prose reflects his dry, rational approach to life and contrasts sharply with Antony's musical verse, his use of dramatic effects, and his moist appeal to emotionality which is the secret of his rhetoric.

Caesar or the spirit of Caesar is the subject of both orations. From Brutus's point of view, we hear that Caesar was ambitious; from Antonys' that he was glorious, victorious, tender, generous. Caesar speaks to the people once more when Antony reads his will aloud. Although dead in body, Caesar's spirit remains, and his shrewd political judgment is revealed in his final bequest. The good that Caesar does will live after him in the gift of money, parks, and pleasures that he bequeathes the people.

At the close of the scene, the meeting of Antony, Lepidus, and Octavius hints at the force which is mustering to destroy the conspirators and prepares us for the action of Acts IV and V.

. . . a bachelor." An enraged citizen interprets this as an insult to married men and promises to beat Cinna for calling him a fool. Cinna then reports that he is going to Caesar's funeral as a friend. When he answers that his name is Cinna, one citizen cries, "He is a conspirator, tear him to pieces." Cinna protests that he is Cinna the poet, not Cinna the conspirator. But another citizen, completely unreasonable, shouts, "Tear him for his bad verses." When Cinna again pleads that he is the poet, still another plebeian answers, "It is no matter, his name's Cinna! Pluck but his name out of his heart, and turn him going." Madly they set upon the helpless poet, and when they have finished rending him, they charge off to burn the houses of Brutus, Cassius, Decius, and the rest.

COMMENT: Cinna was a distinguished poet, a close friend of Caesar, and a tribune of the people. He is not portrayed here in his historical personage but as the Elizabethan stereotype of the court poet of ancient Rome. The poet, it was held among the ancients, had powers of prophecy and the ability to envision the future in their imaginations. Cinna the poet, musing over his ominous dream, shows these legendary powers.

The ancient poet was also a satirist of the people and his times. Cinna in this scene indulges in some trivial foolery over the wisdom of remaining a bachelor, a familiar jest both in ancient times and in our own.

The crowd is in no humor to be amused, and Cinna's wit is taken as an insult to married men. Even so, no reason is necessary to turn the inflamed mob against the first victim they find in the streets. Antony had promised Caesar revenge and a quota of horrible slaughter, which the plebeians are now prepared to take. The spirit of the mob, created in the preceding scene, is dramatized in the tearing of Cinna. In addition, Cinna's ominous dream introduces the theme of murder just as Calpurnia's dream anticipated Caesar's slaughter. Omens will continue to be used as forecasts of death and destruction for the remainder of the play.

Act III: Scene iii

Later that day on the ides of March, Cinna the poet is seen on a street near the Forum. As he walks along, he muses over a dream he has had in which he feasted with Caesar. Now omens of evil are charging his imagination. He does not wish to go out of doors, but something leads him forward. A band of citizens suddenly appears and question Cinna; asking his name, where he is going, where he lives, and if he is married or a bachelor. Wittily Cinna replies that he is "wisely

Act IV: Scene i

The scene now shifts to a room in Antony's house where Antony, Octavius, and Lepidus are holding council. They are found in the middle of their discussion, deciding who is to be killed in the reign of terror which they are about to begin. Octavius tells Lepidus, "Your brother too must die. Consent you, Lepidus?" Lepidus consents "upon condition that Publius shall not live,/ Who is your sister's son, Mark Antony." Antony calmly agrees to this. Antony then sends Lepidus to Caesar's house to fetch Caesar's will to see if they can eliminate some of the heirs.

COMMENT: The meeting of the Caesarist party parallels the earlier meeting held by Brutus' faction. Here as there, an elimination list has been proposed; it is being decided who may be hostile to the party and must die because of it. Unlike Brutus, Antony is calmly prepared to execute his enemies, even his own sister's son, Publius.

(Historically, it was Lucius Caesar, Antony's uncle, who was marked for death in this way. Shakespeare's distortion of this historical fact serves the special purpose of emphasizing the inhumanity and villainy which insurrection fosters. By making Antony condemn his own nephew, Shakespeare shows the cruelty of which Antony is capable, for in ancient Rome, a sister's son was generally raised and adopted by men of repute and often became the heirs of their uncle's great estates. Hence, Antony's consent to Publius' death is as unnatural as a father's execution of his own son.)

In view of Antony's Machiavellian behavior, the deals he makes over the lives of Lepidus' brother and his own nephew calls Antony's honor into question, and his ironic regard for Brutus who "is an honorable man" begins to suggest this double irony that Brutus is really honorable, and that Antony does think so, although he pretends not to for the political purpose of rabble-rousing.

As Lepidus leaves, Antony tells Octavius that Lepidus has little merit as a man and is only fit to do errands. He asks if it is right that this man should get a third part of the world. Octavius answers that Antony seemed to think well of Lepidus when he asked his advice about the proscription lists. But Antony replies he has been using Lepidus as a scapegoat on whom the blame for the murders may be placed later on. Lepidus follows where they lead, or leads where they tell him to go. He will be discarded like an ass set to pasture when it has delivered its burden. Octavius leaves these plans up to Antony, but interjects that Lepidus is a tried and valiant soldier. Antony insists once more that Lepidus can only be regarded as property like a horse. Then he reports that Brutus and Cassius are beginning to gather their forces and that now is the time for unity and for taking council. Octavius assents and they leave to make plans.

COMMENT: The meeting of Antony's party, which has been taken up at mid-point, is to be understood as the one in which the second triumvirate was formed. That is, the three men were to govern Rome with the advice of the Senate.

Antony's machine-like mind continues to be portrayed in his feelings over Lepidus. He shows how little he values men, even those whose service has been courageous and loyal. He believes in using men as he uses animals to serve his own ambitions and needs.

In contrast to Brutus' meeting with the conspirators earlier in the play, Antony has his cohorts well in hand. When suggestions are raised, he yields and consents to them. There are no half-way measures for the practical ruler. At the same time, Lepidus agrees fully to Antony's proposals, and Octavius accedes to Antony's plan to discard Lepidus even though he regards him as a tried and valiant soldier. However brutal the triumvirate may seem, there is far more unity and promise of success in their alliance than was seen among Brutus' conspirators.

SUMMARY: In this scene, Antony is revealed as a cruel, conniving and ambitious man, an opportunist who will seize the first chance he gets to gain full control over Rome. The cruelty of the entire triumvirate is manifest in the ambitious nature of each of its members, and their plan to attack Brutus and Cassius is motivated as much out of the desire for power as for revenge. Thus, Antony, once the friend and pupil of Caesar, is now seen in the light of his unscrupulous ambition; Octavius who is docile for the moment is shown as the willing accomplice in the quest for power; Lepidus who goes off on his errand like the mule Antony calls him promises to be little competition to the two dominant members of the triumvirate. Caesar's ambition, the spirit of Caesarism, lives on in these two.

The triumvirate's council works as a contrast and balance to the meeting of the conspirators in Brutus' garden. The differences to be noted are that Antony shows the powers of calculation which Cassius has, but he has the power to influence his cohorts which Cassius does not have. Octavius takes things at face value as Brutus does, but he is acquiescent to the political wisdom of the acknowledged leader of the triumvirate.

Two new characters are introduced in this scene as complements to Antony and as a balance and contrast to Brutus' team. Antony's cool nature resembles that of Cassius; Octavius' naivete is balanced by Brutus'; and Lepidus' fatuity parallels Casca's.

Act IV: Scene ii

The scene now shifts to a camp near Sardis where Brutus' army has pitched its tents. Drums are sounded as Brutus arrives before his tent accompanied by Lucilius, Titinius, and other soldiers. Lucius, Brutus' servant, is also present. Lucilius has just returned from a visit to Cassius' camp, accompanied by Pindarus. Brutus tells Pindarus that his master Cassius has given him some cause to wish "things done, undone." Pindarus replies that his master will appear "such as he is, full of regard and honor." Brutus then asks Lucilius how he was received by Cassius, and Lucilius explains that he was received with courtesy and respect, but not with the old familiarity that Cassius used to show. Brutus tells Lucilius that he has witnessed a "hot friend cooling," and he compares Cassius to a horse which seems spirited at the start but quickly falls under trial of battle. He then learns from Lucilius that Cassius' army will be camping at Sardis that night.

COMMENT: Attention is shifted from the triumvirate planning its action against Brutus to Brutus' camp, where the insurgents are preparing to fight Antony's forces. Servants arrive to report Cassius' arrival and information is exchanged which suggests that discord between Cassius and Brutus has grown since our last view of them. Brutus' feelings toward Cassius are expressed when he compares his ally to a horse, hot at the start, unreliable in the finish, and the comparison works as a link to the previous scene in which Antony compared Lepidus to a horse and as a foreshadowing of subsequent events in which Cassius will prove unreliable in battle, quick to admit complete defeat, and overly hasty in suicide. Such figures of language force comparisons to be made, work as binding elements among the scenes, and supply much of the unity of the play, which is often difficult to see on the surface. It is intended next that the conflict between the Republican conspirators be compared and contrasted with the momentary harmony of the triumvirate.

Cassius enters with several soldiers and greets Brutus with the words, "Most noble brother, you have done me wrong." He accuses Brutus of hiding his wrongs under "this sober form of yours." Brutus reminds Cassius of his hasty temper and tells him not to wrangle in front of their two armies. Both armies are led off some distance as Brutus and Cassius enter the tent where Brutus regally promises, "I will give you audience."

COMMENT: The argument which ensues in the next scene is anticipated by Cassius' greeting to Brutus and his charge that Brutus hides his wrongs under the appearance of virtue. Cassius has changed since his last appearance; his irascible behavior during the subsequent argument is predicted when Brutus alludes to Cassius' rash temper and urges Cassius not to speak before their men. Brutus is seen to be in control of the situation; he is more confident and self-assured than ever, but his political naivete shows no improvement here or in the subsequent scene. This hint of discord between the conspirators will be confirmed and the suggestion of defeat, which accompanies discord, will prevail from this point on.

Act IV: Scene iii

Inside the tent, Cassius tells Brutus he has been wronged because Brutus has condemned Lucius Pella for taking bribes from the Sardians, even after Cassius had sent letters entreating him not to dismiss Pella. Cassius adds that this is not the time to scrutinize and rigidly censure every petty or trifling offense. Brutus reproaches Cassius for selling offices to undeserving men for gold. At this, Cassius becomes infuriated and says that if anyone but Brutus had told him this, he would have been killed on the spot. Speaking of corruption, Brutus says that Cassius himself has set the example among his men and has escaped punishment only because of his high position. Brutus reminds Cassius of the ides of March, how they had struck down Caesar, the foremost man of all the world, for the sake of justice. He asks if they should now "contaminate our fingers with base bribes." Brutus argues, "I had rather be a dog, and bay the moon,/ Than such a Roman." "Brutus, bait not me;/ I'll not endure it," Cassius warns. He adds that Brutus forgets himself when he attempts to restrain Cassius' actions, for Cassius is a more experienced soldier and more able "to make conditions," that is to make bargains with men and officers. Indignantly, Brutus retorts that Cassius is not more able; Cassius insists he is; Brutus contradicts. Cassius warns Brutus to provoke him no farther, but Brutus insists that Cassius had better listen, since he will not be silenced by Cassius' rash temper. When he asserts that he cannot be frightened by a madman, Cassius exclaims, "O ye gods, ye gods! Must I endure all this?" Viciously, Brutus warns Cassius that he will defy him until "you shall digest the venom of your spleen," and he promises that Cassius will be the object of his ridicule from this day forth. Sarcastically, Brutus urges Cassius to prove he is a "better soldier," for he is anxious to learn from "noble men." Cassius protests, "I said, an elder soldier, not a better." He asserts that Caesar dared not treat him so, and Brutus replies that Cassius had not dared to provoke him as he dares Brutus now. Now at the peak of his anger, Cassius threatens, "Do not presume too much upon my love;/ I may do that I shall be sorry for." Brutus replies arrogantly that Cassius has already done what he should be sorry for and that his threats have no terror for Brutus, "for I am arm'd so strong in honesty/ That they pass by me as the idle wind." Next Brutus complains that Cassius did not send him any of the gold which he had badly needed, for he cannot raise money by vile means, that is, by extorting it from local peasants. Cassius claims that he did not deny Brutus the gold but that the messenger who delivered his reply was a fool. Cassius charges that Brutus no longer loves him, for he refuses to tolerate Cassius' weaknesses and makes them even greater than they are. Cassius unsheathes his dagger, and, handing it to Brutus, he says, "I, that denied thee gold, will give my heart:/ Strike, as thou didst at Caesar, for, I know,/ When thou didst hate him worst, thou lovedst him better/ Than ever thou lovedst Cassius."

COMMENT: During the entire argument, Brutus shows that he is still incapable of managing men. He is too truthful, too "sober," too noble to resort to practical necessities of war. He has become arrogant and overconfident, on the one hand, denying Cassius' superiority as a soldier and as a raiser of funds, and on the other hand admitting that he is unable to raise his own money, which he regards not as a soldierly weakness but as a sign of his noble nature. Cassius' methods of appointing officers and raising money are corrupt but practical. The incorruptible Brutus, however, will not engage in practical immorality.

The argument of the two men follows the childish pattern of insistence, denial, insistence, denial. "You did," "I didn't," children might say. The heroic assassins of the mighty Caesar behave like children who have lost a tyrannical father and unconsciously suggest that Caesar, at least, had maintained harmony among these children. The irrational argument, furthermore, displays both men in a state of angry madness, which, the ancients believed, was inflicted upon men whom the gods would destroy.

The pride Brutus takes in his unassailable honesty is reminiscent of Caesar's pride in his unassailable constancy just before he was killed and presages the imminent destruction of Brutus himself. Brutus taunts Cassius with his own virtuous honesty and his immunity to threats: "I am arm'd so strong in honesty," etc. To the audience, the effect is shocking; to Cassius, it is maddening. Pressed to his limit, Cassius bares his breast and, like Caesar, is prepared to die because he has lost Brutus' love. The harshness Brutus had displayed in his ability to subordinate his personal feelings to his ideal of good in the slaying of Caesar is reasserted in his cruel abuse of his friend Cassius.

This famous Quarrel Scene is one of the best exhibits in Shakespeare of his knowledge of human nature; it has won the praise and interest of critics through the ages and has moved even those who did not like *Julius Caesar* as a whole.

Seeing Cassius with his bosom bared and his dagger offered for his death, Brutus apologetically tells Cassius to sheathe his dagger and "be angry when you will." Brutus compares himself to a lamb that carries anger only briefly as a flint afire one moment is cold the next. Brutus is sorry he has laughed at Cassius' weakness of temperament, promises to tolerate it in the future, and the friends are reconciled.

Suddenly, there is a disturbance outside the door. A poet is trying to gain admittance to the tent on the grounds that he must stop the quarrel within, for the two generals should not be alone at such a time. Lucilius, who has been guarding the entry, refuses to admit the poet, but the poet insists, "Nothing but death shall stay me." Cassius appears and inquires the poet's errand and learns, through some doggerel verses, that someone who is older than either of the generals knows it is not fitting for them to fight. Cassius laughs at the poet and at the inferior quality of the rhymes, but Brutus is annoyed and says that foolish poets are out of place in war. Although Cassius is tolerant of the new fashion of taking poets to war, Brutus orders the poet to be gone. Then Brutus orders Lucilius and Titinius to bid the officers to make camp for the night, and Cassius adds that Messala is to be brought to them immediately.

COMMENT: The reconciliation having been effected when both parties admit they have been ill-tempered, the tension is released by the poet who bursts in and anti-climactically attempts to effect the reconciliation which has already been made. The poet's exaggerated vow to enter the general's tent or die is funny in itself, and his doggerel verses add to the comedy of the moment. However, the gist of the verses suggests the childishness which has been displayed during the quarrel, for the poet affects a kind of paternal authority over the disputants by claiming to "have seen more years" than they.

Cassius' response to the poet is characteristic. Although we have been told that Cassius rarely smiles, we have also learned that when he does, he smiles as if in self-mockery. The poet, whom Cassius calls a cynic (one who satirizes men), has enabled Cassius to smile at himself. Brutus, however, is a Stoic of sorts, who has never been "gamesome." Here he shows his complete lack of humor and his priggish sense of decorum when he orders the "saucy fellow, hence."

The poet gone, Brutus asks Lucius, his servant, for a bowl of wine. Cassius remarks that he did not think it was possible to make Brutus so angry. But Brutus explains that he hears many griefs. Cassius reminds Brutus to make use of his philosophy in facing evil events. Then calmly Brutus tells Cassius that Portia is dead. Amazed at this news, Cassius wonders how Brutus prevented himself from killing Cassius when he had crossed him so. He asks of what sickness Portia had died. Brutus replies that, impatient of his absence and seeing Mark Antony and Octavius grow strong, she killed herself by swallowing fire. Appalled, Cassius cries, "O ye immortal gods!"

COMMENT: The philosophy to which Cassius refers is Stoicism, a creed by which men accepted human events with resignation and quietude. Brutus' uncharacteristic anger is thus explained as the diversion of his grief over Portia's death. This is the first sign that Brutus is in a state of mental deterioration. Soon he will see spirits, which is how Shakespeare commonly dramatized the condition of the unhealthy mind.

Lucius reenters with wine and tapers. Brutus says he buries all unkindness in a bowl of wine, while Cassius says, "I cannot drink too much of Brutus' love." Titinius and Messala arrive and are told that Brutus has received letters saying that Octavius and Antony are marching with a mighty force toward Philippi. Messala says he has had letters to the same effect and adds that Octavius, Antony, and Lepidus have murdered a hundred senators. Brutus remarks that their letters differ in this point, since his report says seventy senators had been killed, Cicero among them. Messala asks if Brutus has received any news from his wife. Brutus replies he has not and asks Messala if he has heard anything. Messala reports that Portia is dead. Brutus, with philosophic quietude, states, "With meditating that she must die once,/ I have the patience to endure it now."

Messala compliments Brutus on his stoical acceptance of Portia's death; this is the way great men should endure their losses, he says. Cassius states that he knows as much about the theory of Stoicism as Brutus does, but his nature (rash and choleric) could not bear grief with the resistance of the Stoic.

COMMENT: The discrepancy in the reports over the number of Senators killed by Antony is a realistic device frequently used by Shakespeare to suggest the confused nature of things during time of war and to introduce the theme of false report which later will be so vital to the tragedy of Cassius.

Brutus allows Messala to tell him Portia has died, although he has already heard this news. We have been shown that messages delivered over long distances are often unreliable and contradictory. Brutus realizes this when he patiently listens for confirmation of Portia's death. When the first report is confirmed by the second, Brutus' response is, "Why, farewell, Portia." This may be taken to mean that Brutus was reluctant to bid farewell until he was absolutely certain of her death.

Other explanations have been offered for the double report of Portia's death. One attributes it to the carelessness of the compositor, who failed to remove the second report, which was marked for deletion. Another, within the context of the play, claims it to be the consideration of Brutus, who lets Messala deliver his report out of respect for his office.

Brutus' reaction to Portia's death is reminiscent of Caesar's belief that "the valiant never taste of death but once." A comparison is forced upon the reader who recalls the verbal and philosophic resemblances between Caesar's statement and Brutus' stoical idea that Portia "must die once." As Messala observes, this stoical resignation to death is the mark of a great man. Cassius, purportedly an Epicurean at this point in the play, admits that he is unable to bear grief like a Stoic, suggesting that he is not a great man. However, he will shortly renounce his Epicurean philosophy and die a Stoic. The implication is that Cassius' character becomes ennobled as the play progresses.

Anxious to leave the subject of Portia's death, Brutus suggests that they march to Philippi with their armies, but Cassius is against this plan. He feels it is better to let the enemy come to them, wearying their troops in the long march, while Brutus and Cassius' men are rested and ready to defend themselves. Brutus counters Cassius' suggestion by asserting that the enemy will gather fresh troops along the way among the people Brutus and Cassius have antagonized by extorting their money. Silencing Cassius, Brutus argues further that the morale of their troops is at its highest, and that if they wait, the morale will decrease. Cassius reluctantly agrees to march to Philippi. Brutus announces that it is time for rest, and Cassius begs Brutus that such a disagreement as had begun that night may never again come between their souls. Brutus replies, "Everything is well," and as Cassius, Titinius, and Messala leave, each in turn addresses him as "my lord" or "Lord Brutus."

COMMENT: Brutus' will has been asserted among his allies, who are forced to accept his decision to march against the enemy rather than wait for the enemy to attack. Cassius offers some feeble opposition to this plan, but, anxious to prevent any further discord, he quickly concedes to the stronger man. By the time the council is over, Cassius acknowledges Brutus as "my lord," as do Titinius and Messala. Thus, Brutus' poor judgment in military affairs prevails over the sounder advice of Cassius, the more experienced soldier, and draws closer the tragic end that awaits the two men.

Preparing for rest, Brutus calls for his gown and asks Lucius to find his instrument (lute). Paternally, he notes that Lucius is drowsy from having served all day. He sends for Varro and Claudius to sleep in his tent in the event that messengers to Cassius are needed during the night. The two soldiers offer to stand guard all night, but Brutus considerately insists that they sleep until they are called. From the pocket of his gown, Brutus produces a book he had blamed Lucius for misplacing and apologizes to his servant for being so forgetful. Still apologetic, Brutus asks the tired boy to play a tune and promises to reward him if Brutus lives. Music and a song follow before Lucius falls asleep. Tenderly, Brutus removes the lute from Lucius' hands. Then, finding his book, Brutus begins to read.

COMMENT: Brutus' obstinate will and his poor military judgment give way to another side of the man. Here he is considerate of his men, who, in return, serve him loyally. To Lucius, his young servant, he is paternal and tender, and his promise to be good to Lucius if he lives is unquestionably a sincere one. The qualification to the promise, however, introduces a new idea. There is doubt in Brutus' mind and, perhaps, fear of death. The contrast between Brutus' treatment of his men and Antony's attitude toward Lepidus may be noted at this point.

As Brutus picks up his book to read, the ghost of Caesar, unnoticed by Brutus, appears in the tent. Brutus observes that the taper burns poorly. Then, suddenly, he sees the apparition, which he tries to attribute to the weakness of his eyes. As the spirit draws closer, Brutus asks, "Art thou some god, some angel, or some devil,/ That mak'st my blood cold and my hair to stare?"/ Speak to me what thou art."

The ghost answers, "Thy evil spirit, Brutus." Brutus asks why the spirit has come, to which the ghost replies, "To tell thee that thou shalt see me at Philippi." Then I shall see you again? Brutus asks. "Ay, at Philippi," the ghost replies. The ghost disappears as suddenly as it has come. "Now that I have taken heart, thou vanishest," Brutus exclaims.

COMMENT: The taper flickers; Brutus is not certain what he sees, but he is frightened by the apparition, whatever it may be. His blood runs cold, his hair stands on end. The question of whether or not the spirit is an angel or devil reflects the divided opinion held during the Renaissance on the existence and the nature of ghosts. Physicians and realists of the age attributed apparitions to an excess of the melancholic humor or the "melancholy adust," produced under the influence of a hot passion like anger. Others who believed in the supernatural thought that ghosts were spirits of the dead released from purgatory. Some thought they were good angels sent by God; still others that they were evil angels sent by Satan.

The fact that the ghost speaks should not be taken as proof that it has objective existence. It may simply be a superstitious projection of Brutus' mind, which has recently been heated by a passionate anger against Cassius and turned melancholy by grief over the death of Portia. Brutus himself admits that his mind has been disordered of late

when he apologizes to Lucius for forgetting the book, and he seems to be in doubt over whether or not he will live. (The book, incidentally, is an anachronism; Romans used scrolls.) Caesar too had become superstitious in his declining days. The appearance of ghosts and the occurrence of supernatural events is repeatedly associated in Shakespeare with diseases of the mind, sometimes accompanied by somatic disabilities, as in Caesar.

That the ghost tells Brutus he is his "evil spirit" may be taken as a foreshadowing of the tragedy at Philippi; it is also a reflection of Brutus' subconscious misgivings over the death of Caesar and his present venture, which Brutus may consciously be incapable of acknowledging. Those in Shakespeare's audience who regarded the ghost as an objective spirit would have seen that supernatural forces were united to the natural ones of Antony to work against Brutus for Caesar's revenge.

In either case the spirit of Caesar, whether real or imagined, has come to plague Brutus. The effect of the ghost is the same; Brutus is frightened, and the death he fears is foreshadowed by the ghost. When Brutus exclaims that the ghost vanishes "now that I have taken heart," the balance swings in favor of a subjective ghost, which is conjured up in the imagination of a troubled mind and disappears when Brutus pulls himself together.

Brutus wakes Lucius, Claudius, and Varro. Lucius, dreaming he is still playing, says, "The strings, my lord, are false." Brutus asks him if he had dreamed and cried out in his sleep, but Lucius says he did not know he cried out and that he saw nothing in the tent. Brutus asks the same questions of Varro and Claudius, and their replies are as negative as Lucius'. Immediately, Brutus sends Varro and Claudius to tell Cassius to set out with his forces promptly and that Brutus will follow close behind.

COMMENT: Brutus' first reaction to the ghost is to find out whether it was real or imagined. He questions his men to see if any of them spoke in his sleep or saw anything. Since they have perceived nothing, Brutus may suspect that the ghost is a figment of his disturbed imagination, or he may believe that the ghost has made its appearance only to him, as was reportedly the case in a good deal of Renaissance demonology.

Brutus' decision to go to Philippi at once may be explained as characteristic of the behavior which Brutus has revealed earlier in the play during his inner struggle before the murder of Caesar (II.i). At that time, the anticipation of action against Caesar had made him sleepless, and his mind in turmoil was described by Brutus himself as a kind of nightmare, a state of insurrection: "Between the acting of a dreadful thing/ And the first motion, all the interim is/ Like a phantasma or a hideous dream./ The genius and the mortal instruments/ Are then in council, and the state of man,/ Like to a little kingdom, suffers then/ The nature of an insurrection." Now, in IV. iii, Brutus has decided to march to Philippi. Having made the decision to do so, he must await the time of action; but for Brutus this is a time of nightmare, a time of mental insurrection. Brutus is anxious to get to Philippi. His troubled mind seems to conjure up a nightmare, a ghost who will appear at Philippi. When he rouses from his vision or visitation, he orders Cassius to march at once, because, whether he realizes it or not, Brutus cannot bear the state of suspense "between the acting of a dreadful thing,/ And the first motion . . . ."

SUMMARY: This lengthy scene, which takes place in the rebel camp, may be divided into four stages. In the first stage, Brutus and Cassius engage in a heated argument which stems from the essential differences between the two friends; Brutus' stoical virtue and incorruptible idealism is opposed to Cassius' cynical and practical militarism. The quarrel, however, turns into a childish battle of wills over who is the better man and ends with the total capitulation of Cassius to Brutus, who has shown the stronger will. The theme of discord among the assassins is intended as a contrast to the cold-blooded harmony of the newly-formed triumvirate, which is masterminded by Antony. Brutus' character, during the argument, shows several unfortunate changes. He has become petty and arrogant, self-confident and obstinate in asserting his misguided judgments on his cohorts. Cassius has become a rash, fearful, and beaten man. By the end of the argument, the man who loved freedom so much calls Brutus "my lord."

The second stage of the scene deals with the reconciliation of the quarrelers and the double disclosure that Portia is dead. Cassius now interprets Brutus' anger as having stemmed from grief over Portia, but Brutus is a Stoic, who remains unaffected by the external events of life, and he seems to accept his loss with resignation, as becomes a great man.

The third state of the scene concerns the decision to attack the enemy at Philippi. Cassius' sensible opposition to Brutus' plan is feeble, and it is quickly dropped when it seems that dissension may be renewed between himself and Brutus, whom he loves.

The fourth stage of the scene is marked by the appearance of Caesar's ghost, which Elizabethans interpreted variously as an objective or subjective spirit, angelic or diabolic, or simply as the spirit of the dead risen from purgatory. The ghost vanishes when Brutus' courage returns, so that it seems to be a projection of his troubled mind, heated from the argument with Cassius, depressed by the news of Portia's death, and fearful of the outcome of the battle of Philippi. Rather than endure the nightmare of a delayed departure, Brutus orders Cassius to march at once toward Philippi, and he himself prepares to follow shortly to meet his destiny.

Act V: Scene i

The action now shifts to the plains of Philippi where Antony, Octavius, and their armies are encamped. Octavius tells Antony that their prayers are answered since the enemy is coming to meet them on the plains rather than keep to the hills as Antony had imagined. Antony replies that he knows why the conspirators do this. They are trying to make a show of courage, which Antony does not believe they really have. A messenger enters to announce the enemy's approach. Antony tells Octavius to take the left side of the field, but Octavius demands the right. Antony asks, "Why do you cross me in this exigent?" Octavius ominously replies, "I do not cross you; but I will do so."

COMMENT: Antony's tone is marked with confidence here; he gives orders to Octavius who is technically his peer, and Octavius shows signs of balking at Antony's command. He demands the right side when ordered to the left and concedes with an ominous warning that while he does not cross Antony now, he will do so in the future. (See Shakespeare's Antony and Cleopatra, where the central conflict concerns Octavius' pursuit and victory over Antony.)

The fact that Brutus has forsaken his vantage point in the hills to fight the enemy on the plains is another mark of his poor military judgment and a foreboding of his defeat.

At the sound of drum, Brutus and Cassius lead their army to the field. Lucilius, Titinius, and Messala join them. Brutus notes that Antony and Octavius stand as if to invite a parley. Antony, observing the same hesitation on Brutus' part, decides to answer the enemy's charges before doing battle. Cassius and Brutus advance to meet Antony and Octavius, while the armies wait for a signal from their generals to begin the fray. The rivals exchange insults over Brutus' love of good words and Octavius' penchant for giving bad strokes (in fighting). A master of the discourteous retort, Antony tells Brutus, "In your bad strokes, Brutus, you give good words;/ Witness the hole you made in Caesar's heart,/ Crying 'Long live! Hail, Caesar!'" Antony gets as good as he gives when Cassius reminds him that Antony is yet untried in battle, although his speech is gifted and his honeyed words rob the bees of Mount Hybla. Parrying Cassius' thrust neatly, Antony replies, "Not stingless too." Antony becomes angry as the insults continue, and his taunts become more venomous. "Villains!" he cries. "You did not waste words when your daggers struck Caesar while some of you smiled like apes, fawned like hounds, bowed like bondmen, kissing Caesar's feet, while damned Casca". . . stabbed him in the back. "O you flatterers!"

Failing an answer, Cassius turns to Brutus, arguing that if his advice had been followed instead of Brutus', they would not now be listening to Antony's abuses. Octavius draws his sword and swears that he will not sheathe it, "Never, till Caesar's three-and-thirty wounds/ Be well aveng'd; or till another Caesar/ Have added slaughter to the sword of traitors." Brutus replies that Octavius cannot die by traitors' hands unless he himself brought those hands with him. When Octavius says that he was not born to die on Brutus' sword, Brutus replies that he could not die more honorably if he were the noblest of his strain, that is, if he were his uncle, Julius Caesar. In a final insult, Octavius bids Cassius and Brutus to come to the field if they dare to fight that day; if not, they may come when they have the stomachs for a fight.

COMMENT: This verbal battle in which the rival generals engage before entering physical combat was a medieval rather than a Roman practice, but it serves an important function in this scene, which overrides any annoyance the anachronism may cause. It establishes the animosity between the two armies and substitutes verbal combat for physical combat which is difficult to enact on-stage. The generals' abusive wit, moreover, was a source of delight to the Elizabethan audience, which regarded the clever insult as a form of art.

Cassius shows that he still resents Brutus for rejecting his battle plan; Antony and Octavius make it clear that they plan to avenge Caesar, and Brutus still insists on the merits of Caesar's murder.

As Antony, Octavius, and their armies leave the field, Brutus and Lucilius, his lieutenant, go aside to talk, while Cassius and Messala confer in the foreground (downstage). Cassius says that this day is his birthday, and he calls Messala to witness that he is compelled, against his will, to risk everything on one battle, just as Pompey was. Cassius confides that although he had formerly believed in Epicurus, he has now changed his mind and believes, to some extent, in portents and omens. He relates how, on their way from Sardis, two eagles swooped down, ate from the hands of the soldiers, and followed them all the way to Philippi. Now, however, the eagles have flown away, and in their stead, ravens, crows, and kites look down upon them as if they were sickly prey. Advised not to believe in the omen, Cassius admits that he only partly believes in it, for at the same time, he is "fresh of spirit and resolved/ To meet all perils very constantly."

COMMENT: At the battle of Pharsalia (48 B.C.), Pompey was persuaded against his will to fight Caesar and was decisively defeated. Cassius feels that, like Pompey, he is being forced by Brutus to stake everything on one poorly planned battle and that he too will be defeated by a Caesar, that is, Octavius Caesar.

Cassius explains that he had formerly believed strongly in the philosophy of Epicurus (a materialist who believed that the gods did not interfere in human events so that omens were to be ignored). Now, however, his deep forebodings of doom in the coming battle have led him to discard his former philosophy. On the other hand, although he senses his forthcoming defeat, he is "fresh of spirit and resolved/ To meet all perils," that is, he has purged his mind of fear and anxiety and has apparently taken the Stoic position of resignation to one's fate. In his conversation with Brutus, which follows, Cassius remarks that "the gods today stand friendly," indicating that he does, indeed, believe that gods concern themselves with human events.

Brutus and Cassius finish their conversations with their respective lieutenants and rejoin each other. Cassius suggests that although the gods are favorable, he and Brutus might hold a final conversation before battle. If the worst befalls them, this conversation will be their last, Cassius states; therefore, he asks Brutus what he proposes to do should they lose the day. Brutus replies that he would arm himself with patience and live by the same rule of philosophy he had followed when he had condemned Cato for his "cowardly and vile" suicide. Cassius asks if this means Brutus would be content to be led captive through the streets of Rome, and Brutus arrogantly replies, "No, Cassius, no. Think not, thou noble Roman,/ That ever Brutus will go bound to Rome./ He bears too great a mind." Without revealing how he could escape humiliation and still avoid suicide should he be defeated and taken prisoner, Brutus asserts, "But this same day/ Must end that work the ides of March begun." He bids a final farewell to Cassius and the two part friends. As they go off to battle, Brutus impatiently wishes, "O that a man might know/ The end of this day's business ere it come!"

COMMENT: Cato, Portia's father, committed suicide at the battle of Utica (46 B.C.) rather than fall into Caesar's hands. In Stoic doctrine, which Brutus presumably follows, suicide in the interest of the public good was condoned. The philosophic principle which Brutus lives by and which holds that suicide is a transgression against the high powers that govern men's lives is really a Platonic (and Christian) one. According to Shakespeare, Brutus has combined Platonism with Stoicism to form his philosophy.

Cassius tries to make Brutus realize that the alternative to death is to be led through the streets of Rome in triumph, but Brutus asserts that he will never face this indignity. At the moment, he is not contemplating suicide, which he regards as "cowardly and vile." He believes that the Fates will pass final judgment at the battle of Philippi for the work that was begun on the ides of March. On that day, just after the assassination, Brutus had called upon the goddesses of destiny: "Fates, we will know your pleasure./ That we shall die, we know, 'tis but the time,/ And drawing days out, that men stand upon." Convinced that the Fates will grant him victory or death, Brutus refuses to face the possibility of defeat and capture, which would force him to choose between humiliation and the betrayal of his philosophic idealism.

The talk of suicide and of parting forever reflects the general pessimism the two men feel and foreshadows both their deaths by suicide. Each man faces possible defeat with characteristic resolution. Cassius, practical and realistic, gives up his former philosophy and embraces a form of Stoicism. He is prepared to commit suicide rather than be taken captive. Brutus still impractical, unrealistic, immutably idealistic, refuses to face the real possibility of defeat without death. Ironically, Brutus will betray the principles he holds so strongly when he commits suicide at last, but he will be honored, nevertheless. Cassius will be honored somewhat less, but his expedient change of creeds before his death allows him to maintain his integrity and die by the principles he has newly embraced.

SUMMARY: This scene juxtaposes the rival generals and shows the prevailing mood in each of the two camps. Antony and Octavius are optimistic and united, although the shadow of disagreement passes over their camp. Their mood foreshadows victory. Brutus and Cassius are also united, but pessimistic; they still disagree both in their military and philosophic decisions, but they exchange farewells in perfect harmony and friendship. The talk of omens, suicide, and philosophy foreshadows the death of Cassius and Brutus by suicide.

Act V: Scene ii

On the battlefield at Philippi, Brutus and Messala exchange hasty words. Brutus orders Messala to ride to the legions on the other (right) side of the field to deliver written orders to Cassius. He is to make an immediate attack on Antony's wing. Then Brutus observes that Octavius' wing shows signs of weakening and orders a sudden attack to overthrow it completely.

COMMENT: Since it is impossible to depict a fullscale battle onstage, playwrights in various eras have used a variety of devices to convey the idea of battle without actually showing it. In ancient dramas, battles took place offstage, and messengers relayed information concerning the outcome of the battle. Shakespeare uses this classical method of establishing the atmosphere of battle without

actually showing it, but he combines it with several other devices: short scenes, shifting from place to place on the field of battle to produce the effect of confusion and rapid action; some hand-to-hand combat enacted onstage; and verbal dueling, as among the generals in the preceding scene. The entire battle of Philippi is presented from the conspirators' point of view. In this scene, only Brutus and Messala are seen, but Brutus' orders describe what is taking place elsewhere on the field.

Act V: Scene iii

Cassius and Titinius appear on another part of the field of Philippi. Cassius, seeing his men deserting, tells Titinius how he slew his ensign who was turning to run. Titinius cries that Brutus gave the word to attack Antony too early. Meanwhile, Brutus' men, having overcome Octavius, were busy plundering the enemy's camp instead of assisting Cassius' flank, which was surrounded by Antony's soldiers. Pindarus enters to warn Cassius to flee, for Antony and his men have reached his tents. Cassius answers that he has retreated far enough. Looking across the plain, he asks, "Are those my tents where I perceive the fire?" Titinius replies, "They are, my lord."

COMMENT: The attack ordered by Brutus has been a failure for Cassius, who has slain his own flag-bearer for deserting the field. Now Cassius rests on a hill at one end of the Philippian plain. He shows his courage and resignation by refusing to retreat farther even though the enemy is in close pursuit.

Cassius sees a body of horsemen in the distance and asks Titinius to ride to them and learn whether they are friends or foes. As Titinius rides off, Cassius orders Pindarus to climb higher on the hill to watch what is happening to Titinius, for his own "sight was ever thick" (near-sighted). As Pindarus climbs the hill, Cassius expresses his complete resignation to death: "This day I breathed first; time is come round,/ And where I did begin, there shall I end;/ My life is run his compass." Pindarus yells back to Cassius that Titinius has been surrounded by horsemen and exclaims, "He's ta'en! And hark! They shout for joy." Cassius bids Pindarus to come down, grieving that he is a coward to live so long and to see his "best friend" captured before his face. When Pindarus returns, Cassius reminds him how he had spared his life in Parthia when he had taken him captive on the condition that Pindarus swore to do whatsoever Cassius demanded. Cassius declares Pindarus a free man and orders him to take his sword, the same which ran Caesar through, and strike him in the bosom. As Pindarus guides the sword into his heart, Cassius cries, "Caesar, thou art reveng'd Even with the sword that kill'd thee." And with these words, Cassius dies. Pindarus sighs, "So I am free; yet would not so have been,/ Durst I have done my will. O Cassius!/ Far from this country Pindarus shall run,/ Where never Roman shall take note of him."

COMMENT: Cassius has already resigned himself to death before he is misinformed that Titinius has been captured. Ironically, he has set Pindarus to watch because his own sight is short. Equally ironic is his grief over having lived to see his best friend captured "before my face," when, in fact, he has not seen a thing. It is Cassius' pessimistic resignation and his short-sightedness which moves him to commit suicide before he has confirmed Pindarus' report. The emphasis on the fact that Cassius dies with the same sword that pierced Caesar expresses the theme of retribution and is an example of poetic justice, in which an ironic ending, suitable to the crime committed, is provided for the wrong-doer. Still another irony is suggested by Cassius' suicide, which shows his complete and misguided rejection of Epicureanism, a philosophy which held that the senses were often deceptive and created illusions which, if they produced pain, were to be rejected. Cassius as an Epicurean would have been forced to reject the false report of Titinius' capture, at least until it had been confirmed absolutely. In his final words, Cassius addresses Caesar, leaving the impression that the spirit of Caesar hovers over the field of death and has participated in his own vengeance.

Pindarus' final words before parting adds a touch of bitter humor to the somber scene by suggesting that the civilized Romans are far more barbaric than the semi-civilized Parthians.

As Pindarus leaves the Roman world for good, Titinius returns with Messala. Messala tells Titinius that they have exchanged Brutus' victory over Octavius for Antony's victory over Cassius, leaving the situation the same as at the start of the day. Titinius remarks that these tidings will comfort Cassius. Messala asks where Cassius is and learns that he is on that same hill, just as he discovers a body on the ground. When Titinius sees that it is Cassius', he cries, "Cassius is no more. O setting sun!/ As in thy red rays thou dost sink to night,/ So in his red blood Cassius' day is set;/ The sun of Rome is set. Our day is gone;/ Clouds, dews, and dangers come;/ our deeds are done./ Mistrust of my success hath done this deed." Messala, however, blames Cassius' suicide on his lack of confidence in their victory for Rome and on the imaginary fears produced by Cassius' melancholy and despondent nature. Titinius then asks where

Pindarus is. Messala tells him to look for Pindarus, while he returns to tell Brutus the bad news.

When Messala leaves, Titinius addresses the body of his noble lord Cassius, mourning, "Alas, thou has misconstrued everything." He takes the victory garland which Brutus had given him for Cassius and places it as a sign of honor on the head of the corpse. Then, asking leave of the gods (for ending his time before their appointed hour), he expresses his duty as a Roman, picks up Cassius' sword, and kills himself.

COMMENT: Titinius has taken personal blame for the death of Cassius, who upon learning that Titinius his "best friend" had been captured, ended his own life. Following Cassius' example, Titinius takes the death of his friend as a sign that all is lost for their cause. He shows the loyalty and personal devotion of a true friend and proclaims it his duty as a Roman to die with Cassius. The theme of friendship even unto death is not a major one in this play, but it crops up from time to time as a sign of the great interest the Renaissance audience had in the concept of friendship among the ancients.

Messala returns bringing Brutus, young Cato, Strato, Volumnius, and Lucilius. Brutus asks where Cassius' body lies, and Messala points to where Titinius kneels in mourning. Brutus discovers that Titinius is dead and cries, "O Julius Caesar, thou art mighty yet!/ Thy spirit walks abroad, and turns our swords/ In our own proper entrails."

COMMENT: The theme of vengeance for Caesar's murder, echoed in Cassius' dying words, is expressed again in Brutus' cry. The battle and destruction which Antony had prophesied at Caesar's death, has, indeed, come to pass, and the spirit of Caesar has relentlessly tracked the murderers "and turns our swords/ In our own proper entrails." Brutus' own death by suicide is now ominously predicted in his last remark.

In a final tribute to his dead friends, Brutus exclaims, "Are yet two Romans living such as these?/ The last of all the Romans, fare thee well!" Brutus then orders that Cassius' body be sent to Thasos for the funeral, lest his funeral at Philippi destroy the morale of the soldiers. He bids young Cato, Lucilius, Labeo, and Flavius prepare for another battle before the night, since it is only three o'clock.

SUMMARY: The importance of this scene is the death of Cassius as the result of his own nature and his ironic misunderstanding of events. Cassius' last hours are courageous and noble ones. He has rescued his battle flag, killed a coward, refused to retreat, and grieved over a captured friend. He dies not as a coward or base murderer but as a noble if misguided man, the victim of an avenging spirit, his own melancholy fears, and his own tragic flaws. The work begun on the ides of March is nearing its end. The man who devises the conspiracy against Caesar is dead. The monster of "domestic fury and fierce civil strife which Antony had set loose (III. i) is writhing to its end. Brutus and Labeo (who, according to Plutarch, had also stabbed Caesar) are the only conspirators left alive. We can expect to see the end of them in the remaining two scenes of the play.

Act V: Scene iv

Brutus, Cato, Lucilius, Messala, and Flavius are seen on another part of the battlefield of Philippi. In the midst of battle, Brutus passes quickly across the stage, encouraging his men to fight bravely.

As Brutus goes off, young Cato stoutly proclaims he is the son of Marcus Cato, "a foe to tyrants, and my country's friend."

Enemy soldiers appear and engage Cato and Lucilius in single combat.

Echoing young Cato's cries, Lucilius shouts, "And I am Brutus, Marcus Brutus, I." The fighting continues. Lucilius sees young Cato fall. As he continues to fight, Lucilius pays tribute to his comrade, "O young and noble Cato, art thou down?/ Why now thou diest as bravely as Titinius."

Commanded to yield, Lucilius ceases to do battle and offers his captors gold to kill him instantly and to be honored by having slain Brutus in battle. The soldier declines the bribe, for it is a far greater honor to take the noble Brutus prisoner.

Antony arrives at this point and is told that Brutus is captured. Addressing Lucilius, Antony asks where Brutus is. Loyally, Lucilius answers, "Brutus is safe enough," He adds, "When you do find him, alive or dead,/ He will be found like Brutus, like himself" (that is, as noble as ever).

Antony informs his men that Lucilius, although he is not Brutus, is a worthy prize. He orders them to take Lucilius prisoner and to treat him kindly, for Antony would like to have him as a friend. Then others are ordered to pursue Brutus and to report to Antony at Octavius' tent.

COMMENT: The second engagement in the battle of Philippi is portrayed with a good deal of physical movement. Brutus rushes across the stage. There is hand-to-hand combat. Cato falls. Lucilius is captured. Lucilius follows a pratice to medieval warfare in proclaiming he is Brutus. He does not wish to assume honors that are not rightfully his,

but attempts to protect his generals by confusing the enemy and preventing their pursuit of the real target, Brutus. In some editions of the play, this speech is attributed to Brutus, in which case, Brutus makes an exit just before Cato falls. Plutarch makes it clear that Lucilius does impersonate Brutus.

Brief as it is, the scene shows that Brutus' men are loyal, fight courageously to the end, and are still devoted to the cause of the Republic. It shows that Brutus is slowly being defeated. His brother-in-law, young Cato, is killed; his lieutenant, Lucilius, is captured; and he himself is in flight with the enemy in hot pursuit. Antony appears briefly as shrewdly politic as ever and attempts to sabotage the rival army by expressing his desire to have Lucilius for a friend.

Act V: Scene v

Brutus, Dardanius, Clitus, Strato, and Volumnius appear in another part of the field. Brutus and the remnants of his army rest on a rock. Clitus reports that Statilius has sent a signal, but since he did not come back he has evidently been captured or slain. Pessimistically, Brutus replies, "Slaying is the word;/ It is a deed in fashion." Leaning closer, Brutus whispers into Clitus' ear, and Clitus responds to the message, "What, I, my lord? No, not for all the world!" Brutus then turns to Dardanius, who replies, "Shall I do such a deed?"

Clitus and Dardanius compare notes and reveal that Brutus has requested each of them to kill him. They watch him as he meditates quietly apart. "Now is that noble vessel full of grief,/ That it runs over even at his eyes," Clitus observes.

Brutus calls Volumnius to him and tells him about the ghost of Caesar, which has appeared to him twice, once at Sardis and again last night at Philippi. "I know my hour is come," Brutus declares. Volumnius tries to argue Brutus out of his depression, but Brutus is convinced that the enemy has beaten them to the pit like wild beasts. It is better, he decides, "to leap in ourselves/ Than tarry till they push us."

An alarm is sounded and Clitus warns Brutus to fly. Brutus bids his men farewell, declaring, "My heart doth joy that yet in all my life/ I found no man but he was true to me." Now he is tired and his bones crave rest. The alarm is sounded again, and warnings to fly are shouted from within. Brutus sends the others off, promising to follow. Only Strato is asked to remain.

Brutus confronts his servant Strato with the same request he had made of his friends, and Strato agrees to hold the sword and hide his face, while Brutus ends his life.

Servant and master take hands and say goodby. Then, with the words "Caesar, now be still;/ I killed not thee with half so good a will," Brutus runs upon his sword and dies.

A retreat is sounded as Brutus dies. Antony and Octavius arrive on the scene. They have with them Messala and Lucilius who have been taken prisoner. Octavius speaks first, "What man is that," he asks, pointing to Strato. Messala identifies Brutus' servant and asks Strato where Brutus is. "Free from the bondage you are in, Messala," Strato replies. Brutus has killed himself, "and no man else hath honor in his death." Lucilius praises Brutus' suicide, which proves to him that Brutus was as honorable as he had thought.

Octavius offers to take Brutus' men into his service, and Strato agrees to go if Messala gives him a recommendation. Learning that Strato held the sword for Brutus, Messala urges Octavius to take this good servant as his follower.

Antony, who has been silent all the while, speaks now over the body of Brutus: "This was the noblest Roman of them all./ All the conspirators save only he/ Did that they did in envy of great Caesar;/ He, only in a general honest thought/ And common good to all, made one of them." Antony concludes his eulogy of Brutus by describing his nature as gentle "and the elements/ So mixed in him that Nature might stand up/ And say to all the world, 'This was a man!'"

It is Octavius who has the last words in the play. He orders that Brutus be given "all respect and rites of burial" and that within Octavius' tent "his bones tonight shall lie,/ Most like a soldier, ordered honorably."

COMMENT: The last climax of the play is reached with Brutus' death. His presumptuousness and arrogant virtue disintegrated in death, Brutus has honor and dignity restored to him in his last hours. He has fought courageously and has faced death with the resignation becoming of a great man. In the last scene, he is seen as the object of devotion of his surviving friends, who refuse to hold the sword on which he dies. He is rid of his obstinate constancy to impracticable ideals and acts by human impulse when he decides on suicide. Lucilius, Messala, and Strato applaud his honorable death, and Octavius promises funeral rites in which Brutus' honor as a soldier will be recognized. Antony sums up the character of Brutus as it has been seen throughout the play. Brutus was "the noblest Roman of them all," the only one of the conspirators who killed Caesar out of a concern for the public good and not for envy or in the hope of personal gain.

The avenging spirit of Caesar is never seen again, except as Brutus reports it as an omen of his defeat. Clearly, it is Brutus' belief as he dies that the work begun on the ides of March has been finished, the pleasure of the Fates has been decided, and the spirit of Caesar has been avenged.

The final episode of the play is like a prologue to another. It shows Octavius emerging as the most dominant member of the triumvirate. He speaks first and last and gives all the commands for the disposition of Brutus' men and his body. Then, for the first time in the entire play, Antony praises Brutus. There is a touch of pathos in the fact that his eulogy of the man he had pursued to his death had its counterpart in previous and subsequent events. Brutus has so praised Causer, the man he had slain; now Antony praises the man he has hunted to the pit; and later, Octavius praises Antony after he has hunted him to his death. This eulogy over his victim suggests that Antony will take over Brutus' role as the man marked for extinction by the gods, just as Brutus had taken over Caesar's, and the clash between Antony and Octavius, which is dramatized in Shakespeare's *Antony and Cleopatra*, is foreshadowed in this closing scene of *Julius Caesar*.

Character Analyses

JULIUS CAESAR in Shakespeare's play is not the Caesar of the Gallic wars, described in Plutarch's *Life of Caesar* and reflected in Caesar's own *Commentaries*. He is the aging Caesar, physically infirm, but successful and overconfident, who, according to Plutarch, had overreached himself, insulted his peers, and incurred the wrath of patricians, Republicans, and the gods. According to the dramatic chronology and Cassius' reports, Caesar has recently suffered from fever in Spain and is now deaf and epileptic. At the opening of the play, apart from his costume and the pomp and circumstance which accompany his appearance, Caesar displays few of the special virtues which had made him a conqueror and dictator and favorite of the common people. Of late, he has begun to stand on ceremony (religious ritual and superstition), which is a sign of his mental deterioration. He is concerned with sacrifice and augury, with prodigies, and with Calpurnia's dream. He is subject to flattery and is vain and boastful. But to call him a coward is to do him an injustice. He agrees to stay home from the Senate out of consideration for Calpurnia's fears, but when he is told the decision would be misconstrued, or ridiculed, or that he might never be offered the crown again, he alters his decision. His human tenderness is subordinated to his public image and his ambition.

Despite his shortcomings, some of the heroic traits and gracious attributes which belonged to the historical Caesar come through in Shakespeare's characterization. His insight into Cassius shows he is still a shrewd judge of men, and his public bequests betoken his political wisdom even after his death. His friends attest to his military powers, his justice, and his generosity; Brutus, his murderer, finds no fault in his past actions; and even Cassius, his worst enemy, admits that Caesar never abused him as Brutus has. Caesar is almost tender in his dealings with Calpurnia and Decius; he is paternal to Antony when he instructs and praises him, and he is urbane and hospitable to the conspirators when they call at his home.

In the Senate, on the day of his death, Caesar reaches the height of his ruthlessness and self-assurance, which had once made him a hero. He has forgotten his human limitations in his rise to power. He tempts the gods when he declares himself above "ordinary men," comparing his own constancy with that of the North Star, and he enrages his friends when he obstinately refuses their petitions, although they implore him on their knees to grant mercy to a banished Roman.

After he is stricken, his humanity is restored to him. The dying Caesar is not the infatuated man who has just spoken from the throne. For a moment, he is an Elizabethan idealist who cherishes the noble love of a friend more than anything in the world. When he sees Brutus, whom he loves best, among his betrayers, he relinquishes his hold on the world: "Then fall Caesar."

BRUTUS is first seen in the play as the bemused observer of Caesar's procession as Caesar marches to the Lupercalia. He is not a "gamesome" fellow and does not choose to join the festivities. Of late, he has shown ungentle looks and has made Caesar fear he has lost his love. Upon hearing shouts from the market-place where Caesar is presiding, Brutus inadvertently expresses his fear that Caesar has become king. From that moment on, he is forced to end his contemplations and make a decision for action.

His conflict consists of his love for Caesar on one hand, and his concern for the public good and the welfare of the Republic on the other. Persuaded by Cassius to join a conspiracy against Caesar, Brutus spends a restless night making his decision. He can find no justification for Caesar's murder in Caesar's past actions; therefore, he finds justification for it in what Caesar might become. He assumes that Caesar will become an unbearable tyrant if he is made king, and on the basis of this assumption he decides to murder him. The flaw in his reasoning is that Brutus does not raise the question of whether or not a moral end justifies immoral means, nor does he consider that his action may be met with public disfavor. He is blindly convinced in the power of reason and believes that the public, when they have heard his reasons, will support his action.

Because he has little practical knowledge of life, he is blind to the real motives and characters of men and is ignorant of the practical means of conducting a war. He trusts Antony who betrays him, rejects Cicero who is as loyal to the same Republican cause as he, and mistrusts Cassius who loves him. He refuses to obtain money by unjust means at Sardis, yet becomes indignant because Cassius has not sent him some of the tainted money that Cassius has obtained. He even falsely accuses Cassius of personal corruption.

He is seen at the height of his arrogance and self-confidence, obstinate idealism, and incorruptibility when, like Caesar, he is being least merciful, least human, least yielding to his friend, Cassius. Despite his show of confidence during this quarrel with Cassius, Brutus spends a restless night in his tent. Disturbed over the reaction of the mob to the murder of Caesar, empassioned by the argument he has had with Cassius, and grieving over the death of his noble wife, Portia, Brutus sees an apparition. The ghost, which is either a subjective projection of Brutus' disturbed mind, or the existing spirit of the unavenged Caesar, tells Brutus that he is his "evil spirit" and will see him again at Philippi.

Courageously, Brutus decides to meet his destiny at once. He is no longer in torment when he sets out for Philippi, for the resolution of his conflict is in sight. Either he will be victor of the day or he will be killed in battle, and the work begun on the ides of March will have been done. It is this impatience to see the end which causes Brutus to act impetuously, bringing about destruction to Cassius, to the cause of the Republic, and finally to himself.

His death by suicide is in opposition to the philosophic principles he has professed all his life, and which he claimed he would continue to follow even if defeated. This suicide is the one compromise with his ideals that Brutus is known to make in the play, for it is an act which he had previously regarded as "cowardly and vile." Yet this act wins him continued honor among his friends and the praise of his enemy, Antony, for the first time in the play.

CASSIUS is an able soldier and a shrewd politician. He is the real organizer of the conspiracy against Caesar, which he enters out of his love of freedom as much as out of his hatred for Caesar and tyranny. When he is first seen in the play, he expresses his fear that he has lost the friendship and approval of Brutus, whom he loves and respects. Assured of Brutus' continuing love for him, Cassius tries to persuade his friend to join the anti-Caesarist cause. Cassius' imprecations against Caesar show a certain blindness to the spirit of leadership, which Caesar still has, and an overemphasis on physical strength, which Caesar no longer possesses.

Seen next from Caesar's point of view, Cassius "has a lean and hungry look;/ He thinks too much." He is a man to be feared because "he reads much,/ He is a great observer, and he looks/ Quite through the deeds of men. He loves no plays,/ . . . he hears no music;/ Seldom he smiles, and smiles in such a sort/ As if he mocked himself and scorned his spirit/ That could be moved to smile at anything./ Such men as he be never at heart's ease/ Whiles they behold a greater than themselves,/ And therefore are they very dangerous." Caesar's description is that of a melancholy man, who is also a cynic (in our sense of the word). Cassius is a silent type, observant, penetrating, quick to anger, slow to smile. He abjures the sensual pleasures of life such as Antony enjoys, but he is well-read and thoughtful. He knows the philosophy of Stoicism, but claims he could never live by its ideals, and he knows that he cannot accept Portia's death with stoic resignation as Brutus does. He is by admission (and historically) an Epicurean, who believes in friendship as one of the highest forms of good and disbelieves in the divine intervention in human affairs. His interpretation of the amazing prodigies on the eve of the ides of March must be regarded as a ruse to attract Casca to the conspiracy, for surely, as an Epicurean, he cannot believe in omens. On the other hand, Cassius announces late in the play that he has discarded Epicureanism and now accepts omens as warnings from the gods to men. Perhaps the conversion is supposed to have taken place prior to the events of the play. (Although Shakespeare does not provide this information, Cassius' philosophic conversion is said to have taken place just before the assassination of Caesar (see Plutarch). If this is true in the play as well, then, as the play progresses, Cassius' character changes philosophically as well as psychologically.)

Early in the play, Cassius' plan to persuade Brutus to join his cause makes him seem like a Machiavellian villain who seduces the noble Brutus in order to use him as a puppet; thus, Brutus appears to be exalted by this contrast with the conniving Cassius, and when he wins decisions over Cassius, his victories seem to be just. Shakespeare makes it clear, however, that Brutus' decisions are based on impractical ideals and Cassius' suggestions, although ignoble, are workable ones. As the play progresses, Brutus' character deteriorates; he becomes overconfident, obstinate, cruel, and taunting.

Cassius, meanwhile, begins to display the "rash choler" of his melancholy nature. At the same time, he reveals that the love, a respect, and honor he shows for Brutus are unquestionably real. Cassius ultimately submits to chastisement for practicing certain military expediencies which Brutus regards as corrupt, and acknowledges his subordination to Brutus by calling him "my lord." His submission is so complete that he follows Brutus to Philippi against his better judgment, changes his philosophy to Stoicism in order to meet his destiny with greater resignation, and ends his life in a burst of melancholic depression in which imaginary fears and delusions of imminent defeat overcome him entirely. Already depressed over the ill-timed venture at Philippi, Cassius seizes upon the supposed capture of his "best friend" Titinius as a final reason for ending his life. His trusted slave Pindarus "guides" the sword, which had killed Caesar, and Cassius dies, guiltily crying, "Caesar thou art revenged."

MARK ANTONY was one of the foremost opportunists of his day. Historically, he was interested in only one thing, political power. In the play, however, Antony is portrayed as a well-rounded Roman or a perfect Elizabethan gentleman. He is an athlete, likes music, and enjoys plays. He is given to all-night carousing, but does not shirk his duties by sleeping late. He is loyal and devoted to Caesar, almost subservient to the man he loves, honors, and fears. He is misjudged by Brutus as a harmless fellow and a mere lover of pleasure, but he is seen as shrewd and dangerous by the more perceptive Cassius. Antony wisely pretends to throw in his lot with the conspirators in order to gain time and favors, but as soon as he can, he plans to let loose an unholy reign of terror to avenge the death of his beloved lord. The mischief he sets afoot is so clever and cruel that he becomes a Machiavellian figure for a time. His gifts of oratory, his political acumen, and his knowledge of mob psychology have been hidden from men, but they are all disclosed during his famous funeral oration, delivered in verse over the body of Caesar. It is seen during the oration that Antony's indulgence in the company of men and in the arts, especially poetry and drama, has served as an education in political leadership.

Antony is next seen ruthlessly signing death warrants of political enemies-seventy or one hundred, according to the reports, including Cicero and his own nephew. He displays Machiavellian statesmanship in these political murders and in his plan to get rid of Lepidus when he has finished using him. His ambition and greed come forward when he flinches at sharing a third of the world with a mulish dullard like Lepidus.

At the end of the play, Antony shows his skill in verbal and physical combat. He is confidently, even smugly, assured of victory over the conspirators, and he still speaks of avenging Caesar, despite his previously expressed interest in gaining control over Rome. Octavius begins to show his teeth, however, and in the final scene of the play, takes full command over the business at hand. Antony is silent in Octavius' presence, but he delivers a final eulogy over the body of Brutus in which he praises his enemy for the first time in the play, suggesting that since Octavius has taken over, Antony has had some cause to sympathize with Brutus' fight against tyranny.

OCTAVIUS, the grand-nephew of Caesar, was adopted as Caesar's son and heir, inheriting Caesar's name, three-fourths of his estate, and Caesar's lust for power and control over Rome. Octavius first appears in the play after Caesar's death. He joins the triumvirate formed by Antony and Lepidus and follows the plans and directions of Antony, even agreeing to eliminate Lepidus. Privately, however, he feels that Lepidus is a tried and valiant man, who deserves to be rewarded for good service. At his second appearance at the battle of Philippi, Octavius is beginning to balk at Antony's command, accepts orders this time, but threatens to cross Antony at a later date. By the end of the battle and the play, Octavius is in full command. He does most of the talking, gets no opposition from Antony, gives orders for Brutus' funeral, recruits men from Brutus' ranks, and calls the field to rest, all in the presence of Antony, who remains silent except for a final, pathetic eulogy over the body of Brutus.

PORTIA is a heroic example of the devoted Roman wife. She has a noble husband, Brutus, and a noble father, Cato, whose courage and wisdom she feels she has inherited. Concerned for her husband, she explains in great detail the reasons for her anxiety and implores him to tell her the cause of her grief. She is not put off by pretexts and uses reason and flattery to get to the truth, which she claims it is her right to know.

As she says, she is more than an ordinary woman, for she is Brutus' wife and Cato's daughter, and has proved her constancy and resolution by spilling her own blood when she thought it necessary. Although she wins the argument and learns of Brutus' plans, she has great difficulty the next day in keeping herself from divulging the plans inadvertently. She admits that it is hard for women to keep counsel, but manages to do so. She becomes a study in anxiety as she awaits news of the outcome of the assassination. Later, her anxiety over Brutus' absence causes her to commit suicide. Her death is received with stoic resignation by Brutus.

Because of her spirited and intelligent argument, her occasional use of legal terminology, and her delicate sexual conversation, Portia's characterization is sometimes taken as a prototype of the later Portia, heroine of *The Merchant of Venice*.

CALPURNIA is the superstitious and barren wife of Julius Caesar, whom she loves and obeys. Her fears of omens is recently acquired, for she "never stood on ceremonies" in her earlier days. Now, however, strange dreams, ominous prodigies, and fateful augurs have frightened her. She fears for her husband's life and implores him to stay at home and guard his safety on the ides of March. She thinks of Caesar as a prince and believes that the falling meteors are warnings of a prince's death. When she hears her husband boast that he is more dangerous than danger itself, she recognizes that this is foolish arrogance and tells him so; "Alas, my lord/ Your wisdom is consumed in confidence." In response to her criticism and humble petitions, Caesar momentarily agrees to satisfy her whim. However, she is last seen accepting chastisement silently ("How foolish do your fears seem now") and obediently fetching Caesar's robe as he flouts her wishes and leaves for the Senate.

DECIUS BRUTUS is a member of the conspiracy against Caesar. His real name was Decimus Brutus, but Shakespeare followed North's translation of Plutarch where Decius had appeared. Decius volunteers to assure Caesar's arrival at the Senate on the ides of March. He is aware of Caesar's assumed disgust for flattery and plans to flatter Caesar by praising this disgust. He uses his friendship with Caesar and Caesar's love for him to elicit Caesar's excuse for absenting himself from the Senate. Then he cleverly reinterprets Calpurnia's dreams, which prevents Caesar from going out, and shrewdly converts it to an auspicious one. Decius manipulates Caesar through the latter's fear of ridicule, his ambition for the crown, and his fear of insulting the Senate. When he finally gets Caesar on his way, Decius contrives to keep him from reading Artemidorus' warning by interposing another letter, purportedly from Trebonius. Thus, he prevents Caesar from reading one letter by giving him a second, and seems to know that Caesar will be easily confused and decide to read none. After the assassination, he disappears from the play, but it is presumed here, as it occurred in history, that Antony has Decius murdered.

CASCA is an amusing and informative conspirator. He first appears as a member of Caesar's train who has attended the Lupercal and observed the attempted coronation and Caesar's reactions to it. He describes these events to Cassius and Brutus in a ludicrous satirical style with more than a hint of rudeness and vulgarity.

The whole coronation episode, to Casca's thinking, is "mere foolery," a phrase he repeats more than once during his description. Brutus views him as a "blunt fellow" who used to have a "quick mettle" when they went to school together, but Cassius explains that Casca still has a lively disposition when it is needed for some bold or noble enterprise. (It is Casca, in fact, who strikes the first blow at Caesar.) According to Cassius, Casca's rudeness and sluggish appearance are donned to disguise his good intelligence so that when he speaks the truth, men will be slow to take offense at an apparent fool.

Not long after this, however, Casca is seen as a trembling clown, amazed, confused, and frightened by the wonders of the night and unable to make sense out of the portents. He fears that the gods are angry and that the end of the world had come. Cassius easily persuades Casca, whom he calls "dull," that the impatience of heaven is a warning of the abnormal state of affairs in Rome, and that an ordinary man like Caesar has become a fearful monster.

Fear and Casca are often found together. Casca believes "it is the part of men to fear and tremble," and he regards one who dies early as one who "cuts off so many years of fearing death." Casca is associated with cowardice when Cassius tells him that he lacks courage ("those sparks of life / That should be in a Roman,") or else that he does not use it, and again when Antony sarcastically calls him "my valiant Casca" and when Antony claims that Casca stabbed Caesar in the back. Although Casca signals the attack against Caesar and strikes the first blow, it may be inferred that Casca's participation in the "bold or noble enterprise" of Caesar's assassination is the act of a coward. (Shakespeare does not reveal Casca's fate after the assassination, but history records that he killed himself after the battle of Philippi.)

OTHER CONSPIRATORS are *Trebonius* who lures Antony away from the Senate while Caesar is being murdered; *Metellus Cimber* who had a personal grudge against Caesar for exiling his brother, Publius Cimber; *Cinna*, a messenger for the conspirators, who had the same name as Cinna the poet; *Ligarius* who gets out of a sickbed to join the conspiracy.

CICERO has a minor role in the play and is used mainly to create the atmosphere of the period in which the play takes place. Cicero was well known to Elizabethans as a famous orator and an ardent Republican; his absence from the conspiracy is given some explanation in the play.

LEPIDUS is the third and weakest member of the triumvirate, consisting also of Antony and Octavius. He appears only briefly, and is rather a subject of discussion

between Antony and Octavius than a character in the play.

MEMBERS OF BRUTUS' ARMY AND HOUSE-HOLD include *Lucilius*, a trusted and loyal lieutenant; *Lucius*, a devoted young slave and luteplayer; *Strato*, the slave who assists in Brutus' death; *Volumnius*, *Cato the Younger*, *Varro*, *Clitus*, *Claudius*, *Dardanius*, and *Messala*, a loyal follower who joins Antony after Brutus' death.

MEMBERS OF CASSIUS' TROOP AND HOUSEHOLD include *Titinius*, Cassius' "best friend," whose capture is the immediate cause of Cassius' suicide; and *Pindarus*, the Parthian slave of Cassius, who assists in his death.

OTHER MINOR CHARACTERS include *Publius*, the venerable Roman senator, who is terrified by the assassination and says not a word in the play; *Flavius* and *Marullus*, tribunes of the people, followers of Pompey, and defenders of the Republic who chastise the mob for celebrating Caesar's triumph; *Cinna the Poet*, a friend of Caesar's who is torn apart by the mob for having the same name as Cinna the conspirator; *Artemidorus*, a teacher of rhetoric who tries to warn Caesar; the *Soothsayer*, who also tries to warn Caesar of the conspiracy; *Popilius Lena*, the senator who wishes Cassius good luck on his venture and then walks off to speak to Caesar, terrifying the assassins with possible betrayal; and a cynical poet who attempts to reconcile Cassius and Brutus after their quarrel.

THE MOB has an important role in many of Shakespeare's plays, especially *Coriolanus*, but is nowhere more significant than in *Julius Caesar*. Here they are seen as an Elizabethan rather than as a Roman mob. They are a capricious lot who love holidays and pageants. They turn out early, climb high towers with babes in arms, and sit all day waiting for a procession to go by. They hiss what offends them and cheer what they like. They have a mass will and a mass mind which can easily be persuaded and easily enraged. Once it is enraged, it is impossible to reason with the mob. Then they are quick to take insult and merciless in their punishment of slight offenses. No individual in the mob would kill a man because of his name, but as a mob, they kill for a name or for no reason at all. They have "chopt hands" and "sweaty night-caps," and utter such a deal of stinking breath (onions were staples in the diet of lower-class Elizabethans) because Caesar refused the crown, that it almost choked Caesar; "for he swounded and fell down at it."

King Lear

Scene-by-Scene Summary and Comment

Act I: Scene i

The play opens in a room in the palace of King Lear, a legendary ruler of Britain in the time before Britain became fully Christianized. Two noblemen, the Earl of Kent and the Earl of Gloucester (pronounced Glos'ter), are chatting about court politics. From this gossip we discover that Lear—who we later learn is about 80 years old—has decided to divide his kingdom and give up his throne before he dies. He intends to divide Britain among his three daughters, who are named Goneril, Regan and Cordelia.

COMMENT: The oldest daughter, Goneril, is married to the Duke of Albany. The middle daughter, Regan, is married to the Duke of Cornwall. British dukes were second in power only to princes. They generally ruled the area which goes by their name. Thus the Duke of Cornwall rules the southwestern part of England known as Cornwall. Dukes are of much higher rank than earls, like Kent and Gloucester. Cordelia is not married when the play opens, but she is being courted by two French noblemen, the Duke of Burgundy, and the actual King of France, who is, at the time the play opens, at peace with Britain.

Kent expresses surprise to Gloucester that the kingdom is to be evenly divided. He had thought that Lear liked Albany, Goneril's husband, better than he liked Cornwall, Regan's husband.

COMMENT: This shows that Lear had made up his mind about how Britain was to be divided before the play has opened. As it will turn out later in the play, Lear should have liked Albany better than Cornwall, because Albany is by far the more decent man of the two.

In the middle of the discussion between Kent and Gloucester, Kent notices that Gloucester has Edmund, the younger of his two sons, with him. Gloucester tells Kent that Edmund is a bastard whom Gloucester begot with a mistress a year after his legitimate son, Edgar, was born. Kent barely recognizes his friend Gloucester's son, because Edmund has been away from court for

nine years. Gloucester jokes lewdly about the fun he had the night Edmund was conceived. He tells Kent that although his property will go by law to the older, legitimate Edgar, he loves Edmund no less, and "the whoreson must be acknowledged."

COMMENT: The tone of this conversation is light and often lewd. Kent and Gloucester establish themselves immediately as two men of the world. There is no sense that Kent either approves or disapproves of Gloucester for the adulterous affair in the past which produced Edmund. The remarkable thing is that neither Kent nor Gloucester is in any way embarrassed at talking about Edmund in his presence. Coleridge thought that this conversation about Edmund's bastardy was embarrassing to him. There seems to be no hint of this in the text. Edmund, like his father, is "brazed to it." See his soliloquy in Scene ii, where he seems to celebrate his bastardy.

The worldly, realistic tone changes abruptly when a trumpet flourish announces the entrance of Lear accompanied by his three daughters, his two sons-in-law, and various courtiers, or nobles who serve the king in his palace. Lear reaches for a map of Britain and announces his intention to divide the kingdom so that he can "Unburthen'd crawl toward death." (This is ironic, as the play turns out, because the division of the kingdom increases, rather than decreases, Lear's burdens.)

COMMENT:

1. There is a fairy tale quality in this scene. There are three daughters, one virtuous, two evil (as in Cinderella); the kingdom is to be divided into three parts; Lear makes something of a ritual of his division.

2. Note the contrast between the rich court, the foreign notables, the many courtiers, and the scene on the heath in Act III, where Lear has only a fool and a madman to attend upon him.

3. The pomposity and long-windedness of Lear's abdication speech.

4. The proposed division of the kingdom into three parts —three being a magic number in myth and fairy tale.

5. The gorgeous court pageantry, complete with shining trumpets and many-colored flags.

6. The ritualistic way in which Lear goes about dividing the kingdom. The whole structure of the scene is absolutely symmetrical until Cordelia upsets the apple cart.

Lear announces the way in which he will divide his lands. There is a catch to it, although he doesn't think of it as a catch. Before Lear gives each daughter her third of the kingdom, she must tell him how much she loves him. Goneril, the oldest daughter, is called on first. She has no trouble making a glib, hypocritical speech. She tells Lear that she loves him "Dearer than eyesight, space and liberty," and, indeed, "no less than life" itself. Regan makes a similar speech. But while Lear is lapping up Goneril's and Regan's praise of him, Cordelia is nervously wondering what will be left for her to say when her turn, as youngest daughter, finally comes. (Her problem stems not from lack of love for Lear, but from her embarrassment at making flowery, ceremonial speeches.)

Finally Lear turns to Cordelia, and calling her his joy (she has always been his favorite daughter), asks her what she has to say about her love for her father. Can her speech draw the richest third of Britain? But all Cordelia says is "Nothing, my lord." Lear is thunderstruck at this blow to his ego. "Nothing?" he asks. "Nothing will come of nothing," he warns her. In other words, she will be disinherited if she can't find some praise for her father.

Cordelia, wretched, says she can't make flowery speeches the way her sisters do. She loves her father as much as daughters are supposed to love their fathers: no more, no less. This perfectly reasonable answer infuriates the proud old king. He warns Cordelia that she will lose her dowry: he will disinherit her. (It is interesting that he assumes that without a money settlement on her marriage, Cordelia won't be able to get anyone to marry her.)

At this point Kent tries to butt in, but Lear warns him not to come "between the dragon and his wrath." Lear banishes Cordelia from his sight, and announces that the third of Britain that was supposed to go to her will instead be divided between Goneril and Regan. Lear, accompanied by a retinue of 100 knights, will spend one month alternately with each daughter.

Again Kent intervenes. He has always loved Lear and been faithful to him, and now that Lear is acting rashly and foolishly in disinheriting the daughter who loves him most, Kent feels he must warn the King. Lear furiously orders him out of his sight. Kent replies, "See better, Lear."

Driven to a peak of anger by Kent's blunt reply, Lear gives him five days to pack his belongings and leave England. Lear warns him that if on the sixth day Kent is found anywhere in his realm, he will be executed on the spot. Kent answers that as long as Lear is going to be so unreasonable, freedom is outside England and banishment is in England. (Normally banishment was considered a very severe punishment.) Kent asks for blessings on Cordelia, warns Goneril and Regan that they had better live up to their words of love, and leaves the court.

Now Gloucester enters with the two suitors for Cordelia's hand, France and Burgundy. Lear announces to Burgundy that if he wants to marry Cordelia, he will have to accept her without a dowry.

When he hears that Cordelia has been disinherited, Burgundy quickly backs out. But the King of France is made of better stuff. He tells Lear he is shocked at this disinheriting of Cordelia, and then announces that he will be glad to marry her even if she comes to him without a penny, for she is "most rich, being poor." In other words he sees that her spirit is rich, and her spirit is what counts. He will bring her back to France with him to live. Lear agrees to the marriage, and leaves.

Cordelia now says goodbye to Goneril and Regan. She tells them that she hopes they will be as good as their words to Lear. Regan's answer is that, being disinherited, Cordelia had better worry now about satisfying her new husband, France, who has taken her without a cent of dowry. (The catty cruelty of Goneril and Regan to Cordelia is very much like the behavior of the older sisters to Cinderella.) Cordelia and France leave. Now that they and Lear are gone, Goneril and Regan discuss the situation cynically and selfishly. Goneril points out to Regan how unreasonable Lear's behavior has been. She is shrewdly worried that everyone in court will notice how peculiar his action was in disinheriting his favorite daughter. Regan answers that their father is probably senile, but, in fact, she says, he never really knew his own mind. Both sisters are worried by Lear's "unruly waywardness" and "unconstant starts," in short, his eccentricity. They talk clearheadedly and unsympathetically about him, as the scene ends.

SUMMARY: This opening scene does the following important things for the play:

1. We are shown all the major characters in action except Gloucester's legitimate son, Edgar, and the Fool, or court jester.

2. The scene shows that the moral slackness of Gloucester in fathering a bastard is considered a matter for joking in the court, instead of something of serious concern. The moral level of the courtiers is not very high. Gloucester will later pay heavily for his lapse of virtue, which took place years before the play begins.

3. It shows that Lear is a rash and self-centered old man. He stages a whole contest to see who loves him most after he has already decided how to divide his kingdom. It also shows the blunt honesty of Cordelia and Kent—an honesty that borders on the tactless.

4. It shows, in the dialogue between Goneril and Regan at the end of the scene, how hypocritical their earlier professions of love to Lear really were. Already we get a sense that they are evil and self-serving women who will stop at nothing to get what they want.

5. It shows Lear's moral blindness as to which of his daughters really loves him and which only pretend to love him. He makes the basic tragic mistake of taking the appearance for the reality. Kent has made the same mistake earlier in the scene, when he comments on how handsome the bastard, Edmund, looks. But ironically, it is Kent who points out to Lear that he should "see better." Much of the play will be concerned with true vision, or insight into character, as opposed to surface vision which can only see the outward shows of character.

6. But Cordelia in her own way is as proud and unbending (to a fault) as is Lear.

7. This scene is the longest of the play and from its conflicts comes the action of the entire play. This is unusual in the first scene of any play.

Act I: Scene ii

We are now in Gloucester's castle. Edmund enters carrying a letter which he has forged as part of a plot to get his brother, Edgar, disinherited. Before we find out the contents of the letter, however, Edmund reveals himself to the audience in the first soliloquy of the play.

COMMENT: The soliloquy is a device used by dramatists to let the audience know directly what is going on in the mind of a character. It does not mean that the character is actually talking to himself. Nor does it mean he is addressing the audience directly. The soliloquy is what is in the character's mind, spoken aloud so that the dramatist can get across to us what the character is thinking about. Because no one else is on stage or able to overhear during a soliloquy, the dramatic convention is that the character is telling the absolute truth as he knows it. He doesn't feel he has to conceal anything from himself as he would from another character, if one were present. Shakespeare uses the device most effectively for revelation of character. Modern dramatists rarely use it.

Edmund calls Nature his goddess, saluting her here as the divinity of lust and as one who would crown his efforts (illegal) to get his brother's land away from him. This is not the nature to whom Lear later appeals and whom Cordelia, Edgar, and Kent obey, but a naked, selfish individualism, given over to lust and greed. Edmund renounces both religion and the laws of human society, seeing nature in opposition to them. Also, as a bastard, Edmund is a "natural child," meaning he was not born as a result of marriage, a social convention. Edmund is haunted in this soliloquy—and later in the play —by the fact that he is a bastard. He tells himself he is as good a man as his brother, Edgar, and probably a better man. The reason he gives is that more energy is required in an adulterous affair than in normal marriage, so that he was conceived when his father, Gloucester, was really lusty.

"Well then,/ Legitimate Edgar," Edmund sneers, "I must have your land." The letter Edmund has just forged should get it for him. Filled with evil confidence he shouts, "I grow, I prosper;/ Now, gods, stand up for bastards!"

COMMENT: This soliloquy shows that Edmund is

1. Ruthless and determined to have his way.

2. Clever and witty.

3. Ashamed of being a bastard; but

4. Genuinely scornful of his legitimate, kindly brother, Edgar.

5. Aware that he is evil by choice, not by necessity. He makes no excuses to himself for his evil.

Now Gloucester enters, musing distractedly about the speed of the unhappy events in the previous scene. Edmund cleverly pretends to hide the letter that is in his hand, knowing that doing so will only make his father more curious to find out what is in it. Edmund refuses to hand the letter over, saying it isn't fit for his father to read. The more Edmund refuses, the more Gloucester insists. Finally Edmund gets his real wish—the counterfeited letter is read by Gloucester, who is horrified at its contents.

The letter, supposedly written by Edgar to Edmund, says that Edgar wishes his father would die soon so that he could inherit his estate. Edmund adds fuel to the fire now raging in his father's breast by saying he has often heard Edgar complaining about this point. Gloucester gullibly believes him, and Edmund's plot is well-launched.

COMMENT: This is the first of several important letters in the play. Many plot-points are made by means of letters.

Gloucester, shouting that Edgar is an "Abominable villain," asks Edmund where he is. Edmund says he doesn't know, but will search Edgar out, and bring him to Gloucester.

Gloucester blames some recent eclipses of the sun and moon for the divisions between parents and children and between friend and friend that he has just seen in the court and now in his own life. First, Lear has been alienated from his daughter, Cordelia, and his friend, Kent. Second, Gloucester himself is now alienated from his son, Edgar. Gloucester says the best part of his life is now over: all that awaits him is "hollowness, treachery, and all ruinous disorders." When Gloucester leaves, shaking his head sadly, Edmund, in another soliloquy, makes fun of his father's gullibility and superstition.

COMMENT:

1. Gloucester is superstitious, but he understands the moral law and grieves genuinely over the chaos which enters into human relationships when nature or order is upset by the failure of natural relationships.

2. Edmund is a skeptic, for he does not believe that the "late eclipses" have any effect on human affairs. Shakespeare would probably have questioned such complete skepticism.

Edgar now enters, and Edmund asks him if he can remember offending their father recently. Edgar says no. Then Edmund, playing a cat-and-mouse game

with his naive brother, says that apparently someone has slandered Edgar to his father, because Gloucester is furious with him. He warns Edgar that he had better fly for his life; if Gloucester sees him, he will kill him. Edgar doesn't understand what Edmund is talking about, but being as credulous as his father, he agrees to flee for his safety.

SUMMARY: In this scene the following things happen:

1. The sub-plot is set in motion. The sub-plot is about the fortunes of Gloucester and his sons, Edmund and Edgar. It parallels closely the main plot about Lear and his daughters, Goneril, Regan and Cordelia. Thus two fathers are deceived by their children. Toward the end of the play the two plots will merge.

2. Edmund reveals himself as a complete schemer and villain. He is like Iago in *Othello*, or Richard III, or the Satan of Milton's *Paradise Lost* because he is a conscious villain. Edmund enjoys being a villain and knows just how evil he is. He is also witty, like the above-mentioned villains.

3. We see that Gloucester, like Lear, is too ready to believe what people tell him. Just as Lear is foolish to accept at face value Goneril's and Regan's claims of love, so Gloucester is foolish and blind to accept one son's (Edmund's) slander of another son (Edgar).

4. Gloucester is shown to be religious to the point of superstition, while Edmund is coldly rational and materialistic.

Act I: Scene iii

The scene shifts to the palace of Albany and Goneril. Goneril is complaining to her servant, Oswald, that Lear's retinue of 100 knights is annoying her and upsetting her household. Lear is apparently spending the first month after abdicating the throne with his eldest daughter and her husband. He has brought with him a band of knights to serve him, and they are not getting along well with the regular household staff. At the moment, Lear is out hunting. Goneril takes this opportunity to tell Oswald that she's had enough of her father and his "riotous" followers. When Lear comes back from his hunting expedition, Goneril wants Oswald to tell him that she's sick and can't speak with him.

Calling Lear an "idle old man," Goneril furthermore tells Oswald that in the future the steward is to ignore any requests her father may make. If the old king objects to this treatment, he can go visit with Regan for a while. Also, she tells Oswald, "let his knights have colder looks among you." In other words, Lear and his retainers are to be totally ignored, if not actually snubbed by Goneril's own servants.

SUMMARY: This is a very short scene—only 27 lines in length. In it, we learn that Goneril is already sick of having her father with her and is planning to make him feel as ill-at-ease as possible.

An easy way to remember which evil daughter is married to which duke, and which pair Lear visits first, is to remember them alphabetically, as follows: Goneril's name begins with a G, which comes before the R of Regan's name in the alphabet. Goneril is married to Albany, whose name comes alphabetically before Cornwall, Regan's husband. Lear visits first the pair whose names come first in the alphabet: Goneril and Albany.

Act I: Scene iv

Lear returns from the hunt, and finds Kent, disguised, waiting to see him. Lear does not recognize his old friend and retainer, whom he banished from England in Scene i. He asks Kent what he wants, and Kent replies that all he wants is to serve Lear. Kent says he recognizes "authority" in Lear's face and would like to be a loyal retainer. He tells Lear he is 48 years old, much younger than he really is. Lear accepts his services.

COMMENT: In recognizing "authority" in Lear's face, Kent is seeing a good deal more than either of the old king's evil daughters can see. His offer of service does much at this point to bolster Lear's sagging spirit.

One of Lear's knights says that he has noticed "a great abatement of kindness" to the old man lately. Lear agrees that he, too, has perceived "a most faint neglect of late," but blames it on his own jealousy and desire for attention. He cannot believe that he is being purposely neglected by Goneril. Then he adds that he "will look further into" the matter.

COMMENT: This turns out to be very ironic, because Lear does indeed look further into his neglect—much further than he ever thought he would have to, or ever wanted to look when he made the statement. Lear's awareness that he is jealous is the first time in the play that he shows any self-criticism.

Then Lear calls for the Fool, or court jester, to cheer him up. The knight tells him, however, that the Fool has been keeping to himself lately, pining for Cordelia, whom he loved, and who is now in France with her husband. The Fool never really recovers from the blow of Cordelia's banishment.

Now Oswald enters. He speaks insolently to Lear, and Kent trips him up and sends him sprawling on the floor for his insolence. This act immediately draws Lear together in a new bond with his old, wronged friend, even though he still does not recognize him. He gives Kent some money as a kind of tip. At this point the Fool enters the room.

COMMENT: The Fool is the most mysterious figure in the play. Essentially he is a court jester, and not "foolish" at all. Sometimes, however, he does seem to be on the verge of madness. His functions in the play are as follows:

1. To teach Lear wisdom that the King lacks. He can do so by means of wit because of a court convention, or custom, which allows the Fool to say anything he likes to his monarch, even things which would be treasonous coming from anyone else.

2. To cheer the old King up. At the same time, though, the Fool is often cruel to Lear in much the same way as Goneril and Regan are, that is, in their insisting on showing him to himself for what he is. Probably this cruelty stems from the Fool's love for the banished Cordelia.

3. To comment on the behavior of all the characters he meets in the play. He can do this because he is not involved in any of the intrigues.

4. He also states the themes of the play.

Once the Fool performs these actions he disappears from the play and is never heard from again. The Fool always talks in riddles and puns. It is often extremely difficult to understand exactly what he is saying at any given moment because:

1. His mind is very complex.

2. The language he uses has become obscure by now. Many words have changed meaning or lost their original meaning entirely over the years.

3. He is fond of singing snatches of archaic nonsense songs.

In this scene the Fool's jests with Lear all come to one thing: Lear, not the Jester is the real fool. For Lear has upset the natural order of things by putting himself in his daughters' care. He did the opposite of what Nature intends parents to do with their children. For upsetting this balance of Nature, in which children must obey their parents, and not vice versa, Lear will suffer. For instance, when Lear asks the Fool if he is calling his master "fool," the Fool answers: "All thy other titles thou hast given away; that thou wast born with." Kent recognizes the truth behind this remark, and tells Lear, "This is not altogether Fool, my Lord."

(This is like Polonius, saying of Hamlet that if he is mad, there's a method to his madness.)

Now Goneril enters, in a bad mood. She upbraids her father for what she considers the wild and boisterous behavior of his retainers. Lear cannot believe his own daughter could be so harsh with him. He asks, with tragic irony, "Who is it that can tell me who I am?" In other words, if Goneril is talking to me in this manner, can I possibly be the King and her father? The Fool answers, appropriately enough, "Lear's shadow." Goneril persists in her scolding. She complains that Lear's followers have made her palace into a "tavern or a brothel" by "not-to-be-endured riots." This is the final touch. Calling his daughter "Degenerate bastard," Lear orders that his horse be saddled. He will leave the house before his month is up and stay with Regan.

COMMENT: Lear's calling Goneril a bastard, although technically she is his legitimate daughter, links his problem with Gloucester's problem in the subplot.

Albany enters and tries to calm down the enraged king, but succeeds only in making Lear even angrier. Lear shouts at Goneril that she is lying about his knights; they are "of choice and rarest parts." He begins to regret his impatience with Cordelia for a relatively small fault. Beating at his head with his fists, Lear cries, "Beat at this gate, that let thy folly in, / And thy dear judgment out!" Then in tones like those of an Old Testament prophet, he denounces his daughter, at first praying that she be childless. But then he changes his mind and asks Nature to make her bear a child, so "that she may feel / How sharper than a serpent's tooth it is / To have a thankless child!"

COMMENT: This ferocious speech is one of the most magnificent in the play, but Goneril is totally unmoved by it. To her, all it means is that her father is senile. Albany, however, is beginning to sympathize with his father-in-law, and he wonders whether the woman he married may not really be the monster her father claims her to be.

Lear has rushed out of the room after making his great speech. While he is out, he evidently learns that Goneril intends for him to dismiss 50 of his knights— half his retinue—for he returns in an even greater rage.

This time he even weeps, although in the speech just before he had begged Nature to make Goneril weep with a parent's sorrow. Instead, against his will, the tears start rolling down his cheeks. Goneril, still unmoved, stands coldly by while Lear threatens that he will get Regan to right the wrong that has been done to him. He keeps saying "I have another daughter" who will be kind to him.

COMMENT: This is ironic because indeed Lear does have another daughter who will be kind to him: Cordelia. But while the audience knows the truth, Lear means Regan when he says it. If anything, Regan will be crueler to him than Goneril. Thus he persists in his misunderstanding of his daughters. The irony consists of the audience knowing something that a character on stage does not.

After Lear storms off, accompanied by Kent and some retainers, Goneril sends Oswald with a letter to her sister, Regan, informing her of the day's events, and warning her of the temper she will find her father in when he arrives at her house.

SUMMARY: This is one of the most important scenes in the play for the following reasons:

1. It shows just how bitter the conflict will be between Lear and his evil daughters. This conflict was hinted at toward the end of Scene i, when Goneril and Regan cold-bloodedly discussed their father. Again, in Scene iii, when Goneril instructs Oswald to ignore Lear, we get some hint of the conflict. But now it really erupts, and Lear abuses Goneril in no uncertain terms.

2. At the same time that Lear begins to reap the fruits of his folly in giving his kingdom to Goneril and Regan, he begins to gather around him three important friends. They are:

  a. The Fool. He has been estranged from Lear ever since the banishment of Cordelia, whom he loved. Now he will try to comfort the King in his anguish, and lead him to a true vision of life.

  b. Kent. In his loyalty to Lear, Kent has refused to accept the banishment meted out to him in Scene i. Risking his life by remaining in England against Lear's orders, he disguises himself and rejoins Lear. He demonstrates his old loyalty again in this new disguise by tripping up Oswald, Goneril's insolent servant, when Oswald speaks curtly to Lear.

  c. Albany. When he married Goneril he was in love with her. In this scene, however, he begins to get some inkling of what a monster Goneril is. Although he is generally ineffective, Albany eventually does come over to the side of the good people in the play.

3. The tension reaches its highest pitch so far in the play. This is accomplished by the magnificent poetry of Lear's speeches to Goneril. The speeches are filled with the angry denunciations and moral fervor of the Old Testament prophets, whom Lear physically resembles with his snowy-white beard and heroic stature.

4. As relief from Lear's speeches we get the jokes, puns and songs of the Fool. Often they are obscure, or lewd, or both. But always they are filled with wisdom about the true order of things. Although the Fool is sarcastic to Lear, it is for the

King's own good, and Lear recognizes the friendly intention behind the Fool's caustic jests.

Act I: Scene v

In this brief scene, Lear asks Kent to deliver a letter explaining to Regan what has just happened at Goneril's house. The letter also says that Lear will be arriving to visit Regan soon. Lear very fair-mindedly tells Kent not to add any details about Lear's miserable reception at Goneril's house to whatever is already in the letter. He warns Kent that if he doesn't hurry, the letter will get to Regan only after Lear arrives.

Kent rushes off with the letter, and the Fool continues his riddles and jokes. Typically, he asks Lear if he knows why a snail has a shell. The answer is that a snail has a shell to keep his head safe, and not to give it to his daughters. Lear is distracted with grief, mixed with a tinge of self-pity. He says of himself, "So kind a father!" The Fool says that if Lear were his fool, he would have him beaten for being old before he was wise. In the midst of this joking, Lear prays tragically: "O! let me not be mad, not mad, sweet heaven."

COMMENT: This is Lear's first inkling that his misery may drive him insane, and there is nothing he can do about it. The fact that Lear is aware of his growing madness makes it all the more tragic.

Characteristic of Shakespeare's love for mixing the tragic with the comic, after this solemn prayer, the scene ends with the Fool making a lewd joke.

SUMMARY: In this short scene, the following things happen:

1. Kent again shows his loyalty by promising to deliver Lear's letter to Regan.

2. Lear shows how deeply he has been hurt in the preceding scene by Goneril.

3. Lear's sending the letter to Regan shows that he expects a kindlier reception from his second daughter.

4. Lear's fear of madness is established.

5. The Fool continues his treatment by wit of what he considers Lear's folly in giving everything to his daughters.

Act II: Scene i

We are now in Gloucester's castle. Edmund meets the courtier, Curan. Curan tells him that Cornwall and Regan will be visiting Gloucester tonight. Curan adds that Cornwall and his brother-in-law, Albany, are feuding, and open war between them is likely to break out.

COMMENT: There is no rational explanation for this feud, except that Goneril and Regan are vicious not only to Lear and Cordelia, but to each other as well. They are involving their husbands in a greedy fight over who is to get more land. The point is that evil is self-defeating because evil people don't know when to stop. They attack each other as well as attacking the innocent, ultimately destroying themselves.

Now Edgar appears. Edmund warns him that Cornwall and Regan are due to arrive at any moment, and rumor has it that Edgar has spoken against them. Gullible as ever, Edgar doesn't understand how this rumor could have gotten started. He still doesn't realize that Edmund is plotting against him. Edmund hears Gloucester approaching, and fools Edgar into drawing his sword and entering a mock duel. Then he tells Edgar to leave, and scratches his own arm with his sword. Now, when Gloucester appears, Edmund complains to him that he just got the wound from Edgar. He thus further angers Gloucester against his one good son, Edgar. Gloucester says that Edgar may have escaped just now, but swears he will be caught and punished.

At this point, Cornwall and Regan arrive at Gloucester's castle. Gloucester appeals to them for sympathy, crying that his "old heart is crack'd" about his son's "treason."

COMMENT: This line identifies Gloucester with Lear, whose old heart is also cracked because of his children's behavior. Thus the Lear plot and the Gloucester subplot begin to merge.

Edmund has joined with Regan and Cornwall. He uses every means to frighten Edgar and make him flee. Also, he turns his father still more against Edgar by reporting that he was "mumbling of wicked charms"— which would especially alarm the superstitious Gloucester. Gloucester actually believes that Edgar wanted to kill him and is ready to catch and "dispatch" him.

Regan asks Gloucester if Edgar had been keeping company with her father's "riotous knights." Gloucester says he doesn't know, but Edmund quickly butts in and says yes, "he was of that consort." (This seals Edgar's doom as far as Regan and Cornwall are concerned.) Cornwall compliments Edmund on his devotion as a son in uncovering Edgar's "plot" against his father. Edmund answers smugly and hypocritically, "It was my duty." Neither Regan nor Cornwall show much

sympathy for Gloucester's misery as a father, although Regan, calling Gloucester her "good old friend," tells him not to worry. She and her husband will take care of his treacherous son, Edgar.

SUMMARY: This scene establishes the following points:

1. Edmund is determined to continue the plot against Edgar.

2. Regan and Cornwall are well-mated. Each is ferociously evil.

3. Regan, Cornwall and Edmund have power over the gullible, easily fooled Edgar and Gloucester.

4. Regan's reception of Lear will be no kinder than Goneril's was.

Act II: Scene ii

This scene takes place before dawn, in front of Gloucester's castle. The two servants, Lear's Kent and Goneril's Oswald, enter separately, each carrying a letter for Regan. Oswald, pretending not to recognize Kent as the man who tripped him for his insolence to Lear in Act I, suavely asks him where he may leave his horse. But Kent, who can't stand Goneril's hypocritical servant, replies with a torrent of abuse, calling Oswald, among other names, "A knave, a rascal . . . a lily-livered whoreson" and a "beggar, coward, pandar, and the son and heir of a mongrel bitch." Kent demands that Oswald draw his sword and fight like a man. When Oswald refuses, Kent starts beating him. Oswald's cries of "murder, murder!" bring Edmund, rapier drawn, to the scene. Edmund asks what the matter is, and Kent offers to teach him a lesson in swordsmanship, too.

By now the whole castle is aroused by the commotion. Cornwall, Regan and Gloucester come out to learn what the matter is. Cornwall asks Kent why he is so furious, and he answers that he is angry that "such a slave as this (Oswald) should wear a sword, / Who wears no honesty." Cornwall's answer is that Kent is the kind of insolent boor who disguises his bad manners as blunt honesty. He calls for the stocks, a device which locks the prisoner's feet so that he cannot move, and makes him an object of mockery to all who see him. He says that Kent will be locked in the stocks until noon, but Regan, typically even more vicious than her husband, changes this order to night. Kent protests that he doesn't mind for himself, but that it is an insult to the King to put his servant in the stocks, which are usually reserved for petty criminals and offenders. Gloucester also begs Cornwall not to punish Kent this way, but to no avail. Kent resignedly whistles himself to sleep in the stocks, bidding "Fortune, good night; smile once more; turn thy wheel!"

SUMMARY: This scene doesn't establish many new points, or advance the action of the plot very far, but it does stress the following aspects of certain characters in the play:

1. Kent's rough, blunt, fierce loyalty to Lear. Kent shows himself unwilling and unable to indulge in the usual court hypocrisy. He says what he means with no flourishes, and no desire to spare anyone's feelings.

2. Oswald is Kent's counterpart in the Goneril-Albany household. While he is loyal to Goneril, as Kent is to Lear, he is sneaky and cowardly, for he calls for help when Kent challenges him to a duel.

3. Regan is shown as even crueler than Cornwall. When he wants to put Kent in the stocks only until noon, she insists that the messenger be kept there until night.

4. Gloucester wants to help Kent, but he is too weak to go against the orders of Cornwall and Regan, even though it is in his own house that they are giving their orders.

5. Placing Kent in the stocks is not only an insult to him, but, more important, an insult to Lear, his master. Cornwall and Regan, hence, are willing to go to any lengths to insult the King.

Act II: Scene iii

This very brief scene (only 21 lines long) consists of a soliloquy by Edgar. He is alone in a wood. He reveals that he knows he is being pursued and decides to adopt a disguise. He will pretend to be a harmless idiot beggar, named Tom Turleygood, or Tom of Bedlam.

COMMENT: Bedlam was an insane asylum. The name is an English corruption of Bethlehem. It is ironic that a hospital named after Christ's birthplace should have been filled with miserable, cruelly treated lunatics. A favorite diversion of Londoners used to be to go to Bedlam and make fun of the inmates, sneering at their peculiar behavior. Bedlam was so crowded that almost any harmless lunatic who preferred to beg alms outside was permitted to do so. The idiot or crippled beggar was a common figure in Shakespeare's day because after Henry VIII closed the monasteries, there was no place for these poor people to seek alms but on the open road. Thus Edgar's choice of a disguise is a reasonable one.

SUMMARY: This scene shows Edgar for the first time taking some action to save himself from his brother's plot. His idea of disguising himself as a mad beggar is that nobody will take a lunatic seriously enough to be suspicious of him. In disguise, he can bide his time until the slander against him has been straightened out. His decision is roughly like Hamlet's decision to act insane in order to avoid the suspicions of his uncle, Claudius. Edgar's disguise as a lunatic has two parallels so far in the play:

1. He is now in disguise, as Kent is.

2. He is pretending to be mad, as Lear is actually going mad.

Act II: Scene iv

We are in front of Gloucester's castle again. Lear, accompanied by the Fool and an unnamed Gentleman, comes upon Kent in the stocks. At fist Lear assumes the Kent is just playing a joke by sitting there. When Kent assures him that he was placed in the stocks by Cornwall and Regan, Lear can't believe what he hears. He is sure that they wouldn't dare treat his own servant in this shameful manner.

Kent, however, tells Lear about his encounter with Oswald, and how Goneril's messenger got a much more welcome reception than he did. Lear, in his anguish on hearing this, cries out, "Hysterica passio! down, thou climbing sorrow!" (Hysterica passio is a disease marked by suffocation or choking.) Lear goes into the castle to find out what has happened, leaving the Fool and the Gentleman to comfort Kent in the stocks. Lear soon comes out of the castle again, amazed that Regan and Cornwall have left word they do not wish to be disturbed. They've said they are tired from their journey to Gloucester's castle and aren't feeling well. At first, Lear is angry, but then is willing to accept the excuse. Still, he is furious that Kent is in the stocks and wants some explanation.

Finally, Gloucester emerges from the castle with Cornwall and Regan. A servant sets Kent free. Lear immediately begins unburdening himself to Regan. He tells her that Goneril "hath tied / Sharp-tooth'd unkindness, like a vulture here," pointing to his heart. Regan's answer is that Lear should be patient; she can't believe her sister would "scant her duty" to him. She tells her father that he is old, and should be more discreet. He should return to Goneril and let her take care of him. Lear again can't believe what he hears. Should he return and ask Goneril's forgiveness? Should he kneel before her and say "Dear daughter, I confess that I am old; / Age is unnecessary: on my knees I beg / That you'll vouchsafe me raiment, bed, and food"? Never!

He begins to curse Goneril, and Regan rightly says that someday he will curse her too, "when the rash mood is on." Lear says he never would, because Regan is kind where Goneril is cruel. He is about to ask her again why Kent was put in the stocks when he is interrupted by a trumpet announcing the arrival of Goneril. When she enters, Lear asks her if she is not ashamed to look upon his old white beard. But Regan takes her sister's hand, and Lear feels completely

betrayed. He gets Cornwall to admit that he was responsible for putting Kent in the stocks. Regan pleads with her father to dismiss half his retinue and return to Goneril. Lear cries out that rather than do that he would live out in the open air, or even beg France for a pension.

COMMENT: As usual, Lear doesn't realize how true are the words he speaks. Before the play ends, he will do both: live in the outdoors, in a storm, without a roof to his head, and receive mercy from France and Cordelia.

Lear tells Goneril that he will stay with Regan, and keep his 100 knights. But now Regan tells him he can't. She isn't prepared to receive him yet, as he wasn't supposed to come to her until the end of the month. Again she urges him to return to Goneril. She asks him why he needs even 50 knights. If he stays with her, he'll have to do with 25. Lear answers tragically, "I gave you all." Regan cruelly counters that he certainly took his time about it. She and Goneril keep arguing with him and finally doubt that he needs even one attendant, and Lear cries, "O! reason not the need."

COMMENT: In a way the sisters are right. They have sufficient servants to take care of Lear's needs. What they don't realize, or ignore, is that he is arguing for retaining his knights as a matter of principle. Also, he still wants to keep some of the grandeur he had as King, even after giving up his kingdom. This desire is part of his folly, but it is more understandable than his folly in banishing Cordelia. Lear is arguing for distributive justice. He will distribute superfluity to beggars in the storm scene. The sisters' argument is that retributive justice—what would legally be sufficient—is enough.

Lear cries to the heavens for patience: "You see me here, you Gods, a poor old man, / As full of grief as age; wretched in both!" He vows that he will not weep; instead he'll take revenge on both daughters.

COMMENT: He threatens them with revenge in such a broken and incoherent way that we can see it is a hollow threat.

For the first time, from a distance, we hear the storm which will unleash all its fury on Lear in the next act. Crying again to the Fool that he will "go mad," Lear leaves, followed by Gloucester, Kent and the Fool.

Cornwall, hearing the storm, asks Regan and Goneril to come back into the castle with him. Regan says the castle is too small to house Lear and all his retainers. She will receive him gladly, "but not one follower." Goneril agrees that he has only himself to blame if he is left outdoors in the storm. Gloucester returns, and tells the sisters that their father is in a towering rage. Regan cooly answers that this will teach him a lesson: "He is attended with a desperate train" who would abuse her hospitality. Regan orders the doors of the castle to be shut as the storm finally breaks, and the act ends.

SUMMARY: This is a crucial scene in the play for the following reasons:

1. Both daughters behave their worst yet to Lear. His sense of betrayal, when Regan backs up Goneril in her demands that he get rid of his retinue, affects him both mentally and physically:

   a. Mentally, it sends him closer to the brink of madness.

   b. Physically, it sends him out into a deserted, desolate heath just as a storm is breaking. A heath is like a moor: it is a vast area of waste land, with only low, scrubby vegetation growing on it. Heaths figure prominently in *Macbeth*, *Wuthering Heights*, and *The Return of the Native*, as well as in *King Lear*. They always symbolize man's puniness in the face of a hostile, or at least indifferent universe.

2. The scene separates Cornwall from Albany in the extent of their villainy. Albany, when last seen, had begun to sense how evil his wife was. Cornwall, on the other hand, in this scene aids Regan in her nastiness to Lear.

3. It brings the audience's sympathy completely over to Lear's side. Where he might have seemed arbitrary and unjust in earlier scenes, the terrible treatment he receives from both daughters here makes us forget that. Lear becomes like a ping-pong ball being battered from one daughter to the other. Even his haggling over how many knights he is to keep obviously stems more from a desire to hang on to some remnant of the respect he enjoyed as a King than from mere willful pride. Although one can see how irritating he must have been to have around, the degree of his mental suffering at the hands of his daughters far exceeds any annoyance he may have given them.

4. It must be remembered that technically, neither Goneril nor Regan has the right to shut the doors of Gloucester's castle on anybody. But Gloucester, although basically a good man, is too weak to stand up to them.

Act III: Scene i

Kent and a Gentleman meet out on the heath. The storm by now has reached full fury. Both men are searching for Lear. The Gentleman tells Kent that he last saw the King "contending with the fretful elements." Lear was shouting that the wind could blow the earth into the ocean, as far as he cared, if only the world as it now exists would change or cease to be. The Gentleman also tells Kent that Lear is accompanied only by the Fool, who is trying to keep his spirits up. Kent, in turn, informs the Gentleman of two important developments:

1. Albany and Cornwall are vying for power and are bringing England to the brink of civil war.

2. France, hearing of the mistreatment of his father-in-law, has launched an invasion of England.

COMMENT: The hint of the invasion of England shows that though all has gone well up to now with Regan and Goneril, retribution in the form of an invasion from France may be at hand. It is often noted as an inconsistency that the King of France could not have heard of the sisters' treatment of Lear. On stage this would not be noticed.

Kent tells the Gentleman to make his way to Dover, where he will find the invasion force. Giving him a ring which will identify him to Cordelia, he tells the Gentleman to inform her of recent developments.

SUMMARY: In this brief scene the plot is advanced in the following ways:

1. We realize anew that the evil sisters are also greedy. They are egging their husbands on to fight each other for more land.

2. All is not lost for Lear. Cordelia and her husband are planning an invasion to set him back on the throne and banish the evil sisters and their husbands. This was a delicate matter for Shakespeare, because his audience would naturally react strongly against any invasion of England by France. He shows in this scene, however, that the King of France has no interest in capturing and ruling England. He merely wants to make Cordelia happy by rescuing her father from the clutches of Goneril and Regan.

3. The scene also functions as a quiet interlude between two scenes of immense emotional force. Plot is more important in it than passion.

Act III: Scene ii

On another part of the heath, we find Lear raging against the storm. He defies the winds to crack their cheeks with blowing and calls out for cataracts to drown the earth and for thunderbolts to singe his white head. In this great speech, interrupted only briefly by some sardonic remarks by the Fool, Lear says that Nature, even at her most violent, is not so cruel as his daughters. The elements, indeed, are merely "servile ministers," because they combine with Lear's daughters to make him wretched. If the storm could accomplish just one thing—destroy the mould of Nature from which "ungrateful man" comes, it would be justified in Lear's eyes, even though he suffers in the process.

COMMENT: The great storm could be taken as a metaphor, or symbol, of the storm which is really going on in Lear's mind. Because he is a king, a great man on whom the good of his people depends, his stormy moods are reflected in Nature. Also the storm represents the upsetting of the order of Nature which Lear caused by making his daughters his masters. This storm scene is the first of several key scenes in the play which are very difficult to stage believably. The power of Lear's language makes any physical storm, produced by wind machines and other sound and lighting effects, seem puny by comparison.

As Lear raves, the Fool keeps trying to comfort him with jests and snatches of song. Then Kent enters. He is shocked to see his sovereign out in this weather, bareheaded and accompanied only by his Fool. Even "things that love night / Love not such nights as these," Kent says. Since he reached manhood, he has not seen "Such sheets of fire, such bursts of horrid thunder,/ Such groans of roaring wind and rain."

To Lear, however, the storm represents a kind of wild justice taken by the "great Gods" against sinful man. Nevertheless, he himself, he feels, is a man "more sinned against than sinning." (Ironically, the real sinners, of course, are comfortably indoors.) Kent tries to persuade Lear to take temporary shelter in a hovel or hut nearby, while he attempts to force Regan and Cornwall to open their gates to Lear. The King, in his misery, feels his "wits begin to turn"—in other words, he is going mad. However, he agrees to find temporary shelter, even in a peasant hovel, because necessity "can make vile things precious." He goes off with the Fool, who sings an adaptation of the popular Elizabethan song. "The rain it raineth every day," which Feste also sings in *Twelfth Night*.

COMMENT: By accepting the proposal that he seek shelter in a lowly hut, Lear shows that he is beginning to learn to divest himself of worldly pomp and possessions. At the beginning of the play, in all his courtly splendor, he would never have dreamt of taking shelter in a peasant's hut.

SUMMARY: The value of this scene is essentially poetic. Unlike the preceding scene, in which important plot points were given, here nothing "happens," except in Lear's tortured mind. Although Lear is not yet totally mad, his mind is failing. He and Kent and the Fool talk at cross-purposes. Among the points stressed in this scene are the following:

1. Man's puniness and isolation in the face of an overwhelming Universe which is indifferent to what goes on in it.

2. The fact that, cruel as Nature can be, it is not nearly so cruel as human beings.

3. The stubborn, practical loyalty of Kent.

4. The loyalty of the Fool. Although he continues his jests at Lear's expense and is himself terrified of the storm, he sticks by his master.

5. The great poetic effect of the storm itself, which is:

    a. A metaphor for the stormy emotions within Lear.

    b. A demonstration of the chaos produced in Nature when any part of it is upset or overturned. This happened when Lear attempted to buy the love of his daughters, disowned Cordelia, and ultimately allowed his children to rule him instead of his ruling them. This upsetting of the balance of nature was discussed in Act 1, Scene ii, by Gloucester, when he noted that the "late eclipses in the sun and moon portend no good to us."

The difficulty of staging this storm scene has led to one of the most famous critical comments about *King Lear*. This is the statement by Charles Lamb, the 19th century English essayist, that Lear is more effective when read to oneself in the study than when seen on the stage, because "the Lear of Shakespeare cannot be acted. The contemptible machinery by which they mimic the storm which he goes out in, is not more inadequate to represent the horrors of the real elements, than any actor can be to represent Lear...." Even today, with more ingenious stage machinery, the actual storm is never as effective as Lear's words about it. In Shakespeare's day the scene was performed in broad daylight on an open stage, with no attempt at sound or lighting effects.

Act III: Scene iii

We move, in this scene, from the heath to a room in Gloucester's castle. Gloucester is bemoaning to Edmund the fact that he was forced by Regan and Cornwall to lock the doors of his own house against Lear. In addition, they warned Gloucester "on pain of perpetual displeasure, neither to speak of (Lear), entreat for him, or any way sustain him." Edmund hypocritically calls this behavior "most savage and unnatural."

Then Gloucester makes a fatal mistake. He tells his son the news that there is a rift between Albany and Cornwall, and, more important, that he has a letter announcing the invasion of England by France to "revenge" the "injuries the King now bears." Realizing how dangerous it is to have such a treasonable letter in his possession, Gloucester has locked it up for safekeeping. He then tells Edmund that he is going out to search for Lear, even if he is killed for doing so. If Regan and Cornwall should ask Edmund where Gloucester is, Edmund is to tell them that he is ill and has gone to bed.

No sooner does Gloucester leave than Edmund decides to retail the information he has received to Cornwall. Gloucester will be a double traitor in Cornwall's eyes, because:

1. Cornwall has forbidden him to help the King.
2. Gloucester has a treasonous letter in his possession telling about the invasion from France.

Edmund soliloquizes after his father leaves that "the younger rises when the old doth fall." In other words, he is perfectly coldblooded about betraying his father. If Gloucester is executed for "treason," Edmund will inherit his property.

SUMMARY: In this short scene we are shown the following things about Gloucester and Edmund:

1. Gloucester's essential soft-heartedness. He is miserable about allowing Lear to be locked out of his house. Now he will try to make it up to Lear by going in search of him.

2. Gloucester's continued naïvete. He tells his son secrets which could get him in trouble with Cornwall. These secrets are:

    a. That he is going out to search for Lear against Cornwall's orders.

    b. That he has heard of a civil war brewing between Albany and Cornwall.

    c. That he has in his possession a letter telling of the invasion from France to right the wrong done to Lear. Although Gloucester is sufficiently prudent to keep the letter from France hidden under lock and key, he is extremely foolhardy in letting Edmund know that he has it.

3. Gloucester's weakness is shown in two ways:

    a. He has allowed his own castle to be taken over by Cornwall.

    b. He is allowing Cornwall to dictate to him what his behavior ought to be to Lear.

4. Another aspect of Edmund's villainy. He is now plotting not only:

    a. To get his brother disinherited by slandering him to Gloucester, but

    b. To get his father into grave trouble by telling Cornwall he is a traitor. His justification for so callous an act is that Nature—his "goddess," we remember—dictates that the old must fall while the young rise in fortune. By possibly getting his father executed, he is merely speeding up the inevitable processes of Nature.

Act III: Scene iv

We are now in front of the hovel to which Kent has led Lear and the Fool. The storm is still raging. Kent tries to persuade Lear to enter, saying "the tyranny of the open night's too rough / For nature to endure." But Lear answers that it would break his heart to take shelter from the storm because then he would be free to think about his ungrateful daughters. He prefers to endure the storm, he says, because at least that keeps his mind off Goneril and Regan. "Pour on," he defies the storm, "I will endure." But then his resolution begins to weaken, and he cries, "O Regan, Goneril! Your old kind father, whose frank heart gave all. . . ." He then breaks off, realizing that brooding about how his daughters have wronged him will lead him directly to madness.

COMMENT: There is more than a trace of self-pity in Lear, as his reference to himself as a kind father shows. He has also claimed, we remember, that he is "more sinned against than sinning." This self-pity does not detract from his grandeur or make his situation any less genuinely tragic; it merely makes him more believable as a human being.

Lear tells the Fool to go into the hovel first, while he waits outside. He will pray and then sleep. After the Fool enters the shack, Lear voices a magnificent prayer for all the "poor naked wretches," wherever they are, who must "bide the pelting of this pitiless storm." He realizes now, in his own wretchedness, that when he was King, he had taken too little care of his poverty-stricken subjects. Now he has learned true compassion for the physically miserable of the world. "Take physic (medicine), Pomp," he cries, "Expose thyself to feel what wretches feel."

Lear's meditation is abruptly broken by Edgar, who, dressed as the madman, Tom of Bedlam, shouts from within the hut. Apparently he had taken shelter there before Lear arrived. In a minute the Fool comes rushing out shouting that he's seen a ghost inside the hut. Kent takes command of the situation, calling into the hut for whoever it is to come out. Edgar finally emerges, and, pretending to be mad, cries, "Away! the foul fiend follows me."

COMMENT: Edgar's feigned madness takes the form of a religious persecution mania. He is always fretting about "the foul fiend," meaning Satan. And in reality he is being pursued by a genuine, human "foul fiend," his brother Edmund.

Lear's immediate reaction to the spectacle is that Edgar, too, must have given everything he had to his daughters. Otherwise he couldn't have fallen into such a sorry state. Edgar answers Lear's questions about himself with mad gibberish, frequently referring to the fact that "poor Tom's a-cold." Again Lear comments, with tragic irony, "What! has his daughters brought him to this pass?" He cannot imagine that there could be any other reason for going mad than the ingratitude of children. When Kent assures Lear that Edgar has no daughters, Lear refuses to believe him.

The Fool rightly comments that "this cold night will turn us all to fools and madmen." Indeed, a good deal of the eerie atmosphere of the scene is produced by the fact that Edgar is pretending to be mad, Lear is really going mad, and the Fool, speaking as usual in puns, riddles and snatches of songs, often seems to be mad. Only Kent miraculously retains his sturdy sanity. Lear, listening to Edgar's prattle and seeing him in rags, asks, "Is man no more than this? . . . unaccommodated man is no more but such a poor, bare, forked animal as thou art." (By "forked," Lear means two-legged, like a two-pronged fork.) Again he thinks of the puniness of man in a hostile, or at best indifferent universe. The sheep at least has wool to keep it warm, but without clothing man is a miserable, exposed animal. Indeed, as if proving his point, Lear starts tearing his clothes off, to identify himself with all suffering humanity. The Fool prevails on him, though, to keep some clothing on, because it's "a naughty night to swim in."

Now Gloucester, who has been searching for Lear, enters carrying a torch. Edgar pretends to think he is the devil, because of the eerie light which surrounds him. Actually, of course, he is afraid his father will recognize him. It is so dark, though, that at first Gloucester does not see who is there. Nor does he ever recognize Edgar, his own son, in the wretched disguise he has assumed. When Edgar treats him to a typical raving monologue, Gloucester sadly asks Lear, "What! hath your Grace no better company?" He explains to Lear that he is disobeying Regan's and Cornwall's orders to keep his doors barred against the King. He has come to bring Lear to "where both fire and food is ready."

Lear, however, ignores Gloucester's offer, even though Kent, too, urges him to accept. Instead, Lear keeps questioning Edgar, as if he were a learned man. Kent notices this, and asks Gloucester to repeat his offer, because Lear's "wits begin t'unsettle." Gloucester says

he can't blame Lear for going mad; his daughters seek his death. Then he thinks of his own situation, and says he is almost mad, too, because he has a son, who though Gloucester loved him dearly, sought his life.

COMMENT: Gloucester is referring, of course, to Edmund's slanderous story about Edgar. It is ironic that he repeats it in Edgar's actual presence, not recognizing:

1. His own son in disguise.

2. Edgar's innocence and Edmund's guilt.

3. But note his subconscious reaction to his son. There is no reason so strong as Edgar's actual presence for Gloucester to refer to him at this point.

Seeing that he can't get Lear to stir, Gloucester at last persuades him to take shelter inside the hovel, and they all go in as the scene ends.

SUMMARY: In this weird scene, the following things happen:

1. Lear has finally gone completely mad.

2. In his madness, his humanity begins to emerge, as he prays for the poor and wretched of the whole world. When he was King, he was too powerful to bother much about his miserable subjects. Now that he is reduced to their state, he realizes the cruelty of his former pomp and power. He has developed a social conscience. This is symbolized in the play by clothes. In Act I, Scene i, Lear was magnificently dressed, complete with crown and sceptre. Now, in this scene, he tries to tear off his few miserable rags. One of the things he is being forced to learn the hard way is that material possessions are worse than useless and must be gotten rid of if he is to attain any spiritual grace.

3. Gloucester's essential goodness is brought out by his disobeying the orders of Regan and Cornwall and coming out in the storm to try to protect and comfort Lear.

4. We see Edgar for the first time since he has decided to adopt the disguise of a mad beggar. It is so effective a disguise that even Gloucester, his own father, doesn't recognize him in it. In this scene, not only is Edgar disguised, but, we remember, Kent also had disguised himself because Lear had banished him from England on pain of death, but Kent is determined still to serve him. Thus, evil goes about openly in the characters of Goneril, Regan, Cornwall, and Edmund. But the good must go in disguise.

5. The scene has a weird, surrealistic quality derived from the wild storm and from the various degrees of madness, real and feigned. These are:

   a. The real madness of Lear, which is getting progressively worse, even though he fears insanity more than anything else. His insanity has a brooding, compassionate quality to it that makes him a much more decent man than he was in the first scene of the play, when he was in full possession of his faculties. Although he cannot concentrate on what people are saying and has no desire to look after his own physical well-being, the things he himself says are magnificently compassionate, rather than truly mad.

b. The Fool, for all his wisdom, seems partially mad himself. He always speaks so cryptically and obscurely, anyway, that he sounds quite mad in this scene.

c. Edgar is doing a very good job of feigning madness.

Act III: Scene v

We shift back to the "sane" world of a room in Gloucester's castle. Edmund and Cornwall are alone together. Edmund has just told Cornwall that his father, Gloucester, has been plotting treason. The scene opens with Cornwall saying "I will have my revenge ere I depart this house." (Notice that it never strikes Cornwall as poor behavior for a guest to have "revenge" on his host while in the host's own house.)

Edmund hypocritically says that he is afraid that his loyalty to England will bring him the censure of people because it has been at the expense of his natural loyalty as a son. Edmund shows Cornwall the letter telling of the invasion plans from France. (This is the letter Gloucester had foolishly told his son about in Act III, Scene iii.) "O Heavens!" Edmund hypocritically cries, "that this treason were not, or not I the detector!" Cornwall assures Edmund that whether the report of the invasion in the letter is true or false, Gloucester is still guilty of treason for receiving the letter and, as a traitor, has forfeited his earldom. Cornwall makes Edmund the new Earl of Gloucester and tells him to find his father so that Cornwall can arrest him. In an aside, Edmund says that he'll try to catch his father in the act of comforting Lear, which will make Gloucester even more treasonous in the eyes of Cornwall. But aloud to Cornwall all he says is that he will "persever in my course of loyalty, though the conflict be sore between that and my blood." In other words, he will be loyal to Cornwall, even though his blood, or natural filial loyalty, tells him not to be. Cornwall assures him that he will find "a dearer father (than Gloucester) in my love," and the scene ends with each hypocrite giving assurances of loyalty to the other.

SUMMARY: This scene pushes ahead the subplot, preparing us for its climax in Scene vii. It does this by:

1. Showing Cornwall increasingly involved in evil. So far he has

a. Backed up Regan and Goneril in their mistreatment of Lear.

b. Barred the doors of Gloucester's castle against Lear during a storm, and now

c. Vowed to arrest Gloucester as a traitor.

2. Showing Edmund smoothly and coldly snatching the earldom from his father while Gloucester is still alive, and adding still another dupe—Cornwall this time—to his list. He has so far:

a. Persuaded Gloucester that Edgar is plotting against him.

b. Persuaded Edgar that since for some mysterious reason Gloucester is angry at him, he had better flee.

c. Now persuaded Cornwall that Gloucester is a traitor to England.

Act III: Scene vi

We are now in a room in a farmhouse near Gloucester's castle. Gloucester and Kent enter. Gloucester tells Kent that he will try to get some food and additional supplies to make the room more comfortable for the King, and off he goes. Now Lear, Edgar and the Fool come in. Edgar is still muttering gibberish and warning everyone to "beware the foul fiend." The Fool asks Lear one of his typical riddles: "Tell me whether a madman be a gentleman or a yeoman (a farmer)." Lear's answer is that a madman is a king. He is getting good at solving the Fool's riddles.

For a moment Lear thinks of taking military revenge on his daughters ("red burning spits / Come hissing in upon 'em"). Then he abandons this idea and decides to try his daughters for their cruelty. This is another and more pathetic way of revenging himself on his daughters. Calling Edgar "most learned justicer," and the Fool "sapient (wise) sir," he tells them to be seated, for the trial is about to begin. Kent tries to bring him to his senses, begging him to lie down and rest, but Lear insists on holding his "trial" first. The first to be arraigned is Goneril, about whom Lear says that "she kick'd the poor King her father." Then Lear "tries" Regan. Meanwhile Kent is appalled at Lear's madness, and Edgar is so much moved by the spectacle of the old man trying two daughters who aren't even there that he begins to weep. He fears his tears will be noticed and his disguise discovered. Lear asks tragically in his "anatomizing" of Regan, "Is there any cause in nature that makes these hard hearts?"

Tiring finally of the mock trial, Lear prepares to go to bed, asking Kent to "draw the curtains." (Evidently in his madness he thinks he is back in his own castle, not in a rude farmhouse.) Then he says, "We'll go to supper i' the' morning," because Gloucester has not yet returned with food, and Lear must go without eating that night. The Fool adds, "And I'll go to bed at noon."

COMMENT: These are the last words we hear from the Fool. After this he disappears mysteriously from the play. Some critics have thought these words have a double meaning, namely, that "bed" means "grave" and that the Fool has a premonition of an untimely death.

Now Gloucester finally gets back. He asks Kent where Lear is. Kent answers that he's there in the hut, but asks Gloucester not to trouble him, because "his wits are gone." Gloucester replies that he has overheard a plot to kill the King. He tells Kent to place the sleeping Lear on a stretcher and carry him to Dover, where he will meet Cordelia and France. He warns Kent to hurry. If he wastes even half an hour, Lear's life, as well as Kent's "stand in assured loss." Kent regrets that Lear can't be allowed to rest undisturbed, but he orders the Fool to help him carry the stretcher away. Kent, Gloucester and the Fool all leave, bearing the King and leaving Edgar alone in the hut to soliloquize that because Lear's sufferings are even greater than his own, they help him to bear his own better. (Because Edgar is alone, his soliloquy is spoken in his own voice, not in the disguised voice of Tom of Bedlam.)

SUMMARY: This scene has the following functions:

1. It shows us Lear at his maddest so far in the play. The "trial" he conducts of Goneril and Regan is both a deadly serious and true indictment, and, at the same time, ridiculous because:

    a. The defendants aren't there, but are represented by farmstools.

    b. The lawyers are either mad or pretending to be mad.

2. It shows that Regan and Cornwall are determined to have Lear killed. If Lear were dead, the expedition of Cordelia and France to restore him, or at least to aid him, would be robbed of its purpose.

3. It shows that not only is Lear in mortal danger—increased now by his inability to care for himself—but so is anyone caught aiding him. This fact prepares us for the horrible blinding of Gloucester in the next scene. Obviously, Regan and Cornwall will stop at nothing to make sure that justice, in the form of France and Cordelia, will not catch up with them. The greater the threat of invasion, the crueler and more reckless they become.

Act III: Scene vii

This is the most terrifying and blood-curdling scene in the play. It opens in a room in Gloucester's castle on the morning after the storm, with Cornwall telling Goneril to deliver a letter to her husband, Albany. The letter, which is the same one Edmund had stolen from Gloucester, informs Albany that the army of France has landed at Dover. Cornwall is obviously anxious to end the feud with his brother-in-law, and unite with him against France. Cornwall also orders a servant to find the "traitor," Gloucester. On hearing Gloucester's name, the bloodthirsty Regan cries, "Hang him instantly." Goneril adds, "Pluck out his eyes." But Cornwall tells the vicious sisters to let him handle the matter in his own way. He asks Edmund to accompany Goneril on her trip home, because the punishment he is about to mete out to Gloucester is "not fit for your beholding"; in other words, it will be too horrible for the victim's son to witness.

COMMENT: This desire of Cornwall's to observe all the proprieties by not letting Edmund witness his father's punishment is doubly ironic, because:

1. It is Edmund who is solely responsible for Gloucester's being in peril in the first place. Nothing Cornwall will do to Gloucester can be as cruel as Edmund's betraying him.

2. If Cornwall is so proper that he doesn't want Edmund to see what he is going to do to Gloucester, why do it in the first place?

Now Oswald enters and Cornwall asks him where Lear is. Oswald tells him that the King has been spirited away by Gloucester. Followed by some of his loyal knights, he is now headed for safety in Dover, where France and Cordelia are. Saying hasty farewells to Goneril and Edmund, Cornwall orders some servants to capture Gloucester and bring him back to the castle. He reflects to himself that although he can't give Gloucester a fair trial, his power in the land is so great that while men may blame what he is doing, they can do nothing about it.

In a minute the servants re-enter, bringing in Gloucester as a prisoner. Cornwall orders his arms bound, and the servants tie Gloucester into a chair. The old man cannot understand why he is being treated this way. He reminds Cornwall and Regan that they are his guests in his own castle. Regan's reply is to call Gloucester a "filthy traitor," and to pluck his beard in a traditional gesture of contempt. Gloucester protests his innocence and tells Regan that the white hairs she has just plucked from his beard will come to life and accuse her. Cornwall and Regan now question

Gloucester viciously about his alleged treachery, and demand to know why he has sent Lear to Dover.

Gloucester answers that he has sent the King to safety because he "would not see thy cruel nails / Pluck out his poor old eyes." (Ironically, this is just what is about to happen to Gloucester himself.) He tells Regan that if wolves had howled at her gate for shelter from the storm the night before, she would have given it to them, yet she turned out her own father. Gloucester takes comfort in the thought that he "shall see / The winged vengeance overtake such children." But Cornwall, ordering his servants to hold fast the chair to which Gloucester has been tied, assures him he will never see anything again, and proceeds with his thumbs to gouge out one of Gloucester's eyes. The blood-thirsty Regan insists that he gouge out the other eye, too. But before Cornwall can do so, one of his servants, unable to stand the spectacle, begs him to cease. He tells Cornwall that he served him since childhood, but the best service he can do him now is to beg him to let Gloucester alone. Cornwall and the servant now draw swords and begin to fight. The servant wounds Cornwall seriously, but before he can finish him off, Regan grabs a sword and stabs the servant in the back, killing him instantly. Then Cornwall, even though he is in mortal pain, cries, "Out, vile jelly!" and gouges out Gloucester's other eye.

In the depths of his agony, Gloucester cries out for Edmund. But with vicious satisfaction Regan informs him that Edmund hates him and that it was Edmund who let them know of his treachery. Suddenly Gloucester perceives the whole plot against him and cries out at his folly. He begs the gods to forgive him for abusing his one good son and begs them to bring Edgar to prosperity. Regan orders the servants to thrust Gloucester out of his castle, and, since he is now blind, to "let him smell / His way to Dover."

When a servant leaves, leading Gloucester with him, Regan asks her husband how his wound is. Cornwall first orders Gloucester to be turned out of the castle grounds and the servant who revolted against him to be thrown on a dunghill. Then he replies that he is bleeding badly. Regan helps him out of the room. The two remaining servants comment on the viciousness of their lord and lady and vow to help Gloucester. One of them will find Tom of Bedlam, who will lead Gloucester to Dover, and the other will apply some ointment to his bleeding wounds.

SUMMARY: In this ferociously barbaric scene, several important things happen:

1. Cornwall has obviously become panicky about the news of an invasion from France. He is trying to enlist the aid of Albany in fighting it, although he himself had been on the brink of civil war with Albany.

2. The two sisters are shown to be at least as vicious as Cornwall. Regan is even more insistent than her husband is about taking fierce revenge on Gloucester.

3. Edmund is shown to be quite willing to desert his father now that he has delivered him into the hands of his bitter enemies.

4. The actual blinding of Gloucester is significant in at least three ways:

   a. It underscores the violence and savagery of the time in which the play takes place.

   b. It shows the absolute depths of despotic cruelty of which a tyrant like Cornwall is capable.

   c. Most important, as soon as Gloucester is physically blinded he "sees the light" spiritually. That is, when his eyes are put out and he can no longer see the physical world about him, he "sees" inwardly that Edgar is actually his good son and that Edmund is evil. He sees the injustice he has done Edgar in believing Edmund's slanders against him. Recognizing his folly, he understands that he is being punished. Thus, just as Lear begins to gain insight as he goes mad and when, in the storm, he is deprived of all the physical comforts of the world, so here Gloucester, in the moment of his utmost agony, sees truly for the first time. In this way he is very much like another great tragic figure, Oedipus, who is told of his guilt by a blind soothsayer, and only truly believes it when he puts out his own eyes. One difference, however, between the tragedy of Sophocles and that of Shakespeare, is that Shakespeare has the actual blinding take place on stage. In the Greek play, we only see Oedipus after he has blinded himself.

5. Regan's nasty comment—that now Gloucester can "smell his way to Dover"—has a deeper meaning than she realizes. The moral stink that she and her husband have made in England can indeed be smelled. The country reeks of crime, treachery and betrayal. The nose, therefore, can prove a more accurate guide to its moral geography than the eyes.

6. For all the human vileness displayed before the audience's shocked eyes in this scene, certain characters display great nobility. These are:

   a. The first servant. After serving Cornwall all his life, he now turns on him and tries to prevent him from gouging out Gloucester's remaining eye. Shakespeare seems to be saying that even the lowest and most passive people in society will assert themselves for good if pushed far enough by evil power. For Cornwall to be mortally wounded by one of his own servants is most ignominious for him, because of the rigid class structure of the time. It was almost unheard of for a servant to disobey his master, let alone turn against him.

b. The second and third servants. Although they have been silent throughout the scene, they vow at the end to do all they can to aid Gloucester.

c. Lear's retainers. According to Oswald, at least 35 of them are loyally trying to help him get to Dover.

These good people, Lear's retainers and Cornwall's servants, maintain the shaky cause of humanity during the darkest part of the play. They help prepare us for the ultimate humanity of Cordelia while she is off stage. In addition, by pitting the servants against Cornwall and Regan, Shakespeare heightens the element of the conflict between good and evil which dominates the play.

Act IV: Scene i

This scene, one of the most philosophically rich in the play, takes place on a heath near Gloucester's castle, immediately after the barbaric events of the preceding scene. Edgar enters alone, still disguised as Tom of Bedlam. He philosophizes in a soliloquy that since he has reached the lowest ebb in his fortunes, things can only improve for him. Normally a hopeful and active young man, Edgar refuse to despair. Having hit bottom, he feels he can only rise: "the lamentable change is from the best," he says, "The worst returns to laughter."

But Edgar's hopeful philosophy is shattered by the sight of his father, the blinded Gloucester, who enters at this point. Gloucester, whose eyes are still bleeding, is led by a humble old man, who has been a tenant on the Gloucester estate for 80 years. When Edgar sees the pathetic pair, he cries, "World, world, O world! / But that thy strange mutations make us hate thee, / Life would not yield to age." This is an extension of the philosophical position which he had just taken in his soliloquy. Here Edgar feels that it is only the changes in fortune that chance brings to our lives which reconcile us to growing old and dying. These changes make us hate life so bitterly that we do not mind leaving the world when our time has come. Meanwhile Gloucester, who of course cannot see his son and who doesn't recognize his voice, which Edgar has disguised, tries to get rid of his old tenant. He tells the old man that he can no longer comfort him, and to be seen with Gloucester would be dangerous to him. When the old man protests that Gloucester cannot see his way alone, Gloucester bitterly replies, "I have no way, and therefore want no eyes; / I stumbled when I saw."

COMMENT: This supports the point made in the previous scene, in which the difference between mere physical sight and true inward vision was dramatized by the putting out of Gloucester's eyes followed by his realization of Edmund's guilt and Edgar's innocence. He means here that he stumbled in his attitude to his two sons, as well as in his whole philosophy of life. Now that he is blind he sees truly, and what he sees is that he has no place to go but to death. Gloucester has been contemplating suicide ever since Regan's revelation to him that Edmund, whom he had loved and trusted, had hated and betrayed him.

Gloucester pathetically wishes he might live just long enough to "see" his son Edgar, if only with his sense of touch. (The irony is that he is standing right before Edgar, but doesn't know it. Edgar wants to retain his disguise until he is able to set things right again in his family. It is the only chance he has to defeat his unscrupulous brother.)

The sight of his father plunges Edgar into the depths of pessimism. He has just said that his fortune could only improve. Now he realizes that it has taken a turn for the worse, and may get worse still. In fact, he says, "the worst is not / So long as we can say 'This is the worst.'" In other words, as long as we still have the power of mind to say anything like "this is the worst that can happen," our fortunes can still take a plunge. We can still go mad, or die, and above all, we are not yet entirely without hope.

The old man asks Edgar where he is going, and Gloucester asks whether this stranger (Edgar) is a beggar. When the old man tells Gloucester that Edgar is both a madman and a beggar, Gloucester replies that he must still have some shred of sanity left, or he wouldn't be able to beg. He says he saw a man the night before, in the storm, who reminded him of his son, and who reminds him too of this beggar. Gloucester says that the mad beggar he had seen in the storm (who was, of course, Edgar) was so miserable that he "made me think man a worm." Then Gloucester makes one of the most crushing philosophic statements in the play: "As flies to wanton boys, are we to th' Gods; / They kill us for their sport." The point is that man is destroyed not merely because the gods are indifferent to him; he is destroyed because the gods take a cruel, sadistic glee in crushing him, just as boys enjoy tearing a fly to pieces. This is the most pessimistic religious position taken in the play because it states that evil and suffering in the world are not merely the result of passive indifference, or of chance, but are the result of active, positive cruelty on the part of the gods.

Gloucester again asks the old man to leave him. If he likes, Gloucester says, he may rejoin him further along the road to Dover. But first he asks the old man to procure some clothes for the poor Tom of Bedlam. Meanwhile Gloucester will entrust himself to Tom's care. When the old man protests that the beggar is mad, Gloucester bitterly comments that it is typical of the times that "madmen lead the blind." Finally the old man consents to find some clothes for the almost naked, shivering Edgar. Left alone with his father, Edgar resumes the "mad" patter that he used to disguise himself in the hovel during the storm. Gloucester asks him if he knows the way to Dover and, out of pity for Edgar's mad replies, gives him some money. Gloucester, contemplating suicide, asks Edgar to lead him to one of the high cliffs of Dover. Beyond that point he will not need to be led any further. The pathetic pair leave the stage together.

SUMMARY: The importance of this scene is mainly philosophical. The basic positions taken are as follows:

1. Edgar at first says that once we have reached the lowest ebb in our fortunes, we can be comforted by the thought that they can only improve. This is again the medieval "wheel of fortune" idea which Kent referred to when he was placed in the stocks by Cornwall in Act II, Scene 2. The idea is that a man's life occupies a set position on a great wheel. As the wheel turns, his fortunes rise or fall accordingly. If he starts off at the top, he must inevitably fall; if he starts off at the bottom, he will rise before his inevitable fall, because the wheel is constantly turning.

2. The sight of his father, blind and led by an ancient retainer, makes Edgar modify this view. He now feels that it is good that our fortunes are constantly changing—his own apparently always for the worse—because this makes us hate the world so much that we don't mind leaving it.

3. Then, seeing the full horror of his father's position, Edgar realizes that he was foolish to think he had reached the lowest ebb of his fortunes. As long as we can say, "this is the worst," we can still hope for improvement, so that it is not really the worst that can befall us. The worst comes when we can no longer hope, through madness, despair or death.

Gloucester's philosophy is even more bitter than his son's. He states that:

1. Since he "stumbled when he saw," in relation to his family, he has no need of eyes. Having sight implies that he has a road to travel in life, but Gloucester is tired of life and wants only to die. He is miserable not only at having had his eyes gouged out, but from the guilt he feels at having disinherited Edgar and trusted Edmund.

2. Man is just a puny worm, at the mercy of the elements, as he realized in the storm the night before. Also, the gods who rule man's fate are not only not benevolent to him, they are not even indifferent or uncaring. Instead they are

consciously and actively sadistic: eager, like boys torturing a fly, only to inflict pain.

3. The world of men, by which Gloucester means mainly the political and social world, consists of the mad leading the blind.

4. Nevertheless, the extreme pessimism of Gloucester's position does not make him cruel or cynical. When he asks the old man to find clothes for Edgar, it is from a compassionate feeling for all suffering humanity. In this he is very much like Lear, who prayed in Act III, Scene 4, for all the "poor naked wretches," wherever they were, who were exposed to the fury of nature. In that scene Lear regretted his former indifference to the suffering of his people. In this scene Gloucester's only care before he tries to commit suicide is to help out the equally wretched Tom of Bedlam.

5. Gloucester's moving concern, in his misery, for the misery of Tom is reflected, too, by the old tenant of his estates, who tries to comfort Gloucester. Even though it is dangerous to be seen aiding Gloucester, the old man refuses to desert him. He is one of the simple, humble people, like Lear's loyal retainers and Cornwall's mutinous servants, who are innately decent and good.

6. The help that Edgar gives to his father parallels the main plot, where Cordelia helps Lear.

Act IV: Scene ii

This scene takes place the following day, in front of the Duke of Albany's palace. Goneril and Edmund have just arrived after their trip from Gloucester's castle. Goneril welcomes Edmund to her home, but expresses surprise that Albany is not on hand to greet them. She asks Oswald, who enters at this point, where his master is. Oswald tells her that a great change has come over Albany. When Oswald told him that France had landed an army at Dover, Albany merely smiled at the news. When told that Goneril was coming home, Albany had curtly commented, "the worse." In short, Oswald complains, "What most he should dislike seems pleasant to him; / What like, offensive."

Goneril's response to this news is that her "mild husband" is probably too frightened to fight against the French invasion. She scornfully tells Edmund about the "cowish terror" of her husband's spirit, and asks Edmund to return to Gloucester's castle and hasten Cornwall's war preparations. Hinting that she would not take it amiss if Edmund were to murder Albany some day, she gives him a "favor," or souvenir, and a kiss, and speeds him on his way.

COMMENT: Obviously Goneril's latent love for Edmund has blossomed during their journey alone from Gloucester's castle to her home. In Albany's moral scruples about the plot she has involved him in, she sees only weakness and effeminacy. The contrast between her dull, sedate husband, and the virile, unscrupulous Edmund has begun to grate on Goneril's nerves, and she is about to add marital infidelity to her other sins.

As soon as Edmund is gone, Albany enters. Goneril sarcastically comments on his delay in greeting her, sneering, "I have been worth the whistle." Albany, however, loses no time, in upbraiding her for her behavior. "O Goneril!" he cries, "You are not worth the dust which the rude wind / Blows in your face." He accuses her and Regan of being "Tigers, not daughters" for their behavior to their father. He is amazed that Cornwall allowed them to lock Lear out in the storm (obviously he doesn't know Cornwall), and foretells that if the heavens don't tame such wild offenses, then "Humanity must perforce prey on itself / Like monsters of the deep." (This, of course, is precisely what is happening throughout the play.)

Goneril's only reply to this richly deserved tongue-lashing is to accuse Albany of being a "milk-liver'd man," in short, a coward, for not arming against France. The argument heightens in intensity, with Albany finally shouting that if he were not a man and Goneril were not a woman, he would tear apart her flesh and bones. Goneril sneers at this statement, coolly and contemptuously like a great cat, "Marry, your manhood—mew!"

At this point a messenger enters with the news that Cornwall has died of the wounds inflicted on him by his servant. It is the first Albany has heard of the putting out of Gloucester's eyes. He is torn between horror at that monstrous act and relief at the swift justice that overtook Cornwall for committing it "This shows you are above, / You justicers," Albany exults, "that these our nether crimes / So speedily can venge!" In other words, to him the stabbing of Cornwall by the servant is a demonstration (1) that the gods are just, and (2) that they act speedily to punish the criminal, even if, ironically, they do it through a mere servant. This is one of the more optimistic statements of belief in the play.

The news of Cornwall's death has a very different effect on Goneril. To her, it is both good and bad. The good part is that with Cornwall dead, she may be able to usurp his and her sister's part of the kingdom. The bad part is that now Regan as a widow may be able to marry Edmund. To make matters worse, Goneril herself has just sent Edmund to Regan, thus allowing them plenty of opportunity to scheme against her, while she is stuck with her now distasteful husband, Albany. She must have time to think; hence, she takes a letter the messenger has brought her from her sister and retires within the palace with the excuse that she must read and answer it.

Albany asks the messenger where Edmund was all the time that Gloucester was being tortured. The messenger replies that Edmund was escorting Goneril home and has since departed again. Did he know what was being done to his father, Albany asks? Not only did he know, the messenger replies, but it was Edmund who betrayed Gloucester in the first place. Albany swears to "revenge" Gloucester's eyes and to thank him for the love and loyalty he showed to King Lear.

SUMMARY: Several new plot developments take place in this scene. They are:

1. The arrival at the Duke of Albany's castle of Goneril and Edmund, after a trip which has apparently solidified their adulterous love for each other.

2. Albany has by now evidently gone over completely to the "good" side in the play. He refuses to arm against the French invasion, and he swears to avenge the tortures undergone by Lear and Gloucester. He has come to the vision that humanity will prey on itself like sharks unless the evil train of events is stopped. This is the true Shakespearean vision of the power of one crime or sin, left unchecked, to bring moral chaos and anarchy on the world.

3. Albany and Goneril are now quite openly at war with each other.

4. Goneril is frantic at the thought that the death of Cornwall will leave the way open for Edmund and Regan to marry. What she wants is for Edmund to kill Albany and marry her. Then they can take over Regan's portion of the kingdom for themselves. This scene launches the complex and vicious infighting among the three major evil characters left alive: Goneril, Regan and Edmund. Their passionate scheming will eventually lead to their own deaths.

5. The balance of power against Lear has been diminished by two important characters: (a.) Cornwall is dead, and (b.) Albany's sympathies are now on Lear's side.

6. Oswald, however, remains in character by being loyal to Goneril and treacherous to Albany. He tells Goneril of her husband's shift of sympathies with smirking satisfaction.

7. The animal imagery which runs through the play reaches a peak of savagery here. Goneril compares Albany to a cow, and Albany, in turn, compares Goneril and Regan to tigers and to sea-monsters. Finally, Goneril actually mews at her husband like a great cat. The significance of the imagery is that when human beings lose their humanity and begin behaving like animals, they turn the normal social world into a beastly jungle, where no code of ethics or morality reigns except vicious self-interest.

Act IV: Scene iii

This scene provides necessary relief and contrast from the squabbling between Albany and Goneril in the preceding scene. It consists of a quiet conversation between Kent and a Gentleman in the French camp near Dover. Kent learns from the Gentleman that the King of France has had to return home on urgent business which required his personal attention. He has left behind him in Dover Cordelia and a Marshal of France, one Monsieur La Far, to conduct the campaign in his absence. The Gentleman is the same one who was sent by Kent to Cordelia in Act III, Scene i, bearing letters telling her of the mistreatment of Lear. Kent now asks him what her reaction was to the news of Lear's suffering. The Gentleman reports that she simultaneously wept with sorrow and smiled with patience, shaking "holy water from her heavenly eyes." Kent, marvelling at the difference between Cordelia and her sisters, muses that "It is the stars, / The stars above us, govern our conditions; / Else one self mate and make could not beget / Such different issues." In other words, man is ruled by an unalterable destiny which he cannot understand. Otherwise how can one explain a Cordelia and a Goneril or Regan being born to the same parents?

Kent then tells the Gentleman that although Lear has arrived in Dover, he refuses to see Cordelia for shame at having given "her dear rights / To his dog-hearted daughters." The Gentleman says that Albany's and Cornwall's armies are on the March, and the scene ends with Kent begging the Gentleman to put up a little longer with his disguise—he will reveal himself when the time is ripe.

SUMMARY: This brief scene, in addition to providing emotional relief, contains the following plot points:

1. After successfully landing an invasion army at Dover, the King of France had to return on urgent business, leaving behind him Cordelia and a Marshal in charge of the army.

2. Cordelia has demonstrated her saintly nobility and forgiveness on hearing the ill treatment her father had received at the hands of Goneril and Regan.

3.   Although Lear has arrived safely at Dover, he is too embarrassed to meet Cordelia, fearing she will not forgive him for the wrongs he has done her.

4. Although Cornwall is dead, his army is still marching with Albany's against the Dover encampment.

Act IV: Scene iv

Amid a flourish of drums and flags in the French camp, Cordelia enters, accompanied by a doctor and some soldiers. Apparently some time has elapsed since the last scene. In that time, Cordelia has received a distressing report about her father. Lear has managed to wander away, in his madness, from the attendants who were supposed to guard him. Cordelia tells the doctor that her father was seen, completely mad, singing aloud and dressed with a variety of flowers. She tells a soldier to send out a hundred troops to look for the King and bring him back to the camp. Then she asks the doctor if there is anything he can do to restore Lear's senses to him. Whoever can do that, Cordelia says, can have all her possessions. The doctor replies that the only treatment he can prescribe for Lear is rest, the "foster-nurse of nature." Cordelia again begs the troops to go in search of Lear, lest, in his insanity, he come to some harm.

Now a messenger arrives with the news that the armies of Albany and Cornwall are fast approaching. Cordelia answers that she is prepared for them. She stresses the point that if there is war, it will be to save her father, not because of any "blown ambition" on France's part. With a prayer that she may soon see her father again, the scene ends.

SUMMARY: In this short scene we learn that Lear, no longer capable of taking care of himself, has escaped from his guards. The news brings out Cordelia's deep concern for her father, and shows a new maturity in her love for him. Other important points in the scene are these:

1. Cordelia's statement that the armies of France are in England not for any territorial ambition, but to restore Lear to his rights. This is very important because Shakespeare's audience was fiercely patriotic and would have been highly suspicious of Cordelia because she was connected with a foreign invasion of England. Patriotism is the reason for Albany's joining his army with Cornwall's, even though he now despises Cornwall, Edmund and their whole plot. Nevertheless Albany feels required, as a loyal Englishman, to help repel any French invasion, however noble its purpose.

2. There are at least two echoes of incidents in other Shakespeare plays in this scene. They are:

   a. Lear decking himself with flowers in his madness is like the mad Ophelia wearing flowers in her death scene in *Hamlet*.

   b. The doctor's recommendation of rest as the only possible cure for madness is like the doctor recommending rest for the sleep-walking Lady Macbeth.

Act IV: Scene v

We are back in Gloucester's castle, where Regan has remained after Cornwall's death. She is questioning Oswald, who has just arrived with Goneril's letter for

Edmund. Regan asks Oswald if Albany's troops are on the move, and if Albany is leading them. Oswald snidely tells her that while the army is indeed marching, with Albany at the head, Goneril is "the better soldier" than her husband. Then Regan tries to pry loose from Oswald some information about the letter which was given him in Act IV, Scene ii. Oswald pretends ignorance out of loyalty to his mistress. Regan tells him he can't deliver the letter to Edmund there anyway, because Edmund has gone off to kill Gloucester and to find out how strong the French army is. Letting Gloucester live after blinding him, she tells Oswald, was a great mistake. Wherever he goes in his wretchedness he arouses "all hearts against us." According to her, however, Edmund's motive in killing his father will be "pity of his misery."

Then Regan tries desperately to keep Oswald at the castle, thus making sure that he can't deliver the letter from her sister. She tells him that the roads are dangerous now, with all the troops marching about, but Oswald remains loyal to Goneril and insists on leaving in search of Edmund. Regan then tries to win Oswald over to her side by assuring him that she knows what is going on in the Albany household anyway. "I know your Lady does not love her husband," she tells Oswald. (How much she loved her own husband is shown by her running after Edmund the minute Cornwall is dead.) She assures Oswald that it is "more convenient" for Edmund to marry her, now that she is a widow, than for him to wed the still-married Goneril. Finally, despairing of ever getting Oswald over to her side, Regan tells him he will benefit greatly if he should happen to encounter Gloucester and kill him, and she sends him on his way.

SUMMARY: This brief scene is mainly concerned with the passionate rivalry between Goneril and Regan for the hand of Edmund:

1. Regan remained at Gloucester's castle after her husband's death, probably in order to be with Edmund, who is the new Earl of Gloucester. She is consumed with desire for Edmund, who has temporarily left in order to:

  a. Find and kill Gloucester, who has been arousing too much sympathy among the people who see him, and

  b. Spy on the French army at Dover to see how powerful it is.

2. Goneril, also desperately wanting Edmund, has sent Oswald to find him at Gloucester's castle, not knowing that he had already left.

3. Oswald remains loyal to Goneril, although certainly not to Albany, of whom he speaks in disparaging terms. This steadfast loyalty to his mistress is the one good thing about

Oswald, although one wonders what it is in Goneril that can inspire it. Oswald will suffer in the next scene for placing his loyalty in the wrong hands.

4. Some pretense to goodness is still kept up by Regan when she tells Oswald that Edmund is out to kill Gloucester, his own father, for reasons of "mercy."

Act IV: Scene vi

This is one of the most crucial and difficult scenes in the play. We are in the countryside near Dover where Edgar, disguised as a peasant in the clothing Gloucester's old tenant had found for him in Act IV, Scene i, is leading his blind father. Gloucester's only thought now is of suicide. He wants Edgar to lead him to the top of one of the steep cliffs of Dover, where he will leap into the sea below. But Edgar has other plans. He will tell his father they have reached the cliff's edge when, in fact, they are on level ground. Then, when his father jumps, and, of course, doesn't die, Edgar will tell him that he has been spared because the gods want him to live. Given Gloucester's superstition, Edgar hopes that this "miracle" will give him the strength to continue existing and to recognize his son.

As father and son progress, though, Gloucester's suspicions are aroused. Edgar tells him that they are climbing a "horrible steep" hill, but Gloucester rightly maintains "the ground is even." Edgar asks him if he can't hear the sea roaring below them, and when Gloucester says he can't, Edgar replies that his sense of hearing must be affected by his loss of sight. Then Edgar paints a most ingenious picture of how tiny everything below them is. The crows seems as small as beetles; the fishermen on the beach look like mice, and so forth. Gloucester finally seems convinced and bids Edgar leave him there, giving him his purse as a reward for leading him this far.

Then Gloucester kneels and prays to the "mighty Gods," renouncing the world and saying he cannot bear to be in it any longer. He throws himself forward and falls, fainting with the thought that he has leapt off a cliff. Edgar rushes up to him, awakens him, and says he has fallen "many fathom down." It is a miracle he is still alive, Edgar says. He should have been broken like an egg. Gloucester is merely disappointed that he hasn't in fact died. Edgar helps him to his feet, saying that the beggar who led him to the edge of the cliff was some fiend so that Gloucester can attribute his life to the fact that the gods wished to preserve him. Gloucester vows to bear his affliction until the end and not try to commit suicide again.

COMMENT: Gloucester's attempted suicide is one of the three most difficult scenes in *Lear* to stage effectively. (The other two are the storm scene and the blinding of Gloucester.) The problem is that the audience sees that Gloucester is not really leaping off a cliff, but is merely falling on level ground. For this reason it is difficult to keep the scene from becoming unintentionally funny. The illusion is helped, however, by Edgar's ingenious poetic description of the imaginary tiny figures on the beach below. Furthermore, some modern directors see the scene as intentionally comic, in the tradition of mad, pessimistic humor that is now called "theatre of the absurd."

At this point Lear enters, dressed in wild flowers, as Cordelia had described him in Act IV, Scene iv. He has eluded his attendants, and is wandering madly about, claiming at one point to be a counterfeiter, at another a recruiting officer, then an expert bowman and a sentry. Beneath all his incoherent babble, however, there is a good deal of sane comment on the state of the world. Edgar and Gloucester are struck with horror at the spectacle of the mad King. Gloucester seems to recognize Lear's voice, and asks, "Is't not the King?" Lear answers magnificently, "Ay, every inch a King." But then he ironically adds, "When I do stare, see how the subject quakes." Again, as in Act III, Scene vi, he holds a kind of mock trial, but this time all nature, not merely his daughters, is arraigned. No one shall be executed for adultery from now on, Lear maintains, because the whole natural world, down to the tiniest wrens and flies, is promiscuous. Besides, Lear says bitterly, "Gloucester's bastard son / Was kinder to his father than my daughters / Got 'tween lawful sheets."

COMMENT: Lear is constantly obsessed with the idea that his daughters cannot be legitimate, because he can't understand how he could have begotten such vicious creatures. Here he turns the idea around, and realizes that legitimacy is no guarantee of decency: the bastard Edmund was kinder to his father than Lear's legitimate daughters were to him. Of course, we know what Lear doesn't know, that Edmund is just as vicious as Goneril and Regan.

Then Lear rages against women and sex in general; the "riotous appetite," as he calls it. In sex, he says, is "hell, there's darkness, / There is the sulphurous pit." He is totally revolted by the constant sexual maneuverings throughout all nature, and holds women especially responsible for them. Gloucester, moved deeply by Lear's words, cries, "O! let me kiss that hand." But Lear replies, "Let me wipe it first; it smells of mortality."

COMMENT: "Mortality" has two meanings here:

1. Death, in which case Lear foresees his impending death, with all the attendant stink of corruption, and

2. Life, in the sense of being mortal; being human and alive. Here he means that just being alive involves moral stench and corruption. In this sense, the smell of Lear's hand may be considered one of the ways in which Gloucester can "smell his way to Dover."

Calling Lear a "ruin'd piece of Nature," Gloucester asks if the King recognizes him. Lear says that Gloucester must be blind Cupid, and warns Gloucester that he will never make him love. Lear adds that Gloucester doesn't need eyes to "see how this world goes." The law of the world, Lear explains, is that there is no difference between judge and criminal. It is just a matter of who is in the more powerful position, for we are all guilty. In his disgust with the world, Lear catalogues all the injustices, all the ways in which people in power get away with the same crimes for which they savagely punish the less powerful. Such is the eloquence of his speech that Edgar turns aside and comments, "O! matter and impertinency mix'd; / Reason in madness."

Then Lear tells Gloucester that he really does know him, and says he must be patient about dying; we can no more control the time of our death than the time of our birth, and "when we are born," Lear adds, "we cry that we are come / To this great stage of fools." Lear then abruptly thinks of his sons-in-law (he doesn't yet know of Albany's sympathy for him) and cries, "kill, kill, kill, kill, kill, kill!"

At this point Lear's attendants catch up with him and try to reason with him to go to Cordelia. But Lear thinks he is being taken prisoner and tells them that if they treat him well, they will get ransom. Then he mockingly bids them catch him and dashes off, leading the attendants quite a chase. Edgar asks the Gentleman who has come with Lear's attendants how near the armies of Albany and Cornwall are. The Gentleman says that they are very close and are about to engage in battle with the French army.

Suddenly Oswald enters, overjoyed that he has found Gloucester, so that he can kill him and gain the prize Regan promised him. But Edgar steps forward in defense of his father and speaks insultingly to Oswald in broad peasant dialect. Oswald is infuriated that a lowly peasant should interfere with his killing of Gloucester, and he begins to duel with Edgar. But Edgar quickly knocks him down, fatally wounding him. Before Oswald dies, he begs Edgar to deliver his letter to Edmund. But, once Oswald is dead, Edgar of course rips open the letter and discovers in it that Goneril is proposing to Edmund that he kill Albany and then marry her.

Suddenly the drums of war are heard in the distance, and Edgar leads his father off the stage.

SUMMARY: In this long and complex scene the following important events take place:

1. The Lear plot and the Gloucester plot finally merge, as the two old men, each in direst wretchedness, meet. Lear, the more commanding figure of the two, is still eloquent in his madness, while Gloucester is just mutely unhappy.

2. Gloucester's gullible superstition—which was played on for evil purposes by Edmund in Act I—here is played on by Edgar for the old man's own good. By tricking Gloucester into thinking he has escaped death from a great fall off a cliff, Edgar hopes to accomplish two things:

    a. Convince Gloucester that the gods are on his side, thus bringing him out of his suicidal gloom.

    b. Give him the strength to recognize Edgar as his son.

3. The scene of Edgar's convincing Gloucester that he is on a steep cliff shows Edgar's poetic ingenuity at its finest. Edgar is no longer the gullible, easily fooled youth of the beginning of the play, but has become cunning and resourceful. Like Cordelia, he has matured considerably as a result of his terrible experiences in the world.

4. Lear, in his madness, is most magnificent in this scene. His mind seems to flit back and forth between reason and insanity, as Edgar observes. But beneath the wild banter, Lear, like the Fool in earlier scenes in the play, tells several homely truths about life. Among his obsessions in this scene are:

    a. How he mistook false court flattery in his youth for real respect and love.

    b. The general sexual rioting throughout all nature, for which Lear holds the female of the species most responsible, and which is continually upsetting any concept of law and order.

    c. The great injustices of the universe. A rich man gets away with the very crimes for which the poor are cruelly punished.

    d. His own former set of values which was false in that he was too much impressed with wealth, pomp and power, and ignored the humble and decent people of his kingdom.

    e. Legitimacy of birth is no guarantee of decency of conduct.

    f. We somehow know when we are born that we are in for a life of folly and suffering, so that "the first time that we smell the air / We wawl and cry."

5. In his madness, Lear mistakes the guards who are trying to take him to Cordelia for enemy troops, and, with surprising strength, eludes them again.

6. Oswald shows several of his major characteristics in this, his final scene. They are:

    a. Complete, vicious unscrupulousness. (He is perfectly willing to slaughter the defenseless Gloucester for money and to please Regan, and, presumably, Goneril. He is prevented from doing this only by Edgar's presence.)

    b. Snobbery. (A household servant and privileged messenger, it offends him that he should have to fight with a mere peasant, as Edgar ingeniously pretends to be.)

    c. Utter loyalty to Goneril. (His dying words are a plea to his slayer to deliver the letter Goneril had given him to take to Edmund.)

In the character of Oswald Shakespeare is showing that mere blind loyalty is not enough, when it is devoted to an evil person or cause. Thus Oswald becomes a commentary, 350 years after he was conceived, on the blind loyalty, say, of the Nazi petty functionaries who were "just doing their duty." For Shakespeare a man must decide for himself between right and wrong in every given instance, and act accordingly. He must have the moral stamina to be disloyal to an evil master. An example of such virtue in the play is Cornwall's servant who slew him during the blinding of Gloucester.

7. The letter from Goneril to Edmund, now read by Edgar, places in writing the plot between the two to kill Albany and get married. Now the once easily misled Edgar finally knows everything about his evil brother.

Act IV: Scene vii

This great scene of the reunion of Cordelia and Lear takes place in Cordelia's tent in the French camp. Lear has evidently been recaptured by the attendants and has been returned to the camp, put to sleep, and dressed in fresh clothes while he slept. Cordelia tells Kent of her deep gratitude to him for all he has done for her father, begging him to come out of disguise and reveal himself to the others. Kent, however, asks her to wait until he thinks it is the proper time to show himself. Then Cordelia asks the doctor how her father is doing. The doctor says that since he has been sleeping soundly for a long time, they might wake him now. So Lear is borne in on a chair and placed before Cordelia, Kent and the doctor. Music is played to wake Lear as gently as possible, and Cordelia, staring at her father's sleeping face, reflects in wonder that her two sisters could have mistreated him. "Was this a face / To be oppos'd against the warring winds?" she asks, and makes the observation, made so often before in the play, that "Mine enemy's dog, / Though he had bit me, should have stood that night (of the storm) Against my fire." Cordelia is amazed that her father was able to survive the experience at all.

As Lear begins to awaken, the doctor bids Cordelia speak to him. She asks her father how he is, but Lear, still half asleep, thinks she is "a soul in bliss" descended from heaven to mock him in hell, where he is "bound / Upon a wheel of fire, that mine own tears / Do scald like molten lead." When Cordelia asks him if he knows her, Lear repeats that she is a spirit, and asks in turn when she died. Finally Lear is fully awake. He is overcome with guilt when he confronts the daughter he had wronged and who, he thinks, still hates him. He tries to kneel before her for forgiveness, but Cordelia begs him to get up. Lear confesses tragically that "I am a very foolish fond old man, / Fourscore and upward, not an hour more or less; / And, to deal plainly, / I fear I am not in my perfect mind." He begs Cordelia not to weep, but says that if she has poison for him, he will drink it. He is sure she does not love him, because he has wronged her, and her sisters, who benefited from him, hate him. "You have some cause" to hate me, Lear says, "they have not." But with simple nobility Cordelia assures him, "No cause, no cause." Then Lear asks her if he is in France, and Cordelia assures him he is in his own kingdom. Again Lear thinks he is being mocked. The doctor intervenes, telling Cordelia that Lear ought to rest again; he is still too weak to learn the whole history of where he is and how he got there. Lear, repeating that he is "old and foolish," leaves with Cordelia, the doctor and some attendants.

This immensely touching scene ends with a brief discussion between Kent and the Gentleman about the death of Cornwall and Edmund's taking the title of Earl of Gloucester. The Gentleman, not knowing who Kent is, mentions a rumor that Edgar and Kent are together in Germany. Kent evasively answers that rumors are not to be trusted; what is to be done now is to arm properly against the oncoming armies of Albany and Cornwall.

SUMMARY: This is one of the most moving scenes in the play because it deals with the emotionally-charged reunion of Lear and Cordelia in the simplest possible terms. It is the complete antidote to the poisonous atmosphere of greed, betrayal and generally monstrous behavior which has preceded it in the play. Each character seems transfigured in an almost holy light:

1. Lear, when he awakes, although he is feeble, has come to a full understanding of himself. He realizes his disabilities: that he is over eighty years old and not in his right mind. The one thing bothering him at this point is the guilt he feels towards Cordelia. He knows he has wronged her and feels she must hate him even more than Goneril and Regan do.

2. Cordelia, however, is all-forgiving, concerned only to see her father restored to health. Although her speeches are still brief and unflowery, they are immensely moving. Cordelia got into trouble originally, in the first scene of the play, because she could not speak her love for Lear. Yet a line like her "No cause, no cause" is deeply affecting precisely because it is not fancy or rhetorical, but obviously expresses genuine feeling.

3. Kent, ever loyal and trustworthy, wishes to remain anonymous until it is perfectly appropriate to reveal himself. The nobility of the scene is established in the opening dialogue between Cordelia and Kent, which is filled with gratitude and humility.

4. Lear's long rest has apparently cleared his mind sufficiently to recognize Cordelia, but he cannot bear up under too much discussion. Note the contrast in his words with her in this scene to those in Act I, Scene i. He has learned to have some humility; she has lost her unwillingness to reveal her love for him.

Act V: Scene i

After the brief interval of affection and forgiveness in Act IV, Scene vii, we are plunged once again into a scene of monstrous plotting and intrigue. The scene shifts to the British camp near Dover, where Edmund and Regan enter, accompanied by soldiers and a flourish of drums. Edmund asks an officer to find out whether Albany is still on their side or if he has deserted them, since "he's full of alteration / And self-reproving." When the officer leaves on his errand, Regan comments that Albany certainly is untrustworthy. Then she gets to the matter which most closely concerns her: does Edmund in fact love her sister? Edmund answers cagily that he loves Goneril honorably, but to think that he has seduced her is unworthy of Regan. He assures her that they have not had an adulterous affair. Regan begs Edmund not to be "familiar" with Goneril, and Edmund reassures her that he cares equally little for Goneril and "the Duke her husband."

Albany and Goneril themselves arrive, also accompanied by soldiers, drums and flags. Goneril's first remark (made aside) on seeing Edmund once more, is that she would rather lose the battle than that Regan should get Edmund for herself. Then Albany informs Regan and Edmund that he has heard that Lear and Cordelia are reunited, along with "others whom the rigour of our state / Forc'd to cry out." He points out that the only reason he is there to help out in the fighting is that "France invades our land." Goneril and Edmund are all for making peace with Albany because they need his army. A council of war is decided upon, but Edmund holds back a moment. Then Goneril and

Regan argue about who is going to remain outside with Edmund. Neither is willing to trust the other alone with him for a second. Meanwhile Edgar, still disguised, enters. He asks Albany if he may have a word with him alone. The others all leave the stage for their council of war.

Edgar now hands Albany the letter which was given him by Oswald. "Before you fight the battle," Edgar tells Albany, "ope this letter." The letter, we remember, contains the plot between Goneril and Edmund to slay Albany and then get married. If Albany should be successful in battle, Edgar tells him, he is to let a trumpet sound, and a champion will come who will give proof of what is in the letter. If Albany falls in the battle, of course, it won't matter. Albany tries to get Edgar to stay until Albany has read the letter, but Edgar says he must leave, and he does.

Edmund re-enters and tells Albany that he has been successful in his spying on the French camp, but that they must hurry off to battle. When Albany leaves to rally his troops, Edmund remains behind for another of his cynical, witty and unscrupulous soliloquies. He has sworn his love to both Goneril and Regan, he says, and each is madly jealous of the other. "Which of them shall I take?" he asks himself. "Both? one? or neither?" One thing is certain; he can enjoy neither sister if the other remains alive. Coldly and cynically he weighs the advantages and disadvantages of each sister in his mind. The chief obstacle in his way right now is Albany. He will let Albany fight in the impending battle because he can use his army. If Albany is killed, then all is well. If he survives, let Goneril kill him. In any case, one thing is clear: the merciful treatment which Albany intends for Lear and Cordelia must be vetoed after the battle. Edmund is concerned only with defending his state, not with debating about it. No enemies can be left alive, and Lear and Cordelia, although they are not active enemies, would be a rallying point for the now numerous people in Britain who hate Edmund.

SUMMARY: Two parallel strands run through this scene: the military situation and the sexual situation. The military situation is as follows:

1.   The army of Cornwall and Regan has been placed under Edmund's command, even though Edmund is only an earl, and Cornwall was and Albany is a duke. There is even some question as to whether Edmund is an earl, because his father, Gloucester, is not dead yet, but has only been branded a traitor by Cornwall and Regan. Edmund, however, is mainly worried about his ally, Albany, and how trustworthy he is. He knows that Albany is deeply sympathetic to Lear and Cordelia.

2.   Neither Edmund nor Regan is sure of Albany's loyalty. He is much weaker than his wife, Goneril, and so is constantly shifting between a desire to help Lear and Cordelia, and a sense of his duty to repel any foreign invasion of England.

3.   Albany has received from Edgar the letter that was meant for Edmund, setting forth Goneril's plan for him to murder Albany and marry her. This is the letter that Oswald was bringing to Edmund when he was killed by Edgar.

Running parallel to the military situation is the sexual triangle, which at the moment stands as follows:

1.   Goneril is in love with Edmund, but must somehow get Albany killed before she can marry him.

2.   Regan is also in love with Edmund and has the advantage of being a widow.

3.   Edmund can't make up his mind which sister to take. What always motivates him is pure, calculating ambition. He has no emotional concern for either sister, and is rather flattered and amused at their constant, embittered struggle for him. Three things are certain to him at this point:

   a.   He is not going to bother killing Albany. If the impending battle doesn't accomplish that, he will let Goneril kill her husband.

   b.   Whichever sister he does marry, the remaining one will have to be killed. The major problem for Edmund at this point is to decide which sister can bring him the most power with the least trouble.

   c.   Albany's plan for showing mercy to Lear and Cordelia once the French forces have been routed is no good as far as Edmund is concerned. Edmund is concerned only with expediency, not mercy. It is inexpedient to leave alive any possible rallying point for an opposition force. So Lear and Cordelia must die.

Act V: Scene ii

This brief scene takes place on a field between the British and French camps. Lear, Cordelia and the French forces enter and quickly leave the stage for the battle, amid flourishes of trumpets and drums. Then Edgar enters, leading Gloucester. He tells his father to rest in the shade of a tree until the battle is over. All Gloucester can do for the cause is "pray that the right may thrive." Then Edgar also races off for the battle. Suddenly the trumpets sound again to announce the retreat of the French forces. Edgar dashes in to tell his father the bad news that Lear and his daughter have lost the battle and are taken prisoner. He begs Gloucester to seek shelter with him, but the old man hasn't the heart to wander any further. Gloomily he tells Edgar that "a man may rot even here." Why keep running from death when that is all he wants? But Edgar tries to cheer him up again, in terms of stoic philosophy: "Men must endure / Their going hence, even as their coming hither": he tells his father, "Ripeness is all." He convinces Gloucester of this truth, and together they leave for safety.

SUMMARY: Although this scene is very short, it raises many problems. Some of these are:

1. The battle seems too short, compared with all the preparations for it in the play. It also seems inadequately described, as it takes place offstage, and the French apparently lose it in barely a minute. One possible answer is that the King of France is away, having been called home on urgent business. A more important answer is that since none of the major characters in the play is a soldier, we are not really interested in how they behave in battle, as we are, say, with Macbeth or Mark Antony. We only need to know the result of the fight, not the manner in which it was fought.

2. Still another reason for the brevity of the battle scene is that the sympathies of Shakespeare's audience were divided between Lear and Cordelia on the one side, and desire for a British victory on the other. Shakespeare thus is minimizing the embarrassing fact that Lear and Cordelia are on the side of Britain's traditional enemy, France.

3. Why does Edgar still express hope to his father after the forces of Albany and Cornwall have won the battle? The reason is that he is hoping Albany will read the damning letter which Edgar gave him in the preceding scene. Once he has done that and learned of his wife's treachery, Edgar thinks Albany will bring over his army to Lear's side, and help the French army defeat Cornwall.

4. Edgar's statement to his father that "Ripeness is all" is one of the major philosophical lines in the play. It means that the only important thing about life is to become ripe; to reach some sort of fulfillment and maturity. Then death doesn't matter. We have, of course, no more to say about the time of our death than we do about the time of our birth. We are born and we die when we are ripe to do so, like everything else in nature. The point is to achieve philosophical maturity—man's "ripeness"—before we die. Here, as elsewhere in the play, Shakespeare is drawing on the philosophy of Montaigne, the great French 16th century essayist, who says "that to philosophize is to learn how to die."

Act V: Scene iii

The final scene of the play takes place in the British camp near Dover. Edmund enters, bringing with him Lear and Cordelia as prisoners. He orders a group of officers to take them away until it is decided what to do with them. Cordelia tells Lear that she doesn't care what happens to her, but is unhappy for him. She tries to comfort the old man by telling him that now they will be reunited with Goneril and Regan, but this is slim comfort, indeed, for Lear cannot bear to see his two evil daughters again. Instead, he is quite content to live out the rest of his days in prison with Cordelia, where, he says, "We two alone will sing like birds i' the' cage:/ When thou dost ask me blessing, I'll kneel down, / And ask of thee forgiveness." In the prison they will gossip about court life, "and pray, and sing, and tell old tales." They will be utterly removed from the cares of the world, from "who's in, who's out" in court politics.

Edmund harshly breaks in on Lear's idyllic picture of prison life, and again orders a guard to take the prisoners away. Lear finally comforts Cordelia, telling her that "Upon such sacrifices, my Cordelia, / The Gods themselves throw incense." (In other words, when human beings have suffered and sacrificed as nobly as they have done, the gods must worship them, instead of their worshipping the gods. There are two major interpretations of what Lear means by "sacrifices." A. C. Bradley says he means his own and Cordelia's renunciation of the world. G. L. Kittredge thinks Shakespeare means specifically the sacrifices Cordelia has made for Lear's sake.)

As Lear and Cordelia are taken away to prison by the guard, Edmund hands one of his captains a secret note to bring to the jail with them. The note orders that Lear and Cordella be executed in prison. Even that last bit of happiness is to be denied them. Edmund feels he has the authority to issue this death warrant because he is commander-in-chief of the British army, in place of the dead Cornwall. Cordelia is to be hanged, and then the rumor will be spread that she committed suicide out of despair. Edmund is quite aware of the bloodthirstiness of his order. He prepares the captain for this cruel mission by telling him that "to be tender-minded / Does not become a sword." These are hard times, Edmund says, and a man must be prepared to act ruthlessly in them if he hopes to get ahead. The officer promises to carry out the order, and Edmund sends him off, asking him to "write happy" when the execution has been carried out.

Now, amid a flourish of trumpets and drums, Albany, Goneril, Regan and some soldiers enter. Albany congratulates Edmund on his "valiant strain" which won the day's victory. But then he asks him for the royal prisoners he has taken, "so to use them / As we shall find their merits and our safety / May equally determine." Edmund tells Albany that he has sent them to prison, but holds back the information that he has secretly ordered their execution. Instead he says they will be ready for trial tomorrow. He and the rest of the army are too tired from the battle to think about Lear and Cordelia right now.

Edmund's high-handed behavior in sending Lear and Cordelia to prison without consulting him irritates Albany, who reminds Edmund that he is merely a commander in the war, but not really Albany's equal as far as civil authority is concerned. Albany is, after all, a duke, while Edmund, even if he has a right to his father's title, which is dubious while Gloucester is still alive, would only be an earl. But Regan intercedes for the man she loves and tells Albany that since Edmund led the army in the dead Cornwall's place, he has every right to order things as he pleases. Now open warfare breaks out between Regan and Goneril over Edmund. So inflamed is Goneril at her sister's standing up for Edmund that she forgets that her own husband is present, and she passionately begins to insult Regan. Unaware that Goneril has secretly poisoned her (this happened offstage), Regan begins to feel the first symptoms in her stomach. She defiantly gives Edmund all her "soldiers, prisoners, patrimony," and calls him her "lord and master." Relations between the sisters and Edmund and Albany become very tense. Enjoying the onset of Regan's death agony, Goneril bitchily asks her, "Mean you to enjoy him (Edmund)?" Albany angrily reminds his wife that it is not up to her to decide whom Regan shall marry, and Edmund, who all this time has been cynically enjoying the fuss made over him, sides with Goneril and tells Albany it isn't up to him to decide either.

Finally, Albany can stand the squabble no longer. He has read the letter given him by Edgar in Act V, Scene i, and his fury at the treachery of Goneril and Edmund has been growing ever since. Now he breaks into the argument to inform Edmund and Goneril that they are both under arrest for "capital treason." With bitter humor he tells Regan that her claim on Edmund is barred: Edmund is apparently already promised to Goneril. If Regan wants to marry again, Albany tells her, she will have to marry him, for his lady has first claim on Edmund. Goneril laughs off Albany's bitter sarcasm, calling it "an interlude," i.e., a little bit of farcical drama, like a short comedy. Ignoring his wife, Albany challenges Edmund to a duel. He calls for the trumpet to sound, as Edgar had told him to do when he gave him the letter. Then, throwing down his glove in the standard gesture of challenge, he tells Edmund that if a champion does not appear to fight him, he will lower himself to duel with him. Edmund throws down his glove, too, and replies that he will maintain his "truth and honour firmly" against anybody. Meanwhile the effects of the poison Goneril gave Regan have been increasing, and now, feeling mortally sick, Regan is led into Albany's tent.

A herald enters, sounds the trumpet, and reads the following proclamation: "If any man of quality or degree within the lists of the army will maintain upon Edmund, supposed Earl of Gloucester that he is a manifold traitor, let him appear by the third sound of the trumpet." Three times the trumpet is blown, and on the third call it is answered by Edgar's trumpet. Edgar enters, fully armed, his face concealed behind a visor. The herald asks him who he is, what his rank is, and why he has come to answer the summons. Edgar replies that his "name is lost" but that he is of noble blood, as noble as his adversary's. Then, calling Edmund "False to thy gods, thy brother and thy father," Edgar challenges him to combat as a "toad-spotted traitor." Edmund replies cooly that according to the rules of knighthood, he ought to demand his challenger's name, but since the stranger seems well bred and warlike, he will consent to fight him.

The two brothers duel, and Edmund eventually falls, mortally wounded. Albany calls for a doctor to save him (because he wants Edmund to live long enough to be tried for treason), and Goneril cries out that he should not have fought because the laws of chivalry do not require a noble to fight "an unknown opposite." But Albany abruptly tells her, "Shut your mouth, dame," or he will stuff it with the incriminating letter he has. He even tries to get the dying Edmund to read the letter. After exchanging insults with her husband, Goneril leaves the stage, followed by an officer sent by Albany because he fears what she may do in her desperation.

Now Edmund, in his death agony, confesses to all the charges brought against him. Indeed, he says he is guilty of "more, much more; the time will bring it out." (Presumably Edmund means his secret order to execute Lear and Cordelia. Why he doesn't send a messenger to stop the execution at this point, when he does later, is a mystery in the play.) Then Edmund asks Edgar again who he is, saying that he forgives him if he is a nobleman. Now is the time that Edgar decides finally to reveal himself. "My name is Edgar," he says proudly, lifting the visor, "and thy father's son. / The Gods are just, and of our pleasant vices / Make instruments to plague us." He adds that Gloucester had to pay with his eyes for begetting Edmund in a "dark and vicious place," i.e., illegitimately. Albany embraces Edgar, and wants to know where he managed to hide himself all this time, and how he knew of the miseries of his father. Edgar tells the story of his disguise as Tom of Bedlam and of his nursing the blinded Gloucester. He didn't reveal himself to his father until just a half hour ago, he says, and he did it then only because he wasn't sure that he would survive the combat with Edmund. When he told Gloucester who he was, and asked for his blessing, the old man's "flaw'd heart, / Alack, too weak the conflict to support! / Twixt two extremes of passion, joy and grief, / Burst smilingly." Albany and even Edmund are moved by the story of Gloucester's final reconciliation with his son and his ensuing death. Edgar goes on to tell how he met with the banished Kent and joined forces with him.

Edgar's tale is interrupted by the frantic entrance of a Gentleman, carrying a bloody knife. The Gentleman tells Albany that the knife is hot from the heart of Goneril, who stabbed herself after poisoning her sister. Both are now dead. Edmund comments, with typical wit, even in his death throes: "I was contracted to them both: all three / Now marry in an instant." Edmund also expresses here perhaps the only genuine emotion he has had throughout the play: "Yet Edmund was belov'd." This suggests that his whole vicious career may have been caused by his feeling that he wasn't loved, a feeling relieved here by the death of the two sisters for love of him. Albany's attitude, however, is that their death was the judgment of heaven, for which he can't feel any pity. At this point Kent enters, seeking Lear. Albany remembers that he doesn't know where Lear and Cordelia are. But before anything can be done about it, the bodies of Goneril and Regan are brought onstage. Edmund tells Kent what happened, and then decides, since he is dying, to do at least one good deed in his life. He tells Albany of his secret execution warrant, and bids him send a messenger to prevent the deaths of Lear and Cordelia. Albany does so, and the dying Edmund is borne offstage.

But Edmund's last bit of mercy comes too late, for now Lear enters, with the dead Cordelia in his arms. Howling with horror, Lear begs for a looking glass to see if Cordelia has any breathe of life left in her. He places the glass to her lips, and convinces himself that she does still breath. He is too absorbed in trying to revive Cordelia to notice that Kent has knelt by his side to reveal himself to his King at last. Although later he does recognize Kent, at this moment Lear has no mind for anything but his Cordelia, whom he begs to "stay a little." Of her he says, "Her voice was ever soft, / Gentle and low, an excellent thing in woman." (And very different from the shrill, grating, fishwife voices of Goneril and Regan heard earlier in this scene.) Then Lear remembers that in a last surge of royal power he had killed the executioner who was hanging Cordelia. An officer confirms this story of Lear's last heroic action. Kent, Albany and Edgar try to tell Lear the bits of the story that he doesn't know, but his mind has completely gone now, in sorrow for Cordelia. Even the announcement by an officer that Edmund has just died, causes Albany to say, "That's but a trifle here," in the face of the overwhelming tragedy of Cordelia's death and Lear's final suffering. Lear gazes raptly at his daughter, trying to convince himself that there is still a stir of life

in her. "Why should a dog, a horse, a rat, have life, / And thou no breath at all?" he asks bitterly. Finally the majestic old King begs someone to undo a button that is constricting him, and, with a final hope that Cordelia may yet be alive, dies of a broken heart.

Edgar tries to revive him, but Kent wisely says: "Vex not his ghost: O! let him pass; he hates him / That would upon the rack of this tough world / Stretch him out longer." The wonder, Kent says, is that he managed to endure so long. Albany commands that the body of Lear be borne away, and asks Kent and Edgar to rule the kingdom. But Kent refuses: he is too broken-hearted at the death of his master, who he says calls him. Edgar will rule alone. The final words of the play, given in some editions to Albany, and in others to Edgar, aptly summarize, whoever speaks them, the feelings of the survivors:

> *The weight of this sad time we must obey;*
> *Speak what we feel, not what we ought to say.*
> *The oldest hath borne most: we that are young shall never*
> *see so much, nor live so long.*

Then the survivors leave the stage, to the solemn music of a funeral march.

SUMMARY: In this titanic final scene, one of the richest in the play in action, passion and poetry, all the tangled threads of the drama are tied together.

1. Lear and Cordelia, in their imprisonment and death, reach their highest peaks of grandeur. Completely forgiving each other and prepared to renounce the world, they desire at the beginning of the scene only to be left in peace together in prison. But even this small mercy is denied them by the cold, ambitious villainy of Edmund. He does repent, on the point of his own death, but it is too late to save Lear and Cordelia.

2. Lear's death is foreshadowed by Gloucester, who also dies of a broken heart. Each has been restored to his one loving child, but in both cases it is too late. It is significant that Gloucester's death occurs offstage. We are only told about it by Edgar so that it won't detract us from the death of Lear. For although Gloucester is like the King in situation, he is a much shallower and more superficial man, incapable of the poetic grandeur of feeling which Lear expresses.

3. Edgar's challenge and duel with his brother Edmund show how far he has progressed from the gullible, ineffectual young man who was tricked into fighting a mock duel to further Edmund's plot in Act II, Scene i. All the ingenuity and stamina involved in his disguise as Tom of Bedlam, and, later, as the peasant who guides and protects his blinded father, now come into play. By the end he has indeed become a knight in shining armor, whom even Edmund must respect.

4. Edmund behaves in character throughout the last scene, allowing Goneril and Regan to fight over him, but then rather grandly accepting the challenge from the disguised Edgar. As he is dying, Edmund has two moments of glory:

- a. His jest about marrying both sisters in death.
- b. His last-minute attempt to save Lear and Cordelia.

Edmund is a very complex villain indeed.

5. Albany, like Edgar, has grown during the play. Where earlier he was overshadowed and somewhat henpecked by his ambitious, unscrupulous wife, here in the last scene he is in complete command.

6. Goneril and Regan, scheming to the last like the vicious animals they have been compared with throughout the play, meet their just ends. Goneril secretly poisons her sister, and then stabs herself when it is evident that Albany knows of her treachery, has written proof of it, and will punish her for it. Not many tears are wasted on their deaths.

7. Kent, loyal to the end, finally reveals himself to Lear. He is unwilling to receive any power in the kingdom after Lear's death. In his loyalty he can think only of joining his King in death.

Character Analyses

KING LEAR   Lear is basically a generous and unsuspicious man, but he is too used to getting his own way after a long lifetime of absolute rulership. He is also hot-tempered and self-willed. Despite his age he is in top physical condition at the beginning of the play (he goes out hunting when he is staying with Goneril). His disinheriting of Cordelia is not an act of senility but the act of a man who will stand no opposition to his slightest whim. What the opening scene does prove is that he lacks common sense and insight into people and that he puts too much faith in outward show. He seems to have known enough about his daughters before to have preferred Cordelia to the others, but his folly consists in his accepting at face value the hypocritical protestations of love by Goneril and Regan.

Lear is like a man who wants to eat his cake and also have it. Having given away his kingdom, he expects to retain the dignity and power of kingship and refuses to accept a lesser role in life. This first scene, however, is the only one in the play in which Lear is shown in an unsympathetic light. Immediately afterward, when he goes to stay with Goneril, his suffering begins. It is so intense that we can only sympathize with him. We learn, too, that Lear has attracted the intense fidelity and devotion of Cordelia, Gloucester, Kent, the Fool and, later, Albany. He must have had good qualities to do so. Hurt deeply by his daughters' ingratitude, Lear throughout the play is desperately fighting a losing battle with madness. He is determined to remain "every inch a king." His deep-rooted pride will not allow him to diminish his retinue by one knight. He would rather go out into the storm. There, as his trials increase in intensity, a transformation seems to overtake Lear. He loses his temper less and less and begins to learn patience and humility. His suffering makes him aware of the suffering of all humanity—something he had been protected from by court flattery when he was a King.

There is also a streak of self-pity in Lear. He feels himself "a man more sinned against than sinning," and keeps reminding his daughters that he "gave them all." This self-pity, too, is purged from his character, and he comes to realize that the world owes him nothing. In his madness, Lear comes paradoxically to a true vision of the workings of the universe and of man's place in it. He rebels, with puritanical disgust, against the lust, greed and hypocrisy which run the world. Toward the end of the play, under the love of Cordelia and the care of her physician, Lear achieves a degree of serenity until the final blow—the death of Cordelia—deprives him of all reason for living.

GLOUCESTER   Like Lear, Gloucester is an old, white-haired man, a widower, whose children are still comparatively young. He, too, has been guilty of folly and injustice. He, too, is normally affectionate, but over-hasty in his actions. Like Lear, he cannot distinguish between his good child and his wicked one. His son Edmund, as a bastard, is an embarrassment to Gloucester, and he keeps him away from court for several years. But then, when Edmund returns to court, Gloucester is all too willing to believe his slander against Edgar. He is far more superstitious and credulous than Lear. In fact, he is the only completely superstitious character in the play, giving great credence to such things as eclipses and the movement of the stars as forces in human behavior. He is also a very weak, though good-hearted man. Although he disapproves of what Cornwall and Regan are doing to Lear and although they are doing it in Gloucester's own castle, all he can do is chide them for it; he can't stop them. This is partly because he is only an earl, whereas Cornwall is a duke. But partly it is because Gloucester doesn't have the strength of character necessary to put a stop to rampant evil. His life, too, has been more devoted to the enjoyment of sensual pleasure than Lear's, as the begetting of the illegitimate Edmund shows. In his suffering, Gloucester seems like Lear, but not nearly so impressive. He tends more to whimper than to lash out at his oppressors as Lear does in his great biblical tirades. His blinding by Cornwall makes him pessimistic to the brink of suicide. Even then he is gullible, believing Edgar's story that he is on the brink of the cliffs of Dover, instead of simply on level ground. It is harder for Gloucester to learn what Lear and Edgar know: that a man must endure whatever horrors the fates may heap on his shoulders. He doesn't have to grin and bear it, but he must bear it.

GONERIL   Lear's oldest daughter is a supremely evil woman. She understands her father very well and plays up to him with her hypocritical avowal of love in the first scene. But she knows that he is willful and changeable and decides to play him for all that she can get. She knows, too, that Cordelia has always been Lear's favorite and is jealous of her, as Edmund is jealous of Edgar. She is highly intelligent, but has no sense of proportion. She despises her husband, Albany, for being weaker-willed than she is, but fails to see that if he is, it is a sense of decency which makes him so. She fails utterly to see Lear's inherent nobility. She is also very thick-skinned and callous. It doesn't bother her that her bargaining with Lear about how many knights he is to retain is for him the most inhuman degradation. His justifiable tirades against her just slip off her like water off a duck's back. She is determined to reduce Lear to beggary, to utter dependence on her charity for the means to live, and doesn't care about the devastating psychological effect such an attitude would have on a man used to being an absolute ruler all his life. Her "love" for Edmund is pure lust for sex and power. It is based on Edmund's handsome exterior and on his temperamental likeness to herself. He, too, will stop at nothing to get his way. Far more ambitious and unscrupulous than Albany, Edmund appeals to Goneril as the kind of man who is worthy of her.

REGAN   Like her older sister, Regan is intelligent, grasping and cruel. The only thing she lacks is initiative. She is always following Goneril's footsteps, sometimes even outdoing her in cruelty, but never originating anything. Typical of Regan is her remark when Cornwall orders that Kent be placed in the stocks until noon. "Till noon!" Regan exclaims, "Till night, my lord; and all night too." She is always going others one better in cruelty, but she doesn't poison anybody, commit adultery or plot against her husband's life, as Goneril does. She is presumably more "happily married" than Goneril because her husband, Cornwall, is just as vicious and strong-willed as she is. She even slays the servant who

kills Cornwall. Nevertheless, when Cornwall is killed, Regan immediately transfers her affections to Edmund, for the same reasons that Goneril loves him. Regan shamelessly throws all her possessions at Edmund after he wins the battle against France. It is typical of Goneril's power over Regan, however, that it is Goneril who poisons Regan and not the other way around.

CORDELIA   The youngest sister is almost like the Virgin Mary in her meekness and gentleness. As good as her sisters are evil, Cordelia is a unique portrait in literature. Only Shakespeare could draw a picture of such utter goodness in so few lines and not become sentimental. Although Cordelia is present in only four of the 26 scenes of the play, we never forget her during the long stretch when she is offstage. Her character is based on three traits: reverence, pity, and absolute devotion to the truth. It is this latter trait which gets her into trouble at the beginning of the play. She lacks any of her sisters' hypocrisy, but is too severe and unyielding in her insistence on telling Lear the truth. She tells him, "I love your Majesty / According to my bond; no more no less." This shows that although Cordelia had always been Lear's favorite daughter, she understands him as little as he does her, and much less than Goneril and Regan understand him. During the course of the play the two come to a mutual understanding, and Cordelia learns the same lesson of humility that Lear must learn. She is married to the King of France at the beginning of the play, and is able to arouse enough love in him for him to take her without a dowry and to bring his whole army to Dover to re-establish her father on his throne. She also has aroused intense devotion in Kent, who gets himself exiled for speaking out in her favor, and in the Fool, who pines away for her when she is in exile. When she is reunited with her father, she looks out anxiously for his welfare, and assures him of her undying devotion to him in words of noble simplicity. Most critics and spectators of *Lear* find Cordelia's death the most unbearably poignant episode in the play.

EDGAR   Edgar undergoes one of the most marked developments of any character in *King Lear*. At the beginning he is as credulous as his father, Gloucester. It is ridiculously easy for Edmund to fool him. He cannot suspect evil because he is wholly good himself. Also, Edgar is the most religious character in the play, who believes that the gods are always just. Edgar learns, however, to be resourceful and ingenious in order to survive. He adopts the disguise of Tom of Bedlam because he knows that since nobody will take a mad beggar seriously, he will be able to survive while Edmund is plotting against him. Later, his disguise as a peasant is good enough to fool even his own father. He learns to be cheerful in adversity and helpful in a practical way. When the Fool drops out of the play, it is up to Edgar to cheer and comfort Lear and look after his welfare. He is reliable, and the state is in good hands with him at the end of the play. By the time of his duel with Edmund, he has become a strong, self-reliant man. He is still deeply good, sometimes even priggish, as when he tells Edmund that Gloucester was blinded because of his "pleasant vices." Edgar is no longer taken in by evil, and yet has not become hard-hearted or cynical.

EDMUND   Edmund is the complete opposite of his brother. Where Edgar is religious, Edmund is a complete atheist and materialist. He believes that men just use the gods as excuses for their own bad behavior. "Thou, Nature, art my goddess," he proudly proclaims, meaning that he thinks of himself as a natural man, not bound by any moral or ethical considerations. The gods are to Edmund merely "an admirable evasion of whoremaster man, to lay his goatish disposition to the charge of a star!" Edmund is highly intelligent. He plots coldly and brilliantly to gain first his brother's inheritance, then his father's title, and finally the entire kingdom. He is, in short, an ambitious adventurer. He lets nothing stand in his way. He even betrays his father to his enemies. Although Edmund is physically handsome, he suffers deeply from the fact of his illegitimacy and the mockery he has had to endure because of it. At the very beginning of the play his being a bastard is discussed in his presence, with cynical wit by his father and Kent. In his first soliloquy he reflects, "Why bastard? Wherefore base? / When my dimensions are as well compact, / My mind as generous, and my shape as true, as honest madam's issue?" Then, thinking over his plot, he concludes, "I grow, I prosper; / Now, gods, stand up for bastards!" Edmund's psychological suffering for being a bastard provides him with at least a speck of motivation for his evil in the play. Other sympathetic aspects of Edmund are his subtle humor and his refusal to fool himself. He says, while dying, of Goneril and Regan, "I was contracted to them both: all three / Now marry in an instant," and we feel a pang of sympathy for him when he says, "Yet Edmund was belov'd." Also, at the point of death he tries to save Lear and Cordelia from his own cruel death warrant. In these ways, Edmund is a much more appealing villain than Cornwall, but he is still a coldly calculating villain, much like Iago in *Othello*, or Richard III. The one thing his intelligence fails to comprehend is that evil is self-defeating, a failure of comprehension that is his destruction.

KENT   The key to Kent's character is his absolute devotion to Lear. An old man, although not as old as Lear or Gloucester, Kent puts himself to endless trouble to be with Lear and to help him whenever he can. What makes his behavior all the more admirable is that since Lear banished him in the first scene for defending Cordelia, Kent is in England on pain of death, should he be recognized and captured. Hence he must maintain his disguise throughout. He is blunt and eccentric, utterly lacking any of the smoothness and suavity of the usual courtier. He is a plain, honest man, who, like Lear, acts hotly and rashly. To Cornwall he is merely "some fellow / Who, having been prais'd for bluntness, doth affect / A saucy roughness" - in other words, he is putting his bluntness on. But this is untrue. Kent simply cannot control his temper when he sees the ingratitude and injustice of Lear's daughters, or the lack of respect for Lear that Oswald shows. He is the typical warrior, rather than courtier: unthinking, hot-tempered, but profoundly loyal and unselfish. He is also a fatalist. When he is placed in the stocks and there is nothing more he can do, he simply says, "Fortune good night; smile once more; turn thy wheel!" and promptly goes to sleep. His devotion to Lear is such that when Lear dies and Kent is offered a share in ruling the kingdom, he refuses, because "My master calls me, I must not say no." In short, he must die, too, once Lear is dead.

THE FOOL   Another devoted servant of Lear's. In happier days he entertained the king and court with his quips and riddles. When we first see him, he is unhappy because his favorite, Cordelia, has been exiled. He alternately cheers and torments Lear with his witty insights into Lear's folly and the ingratitude of his daughters. Like Kent, he cannot be separated from Lear, but he is not so brave as the old warrior. Goneril and Regan stun him into silence, and he is so terrified of the storm that Kent has to comfort him. The Fool has true insight into what is going on in the world, but he is also more than a touch insane. This is part of the convention of court jesters, however, and is not original with Shakespeare's Fool. The Fool is someone who is so far outside the realms of political and social power that he is privileged to make any comments on his superiors that he chooses, as long as he is witty and amusing. In *Lear*, the Fool sings songs, speaks in puns and riddles, and is often rather difficult to understand. He is apparently quite young, and the suffering he has endured and seen around him has been too much for him. He disappears mysteriously half-way through the play, after he has taught Lear all he can about the ways of the world.

ALBANY   A vacillating man, but not nearly so weak as Goneril thinks him. It merely takes him a long time to make up his mind because he is the kind of man who has to weigh allegiances very carefully. Albany at first doesn't interfere with Goneril's cruel treatment of Lear, and Lear makes no distinction between him and Cornwall. He is obviously in love with his wife for her physical beauty. But as the play progresses, Albany's essential decency emerges. He cannot bear the cruelty that has been shown Lear, and at the risk of losing his wife to Edmund he defends the old King. He roundly upbraids Goneril as "Most barbarous, most degenerate," and when he hears that his brother-in-law Cornwall was slain while gouging out Gloucester's eyes, Albany cries out in exultation: "This shows you are above, / You justicers, that these our nether crimes / So speedily can venge!" Nevertheless, Albany is a patriotic man, and leads his troops in the war against the French, although he must fight on Edmund's side against Lear and Cordelia. He is a man who can be pushed around only so far, and when he learns of Goneril's plot to have him killed and to marry Edmund, he has the plotters arrested for treason. He has learned that there is no compromise with evil.

CORNWALL   Cornwall seems at first to be as much under Regan's thumb as Albany is under Goneril's. It soon becomes obvious, however, that Cornwall is at least the equal of the sisters in cruelty. He thinks nothing of putting Kent in the stocks for insulting Oswald, taking over Gloucester's castle completely, siding with Regan against Lear and even locking Lear out in the storm. Cornwall's crowning moment of villainy comes when he gouges out Gloucester's eyes with his own thumbs. It is for this last outrageous deed that Cornwall's own servant stabs him (an unheard of act in those days). As another servant says, "I'll never care what wickedness I do / If this man come to good." Regan wastes no time mourning for him, and neither do we.

OSWALD   Oswald, like Kent, is fiercely loyal, but to the wrong person. He will do anything for Goneril. But unlike Kent, instead of being blunt and outspoken, Oswald is an oily and suave snob, which is why Kent despises him. When Oswald speaks disrespectfully to Lear at Goneril's house, Kent immediately trips him up and sends him sprawling for his insolence. Later, at Gloucester's castle, Kent rightly calls Oswald "a lily-livered . . . super-serviceable, finical rogue," and "a knave, beggar, coward, pandar, and the son and heir of a mongrel bitch." Oswald is loyal, however, and even performs Goneril's evil missions with more zest than is necessary because he has a taste for cruelty himself. His loyalty is shown when Regan tries to worm out of him the contents of the letter he is carrying from Goneril to Edmund. He steadfastly refuses to let her see it. His cruelty is shown by his willingness to stab the defenseless Gloucester in the back. When he is prevented from doing so by Edgar, disguised as a peasant, Oswald, the

complete snob, is insulted that a social inferior should dare to fight him. But his final action is a loyal one: he begs Edgar to deliver the letter with which he had been entrusted. Oswald is the kind of man who might have been decent if he had attached himself to a decent master, but with no conscience of his own, he is a complete villain in the pay of a Goneril.

FRANCE   The King of France is a generous, intelligent man, who sees enough in Cordelia to be willing to marry her without a dowry. He goes to immense trouble to launch an invasion of England in order to rescue Lear. But then he makes what may have been a fatal mistake by returning to France just before the battle because of urgent business at home. By leaving his army in the command of a marshal, he may have forfeited the victory. His motives in landing an army at Dover are completely honorable. He desires no territorial conquest, but merely to see Cordelia happy again.

THE DUKE OF BURGUNDY   We see Burgundy only briefly in the first scene. He is the other suitor for Cordelia's hand. Apparently he has priority over France, but he loses out on marrying Cordelia because he is too cold and materialistic to wed her without a dowry. France puns on his name and character by calling him "wat'rish Burgundy." Even Lear doesn't seem to think much of him in the scene, although he has no sympathy for Cordelia either, then.

THE PHYSICIAN   A quiet, obedient and intelligent practitioner, the physician realizes that the only hope of restoring Lear to a degree of sanity is to let him rest after his great travail. "Our foster-nurse of nature is repose," he says, "The which he lacks; that to provoke in him, / Are many simples operative, whose power / Will close the eye of anguish." The physician probably represents the best Elizabethan medical practice. He intelligently asks Cordelia to be the first to speak to Lear when he awakens, and his idea of awakening Lear to the sound of music is highly interesting because this was the way in which the essayist Montaigne, who greatly influenced Shakespeare, used to be awakened. He very much resembles the doctor in *Macbeth*.

MINOR CHARACTERS   Other minor characters, with the exception of Curan, Edmund's servant, tend like the physician to be good, simple men. The Gentleman who keeps Kent abreast of latest developments, and Cornwall's servants who revolt against their master and try to comfort the blinded Gloucester, are humble, decent men who do much, in their small ways, to offset the aggressive evil of half the major characters.

Macbeth

Scene-by-Scene Summary and Comment

Act I: Scene i

The play opens with a meeting of Three Witches in some sort of deserted place. The Witches tell us that the next time they meet it will be with Macbeth. The meeting will take place when the tumult ("hurlyburly") is ended, when a battle has been "lost and won," and that this will occur before the sun goes down. After having said this, the Witches hear the cries of their "familiar spirits," two of whom are called Graymalkin and Paddock, recite an ambiguous couplet ("Fair is foul and foul is fair:/ Hover through the fog and filthy air"), and exeunt.

COMMENT: Shakespearean scenes at their beginnings plunge into the midst of things, leaving the reader to gather what has immediately preceded; the opening of *Macbeth* is an instance. The Witches have had a consultation and are about to depart. The question of the First Witch about whether to meet "In thunder, lightning, or in rain" (l. 2) suggests that these witches by their spells cause bad weather, an idea confirmed in I.iii.20–25 and IV.i.52–60. One may say that *Macbeth* gains in dramatic force if the *reader or spectator makes the imaginative effort of taking the Witches seriously.* The "battle" that the Second Witch refers to is that taking place this day between the forces of Duncan, King of Scotland, and those of Macdonwald, the Hebridean rebel, and Sweno of Norway. The battle is lost from the Witches' point of view when Macdonwald is slain by Macbeth, and it is won when Sweno is driven from Scotland: it is not difficult to understand why the Witches would sympathize with rebellion, but why the Witches are opposed to Sweno's invasion of Scotland—the point is H.N. Paul's—is unclear. "The battle's . . . won" would not allude to the death of Duncan or the flight of his sons because these are events of the night.

Macbeth here presents the "weird sisters" in the character of the three Fates, but the play does not always sustain this conception of their role. As M.C. Bradbrook, points out, *Macbeth*'s witches derive from many different traditions: the "weird sisters" of Holinshed; the North Berwick coven of witches (in their control of weather, sailing in a sieve); the magician's power to command spirits and foretell the future; English witches (beards, animal familiars, petty

revenge against the sailor and his wife); the ability to vanish like bubbles (herein they differ from common witches); and freedom from subjection to superior demons (though spirits raised in the cauldron are called "our masters" [IV.i.63]).

Whether the Witches are human or not is unclear. The Third Witch mentions meeting Macbeth, establishing the supernatural control of the play, especially the force of metaphysical evil upon Macbeth in *this first of English plays to treat witchcraft seriously.* Then the First Witch, hearing a cat, says, "I come Graymalkin," naming her familiar spirit, *i.e.,* demonic servitor. The Second Witch hears her familiar spirit, whom she names "Paddock," presumably the "hedge-pig" or hedgehog of IV.i.2. Because toads cry out under torture may be (in part) why G.L. Kittredge and G.B. Evans think Paddock to be a toad when the Second Witch says, "Paddock calls." The Third Witch's familiar is named "Harpier," as we learn from IV.i.3, presumably from harpy. Harpier's shape is not indicated here or elsewhere, but it is probably that of an owl since this bird hooted during the night of Duncan's murder. The Third Witch hears his distinctive note just before l.10 and answers "Anon." There is no stage direction to indicate that the audience hears anything, but a producer of *Macbeth* may call for the sound of an owl.

Moral relativity. "Fair is foul, and foul is Fair" (l.11) introduces the idea of moral relativity, of deceptiveness of appearances, and, as L. Veszy-Wagner says, of Macbeth's "uncertain identity" *e.g.,* whether to be loyal or disloyal to the King, whether he is a manly or an effeminate man. Here *Shakespeare's master-theme for all his dramatic work*—the deceptiveness of appearances—is in view. In Roman Polanski's filmed version of *Macbeth,* one of the Three Witches is "fair" and youthful, her two companions being traditionally "foul." One gathers from this that somehow witches go on forever.

"Hover through the fog and filthy air" (l. 12) presents a chief image of *Macbeth*—darkness—and suggests that evil spirits are invisibly carrying witches in great numbers through the air. The Witches are "posters of the sea and land" (I.iii.33) and "made themselves air" (I.v.5). The Bleeding Sergeant of I.ii probably refers to this when he says that Macdonwald was a rebel because "the multiplying villainies of nature/ Do swarm upon him."

This first scene of *Macbeth*, with its emphasis on *thunder*, *lightning*, and *darkness*, suggests that George Schaefer's filmed version of I.i was a mistake because in this the wasteland becomes the blue-skyed, bonny Scotland of the postcards and the calendars. At the end of the scene Polanski has two of the Witches diverge from the third in a V pattern intimating that these beings cover a wide sweep of earth.

Act I: Scene ii

This scene takes place in a military camp. The following characters enter: Duncan, king of Scotland; Malcolm, Duncan's elder son; Donalbain, Duncan's younger son; Lennox, a nobleman of Scotland; and attendants. They meet a wounded man referred to by Malcolm as "the sergeant." The Sergeant has been wounded apparently in the battle referred to by the Witches in the last scene, and Duncan decides that because the Sergeant has been wounded he must know how the fight has been going. We also learn from Duncan's remarks that the battle is part of a revolt against Duncan. Malcolm asks the Sergeant for news of the battle, and the wounded man tells this story. The fight was such that it was difficult to tell which side would win, the rebels' troops headed by Macdonwald or the forces loyal to Duncan, which, we learn in the course of the scene, are headed by Macbeth and Banquo. Added to Macdonwald's troops were Irish foot soldiers and horsemen ("kernes and gallowglasses"). Fortune seemed to be all on the rebels' side, but to no avail. For "brave Macbeth" despite fortune, made a passage for himself to Macdonwald by killing everyone between him and the leader of the rebels. When Macbeth came face to face with Macdonwald, he immediately ripped the rebel open from the navel to the lips, cut off his head, and placed it on the roof of the loyalists' castle.

Unfortunately, continues the Sergeant, that did not end the difficulties. No sooner did Macdonwald's Irish soldiers run away than the king of Norway, whose name is Sweno, in league with the rebels, took advantage of the situation, and "began a fresh assault," with new supplies of men and guns. But this did not make the loyalist leaders, Macbeth and Banquo, despair. They redoubled their strokes upon the enemy. As the Sergeant is about to continue, he finds he cannot, for he feels faint. When Duncan sends off the Sergeant to the doctor, Ross and Angus, two more noblemen of Scotland, enter. They have come from the battlefield, and Ross proceeds to finish the story broken off by the Sergeant's weakness. The king of Norway (referred to simply as "Norway") with his great number of troops was assisted by another traitor, the Thane of Cawdor. (Thane is a Scotch title approximating that of earl.) Ross says the conflict was "dismal." However, the conflict was dismal only until "Bellona's bridegroom" (almost certainly meaning Macbeth) with equal strength met the strong king of Norway and beat him. Now Sweno, the king of Norway, wishes to come to terms with Duncan. Duncan says that the Thane of Cawdor will no longer deceive him, for Cawdor will be sentenced to death. And Macbeth, Duncan announces, will be the new Thane of Cawdor. Duncan sums up the situation in the last line, "What he [the Thane of Cawdor] hath lost, noble Macbeth hath won."

COMMENT: The speeches of the Bleeding Sergeant, who is unnamed because Shakespeare wishes not to individualize him but to employ him as a spokesman, are in the Senecan tradition of the 1590s. A richer example is Shakespeare's account of "Aeneas' tale to Dido" in *Hamlet*, II.ii.472 ff. Similarities between the Sergeant's speeches and Senecan drama are: *slave* as a term of abuse, adjectives such as *direful* and *dismal*, the phrase "curbing his lavish spirit," and the personifications "Fortune" and "Bellona." J. M. Nosworthy thinks that Shakespeare was patronizing Senecan style.

This scene is now usually regarded as authentic Shakespeare, Nosworthy's "The Bleeding Captain Scene in *Macbeth*" having decisive influence; but *the faults remain* that caused some editors to regard I.ii as non-Shakespearean. *Bombast* is seen in the Sergeant's beginning three speeches with similes introduced by *as* (cf. Hamlet's "As's of great charge," V.ii.43). The bombast is dramatically functional, however, in that it provides contrast to the clear and unburdened speech of the King, which is just the kind of speech that James commended in *Basilikon Doron* to his son. Three of the Sergeant's speeches that should be worked into the rhetorical structure are set off in parentheses. L. 20 is a half line. L. 21 presents *which* with a doubtful antecedent. Ll.20 and 22 both begin with *till*. There is no verb at the end of 1.26; so editors supply *break*. L. 38 in First Folio reads "So they doubly redoubled stroakes upon the foe"—twelve syllables instead of ten. The meter is faulty in Ll.50, 58–59. Ll.7–9, which Holgar Norgaard thinks to be derivative from Daniel's *Cleopatra*, are puzzling.

The Sergeant regards Macdonwald as a compendium of human villainy because he is a rebel; on this account Macdonwald is assumed, in medieval fashion, to be stained with all vice. Rebellion against a lawful king in the *Mirror of Magistrates* and the Elizabethan *Homilies* was reckoned to be tantamount to rebellion against God. The introduction of Macdonwald was topical inasmuch as James is on record as believing the Hebrideans to be utterly barbarous and averse to law, and in 1605 one Angus Macdonwald of the southern Hebrides rebelled against him. One should avoid reading into *Macbeth* suggestions of the glamor that since the eighteenth century has invested the Hebrides, what with the defeat of Prince Charles Stuart in 1745, the official subjugation of the clans, and the romanticizing of the Western Islands seen in Collins, Scott, Wordsworth, Keats, and other writers. The view of the Hebrideans held by James and reflected in *Macbeth* appears to have been usual in the earlier seventeenth century.

Is Duncan a coward? Some critics, such as Archibald Henderson, suggest that Duncan is guilty of cowardice in not taking part in the battle. Although, as Shakespeare conceives him, Duncan does not lack vigor, he is too old (V.i.45) to fight personally. He sees to it that his elder son takes part in the battle; and he is near the scene, not mewed up in a castle. Admittedly he asks the naive question, "Dismayed not this/ Our captains, Macbeth and Banquo?" Certainly Shakespeare in preparing this play to be exhibited before James, who was descended from Duncan as well as Banquo, cannot be imagined, having offered incense to his sovereign at several places in the play, as intending to present a royal poltroon. One may note that Shakespeare changes Sweno from a Dane, as in Holinshed, into a Norwegian in deference to James's brother-in-law, King Christian of Denmark, present with James at the first performance of *Macbeth*.

Macbeth as butcher. The "bloody man" who is the Sergeant opens the play, John Holloway says imaginatively, "with an 'image of revolt,' the image of an actual deed of overturning, which serves from the start as emblem both of the central character, and of the course of the action." The Sergeant by his bloodiness foreshadows Malcolm's description of Macbeth as a "butcher," and Ll. 22–23 anticipate bringing Macbeth's head onstage.

This scene presents some instances of the lesser carelessness of which Shakespeare was often guilty, perhaps cheerfully so. "Dollars" and "cannons" are mentioned— both anachronisms in the eleventh century. From Fife (I.ii.48) to Forres (I.iii.39) is about one hundred miles, an impossibly long way for the Bleeding Sergeant, and an instance of Shakespeare's indifference to details of Scottish geography.

Act I: Scene iii

The scene opens with the appointed meeting of the Three Witches. The First Witch gives an account of what she has been doing since their last meeting. She tells us that she has met a sailor's wife munching on chestnuts. When the Witch asked the wife for some nuts, the latter refused them to her. The Witch will therefore soon take revenge, the revenge to be taken through the wife's husband, the sailor, who is the captain of the ship *Tiger*. She will cause the wind to blow so that he will never be able to sleep. He will be so weary that he will "dwindle, peak, and pine." However, the Witch, much as she can cause the captain of the *Tiger* to suffer, cannot make him lose his ship ("his bark").

The Witches then hear the sound of a drum, which announces the arrival of Macbeth and Banquo, who now enter. Macbeth's first words, spoken to Banquo, apparently comment on the weather, "So foul and fair a day I have not seen." They then see the Witches, who greet Macbeth with three titles, those of the Thane of Glamis, the Thane of Cawdor, and the future king. We learn from Banquo's speech immediately following the Witches' greeting that Macbeth is visibly shaken by the Witches' words, for Banquo says, "Good Sir, why do you start, and seem to fear/ Things that do sound so fair?" But Macbeth is not only shaken; he is so involved with his thoughts that he does not hear Banquo and therefore does not answer Banquo's question. Returning to the Witches, Banquo asks them whether they have any predictions for his own future. They reply that he will be "lesser than Macbeth and greater" and "not so happy, yet much happier." They also tell him that, although he himself will not be a king, he will be the father of kings. Macbeth, coming to himself, asks the Witches questions, but they vanish. As Macbeth and Banquo are speculating about the Witches, Ross and Angus enter to tell Macbeth that he has been granted the title of Thane of Cawdor. "The Thane of Cawdor lives," says Macbeth, "why do you dress me in borrow'd robes?" That is, Macbeth asks why the title should be given him when the man to whom it belongs is still alive. Macbeth is told the story of Cawdor's disloyalty; he then privately asks Banquo whether Banquo does not hope for the fulfillment of the prophecy for Banquo as the prophecy for Macbeth has in part been fulfilled. Banquo indicates a distrust for the Witches. He tells Macbeth that the tools of Satan ("instruments of Darkness") often fool us in the final result ("betray's in deepest consequence") by first telling us truths as thereby appearing honest.

As the other characters are involved in conversation, Macbeth speaks an aside. (An aside is a speech spoken by one character and heard by no one else on stage except those actors whom he may be addressing. In this case Macbeth is speaking to no other characters.) Macbeth tells himself that this beckoning him on (to greater things) by beings who know more than ordinary men ("supernatural soliciting") is ambiguous. That is, it is difficult to decide whether it is good or evil. The fact that he is made Thane of Cawdor seems to indicate that they tell the truth, and that appears to show that the beings are good. On the other hand, how can they be good when he allows himself to see a picture so horrible that it makes his hair stand on end and his heart beat unusually hard. Macbeth goes on to say that immediate dangers ("present fears") are less frightening to him than horrible things which he imagines. Exactly what makes his hair stand on end and heart beat wildly becomes a bit clearer in the following line: "My thought, whose murder is but fantastical . . . ." Apparently he has been thinking of murdering someone. The picture of himself as a murderer has been so vivid that he has been thoroughly shaken and caught up completely by his inner thoughts. He is incapable of seeing anything around him. Banquo remarks to his companions on Macbeth's self-absorption. But Macbeth continues his speech. If fortune ("chance") wants him to be king, he says, fortune may find a way to make him king. The implication is, of course, that Macbeth then will not have to do anything. (Almost certainly, he is thinking of the murder he has just been imagining.) Banquo, still watching Macbeth, remarks that Macbeth apparently is not yet accustomed to his new honors; they fit him "like our strange garments [which] cleave not to their mold." Macbeth ends his deliberations with "Come what come may, / Time and the hour runs through the roughest day." Banquo tells Macbeth that the group is waiting for him, and Macbeth begs their pardon. He also tells them that he appreciates the trouble they have taken to inform him of his good fortune. Then in an aside to Banquo, Macbeth advises Banquo to think about what has occurred, which they will sincerely discuss at their leisure. Banquo replies, "Very gladly."

COMMENT: From l.77 one gathers that this scene is set on a "blasted heath." The Witches, who seem more human in Act I than they will later, here speak among themselves in *headless octosyllabic couplets, i.e.,* in eight-syllabled lines that lack the first syllable and are rhymed in pairs.

> *Weary sev' nights, nine times nine,*
> *Shall he dwindle, peak, and pine.*
> *Though his bark cannot be lost,*
> *Yet it shall be tempest-tost*

This verse form differentiates them from the strictly human characters who speak mainly in unrhymed ten-syllabled lines called *blank verse.*

> *If you can look into the seeds of time*
> *And say which grain will grow and which will not,*
> *Speak then to me, who neither beg nor fear*
> *Your favors nor your hate.*

In their killing of the swine, the Witches behave like witches of English provenance. In their interest in affairs of state and in plotting the fall of kings, evident later in this scene, they are like Scottish witches; and they are therefore closer in conception to the witches of the continent,

especially France. Line 7 may be a topical allusion: a *Tiger* sailed for the East in December 1604 with John Davis as master; many of the crew were killed by pirates, but the ship did manage to return to England. The rat of l.9 is without a tail because Satan's creatures should not be so perfect as God's. We gather that the *Tiger* is fated to reach port and that *some things are beyond the powers of the Witches, a point suggesting Macbeth's freedom of the will.* The First Witch, as Dennis Biggins observes, by the repetition of "do," a sexual euphemism, and by the assertion that she "will drain him [the sailor] dry as hay," is rendered in this instance as possessing one of the ordinary trappings of witchcraft. In ll.35 ff. this coven of Witches ceremoniously adores their devils three times to each, intimating their mockery of the Trinity: *this is as far as Shakespeare ever goes in the depiction of devil-worship.* If Harpier, Graymalkin, and Paddock were physically present onstage, the scene would become more sinister because it would be more obviously idolatrous. Sir William Davenant's "improvement" of *Macbeth,* by making the Witches comic, made a dignified presentation of the title role more difficult for the great Thomas Betterton, the leading actor of Restoration London.

Sympathy between Witches and Macbeth. Then Macbeth and Banquo enter. Simon Forman, who saw Macbeth at the Globe in 1611, suggests that Macbeth appeared first on horseback, a piece of business unsupported by the Folio text. But since horses are restless and intimate nightmare, this action reflects Macbeth's state of mind. Furthermore, a horse indicates Macbeth's class as noble and as "Bellona's bridegroom," his interest in power. *In Polanski's filmed version the difficulty of distinguishing Macbeth from Banquo until the Witches address Macbeth enhances the ambiguity inherent in the play.* Since Macbeth and Banquo are marching from a double victory toward Forres with some of their troops (l.30), we presume the troopers to be in the rear of the stage during the interview with the Weird Sisters. Macbeth says, "So foul and fair a day I have not seen," meaning that the weather is foul, and the victory is fair and, thematically, the ambiguity of appearances. Furthermore, *this line of Macbeth's suggests,* by its reminiscence of the Witches' "Fair is foul, and foul is fair," *a secret sympathy between Macbeth and the Witches before he has seen them.* With their repulsive beards, their choppy fingers, and their skinny lips, the Sisters are like English witches (Scottish witches could be beautiful), but Banquo's description in ll.40–41 intimates their extraordinary dress. In the interview Banquo appraises their appearance objectively whereas *Macbeth finds the Sisters secretly sympathetic to the baser instincts of his heart.* When the Witches speak, they oracularly announce; they do no "soliciting" (l.130) by foretelling the murder of Duncan. If Macbeth is innocent of musing on opportunities of sending Duncan somewhat early to his Maker, one wonders why he starts with fear at the mention of a crown, and why, a little later (l.139), he soliloquizes on murder. Hearing the prophecies does not in a practical sense remove Macbeth's free will, but in theory (since theory generally favors determinism) they do: *Shakespeare in any case* (unlike Chaucer) *was not interested in questions of free will and determinism*. The prophecy to Banquo "Thou shalt get kings" may certainly be regarded as *a topical allusion* what with King James in the first audience, since the Stuarts believed themselves to be descended from Banquo. Macbeth and Banquo receive the prophecies differently partly because Macbeth is announced by utter strangers to be Glamis and shortly becomes Cawdor, whereas the prophecies relating to Banquo pertain to the distant future after his death. In Ll. 75–76 Macbeth is striving to discover whether the prophecies derive from good spirits or evil ones. He cannot learn this because the Witches exeunt—a business that should be managed without a trapdoor because they are linked to the Prince of the power of the air, *i.e.*, Satan, because the air over Scotland is filthy, and because Macbeth says (l. 81) they have vanished "into the air."

The question of Cawdor. We come now to consider the vexed matter of the Thane of Cawdor. Dr. Johnson wrote, "The incongruity of all the passages in which the Thane of Cawdor is mentioned is very remarkable": "Neither Ross knew what he had just reported, nor Macbeth knew what he had just done." Dugald Murdoch points out that a careful reading of the text reveals that Cawdor was personally engaged in battle and that Macbeth did not fight him *vis-à-vis* in the field. Cawdor was a traitor, not a rebel. Furthermore, the text does not indicate that either Ross or Angus supervised Cawdor's execution. Murdoch thinks Cawdor's treason to have been purposely created to be opaque and thus a part of *Macbeth's* ambiguities. Daniel A. Amneus in "The Cawdor Episode in *Macbeth*" contends that the real difficulty (Murdoch disagrees) is Ross's ignorance in scene iii of what he knows in scene ii: the problem, he opines, lies in the time scheme; and he suggests that *scene ii, reconstructed from its confusion, would present sequentially*: a report by the Bleeding Sergeant on the first battle; a report (probably by Ross) of Sweno's landing at Fife; a report (in a new scene perhaps) of Cawdor's treachery; and a report of Macbeth's victory over Sweno.

Macbeth's "greater honor." Ross and Angus enter to convey the King's pleasure in Macbeth's prowess as demonstrated against the Hebridean rebels and the Norwegians. Ross says to Macbeth, "And for an earnest of a greater honor,/ He bade me, from him, call thee Thane of Cawdor" (Ll. 104–05). The "greater honor" must be the title "Prince of Cumberland." That would make Macbeth the succesor to the kingship, according to the *law of tanistry*, which permitted selection of the successor from *any* member of the "royal blood" line. (King James disapproved of tanistry; he preferred direct succession by the king's oldest son.)

But later King Duncan, perhaps forgetful of this promised "greater honor" for Macbeth, names his own son Malcolm as Prince of Cumberland! That gives Macbeth a motive for killing Duncan.

Of course, if Macbeth were to be named Prince of Cumberland, it would be unnecessary for him to undertake the murder of Duncan, and the complicity of Banquo in knowledge of the prophecy and of Macbeth's supposed intentions is removed, as Daniel Amneus has pointed out in "Macbeth's 'Greater Honor.'"

Some reasons to support this view are the following. In II.i.20–30 Banquo indicates willingness to cooperate with Macbeth and to win honor from him if Banquo can "still keep / My bosom franchis'd and allegiance clear": presumably he means that he will be "counsell'd" if Macbeth is to be named Prince of Cumberland. However, when Malcolm is given that title, and Duncan is dead, Banquo would be loyal to Malcolm. Another reason is that this supposition gives Macbeth a cause to decide against the murder; his proceeding with the regicide would be occasioned by Malcolm's unexpected accession to the title of Prince of Cumberland. A third reason is *Simon Forman's report of what he saw in the Glove performance of Macbeth* in 1611: "And Duncan bade them both kindly welcome and made Macbeth forthwith Prince of Northumberland [*i.e.*, Cumberland]." One point is certain: it is impossible to reconcile Macbeth's "greater honor" with Malcolm's being made heir apparent unless we know more than we do about Duncan's motivation. Scholars like A. C. Bradley, J. Q. Adams, and Dover Wilson have suspected omission, curtailment, or textual dislocation.

Macbeth, hearing himself addressed as Thane of Cawdor, replies, ". . . why do you thus dress me / In borrowed robes?" (Ll. 108–09), preparing the *imagery*, discussed by Caroline Spurgeon, *of over-large clothing which Shakespeare employs as a visualization of Macbeth's tyranny*.

Macbeth's habit of repetition. Macbeth then in an aside (not a soliloquy because others are onstage) muses on the meeting of his being named Thane of Cawdor and wonders whether the two truths told him guarantee the truth of the *third* truth—that he is to be King of Scotland. *His language from l. 134 to l. 141 is remarkably unclear.* On the one hand, *he has reason to believe that he may honestly become king:* he is of royal blood, Duncan is old, the princes are young, Duncan has promised him "a greater honor" than Thane of Cawdor. On the other hand, these verses could mean that Macbeth has an inchoate intention of murdering Duncan even before Duncan nominates his successor: "My thought, whose murther yet is but fantastical," by employing bad grammar, suggests that Macbeth is in the process, as L. C. Knights observes, of forming his thought. "Smother'd in surmise" anticipates Lady Macbeth's "blanket of the dark" and Ross's choric comment in II. iv. 6–10. *Here we see a habit of Macbeth which manifests itself when he is under pressure,* as Walter Gierasch has also remarked in II. ii. 35–40; IV. i. 144–48; V. iii. 40–42; and V. v. 9–15—*repetition by reformulation*—*"the hero's rhetoric in intense moments is characterized by saying a thing over again, usually three times."*

"The imperial theme" (l. 129) is a pregnant phrase that requires glossing. It did not suggest to the Jacobean audience an empire in the nineteenth-century sense. For the unschooled of that audience, *imperial* would probably have suggested Macbeth's hubristic imagination, *royal* being too weak a word for him. To the learned it might well call to mind, according to Henry N. Paul, the *Aeneid* as quoted in Gwinn's *Tres Quasi Sibyllae,* acted for King James's pleasure at Oxford on Aug. 27, 1605: "Imperium sine fine tuae, rex inclyte, stirpis" (rule of your dynasty without end, renowned king). In this association the line phrases the Stuart theme—the endless line of James's descendants (IV. i. 117) and the imperial expansion of his country (IV. i. 121). In the *Aeneid,* Jove promises to the descendants of Aeneas rule without bounds in time or space.

Macbeth ends the scene by excusing his fit, saying that his "dull brain was wrought / With things forgotten." The remark is improbable because it would be expected that his mind would be occupied with his new honor and its meaning.

Act I: Scene iv

We have here another short scene (58 lines), but one of great significance. Duncan, his two sons, Lennox, and some attendants enter. In the first two speeches we learn that the rebellious Thane of Cawdor has been executed. Malcolm tells us that a witness of the execution has reported that Cawdor confessed his treason and repented of it. He therefore died well: "Nothing in his life / Became him like the leaving of it . . . ." Duncan talks of the difficulty of knowing from a man's face what is going on in his mind. Cawdor, Duncan says, "was a gentleman on whom I built / An absolute trust." He breaks off because Macbeth enters.

Banquo, Ross, and Angus enter with Macbeth. Duncan greets Macbeth with an elaborate speech, the essence of which is that Macbeth has done more for Duncan than Duncan can ever repay. Macbeth replies courteously and formally, saying in effect that the services that he, Macbeth, has given Duncan are their own reward and need no thanks from Duncan, for Macbeth owes these services to Duncan since Macbeth is a subject and Duncan a king. Macbeth states his reply thus in part: ". . . our duties / Are to your throne and state, children and servants," and Macbeth is only

behaving properly "by doing everything / Safe toward [for the safety of] your love and honor."

Duncan now says, "I have begun to plant thee, and will labor / To make thee full of growing."

Duncan ends with: "let me infold thee, / And hold thee to my heart." That is, "Let me embrace you," which, of course, tells the actors what to do. Duncan says that his joys are so many that he is beginning to weep. Apparently when he recovers from weeping, he makes an important announcement. Malcolm, his eldest son, will hereafter have the title of Prince of Cumberland. But Malcolm will not be the only one newly honored. Other nobles will also receive greater honors. He then says that he will proceed to Inverness, Macbeth's castle. By becoming Macbeth's guest, he tells his host-to-be, he will put himself in even greater debt to Macbeth. Macbeth replies to Duncan, that he, Macbeth, will now put forth an effort which is not for Duncan's pleasure but for Macbeth's. Macbeth will hurry forth and he himself will be the messenger who will announce the news of Duncan's arrival, which will make Lady Macbeth, Macbeth's wife, "joyful." "My worthy Cawdor," says Duncan, thus at once thanking Macbeth and giving him permission to leave.

But before Macbeth exits, he has an aside. "The Prince of Cumberland!" he says, "that is a step / On which I must fall down, or else o'erleap. / For in my way it lies."

The reason Malcolm's becoming the Prince of Cumberland is an obstruction in Macbeth's way to the kingship is explained by George Steevens, the eighteenth-century Shakespearean scholar. "The crown of Scotland was originally not hereditary. When a successor was declared in the lifetime of a king, as was often the case, the title of Prince of Cumberland was immediately bestowed on him as the mark of his designation." Malcolm, therefore, in being given the title of Prince of Cumberland is being designated as the next king of Scotland. It is this obstruction that Macbeth must overcome.

Macbeth continues the aside by telling the stars to hide their light ("fires") so that their light will not discover Macbeth's "black and deep desires"; nor must their light show the eye shut in refusal to see [the action of] the hand. Yet he wants that deed to be done which, having been committed, the eye would be afraid to see.

After the speech Macbeth exits. During the speech Duncan had been talking with Banquo, and we hear the last part of their conversation. They have been apparently discussing and praising Macbeth, for Duncan agrees with Banquo that "he" is extremely brave. Duncan also says that when Macbeth is praised, Duncan is "fed." Commendations of Macbeth are "a banquet to me." And they exeunt to follow Macbeth. Duncan's last words are that Macbeth "is a peerless kinsman."

COMMENT: Duncan is informed of the death of Cawdor. *His inability to judge Cawdor and Macbeth is not caused by senility.* Duncan, although often played as an old man, might be fifty. His mistakes are due, J. W. Draper thinks, to his sanguine humor—his physiological system has an excessive amount of blood: a defect of this kind of temperament is lack of caution to foresee and avoid pitfalls. There is some textual support for the view—Duncan weeps in this scene, tears being derived from blood; and in V.i Lady Macbeth will recall the incredible amount of blood that flowed from his aged body at the time of stabbing.

Macbeth, Banquo, Ross, and Angus enter. Duncan heaps praise on Macbeth not, as has been thought, to compensate him for naming Malcolm Prince of Cumberland, but out of the generosity of his nature. His repeated use of "thou" in addressing Macbeth (l.16) is a sign of affection. The King's speech is so excessively laudatory that it might conceivably, as Edwin Thumbo notes, contribute something to Macbeth's self-esteem and want of regard for the proper relationship of king to thanes. Macbeth replies formally: his speech should not be delivered with histrionic hypocrisy that would distort the dramatic motive at this point even though it would provide (for some) "good theater." The King responds, "I have begun to plant thee, and will labor / To make thee full of growing." Critics often note that the *idea of planting is in the Bible usually associated with God, and the effect of the speech is to render Duncan sacrosanct, God's representative on earth.* In l. 37 Duncan shifts from *I* to *we*, signifying royal purpose and ceremony; and *he proceeds in a manner extraordinarily gauche* to declare Malcolm Prince of Cumberland. But the audience has now been prepared for Duncan's ineptitude, most notably seen in his misreading of Cawdor.

At this point there is conflict between the primary source and Shakespeare. Holinshed stated that the Scottish crown was not strictly hereditary, and that Macbeth, by the naming of Malcolm, had "a just quarrel so to do [to kill Duncan] (as he took the matter) . . . ." Shakespeare does not enlarge upon this hint and indeed, as Bradbrook says, suppresses notice of the *opposition between tanistry (an elective monarchy within the limits of the descendants of Macalpine) and the elective principle,* established by Malcolm Canmore. *The play emphasizes the hereditary principle to which James fondly referred in his speeches to Parliament and in his writings.* So Macbeth in Shakespeare does not muse on the justice of his murder of Duncan. At the investiture of Malcolm it would be unwise for Macbeth to take or kiss the hand of the new heir apparent. Macbeth's aside in Ll. 48–53 shows by the phrase "my black and deep desires" that the thought of murdering Duncan has become firm.

Act I: Scene v

The scene takes place at Macbeth's castle at Inverness. Lady Macbeth enters reading a letter from Macbeth. *The letter itself is the first piece of prose in the play.* Lady Macbeth's comments following the letter and the ensuing dialogue return to poetry. Lady Macbeth is reading apparently the last part of the letter. Macbeth has been writing her about the Witches, who, he says, met him on "the day of success," that is, the day of victory. He has learned dependably that they have more knowledge than ordinary mortals. Macbeth wanted very much to question them further, but they dissolved into air. As he "stood rapt in the wonder of it," the news came that he was the Thane of Cawdor, by which title the Witches had previously greeted him, and they also greeted him with "Hail, King that shalt be!" that is, hail, future king. Here the letter ends its account of his meeting with the Witches and addresses Lady Macbeth directly. This news of the meeting with the Witches, he thought it "good" to tell her so that her ignorance of her future greatness would not keep her from rejoicing at the prospect of her greatness ("that thou might'st not lose the dues of rejoicing, by being ignorant of what greatness is promised thee"). Immediately before the last remark Macbeth calls Lady Macbeth his "dearest partner of greatness." He ends by telling his wife to put the letter to her heart, and he bids her farewell.

Lady Macbeth now comments on the letter. She says that Macbeth shall attain the goal he has been promised, that is, the kingship. But she is afraid that his character is "too full o' the milk of human kindness, / To catch the nearest way." She continues by saying that although he is ambitious, he does not have that evil in his character that will permit him to reach his great goal: ". . . what thou wouldst highly, / That wouldst thou holily." Then, as though she were addressing him directly, she says, "Hie thee hither . . . ." She wants him to come quickly so that she can fill him with her spirit and disperse with a tongue-lashing all of his character which prevents him from attaining the crown ("the golden round") promised him by fate and supernatural help ("metaphysical aid").

A Messenger interrupts Lady Macbeth's thoughts to inform her that the king will arrive at Inverness that night. "Thou'rt mad to say it," cries Lady Macbeth. Would not Macbeth, who is with the king, have warned them beforehand so that the castle could be prepared for the king's arrival? The Messenger replies that one of his fellow servants had indeed been sent beforehand and is completely out of breath from rushing with the news. He precedes Macbeth, who will arrive before Duncan. When the Messenger leaves, Lady Macbeth has a soliloquy of some fifteen lines. In the first line and one-half she imagines a raven greeting the "fatal" arrival of Duncan to her castle ("my battlements"). She says that a raven greeting this arrival would have a voice even more harsh than usual (obviously because the entrance will be "fatal" to Duncan). She then invokes (calls on for aid) "Spirits/ That tend on mortal thoughts . . . ." That is, she asks the spirits that are the servants of murderous ("mortal") thoughts to come to her aid. She wants them to "unsex" her, that is, to take away her womanliness, which makes her soft-hearted. And she wants these spirits to fill her from head to toe with the worst sort of cruelty. She wants the spirits to make it so that nothing in her nature will prevent her from carrying out her "fell" (cruel) purpose. She continues the invocation, "Come to my woman's breasts . . . ." She now wishes the servants of murderous thoughts (whom she this time calls "murdering ministers") to act as her children sucking at her breasts. But instead of taking milk from her breasts as children normally would, the "murdering ministers," she hopes, will take milk and inject in its place gall (bitterness). She now invokes "thick night" and tells night to cover itself with the gloomiest smoke of hell. She wants this done so that her knife (she means, of course, the eye that is guiding her knife) will not see the wound it makes and heaven will not be able to peep through the dark to tell her to stop.

The entrance of Macbeth brings us to the first dialogue between the play's two main characters. Lady Macbeth greets her husband with his two current titles, Glamis and Cawdor. He will have a title, she continues, greater than both in the future. His letters have made her feel the future in this moment. She obviously means that she feels now like the queen. Macbeth replies with a statement that apparently does not follow logically, "My dearest love / Duncan comes here tonight." Lady Macbeth asks her husband when Duncan is leaving, and he replies, "Tomorrow, as he purposes [intends]." Her response is that the sun will never see the morning (when Duncan leaves their castle). Macbeth apparently looks disturbed at his wife's remark, for she says, "Your face, Thane, is as a book, where men / May read strange matters." Then in a series of images which mean more or less the same she advises him not to give away his thoughts by the expression on his face: "To beguile [cheat] the time [that is, the men of the time], / Look like the time . . . / . . . look like the innocent flower, / But be the serpent under't." She adds ironically, "He that's coming / Must be provided for [prepared for] . . . ." She concludes by saying that he shall turn over to her the management of the affair, the results of which shall give to the rest of their days "sovereign sway and masterdom." Macbeth answers only, "We will speak further." She tells him again to keep a face that indicates an undisturbed mind, "Only look up clear . . . ." To

change one's face (an indication of disturbance in the mind) is always to be afraid. Lady Macbeth ends by saying, "Leave all the rest to me."

COMMENT: Lady Macbeth reads a letter from Macbeth which—being composed between I. iii and I.iv—gives no intelligence of the King's purpose to visit Macbeth's castle and no notice of Malcolm's being named Prince of Cumberland. Macbeth, in short, has not at that point consciously determined to kill Duncan. Lady Macbeth should not read the letter in the manner of a fiend lest it spoil the contrast between her present mood and the black mood that develops later in the scene. She does not burn, as Holinshed says, "in unquenchable desire to beare the name of a queene"; but since Macbeth writes "that thou mightest not lose the dues of rejoicing by being ignorant of what greatness is promis'd thee," we gather that being Queen of Scotland is quite to her taste. By employing the correct name for the Witches, *i.e.,* "weird sisters," Macbeth suggests that he has learned something by investigation. They said to him, "Hail, King that shalt be." "Shalt be," Lady Macbeth thinks, does not mean determination in the full sense of the word because Macbeth is only a murderer in his thought-life, a hypocrite, and a man whose conscience is almost exclusively prudential. When Lady Macbeth says that he is "too full o' th' milk of human kindness / To catch the nearest way," she means that although he would assuredly enjoy the fruits of killing Duncan, *i.e.,* the crown, his nature is averse to the unnatural act of regicide, and his imagination is burdened with thoughts of the horror with which his compatriots would view a king-killing tyrant. Lady Macbeth habitually refers to the killing of Duncan in *periphrasis* (or roundabout speech), *e.g.,* "the nearest way," because she shrinks from the bloody deed itself; nevertheless, *unlike Macbeth, she is ruthless in pursuit of ambition, and she promises to goad him into achieving by direct action (rather than by awaiting) what has been promised him.*

When the Messenger enters to give news on Duncan's intention to stay the night, Lady Macbeth in a soliloquy invites "spirits" to "unsex" her and fill her "topful / Of direct cruelty." *If she is depicted as young and attractive,* as in Polanski's filmed version, *this line has more meaning than if she is played as a middle-aged, "bitchy," hatchet-faced woman: it underlines the theme of fair on the outside, foul within. The usual view of the speech,* as seen in the Variorum edition—John Dover Wilson, George L. Kittredge, and W. C. Curry—is that she is inviting demon-possession. *A contrary view,* expressed by Paul H. Kocher, is that "the spirits that tend on mortal thoughts" are animal spirits that communicate the mind's decisions to the body. Thick melancholy blood, reinforced by fresh supplies of melancholy from the spleen, would thus flow towards the heart and make it colder and heavier. By this means the pronouncements of conscience drawn from its reading of the engraved moral law of nature ("compunctious visitings of nature") will be blocked from the will and from bodily organs that would put them into effect. In this state the other kind of nature ("nature's mischief"), meaning the corrupt passions of fallen mankind unpurified by divine grace, is to predominate. *Another view*, advanced by Alice Fox, is that "visitings of nature" was commonly euphemistic for menstruation, and that Lady Macbeth uses blocked menses, causing thick and gross blood, as a metaphor for a blocked conscience.

Demon possession. The idea of demon possession better suits the atmosphere of *Macbeth* and the predilections of King James. On the other hand, II.43–47 lend color to Kocher's interpretation because here Lady Macbeth, contrary to the Christian position, takes a purely materialistic view of conscience, as something, that is, that can be stifled by thickened blood; and in this way of thinking she may be likened to Iago and Edmund. Lady Macbeth asks the demons or animal spirits to exchange her woman's milk for gall—a line that, one thinks, interested James because of his belief, common in the time, that the morals of nurses affected their babies through milk. James attributed his Protestantism (his mother was a Roman Catholic) to his nurse, Helen Litell. Lady Macbeth concludes the soliloquy by invoking night to invest the projected murder with "the dunnest smoke of hell."

Incidentally, *peep* in l.53 was not in 1606 a word with comic overtones as today.

Macbeth enters not knowing that his wife has learned of Duncan's coming. One notices that Lady Macbeth's "the all-hail hereafter" (I. v. 55) is like the Third Witch's greeting to Macbeth in I. iii. 50, from which we gather an obscure connection between Lady Macbeth's present mood and the Witches. "All hail" to Shakespeare is enriched by reminiscence of Judas's kiss in the Gospels (*III Henry VI*. V. vii. 33; *Richard II*. IV. i. 169). An illustration of how acting can bring Macbeth to life is observed in the actor Edmund Kean's employing a pause and stress in l. 60 — "Tomorrow, as he . . . purposes"— to suggest that the idea of killing Duncan at Dunsinane has already occurred to Macbeth. Lady Macbeth now begins to chastise Macbeth with the valor of her tongue, counseling him in a line suggesting the story of Adam and Eve, "look like th' innocent flower, / But be the serpent under't." She never tries to banish the thought of killing Duncan, and she never thinks of an alternative. Her utterance of l. 70—"Give solely sovereign sway and masterdom"—has a roll that somehow conveys the juicy, full-blooded relish that she takes in the thought of being translated to the crown.

Act I: Scene vi

The scene occurs in front of the castle at Inverness. Duncan and his party enter. The characters in the party whose presence interests us are Malcolm and Donalbain (Duncan's two sons), Banquo, Lennox, Macduff, Ross, and Angus, all of whom are Scottish noblemen, or thanes. The scene is a formal one consisting in large part of the elaborate and courteous language used in ceremony, in this case the ceremony of greeting the arrival of a guest. Here, of course, it is a special guest, the king. When Duncan enters, he remarks upon the pleasantness of the air around Macbeth's castle. Banquo agrees with Duncan by saying that the presence of a martlet's nest in every possible corner of the face of the castle proves that "the heaven's breath / Smells wooingly here," that is, that the air smells enticingly here. The presence of so many martlets' nests shows the air's pleasantness because the martlet is "templehaunting." That is, the martlet ordinarily nests in churches. If he chooses to rest elsewhere, it is because the air is as soft and pleasing as the air about the churches. Banquo ends his speech by saying that he has observed that where "they most bred" the air is "delicate," that is, soft.

Lady Macbeth enters, and Duncan greets her in an elaborate and complicated way. The point of the speech is that Lady Macbeth really does not mind the extra pains she takes in having Duncan as a guest, because she loves Duncan. Lady Macbeth replies as elaborately as Duncan has spoken. She says that double all of the service which Macbeth and Lady Macbeth have done for Duncan does not compare to the "honors deep and broad" which Duncan has given their house. For both the old honors and the recent honors Macbeth and Lady Macbeth will pray to God for him ("We rest your hermits"). Duncan asks for Macbeth, who, he says, has ridden faster than Duncan. Duncan had hoped to precede Macbeth. Duncan concludes with "Fair and noble hostess, / We are your guest tonight." The hostess replies that everything in the house is really Duncan's. He asks her to conduct him to Macbeth, whom he loves and whom he will continue to honor, and they exeunt.

COMMENT: Banquo, we gather, has declined to tell Duncan of what he and Macbeth have heard from the Sisters and of what he may suspect concerning Macbeth. It would, after all, be embarrassing for Banquo—since his descendants are to inherit the crown, according to the prophecy—to speak to the King in this sense. One may also say that Banquo has no occasional motive to be thus confidential with the King inasmuch as, although he appears to be as worthy as Macbeth, he is not rewarded with the thaneship of Cawdor or any other material honor or title.

There is *tragic irony, the kind for which Sophocles is famous*, in Duncan's remark "The air / Nimbly and sweetly recommends itself / Unto our gentle senses" because nowhere is Scottish air more infected, though sightlessly, than at Macbeth's castle. The hill air, sweet and fresh, contrasts with "the blanket of the dark," and suggests in its hospitality to martlets (house *martins* or swallows) that Duncan, too, is born from Heaven.

Banquo's speech on martins (ll.33 ff.) is pregnant with dramatic significance: it continues the irony of the King's first speech; it contrasts a temple to Macbeth's bloody hall; it exhibits the composure of Duncan and Banquo; it juxtaposes martins and the ravens on the battlements; and it points up an ironic difference between the martins' "procreant cradle" and the childlessness of the Macbeths (and almost all other villains in Shakespearean drama). Martins were traditionally supposed to know when a house was on the verge of some great collapse and to leave it. Peter M. Daly says, "By not abandoning the castle Banquo's martlets ironically underscore the theme of deception; they reflect in the world of nature the human misreading of the situation."

Lady Macbeth's hypocrisy. It is better dramatically for Lady Macbeth to greet Duncan first, for she is at this stage a better actor than Macbeth. *Duncan's speech* (ll. 10–14) *is thus paraphrased by Henry N. Paul:* "The modest Duncan dislikes the pomp and ceremony of a royal visit. The visit is therefore a 'trouble' to both the host and the royal guest. But it is also the means by which both show their love. Therefore, the king thanks his host for his trouble, because showing love, and so teaches his host to thank the king for his trouble for the same reason." Paul makes the point that the King finds the royal "we" troublesome. Lady Macbeth responds with gratitude for the honors the King has done her house, concluding "We rest your ermites." *In this piece of arrant hypocrisy she alludes to Duncan's preceding religious adjuration and resorts to the hyperbole of describing herself and Macbeth as religious hermits praying in solitude for Duncan's welfare.*

Of the scene as a whole Sir Joshua Reynolds wrote in his *Eighth Discourse at the Royal Academy*, "The subject of this quiet and easy conversation gives that repose so necessary to the mind, after the tumultuous bustle of the preceding scenes, and perfectly contrasts the scene of horrour that immediately succeeds." Sir Joshua failed to note that horror is increased by Duncan's cheerful confidence amidst the scene of his impending doom.

Act I: Scene vii

The scene opens with servants serving the dinner in honor of Duncan's visit. Macbeth enters and speaks a soliloquy, which begins, "If it were done when 'tis done, the 'twere well/ It were done quickly . . . ." *It*, of course, refers to the murder. He continues in a series of images the essence of which is: If the murder should be successful here on this earth and have no dangerous consequences, the risk of punishment in the next world would be worth it. But in cases such as the murder of

Duncan, Macbeth goes on to say, we are sentenced for our crime in this life. The sentence is this: when we commit an assassination, we in effect teach others to commit the same act. It is "even-handed justice." Macbeth now turns from the practical reasons why he should not kill Duncan to the moral reasons. He says that Duncan is in his house "in double trust." First, Macbeth is both Duncan's relative and Duncan's subject. Both of these ties to Duncan make the murder reprehensible. Second, Macbeth is Duncan's host; as Duncan's host Macbeth should shut the door against Duncan's murderer, not carry the murder knife himself. Macbeth goes on to a political reason why he should not murder Duncan. Duncan, he says, has been so mild and guiltless as king that Duncan's virtues will cry out like a trumpet against his murder ("taking-off"). And pity, as though it were "a naked new-born babe," or some member of an order of angels ("heaven's cherubins") riding the wind, "Shall blow the horrid deed in every eye"; there will then be a tremendous amount of weeping ("tears shall drown the wind"). Macbeth continues with an image from horsemanship, which says he has no reason to murder Duncan except ambition.

Lady Macbeth interrupts Macbeth's thoughts with her entrance. We learn that Duncan has almost finished supper and that he has wondered why Macbeth has disappeared from the table. Macbeth then says that he and his wife will no longer continue with the business of killing Duncan. The reason is that Duncan has recently honored Macbeth, and Macbeth has "bought/ Golden opinions from all sorts of people,/ Which would be worn now in their newest gloss,/ Not cast aside so soon." At Macbeth's remarks Lady Macbeth pours out a torrent of contempt, the main idea of which is this: you do not really love me when you are not man enough to go out and get what you want. Macbeth replies, "I dare do all that may become [is appropriate to being] a man . . . ." To this his wife says, "What beast was't, then,/ That made you break this enterprise to me?" That is, as she explains in the next line, when you dared to plan the murder, you were a man; so that if you dare do all that is appropriate to being a man, you would dare do the murder. By breaking the promise to commit the deed you are behaving like a creature lower than a man, which is a beast. She goes on to say that when Macbeth promised her to kill Duncan the best possible occasion for the murder had not presented itself ("Nor time, nor place,/ Did then adhere") and in fact he had said that he would have created a good occasion for the deed. But now that the best possible occasion has presented itself, he is unmanned. She then follows with *one of the most blood-curdling images of the play.* She knows, she says, "How tender 'tis to love the babe that milks me [feeds at my breast]." But rather than break the kind of promise that Macbeth wants to break now, she would, while the baby at her breast was smiling up at her, pull her nipple from the baby's mouth and crush out the baby's brains. Macbeth has no answer to this and turns to the practical problem of possible failure. Lady Macbeth tells him that as long as he has courage, they will not fail. She the recounts the plan for the murder. When Duncan is sound asleep, as he will be after his hard day of travel, she will so fill with drink his bedroom attendants that they will sleep as though they were dead. Then Macbeth and his wife can do anything they wish to Duncan, who will be unwatched. And they can put the guilt upon the drunken ("spongy") guards. Macbeth says that his wife ought to bear only boys because her courageous spirit should go into the making of men. He then turns back to the murder plan and, as though he had not heard his wife's last words, he repeats in the form of a question what she had said about the guilt being put upon Duncan's drunken attendants. She replies that since she and Macbeth would be loudly grief-stricken over Duncan's death, no one would dare put the blame anywhere but on the drunken attendants. Macbeth says that he has decided to go through with the deed. And now Macbeth repeats his wife's advice of a previous scene: the expression on the face must be innocent although the heart intends murder.

COMMENT: While Duncan and the others are dining, Macbeth muses alone on the heinousness of killing the King, but this is perhaps not the first time such thoughts have circulated in his head. Lady Macbeth, upon reading his letter, immediately assumed that Duncan would be murdered. As soon as Macbeth met her, he knew what was in her mind. Later in scene vii Lady Macbeth will state that Macbeth swore to carry out such a murder, and this swearing occurred when there was neither time nor place for it: Macbeth would make time and place. On the other hand, Macbeth is violently shaken when he thinks of the murder; and *Shakespeare does not make this point quite clear* to the audience although he might have done so in I.iii. If Macbeth harbored before the beginning of the play the idea of killing Duncan, the play would be something nearer melodrama than it is.

According to Paul, what happens is this: Duncan was incompetent to control his rebellious subjects. Macbeth offered his services *in propria persona* to crush this rebellion (I.iii.91). His pride grew in this work, and he offered his wife the thought that because of Duncan's ineptitude he should be disposed of (I.vii.48). Lady Macbeth embraced the thought, but Macbeth put it away because it amounted to "murder" (I.iii.139) and therefore involved his own damnation (I.vii.20).

Modern criticism, however, generally cannot credit the idea that a man like this would commit so great a crime and therefore sees Macbeth as diseased from the start of the play. Macbeth delivers the opening soliloquy not as if he had made up his mind: he is debating here. The first line thus means that if it were ended when it is performed, it would be well. Macbeth does not dismiss the thought of judgment in another world as if it were a chimera; he entertains it as a possibility that he is willing to risk in the interest of his worldly ambition. He argues that he should not kill the King because of prudence, loyalty (kinship, allegiance, hospitality), and pity. But if one looks hard at pity, which from its position should constitute the climax of his argument, one finds, à la Cleanth Brooks, that the pity that influences Macbeth is the pity of the public for their murdered king.

Naked babes and the four horsemen. Lines 21 ff. thus mean that pity, when born, is helpless as a babe; but when blown into many hearts, it becomes stronger than the wind. Grover Smith suggests that Shakespeare may have been influenced by emblematic naked infants fast riding the wind over the ocean spaces of decorated Renaissance maps. S. R. Swaminathan thinks that a Flemish *Book of Hours*, owned by Henry VIII, might have relevance inasmuch as the human soul at death is "symbolized by a naked infant in an oval glory." This point has color in the quasi-universality of the motif. ". . . or heaven's cherubin, hors'd/ Upon the sightless couriers of the air/ Shall blow the horrid deed in every eye." Whether the invisible "cherubin" are powerful angels or tender babes (on this debate see Grover Smith), these lines, Holloway assures us, would have reminded the first audiences of the Four Horsemen of the Apocalypse (Rev. 6, 2–8), "bringing, as they ride over the earth, the disasters which are the proper result of, proper retribution for, human evil." In short, Macbeth's conscience counsels him to fear the consequences of sin rather than to love the fruits of righteousness. Although active, his conscience is not altogether admirable, for it is negative in the guidance it gives him. *So he begins his course of evil with complete knowledge of what he is doing and with the evident willingness to exchange a heavenly crown (Rev. 2, 10) for an earthly one. He is deceived by the prophecies of the Witches, but he is not deceived by them into believing that evil is good or that evil is beautiful.*

Sexual blackmail. When Lady Macbeth enters full of determination to dispatch Duncan this night, and Macbeth proves averse in order to enjoy the "golden opinions" he has won, Shakespeare exploits the contrast between a feminine-looking woman with great strength of will and a masculine-looking man with a sufficiency of courage but with feminine fancy and weak resolution. In saying "From this time/ Such I account thy love" (ll. 38–39), Lady Macbeth goads her husband with something like sexual blackmail. She parallels Macbeth's unwillingness to kill the King with sexual nonperformance. The upshot of all this, as

Dennis Biggins points out, is that Shakespeare metaphorically identifies Macbeth's impulse to murder with perverted sexual passion. She chides him with cowardice, alluding to the proverb that "the cat would eat fish but would not wet her feet." As Eugene Waith has pointed out, Lady Macbeth's conception of manhood emphasizes valor and resolution but excludes moral purpose: in the Renaissance word she identifies masculinity with *virtú*, and, of course, fantasizes dreadfully about what it is to be a man. To pump courage into Macbeth, she tells of her willingness to dash out the brains of her nurseling if she had sworn as he had done. For those who (with some reason) believe that Shakespeare shrinks from the horrible, one may point out that Ovid has an account, as James Wood notes, of a mad father, Athamas, who brains his child; so Shakespeare may have borrowed this repulsive conception.

Whether Lady Macbeth had a child is a vexed critical question. We simply do not know. One may say in passing that in Shakespeare's plays, persons of villainous inclinations (except Aaron in *Titus Andronicus*) do not have children; and although Macbeth and Lady Macbeth must often attempt to have a child, for Macbeth's ambition is dynastic more than personal, they never succeed. *The language of the play, as Alice Fox has especially noted, is much concerned with pregnancy, miscarriage, normal and abortive births.*

Macbeth asks, "If we should fail?" *Lady Macbeth's response "We fail" should be followed by a question mark rather than an exclamation point,* for her sense is "How can we fail? If only you act resolutely we cannot fail." Taking a figure from the crossbow, she advises him to "screw your courage to the sticking place." Ernest Schanzer, taking *warder* in I.65 to be a misprint for "warden," as against Kittredge, paraphrases II.64–67 thus: "The full meaning of the image is therefore that the receptacle which should collect only the pure drops of reason, the final distillate of the thought process, will be turned into the retort in which the crude undistilled liquids bubble and fume." In this elaborate figure Lady Macbeth explains how soporific wine will put Duncan's chamberlains into "swinish sleep" and permit both the murder of the King and the assumption of their guilt for regicide. Thus Lady Macbeth, sketching the practical details of the murder, changes her lord's reluctance to enthusiasm for the deed.

Act II: Scene i

The scene is still Macbeth's castle at Inverness, this time, the stage directions tell us, a court of the castle. Banquo is talking with his son, Fleance. We learn from their first lines that the night is dark. "There's husbandry in heaven"; says Banquo as a mild joke, "Their candles are all out." He means there must be economy in heaven because the lights of heaven (the stars) are shut off. Banquo goes on to say that, although he is very tired,

he does not want to sleep because of the "cursed thoughts," that is, bad dreams, he has in his sleep. Apparently because he hears someone coming, he asks Fleance for his sword. With his sword in hand he shouts, "Who's there?" Macbeth enters and answers, "A friend." Banquo wonders why Macbeth is not yet asleep. The king, Banquo says, has already gone to bed having had "unusual pleasure," and he has bestowed many gifts in Macbeth's servants' quarters ("your offices"). Banquo also shows Macbeth a diamond that Duncan has left for Lady Macbeth because she has been such a "kind hostess." And, Banquo says, Duncan is "shut up in measureless content," that is, had concluded the day with a satisfaction so great that it cannot be measured. Macbeth says courteously that he and his wife were unprepared, and therefore they could not do as much for the king as they would have liked. Banquo then tells Macbeth that he dreamt last night of the "three weird sisters," whose predictions have partially come true for Macbeth. The latter replies, "I think not of them . . . ." However, he continues, Banquo and he, when they have leisure and if Banquo wishes to give the time, might talk about the matter. Banquo agrees. Macbeth goes on, "If you shall cleave to my consent, when 'tis,/ It shall make honor for you." That is, if you go along with me when the time comes, you will be rewarded. Banquo picks up the word *honor* from Macbeth's remark and uses it first in another one of its senses. (Actually, he does not use the word *honor*, rather he uses *none* in reference to Macbeth's using the word, and Banquo means, no *honor*.) He changes its meaning from *reward* (Macbeth's usage) to *honorableness*, or *uprightness*. Banquo's reply, therefore, signifies: As long as I lose no uprightness in trying to add to my rewards ("it" referring to *honor*) and keep myself guiltless and innocent. I shall listen to you. They wish each other good night, and Banquo and Fleance leave.

Macbeth is left alone with his servant to whom he gives instructions for Lady Macbeth. She is to ring a bell when his "drink" (his bedtime drink, his nightcap) is ready. Left alone, he speaks another soliloquy. "Is this a dagger, which I see before me,/ The handle toward my hand?" He thinks he sees a dagger in the air, the handle toward him. He wishes to take hold of the dagger, but since it is an hallucination, he cannot do so. He sees it still as vividly as the one which he now actually draws. He asks himself whether it is real or a creature of his mind, and he says that it leads him the way that he was going (that is, to murder Duncan). And the dagger he sees in the air is the very one he was going to use for the murder. Now he can see drops of blood on the dagger. "There's no such thing," he cries. "It is the bloody business which informs/ Thus to mine eyes." That is, there is no such dagger in the air; the fact that I am going to do the murder ("the bloody business") causes me to imagine I see it. Macbeth goes on to give his impression of the atmosphere of the night. He says that over half the world all activity seems to have stopped, and evil dreams are disturbing sleep. Witches are celebrating the rites of the moon ("Hecate," another name for Diana, the goddess of the moon; but Hecate was considered also the goddess of witchcraft). And "withered murder," that is, murder personified as wrinkled and shrunken, awakened by his guard, the wolf, strides secretly and quietly toward his purpose, like Tarquin. (Tarquin is Sextus Tarquinius, the son of the last Roman king. Tarquin's rape of the virtuous Lucrece caused the expulsion of his family from Rome and the establishment of the Roman republic.) Macbeth then addresses the stones of the earth asking them not to make noise as he walks, for the noise will take from the current occasion the horror which is appropriate to it. The bell sounds which Macbeth had the servant tell Lady Macbeth to ring. Apparently, it is a pre-arranged signal between them, the signal which summons Duncan to heaven or to hell. That is, it is the signal that tells Macbeth that he is to murder Duncan.

COMMENT: In this scene Shakespeare first exploits the *contrasts between Banquo's self-control and Macbeth's bloody thoughts;* then he emphasizes the *contrasts between Macbeth's public manner and his private aims, between the ceremony due him as a king and his unworthy self.* The poet departs from Holinshed's implication of Banquo in the conspiracy *because,* if he did not so, the King's ancestor would be guilty of treason, *because* James believed that rebellion is never justified, even against a wicked king, and *because* the story would then be lacking in inward conflict. Banquo and Fleance prepare themselves for sleep. From Banquo's removal of his weapons (ll. 4–5 contain implicit stage directions) we gather that everyone feels safe in the castle. Incidentally, Shakespeare's explicit stage directions are sparse by comparison with modern practice: this means that actors have more freedom of interpretation in Shakespearean plays. Banquo now prays for grace against "the cursed thoughts that nature / Gives way to in repose," a remark both general and particular in application. Banquo is presumably praying that God will restrain in him thoughts of hastening the day when his issue will become kings.

Macbeth enters, and Banquo delivers to him a diamond, a gift of Duncan to Lady Macbeth, which Banquo has about him undelivered—*seemingly hasty writing on Shakespeare's part.* Banquo, curiously, tells Macbeth, "I dreamt last night of the three weird sisters," yet *it cannot be shown how a night passes between the first appearance of the Sisters and the night spent by Banquo at Macbeth's castle.* Macbeth lies in response, "I think not of them." Then, assuming *the royal "we"* (l.22) in anticipation, he apparently thinks of awarding honors to his supporters. If Macbeth is made king, Banquo can expect to move up the ladder,

perhaps to become Thane of Cawdor. Banquo promises to be receptive to Macbeth's overtures so long as they are within the eye of honor.

How actors "handle" the "dagger." Banquo and Fleance leaving, Macbeth begins hallucinating about the dagger and uttering a soliloquy. It would be dramatically better for Macbeth to view the dagger at first slowly and reluctantly, struggling with belief that it is there and with diminishing skepticism that it is not there. *The best actors —* Garrick, Macready, Irving, and Booth—*did not use daggers onstage because they were able to make the audience see and feel what was not there.* The dramatic critic of the *Daily News,* Sept. 21, 1875, wrote of Irving: "We believe it has always been customary in the dagger scene to confront the audience looking upwards, as if the imaginary dagger was hovering in the air somewhere between the performer and the audience. Mr. Irving on the contrary sees the dagger at a much lower point as he follows it across the stage, drawn as it were by its fascination toward the arched entrance to the chamber of the king—a fine point being his averted hands as if the man 'infirm of purpose,' and conscious of the spell that is around and about him, could not trust himself to clutch the airy weapon save in words." The dagger is Macbeth's imagination leading him on, and his imagination is the fruit of his desires. In ll. 49–60 he allies himself with the wolf, suggesting his intention to destroy the lamb (God), and with less point he likens himself to Tarquin, who was, as Irving Ribner says, "the destroyer of chastity, symbolic in the Renaissance of the perfection of God." Macbeth then goes offstage to murder Duncan. Polanski, unlike Shakespeare, exhibits Macbeth in the act of killing Duncan; while this notable effusion is occurring, the crown rolls from a table to a floor suggesting, again unlike Shakespeare, that its slipperiness will continue to attract ambition beyond the confines of the play.

Act II: Scene ii

The setting is the same as in the previous scene. The beginning of this scene occurs as Macbeth is in Duncan's room committing the murder. Lady Macbeth enters in a state of high excitement. In the last scene of Act I she had said that with "wine and wassail" she was going to make Duncan's two attendants drunk. Apparently, she has not only done so, but she has also taken some of the drink herself, for she says when she enters, "That which had made them drunk hath made me bold . . . ." But despite the daring given her by drink, she is nervous. "Hark!" she cries when she hears a sound, which turns out to be nothing but the shriek of an owl. "He is about it," she then says; that is, Macbeth is committing the murder. She recounts her preparations: the doors are open (so that Macbeth can get in); the attendants ("grooms") are snoring, for she has drugged their nightcaps ("possets"). Macbeth suddenly cries from inside. "Who's there?" Lady Macbeth is afraid that Macbeth's shout means that the grooms have awakened and that the murder has not been committed. The attempt at the deed, she says, not the murder itself will cause their failure. She grows increasingly nervous. She thinks she hears a noise again, for she cries once more, "Hark!" She must now be thinking that Macbeth cannot find the daggers she had prepared: she says, "I laid their daggers ready;/ He could not miss 'em." Then she says, "Had he not resembled / My father as he slept, I had done't." At this point Macbeth enters, and his wife calls to him, "My husband!"

When Macbeth enters, he tells his wife that he has "done the deed." But they are both obviously nervous, for they ask each other a series of quick questions about noises they have heard. The exchange ends with Macbeth's "Hark!" and they both apparently listen, hearing nothing. Then Macbeth asks who was sleeping in the "second chamber," that is, the bedroom behind Duncan's. "Donalbain," Lady Macbeth replies. Macbeth apparently looks at his bloody hands, for he says, "This is a sorry sight." His wife tells him that he is foolish to think so. Macbeth then goes on to recall an incident that occurred while he was in Duncan's chamber. In telling of the incident Macbeth talks of two men who were sleeping in a room. It is difficult to know whether he is talking of Malcolm and Donalbain who were apparently sleeping in the room behind Duncan or the two grooms who were in Duncan's room. It hardly matters which of the two groups he is talking about. It is the story that Macbeth tells that counts, not the participants. In any case, one of the men laughed in his sleep and the other cried out, "Murder!" The sounds each made woke the other, but they said their prayers and returned to sleep. During their prayers one said, "God bless us!" and the other responded with "Amen." The men expressed these wishes as though they had seen Macbeth with his "hangman's hands," that is, with his hands full of blood. Macbeth listened with fright. When the first man said, "God bless us!" Macbeth wanted to reply, "Amen," but he was unable to do so. Lady Macbeth tells him not to think about it. But Macbeth wants to know why he could not say, "Amen." He wants to know why the word stuck in his throat. She says that if they keep thinking that way they will go mad. But Macbeth continues in the same vein. He thought he heard a voice cry, "Sleep no more! Macbeth does murder sleep . . . ." In recalling what the voice had said Macbeth is reminded of the importance in life of "innocent sleep." Sleep, Macbeth says in a series of images, nightly soothes the spirit made sore by the

difficulties of daily life. After a short interruption by Lady Macbeth, to which her husband seems to pay no attention, he continues to talk of the voice he thought he heard. The voice continued to cry, "Sleep no more! . . . Glamis hath murdered sleep, and therefore, Cawdor/ Shall sleep no more, Macbeth shall sleep no more!" Lady Macbeth is rattled by this and asks Macbeth who cried out in that way. But she recovers her composure and tells Macbeth that he makes himself weakspirited to think in this way; he must get some water and wash away the blood from his hands which would reveal his having done the murder. She now notices for the first time the daggers he has brought with him from the scene of the crime, and she tells him to return them and to smear the faces of the grooms with blood. Macbeth refuses to return. It is bad enough that he is afraid to think of his crime; he dares not look at it again. His wife derides his weakness ("Infirm of purpose!"), takes the daggers, tells him that sleeping and dead people are like pictures feared only by children; if Duncan is bleeding, she herself will smear the groom's faces with blood. And she goes to perform her task.

Macbeth is left alone. A knocking can be heard. Macbeth has turned so many ordinary night noises into frightening ones that he thinks the knocking is another ordinary night noise his imagination has turned into a dangerous one. He looks at his hands. They are so bloody, he thinks, that they are blinding him. He wonders whether the ocean can wash his hands clean. They cannot, he says; rather, his bloody hands will make all the seas of the world red. Lady Macbeth re-enters and tells him that her hands are also red, but she is ashamed to have a coward's heart ("a heart so white"). She hears the knocking, which is at the south gate. She tells her husband that they must go to their bedroom. "A little water clears us of this deed: / How easy is it then." That is, once they have washed their hands, how easy it will be not to feel guilty and to fool people into believing that they have not committed the deed. Macbeth apparently remains immobile, for his wife says "Your constancy / Hath left you unattended." That is, your firmness has deserted you. The knocking is heard once more, and she urges Macbeth to move so that he can appear as though he has just awakened. He finally exits showing his regret, "Wake Duncan with thy knocking: I would thou couldst!"

COMMENT: Lady Macbeth has felt the need of wine to make her strong enough for the wickedness of the night. She hears an owl and likens it to the bell-man (or town crier) who, giving the "stern'st good-night," visited London prisoners on the night before execution. The owl and the bell-man, John Orrell notes, were conflated in *Blurt, Master Constable* (1602). Macbeth, she believes, is murdering

Duncan; and she takes pleasure in the thoroughness with which the drugged possets are working upon Duncan's grooms. One might observe in passing that *wine, to which the plebian grooms were unaccustomed, would have a stronger effect upon them,* according Elizabethan thinking, than upon Lady Macbeth. At l. 8 Macbeth calls without hysteria; and Lady Macbeth, not knowing whether it is the awaking grooms, shows a distinct preference, if something should go wrong, for being blamed for the deed itself rather than for attempting the deed. Although she says that she would have killed Duncan herself if it were not for his resemblance, when asleep, to her father, the text indicates that she resolves only to steel her husband for the deed. When she calls on the spirits to unsex her, she is identifying herself imaginatively with the deed. Her only physical part in the murder is the drugging and the smearing of the grooms. We are never sure that Macbeth will kill Duncan until he does it because there is always a chance that a sight of the intended victim will restore him to his senses. The deed is committed, we learn from V.i.35–36, shortly after two in the morning. Suspense collapses at once, but for Jacobean spectators there was still the suspenseful possibility that the remorseful Macbeth will repent.

Human blood and the sea. Macbeth, entering, tells of hearing Donalbain and Malcolm's awaking and praying. So we gather that the King's sons "feel for" his murder. *Macbeth's inability to pronounce the "Amen" should be interpreted as a sign of the assurance of his damnation in the theological sense.* When Lady Macbeth says, "These deeds must not be thought/ After these ways," Kittredge comments,"in such a fashion as this (with an agonizing dwelling on every little detail, and perplexity as to what it means)." But surely she is telling Macbeth not to give heed to religious scruples. Macbeth recounts hearing a voice crying "Sleep no more" — a sign that his mind is beginning to break under the strain of the murder. He then delivers with his usual verbal felicity a short speech (Ll. 33 ff.) on sleep that has, as Jean Robertson shows, a number of classical and Elizabethan parallels. The expression "great nature's second course," a phrase obscure to us, would appear to be a figure referring to the most substantial part of an Elizabethan dinner. Disgusted with Macbeth's being so "brain-sickly," Lady Macbeth grabs daggers and goes herself to place them by the grooms and smear the grooms with Duncan's blood. She is not sure if the old man has any flowing blood; but if he has, she will "gild the faces of the grooms withal,/ For it must seem their guilt"—*a pun exhibiting her self-command or,* conceivably, *her repression of her guilt.* Macbeth, whose rhetorical strength grows in soliloquy, communes with himself on the impossibility of washing Duncan's blood from his hands: ". . . my hand will rather / The multitudinous seas incarnadine, / Making the green one red." The last line, Russell K. Alspach assures us, should be read, "Making the green—one red," a nuance

that goes back to the actors Sheridan and Murphy. The passage is not so hyperbolical as has been thought if it is remembered that Renaissance people were accustomed to seeing analogies between the human body and the earth, specifically between human blood and the sea.

Lady Macbeth enters with bloody hands. She chides her husband for his white heart, meaning that in her view his behavior intimates that he is now totally lacking in virility, which she customarily identifies with the ability to perform bloody deeds of resolution without regard to their morality. *Repeated knocking, significantly at the south entrance (associated in this play with England and in general, with the east, a direction allied with moral goodness), means that the murder will shortly produce moral consequences.*

Act II: Scene iii

The scene is really a continuation of the previous one. The knocking at the gate heard by Macbeth and his wife is still heard after they leave the stage, and soon after the porter, whose job it is to open the gate, enters. His speech is in prose. "Here's a knocking, indeed!" he says. "If a man were porter of hell-gate, he should have old turning the key." That is, if a man were assigned the job of opening the gate of hell for the dead people who were sent there, he would have plenty to do ("should have old") turning the key. He hears the knocking again, and his remark about the porter of hell-gate apparently prompts him to play a game. He imagines himself to be the porter of hell-gate, and he thinks of types for whom he would be opening the gate and the reasons why these types would be coming to hell. The first is "a farmer, that hanged himself on the expectation of plenty . . . ." The farmer, the porter means, hanged himself because he had stored up grain originally expecting bad crops and high prices; but it now appeared as though the crops would be good and the prices would therefore be low; so, on the "expectation of plenty" he hangs himself. The next man is "an equivocator, that could swear in both scales against either scale; . . . yet could not equivocate to heaven . . . ." An equivocator is a man who purposely says something that has one meaning for most people hearing it but another meaning for himself. That is why he can swear on either side of the scale of justice against the other side. The third type is "an English tailor come hither for stealing out of a French hose . . . ." The English tailor had copied what he thought was the current French style just as that had changed. Since Englishmen followed the French style, he thought the copying would make him popular. But he out-smarted himself. The porter hears the persistent knocking at the gate. "Never at quiet," he says. He is about to continue with another type when he remarks, "But this place is too cold for help. I'll devil-porter it no further: I had thought to have let in some of all professions, that go the primrose way to the everlasting bonfire." That is, he was going to show those in each profession who cheat and make it easy for themselves and therefore go to hell. He opens the gate for the men who have been knocking and *asks them for a tip* ("I pray you, remember the porter").

Macduff and Lennox are the men who have been knocking. Macduff asks whether the porter's sleeping late is a sign that he had gone late to bed. The porter answers that the people of the house had gone to bed at 3 A.M. ("the second cock") because they were up drinking. An exchange of shady dialogue about lechery and equivocation follows until Macbeth enters.

There follows some courteous greeting between him and the two thanes. It is Macduff's duty to wake the king, and he goes off to do so. Lennox talks about the stormy night that has just past. Among other things, chimneys were blown down, "strange screams of death" were heard as well as "lamentings . . . i' the air." Macbeth replies, "'Twas a rough night." Macduff then rushes out shouting the news of Duncan's murder: "Most sacreligious murder hath broke ope / The Lord's anointed temple . . . ." Macbeth and Lennox go out to confirm Macduff's report. Macduff rings the alarm bell and wakes the house. Lady Macbeth and then Banquo enter. Hearing of Duncan's murder, Lady Macbeth cries, "What! in our house?" When Macbeth re-enters with Lennox, the former says that if he had died an hour before the accident of Duncan's murder he would have thought of his life as blessed. He goes on to say, "The wine of life is drawn, and the mere less / Is left this vault to brag of." That is, the best part of life is over. Malcolm and Donalbain enter and discover what has happened, and Malcolm asks who has done the deed. Lennox replies that because the grooms were covered with blood it seems as though they had done it. Macbeth says that he is sorry he has killed the grooms. To Macduff's question as to why he did so, Macbeth replies that in the cross-current of violent emotions he felt upon seeing Duncan dead he had killed the attendants "to make's love [for Duncan] known." When Macbeth finishes telling his story about the killing of the grooms, Lady Macbeth faints (indicated by "Help me hence, ho!"). During the excitement brought on by Lady Macbeth's fainting Malcolm and Donalbain decide that in the currently dangerous situation they had better leave in a hurry. Lady Macbeth is carried out, and Banquo says that as soon as they are all properly dressed they will confer as to what to do. They all agree. Everyone but Malcolm and Donalbain exits. The latter decide that, in the situation as it stands, the false man easily shows false sorrow. Malcolm will go to England; Donalbain to Ireland. They will be safer if each goes a different way. Malcolm concludes by saying that, since there is no mercy left, there is good reason to steal oneself away.

COMMENT: *The Porter's soliloquy serves a variety of functions—dramatic irony, comic relief, foreshadowing, theme, the introduction of topical allusions, and a separation between the exeunt of the Macbeths and their re-entrance.* As comic relief, the present scene is analogous to the grave-scene in *Hamlet* and to the representation of the clown with asps in *Antony and Cleopatra*. It would appear that the Porter is guarding a gate locking off one wing of the castle from another. The Porter fancies himself as playing the role of Satan's gatekeeper, who would of course be busier than the Porter himself: *porter* derives from L. "porta," gate. (One might well remember that during the Renaissance words of Latin and Greek origins were closer to their original meanings than the same words nowadays.) Someone has happily remarked, with reference to the Porter's mental state, that his speech reflects "the sea-green clarity of the hang-over, not the crimson fantasies of the debauch." Curiously, the Porter bears some resemblance to Macbeth in that he has a low grade of poetic invention. *In Polanski's filmed version,* which at this point summons up a believable picture of medieval society with animals in the courtyard, men in dirty jerkins, and a sword dance, *the Porter urinates while delivering his speech.* Needless to say, the Porter ought to speak with a lower-class accent. With a number of allusions to the Gunpowder Plot of 1605, the speech may be presumed to have been electrifying to the chief intended victim, King James I.

Allusions to Jesuits. The Porter says, "Here's a farmer, that hang'd himself on th' expectation of plenty." H. L. Rogers thinks that this may be an allusion to Henry Garnet, the chief Jesuit of England, who was tried for complicity in the Gunpowder Plot, found guilty, and executed: one of Garnet's aliases was "Farmer." J. B. Harcourt thinks that the next speech should read, "Come in, Time," "for that relentless figure presides over the action of the play." "You'll sweat for't," in addition to the idea of sweating in Hell, carries with it, Harcourt believes, a sexual jest on *the sweating tub, the standard Elizabethan treatment of venereal disease.* "Faith, here's an equivocator, that could swear in both the scales against either scale, who committed treason enough for God's sake, yet could not equivocate to heaven." This remark is regarded as a clear allusion to Garnet and the Jesuits, who supposedly made ambiguous answers to questions and then swore to their truth. Frank L. Huntley, who has studied the background of the doctrine of equivocation (he has been corrected on a number of points by A. E. Malloch), points out that in *Macbeth* equivocation originates from the Devil, the arch-traitor, and that Macbeth, who has entertained treasonous thoughts before meeting the Witches, accepts the spoken half of their thoughts and acts on the other, unspoken half as completing the "truth." Such thinking involves two times: the present and the future, the latter belonging in the case of the Jesuits to God, in the case of the Macbeths to the Devil. Huntley presents an instance of Jesuitical equivocation from the "bloody question" in *The Treatise of Equivocation* by Henry Garnet, S. J.: "if brigands ask, 'Where is the Queen? We are sent to murder your sovereign,' you must equivocate by, '*Nescio [ut te dicam]*'—I know not *[to the end of telling you]*." *Scale* refers to "the exact balance between the two meanings of the ambiguous assertion."

Meanings of "tailor." "Faith, here's an English tailor come hither for stealing out of a French hose. Come in, tailor, here you may roast your goose." Tailors were proverbially thought to steal material. Since French hose (breeches) were tight-fitting and required little cloth, this kind of thievery would take skill. Rogers is of the opinion that there is an allusion here to an English tailor named Hugh Griffin, who was examined in late 1606 for a possible connection in the matter of Father Garnet's miraculous head of straw that was bothering authorities who feared the political consequences of Garnet's martyrdom, as Catholics conceived it. A very different interpretation, which may of course be held simultaneously, is Hilda Hulme's belief that *tailor* may be a euphemism for "penis," and that Gallic pox, *i.e.*, syphilis, is in view.

Associations with knocking. The Porter opens the gate with a request ("remember the porter") for a tip, and Macduff's insistent knocking is rewarded with a few light but dramatically important moments. J. W. Spargo observes that the knocking on the gate would not have been comic to the first audiences because it would have reminded the learned of Horace's line concerning the equality of death in kicking (Romans kicked doors) the doors of both rich and poor, and it would have summoned up for all ranks the rough knocking made by spade handles of citizens who entered houses to remove the corpses of those struck down by the plague. Glynne Wickham thinks the powerful knocking to be an overlay of the Harrowing of Hell scenes in certain English miracle (*i.e.*, mystery) plays. If so, Macduff suggests Christ knocking at the door of Hell to release the souls of patriarchs and prophets; and one with this memory would expect Macduff to be the avenger of Duncan's murder.

The Porter says to Macduff, ". . . drink, sir, is a great provoker of three things." It is difficult indeed to imagine this Scottish laird Macduff playing straight man to the Porter, "What three things does drink especially provoke?" The Porter punningly responds with application to drink as an "equivocator" who gives its user the "lie." ". . . though he [much drink] took up my legs sometime, yet I made a

shift to cast him"—*here the Porter* employing language suggestive of uroscopy, *i.e.*, detection of illness by examination of urine, combined with the language of a purge or vomit, *grossly puts forward a thematic idea* in *Macbeth* that *evil will be expelled from the body politic.* Harcourt points out that the Porter's dealing with fornication and drunkenness—sins possessing a degree of human warmth—and his noting of the coldness of Macbeth's castle help to call our attention to Macbeth's monstrosity in evil. Frederic B. Tromly, however, thinks of *the Porter as a metaphor for Macbeth*: he points out that the Porter takes Macbeth's crime and translates it to "the familiar realm of diminished moral expectation." Both men lose themselves in "brainsickly" thoughts; both are reluctant to perform their offices; the Witches' equivocations are in effect like the Porter's drink. Tromly sees correspondences between Macbeth and the Porter in virtually every detail of the scene. On the other hand, M. J. B. Allen regards *the Porter as Macbeth's evil genius*: the drunk's tumescence is an analog of Macbeth's inability to beget children; Macbeth from this point on becomes spiritually degenerate; and the Porter, by letting in Macbeth's executioner, betrays Macbeth's soul to Hell.

Macbeth enters, and Macduff indicates that he has been commanded to waken the King. Macduff leaves for this purpose. Lennox and Macduff, we apprehend, have slept in a place separated by the gate from the King's wing, a point that absolves them from complicity in the murder, and one that makes it possible for them, whose quarters were in a more exposed part of the castle, to have heard the strange prodigies of the night. Prodigies announce or accompany the death of a great man also in *Julius Caesar*, II.ii. 17–24.

Macbeth's low tolerance of suspense. Macduff bursts in with the horrendous report of regicide, set forth in terms combining language from Biblical verses like II Cor. 6, 16— "Ye are the temple of the living God" and I Sam. 24, 10, "the Lord's anointed." Showing that he cannot endure suspense, Macbeth leaves to murder the grooms, a crime not part (see II. ii. 45–47) of the original plan. Macduff bawls out to awaken the sleepers, "Rise as at Doomsday and walk like white spirits to give the right setting to this horror." *The clang of the bell, as well as the earlier knocking on the gate, has been thought to symbolize Macbeth's agitation and convulsion in the murdering of Duncan.*

Lady Macbeth enters, Shakespeare here being wisely in defiance of an old acting version that required the Lady's absence from II.iii. She should be in the middle of the clamorous hall, *not* in her room, so that her self-possession might regard the nervous Macbeth and, if need be, take command. She does make a slip in her role as gentle hostess when she says, "What, in our house?" for which she is checked by Banquo, "Too cruel anywhere."

Macbeth re-enters, and by the eloquence of his lines (Ll. 91–96) suggests that a politician is never more emotionally sincere than when commemorating a fallen rival.

"Discovering" that Duncan's grooms have killed the King, Macbeth confesses that he has killed the grooms in an orgy of emotion and has not questioned them. *Macduff's response, "Wherefore did you so?" does not, one thinks, indicate either anger or suspicion but rather a desire to interrogate the grooms.* Macbeth vividly describes the stricken Duncan, "His silver skin lac'd with his golden blood." Duncan's blood differs from other blood—a pervasive image in the play—in that it is not thick and fearfully colored. W.A. Murray connects Duncan's "golden blood" with an alchemical agent capable, because of its perfections, of transmuting baser substances into something like itself.

Why Lady Macbeth faints. Lady Macbeth then faints, and a glance at the Variorum *Macbeth* is sufficient to gather that her motive has excited much discussion: is it genuine or histrionic? On the one side several considerations may be adduced. Her blunder about "What, in our house?" puts her under strain. She may be nervous about Macbeth's magniloquent prating upon something that a few minutes before he was afraid to look upon. She is quite unprepared for her husband's murder of the two grooms. She is constitutionally averse to bloodshed. She has not been able to relieve her mind with words. Madness and destruction seem to lie at the back of her mind (cf. II.ii.31). On the other hand, her fainting may be a feint to divert attention from the murder and to make herself appear innocent. Donalbain, in an aside "Our tears are not yet brew'd," suggests that the young princes may think the lamentation of the host and hostess to be synthetic. Malcolm perhaps means by Ll. 139–40 that *we who are near in blood to the murdered King are nearer to being made bloody, i.e.,* murdered. Malcolm and Donalbain do not even trust Banquo or anyone else who is present: *one should note Malcom's suspicion of Macduff in IV.iii.*

Act II: Scene iv

The scene occurs outside Macbeth's castle. Ross and an old man enter. The old man says that he can remember things for seventy years back, but he cannot remember a night as stormy as this has been. Ross replies by saying that the heavens are behaving as though they are troubled by "man's act," that is, last night's murder, and are threatening man. He goes on to say that, although the clock says that it is daytime, yet it is as dark as night. The old man answers, "'Tis unnatural,/ Even like the deed that's done." And the old man and Ross talk of other unnatural events that have recently occurred, which fit with the last night's event and the present day's darkness. For example, Duncan's horses, previously tamed, turned wild and ate each other. Macduff now enters and tells the two who have been on stage the

common belief concerning the murder. Malcolm and Donalbain, who have fled, hired the grooms to kill Duncan. He continues with the news that Macbeth has already been named king and has gone to be crowned at Scone, where Scottish kings are crowned. Duncan has been taken for burial. Ross asks Macduff whether he is going to the coronation at Scone, and Macduff replies, "No cousin; I'll to Fife." (Fife is Macduff's home; he is the Thane of Fife.) Ross says that he will go to Scone, and Macduff replies, "Well, may you see things well done there . . ./ Lest our old robes sit easier than our new!" And each leaves on his own way.

COMMENT: Between II.iii and II.iv the princes escape, the electors choose Macbeth as king, and Macbeth and his lady leave for Scone to be crowned. The chief purpose of this scene is to keep before us the connection between the material storms and the spiritual storms. The dramatic function of the nameless Old Man is to deliver *apocalyptic omens, the earthquake and eclipse reminding one of Christ's crucifixion and tending, therefore, to make Duncan a Christ-figure.* Another of the Old Man's prodigies is Duncan's horses eating each other: here we see *the most monstrous example of the pervasive horse-and-rider imagery of the play.* Horses were viewed in Elizabethan times as illustrations of unbridled violence: the *Homily against Wilful Rebellion,* for example, states that unmarried men when they revolt "pursue other men's wives and daughters . . . worse than any stallions or horses."

Macduff, entering, informs Ross and the Old Man of the "official theory" of the murder: the guilty grooms were bribed, suspicion says by Malcolm and Donalbain, to do the deed. Macduff apparently accepts the theory; but his answers are short, and he declines to attend the investiture of Macbeth. The crown goes to Macbeth, we apprehend, because Malcolm, the legal claimant, has repudiated the duty of claiming it. Macduff at Ll. 36–37 fears that Macbeth's reign may not be so agreeable to the nobility as Duncan's. In the last lines of the scene the seerlike Old Man, speaking to Macduff and Ross, may harbor some suspicion of Macbeth.

Act III: Scene i

The scene takes place in the palace of the king of Scotland at Forres. As we learned in the last act, Macbeth is now king. Banquo enters and speaks a soliloquy. As though he is talking to Macbeth, he says, "Thou hast it now, King, Cawdor, Glamis, all / As the weird women promised . . . ." That is, you now have all the titles promised you by the Witches. And Banquo goes on to say that Macbeth attained the titles "most foully." But Banquo remembers the rest of the prophecy. No descendants of Macbeth would be kings; yet

Banquo himself would be the forebear of a line of kings. If the prophecy for Macbeth came true, why should not the prophecy for Banquo come true and make him hopeful. But he sees Macbeth, Lady Macbeth and their party enter and he must be quiet.

Among the attendants of the king and queen are Lennox and Ross. Macbeth's first words refer to Banquo, "Here's our chief guest." Lady Macbeth adds that to forget Banquo is to have a "gap in our great feast." Macbeth formally announces the "solemn supper" they will hold tonight, and he formally invites Banquo. Banquo accepts the invitation. In the course of apparently casual conversation, Macbeth finds out from Banquo that Banquo and his son, Fleance, are going horseback riding and that they will not be back until after dark. During this conversation we also learn that Malcolm and Donalbain, whom Macbeth calls "our bloody cousins," are in England and Ireland. They do not confess "their cruel parricide," that is, the murder of their father, and they make up strange stories. Banquo leaves and Macbeth tells everyone to do as he wishes until the feast that evening. Macbeth commands a servant to bring in some men who are waiting for him. While he waits for the men, Macbeth is left alone on the stage, and he speaks a soliloquy.

"To be thus is nothing, but to be safely thus . . . ," says Macbeth. That is, to be king has no meaning unless one is securely a king. Macbeth is afraid of Banquo. Banquo has the character of a king, which contains something to be afraid of: Banquo is daring, fearless, and wise enough to act safely. Macbeth is afraid of no one but Banquo, for Macbeth's angel ("My Genius") is always put down by Banquo. Banquo chastised the Witches when they first called Macbeth king and asked them to speak to him, Banquo. They told Banquo that he would be the forebear of "a line of kings" and upon Macbeth's head they placed "a fruitless crown,/ And put a barren sceptre in my gripe . . . ." That is, since Macbeth would be childless no descendants of his would be kings. If this is so, Macbeth has given up his immortal soul ("eternal jewel") to the devil ("the common enemy of man") only to make kings of Banquo's descendants. Rather than allow this to be the case, Macbeth challenges fate. But he is interrupted in his thoughts by the entrance of the servant bringing his two visitors.

The servant enters with the two men whom the stage directions call Murderers. In the course of Macbeth's conversation with them we learn that they have had a previous interview with him. He told them in that interview that where they had thought it was Macbeth who had deceived them with false promises, it was in actuality Banquo. Macbeth then goes on to the point of the current meeting. He tries to persuade them that if they are men, they will not take their betrayal

lying down. The First Murderer has answered only very briefly until this point. Now he says in a speech of three lines that his luck has been so bad that he is desperate and does not care what he does. The Second Murderer in a speech equally long agrees with the First. Macbeth tells them that Banquo is also Macbeth's enemy. Although he could kill Banquo with "bare-faced power," yet he dare not do it because of the mutual friends that he and Banquo have, whose love he is afraid to lose. Therefore, he asks the two men to take care of his business privately. They give their consent. Macbeth will advise them as to the place. And they must kill Fleance also, for Fleance's death is as important to Macbeth as Banquo's. The Murderers agree and leave. Macbeth concludes with "Banquo, thy soul's flight,/ If it find Heaven, must find it out tonight."

COMMENT: The unclear time lapse between Acts II and III permits us only to gather that Macbeth has been crowned for some time. Banquo in soliloquy shows awareness that Macbeth may have engineered his becoming king; but although Banquo is, by analogy with Macbeth's rise, inclined to place some credence in the Witches' prophecies, he is not inclined to criminal action himself, partly because he does not know whether his immediate or his remote descendants will become kings. He does not feel a need to hide himself, as Macduff does, from Macbeth's administration partly because, unlike Macduff, he has no great estate or fief. *It is not customary to decline support to an able politician who has perhaps used unfair tactics in putting down the opposition and who now promises a fair administration!* Bradley opines that Banquo is in this speech yielding to evil, but Kirschbaum with more cogency argues that "But hush, no more" is not said to dismiss "cursed thoughts," but merely to register Banquo's *hearing the sennet* announcing the entrance of the King and Queen.

Macbeth, entering, shows his graciousness to Banquo by employing, in l. 15, *the personal "I" rather than the royal "we" in issuing a command* for Banquo to appear at a "solemn supper" this evening. Banquo in response mentions "a most indissoluble tie" between Macbeth and himself, alluding to the prophecies of the Witches and his suspicions of Macbeth's making himself king, neither of which Banquo seems ever to have communicated to anyone else. Macbeth shows much interest in the details of Banquo's riding forth with Fleance because he wants to murder them both. Curiously, Banquo exhibits no suspicion about this line of inquiry. It would be a mistake, should Fleance be onstage, for the actor playing Macbeth to fondle him in a catlike manner at l. 35, for Macbeth is not a sadist. He fears Banquo because of what Macbeth knows of Banquo's character and of the prophecy; and he wants Banquo out of the way at once, rather than later, because at the council of state indicated in ll. 32–34 he will have to confront Banquo publicly on what "our bloody cousins" are putting forth in the way of "strange invention."

A great soliloquy and its symbolism. In the great soliloquy that follows, Macbeth fears not so much Banquo the man as Banquo the symbol, as Kirschbaum points out, of virtues that Macbeth wants but cannot have. In saying ". . . under him,/ My Genius is rebuk'd," Macbeth is in effect saying, "My genius of intemperate ambition for the crown rebuked by his steadfast loyalty even in the face of provocation." Although Shakespeare is sometimes credited with causing characters who speak in soliloquy to tell therein the straight truth, it is not true that Banquo "chid the sisters/ When first they put the name of king upon me,/ And bade them to speak to him"; for Banquo spoke to them fairly and dispassionately. Macbeth reports (ll. 60–63) the Witches as prophesying that he would be childless; the fact of the matter is that they did not say this. The prospect of kingship must seem absolutely good to Macbeth when it is first offered. By III.i Macbeth realizes that he has gained nothing by the murder of Duncan; and now the prophecy of his lack of progeny is brought in as it were by stealth. In l. 69 "seeds" rather than "seed" should be used because Shakespeare wrote it that way, and this emendation that Alexander Pope made does not so well convey the multiplication of Banquo's issue. Macbeth thinks that he has made a bad bargain—he has entered the ranks of the damned for no better reason than to make Banquo's posterity kings. Ll. 70–71 mean "Let fate fight as my champion until I am killed," not as Dr. Johnson thought, "let fate enter the lists against me."

Motivating the Murderers. The two Murderers enter: they are Scottish gentlemen, maddened by despair, previously enemies of Macbeth but now convinced that Banquo has wronged them; by contrast Lady Macduff's Murderers are common cutthroats. Macbeth endeavors to steel the murderers for the killing of Banquo by asking them whether they are so full of Christian grace that they can pray for their wrongdoers. Macbeth's "dog" speech, ll. 91 ff., exhibits moral confusion from the point of view of Renaissance orthodoxy because it confuses dogs and men; and one might add, it shows Macbeth not far removed from his wife's conception of manhood. Both Murderers are utterly reckless, but Macbeth is willing to use them to make it appear that Banquo's death is the result of a feud. Macbeth says, honestly enough, that he must not sweep Banquo into death in an open manner lest doing so should aggrieve certain mutual friends. The Murderers appear resolved although *we learn later that they are reluctant:* Macbeth sends a Third Murderer in III.iii. One might think of ending this scene with the following business: "At the close of Macbeth's colloquy with the villains whom he employs to murder Banquo, those wretches try, with fawning servility, to seize the hem of his regal robe, and thereupon he repulses them with a deportment of imperial disdain and a momentary shudder." But this interpolated action would reduce these decayed gentlemen to the level of hired thugs.

Act III: Scene ii

We are still in the king's castle at Forres. Lady Macbeth enters with a servant. Lady Macbeth asks the servant whether Banquo has as yet left the court, that is, has he yet gone riding. The servant replies that he has but that he will be back in the evening. The mistress sends her servant for Macbeth, and Lady Macbeth is left alone. She has a short speech before Macbeth enters. "Naught's had, all's spent/ Where our desire is got without content . . . ," she says. That is, when one has attained one's goal without mental ease and satisfaction, all the effort used to attain the goal has been put forth for nothing. She continues by saying that it is safer to be the murdered person ("that which we destroy") than to be the murderer living in uncertain happiness ("dwell in doubtful joy").

Macbeth enters, and his wife berates him. Why, she asks, does he isolate himself with his unhappy thoughts? Those thoughts about the dead should have died with them. Things that cannot be helped should not be thought about. "What's done is done." Macbeth replies that they have slashed the snake in two; they have not killed it; the snake will re-form into a whole. Macbeth uses figurative language to say that in killing Duncan and his two grooms Macbeth and his wife have not completely eliminated their danger; because the danger has not been completely eliminated, it will again be as great as once it was. He goes on to tell Lady Macbeth that he will let the entire universe disintegrate before he and his wife "will eat our meal in fear, and sleep/ In the affliction of these terrible dreams,/ That shake us nightly." It is better, he says, to be with the dead whom they have killed to gain peace (for the ambitions) than to be in constant mental anguish. Duncan is dead, and nothing in this life can hurt him any more. Lady Macbeth tells her husband to take it easy and to be happy at the feast that evening. He says that he will be happy and that she should be happy too. She ought to pay special attention to Banquo: while they are unsafe, their faces must mask their hearts. "You must leave this," says Lady Macbeth. "O! full of scorpions is my mind, dear wife!" answers her husband. That is, my mind is full of evil thoughts. Macbeth adds, "Thou know'st that Banquo, and his Fleance, lives." She replies that they do not live forever. "There's comfort yet," says her husband. He tells her that Banquo and Fleance are vulnerable. He adds that before night a dreadful deed shall be done. "What's to be done?" she asks. "Be innocent of the knowledge, dearest chuck,/ Till thou applaud the deed." That is, you do not have to know about the deed, darling, until it is over, at which time you can praise me for it. Macbeth now makes an invocation to night. He asks night to come and to blindfold the eye of day, which is full of pity; and night, he continues, with its "bloody and invisible hand," will then destroy "that great bond/ Which keeps me pale!" (the lives of Banquo and Fleance). Apparently, night once more answers Macbeth's command, for he now says, "Light thickens," and he goes on to describe the onset of night, which again reflects the state of his mind: ". . . night's black agents to their preys do rouse." Lady Macbeth evidently gazes at her husband in astonishment, for he remarks to her, "thou marvell'st at my words . . . ." He goes on to observe that things begun badly improve themselves by continued evil. "So pr'ythee, go with me," says he as they exeunt.

COMMENT: In this scene Macbeth is brooding about Banquo's still being alive. Lady Macbeth, in language equating Banquo's continued life with unsatisfying sexual performance, shares her husband's fear. Macbeth, entering, observes that although his enemies have been wounded, there is still life and menace in them. Amneus argues that this passage strongly suggests, and Forman's report of the Globe performance confirms, that Banquo's murder has already taken place: the Folio text has been cut. (The word should be "scotched" the snake, not "scorched" it.) He expects "Malice domestic" from Banquo and Macduff, "foreign levy" from Malcolm in England and Donalbain in Ireland. Lady Macbeth advises him to take his mind off his sleeplessness and Duncan's sleeping in his grave; he should prepare, she says, for the feast tonight. He replies. "O, full of scorpions is my mind, dear wife!" *The scorpion image may be derived from the traditional inconography that made the scorpion a symbol of Judas, a view that enriches analogies with the betrayal of Christ and Macbeth's murder of Duncan.* However, Dennis Biggins is disposed to *regard the scorpion on the basis of medieval and Renaissance thought as a secular emblem of flattering treachery:* as such, the word brings to focus the theme of false appearances. *Scorpions were in Shakespeare's time thought to be serpents,* and Macbeth is adjured by his wife in I.v to be the serpent under the innocent flower. There is notable irony in Macbeth's playing the snake and acting the scorpion *vis-à-vis* Duncan and then finding serpents under every innocent flower. Macbeth continues, "Thou know'st that Banquo, and his Fleance, lives." Lady Macbeth replies, "But in them nature's copy's not eterne." *The meaning of "nature's copy" has occasioned much discussion.* Matti Rissanen points out that there are two chief interpretations: *copy* in the sense of "copyhold," thus linking this metaphor with the idea (cf. III.ii.49; IV.i.99) that man holds his life from nature until death; *copy* in the sense of the human body as "a thing to be copied" or "the result of imitation." Recent editors of *Macbeth* tend to accept the second interpretation as primary. Macbeth responds, "There's comfort yet," in which *"There's"* should be emphasized. Macbeth's last speech sounds consciously literary and melodramatic as if, speaking a private incantation, he is trying to build his

confidence. One may wonder why Macbeth does not here disclose to Lady Macbeth his plot against Banquo. There is no clear answer. He may wish to shield his wife from further guilt, or he may wish to avoid her further chiding. The former possibility, since he has grown bolder since the murder of Duncan, seems stronger. At any rate, Lady Macbeth knows at the end of the scene that Banquo and Fleance are to be killed.

Act III: Scene iii

The scene occurs in a park near the palace. Three Murderers enter. Two of them we know; they had the interview with Macbeth in the first scene of this act. The third one is known neither to us nor to the first two Murderers. The First Murderer asks, "But who did bid thee join us?" The First Murderer is apparently suspicious of the Third. The latter says that Macbeth told him to come. The Second Murderer says, "He needs not our mistrust . . . ." That is, we need not mistrust him. The reason why they need not distrust the Third Murderer, he says, is that the Third Murderer gives them all the directions Macbeth had promised they would receive. The First Murderer agrees and then describes the coming of night in lovely language. When he ends, the Third Murderer hears their victims. Banquo enters with Fleance, who is carrying a torch. Banquo says, "It will rain tonight." The First Murderer responds with "Let it come down." The First Murderer apparently then puts out the torch being carried by Fleance. The Murderers attack Banquo, who cries, "O, treachery! Fly good Fleance, fly, fly, fly!" He dies, and Fleance escapes. The Third Murderer asks who put out the light. The First Murderer returns with the question, "Was't not the way?" That is, was not that the arrangement. They realize that Fleance has escaped, and the Second Murderer says, "We have lost/ Best half of our affair." The First Murderer says that they ought to report to Macbeth, and they exeunt.

COMMENT: Macbeth wishes to murder Banquo, his chief counselor, because Banquo stands ready through his children to take the throne. He does not himself murder Banquo for the apparent reason that if others do it, he feels that he will not be haunted by guilty thoughts: Macbeth says later to Banquo's Ghost, "Thou canst not say I did it" (III.iv.49). The Third Murderer is sent to give final orders to the other assassins in accordance with Macbeth's promise (III.i.127 ff.); so the Third Murderer's appearance has been prepared for. We gather that the Third Murderer has Macbeth's confidence because he does not require briefing. As the Variorum edition testifies, *there has been* discussion, pro and con, *about the possibility that Macbeth is the Third Murderer. This view is incorrect for at least three reasons.* The interview between Macbeth and the First Murderer in III.iv.13 ff. would then become useless. This view transforms down-at-the-heels gentlemen-murderers into hireling assassins. If this view is held, as George W. Williams has shown, it violates *"The Law of Re-entry,"* i.e., Shakespeare's habitual adherence in plays at and before this time to the rule that a character who exits in the last line of a scene does not immediately re-enter at the first line of the following scene.

Cooling the hot horses. The First Murderer in Ll. 5–8 gives a poetic chronological indication: he can do this because he has no "character" at all, *i.e.,* he is a personified set of functions. Banquo tells us, "It will rain tonight," intimating that the night is cloudy, ripe for murder, and that it therefore suits the mood of the Murderers. Act III, Scene iii suggests, according to Joan Blythe, that Banquo and Fleance are walking their horses the last mile through the park to the palace presumably to cool the hot beasts. When they are beset by the Murderers, who are on foot, Banquo cries to Fleance to "fly," meaning that Fleance is to remount and escape.

Bradley on Banquo. Banquo is killed onstage, one surmises, partly for the reason that the audience is thus prepared for his Ghost at the banquet. If his death atones for anything it is for the ambitious curiosity to know what the future has in store for him, for he thus incurs the jealousy of Macbeth. Bradley remarks, "When next we see him [Banquo], on the last day of his life, we find that he has yielded to evil. The Witches and his own ambition have conquered him. He alone of the lords knew of the prophecies, but he has said nothing of them. He has acquiesced in Macbeth's accession, and in the official theory that Duncan's sons had suborned the chamberlains to murder him. Doubtless, unlike Macduff, he was present at Scone to see the new king invested." But there is no hint that Banquo will play "most foully" to make the prophecy come true. One may think that Banquo is necessary for dramatic contrast, as a foil to Macbeth. After all, Macbeth is king, and subjects are to be loyal. Furthermore—the point is crucial—Banquo has no real evidence: it is not prudent to accuse any man, still less a king, of murder unless one has solid evidence. Fleance, in escaping, underscores the truth of the Witches' prophecy to Banquo.

Act III: Scene iv

This scene takes place in a room of the palace set for a banquet. Macbeth, Lady Macbeth, Ross, Lennox, other lords, and attendants enter. Macbeth says, "You know your own degrees, sit down . . . ." He tells them, in effect, that since they know their proper ranks, they can seat themselves according to rank without the formality of Macbeth's having to place them. After being thanked Macbeth goes on to say that he himself will mingle with the guests while the hostess (Lady Macbeth) remains on the throne. As the formalities of welcome continue, the First Murderer appears at the door. Macbeth continues talking but meanwhile making his way to the door. Presumably, the guests cannot see the First Murderer. Macbeth says to him, "There's blood upon thy face." The First Murderer replies that it is Banquo's blood. To this Macbeth says that he prefers Banquo's blood on the Murderer's skin than inside Banquo's body. The First Murderer assures Macbeth that Banquo is dead. Macbeth asks whether Fleance is also dead. The Murderer replies that Fleance has escaped. "Then comes my fit again: I had else been perfect . . . ," says Macbeth. That is, because Fleance has escaped, I am once more in a fit of fear; if he had not escaped, I would now be healthy. He continues in the same vein in a series of images, which are climaxed by "But now, I am cabin'd, cribb'd, confin'd bound / To saucy doubts and fears." He means that he is not to act normally at ease but subject to doubts and fears. "But Banquo's safe?" he adds. That is, is Banquo safely dead? The Murderer assures him that Banquo is "safe in a ditch . . ./ With twenty trenched [cut] gashes on his head . . . ." Macbeth thanks the Murderer. Then in a metaphor in which Banquo and Fleance are compared to a grown serpent and the child serpent ("the worm") Macbeth says in effect that, although Banquo is dead, Fleance, who has escaped but offers no threat now, will one day present a threat. Macbeth tells the Murderer to leave, that they will have another interview tomorrow. The Murderer exits.

Lady Macbeth now calls to her husband, who has been absenting himself from the table. She tells him that the feast without Macbeth's ceremony of good cheer is like a feast not given. Macbeth becomes aware of his surroundings and begins to act hearty. Lennox asks Macbeth to sit at the table. Macbeth says that all of the men of distinction of the country would be here now if Banquo were present. And Banquo's absence, Macbeth tells his listeners, is due to Banquo's unkindness rather than to accident. While Macbeth has been speaking, Banquo's ghost enters. Now Ross asks Macbeth to be seated at the table. As Macbeth approaches the empty place at the table, the place reserved for him, he sees *his* place occupied by Banquo's ghost. "The table is full," says Macbeth. The others cannot see the ghost. They tell Macbeth that there is a place for him. "Where?" asks Macbeth. "Here, my good lord," replies Lennox, who then asks Macbeth what is troubling him. Macbeth shouts at his guests, "Which of you have done this?" That is, who has killed Banquo? The guests do not know what Macbeth is talking about. Macbeth now shouts at the ghost, "Thou canst not say, I did it [the murder]; never shake / Thy gory locks at me." Ross tells the other lords to leave; Macbeth, he says, is not well. Lady Macbeth, however, intervenes. She tells the lords to sit. She says that Macbeth has had momentary fits since his youth and any attention paid to them extends the fit. She then whispers to Macbeth, "Are you a man?" He says that he is a bold man, for he dares "look on that / Which might appal the devil." Lady Macbeth pours contempt on her husband. He insistently points at the ghost, "Behold! look! . . . ." He then becomes desperate: "Why what care I?" And he challenges the ghost to speak.

The ghost disappears. Lady Macbeth continues to berate him, "What! quite unmann'd in folly?" Macbeth insists that, as he is alive, he saw him. We know of course that it is Banquo; Lady Macbeth, since she does not see the ghost, cannot be certain whom Macbeth sees. Whoever it is, she must set things in order again. "Fie! for shame!" she tells him. Macbeth says that in former times, when a man was murdered, he would stay dead; "but now, they rise again,/ With twenty mortal murders on their crowns [heads],/ And push us from our stools." Apparently the ghost of Banquo has the "twenty trenched gashes on its head" about which the First Murderer told Macbeth. The ghost, then, is all cut and bloody. Seeing that Macbeth is coming to himself again, Lady Macbeth says, "My worthy lord, / Your noble friends do lack you." That is, the guests miss him. Macbeth replies, "I do forget." He goes on to give for himself the same excuse Lady Macbeth had previously given for him, that he has a strange illness which, when it shows itself, does not surprise people who know him. He now offers a toast to everyone at the table, "And to our dear friend Banquo, whom we miss;/ Would he were here!" At this point the ghost of Banquo re-appears. Macbeth sees it and shouts for it to leave his sight. He says, in effect, that since the ghost is only a ghost it ought to let itself be buried. Lady Macbeth tries to smooth things over again. She repeats that Macbeth's peculiar behavior is not extraordinary. "Only it spoils the pleasure of the time." Macbeth continues speaking to the ghost. He dares do anything a man would do: let the ghost appear in any form but that in which it now appears; let it appear in the form of a bear or a tiger or even the live Banquo, and Macbeth would fight with him. "Unreal mockery, hence!" That is, get away, you parody of reality. The ghost disappears. Since it has done so, Macbeth says, he is "a man again." He turns to his guests and tells them to sit still. Lady Macbeth says that he has destroyed everyone's good time. Macbeth, who thinks that the guests have also seen the ghost, cannot understand how they could have looked at such a sight without fear. Ross asks him what he has seen. Lady Macbeth intervenes and requests the lords not to

speak; questions will make Macbeth only worse. "At once, good night": she says to them, "Stand not upon the order of your going,/ But go at once." And all the lords leave.

Macbeth and Lady Macbeth are left alone. Macbeth says that no matter how secretly done, murder will out. He asks his wife the time, and she tells him that it is almost dawn. He now asks her what she thinks of Macduff's refusal to present himself at Macbeth's command. To her question as to whether he had sent for Macduff, Macbeth replies, "I hear it by the way . . ./ There's not a one of them, but in his house / I keep a servant fee'd." He goes on to tell her that he is going to see the Witches the next day. Then he says. "For mine own good,/ All causes shall give way . . . ." He feels that he is so deep in blood "returning were as tedious as go o'er." He has strange things in his mind, he continues, which must be accomplished before they are thought about. Lady Macbeth tells him that he lacks what everyone has, sleep. "Come we'll to sleep," he says. His peculiar self-punishment, he goes on, is the fright that comes from first doing an evil deed. Evil has not yet become customary for them. "We are but young in deed," he says as the scene ends.

COMMENT: *The banquet scene* presents *Macbeth* in microcosm because it *exhibits in Macbeth's mind and in Scottish society the movement from order to chaos* and because Macbeth comes here to a realization that there is a world over which he possesses no control, the world from which the dead return to "push us from our stools." J. P. Dyson divides it into *five parts or "movements"*: from the opening to the appearance of the First Murderer, wherein Macbeth's intentions of order are prominent; the conversation with the Murderer; the appearance of Banquo's Ghost, which is the turning point; the chaotic aftermath of the feast; and Macbeth's awareness of the wasteland of his existence.

Macbeth prepares a banquet for his nobles because he wishes not merely to be king but to have the hearts of his people. Lady Macbeth is seated in a chair of state or on a dais under a canopy. Macbeth is to sit at the head of the table because he is king and the nobles are commanded to sit in strict hierarchical order, and also because he wishes to go to the door easily. Since Banquo is not present, his seat has been removed to relieve awkwardness and to defer to the superstition against uneven numbers.

Macbeth then parleys with the First Murderer, whom he appropriately "thou's," and learns with joy that Banquo is dead and with fear that Fleance has escaped. Lady Macbeth recalls him to the feast.

Is it an objective ghost? At this point the Ghost of Banquo appears—so the stage direction in the First Folio has it—and sits in Macbeth's place. *There has been much debate about the objectivity of the Ghost.* The view taken here is that *for many reasons* — cited by E. E. Stoll and others — *the Ghost is to be viewed as a visual reality, not a hallucination of Macbeth's*. At sighting it Macbeth changes suddenly and totally from composure to frenzy. Macbeth and the Ghost are mutually hostile. Macbeth defies the Ghost. The Ghost is persistently vindictive, being sent to "religiously punish Macbeth." Macbeth brushed aside the appearance of the dagger, but he does not think of brushing aside the Ghost. At IV.i.112 he believes the Ghost to have been a visual reality. *The spectre appears before Macbeth discerns it*, and it is given stage directions. The fact that the Ghost declines to speak is not weighty because its purpose is to be inscrutably menacing, and Stoll cites *other instances in Elizabethan drama of silent and supposedly objective ghosts*. If one argues that the Ghost is subjective because the dagger and the voice, which Macbeth declares to be figments of the mind, have brought him to the point where he believes the Ghost to be real, why is he free from hallucinations after this point? One would expect him to commingle fact and fancy all the more. To be sure, Lady Macbeth and the guests do not see it; but *the nature of ghosts permitted a sighting to one observer and denied this to others* (cf. *Hamlet*, III.iv.101 ff.), and one might add that the guests are not in the position of the audience. *The Ghost sits in Macbeth's seat because Banquo's issue will take over the siege royal.*

In the Kurosawa filmed version Macbeth suddenly draws his sword upon the Ghost, the contrast between ceremony and irrational spontaneity becoming, as Michael Mullin says, "a dramatic metaphor for Macbeth's conflict between duty and ambition."

Macbeth cries, "Which of you have done this?" meaning "Which of you has killed Banquo?" *not* "Which of you has placed this corpse in my chair?" Lady Macbeth learns from this what is bothering her husband. The "gory locks" of Banquo's Ghost, a characteristic shared by his posterity (IV.i.113), suggest, as Blissett points, the virility and procreative quality of the line. At this point Lady Macbeth tries to quiet the shaken assembly, using "frightful smiles, overacted attention, and fitful graciousness" to divert notice from her husband.

The Lady now decides her husband needs disciplining, being "brainsickly" again. Accordingly ll. 57–83 are not meant to be heard by the banqueters. She chastises him again as one wanting manliness. Macbeth replies that he is bold enough to look on what might "appal" the Devil, meaning, according to Biggins, make the black Devil turn to white with fear.

Some traditional business. Macbeth becomes calm again, the Ghost having exited. In an access of hubris he toasts Banquo again, the Ghost having reappeared. Macbeth is here, as G. R. Elliott remarks, doing what politicians often do—he is expressing mock regard for a rival politician whom he has long wished to dispatch or have dispatched. More philosophically, he supposes that by the exertion of personal force he can impose his own order on the vicissitudes of existence. The traditional business here, which goes all the way back to a line in Beaumont's *The Knight of the Burning Pestle* that seems to reflect the way the play was acted, is Macbeth's dropping his cup. The second appearance of the Ghost is not anticlimactic, for this glassy-eyed creature has grown desperate to match Macbeth's growing boldness. It does not prophesy Macbeth's death because Macbeth dies not at the hands of Fleance but in combat with Macduff. The king chides the Ghost for not being a man, "Unreal mock'ry, hence!" meaning not that the Ghost is subjective but that as a shade it lacks substance. The banquet is broken up even to the point of the guests leaving, at Lady Macbeth's command, without regard to "degree."

Macbeth's conscience speaks, editors generally believe, to the effect that the murderer will be identified by means of the *auspicium*, divination of augurs by means of birds. This theory, according to Schanzer, fails to meet two difficulties: divination of murderers by means of birds has not been known anywhere; the birds mentioned here—magpies, choughs, rooks—have never been regarded as "auspicious." The probable meaning is that any ordinary bird might be endowed by the gods with the power of speech for the purpose of disclosing the identity of a murderer (in Chaucer's "Manciple's Tale" a crow reveals adultery), and then *understood relations* means simply "reports which could be understood."

Two Biblical allusions. Macbeth then turns his thoughts to Macduff, who has not been present at the banquet, who has avoided attending the coronation (II.iv.36), remaining on his Fifeshire estate, but who has not positively refused a royal command. Macbeth gets wind of Macduff's intentions from a spy. The king tells his lady, "Returning were as tedious as go o'er." Here "returning" has the Old Testament sense (see Isa. 30, 15) of going back to the Lord and His way—the line should remind us that Macbeth still has the possibility of repenting although modern critics think of him as being "determined" to go on in bloodshed. Macbeth suggests that he will indulge an orgy of bloodshed, but his terms are so general that suspense is not completely removed.

The banquet scene loosely parallels Belshazzar's feast in that it is intended to signal an iniquitous success; it exhibits a supernatural omen presaging doom, and the doom itself. The scene fascinates partly because it moves on several levels. It marks the ending of Lady Macbeth's part of the action.

Act III: Scene v

The point of this scene seems to be that the Witches will make Macbeth feel secure, and his sense of security will lead him to destruction.

This scene and part of Act IV, Scene i, permit the Witches to sing songs, which undoubtedly heightened the interest the Witches held for the audience. These songs are from a play, *The Witch*, by Shakespeare's contemporary, Thomas Middleton. Because the company used the songs from Middleton's play, some critics think that Middleton also wrote the insertions for this play. However, a number of scholars who know Middleton's work well are inclined to think otherwise.

COMMENT: This scene serves by means of fantasy to provide relief from the harrowing banquet just as the Porter does with coarse humor after the murder. The author accounts for Hecate's absence during the preceding part of the play by having her berate the Witches (Ll. 2 ff.) for failing to call her in their dealings with Macbeth. Hecate's appearance, however, has been to some extent prepared for by Macbeth's imagination (II. i. 52; III. ii. 41); but the Hecate of III. v is more fairylike than we should expect. It has been wrongly suggested that ll. 2–13 reach "a climax of unfitness" in the allegation that Macbeth is pretending to be in love with the Witches: l. 13 — "Loves for his own ends, not for you"—means that Macbeth is a lover of his own worldly success rather than of diabolism per se. Hecate says that Macbeth is but "a wayward son," meaning that he is not a true disciple of a demon-worshipping sect. He never goes to "the pit of Acheron" (l. 15), as Hecate says that he will do. Hecate in truth has only a tenuous connection with the Witches of the play. She leaves the scene, we gather, by a machine that lifts her into the "heavens" (ll. 34–35), an area above the balcony of the theater.

The song "Come away! Come away! / Hecate, Hecate, come away" is credited to Thomas Middleton inasmuch as it appears in his play titled *The Witch*. But Nosworthy points out that Middleton's Hecate is coarse, brusque, and colloquial, speaking mainly in blank verse, occasionally in irregular verse, and never in octosyllabic couplets. J. O. Wood believes that the literary quality of the scene rises above Middleton's known powers.

Wood has suggested that "profound" in "There hangs a vap'rous drop profound,/ I'll catch it ere it come to ground" may be a truncated participle deriving from L. *profundere*, "to pour forth," rather than from L. *profundus*, "deep." When Hecate next appears, nothing is said of the "vap'rous drop."

Act III: Scene vi

Most editors locate this scene in the king's palace at Forres. In the original edition of the play it is unlocated, and some critics believe that this conversation could not occur in the king's palace filled with spies. *On the bare Elizabethan stage probably no one would have thought about where the scene takes place; only important was the fact that the scene developed the play's plot, atmosphere and idea.* The surface reality did not matter: the scene obviously occurs somewhere in Scotland, and we learn something about Macbeth and something about Scotland.

Lennox and an unnamed lord enter. Apparently, they are either in the midst of a conversation or they have previously discussed matters. For Lennox says that in his "former speeches" he has said what the lord had been thinking. Lennox then becomes obviously ironic. Macbeth pitied Duncan, and Duncan died. Banquo stayed out too late; it is possible to say that Fleance killed him because Fleance ran away. One must also think how terrible it was for Malcolm and Donalbain to kill their father. This made Macbeth so very unhappy that in religious anger he killed the murderers. He was wise to do it, too, for it would have made anyone angry to hear them deny the deed. Lennox thinks, therefore, that Macbeth has managed things well. And he also believes that if Malcolm, Donalbain, and Fleance were in Scotland, they should know what it is to kill a father. Lennox now changes the subject. He has heard that Macduff is not in the king's good graces because he has spoken "broad words," that is, Macduff has spoken too obviously—of course, too obviously against the king; and because he did not appear at the "tyrant's feast" (Macbeth's banquet). He wishes to know whether the lord can tell him where Macduff is.

The lord replies that "The son of Duncan,/ From whom this tyrant holds the due of birth,/ Lives in the English court...." The lord must be talking about Malcolm, because we know that Malcolm said that he was going to England; and because we know that with Duncan's death, Malcolm should be on the throne. The lord then says that Malcolm lives at the English court of "the most pious Edward" (Edward the Confessor) who treats Malcolm very well. Macduff has gone there to ask Edward to encourage Siward, the Earl of Northumberland, to help Malcolm in an undertaking to overthrow Macbeth. This undertaking (if successful) would once more "Give to our tables meat, sleep to our nights,/ Free from our feasts and banquets bloody knives . . . ." The report of all this has prompted Macbeth's sending for Macduff. Macbeth sent for him, continues the lord, but Macduff replied in a definite negative. When Macduff thus answered the messenger looked threateningly at him. Lennox says that Macduff should be cautious enough to retain a distance. He hopes that Macduff does well in England so that "a swift blessing/ May soon return to this our suffering country/ Under a hand accursed."

COMMENT: Between III.iv and III.vi Macbeth summons Macduff; Macduff flees to England; and the Scottish nobles become suspicious of Macbeth. Lennox ironically argues that Malcolm and Donalbain engineered their father's murder. What is the proof? Their flight. Fleance has killed Banquo. The proof? His flight. Lennox should know whereof he speaks with regard to the slaughter of the drunken grooms, for he was an eyewitness. The English king to whom Malcolm has fled is known to history as Edward the Confessor, who reigned before the Norman Conquest.

An interesting question posed by the flight of Macduff to England is *how Lennox and the anonymous lord in III.vi come by their knowledge of Macduff's whereabouts* when Macbeth learns of this matter only after the cauldron scene (IV.i). The somewhat unsatisfying answer is that these persons know more than their king does. One ought to bear Ll. 39–43 in mind when we later come to the murder of Lady Macduff: the Lady does not know the consequences of Macduff's failure to attend the royal court; she thinks that her husband is animated by irrational fear. If we suppose that Lady Macduff is merely given to complaining we miss much of the dramatic quality of IV.ii.

Act IV: Scene i

The scene occurs in a cavern in the middle of which is a boiling cauldron. The Three Witches enter. As they speak a charm, with which they hope to secure Macbeth, they throw into their boiling pot such parts of repulsive animals as the eye of a newt, the wool of a bat, and a lizard's leg. The refrain of their charm is "Double, double toil and trouble:/ Fire, burn; and, cauldron, bubble." When they are finished, Hecate, the queen of the Witches, enters together with three other Witches. The lines Hecate recites and the song the Witches sing are considered by some scholars to be non-Shakespearean.

After Hecate and the other Three Witches leave, Macbeth enters. He insists that the Witches answer his questions. It makes no difference to him, he says, whether or not the universe is totally destroyed in the process; he will have his answer. They agree, but first they inquire as to whether he would have the answer from them or from their masters; Macbeth prefers the latter. The Witches then throw into the boiling cauldron some unappetizing liquids: the blood of a sow who has eaten her young and the sweat that fell from a murderer as he was being hanged. This addition to the Witches' brew brings forth the apparition of an armed head. Macbeth is about to ask a question when the First Witch informs him that the Apparition knows his thought. The Apparition tells Macbeth to beware of

Macduff, the Thane of Fife. The head then disappears. Macbeth thanks the armed head for cautioning him about Macduff and adds that this warning supports his own fear. Macbeth wishes to inquire further, but the First Witch tells him that the Apparition will not respond again. However, a stronger power will now appear.

The Second Apparition comes forth, and it is in the form of a bloody child. The Second Apparition advises Macbeth to be "bloody, bold, and resolute," for no one who was born of a woman can harm him. The Apparition disappears. Macbeth's comment on this information is that he need not fear Macduff (for Macduff is a man and all men are born of women). Macbeth, however, wishes to make "double sure"; he wishes to obliterate any trace of fear, and he says that he will kill Macduff anyway.

The Third Apparition now comes forth in the form of a crowned child with a tree in his hand. Macbeth asks who the Apparition is, but the witches merely tell him to listen. The Third Apparition advises Macbeth to be courageous ("lion-mettled") and proud, not to care about those who are dissatisfied or those who conspire against him, for Macbeth will never be defeated until the woods (called Birnam Wood) around his castle Dunsinane march toward the castle. The Third Apparition disappears. Macbeth says that it is impossible for a forest to move; the prediction is a good one. Macbeth now feels that he "Shall live the lease of Nature, pay his breath / To time, and mortal custom." That is, he feels he will die a natural death. However, he wishes to know one more thing: will Banquo's descendants ever rule Scotland? The Witches try to dissuade him from inquiring further, but Macbeth insists, whereupon the Witches call for a show; a show, they say, which will "grieve his heart."

There follows a procession of eight kings. The last of them holds a mirror. To anyone watching the procession from the front, the mirror makes it seem as though the line of kings stretches endlessly. Some of the kings carry "two-fold balls and treble sceptres." All of the kings in the procession resemble Banquo, and Banquo himself comes behind the line of eight, his hair caked with blood ("blood bolter'd"). He looks at Macbeth, smiles, and points at the procession; Macbeth takes these actions to mean that Banquo's descendants will, in fact, rule Scotland. Macbeth calls this pantomime a "horrible sight." To cheer him up the Witches perform a wild dance (an "antic round") and disappear. After they disappear, Macbeth says, "Let this pernicious hour / Stand aye accursed in the calendar!"

He calls for his attendant, who turns out to be Lennox. Macbeth asks Lennox whether the latter has seen the Witches. Lennox replies that he has not.

Macbeth says that he heard a horse's gallop, and he wishes to know who went by. Lennox informs Macbeth that word was brought of Macduff's flight to England. "Time, thou anticipat'st my dread exploits," says Macbeth to himself. From now on, he continues, he will immediately do whatever his heart desires. And to turn his current wish into an act, he will make a surprise attack on Macduff's castle at Fife, and kill Macduff's wife, children, and any relative that might succeed him. Macbeth says that he will no longer boast. He will commit this act before his intention diminishes in strength. "But no more sights!" he says, apparently referring to what the Witches have shown him. He then asks to be led to the messengers, and Lennox and Macbeth exeunt.

COMMENT: *In his filmed version, Polanski here presents a cave full of nude witches, most of them old and physically repulsive, and some of them young.* Their number suggests the multiplicity of witches at work in the world; and their varied ages intimate, since witches do not reproduce themselves, that sustained efforts at recruitment ensure the continuity of their kind. *In the Shakespearean text, however, no more than six Witches and Hecate are called for, and there is of course no suggestion of nudity or, for that matter, of varied ages. Another departure from the text occurs in the Schaefer filmed version,* which depicts the inebriated Macbeth sleeping and dreaming the cauldron scene, thus depreciating Shakespeare's emphasis on the supernatural.

Since Shakespeare's supernatural characters employ *shortened verse-forms,* one should note that the Witches speak in *seven-syllabled verse* with accents falling on syllables one, three, five, and seven. The brinded cat, the hedge-pig, and Harpier are animal and bird forms assumed by the familiar spirits of the Witches. One notices that the Witches never use even numbers; they are especially fond of threes, notable in their use of triplets, and when they say four (l.2), it is by "Thrice, and once." *This marked tendency is to be thought of as a burlesque of the Trinity.*

Harpier is mentioned by name since he is leader of three devils. The name, which seems to be of Shakespeare's invention, suggests the harpylike way in which the Sisters hover over the pot. Harpier, we gather, is a large owl that actually sounded on the earlier stage. Harpier is to be connected with II.ii.3: "It was the owl that shrieked." Lennox at II.iii.59–60 says: "The obscure bird / Clamor'd the livelong night." In II.iv.12–13 the owl hoots as Banquo is about to be killed, and the owl is mentioned suggestively in IV.ii.11 when the family of Macduff is endangered. *The owl-business has died down in modern performances of Macbeth* perhaps because of the danger of mimicry in an unruly audience.

In l.3 a light stop, here a comma, after "cries" would mean that Harpier cries, "'Tis time, 'tis time." A heavy stop, *i.e.,* a semicolon (a period would be too heavy), signifies

that Harpier cries; then the Third Witch interprets the cry, probably the sound of an owl. A light stop might be interpreted to mean that the familiar spirit of the Third Witch, unlike the spirits inhabiting the brinded cat and hedge-pig, is calling out his orders in English.

Ovid and Shakespeare. Among the ingredients of the Witches' brew the "Fillet of a fenny snake" (l. 12) is usually regarded as a slice; but Wood shows on the basis of Golding's translation of Ovid, usually acknowledged as influencing Shakespeare in the cauldron scene, that it is "the ribbon of its [a snake's] scarf-skin; and the snake is 'Fenny' because fen-bred."

Eight spurious lines? Hecate enters with three more Witches. She may be thought of as a devil because of the traditional notion that the gods of the heathen became devils. *Some scholars have regarded this part of the play as spurious*—J. Q. Adams, for example—removing from the text the first eight lines from the entrance of Hecate. *Some reasons for this view follow:* the speech is in iambic meter; Hecate does not bring the lunar venom which she mentions as to be used in "raising artificial sprites"; there are no "gains"; and l.43 does not make good sense. The song "Black spirits" is in Middleton's *The Witch,* and it was inserted in Sir William Davenant's Restoration version of *Macbeth.* Wood thinks that the line "By the pricking of my thumbs" derives from Reginald Scot's *The Discoverie of Witchcraft* (1584); if so, Shakespeare changed Scot's "tingling of the finger" into the coarser "pricking of my thumbs," preparing for the inevitable rhyme "comes." The line in any case conveys an ancient means of prognostication and so prepares for the advent of Macbeth.

Macbeth and Nature. Because Macbeth is to be obeyed (within limits) he is not obliged to employ circles and magical ceremonies to conjure devils. He delivers, as Holloway says, a formalized speech (Ll. 50–61) rather like a curse in which he demands answers to his questions even if the cost is to be the destruction of Nature. Macbeth's speech is much like Northumberland's in *Henry IV, Part II,* l.i.153 ff. in theme and magniloquence: both men seem to think themselves outside Nature, which they would willingly let dissolve into chaos for merely selfish reasons. Macbeth thinks of Nature, as Edmund does in *King Lear,* as being in harmony with his career. This unorthodox view of Nature separates God and Nature. "Nature," as John F. Danby says in *Shakespeare's Doctrine of Nature,* "becomes given structure instead of normative pattern." Nature thus conceived excludes human values and reasonable norms. Nature has no intelligence, no connection with reason. Nature does not include man except on his bodily side; his mind is above it and free to manipulate it. Reason, instead of representing the ideal toward which men strive, becomes the means of satisfying men's appetites. *The orthodox Elizabethan view of Nature viewed it as a rational and benevolent arrangement. Nature is "bound to God."* Nature is nonmechanical; it is held together by Reason. Man's duty is to conform to custom, which represents codified Nature. Restraint is identified with Nature. Nature is identified with man's ability to reach, with the cooperation of his fellow men and circumstance, the realization of a large goal.

Richard Hooker's *Of the Laws of Ecclesiastical Polity* is a classic expression of this view, upon which Macbeth turns his back. At this point the Witches give Macbeth his choice between visions and prophecies, and with bare colloquial simplicity and fierce intensity he opts for the latter: "Call 'em; let me see 'em." The fact that these Witches have "masters" (l. 63) is sufficient to indicate that *they are not*, as Kittredge thought, *Norns*. The "masters" may be Paddock, Graymalkin, and Harpier; but one feels that superior devils are here referred to.

The First Apparition, an Armed Head, really means the beheading of Macbeth by Macduff, but the audience is not aware of this until Act V. That Booth had the armed head made up like Macbeth readily brought the matter home to his audience, but it is doubtful Macbeth would notice this. Macbeth never again mentions the First Apparition, but he twists the Second and Third Apparitions to his own purpose. Heaven keeps him from making anything of a connection between the First Apparition and his own head brought in on a pole by Macduff. It will be noticed that Witches thrice in this scene prevent Macbeth from asking questions of the Apparitions: the devils, charmed by the Witches, have shown Macbeth things that will kill him, and they are not bound to tell him the truth.

Necromancy and King James. The Second Apparition represents Macduff though in a character not known to Macbeth at present. The line "More potent than the first" really means that Macduff is "more potent" than Macbeth. Necromancy in the strict sense is used in that devils enter exhumed bodies rather than take the forms of human beings. Such was James's view. The two children are presumably unbaptized infants (cf. ll. 30–31). The dissevered head, the bloody child, and the crowned child should tell Macbeth how to extinguish Macduff's revolt; but actually they ambiguously foretell his death, his killer, and his supplanters. By "assurance double" (l. 83) Macbeth means that by killing Macduff, he will put it out of harm's power to reach him unless Fate breaks the law of birth and the law of death.

The Third Apparition, a crowned child, enters with a tree in his hand signifying not only the later march from Birnam Wood to Dunsinane but also the bloody and unnatural giving way to nature as orthodoxy conceived. The word "Dunsinane," by the way, is pronounced in IV.i.93 with stress on the penult in Scottish fashion; in Act V it is stressed eight times on the antepenult, English fashion. *It is valuable to note the difference between Macbeth at III.iv.122–26, where he as a man of conscience thinks that even stones and trees speak out to expose foul murder, and*

Macbeth in this scene where he is convinced (ll. 94–96) that no one can "impress the forest, bid the tree / Unfix his earth-bound root." He cannot see, as William Free observes, that if a power can move trees to expose murder, it can move a forest for the same purpose. Macbeth is so impressed with the visions and willing to accept the oracles that he falls to rhyming in ll. 94 ff. There follows in l. 97 a choice for editors between "Rebellion's dead," the Folio reading, and Theobald's emendation "Rebellious head." As a reference to Banquo, the original makes excellent sense and links with Banquo in Ll. 100–103: Banquo may rise again in his son, his followers, and supporters.

Macbeth's pleasure in these prophecies is speedily removed by the show of kings and the smiling Ghost of Banquo. A notable difference between the Apparitions and the kings is that the former exist whereas the kings, according to King James, are technically a "sight"—they are "an impression in the air, shown to the eyes, deluding the senses, nonexistent." Bradbrook and Paul emphasize the topicality of the show of kings.

An interesting question is why Shakespeare omits Mary Stuart from the eight—Robert II, Robert III, and the six Jameses—since Mary was sovereign for twenty-five years between James V and James VI, *i.e.,* James I of England. The prophecy to Banquo is "Thou shalt get kings," and Mary was a queen. In *Macbeth* female beings tempt to evil and unwise deeds, and it would be imprudent to introduce a queen into the Stuart dynasty. *For reasons of state and of religion it would have been inappropriate to remind the sovereign of his mother* (executed by order of Queen Elizabeth) *and the audience of the unhappy Mary.*

The kings are connected to Banquo by the family characteristic of abundant hair (cf. III.iv.50). There is a discrepancy between the Folio's calling for Banquo to have a glass, *i.e.,* a magic mirror, in his hand and editorial policy in placing the glass in the hand of the eighth king. Probably the last of the eight kings should enter with the glass, Banquo's Ghost standing by and watching the procession with pleasure. A gauze to "soften the glare of reality" might well be introduced here into a stage version.

Banquo and Elizabeth II. It is interesting to note that the verse "Will the line stretch out to the crack of doom?" has relevance to the current sovereign, for Queen Elizabeth II is descended from King James I. The "twofold balls" perhaps allude to King James's being crowned at Scone and at Westminster, and the "treble sceptres" may allude to King James's being crowned King of Great Britain, France, and Ireland, or perhaps to his rule over England, Scotland, and Ireland. The kings disappear into the exiguous air which is their substance.

The First Witch, speaking in ll.125 ff. (in a manner strongly intimating interpolation by another writer), suggests, contrary to the mood of great tragedy, that Macbeth needs to be cheered up and calls for a dance of the Six

Witches to music. Clifford Davidson and others have conjectured that in the Globe performance of *Macbeth* the dances at this point were adapted from Ben Jonson's *Masque of Queenes* (1609), in which six grotesque hags dance "contrary to the custome of Men." It is difficult indeed to think that Macbeth would patiently sit through the beldam and ballet and then, upon the disappearance of the *danseuses,* exclaim "Where are they? Gone?" Generally, as ll. 138–39 intimate, Macbeth's second interview with the Witches suggests a falling away of his resolution.

Lennox's position in this play needs defining. He is one of Macbeth's most trusted advisors, yet we find in III.vi that he is a ringleader against Macbeth. He has concealed from Macbeth knowledge of Macduff's flight from the king. Macbeth evidently trusts him, for Lennox hears the king's plan for revenge against Macduff.

Act IV: Scene ii

This scene takes place in Macduff's castle at Fife. Lady Macduff, her son, and Ross enter. Lady Macduff is speaking to Ross. She does not understand why her husband has run away from Scotland. "His flight was madness," she says. She implies that even though Macduff is not a traitor, his fear makes him look like one. Ross tells Lady Macduff that she cannot know whether it was fear or wisdom that made her husband run. But, she questions, how can his flight be wise when he leaves his wife and children in a place from which he himself runs away. "All is the fear, and nothing is the love . . . ," she comments. Macduff's flight, she insists, was unreasonable. Ross tells Lady Macduff that her husband is a wise and trustworthy man. He understands the cruel times in which men "float upon a wild and violent sea . . . ." Ross, however, breaks off the conversation to say that he must leave. But he will soon be back. He comforts Lady Macduff by saying that things at their worst will either come to an end or improve. He gives his blessing to young Macduff, whom Lady Macduff calls "fatherless." Ross feels he cannot prevent himself from weeping, and so he departs at once.

An amusingly pathetic dialogue now ensues between Lady Macduff and her son. Lady Macduff says to her son that his father is dead. "How will you live?" she asks. He will live as the birds do, he replies. "Poor bird!" she calls him, and she hopes that he need never fear a trap as birds fear it. The son now reverts to their former conversation and says that he does not believe that his father is dead. His mother insists that his father is dead, and they joke a bit about a consequent search for another husband. The son then asks, "Was my father a traitor, mother?" Lady Macduff replies that his father was. The son now asks, "What is a traitor?" "Why, one that swears and lies," she answers. The question arises whether all that swear and lie must be hanged. To Lady Macduff's affirmative response, the son says that "the liars and swearers are fools." They are fools because there are more of them than there are honest men. If the liars and swearers were smart, they would band together and hang the honest man. Lady Macduff now returns to her former theme: "But how wilt thou do for a father?" The boy still does not believe that his father is dead. If his father were really dead, the boy insists, she would weep for him. A messenger suddenly enters. He is not known to Lady Macduff, he tells her, although he is looking out for her honor. He warns her to run away, for danger is fast approaching her. He blesses her, says that he dare not stay longer, and exits. Lady Macduff exclaims that she does not know where to run. "I have done no harm," she says. But, she reflects, in this world it is often praiseworthy to do harm; to do good is often thought to be "dangerous folly." Why, then, does she bother saying that she has done no harm?

Murderers suddenly interrupt her. "Where is your husband?" one Murderer asks. Lady Macduff replies that she hopes that he is in no place so unholy that he can be found by the Murderer (who, she implies, would ordinarily frequent only places that are damned). The Murderer says that Macduff is a traitor. Macduff's son cries, "Thou liest, thou shag hair'd villain!" At this the Murderer stabs the boy, who tells his mother to run away. The scene ends with Lady Macduff running off the stage crying "Murder!" followed by the Murderers.

COMMENT: This scene advances the plot by showing how swiftly Macbeth carries out his revenge against Lady Macduff and her offspring. The dramatic effect of omitting this scene from stage from representations is unwarrantedly to improve the character of Macbeth and to prevent us from seeing domestic affection. *Little Macduff is rendered interesting by his mixture of insight and naivete, his attempt to confute his mother, his mother's addressing him as if he were a person of importance, his serious response to his mother's facetious touches, and his gallantry.*

At this point Macduff has done nothing treasonable; and Lady Macduff, though thoroughly incensed at his departure, which presumably the husband has not discussed with his wife lest he implicate her, does not really believe that her husband is a traitor. Although she appears to be *an idiot in the Greek sense of being unversed in political affairs,* she has premonitions of disaster. In her conversation with Ross she points to the diminutive wren that, unlike Macduff, will fight for its young: Elizabethans were in the habit of seeing nature, both animate and inanimate, as reflecting human emotions, moods, and attitudes. In saying "All is the fear, and nothing is the love" (l. 12), she draws upon I John, 4, 18 "perfect love casteth out fear." Shakespeare's extensive use of the Bible, by the way, is based upon the popular Geneva Version and the Bishops' Bible. Ross, in trying to comfort her, speaks of "The fits o' th' season," intimating Macbeth's accesses of murderous passion. This kind of imagery suggests that Macbeth's tyranny, manifesting itself by fits and starts rather than by a steady, grinding malevolence, is beginning to ebb. Unsuccessful in his attempts at consolation, Ross abruptly leaves.

Use of you and thou. In the conversation between Lady Macduff and her son, she uses the formal "you" in the mock solemnity of "Sirrah, your father's dead, / And what will you do now?" The boy always responds with the formal "you," indicating his class and nurture. When Lady Macduff is pleased with his answers, she allows her affectionate nature to flow towards him by the use of "thou" and "thee." Generally one apprehends that *since Elizabethan children were thought of as miniature adults*, little Macduff is a worthy scion of his line, what with his common sense and his trust in his father; and his wretched death from an Elizabethan point of view is more pitiable on this account.

Who sends the Messenger? A Messenger enters with a warning to Lady Macduff that she and her children should depart their castle immediately. It is possible, though we do not know it, that he has come from Lady Macbeth, from Lennox, or from some friend of the Macduffs who has learned Macbeth's purposes. Simply his presence and his mission remind one that Macbeth has not been able to suborn even the lowlier elements of the Scottish population. His reference to "little ones" in l. 69 is a reminiscence of Matt. 18, 6 wherein a dreadful retribution is threatened for "whatsoever shall offend one of these little ones which believe in me."

At this point the Murderers enter. *Polanski* has Young Macduff bathing—thus he *connects with effect a nude bloody child previously seen in the Witches' cauldron.* Lady Macduff, seeing them, cries, "What are these faces?" The villains' shaggy hair marks them as being Elizabethan professional ruffians, men of a different class than the desperate gentlemen who dispatched Banquo. Accent would be suitably vulgarized. The First Murderer's question "Where is your husband?" is rhetorical rather than genuine, for he must say something. The gallant Young Macduff attempts to face him down with "Thou li'st, thou shag-ear'd villain," but the boy is horribly murdered in the sight of the audience. Shakespeare as an Elizabethan playwright is not, in the matter of onstage murder, in the tradition derived from the ancient Greeks who declined to represent bloodshed before the eyes of the audience. Macbeth's purpose is apparently an attempt to prevent other thanes from following Macduff's example, and the Macduffs are killed because they share the blood of the husband and father.

Act IV: Scene iii

The scene takes place at the palace of King Edward of England. Malcolm and Macduff enter. To Malcolm's remark that Macduff and he go to a deserted spot and weep out their sadness, Macduff replies that they ought rather to hold in their hands their deadly swords and conquer their native land. There every morning "New widows howl, new orphans cry; new sorrows / Strike heaven on the face . . . ." Malcolm replies in effect that he does not trust Macduff. "He [Macbeth] hath not touch'd you yet" (that is, he has not hurt you yet) continues Malcolm. He suggests that perhaps Macduff is looking for a reward from Macbeth by luring Malcolm to Scotland. Macduff answers, "I am not treacherous." "But Macbeth is," says Malcolm: a good man may not be able to resist orders from a king. But Malcolm then begs Macduff's pardon. Malcolm says that his thoughts cannot change Macduff's nature. Even though some good people may change, not all good people change. Macduff (seeing that Malcolm is hesitant about his proposals) says that he, Macduff, has lost his hopes (for an invasion of Scotland). But it is in Scotland that Malcolm finds his reasons for doubting Macduff. Why did Macduff suddenly leave his wife and children, asks Malcolm. Malcolm begs Macduff not to take the question as implying Macduff's dishonor but rather Malcolm's caution for his own life. Apparently feeling the hopelessness of persuading a suspicious man of one's innocence, Macduff says that his country must continue in its ruin. He adds that he would not be suspected as a deceiver for all of Scotland and the rich Orient combined.

Macduff is about to leave but Malcolm tells Macduff not to be offended, for Malcolm has spoken not merely in fear of Macduff. Malcolm believes his country is suffering, that there would be Scotsmen who would come over to his side. From "gracious England" he has received offers of help. But despite all of this, when he has conquered the tyrant Macbeth, Scotland would suffer more from Macbeth's successor than it is suffering now. To Macduff's question, "What should he be?" Malcolm replies that he is talking about himself, who, in the course of time, would make Macbeth appear pure. Macduff replies that no one could be worse than Macbeth. Malcolm says that he knows Macbeth is "Luxurious [lustful], avaricious, false, deceitful, / Sudden [violent], malicious, smacking of every sin/ That has a name . . . ." However, he continues, not all the women of Scotland can ever satisfy *his* lust; it would be better for Macbeth to reign. Macduff replies that such lust is tyrannical and has caused the fall of many kings; but Malcolm should not hesitate to take the kingdom that belongs to him. For undoubtedly enough women will find the greatness of kingship sufficient lure so that he will be satisfied. But Malcolm goes on to speak of another fault. He is so avaricious that he would invent quarrels with his good and loyal subjects only to obtain their wealth. This is worse than lust, says Macduff; but Scotland has riches enough to quench Malcolm's desire. Lust and avarice are bearable when other virtues ("graces") are taken into account. But, Malcolm answers, he has no other virtues. He has no desire for the virtues which are fit for a king; such virtues as "justice, verity, temperance, stableness,/ Bounty, perseverance, mercy, lowliness,/ Devotion, patience, courage, fortitude." Instead, if he had the power, he would "Pour the sweet milk of concord into hell,/ Uproar the universal peace, confound / All unity on earth."

Macduff replies that the kind of man that Malcolm describes is not only unfit to govern but also unfit to live. He wonders when his nation will once more see "wholesome days." Now a bloody usurper is on the throne and the rightful occupant is self-accused in villainy. Macduff goes on, apparently trying to understand how it came about that Malcolm is so evil, for he talks of Malcolm's parents who were very holy. Macduff bids good-bye to Malcolm and adds that what he has learned of Malcolm's character has in effect banished him from Scotland (for no invasion will occur, and he cannot otherwise return).

Malcolm once more holds back Macduff. Malcolm says that Macduff has shown himself to be a man of integrity and has erased Malcolm's suspicion of him. Macbeth, Malcolm says, had tried to trick Malcolm into returning to Scotland by sending men who acted as Macduff did at first. Malcolm has had to use "modest wisdom" to discern the true man from the false. But he knows now that Macduff is honest, and he says that all the evil character he has given himself is untrue. The first lies that he has ever told have been about himself. His true self is ready to obey the commands of Macduff and of his country. Also, Old Siward, the Earl of Northumberland, has already started for Scotland with ten thousand men. "Now," continues Malcolm, "we'll together . . . ." Malcolm asks Macduff why the latter is silent. Macduff replies that he is confused by the quick reversal of things.

A doctor enters and Malcolm stops the discussion with Macduff; they will continue it later, he says. Malcolm now addresses the doctor, asking him whether the king (King Edward) is coming out. The doctor replies in the affirmative: a group of sick people are waiting to be cured by the king. Their illnesses cannot be cured by the art of medicine, but King Edward's hand has been given such holiness that when the sick people are touched by him, they are cured. Malcolm thanks the doctor, who then exits. Macduff asks Malcolm

what illness the doctor is talking about. Malcolm replies that the illness is called the evil. He has often seen the good King Edward perform this miraculous cure. How Edward has asked heaven for this miraculous power only Edward knows. All Malcolm knows is that people sick with the evil, a disease that causes swelling and ulcers, are cured by Edward and cannot be cured by doctors. It is said that this healing power will be inherited by Edward's successors. With this ability to heal he has the "heavenly gift of prophecy;/ And sundry blessings," which indicate that he is "full of grace."

Ross enters. Macduff recognizes him immediately, but Malcolm has some difficulty in doing so apparently because Malcolm has not seen Ross for a long time. Macduff asks Ross how things are going in Scotland. Ross replies that things are very bad; the country cannot "Be called our mother, but our grave." Violence and death are commonplace. Malcolm asks what has given the most recent cause for grief. Ross answers that anyone attempting to report a crime an hour old as the newest cause of grief would be ridiculed, for every minute brings new ones.

"How does my wife?" inquires Macduff. "Why, well," replies Ross. "And all my children?" is Macduff's next question, to which Ross answers, "Well, too." Macduff then asks whether Macbeth has not harassed Macduff's family. "No," says Ross: "they were well at peace, when I did leave 'em." Macduff tells Ross not to be so stingy in details about the family; he wishes to know how they are. Instead of answering him, Ross says that when he came here to bring his sad news, a rumor went about that many good men had taken up arms against Macbeth. Ross believes this to be true, because Macbeth had his army mobilized. "Now is the time of help," he says. Malcolm's appearance in Scotland would cause many, including women, to fight and rid themselves of their troubles. Malcolm tells Ross about the forthcoming invasion, which will be aided by Siward, than whom no older nor better soldier can be found in Christendom. Ross says that he wishes his news were as good. Macduff asks whether the news concerns all of them or one of them. Ross says that all virtuous men must share the grief of his news, but mainly the news concerns Macduff. The latter requests that it be given to him quickly. After apologizing for the necessity of bringing Macduff such a report, Ross tells him that his wife and children have been "savagely slaughtered."

Probably because he is weeping, Macduff pulls his hat over his eyes. After an expression of shock, Malcolm tells Macduff that the latter should not have pulled his hat over his eyes. If a man does not speak out his grief, Malcolm continues, his heart breaks. Macduff merely asks, "My children too?" To this question Ross replies,

"Wife, children, servants, all/ That could be found."
Macduff cries, "And I must be from thence!" That is,
he is exclaiming over the bitterness of his absence from
his castle at the time of the attack. Evidently unable
completely to absorb the situation, he once more
inquires, "My wife kill'd too?" Ross tells Macduff that
what he has said is true. Macduff tells Macduff to cure
his grief with revenge upon Macbeth. "He has no
children," says Macduff, probably referring to Macbeth.
Still unable to accept the terrible facts, Macduff now
asks whether all of his children were killed. "O Hell-
kite!" he exclaims. "All?" Were all the children and
their mother killed at once? Malcolm tells Macduff to
fight against his grief like a man. Macduff says that he
will do so; "But I must also feel it as a man . . . ." He then
says, "Sinful Macduff!" All his family were killed, he
feels, not for their original sin (for they were so
innocent, it would seem, they had none) but for his.
Having cried out his grief, he can accept the horrible
facts: ". . . heaven rest them now!" he says. Malcolm
tells Macduff to "let grief/ Convert to anger." Macduff
says that he could weep now and brag. Instead, he prays
to heaven to bring him as soon as possible face to face
with the "fiend of Scotland." If Macbeth escapes, may
heaven forgive Macbeth. Malcolm says that Macduff's
words are manly. Malcolm now tells his countrymen to
come along to the king (King Edward); "our power
[army] is ready," he says, all they require is leave from
the king. "Macbeth is ripe for shaking," Malcolm says
in the concluding lines of the scene, "and the powers
above / Put on their instruments." (The last words
mean that the forces of heaven are arming themselves.)

COMMENT: This scene, based on Holinshed's *Chronicle*,
concerns Malcolm's testing of Macduff's loyalty: the fact
that such an examination is necessary shows the far-flung
currents of Macbeth's depravity. *The Romantic view that the
scene is tedious is wrong* because a normal audience would
wish to know whether Malcolm is qualified to be named
King of Scotland and whether or not his relationship with
his chief thane, Macduff, is good. Although Malcolm is
decidedly awkward in depicting himself as a paragon of
vice, he shows that he has learned the Renaissance rule *qui
dissimulare nescit, regnare nescit*, "He who does not know
how to dissimulate does not know how to rule." He presents
evidence that in truly knowing his friends and his enemies,
he will excel his father, who admittedly did not know how
to find "the mind's construction in the face." Since *Macbeth*
is a tragedy and since Shakespeare's tragedies (unlike his
histories) are more basically concerned with morality than
with politics, one should say with Herbert Coursen that *this
scene exhibits a future King of Scotland whose fundamental
virtue is aided and strengthened by his political skill.* Not only
that. The scene is resonant with suggestions that *Heaven

and Malcolm are in alliance*: his return to Scotland with
"goodly thousands" will be by sanction of the indomitable
"powers above" which "put on their instruments" to cleanse
Scotland of Macbeth.

Malcolm's suspicion. Malcolm has a reasonable suspicion of Macduff because of the thane's desertion of his
defenseless wife and children, and it will be observed that
Macduff does not answer the Prince's question on this
point. *Nineteenth-century audiences, regarding this matter as
painful and unnatural, omitted the scene from representation;
but, as Bradbrook suggests, the twentieth century, well acquainted with* agents provocateurs *and the uprooting of
families for political reasons, has a better understanding of this
part of the plot.* In Holinshed the scene loses force because
both Malcolm and Macduff know of Macbeth's murder of
Macduff's family from the beginning. One gathers that
Macduff concealed his intentions of flight from Scotland
from his fellow thanes to prevent them from implication,
which would expose them to Macbeth's rage. Malcolm's
method of testing Macduff is by making provocative remarks such as suggesting that Macduff may have foul
motives for leaving wife and children in Scotland, and by
heaping undeserved obloquy upon himself, such as saying
what he will do with the Scottish nobles' estates if he should
become king.

Malcolm begins by stating the need to weep; Macduff
counters, using the figure of hand-to-hand combat to
protect the body of a fallen comrade, by asserting the need
for military action. Malcolm declares Macbeth a "tyrant":
Elizabethans carefully distinguished, as W. A. Armstrong
points out, *between tyrants who held usurped thrones and
bad kings who by lawful heredity had been rightfully anointed
— the former could be attacked openly or sub rosa, the
latter were to be religiously endured.* Macbeth is clearly
tyrant since he is no son to Duncan and has been wrongly
anointed although the play admittedly offers no intimation
of the latter point. In l.15 the Folio reads "discerne," but
editors, following Theobald, generally read "You may deserve of him through me." But if we assume that Malcolm
would not broach the matter of material advancement to
Macduff, as we should, the Folio reading had better be
retained. Malcolm in the midst of l. 20 reads grief and
horror in Macduff's face — an implicit stage-direction. In ll.
23–24 Malcolm says, in Dr. Johnson's paraphrase, "I do not
say that your virtuous appearance proves you are a traitor;
for virtue must wear its proper form, though that form be
counterfeited by villainy." Malcolm centers his mind on the
never-explained reason for Macduff's leaving of wife and
children to the wolfish Macbeth: specifically he fears an
understanding between the tyrant and Macduff. Since no
explanation is forthcoming, he proceeds to dishonor himself in a highly concrete fashion to observe how Macduff
reacts.

"The man behind Macbeth." Essentially he recites and exaggerates Macbeth's villainies except that, as Bradley has pointed out, lechery and avarice are not properly charged to Macbeth's account. Sir James Fergusson is of the opinion that this coloring may derive from the sixteenth-century James Stuart, whom Sir James styles "the man behind Macbeth." Macduff is not greatly disturbed by Macbeth's lechery or by Malcolm's magnified imputation of himself as being so stained, for princes were commonly given to this vice. What appalls Macduff are the evidences of avarice, pride, ambition, self-seeking, deceit—vices that do not disappear with the disappearance of youth. Malcolm continues in Ll.91 ff. in cataloging his vices, thereby defining by negatives what a good king should be and what Malcolm actually is. Malcolm says that he would "Uproar the universal peace," a line that must have, per contra, pleased King James, who affected himself in the role of peacemaker and who was desirous of Christian unity. Bradbrook suggests that James, who himself practiced dissimulation with the Ruthven gang of kidnappers when he was eighteen, would have watched with personal interest Malcolm's provocation of Macduff. This list, by which Malcolm marks himself a veritable cesspool of villainy, has the improbable effect of causing Macduff to expostulate that Malcolm is not only unfit to govern but even to live: Malcolm's true character must have been known to Macduff when Malcolm left Scotland; more important, Macduff has been told the Confessor trusts Malcolm (Ll.43–44).

Macduff's reactions. It is interesting to note that Macduff shows no ambition to push himself into Malcolm's place when Malcolm admits practicing every crime under the sun. Macduff does not go to the length of denying Malcolm's legal right to the throne: presumably Malcolm would be an evil but legitimate king, in Macduff's view, who would elicit religious endurance from those subjects not in position to exile themselves. Macduff contrasts Malcolm with his "most sainted" father and with his mother, who "Died every day she liv'd," meaning that she died to worldly desires (cf. Paul's "I die daily," I Cor. 15, 31) every day of her life. Since historical record does not warrant the saintliness of Duncan's wife, one gathers that Shakespeare, again desiring to gratify King James, transferred St. Margaret's reputation to her mother-in-law. St. Margaret was Malcolm's wife and had a strong influence on his policy, bringing it about that Scottish kings should be anointed by the Pope. It is chiefly the memory of Malcolm's father and mother that convinces Macduff that Malcolm is not speaking truly of himself.

"An excellent team." Thus Malcolm passes his examination, not trusting at first even the ingenuous Macduff (by comparison with Macbeth); and Macduff passes his. One apprehends that Malcolm and Macduff will make an excellent team because Malcolm lacks force but possesses prudence, and Macduff has force aplenty but is somewhat naive. It must be said, however, that Malcolm has sufficient force to advance on Scotland with Old Siward and ten thousand men. One's estimate of Malcolm's prudence is raised by learning (Ll.117–20) that he has declined Macbeth's blandishments aimed at luring him back to Scotland. Line 118 lengthens the time since Malcolm took refuge at the court of the Confessor. Then Malcolm exonerates himself of the vices he has claimed and makes Macduff commander of the forces against Macbeth.

A Doctor enters with notice that a band of suppliants possessed of scrofula await the royal touch of the Confessor for healing. This passage provides an interval of time before the arrival of Ross with news of the murder of Macduff's wife and children, and it serves as a substitute for the appearance of the Confessor onstage, which could encumber the action. The business of healing "the King's evil" is introduced into the play for several reasons. It shows that Malcolm by virtue of his healing touch is the true King of Scotland even though he has this power only by association with Saint Edward the Confessor and even though he does not use it in this place: since the audience is in no doubt about Malcolm's legitimacy and purity it is not necessary for him to validate this power. *The beneficent supernatural spoken of here contrasts with the evil supernatural of the Witches just as the sainted Edward contrasts with Macbeth.* Knights points out that the healing imagery contrasts with the disease imagery prominent in Act V. Finally, the entrance of Ross with his evil news comes more dramatically after this quiet scene than it would after one with heavy action. Curiously, the matter of touching was viewed with disfavor in contemporary Scotland, and James shared this view. James, upon becoming King of England, was induced to take up touching (in a much modified ceremony) as showing his legitimacy. He used no angel (a coin); he declined to make the sign of the cross; he held the Protestant view that miracles had ceased. The King was supposed to say (the service is found in old prayerbooks) "Le Roy vous touche, Dieu vous guerys" (the king touches you, the Lord heals you). By the use of this expression the King relieved his mind on the score of endorsing superstition, and his patients would not know what he said. The English were trying to persuade the King to resume the Elizabethan practice of touching, and *Macbeth* gave him a nudge in this direction. Malcolm does not say that he has taken Saint Edward as his model, for to do so would be priggish; but he has obviously done so. Edward is not mentioned here by name, for he is a mysterious presence; furthermore, Shakespeare does not wish to throw Malcolm into too much obscurity which would naturally come if Saint Edward is to be too prominent.

Ross's ambiguity. Ross enters. Although Malcolm does not know him by name, he recognizes him by his costume as a Scot. Macduff, who has been away from home for a time before Macbeth started tyrannizing the countryside, asks about his wife and family. Ross is hesitant about conveying the worst news and uses the ambiguous "well," meaning that Lady Macduff and her children are in Heaven (cf. *Antony and Cleopatra*, II.v.32–33). Then he openly states in a manner neither too short nor too long, "Your castle is surpris'd; your wife and babes/ Savagely slaughter'd." For him to have used softness would have been cruel; to have been graphic, in the manner of a messenger in a Greek tragedy, would have been cruel too. *For Ross to pun on "deer" (l. 206) at this tragic moment is something for which Shakespeare was condemned by neoclassicists;* but the ancient Greeks, who sometimes permitted word play on similar occasions, suggest its naturalness. The effect of this shocking news on Macduff is to harden him against Macbeth and to bring closer the final reckoning. Here we learn what previously we have sensed — the Satanic Macbeth has no children, which Macduff assuredly does not utter because of the removal of the possibility of exact retaliation: the child Lady Macbeth mentions in I.vii must have died in infancy. Macduff, saying "Naught that I am" (wicked man that I am), regards the cause of this atrocity as a judgment of Heaven on his sins; yet despite what he says, and remembering Lady Macduff's describing her husband's flight as "madness," we are not expected to blame Macduff. Macduff cries, ". . . if he scape, Heaven forgive him too!" meaning "If I let him escape, I will not only forgive him myself, but I pray God to forgive him also." He is obviously hopeful not only of Macbeth's death but of his condemnation to Hell (cf. *Hamlet*, III. iii. 73–95). The scene ends, as blank-verse scenes in Shakespeare's plays commonly do, with the finality of a couplet.

Act V: Scene i

The scene occurs in a room at Dunsinane. Except for the last nine lines the scene is in prose. A Doctor and a Gentlewoman who waits on Lady Macbeth enter. The Doctor addresses the Gentlewoman. He has stayed awake with the latter for two nights, but he has not seen what she reported to him. He asks her when Lady Macbeth last walked in her sleep. The Gentlewoman replies that, since Macbeth ("his majesty") went into the field to fight, she has seen Lady Macbeth get up from bed, put on her dressing-gown ("night gown"), write on some paper, seal it, and return to bed. All the time she did this, Lady Macbeth was fast asleep. The Doctor says it is a disturbance of nature when one is simultaneously awake and asleep. He then asks what Lady Macbeth has said. The Gentlewoman refuses to tell, even to the Doctor, because she has no witness to support her statement.

As the Gentlewoman speaks, Lady Macbeth enters holding a lighted candle, which, the Gentlewoman informs the Doctor, Lady Macbeth has at her bedside all the time. From the conversation of the two observers, we learn that the queen is sleep walking; her eyes are open "but their sense are shut." She is also making the motion of washing her hands. The Gentlewoman has seen her mistress do this sometimes for a quarter of an hour.

Until she exits, Lady Macbeth speaks a number of disconnected phrases and sentences. Most of Lady Macbeth's remarks refer to incidents which have been dramatized in the play; a listener might infer from her remarks a soul tortured by the guilty acts of its owner. The two listeners do make this inference about Lady Macbeth and express their shock at what they have been forced to conclude. When Lady Macbeth leaves, the Doctor indicates that rumors are flying about of "unnatural deeds" committed by the ruling couple. Guilty minds, he says, will relieve themselves of their secrets by telling them to their pillows, which do not really hear. He asks God to forgive them all. He tells the Gentlewoman to look after her mistress and to remove from the latter any means of self-harm. He ends with "I think but dare not speak." The Gentlewoman bids the Doctor good night, and they exeunt.

COMMENT: Lady Macbeth has been portrayed quite variously in her last appearance in the play. Henry Irving wrote to Ellen Terry, "The sleepwalking scene will be beautiful too the moment you are in it—but Lady Macbeth should certainly have the appearance of having got out of bed, to which she is returning when she goes off. The hair to my mind should be wild and disordered, and the whole appearance as distraught as possible, and disordered . . . ." The Polanski filmed version, sponsored by Hugh Hefner of *Playboy*, presents a nude Lady Macbeth — "Lady MacBuff," as she was described in the London *Times* of Oct. 26, 1971. In the Kurosawa filming entitled *Throne of Blood*, Lady Macbeth's pregnancy, announced when Macbeth is about to take possession of the throne, renders her ambitious; and a miscarriage drives her insane. This notable departure from the text, as Gerlach says, gives "social and biological excuses for what can only be laid to unfathomable greed in Shakespeare's *Macbeth*."

If Lady Macbeth holds herself in hand until the sleepwalking scene, it would have the advantage of surprise except for the brief interchange between the Doctor and the Waiting Gentlewoman. But one could characterize her on the basis of *the hint in III. ii. 4–7* as growing weary, sick of blood, and apprehensive of further murders; this would somewhat blunt the shock of the sleepwalking scene. A headstrong actress would perhaps attempt a *coup de théâtre* here, but it would destroy the *contrast between Lady Macbeth's slow weakening and Macbeth's slow hardening.*

The stain of blood. Lady Macbeth's malaise exhibits the following *symptoms*: she walks, speaks prose, and even writes in her sleep; and her *theme*, as she rehearses fragmentary reminiscences of murders, is her blood guilt seen visibly on her hands which she continually washes without effect. The idea of bloodstained hands probably came to Shakespeare from Pilate's washing his hands of the guilt of the Saviour's death; but Beatrice points out that in *Gesta Romanorum* there is a story of a "woman of queenly station and hitherto of blameless report who in the interests of her own security murders an innocent person. The blood of her victim falls upon her hand, and although she makes repeated efforts to remove the stain, it remains. Oppressed by the burden of her guilty secret, she finally makes confession to a priest and the stain vanishes."

One gathers that Macbeth has been in the field (l. 4) against his rebellious subjects since the time before Ross went to England (see IV.iii.185). The Doctor and the Gentlewoman prepare us for Lady Macbeth's strange entry. She carries a taper concerning which Bradley comments: "The failure of nature in Lady Macbeth is marked by her fear of darkness; 'She has light by her continually.'" Although the Gentlewoman knows that Lady Macbeth cannot see, she tells the Doctor to "stand close": this act is instinctive, and it gives the center of the stage to Lady Macbeth. *Lady Macbeth speaks in prose because Shakespeare uses this medium for abnormal mental states* as, for example, when Hamlet is acting madly, when Ophelia and Lear are insane, and when Othello in IV.i is virtually in this condition. The regular rhythms of verse, Shakespeare may have thought, ill accord with a mind that has lost its balance. It would be dramatically unwise for Lady Macbeth to speak with sepulchral solemnity and to appear the incarnation of Nemesis, for she is a living woman disturbed by fear and guilt.

Evidence of conscience. Her sleepwalking is probably a sign of demonic possession in the form of demonic bloodletting. Evidence for this view is the lines "Come to my woman's breasts, / And take my milk for gall, you murth'ring ministers" (I. v. 47–48). Milk was in Elizabethan physiological thought an alternate form of blood. Shakespeare, who usually shrinks from depiction or suggestion of the utterly abominable, delineated Joan of Arc in *I Henry VI* as a witch who lost blood to demons (V.iii.14). This distressful situation, by its diminution of Lady Macbeth's blood together with the thickening dregs of melancholy, causes her mind to totter. Most of her rords seem to be directed to the absent Macbeth. Her revulsion from the murders, as well as her thinking herself able at some time in her life to have a child, is good evidence of her possession of a conscience however much seared. She says, "one—two—why then 'tis time to do't," which intimates that Duncan was murdered soon after two in the morning. "What need we fear who knows it, when none can call our pow'r to accompt?" appears to mean that law and tyrants have no part with each other.

A new contribution to scholarship. Reference to Duncan's blood is a hitherto uncommented-upon compliment to King James because old men in Shakespeare's time and in his plays conventionally have little blood: Duncan's abundant blood is a testimony to a life blessing and virtue beyond nature's course; it signifies that he could have begotten male offspring who would have closely resembled him (rather than their mother); and, of course, it tends to certify both Malcolm and Duncan's line generally. Whether the Doctor understands the reference to the "old man" is unclear, but he certainly knows that the murder of Lady Macduff is weighing upon Lady Macbeth's conscience. In l. 50 — "Here's the smell of the blood still" — "smell" rather than "blood" should be emphasized because the spot, Lady Macbeth thinks, has been removed at last. The expression is reminiscent of Cassandra smelling blood and vapors from the tomb in the palace of Atrides in Aeschylus' *Agamemnon*, ll. 1306–11. At this point in *Macbeth*, Mrs. Siddons, one of the great actresses in this role, passed her hands before her nose as if she perceived a foul smell, eliciting the following comment from Leigh Hunt, ". . . she should have shuddered and looked in despair, as recognizing the strain on her soul." Alice Fox points out that Lady Macbeth, being a woman, is more aware than her husband of the smell of blood, Macbeth being preoccupied with its sight. Lady Macbeth's dreams reconstruct something of the terror and coloring (hands, water, blood, and darkness) of the entire play. To have a physician hear them, as Kocher suggests, is to show that her death is not caused by natural melancholy, nor by insanity, but by conscience, which is beyond the power of medicine. If the Doctor had been allowed competence, he would have obscured the point that Shakespeare wishes to make. Lady Macbeth would like to confuse conscience and melancholy (I.v.43 ff.), but the Doctor keeps them separate. He believes that her ailment, psychic in origin, is due to guilt, and that she is therefore in need of a divine. He foresees her eventual suicide (l. 76).

Generally this scene shows that the womanly nature (as then understood) of Lady Macbeth has been violated.

Act V: Scene ii

The scene takes place in the country near Dunsinane. Menteith, Caithness, Angus, Lennox, and their soldiers enter. They are Scottish rebels, who have not left their native land, the "many worthy fellows that were out" of whom Ross had told Malcolm and Macduff in the previous act. Menteith reports that the English forces, led by Malcolm, his uncle Siward, and Macduff, are near. They are burning for revenge, and their righteous cause would raise dead to do battle. Angus says that the native rebel army will meet the English near Birnam

Wood. A short discussion follows as to who makes up the English army. Donalbain is not there, but Siward's son is there and many other young men. Menteith asks about Macbeth's situation. Caithness replies that Macbeth is strongly fortifying Dunsinane. Caithness continues, "Some say he's mad; others, that lesser hate him, / Do call it valiant fury: but, for certain, / He cannot buckle his distempered cause / Within the belt of rule." Angus says that Macbeth can no longer escape from his crimes: every minute ("Now minutely") "revolts upraid his faith-breach." His men obey him only by command. "Nothing in love. Now does he feel his title / Hang loose about him, like a giant's robe / Upon a dwarfish thief." Menteith adds in a rhetorical question that Macbeth cannot be blamed for being frightened "When all that is within him does condemn / Itself for being there." Caithness says that they will march ahead "To give obedience where 'tis truly owed." And it is agreed that they will pour out as much blood as is necessary for their country's cure.

COMMENT: Scenes ii through the ending, which were originally continuous, are marked by intermittent drumming which has the effects of unifying this part of the play and of charging the somewhat prosaic character of Macduff as an instrument of Nemesis. A combined Scottish-English army, ardent for revenge and purging Scotland of Macbeth, is marching toward Birnam Wood. Lines 3–5 say that their heartfelt causes would rouse even a paralytic. Mention of Donalbain, certainly irrelevant to a modern audience, would presumably have been understood in earlier days: Donalbain, who succeeded Malcolm, had been brought up, according to Holinshed, in the old Celtic manners and desired to keep Scotland free from English influence whereas Malcolm was striving to unite the two kingdoms and was certainly susceptible to English manners and influences. *Hence Donalbain's absence,* ll. 12—16, prepares us for the desperate madness of Macbeth in the next scene—something which we have not seen before. Macbeth has evidently suffered military reverses, for, having previously been in the field, he is about to retire to a fortified castle, where he does not even command a loyal following. Caithness, Menteith, and Angus seem to think that Macbeth's conscience is bothering him; indeed, Angus at l. 18 says that everytime a follower revolts, this act reminds Macbeth of his own perfidy.

With regard to ll. 20–22, Spurgeon, analyzing clothes imagery, writes that a "small ignoble man encumbered and degraded by garments unsuited to him should be put against the view emphasized by some critics (notably Coleridge and Bradley) of the likeness between Macbeth and Milton's Satan in grandeur and sublimity." (Critics of Milton's *Paradise Lost* are accustomed to seeing many parallels between Macbeth and Satan.) Spurgeon concludes that Shakespeare sees Macbeth as both Bellona's

bridegroom and as a dwarfish thief. Caithness at l. 18 speaks of Malcolm as "the med'cine of the sickly weal" with imagery that would have especially appealed to King James, who learned from his tutor, George Buchanan, author of *De Jure Regni apud Scotos,* to think of a king as the physician of the commonwealth, an image that James employed in his *Counter-Blaste to Tobacco* (1604).

Act V: Scene iii

The scene is in a room at Dunsinane. Macbeth, the doctor, and attendants enter. Macbeth wants to hear no more reports of men deserting him. He cannot fear, for the prophecy had been that no man born of woman will defeat him, and Malcolm has been born of woman. A servant, white-faced with fear, enters. The servant informs Macbeth that ten thousand soldiers of the English power are approaching. Macbeth keeps interrupting his servant's report with scornful remarks because the servant looks frightened and undoubtedly speaks in a frightened way. After the servant leaves, Macbeth speaks a soliloquy, which he twice interrupts with calls for his armorbearer, Seyton. In the soliloquy he says that he is "sick at heart" when he sees . . . and we do not learn what makes him sick at heart, for he interrupts by crying once more for Seyton. Then he says that this attack "Will cheer me ever" or topple him from the throne now. He has lived long enough, he feels; ". . . my way of life / Is fall'n into the sere, the yellow leaf." All that one ordinarily expects of old age, such as "honor, love, obedience, troops of friends," Macbeth must not expect to have. Instead he will receive "Curses, not loud, but deep, mouth-honor, breath"; these who give the mouth-honor know in their hearts that they do not want to give it but dare not withhold it. Seyton enters and says that all reports (probably of the approaching English and of the desertions) are true. Macbeth says that he will fight until his "flesh is hacked" from his bones. Macbeth wishes Seyton to help him on with his armor. Seyton tells him that it is not necessary yet. Macbeth insists. He gives orders to send out men who will hang those who say they are frightened. He interrupts his talk and addresses the doctor, of whom he inquires about his wife. The doctor tells Macbeth that Lady Macbeth is not so much physically ill as she is bothered by illusions which come one after the other and keep her from sleep. "Cure her of that. . . ," Macbeth tells the doctor. He then asks the doctor whether the latter can help a person sick in his mind. The doctor replies that in that situation a person must help himself. "Throw physic [medicine] to the dogs . . . ," replies Macbeth. Macbeth, talking at once to the doctor and to Seyton, tells the latter to help him on with his armor, to send out . . . for something—the order is never completed . . . to take off his armor. To the doctor he says that his nobles are leaving him; and then he says that he would greatly applaud the doctor if the latter could find a cure for his sick country. Has the doctor heard that the English are coming? The doctor replies in the affirmative. But Macbeth is now back to Seyton, commanding him to follow Macbeth with the armor. Macbeth exits saying that he will not be frightened "Till Birnam forest come to Dunsinane."

COMMENT: This scene exhibits a Macbeth not hitherto observed. He speaks for the first time in public that supernatural spirits have guaranteed him against defeat by any "man that's born of woman," and he applies the oracular saying to Malcolm. He raves against "false thanes," bidding them join "the English epicures." Shakespeare perhaps derived from Holinshed the idea that "fine fare" and "superfluous gormandizing" were brought into Scotland by the English. Following George Orwell and extending his thought, one may say that northerners in various countries tend to think of southerners as being stained with "epicurism" (Epicurus would be aghast at this use of his name), as well as softness, untruthfulness, lechery, and so forth. A Servant enters whose appearance Macbeth does not like: he shouts at him "thou cream-faced loon." *Loon* is usually glossed "worthless fellow," but it may conceivably mean, as Weston Babcock thinks, the aquatic bird, a meaning probably current circa 1606 in spoken (though not written) English. Macbeth under the impetus of his anger goes from "cream-fac'd loon" to "goose look" to "lily-liver'd" to "linen-cheeks," all epithets reflecting badly on the Servant's manliness. The Servant bears the bad news of the approach of the English army. Macbeth shrieks, "Take thy face hence," an admirable expression because, like Lady Macduff's "What are these faces?" it presents a concentrated expression. One supposes that the Servant alarms Macbeth's following.

Seyton, the armour-bearer, enters. Macbeth calls three times for armour, and then says, "Pull't off, I say," his indecisiveness suggesting his insecurity. He knows that the English force arrayed against him amounts to "ten thousand," but he does not know how many revolted Scots have joined it. The memorably phrased speech in ll. 22–29 indicates lapse of time, contrasts Macbeth with Duncan, and shows that Macbeth not only wanted the crown but the peaceful possession of it.

Theory of humors. He turns to the Doctor with a question about Lady Macbeth's health, and he understands that his wife's condition is psychosomatic. So he bids the physician erase from her mind "a rooted sorrow," and "Cleanse the stuff'd bosom of that perilous stuff/ Which weighs upon the heart." Physiologically any of the four humors—melancholy, blood, phlegm, and choler—burnt by the extreme heat accompanying passion, was called melancholy adust. This sediment or residue could not be absorbed by the body and tended to choke the veins. It was a cause of madness and would ultimately destroy life. Hence, Macbeth hopes that physical purgation, effected before it is too late, may conduce to the cure of mental illness. The Doctor evidently diagnoses Lady Macbeth's illness as mental in origin and asserts in effect that he does not undertake psychiatry.

In a masterly touch at l.49 Macbeth tells the Doctor, "the thanes fly from me," a remark that suggests at once that Macbeth is under pressure dropping his guard and that physicians by their calling hear secrets. It is evident that Macbeth rests his security, such as it is, upon the prophecies regarding Birnam Wood and lack of fear or a man born of woman. The armed head, which might well jar him, has been cast out of mind.

Act V: Scene iv

The scene occurs in the country near Birnam Wood. With drum, colors, and soldiers marching, enter Malcolm, Siward, Siward's son, Macduff, Menteith, Caithness, Angus, Lennox, and Ross. Malcolm addresses the native rebels, saying that he hopes that soon bedrooms will be safe. (Duncan was murdered in a bedroom.) Menteith replies that his group does not doubt that at all. Siward asks for the name of the wood which they are near. He is told that it is Birnam Wood. Malcolm announces that every soldier is to cut off a bough from a tree so that the army may fool the enemy by camouflage. Siward says that "the confident tyrant" (Macbeth) remains in Dunsinane and will sit out his antagonists' siege in the palace. Malcolm adds that that strategy is Macbeth's principal hope for victory. For whenever Macbeth's soldiers have the opportunity to do so, they revolt against him. Macduff and Siward agree that they should not speculate on such matters; rather they should do their jobs as good soldiers, and time will tell whether or not their speculations are right. The group exits marching.

COMMENT: This brief scene, based on Holinshed, exhibits the combined English-Scottish force marching toward Dunsinane, where Macbeth is on the point of incarcerating himself in his castle for his last stand. Malcolm, seeing Birnam Wood (Americans would say "Woods") before him, orders his force to cut boughs that would disguise their numbers as the army approaches Macbeth. It is important to note that *Malcolm is unaware that he is fulfilling Macbeth's vision of "a child crowned, with a tree in his hand."* It is equally important to observe that Malcolm is unaware that he is implementing the prophecy of the Witches to the effect that Macbeth is in no danger until Birnam Wood come to

Dunsinane. Not coincidence but Providence overrules the action. The moving wood imparts the spectacle not of wild revenge but of order and even ceremony in league with nature advancing to restore kingly dignity to Scotland. John P. Cutts points out that George Sandys, in his commentary to *Ovid's Metamorphosis Englished, Mythologized, and Represented in Figures . . .* (1632), placed the moving of Birnam Wood toward Dunsinane in suggestive parallel with Orpheus' music calming the inebriated Bacchantes.

Malcolm dilates hopefully on the weak state of Macbeth's defensive forces, suggesting that some have revolted and that those who cannot revolt accordingly serve from constraint. In ll. 14–16 Macduff gracefully checks the young man: "Let our opinions, to be accurate, await the outcome, which will disclose the truth." Though confident of vanquishing Macbeth, Macduff is less sanguine and more experienced than Malcolm.

Act V: Scene v

The scene takes place within Dunsinane castle. Macbeth, Seyton, and Macbeth's soldiers enter with drum and colors. Macbeth cries out that he and his soldiers will remain in the castle because the castle's "strength / Will laugh a siege to scorn." He will be able to endure until his enemies are depleted by famine and illness. If his enemies were not reinforced with men who have deserted him, his army might have gone out and met the enemy and beaten them back.

A cry of women interrupts Macbeth. Seyton goes off to discover the cause. "I have almost forgot the taste of fears," says Macbeth aside. At one time, he continues, he would have had chills on hearing a cry in the night; and at a horrible story his hair would have stood on end. "I have supp'd full with horrors: Direness, familiar to my slaughterous thoughts,/ Cannot once start me," he concludes. Seyton re-enters to tell Macbeth that Lady Macbeth is dead. "She should have died hereafter . . ." says Macbeth. *He then speaks one of the most famous Shakespearean speeches,* which begins, "Tomorrow, and tomorrow, and tomorrow . . . ." The main idea of this speech is that all the future and all the past have no significance. The speech ends with Macbeth's saying that life "is a tale / Told by an idiot, full of sound and fury, / Signifying nothing."

A Messenger enters and tells Macbeth of something that seems unbelievable:"... I looked toward Birnam, and anon, methought, / The wood began to move." Macbeth cries, "Liar, and slave!" The Messenger insists upon the truth of his statement. Macbeth says that if the Messenger is lying, the latter will hang on a tree alive. If the Messenger is telling the truth, Macbeth would be indifferent to the Messenger's hanging him. Macbeth says that he begins "To doubt the equivocation of the

fiend, / That lies like truth." He had been told not to fear until Birnam Wood came to Dunsinane, "and now a wood / Comes toward Dunsinane." Macbeth gives the order to fight outside the castle, for if what the Messenger said be true, it does not matter whether or not his army outwait the siege in the castle or wait outside. "I'gin to be aweary of the sun," reflects Macbeth, "And wish the estate o' the world were now undone." Then he cries, "Ring the alarm bell! Blow wind! come, wrack! / At least we'll die with harness on our back."

COMMENT: This scene forwards the plot by reporting the death of Lady Macbeth and by informing Macbeth that Birnam Wood is moving toward Dunsinane. Macbeth shows apathy in learning of his wife's death, anger at hearing of Birnam Wood, and apathy again at the end of the scene.

When a cry of women arises offstage, Macbeth marvels at his present inability to register shock. "I have supp'd full with horrors," he says with a suggestion that as a devouring hell-kite he has surfeited upon innocent victims. Seyton the armor-bearer announces that the Queen is dead. Macbeth responds, "She should have died hereafter," meaning that she was bound to die at some time or other. This remark is not necessarily a reflection of callousness, although it may be: Romeo has almost nothing to say (V.i.24 ff.) when he learns of Juliet's death. There is a rumor that Lady Macbeth committed suicide (V.ix.36–37), but she may have died of a broken heart caused by the slaughter of Lady Macduff. An effect of having Lady Macbeth die before her husband is somewhat to soften the catastrophe: Macbeth becomes more sick at heart and attracts enough sympathy to permit one to view his approaching death as justice rather than to rejoice over it with personal hatred.

"Tomorrow, and Tomorrow . . ." Macbeth's speech "Tomorrow, and tomorrow, and tomorrow" has been finely interpreted by Fitzroy Pyle as imaging a funeral procession through a vault with each day being a mourner that carries a candle. Macbeth thinks of life as nothing but illusions and evanescence. Abruptly changing the imagery, as Shakespeare does in his mature manner, Macbeth in effect says in l.21: "Events by syllables go on, one after another, until the last syllable has been registered; and time is merged with eternity." Conviction grows on Macbeth; and, dropping his interest in the burial vault, he concludes that both life and death are futile—"Out, out, brief candle!" This expression could mean that Macbeth believes in the death of the soul with the death of the body or, less probably, that trust in this life is but trust in a candle and a shadow. Dr. Johnson took the view that the speech broadly means that "life is such that instead of enjoying today we entertain hopes of tomorrow; and when tomorrow comes, then we hope for the next day. Days thus spent bring fools to the grave." Frye has interestingly assembled similar remarks from others, including John Donne, of Shakespeare's

time. In this purple patch the word "poor" in "poor player" should be stressed because the pity of an actor is that he leaves nothing behind him. But "struts and frets" shows contempt chiefly for life rather than for acting because an actor imitates life. Macbeth's despair penetrates us more through the power of the phrasing than from the terrible situation. Irving Ribner finely says: "As his link with humanity weakens, so also does his desire to live, until at last he sinks into total despair, the medieval sin of *Acedia*, which is the surest evidence of his damnation." In the coda of this speech Shakespeare should not be thought to be expressing his personal philosophy, for the fact is that we do not know what Shakespeare thought about anything except such elementary matters as that New Place, Stratford, was worth buying. We know this because his plays lack *raisonneurs*, authorial mouthpieces (except, possibly, Ulysses in *Troilus and Cressida*), and because there is a most plentiful absence of letters, diaries, and reported conversations to document the point that a given character in a given speech is voicing Shakespeare's own sentiments.

From Kemble to Kurosawa. A Messenger, entering, gives an eyewitness report that Birnam Wood seems to be moving to Dunsinane. In the Kurosawa filmed version, birds from Birnam Wood "fly desperately" through the castle of Dunsinane in reminiscence of the verses (III.iv.123–25) of choughs and magpies revealing "The secret'st man of blood." The Messenger slightly individualizes himself by standing up to Macbeth: "I should report that which I say I saw." Macbeth becomes abusive. The actor Philip Kemble found it necessary to argue that a stage direction "Striking him," placed after l. 34 in the acting version, is not found in the Folio. Certainly, however, Macbeth is at this point, as Kemble said, in a "bewilderment of fear and rage," even offering himself to be hanged if the report about Birnam Wood should prove to be correct. Again Macbeth, losing control, quotes the prophecy in public. When he says that he is growing "a-weary with the sun," the sun should be thought as symbolizing light, reason, reality, legitimate kingship, and Christ. The scene ends with a desperate couplet by no wise equal in poetic merit to the speech beginning "tomorrow, and tomorrow, and tomorrow."

Act V: Scene vi

The scene takes place on a plain before the castle. Enter Malcolm, Old Siward, Macduff, and their armies, with boughs. Malcolm says that they are now near enough (to the castle) to put down the branches of Birnam Wood, which they have been using as camouflage. Malcolm then makes the arrangements for battle. Macduff gives the order for the trumphets to sound, which announce the coming of "blood and death."

COMMENT: In this brief scene Malcolm commands his army to throw down their "leavy screens," *one of the last reversals in the play.* The coming of Birnam Wood to Dunsinane, Holloway says, is "a vivid emblem . . . a dumbshow of nature overturning antinature." John Gerlach makes the same point: "When the forest moves in Act V, it is true enough that nature, rampaging beyond control since the murder of Duncan, is now through human bidding restoring order." *A company carrying green branches was a traditional part of Maying processions; so this spectacle would have seemed less unnatural to the first spectators than it does to us.*

Malcolm orders Old Siward to lead the assault on the castle.

Act V: Scene vii

The scene occurs on the field of battle. Macbeth enters. He feels like a bear tied to a stake in the spectator sport of bear-baiting. (In that game the bear is tied to a stake and dogs are sent out to fight him.) Macbeth then refers to the prophecy that is his last hope. He does not believe a man exists who was not born of woman. "Such a one / Am I to fear, or none," he says. Young Siward enters. When he asks Macbeth for the latter's name, Macbeth replies that Siward will be afraid to hear it. "No; though thou call'st thyself a hotter name / Than any is in hell," answers the young man. But on hearing Macbeth's name, Young Siward says, "The devil himself could not pronounce a title/ More hateful to mine ear." Macbeth adds, "No, nor more fearful." But the remark only incites the young man to call Macbeth a liar and to start the fighting. Macbeth kills Young Siward, and this leads Macbeth to the grimly humorous conclusion that Siward was born of woman.

Macbeth leaves the stage. Macduff enters. Macduff has been looking for Macbeth. Macduff feels that if Macbeth dies without Macduff's having a part in killing him, he, Macduff, will be haunted by the ghosts of his family. He does not want to fight with the hired Irish foot-soldiers ("kerns"); he will either fight with Macbeth or not at all. He hears a great noise and believes that should denote the presence of a great person. He exits saying, "Let me find him, Fortune!/ And more I beg not."

Macduff's exit is followed by the entrance of Old Siward and Malcolm. Perhaps because his son's body has been in one way or another removed from the stage; perhaps because the stage arrangement is such that the audience can see his dead son and he cannot, Siward is unaware that his son has been slain. He is telling Malcolm that the castle will surrender without much fight; that Macbeth's men fight on Macbeth's enemy's side as well as on Macbeth's. Malcolm almost has the victory clinched, says Siward. They exeunt as Siward shows Malcolm into the castle.

COMMENT: When Macbeth exclaims that he is now tied like a bear to a stake, the image reduces him to that which he in some respects is, an animal. Polanski's filmed version made the bear-image come alive by having staged a bear-baiting episode as entertainment during the banquet scene: the bear, bloodied and then killed, foreshadows the death of the tyrant, and the remark in V.vii is therefore a flashback. The fact is, however, that Macbeth is not now in his castle but near it.

After an unpleasant exchange with Young Siward, marked by the mutual "thou," Macbeth kills the young man. It must be so because, as the eighteenth-century critic Steevens remarked, "Shakespeare designed Macbeth should appear invincible till he encountered the object destined for his destruction."

Macduff, entering, declares that he will kill no one but Macbeth. In his soliloquy the word "kerns" indicates that Macbeth is depending upon Irish mercenaries as Macdonwald the rebel did before him.

Malcolm and Old Siward, the latter of whom unaccountably fails to spot his son's corpse, enter the castle with conversation suggesting the ease with which it will be taken. Malcolm says, "We have met with foes/ That strike beside us," which could mean that they "deliberately miss us."

Act V: Scene viii

The scene occurs in another part of the field of battle. Macbeth enters and says that he will not behave like the Roman soldier who would commit suicide before he allowed himself to be captured and killed by his enemies (like Brutus or Antony in other plays of Shakespeare). As long as Macbeth sees others alive, he would rather give other wounds than himself. Macduff enters and cries, "Turn, hell-hound, turn!" Macbeth tells his pursuer that he has been avoiding Macduff more than he has avoided any other man, for "my soul is too much charged/ With blood of thine already." He tells Macduff not to fight him. But as an answer Macduff does little more than show his sword ready for battle. In the midst of the fight Macbeth warns Macduff that the latter is wasting time fighting, for Macbeth leads "a charmed life" and cannot be defeated by "one of woman born." Macduff tells his adversary to give up hope, because "Macduff was from his mother's womb/ Untimely ripped." Macbeth cries, "Accursed be that tongue . . .," for it frightens him. Macbeth continues, "And be these juggling fiends no more believed,/ That palter with us

in a double sense;/ That keep the word of promise to our ear,/ And break it to our hope." Macbeth refuses to fight with Macduff. In that case, Macduff says, Macbeth must surrender and must submit to being displayed as a monstrous rarity in the side show. Macbeth refuses to surrender. He will neither serve Malcolm nor "be baited with the rabble's curse." Despite the fact that the conditions of his defeat as foretold in the prophecies have arrived, he will fight to the end. Placing his shield before him, Macbeth challenges Macduff, ". . . lay on, Macduff;/ And damned be him that first cries. 'Hold, enough!'"

COMMENT: The outcome of this battle scene is never in doubt. Macbeth considers suicide after defeat, connecting this course (as Cleopatra does in *Antony and Cleopatra*) with Roman practice; he rejects it.

Macduff, entering and encountering Macbeth *vis-à-vis*, prepares for the moment of prophetic truth in the sense of the Witches and in the larger sense of the Bible that "all they that take the sword, shall perish with the sword" (Matt. 26, 52). *Lines 4–6 are the closest to repentance ever seen in the characterization of Macbeth. Macbeth intellectually understands that he has erred, and in some degree he regrets his error; but he does not repent in the Christian sense.* When Macduff assures him that he is a servant of Satan, he does not even try to gloss over his wickedness with a conventional religiosity. Yet Macbeth's fear of Macduff is chiefly spiritual rather than physical; it is like his fear of Banquo but stronger in degree. Because of prophecy and tenderheartedness, Macbeth wishes to avoid a fight with Macduff, and he does so by informing Macduff of the prophecy to the effect that no man born of woman shall conquer him. Macduff then acquaints Macbeth with his Caesarian birth. *The prophecy of the bloody child, quite unknown to Macduff as Macduff's Caesarian birth is to Macbeth, is fulfilled by an overruling Providence.* Macbeth curses the Witches for their equivocations and declares that he will not fight Macduff. Then Macduff offers Macbeth the option of living out his life in captivity like an animal in a zoo, *a speech not out of character for Macduff but one that is unexpected.* Macbeth should accept this offer if he wishes to repent, but his pride is recrudescent. Like Cleopatra, he cannot bear to present himself abjectly before the jeering rabble. So he fights and dies. Kean, a famous Macbeth in the nineteenth century, is reported by Hazlitt as falling "at last finely, with his face downwards, as if to cover the shame of his defeat." Kean crawled for his sword, and "died" as he touched it. Polanski's death of an excessively villainized Macbeth, by reason of its emphasis on bloodshed, tends to debase tragedy into melodrama.

Differences over staging of Macbeth's death. The action at the ending of this scene is a problem. If one inspects the Variorum edition, he finds that early critics thought Macbeth to have been killed onstage, his body then being dragged offstage, decapitated, and the head brought back on. Davenant, the Restoration "improver" of *Macbeth*, and Garrick brought no head back but rather Macbeth's sword. In the twentieth century, the severed head is sometimes returned (certainly it is in Polanski's gory version) and sometimes not; producers evidently feel awkwardness here. The important point is the identity of the First Apparition: is it Macduff, as most commentators think, or is it Macbeth, as in Hardin Craig's opinion and as in Sir Laurence Olivier's stage version at Stratford, England in 1954? A secondary point, suggesting the soundness of the latter view, is the final reminiscence of Saul in the characterization of Macbeth. W. B. Hunter, Jr., argues that the death of Macbeth occurs "in such a way that the victim can be killed in full view or hidden. The play, that is, can be performed in accordance with the classical principle of decorum, or it can be acted with sufficient blood and guts to satisfy an average Jacobean playgoer." *Thus, King James could be soothed by a decorous play and by one in which he, the chief intended victim of the Gunpowder Plot, would not have to witness the staged killing of a king.*

Act V: Scene ix

The scene occurs within the castle. Malcolm, Old Siward, Ross, and their army enter victoriously. Malcolm says that he wishes that friends who are not present were safely here (that is, not dead). Old Siward replies that (in war) some must die. Yet, from all he can tell, the great victory of this day was achieved at the expense of few lives. Malcolm says that Macduff and Old Siward's son are missing. Ross tell Old Siward that Young Siward "paid a soldier's debt." That is, he died as a man should. After Old Siward is assured that his son had indeed died as a man should and had wounds on his face before he died, the father says, "Why then, God's soldier be he!" If Old Siward had as many sons as he has hairs on his head, he would not wish them better deaths than this one. Malcolm says that he will give the young man more grief than his father has given, for the young man deserves it; but Old Siward insists otherwise: "They say he parted well and paid his score:/ And so, God be with him!" (The idea in "paid his score" is that each man owes God a life, and we pay God our debt when we die.)

Macduff now enters carrying Macbeth's head. He hails Malcolm as king, points to Macbeth's head, and announces that now "the time is free." He then asks the nobility (the "kingdom's pearl") to shout with him, "Hail, King of Scotland!" This the nobility does. Malcolm says that he will not permit a long time to pass before he pays his debt to those present. The thanes shall

become earls, the first earls ever named in Scotland. Whatever else remains to be done, "which would be planted newly with the time," such necessities as recalling Scotland's exiles, finding out the agents of the cruel Macbeth and his "fiend-like queen," who, it is thought, committed suicide—such necessities, Malcolm says, he "will perform in measure, time, and place." Giving thanks to all and inviting them to his coronation, Malcolm leads the actors off the stage in their final exeunt.

COMMENT: Old Siward, receiving news of his son's death, is reassured that the young man has perished in soldierly fashion because his wounds were "on the front." Old Siward appears an ideal soldier: having taken Macbeth's castle, he promptly turns it over to Malcolm and recognizes him as master. Indeed, the characterization of Old Siward, a Dane, may be thought a compliment to Christian, King of Denmark, who with his brother-in-law, James I of England, witnessed the first performance of *Macbeth* at Hampton Court in 1606.

Then the Folio (there was no Quarto) reads, "Enter Macduffe; with Macbeths head." The source is Holinshed's *Chronicles*: "Then cutting his head from his shoulders, he set it vpon a pole, and brought it vnto Malcolme." Malone inserted the stage-direction "on a pole." The textual evidence for the pole is found in ll. 20–21: "Behold where stands/ Th' usurper's cursed head." Macbeth's head is not dragged in by the hair nor is it resting in someone's arms. Julian Mates emphasizes the point that Londoners were familiar with the practice of placing traitors' heads on poles atop the southern gate towers of London Bridge; so the first audiences could easily see not only the fulfillment of the Witches' prophecy of the armed head but also the association with treachery. Macduff, in short, has dragged Macbeth's corpse to decapitate it offstage and impale the head; then he re-enters with the poled head, plants it, and speaks in felicitation of Malcolm as King of Scotland. ". . . the time is free," says Macduff.

Barbara Parker points out that the play's ending sees the restoration of natural time, *e.g.*, that associated with planting and harvesting, as distinguished from that time which sees "the future in the instant." Macduff continues, "I see thee compass'd with thy kingdom's pearl," which Paul explains as the dependent fiefs of the imperial diadem placed or to be placed on Malcolm's head; the primary reference is of course to the crown. *In his filmed version,* Polanski here emphasizes the crown on Malcolm's head, not wanting us to forget that it was for this crown that Macbeth did murder; and he even goes beyond the text to show Donalbain, at the conclusion of the play, riding to the cave of the Witches, and thus suggesting that another Macbeth is in the making. Another extra-textual touch that has been used (not by Polanski) is keeping the Witches aloft during the last scene so that they can join in the concluding cry, "Hail, King of Scotland!" If this insertion is made, the Witches become a mute chorus of Fates and assume a prominence that Shakespeare never intended. "Hail" here, unlike its earlier application to Macbeth, unites ceremony with substance.

The last speech: restoration of order. Malcolm, here as earlier, shows the man submerged in the ruler. Exhibiting neither self-glorification nor condescension, he undertakes himself and magnifies his thanes with the title of "earls." He promises to call home Scottish exiles who fled Macbeth. Malcolm is known in Scottish history as Malcolm Canmore, who with Saint Margaret the English princess, founded on April 25, 1057, his coronation day, the first dynastic succession that Scotland ever had. Because Shakespeare does not wish Macbeth to have any excuse for his deed (there is,

however, the matter of the royal slip seen in I.iii.104), he obscures Malcolm's innovation of hereditary monarchy and suppression of tanist law (*i.e.*, the idea that the monarchy was elective within the descendants of Macalpine). The hereditary principle is apotheosized in the cauldron scene, which must have pleased James immensely with its depiction of eight sovereigns in lineal descent one from the other. *So the play ends with the last speech being assigned Malcolm rather than Macduff in observance of the tragic convention that the highest-ranking character left alive is to speak last, thus showing the restoration of order after the tempest.* It might be remarked that although Shakespeare is here following a pattern of tragedy, the ending of Macbeth is in the atmosphere of his chronicle and history plays.

CHARACTER ANALYSES

MACBETH   When we first hear of Macbeth, he is a man much honored by his countrymen for his leading and courageous part in defense of his good king and native land. However, almost as soon as we meet him, we realize that he is both ambitious and murderous. For as soon as the Witches greet him with the title of future king, Macbeth thinks of murdering Duncan, the current king. But Macbeth is not merely the kind of man who serves his king until he has an opportunity of killing the king. Macbeth, though he may wish to murder Duncan for Duncan's crown, nevertheless also wishes to be a good man. In fact he thinks of himself basically as a good man. This becomes obvious from his fright and his consciousness of his fright that result when he pictures himself murdering Duncan. Nevertheless, the powerful drive of his ambition has dangerously affected him. Macbeth regards the predictions not so much as predictions but as "supernatural soliciting," that is, as requests to him from powers greater than man to attain his goal of the crown. Since Macbeth has mainly homicidal methods in mind, he in effect thinks of the predictions as invitations to murder. Although Macbeth does not understand the trick his mind has played on him, he has in fact been warned away from falling into the very trap laid for him by his ambitions and by the Witches. Banquo warns Macbeth, after the latter has learned that he has ben made the Thane of Cawdor, that the agents of the devil sometimes tell us small truths "to betray's/ In deepest consequence." But the unheeding Macbeth in the very next speech refers to the predictions as "supernatural soliciting."

Now, Macbeth's conscience must contend not only with his powerful ambitions. Macbeth's conscience must also contend with Lady Macbeth, his wife, and Macbeth's love for his wife. Macbeth's love for his wife is so great that his ambitions strive as much for her as for himself. In his letter to her telling of his meeting with the Witches he calls her "my dearest partner of greatness" and he says that he wishes her not to be ignorant of what greatness "is promis'd *thee*." All of his thoughts, when he thinks of the pleasures and prestige of the kingship, include his wife. She on her part loves him equally and wishes to see him king at least as much as she wishes to see herself queen. But she is aware of his prickly conscience, which would make it difficult for him "To catch the nearest way," that is, the murderous way. She therefore uses the most effective method at her command, shame. Macbeth, after all, is a soldier, and he loves his wife. Neither for himself as a soldier nor before his wife would Macbeth want to appear as a coward. So despite his decision not to go ahead with the murder, when Lady Macbeth accuses her husband of cowardice in making his decision, he succumbs to her, and they continue with their plans for the crime.

Why had Macbeth decided against committing violence for the kingship? In a soliloquy in the seventh scene of the first act, he tells us that it is not death in the next world that he fears. Rather, he is afraid that his crime for the kingship will teach others to commit similar crimes when he is king. However, despite Macbeth's apparent indifference to religion and morality, he is really very much involved with both. He gives as further reason against killing Duncan the fact that

Duncan is Macbeth's relative and his guest, both of which relationships urge Macbeth against committing the crime. And a final reason for not killing Duncan is that pity should prevent Macbeth from harming the good man and gentle king that Duncan has been. For most Elizabethans these reasons would have implied a concern with religion and morality, the extent of which Macbeth does not consciously admit.

Macbeth's internal conflict. Yet Macbeth allows himself to be shamed into the crime by Lady Macbeth. But, while she has whipped him into committing the act, she has not succeeded in silencing his conscience or stopping his concern with eternal things. After the murder he is distressed that he has not been able to say "Amen" at the end of prayers he had heard two men reciting. And at the same time his conscience hurts so, that he thinks he hears voices which cry, "Sleep no more! / Macbeth does murder sleep . . . ." He is in fact so hampered in his actions by the conflict between his knowledge that he has committed the crime and his abhorrence of it, that he becomes immobile. After the murder, when the two realize that Macbeth has brought the daggers from the murder chamber, Macbeth cannot return, even though returning means the difference between discovery and success. When Lady Macbeth has returned from placing the daggers near Duncan's attendants and hears the knocking at the gate, she almost has to push Macbeth into their bedroom so that they will look as though they have just been awakened.

The efforts of Macbeth and Lady Macbeth to attain the crown are successful. But Macbeth's awareness that he has given up his eternal soul makes him especially sensitive to his desire to make his kingship secure. Also contributing to his sensitivity is the fear that his crime may be discovered. The two motives make him first turn on Banquo and Fleance, Banquo's son, as the cause of his anxiety. Banquo was present at the Witches' meeting with Macbeth and that fact may make him especially able to discover Macbeth's crime. Also the Witches had predicted that Banquo's children rather than Macbeth's children would be kings. Perhaps Macbeth projects onto Banquo his own turn of thought and presumes that Banquo will attempt to attain the crown just as Macbeth himself had done so. Macbeth says, ". . . to that dauntless temper of his mind, / He [Banquo] hath a wisdom that doth guide his valor / To act in safety." At any rate, even if Banquo himself does not make an attempt, Macbeth's children will not succeed Macbeth and Banquo's will. In that case Macbeth will have lost not only his soul but the fruit of his labor in this world as well. For a man does not work only for his immediate profit in this world but also for the benefit of his children, who will make his name live on in honor. Macbeth therefore decides to have Banquo and Fleance killed.

Although, after the murder of Duncan, Macbeth's conscience had brought him nearly to immobility, he still decides to murder Banquo and Fleance. Nothing must stop him from living securely: "But let the frame of things disjoint, both the worlds suffer, / Ere we will eat our meal in fear, and sleep / In the affliction of these terrible dreams, / That shake us nightly." Despite these desperately resolute words his conscience is still able to attack him. At his state dinner the sight of Banquo's ghost makes him shake with guilt and fear. But this terrible experience causes Macbeth to be only more desperate in his efforts to repress his conscience and stem his fear and guilt. He will return to "the weird sisters," the Witches, whom he now recognizes as evil, so that he may "know / By the worst means, the worst." He repeats his determination that nothing shall stop him in his quest for security. "For mine own good / All causes shall give way . . . ." And all "Strange things" that he thinks of will immediately be acted out. Macbeth has completely committed himself to evil.

Macbeth's confusion of values. Why has Macbeth done this? Why has not the terrifying experience with Banquo's ghost warned him into repentance? Macbeth partially answers that question for us. "I am in blood / Stepped so far," he says, "that, should I wade no more, / Returning were as tedious as go o'er." Macbeth says that he finds it too tiresome to repent. But to someone who understands the worth of repentance, the process of repentance, hard as it may be, is hardly tiresome. What has happened is that in making his first decision for evil instead of good and in accustoming himself to the thoughts necessary to maintain the results of that decision, Macbeth has confused the values of good and evil. That is, he has confused fair and foul, which confusion has all along been the devil's aim. Macbeth, in other words, has forgotten the comfort of a life without a screaming conscience or desperate thoughts. But behind his forgetfulness, at the very heart of his confusion of fair and foul, lies Macbeth's egotism. In order to repent, Macbeth would have to give up the kingship, which is giving him so much trouble. But he is unable to do so. The kingship still means more to him than quiet days and the possibility of heaven. Macbeth would rather rule in the hell he has made of his world than serve a good king and God in heaven. He therefore accustoms himself to his current life of anxiety, forgets the pleasures of easeful days, and finds it "tedious" to repent.

The irony of egotism. This same egotism is in evidence when Macbeth says that nothing will stand in the way of his security. "For mine own good, / All causes shall give way," he says. Earlier he had said that he would "let the frame of this disjoint" before he would live insecurely. Macbeth would destroy the world to gain security in his kingship. Of course, this is the reduction to absurdity which results from completely egotistic thought. Here is a man who would rule the world, yet would destroy it if he could not rule it securely. What world would there then be left to rule? And this foreshadows his later feeling, that he wishes the end of the world would come with his own desperate end. We see the irony of the completely egotistic pursuit. At the beginning of the play Macbeth had a good deal of stature. But his attempts at self-aggrandizement have reduced Macbeth to the size of a small man ineffectively flailing at a large world completely beyond his control. Really knowing this, Macbeth finds it "tedious" not only to repent but also to "go o'er," that is, to go on in his life.

However, he is not yet ready to admit the implication of this remark, which tells us that Macbeth despairs of this life as well as of the next. *And in fact he never does completely despair. No matter how much he comes to hate himself and life, his egotism also prevents him from ever simply surrendering his life.* He therefore works harder and harder to maintain his security. Banquo, his first object of fear, is now dead. But Macbeth is now frightened of Macduff and attempts to kill him. When Macduff escapes, Macbeth capriciously murders Macduff's family. Soon we hear that all of Scotland is frightened of Macbeth. The only way in which Macbeth can cause people to obey him is through fear, for that is the only motive for obedience that Macbeth can understand. *Macbeth has therefore turned Scotland into a reflection of his own mind; he has turned Scotland into hell.* But only devils and Macbeth wish to live in hell. And so his people begin to revolt against him. Macbeth becomes increasingly isolated. Not only are the people within Scotland revolting against him; Scotsmen have fled the land, and they are returning with an army of Englishmen to fight Macbeth. Finally, Macbeth is also isolated from the one person outside himself whom he has loved and for whom he has acted, his wife. She, too, had begun suffering the torments of a guilty conscience. Mainly because he loved her, he stopped telling her about his dire deeds so that she would not have them on her conscience. But she has felt responsibility for them as well as for those she actively helped to commit, and her conscience has increasingly paralyzed her mind. Macbeth, partially because he loved his wife and acting therefore more and more on his own, partially because her own conscience caused a mental breakdown, and finally because his wife dies, finds himself toward the end of the play in total isolation.

Macbeth's implied self-hatred. Thus isolated at the end of the play, Macbeth's final hope is the second set of prophecies of the Witches. They had told him that he would be harmed by no man born of woman and that he would not be defeated until Birnam Wood came to Dunsinane. Macbeth, thoroughly committed to evil and careless in his desperate search for assurance, believed them, although he should have realized from past experience that their promises of hope look good only on the surface. Now that he is isolated, the impossibility of his defeat, which the Witches' prophecies seemed to indicate, seems incredible. Yet Macbeth hopes on. But he only hopes; he barely believes. He is in a fever of anxious activity. He commands his servant to dress him in his armor; then he commands his servant to take it off. But one decision seems firm. He will stay in the castle of Dunsinane, which is easily defended against a siege, and starve his enemies into defeat. But this resolution holds only until he sees Birnam Wood. It seems, he says, as though the Witches were only fooling with him. His desperation grows, and feeling the imminence of defeat, he orders what remains of his army out into the field, for he wishes to die at least actively fighting. But he also says that he is beginning to wish himself dead. Such a wish is not surprising. For when Macbeth wished earlier to see the destruction of the world if he should not be secure, when he found life too tedious to continue, when he felt anxious with guilt and fear, implied always was a hatred for himself and for life. And now in his final, desperate straits he expresses the hatred overtly.

And so Macbeth goes out into the field. Like a bear tied to a stake, he "must fight the course." He has one last hope, that his life "must not yield / To one of woman born." But finally he meets Macduff, who was "from his mother's womb / Untimely ripped." On hearing this bit of information Macbeth does not wish to fight with Macduff. But when Macduff threatens to make him a public show, Macbeth fights. He would rather die than bend to Malcolm or "be baited with the rabble's curse." Macbeth dies, then, not wholly to be scorned. His terrific egotism prevents him from bowing, as he should bow, before the rightful king, Malcolm. But it also prevents him from submitting to the indignity of being "baited with the rabble's curse." Although that indignity would present him as the monster he has become, Macbeth still thinks of himself as a man, and as such would rather die than suffer the indignity. This feeling in him reminds us of the worthy Macbeth at the beginning of the play. We also see that he still has the courage to act on his convictions, desperate though that courage may be. And it is not merely an animal courage. For he knows now that he must die. He fights as a man. *At the conclusion of the play, although we have come to abhor Macbeth, we cannot help but feel a certain admiration for him. But much more we have a sense of irony and waste: irony because some sterling qualities have been put to such evil use, waste because Macbeth was a potentially great man who was lost.*

LADY MACBETH   Lady Macbeth resembles her husband in a number of ways: she honorably and efficiently carries out her duties as a member of the aristocracy; she has powerful ambitions; she loves her spouse and is ambitious at least as much for him as for herself; finally, she also has a strong conscience. The main difference between Lady Macbeth and Macbeth lies in Lady Macbeth's utter refusal to listen to her conscience at the beginning of the play. Actually, we never actually see a conflict in Lady Macbeth between the good and evil parts of her as we do see in Macbeth. We infer her conscience from the strength of her invocation to the "spirits/ That tend on mortal thoughts." She needs so strong and so horrifying an invocation in order to repress an active conscience. Knowing that her conscience would pain her for planning and committing a murder, she calls on the spirits to "Stop up the access and passage to remorse," to "take my milk for gall," and not to permit heaven (another way of referring to her conscience) "To cry, 'Hold, hold!'" Perhaps Lady Macbeth finds it somewhat easier to ignore her conscience than her husband can ignore his because her imagination is less vivid than his. When he thinks of murdering Duncan, the picture of his doing so appears before his eyes blotting out his real surroundings. Macbeth also sees daggers pointing him to the murder and hears voices which cry, "Macbeth does murder sleep." Lady Macbeth does not have the problem of contending with this kind of imagination.

There is another difference between Lady Macbeth and Macbeth: it is in their attitude toward each other. *Macbeth never in the play thinks of manipulating his wife.* Later in the play, in order to save her from the torments of her conscience, he does not tell her of his plans for murder , but that is different from handling someone in such a way as to induce him to do something he may not want to do. *But Lady Macbeth does manipulate her husband.* This is not to say that she does not love him; on the contrary, her care for him and her tenderness toward him show that she does. She believes that her manipulating him into the murder of Duncan will attain for him the crown, which will eventually make him happier than his conscience will allow him to know that he will be. She therefore decides that she will "chastise [him] with the valor of [her] tongue." When the time comes for the fatal decision, she plays upon his manhood and his love for her. *Lady Macbeth is going to get her husband what he really wants, whether or not he knows he wants it.* Love, such as Lady Macbeth's which induces its object to try for more than its object wholly wants, is, we must conclude, influenced by egotism.

Now, when Lady Macbeth made the gigantic effort to repress her conscience, she apparently felt a necessity to do so only for the period in which the murder was

to be committed. She never talks of needing the repression later. It appears as though she felt that once the murder was committed and "sovereign sway and masterdom" was attained, her guilt would be assuaged. Or, perhaps she felt that her conscience, once repressed by this great effort, would stay repressed. At any rate she counted neither on an irrepressible conscience nor on the consequences brought about by a kingship attained through violence, which consequences only brought on further acts of violence, which in turn only strengthened the conscience. The energy Lady Macbeth required to push down her conscience in the first place was great. She would need an ever-increasing energy to repress it, especially when it was always increasing in strength. Expecting only "sovereign sway and masterdom" without increased activity of her conscience, having consumed a tremendous amount of energy in first repressing her conscience, Lady Macbeth finally succumbs to its torments and can escape from them only in madness and suicide.

Her conscience victorious. The line of her deterioration can be traced in the play. In the first place she is not altogether successful in pushing down her conscience even for the period of the murder. She would herself have murdered Duncan "had he not resembled / My father as he slept," a resemblance probably made vivid by her conscience. After the murder, when Macbeth is making excuses for having murdered outright Duncan's attendants, Lady Macbeth faints. This may be a clever ruse on Lady Macbeth's part to take attention away from Macbeth, who seems to be talking too much. It may also be relief from the nervous tension engendered by her great efforts of the last few hours. However, these are just foreshadowings of what is in store for her. The next time we see her alone, she voices her sense of insecurity, "'Tis safer to be that which we destroy, / Than by destruction dwell in doubtful joy." And later in that same scene Macbeth speaks of these terrible dreams "That shake us nightly." The *us* refers to him and Lady Macbeth. However, she still retains enough energy to attempt to keep Macbeth from revealing his fears in the banquet scene. *Yet, once the guests have left in disorder, she is listless, all energy gone. She can speak only in single sentences;* Macbeth is dominant; he makes all the decisions, she none. *When next we see her, her conscience has emerged victorious.* Despite "the dignity of the whole body," which she apparently can maintain during the day and perhaps even in sleepwalking, *at night her conscience rips her with fears and shattered memories of crimes.* Worst of all, the stain and smell of Duncan's blood seems to cling to her hands. When we finally hear of her, it is thought that she has committed suicide. Almost certainly she has. We had heard earlier of her escape into madness, which was probably no escape, for undoubtedly the memories remained; and now suicide has become a final escape. Suicide was the only way in which she could control the conscience she so thoughtlessly and resolutely believed she could repress.

BANQUO   Banquo's function in the play is mainly as a foil to Macbeth. With Macbeth he is co-leader of Duncan's army against the rebel Macdonwald and the king of Norway. Like Macbeth he is an important member of the aristocracy, and he, too, meets the Witches who make prophecies concerning him. *Macbeth and he therefore have enough in common to make their different reactions and responses to events important.* We may first notice their different reactions to the Witches' prophecies. Macbeth regards them as "supernatural soliciting." But it is Banquo who reminds us that the devil tries to "Win us with honest trifles, to betray's/ In deepest consequence." And Banquo's caution is the proper response, not Macbeth's egotistic assumption of "supernatural soliciting." Second, we may notice the images of time and growth so frequently used by Banquo, which indicate his acceptance of God's order and which contrast with Macbeth's attempt to control time for his own purposes. Listen to Banquo: "If you can look into the seeds of time,/ And say which grain will grow and which will not . . ." (I. iii); "There if I grow, / The harvest is your own" (I. iv); ". . . no jutty, frieze, / Buttress, nor coign of vantage, but this bird / Hath made his pendent bed, and procreant cradle . . ." (I. vi); ". . . our time does call upon's" (III. i). And those are samplings. Third, Banquo is wary not only of supernatural temptation but also of human temptation. Macbeth falls not only for the lure of the Witches but also for the temptation offered by his wife. But when Macbeth says to Banquo, "If you shall cleave to my consent, when 'tis, / It shall make honor for you," Banquo indicates in his reply that he will be involved in no dirty work for worldly gain: "So I lose none [honor]/ In seeking to augment it [honor] . . . ."

More than a foil. But while Banquo in large part serves in the play as a foil to Macbeth, he, unlike most of the other supporting characters, interests us in and of himself. For Banquo is ambitious, and the ambition pulls strongly on him. Although he is cautious of the temptation Macbeth may warily have put to him, he is, after all, willing to confer with Macbeth about augmenting his honor—as long as no dirty work is afoot. Banquo strongly wishes to rise, but he wishes to do so without foul play. And his wish for worldly gain is so strong that, though he is not consciously tempted, he may have been unconsciously tempted. At the beginning of Act II he says to Macbeth, "I dreamt last night of the three weird sisters: / To you they have showed some truth." What did he dream about? Was it of a foul way of gaining his ambition? He had said earlier in the scene that he had had "cursed thoughts" in his sleep. His dreams, at any rate, show his powerful interest in what the Witches had forecast for him. Finally, although his soliloquy in Act III, Scene i, begins with a consideration of how Macbeth had attained the kingship, Banquo does not dwell on that subject long. Macbeth's acquisition of the crown only leads him to the thought of the truth of the Witches' prophecy to Macbeth and therefore to the possibility that their prophecy to him may also end in truth. But these revelations of Banquo's ambitious drives, while they make him more interesting to us in that they show him to be a man of conflicting motives, also accentuate his function as a foil to Macbeth. For like Macbeth, he is powerfully driven to worldly goals; but unlike Macbeth, he never confuses fair and foul. Also, no actor playing Banquo should forget what Macbeth says about him, for such an actor must show it in his bearing and in his pantomime. Banquo, says Macbeth, has a "dauntless temper of . . . mind" and a "wisdom that doth guide his valor / To act in safety." That is, Banquo is brave both physically and spiritually, and he has an intelligence that teaches his bravery to act with discretion.

MACDUFF   We first distinguish Macduff from the other members of the supporting cast when with Lennox he knocks at the gate after the murder of Duncan. The knocking itself is like the hammer-blow of fate, which Macbeth has called down upon himself by having committed the murder. Macduff is the instrument of that fate. This idea begins to emerge as Macduff is distinguished from Lennox because the former enters Duncan's chamber to rouse Duncan only to discover Duncan dead. It is then Macduff who returns shouting horror at the fact of Duncan's murder. It is also Macduff who asks Macbeth why the latter has killed Duncan's attendants. Macduff is further impressed upon our consciousness when we learn of his decision against attending Macbeth's coronation. In discussing the coronation with Lennox, Macduff's ironic tone indicates his suspicion of Macbeth: "Well, may you see things well done there . . . ." Thus, with his few brief appearances and few lines Macduff has become rather important to us. While we cannot as yet understand *the full significance of Macduff as one of the knockers at the gate, we do recognize early in the play a basic antagonism between him and Macbeth, an antagonism that begins earlier than that of any other character in the play.*

Why Macduff leaves his family. Whether Macduff has attempted to encourage in others his own distrust of Macbeth, or whether he merely voiced his distrust, or whether he did neither of these, we do not know. We do know that his distrust of Macbeth was great enough for him to refuse a command to appear before Macbeth.

The refusal, of course, makes for an untenable situation and Macduff understandably flees Scotland leaving his wife and children. Lady Macduff perhaps half believes her husband to be a traitor. A man who is not a traitor, she says, would not leave his family to a tyrant from whom he himself is running away. But in her distress and confusion Lady Macduff misses the intention of her husband's action. He has left Scotland without word to his family because he did not wish the family to be implicated. Macduff regarded Macbeth as a tyrant but not a mindless murderer of those who were completely innocent. But not warning his family of his flight, Macduff thought to free them of the possibility of any blame. The family would then live comfortably in its home and not become exiles in England. *This is the only construction that can be placed on Macduff's actions, for Macduff is neither coward, traitor, nor fool. But even Macduff could not see the depths to which Macbeth would sink.*

Symbolic avenger. Until the point at which his family is murdered, Macduff symbolizes the opposition to Macbeth that comes from the good man interested in the welfare of his country. But in England, when Macduff hears of the slaughter of his family, his role changes. He becomes the *determined avenger, symbolic* of those set upon the destruction of Macbeth because they are personally involved. *We can now see why Macduff as the instrument of fate knocked at the gate.* Macbeth, having fatefully murdered Duncan, inevitably ended in murdering innocent women and children. The inevitable avenger, therefore, is Macduff, symbolic of the husbands and fathers of the slaughtered innocents. Macbeth then, in killing Duncan, assured the course for the rest of his life and thus sealed his own doom. His doom is Macduff, for that purpose by fate "from his mother's womb / Untimely ripp'd." That is, Macbeth in killing Duncan in effect made sure that eventually a Macduff would kill Macbeth.

DUNCAN   Duncan is the good king under whom apparently a kingdom flourishes. In his soliloquy in Act I, Scene vii, Macbeth attests to Duncan's virtue and to Duncan's restrained usage of his kingly powers. When Duncan arrives at Macbeth's castle, Inverness, in the brief respite between the outrages perpetrated by Macdonwald and Macbeth, the descriptions of the atmosphere about Inverness given by Duncan and Banquo suggest the healthy, peaceful condition of the land during the rule by such a man as Duncan. That Duncan is aware of "no art / To find the mind's construction in the face" is not a criticism of Duncan. There is, in fact, no art which will do so. Only time will reveal the "mind's construction." The only early antagonist of Macbeth is Macduff, and he may have been suspicious of Macbeth only because he happened to ask

Macbeth why the latter had killed Duncan's grooms and therefore may have been keenly watching Macbeth flounder in the reply. Antagonism to Macbeth grows as time reveals the destructive nature of his mind. That there is "no art/ To find the mind's construction in the face" and that only time can show that construction is part of the tragedy of this play. Duncan, therefore, is the good king at one end of the play just as Malcolm is the good king at the other end of the play; the first has had his reign interrupted, and the second may have his reign interrupted, because in the nature of things some men succumb totally to the temptations of the devil.

MALCOLM   Malcolm is the man who will be the ideal king, and thus he represents all that Macbeth as king is not. Malcolm uses deception only in a time of turmoil, when the values of fair and foul are confused. His deception, as he tells Macduff in IV.iii, is "modest wisdom" and therefore not to be used indiscriminately. When he feignedly denies his possession of the "king-becoming graces," he shows his understanding that these virtues in a king will bring his land "the sweet milk of concord." And when he finally confesses that he has been practicing a deception on Macduff and asserts an unspotted personal integrity, we realize that he does have the "king-becoming graces"; and that his behavior is meant to symbolize what a man in his position should do; and that when he becomes king he will rule with the "king-becoming graces" for the purpose of bringing his land "the sweet milk of concord." That he will in fact return Scotland to "wholesome days" is shown at the end both by his expressed intention and his usage of the imagery of time and growth.

LADY MACDUFF   Lady Macduff is a good woman who loves her husband and her family. When her husband flees Scotland without a word to her, she does not know what to think. Macduff seems to behave as the traitor he is accused of being. Yet, although she accuses him of not loving his family and of being traitor, the prattling tone she uses with her son indicates that she does not quite believe what she says. Rather, her one scene indicates distress and confusion, not certainty of Macduff's motives. But all confusion is dispersed, of course, when the Murderers enter. She shows fierce loyalty to her husband and makes no attempt to save her own life at his expense. "Where is your husband?" demands one of the Murderers as he enters. "I hope in no place so unsanctified,/ Where such as thou may'st find him," replies Lady Macduff without a thought for her life. In her distress and confusion, in her tenderness for her son, in her fierce loyalty to her husband Lady Macduff symbolizes the good and innocent people who are mindlessly slaughtered by the tyrant Macbeth.

Merchant of Venice

Scene-by-Scene Summary and Comment

Act I: Scene i

The scene is a street in Venice. Antonio, a prominent merchant, is talking with his friends Salarino and Salanio. He tells them that he does not know why he is so sad nowadays, and that his sadness wearies him as much as it wearies them.

COMMENT: Antonio is the merchant of the title of the play. The state of depression or "want-wit sadness" which Antonio describes marks him at once as a typical pensive Renaissance man. His show of world-weariness is an inner condition brought about by the idealistic, spiritual, noble nature of the man himself; he has less use for the material realities of the world than for idealistic values he lives by. Antonio's depression is symptomatic of the melancholy man, one whose "humours" or bodily fluids consisted of a preponderance of black choler or black bile. In Medieval and Renaissance physiology, the body was believed to contain four chief fluids: blood, phlegm, choler, and black choler. A predominance of one of these fluids was believed to affect the mental disposition and consequently the behaviour of the man. The behavioral characteristics of the melancholy man were, in addition to an unaccountable gloom (such as Hamlet also displays), sullenness and irascibility. It will be seen shortly that Antonio manifests all these symptoms of the melancholy man. He is taciturn of speech and sullen among his friends; and that he is hot-tempered we may guess from his past treatment of Shylock.

Antonio's companions think that he must be worried about business, since he has several ships out on the ocean where anything might happen to them. Salanio tells Antonio, "Believe me, sir, had I such venture forth,/ The better part of my affections would/ Be with my hopes abroad." He says that he would be constantly plucking the grass to test the wind's direction, and peering into maps to chart the routes of his vessels. Salarino pursues this train of thought, declaring that he, for his part, would connect every part of his experience with the thought of possible dangers to his ships. Thus, his breath cooling his broth would make him worry about storms at sea; sand running through an hour glass would remind him that ships can founder on dangerous sandbars; and the stone walls of a church would make him think of the treacherous rocks in the sea.

COMMENT: In some editions, Salarino and Salanio are called Salerio and Solanio. Early quartos and folios of the play used various similar abbreviations to designate these characters, and some modern editors attempt to clear up the confusion in names by adopting new forms for them.

Salarino describes the process of associating ideas, a tendency frequently found in Shakespeare himself by Caroline Spurgeon in *Shakespeare's Imagery*. Shakespeare repeatedly called up whole groups or chains of ideas by a single word or idea which acted as an emotional or mental stimulus. The meaning of an idea-chain is sometimes clearer in one context than in another and can be used to throw light on some of the obscure passages in Shakespeare. The character's emotional persuasions are often revealed by the explication of an idea-chain, as shall be seen.

Antonio denies that he is melancholy because of business. Not all his fortune is invested at one time and, moreover all his capital is not entrusted in a single ship. It is hardly likely that several vessels will come to a bad end simultaneously. Salanio declares that if it is not business, it must be love that troubles Antonio, but the merchant denies any romantic attachment. With this explanation ruled out, Salanio falls back on the inexplicable ways of Nature, who has made some strange fellows in her time. The best he can say is that Antonio is sad because he is not merry, which, of course, is not to say anything at all.

COMMENT: Salarino and Salanio speak in rich poetry that evokes the wealth and splendor of Venice. Salarino refers to Antonio's ships as "argosies with portly sail," and compares them to the Venetians he knows, "signiors and rich burghers." Their stately sails tower above their petty competitors, past whom they fly "with woven wings." Antonio's ships are engaged in trade with the exotic Orient, and therefore, when Salarino thinks of a shipwreck he naturally thinks of the loss of precious spices and silks. All in all, Venice seems to be a marvelously glamorous world, where familiarity with the beautiful and the exotic breeds a general gaiety and elegance. Antonio's melancholy puts him at one remove from this Venetian world, but we will see in the rest of the scene how he makes up in nobility of soul for want of sprightliness.

Three more gentlemen enter, Bassanio, Lorenzo, and Gratiano. Salarino and Salanio leave the newcomers to cheer up Antonio if they can, but before they depart they assure Bassanio that they will be delighted to make merry in his company whenever he is available. When they have gone, Gratiano remarks that Antonio is not looking well, and chides the merchant for worrying too much about worldly matters. Antonio denies this charge, declaring, "I hold the world but as the world, Gratiano/ A stage where every man must play a part, /And mine a sad one." Gratiano replies that he, for his part, prefers to play the role of the fool, always gay and laughing. He says that he would rather have his liver heated with wine than his heart cold as the marble on a tomb. (Sixteenth-century psychology held that the liver as well as the heart played a part in emotional life.) From this remark about his own predisposition, Gratiano goes on to criticize those men who keep up an appearance of gravity and silence in order to impress the world with their profundity, as if he thought that Antonio were only pretending to be melancholy.

Lorenzo declares that by associating with the loquacious Gratiano he is afraid he will gain the reputation of the kind of false wise man of whom Gratiano was speaking, for he can never get a word in edgewise as long as Gratiano is around. While Gratiano accepts this rebuke with good humor, Antonio promises to make an effort to talk more. The comical Gratiano is happy to hear this, declaring that silence is only commendable in a dried ox's tail and in an unmarriageable girl.

Lorenzo and Gratiano depart, promising to meet Bassanio for supper. When they have gone, Bassanio declares that "Gratiano speaks an infinite deal of nothing, more than any man in all Venice." His reasons are as obscure as two grains of wheat hid in two bushels of chaff, and worth just as little.

COMMENT: Antonio's explanation that he holds "the world but as the world" is another key to his character. The Renaissance gentleman was schooled in neo-Platonic ideas and adopted the position that the world was only a testing place for the soul of man. Far more important than the world of reality or the material world was the world of the spirit to which the pure soul aspired during its sojourn on earth and to which the soul departed after death. Antonio's promise to talk more in the future reveals another of his aspects as a melancholy man, one who is sullen among his friends.

Gratiano, a fool, is offered as a contrast to the grave and silent wise man whom Antonio represents. That Bassanio recognizes Gratiano's absurdity and still remains his friend is a sign of the former's noble spirit. Associations of this kind were thought to be commendable because the gentleman could instruct the fool on how to mend his ways. By setting a good example, Bassanio does just this for Gratiano.

Antonio asks Bassanio to tell him now, as he promised he would, about that lady "To whom you swore a secret pilgrimage." Instead of answering directly, Bassanio talks about the state of his own finances. He reminds Antonio that because he squandered his fortune and lived beyond his means in his youth, he is now heavily in debt, and chiefly to Antonio, his friend and kinsman. Bassanio is deeply distressed at being unable to repay this debt, but now he has an idea of how to win a new fortune. Antonio begs to know how he may be of service to Bassanio and assures him that "My purse, my person, my extremest means / Lie all unlocked to your occasions."

COMMENT: Antonio in this play represents the principle of noble friendship. His offer to Bassanio of his purse, person, and means is the first of a line of acts which mark him as the ideal friend, one who is willing to set aside his Christian scruples to negotiate a loan for his friend, and who is even willing to die in supporting the cause of his friend.

The Renaissance ideal of the perfect friend developed first in the neo-Platonic schools of Italy and was perfected in the narrative *Il Cortegiano (The Courtier)* by Baldassare Castiglione. Published in Italian in 1528, the book was subsequently translated into English by Thomas Hoby and published in 1561 and 1588. It served to fix a standard of manners, not entirely new to England, in which courtesy was based on a beautiful purity of heart and was regarded as a manifestation of the highest good.

The perfect gentleman (or courtier) was a passionate friend, for "that high degree of friendship," Castiglione wrote, "ministereth unto us all the goodness contained in our life. . . . I would have our courtier, therefore, to find him out an especial and hearty friend, if it were possible. . . ." Antonio's friendship is combined with other noble characteristics, as we shall see, all of which add up to a portrait of Antonio as a perfect Renaissance gentleman.

Bassanio hesitates to divulge his plan. By way of introduction he tells Antonio how, when he was a boy, he often lost an arrow by carelessly shooting it without looking to see which way it went. When this happened, he sometimes managed to retrieve the arrow by firing another after it in the same direction, but this time keeping careful watch on its flight. In any case, if he did not find the first arrow, at least he did not lose the second. Turning to the matter at hand, he tells Antonio, " I owe you much, and like a willful youth / That which I owe is lost; but if you please / To shoot another arrow that self way / Which you did shoot the first, I do not doubt, / As I will watch the aim, or to find both / Or bring your latter hazard back again / And thankfully rest debtor for the first."

Antonio chides his friend for this elaborate preparation and tells Bassanio that there is nothing he would not do for him. Thus encouraged, Bassanio reverts to the subject of the lady, which is how their conversation started. He tells Antonio that "In Belmont is a lady richly left;/ And she is fair, and fairer than that word,/ Of wondrous virtues." This lady is Portia, whom Bassanio met some time ago in Belmont and from whose eyes he received "fair speechless messages" that she would not be averse to his suit. Like the Portia of Ancient Rome (daughter of Cato and wife of Brutus), she is an extraordinary woman. Suitors flock to her from all over the world, just as the mythological heroes sought the Golden Fleece. (In Greek mythology the Golden Fleece on the island of Colchis was a precious object for which many men went in quest. Jason finally obtained it after overcoming great danger.) Bassanio tells Antonio that he is sure that if he had the means to return to Belmont he, like Jason, would win the prize so many men seek.

Antonio immediately agrees to help his friend, but, with several ships at sea, he does not have the necessary cash on hand. He therefore asks Bassanio to find someone who will lend the money on the basis of Antonio's.

COMMENT: Antonio and Bassanio are alike in many ways. Both show the virtues and characteristics of the Renaissance gentleman who engages in perfect friendship. Antonio is apparently older than Bassanio since he has been able to lend his friend money in his youth, and he is certainly at this point a more melancholy soul than the gregarious and romantic Bassanio. Like the speaker in Shakespeare's famous sonnet series to a young friend, Antonio appears to idolize Bassanio and shows that he is capable of the extraordinarily devoted and selfless friendship of an older man. Bassanio, still in his prime, is interested in the lady of Belmont whom he describes as a perfect Renaissance lady.

The interests of the two friends are readily explained by the precepts of love described in Castiglione's Courtier. Neo-Platonic Christian philosophy of the Renaissance recognized three stages of love in man. The first and most youthful level was sensual love, a manifestation of youthful appetite, which if directed toward a virtuous lady informed the youth of the nature of love and prepared him for the second stage of development. In the second stage, Reason prevailed and manifested itself in friendship and in the decline of youthful appetite. The third and final stage of love pertained to the Understanding and could only be found among angels in the world of the spirit.

Bassanio is clearly at the first stage of development, and Antonio at the second. His interest in promoting Bassanio's suit with the lady of Belmont would be to direct his friend in the course by which perfect love eventually could be achieved.

In the course of their conversation, we learn about Portia for the first time in the play. The conversation works as a preparation for the following scene in which Portia appears personally. She is both fair and wondrously virtuous and is sought by suitors from all over the Mediterranean world. But first of all, she is a lady "richly left," an heiress of great wealth. Bassanio's interest in the lady's fortune has disturbed critics who are ill-informed about Renaissance social history. Bassanio is simply acting in accordance with the humanist code of behavior (of the sort drawn up by Castiglione in The Courtier), which expected a person of a given rank, education, appearance, and sex to conduct himself in accordance with the rules drawn up for his class. Bassanio is the descendant of a noble Venetian family, and in his schooldays displayed that "certain Recklessness" or nonchalance about money which was the hallmark of gentle birth. Now that he has ended that stage of his youth, it is incumbent upon him to marry a lady appropriate to his class, to restore the fortune he has squandered, and to repay his old debts. It is to Bassanio's credit, therefore, and in accordance with "nature," that he take an interest in Portia's wealth and be concerned over his debt to Antonio.

SUMMARY: The first scene of the first act prepares us for what is to follow. We meet most of the main characters of the play and hear about one other, Portia. We learn the following important things:

1. Antonio is a rich merchant who has many ships embarked on trading ventures on the seas. He is marked at once as a melancholy man, a "humorous" type who is expected to follow a line of behavior already familiar to the Elizabethan audience. He is a reflective man, given to a few words, a devoted friend, an idealist, and one who cares little for the material things of this world. He is also quick to anger (as we shall soon learn) and staunch in his submissiveness to melancholy (and later, to misfortune).

2. Salarino and Salanio's speeches serve to explicate the character of Antonio and to establish the atmosphere of Venice as an opulent city, thriving on commerce.

3. The loquacious Gratiano shows a rather crude and ready wit. What he says appears to be nonsense, but is actually extremely informative satire of the types of mankind. He calls himself a fool and serves as contrast to the much wiser Antonio whom he warns against appearing as a pseudo-wise man.

4. Lorenzo says very little, suggesting that he is a worthy gentlemen. (Garrulous types are obviously comic characters.) He too is contrasted by Gratiano. We shall see more of him later.

5. Bassanio's character is established in connection with Antonio and Portia. He is the worthy object of Antonio's devotion in that, having squandered his fortune and fallen into debt, he is now ready to make amends for his earlier profligacy by forming an alliance with a lady of virtue and wealth through whom his own character and fortune will be improved.

6. The plot is put into motion in this scene. We learn that Bassanio wants to go to Belmont to woo the rich, beautiful, and virtuous Portia, and that Antonio agrees to borrow money to finance his trip to Belmont. The major action of the play will revolve around (1) Bassanio's wooing of Portia and (2) Antonio's borrowing money for his friend from a cruel usurer.

Act I: Scene ii

The scene is Belmont. Portia and her waiting woman, Nerissa, are talking. "By my troth, Nerissa, my little body is aweary of this great world," sighs Portia, but Nerissa, instead of commiserating with her mistress, declares that Portia's unhappiness can only be the result of an overabundance of good fortune. It is a fact, she says, that superfluity can be as oppressive as insufficiency: "they are as sick that surfeit with too much as they that starve with nothing." The ideal in all things is the mean between two extremes. Portia approves of these "Good sentences and well pronounced," but regrets that it is easier to give good advice than to follow it. I can easier teach twenty what were good to be done," she declares, "than to be one of the twenty to follow mine own teaching. The brain may devise laws for the blood, but a hot temper leaps o'er a cold decree." The knowledge that one *ought* to be happy is never the same as actually *being* happy, which Portia says she is not. And the reason that she is not happy becomes clear when she adds that all this talk will not serve to choose her a husband. After all, she sighs, it is not up to her to choose a husband for herself. According to her father's instructions laid down just before he died, suitors for her hand must choose which of three caskets contains her picture. Portia finds it hard to bear that she is "curbed by the will of a dead father," that she may neither accept nor refuse any man on the basis of her own inclination, but Nerissa consoles her with the assurance that dying men often have good inspirations. She tells Portia that her father must have devised the lottery in such a way that only a man truly worthy of her would be able to choose correctly.

COMMENT: Portia is the first lady among Shakespeare's great heroines, one of his "characters of intellect," as Mrs. Jameson called her in *Shakespeare Heroines* (1833). She is a woman of wit, imagination, intelligence, humor, resourcefulness, sensibility, and compassion, a perfect Renaissance lady. In her first scene, we learn that she is "aweary of this great world," which immediately associates her with Antonio, who is so sad that "it wearies me." (I.i). We may understand this weariness to mean that Portia is also a reflective person who values spiritual things above others. Unlike Antonio, however, the source of her disturbance lies in her recognition of her own powers of reasoning, which she feels enable her to choose her own husband, and her virtuous desire to remain obedient to her dead father's wish that her husband be selected by the means he has devised. She learns as the play progresses the wisdom of her father's commandment.

Nerissa is a confidente-servant, a popular type in Renaissance literature. She is companion or lady-in-waiting to Portia and acts as a foil to the heroine of the play. She plays the realist to Portia's idealist, and is bright and witty in the same way but not to the same degree as her mistress. She plays an amusing part in advancing the comic theme of servants who imitate their masters.

Nerissa questions Portia about her feelings towards the numerous suitors who have already presented themselves in Belmont and, while she acknowledges that "it is a sin to be a mocker," Portia takes the opportunity to poke fun at them one by one. First there is the Neapolitan prince, who talks of nothing but his horse and of his own expertise in shoeing him. Portia gaily wonders if perhaps "my lady his mother played false with a smith." Next there is the County (Count) Palatine, whose particular characteristic is a perpetual frown. Since he never smiles now in his youth, Portia concludes that he will undoubtedly be "the weeping philosopher when he grows old." She declares she would rather be married to "a death's head with a bone in his mouth than to either of these."

The Neapolitan and the Palatine are Italian noblemen. The next four suitors are French, English, Scottish, and German. Of the Frenchman Portia declares, I know God made him, and therefore let him pass for a man," but she thinks he has no character at all, for he changes mood and behavior from minute to minute. As for the Englishman, Portia cannot really judge, because he knows neither Latin, French, nor Italian (all of which, presumably, she does know), and she has only a smattering of English. Consequently, they cannot carry on any sort of conversation. His appearance, however, she finds decidely peculiar, for he looks as if he bought his coat in Italy, his breeches in France, his hat in Germany, and "his behavior everywhere." The

Scottish lord is not worth much comment. Portia merely remarks mockingly that he seems to be generous, for when the Englishman gave him a box on the ear he swore he would pay him back. Finally, as for the German, Portia makes fun of his love of drink, but declares she dislikes him as much in the morning, when he is sober, as in the evening, when he is drunk."

COMMENT: It is interesting to note that this scene is in prose rather than in poetry. As a general rule, the characters involved in the main action of a Shakespearean play speak in blank verse (unrhymed iambic pentameter), while the characters of the comic subplot speak in prose. In all her other appearances in the play, Portia speaks in blank verse, but in this scene she engages in satire, drawing verbal caricatures of her suitors, although she knows "it is a sin to be a mocker." Thus, she speaks prose, the language deemed most suitable for satire and comedy, according to Renaissance practice.

Portia's suitors come from all over the world, for her fame has spread throughout Europe, and this gives Shakespeare a chance to poke fun at some national weakspots. Thus, the French suitor is flighty, the German is a drunkard, and the Scotsman is subject to the Englishman. As for the English lord, he is mocked for knowing no foreign languages and for his motley attire. These caricatures, incidentally, are microcosmic prose essays of the sort which were popularized by the "character-writers" early in the seventeenth century. Similar comic national types appeared with some frequency in the comic or antimasque sections of court masques produced during the reigns of King James and Charles.

When Portia has run through the list, Nerissa comforts her with the news that she need not fear marrying any of these gentlemen, who have all decided to return home rather than risk the condition imposed by her father's will on all her suitors. (This condition, we will later learn, is that before he may choose among the caskets, each suitor must swear that if he chooses wrongly he will never seek to marry another woman.) Portia is delighted to hear this, and says. "There is not one among them but I dote on his very absence."

Nerissa asks if Portia remembers one man in particular, "a Venetian, a scholar, and a soldier," who came to visit during her father's lifetime. This man, declares the maid, seemed more deserving than any other of winning a fair lady. Portia does indeed remember him; his name is Bassanio, and he did seem worthy of all praise. At this moment a messenger enters with news that the current batch of suitors is departing and that the Prince of Morocco will arrive shortly as a new suitor. The lady of Belmont wishes she could feel as happy to see the new suitor arrive as she is glad to see the old ones leave.

COMMENT: Portia's criticism of her suitors is both witty and astute. She is too intelligent and well-educated to enjoy the company of humorless men or men with limited interests. Bassanio, on the other hand, is "a Venetian, a scholar, and a soldier." He is the perfect gentleman, in short, and as Nerissa tells us, he is worthy of a fair lady. This description of Bassanio is reminiscent of another admirable hero, which Shakespeare created some years later. Hamlet, the noble Prince of Denmark, had "the courtier's, soldier's, scholar's eye, tongue, sword." (III.i.159), we may recall. The tendency in Shakespeare to associate chains of words and ideas makes it fairly certain that Bassanio, like Hamlet later, was intended as the perfect gentleman.

As a scholar, Bassanio can be expected to use language with great wit, to pun and jest ironically with the best of them (Portia). As a soldier, of course, he has been brave and bold, skilled in the use of weapons, physically alert, admirable in every way in the eyes of the fair lady of the Renaissance ideal. Other courteous traits are implied in Nerissa's description of Bassanio. He will be a passionate friend, a humble suppliant, and a totally dedicated lover. He can be counted on to "hazard all" and choose the leaden casket.

SUMMARY: This scene is important for the following reasons:

1. We meet Portia, and begin to appreciate her fine qualities. She is not very happy in her present position, waiting for one of her numerous suitors to choose correctly among the caskets in order to marry her, but in the meantime she makes the best of her wit by satirizing her suitors.

2. Nerissa, Portia's maid, is also very clever, but her part is decidedly subordinate to that of the mistress. Nerissa's chief function in the drama is being the foil against which Portia's character, particularly her wit, is revealed.

3. In Portia's prose descriptions of her suitors, Shakespeare satirizes the outstanding national foibles of England, France, Germany, and Scotland.

4. We learn that Portia remembers Bassanio very well and with very fond memories. Nerissa agrees with her that he is the kind of man whose suit would be acceptable.

5. The Prince of Morocco is on his way to try his luck. We will see in the next act how well he fares.

Act I: Scene iii

The scene is back in Venice. Bassanio has found Shylock, a Jewish moneylender, and is seeking to borrow three thousand ducats for three months, for which Antonio will be bound. As Bassanio tells him the sum of money required and the length of time. Shylock repeats the words in a noncommittal fashion: "Three thousand ducats, well . . . For three months, well . . . Antonio shall become bound, well." Pressed for a decision by Bassanio, who is becoming impatient, the moneylender finally says, "Antonio is a good man." Bassanio, evidently thinking that Shylock uses the word "good" in its moral sense, asks indignantly if he has heard anything to the contrary about his friend, but Shylock assures him that by "good" he simply meant that Antonio has good credit. However, continues Shylock, Antonio is not a very safe risk, since his fortune is bound up in commercial ventures at sea, which is not entirely safe, for "ships are but boards, sailors but men; there be land rats and water rats, water thieves and land thieves—I mean pirates" (pun on pie rats). On the whole, however, Shylock decides that Antonio is sufficient, but he insists on speaking to the merchant himself.

COMMENT: Shylock is one of the most fascinating and one of the most controversial characters in Shakespeare. Critics at one extreme have argued that Shakespeare intended Shylock as the stereotype of the infidel Jews, and a complete villain. Critics at the other extreme contend that Shylock is a tragic figure, more sinned against than sinning. In this scene we are introduced to him for the first time, and we must watch carefully what he says and how he says it in order to decide what sort of person he really is.

Perhaps, the first thing we notice about Shylock is that he was probably costumed like the conventional comic Jew in earlier morality plays, in which Judas Iscariot, the betrayer of Christ and the most debased of villains, appeared in a red beard, red wig, long nose, and "gaberdine," and was immediately identified by his stereotyped attire. Shylock considers Bassanio's request with slow deliberation, repeating everything that Bassanio says as if stalling for time to weigh the pros and cons within himself. Shylock evidently keeps abreast of the business affairs of the principal merchants of Venice, for he already knows how many ships Antonio has at sea and what their destinations are. He is wary and pragmatic. Thus, when he uses the word "good," his meaning is entirely financial, whereas for Bassanio, whose orientation is neo-Platonic and Christian, the word "good" is primarily a moral category. Another important difference between these two men is their manner of speech. Shylock's repetition of certain words and phrases is partly comic and partly ominous, as is his warning about land rats and water rats. In the light of future developments regarding Antonio's ships, his forebodings are particularly significant. On the whole, in this opening discussion, Shylock appears as a highly cautious and suspicious individual, which the Elizabethan imagined a Jew to be.

Bassanio invites Shylock to meet Antonio at dinner, a suggestion that Shylock takes very badly. "Yes," he says sarcastically, "to smell pork, to eat of the habitation which your prophet the Nazarite conjured the devil into." He declares that he will do business with Christians, walk with them, talk with them, but he refuses to eat with them, drink with them, or pray with them.

COMMENT: The Elizabethan audience had already identified Shylock as the comic Jew of the play by the costume he wore. It was prepared to enjoy jokes at the expense of this character, who, as in Marlowe's well-known *The Jew of Malta*, was a moneylender or usurer, an occupation held only by Jews. It was amusing to Shakespeare's audiences that Shylock only thinks of "goodness" in terms of worldly goods; it was part of the Christian stereotype of the Jew to see him this way. The stereotype is continued in a jest on Jewish dietary law forbidding the consumption of "unclean" meat, which was the subject of vulgar amusement in Christian art and legend throughout the Middle Ages and Renaissance. Shylock displays the scorn of Christian doctrine attributed to the Jews by sarcastically referring to "your prophet the Nazarite" (Matthew 2:23) and to Jesus' exorcism of the devils, which possessed the two demoniacs, by transferring them to a herd of swine, which he then drove into the sea (Matthew 8:28-33). That Shylock refers to Christ by one of his *New Testament* sobriquets is a sign of the Jew's refusal to acknowledge Jesus as the Christ (Messiah, the Lord's anointed). His rejection of Bassanio's dinner invitation is couched in terms of the anti-Christ.

Bassanio's invitation is meant as a friendly gesture, and Shylock's reply (if heard by Bassanio) is hostile and discourteous. One editor of the play suggests that Shylock's remarks about pork and his reference to "your prophet" were probably spoken in an aside (a speech which is intended only for the audience's hearing). In any case, the speech reveals Shylock's hostility toward the Christian world, for he assumes that Bassanio intends to flout his religious traditions.

Just at this moment along comes Antonio himself, and Shylock, noticing him out of the corner of his eye, expresses in an aside that merchant looks like a "fawning publican." "I hate him for he is a Christian; / But more, for that in low simplicity / He lends out money gratis and brings down / The rate of usance here with us in Venice. / If I can catch him once upon the hip, / I will feed fat the ancient grudge I bear him." Shylock goes on to say that Antonio "hates our sacred nation," and concludes, "Cursed be my tribe / If I forgive him."

COMMENT: Shylock's aside continues the unflattering portrait of the Jewish usurer as a greedy, rapacious, revengeful, and proud man. Antonio's humility, his resemblance to a "fawning publican" (Luke 18:10-14), enrages Shylock. In fact, he hates Antonio because he practices Christian generosity and humanity, lends money without interest (see Matthew 5:42), and competes with the professional usurers of Venice. The themes of pride vs. humility, hate vs. love, thrift vs. usury, are introduced at this point.

Other recurrent themes suggested in this speech by Shylock are mercy, revenge, and cannibalism. Shylock plans to take revenge against Antonio if he can "catch him one upon the hip," that is, if he can get him at his mercy, and he swears by his tribe that he will not forgive Antonio for denouncing him to the merchants of Venice. Shylock also promises to "feed fat the ancient grudge," suggesting for the first of many times in this play, the disgusting connotation of cannibalism. (Charges that Jews practiced ritual murder and drank the blood of Christians during their religious ceremonies and that they desecrated the wafer — the body of Christ—for the same purpose, were regularly made during the Middle Ages.)

The hatred and desire for revenge which Shylock reveals, and the humility and Christian idealism which Shylock correctly attributes to Antonio, have their counterparts in medieval and Renaissance Christian doctrine. Pauline Christianity, which formed the basis of this doctrine, ignored the evolution of Hellenist-Judaism from hide-bound literalism to the more spiritual form of worship which anticipated Jesus' teachings and formed the basis of Jesus' precepts. Thus, the God of the *Old Testament* was commonly viewed as a vengeful God who had demanded "eye for eye, tooth for tooth, hand for hand, foot for foot" (Exodus 21:24), while the God of the *New Testament* was seen as a merciful one: "Ye have heard that it hath been said, An eye for an eye, and a tooth for a tooth: But I say unto you, That ye resist not evil: but whosoever shall smite thee on they right cheek, turn to him the other also" (Matthew 5:38-9). Shylock here represents the spirit of the *Old Testament*, while Antonio represents the spirit of the New; they symbolize the doctrines of hate vs. love, revenge vs. forgiveness, usury vs. charity.

While speaking to the audience in an aside, Shylock pretends that he has not seen Antonio but has been thinking about how he can raise the necessary sum of money. He looks up from his reverie and says that, although he does not have the ready cash, his friend Tubal can supply the rest, so there will be no problem. Suddenly he notices Antonio (who has been standing there for several minutes) and greets him in sycophantic terms, addressing him as "Your worship," and saying, "Rest you fair, good signior./ Your worship was the last man in our mouths."

COMMENT: Shylock's last line continues the idea of cannibalism, which had begun in his aside and which suggests that his thoughts are inhuman and evil. Shylock's ability to dissemble his feelings is amply demonstrated in his gracious reception of Antonio, whom he has just been vilifying. We must keep in mind this hypocrisy when we hear Shylock tell Antonio and Bassanio later in this scene that he wants to be friends with them. Shylock's hypocrisy carries on the theme of anti-Judaism (see Matthew 23:28) and is related to the theme of deceptive appearances, which forms the crux of the romantic plot, the choosing of the caskets.

Antonio does not beat around the bush with Shylock but goes directly to the point. Although as a rule he neither lends nor borrows money at interest, he is ready to break his custom in this case in order to help a friend. Shylock justifies his financial practices by citing the story from the Book of Genesis (30:31-43) in the Bible of how Jacob dealt with his uncle Laban. It was agreed between the two men that when Laban's flocks gave birth, Jacob would take as his wages all the multicolored lambs, leaving the solid colored lambs for Laban. While the rams and ewes were mating, however, Jacob used a special magic device to make sure that all the lambs would be spotted and speckled, and in this way he got the best of the bargain. Shylock approves of Jacob's apparent cunning, and declares, "This was a way to thrive, and he was blest;/ And thrift is blessing if men steal it not." Antonio declares that it was beyond Jacob's power to determine the color of lambs before conception, and that their complexion was the work of God, not man. He does not see that this story will justify the practice of usury, and Shylock answers simply that he can make money breed as fast as rams and ewes (which is comic). Antonio remarks to Bassanio apropos of this discussion that "The devil can cite Scripture for his purpose," for Shylock hides his villainous deeds behind the holy words of the Bible, whose meaning he distorts. "O, what a goodly outside falsehood hath!" Antonio observes.

COMMENT: What Shakespeare fails to include in Shylock's story of Jacob and Laban is that Laban deceived and cheated Jacob first by removing all the speckled kine from the flock before Jacob could collect them. The Jewish meaning of this analogy between Laban, Jacob and the usurer is that Christians, like Laban, restricted Jews from ordinary means of earning a living (relegating many of them to the business of usury and despising them for conducting this business on a profitable basis), but the usurer, like Jacob, has foiled his Christian deceivers. Antonio points out that Jacob's profits were achieved by the means of God's intervention and were blessed rewards for years of honest labor as Laban's shepherd. He feels that Shylock, by putting his money to work for him and by charging interest for loans, profits from another man's need, not from his own labor. Jewish and Christian interpretations of the Scriptures differed then, as now, and Antonio's comment about the devil citing Scripture expresses the Christian view of Jewish biblical interpreters. The theme of deceptive appearances in Antonio's last remark applies to Shylock's alleged misuse of the Bible.

Shakespeare also engages in a play on word "kind," using it with different meanings during this scene. The word-play is calculated to associate Shylock with carnality, and Antonio and Bassanio with generosity.

Shylock describes ewes and rams (creatures Shakespeare usually associated with lust) as "doing the deed of kind" ("deed of nature," that is, "breeding"), and he thinks of money as a thing capable of breeding or multiplying. Later in the scene, Shylock will offer "kind" (apparently "generosity," but with lustful connotations), and Bassanio will be suspicious of Shylock's offer.

Returning to the matter at hand, Antonio asks Shylock, who has been computing the rate of interest, whether or not he will supply the money. For answer Shylock complains in a long and bitter speech about the hostile and contemptuous way that Antonio has long treated him in public. "In the Rialto you have rated me . . . you call me misbeliever, cutthroat dog, / And spit upon my Jewish gaberdine, / And all for use of that which is mine own." After such words and such treatment, says Shylock, is there any reason why he should be courteous and obliging? "Hath a dog money?" Shylock asks. Is it not too ironical for him to whisper humbly, "Fair sir, you spit on me on Wednesday last, / You spurned me such a day, another time / You called me dog; and for these courtesies / I'll lend you thus much moneys?"

Antonio replies that he is just as likely to call Shylock dog again and to spurn him again. He tells the moneylender that although he holds Antonio as an enemy, Shylock may still lend him money for his own profit. Friends do not charge interest (which Antonio calls "a breed for barren metal"). It is better to lend money at interest to an enemy, in any case, for then one may exact the penalty later with "better face."

COMMENT: In computing his interest "rate," Shylock is reminded of how Antonio "rated" (berated) him in the marketplace. Shakespeare once again shows (see Salarino's speech in I.i) how any word or idea may serve as a reminder of an emotional or mental preoccupation which has been momentarily forgotten.

Shylock is obsessed by Antonio's vilifications, which, ironically, he calls "courtesies." Four times in a single speech, he repeats Antonio's dog-epithet. Dog was a common Christian metaphor for Jew, and Antonio's abuse is not an unusual one in his world. Shylock's explanation of his hatred, however, is a unique expression; the Jew in earlier literature was never given such an opportunity to state his grievances. In view of Antonio's abuses, it is small wonder that Romantic and subjective critics decide that Shylock was more sinned against than sinning, and it is no surprise that Shakespeare idolaters refuse to believe the great Bard could have approved of Antonio's cruelty to the moneylender.

Antonio's character has been called into question by Shylock's description of his abuses. Antonio admits that he has humiliated the Jew and that he will do it again. But this is not inconsistent with his character as a perfect Renaissance gentleman, which included, among other virtues, devotion to the Christian faith and scorn for "misbelievers." In addition, Antonio is a melancholy man, and it should not be forgotten that his nature had an irascible side too.

The play on "kind" and 'breed" is continued in Antonio's metaphor for "interest," the unnatural profit extracted from "barren metal," which by nature is incapable of breeding. Antonio's argument that money lent to an enemy may be exacted with "better face" is another statement of the theme of hypocricy or deceptive appearances. To Antonio, it is hypocrisy to charge interest and still claim friendship.

After Antonio's outburst Shylock suddenly changes his tone, and declares that he wants to be friends with Antonio, to forget the past, and to supply the three thousand ducats at no interest. "This is kind I offer." Bassanio, suspicious, exclaims "This were kindness," and Shylock goes on to explain that all they need to do is accompany him to a notary to sign a bond "in merry sport" that if Antonio does not repay three thousand ducats in three months he will forfeit a pound of flesh, to be cut off and taken from what part of his body pleases Shylock. Antonio agrees to sign such a bond, "And say there is much kindness in the Jew," but Bassanio is appalled at the proposed condition. Antonio reassures him that the bond will not be forfeited, since his ships will certainly return well before three months with three times the value of the bond. Shylock declares that the bond is just a kind of joke, since he could make no profit from a pound of human flesh, as he would from a pound of mutton or beef or goat flesh. These Christians, he says, suspect the intentions of others because of their own hard hearts. He insists that he is doing this as a favor and in friendship, and says, "for my love I pray you wrong me not." These words settle the matter for Antonio. They agree to meet at the notary's, where Antonio will give instruction for the bond to be drawn up. Shylock returns home to get the money and to check up on his household left in the care of his servant, "an unthrifty knave." When the Jew has left, Antonio cheerfully tells Bassanio, "The Hebrew will turn Christian; he grows kind," but Bassanio, who distrusts Shylock, answers, "I like not fair terms and a villain's mind." Antonio, however, certain that his ships will come home a month before the bond is due, refuses to be dismayed.

COMMENT: The theme of deceptive appearances is augmented by dramatic ambiguity of these last speeches created by Shakespeare's skillfully ironic use of words with double meanings. There is very little doubt, however, about Shakespeare's intentions. Exigencies of the plot and theme, combined with Renaissance Christian values, point to a single plausible interpretation of this section of the scene.

Shylock offers "kind," a word which suggests "generosity and friendship," but which also suggests "engendering in nature." The sort of engendering the Jew is supposed to believe in, however, is the unnatural breeding of gold and silver. By association of ideas, Shylock is an unnatural man (one who interpreted Scriptures with the devil's tongue and one who has already been linked with carnality). Bassanio is suspicious of Shylock's offer of "kind" and rephrases the offer by substituting the conditional verb "were" for Shylock's "is" and a less ambiguous form of the word "kind," that is "kindness." Bassanio means, in effect: Yes, Shylock, your offer would be a kindness if the "kind" you speak of were Christian "kindness." I fear, however, that you are using the word in its carnal sense, for Jews are a fleshly race and have no idea of the spirit of the word which means "generosity." Shylock confirms Bassanio's suspicion when he demonstrates the "kindness" he has in mind; it is the offer of the flesh-bond. Shylock's next speech is full of fleshly imagery: "man's flesh," "flesh of muttons, beef, or goats." The theme of cannibalism or carnality is repeated over and over again, even as Shylock chastises Christians (not just Bassanio) for their suspicious natures.

Antonio is surprised to find "kindness" (generosity and, perhaps, nature) in a Jew, but he is willing to accept it as possible, partly because he is extremely anxious to help his friend Bassanio and partly because, like other Christians of his age, he is still hopeful that "the Hebrew will turn Christian." It is clear the Shylock uses the words "kind" and "kindness" ironically, that he expects the Christians to believe he means "generosity" when he actually has in mind a carnal and cannibalistic transaction involving the flesh-bond.

Bassanio has picked up Shylock's reference to his servant as an "unthrifty knave." We shall see shortly that Bassanio interprets Shylock's "unthrifty" as "Christian generosity" and regards Shylock's ill favor as a good recommendation for Launcelot.

The theme of deceptive appearances is once more asserted in Bassanio's interpretation of Shylock and his offer as "fair terms and a villain's mind," and this may be taken as an instance of dramatic foreshadowing, a device frequently found in Shakespeare, by which subsequent events of the plot are anticipated.

SUMMARY: This scene is extremely important for the following reasons:

1. The plot is advanced when we meet Shylock, the Jewish usurer from whom Bassanio borrows three thousands ducats with a pound of Antonio's flesh as security.

2. The *Old* and *New Testament*, Jewish vs. Christian dispute, which underscores both plots in the play, is introduced in the debate between Shylock and Antonio over the interpretation of Jacob's wand.

3. The characterization of Shylock is presented along the lines of the Renaissance stereotype of the Jew as a "dog," a usurer, an anti-Christ, and a revengeful, hateful, hypocritical, carnal, and cannibalistic "devil."

4. The friendship theme is advanced in the generous behavior of Antonio and Bassanio to each other.

Act II: Scene i

Back in Belmont, the Prince of Morocco (described in the stage direction as a "tawny Moor all in white") is pressing his suit to Portia. He explains that his skin is dark because of the climate of his country and hopes that she will not object to him on that account. The blood that runs in his veins, he assures her, is redder than that of "the fairest creatures northward born," and the most beautiful ladies of Morocco are in love with him. Therefore, he would not change the color of his skin except in order to win Portia's favor.

Portia, for her part, declares that she is bound to abide by her father's order regarding the caskets irrespective of her inclinations. However, she tells him that if the choice were hers to make she would not be led by superficial matters of appearance, and that he would be as likely a choice as any suitor who has yet come to Belmont.

COMMENT: The aspect of the tawny Moor in his flowing white robes appealed to the Elizabethan's interest in exotic places and manners, but it also appealed to their sense of humor. Elizabethans did not distinguish between Negroes and Moors; both were regarded as members of strange barbaric races not far removed from savagery, cannibalism, and carnality, which the red blood symbolizes. Their complexion was both feared and abhorred, and marriage between a Moor and a Christian lady was regarded as unnatural and impossible. If he chooses correctly, however,

Portia will marry the Moor in spite of his appearance, for his correct choice would prove his inner worth. But that this Moor should sue for Portia's hand is a completely ridiculous notion and is characteristic of his shallow, presumptuous, and boastful disposition. The Moor lacks the humility and spiritual sensibilty to choose wisely.

Portia finds the Prince extremely distasteful, although she seems to treat him with courtesy, for her discourteous retort is covered by a witty irony, which the thick-headed Moor is unable to comprehend. Elizabethans shared Portia's distaste for Moors and applauded her ironically witty assurance to Morocco that she likes him as well as her previous suitors, which means not at all.

The theme of deceptive appearances runs through the scene and is expressed, for example, in Portia's assurance to the Moor that she is not led solely by "nice direction of a maiden's eyes."

The Prince thanks her for these words and says he is ready to be led to the caskets to make his choice. He only wishes that his fortune depended on his courage rather than on mere luck (it depends on neither), for he swears that in order to win Portia he would stare down the sternest eyes, outbrave the most daring heart, steal cubs from a she-bear, or mock an angry lion (yet he refuses to hazard the leaden box). He brags about having slain the Shah of Persia as well as a Persian prince and about having won three victories over the Sultan Solyman. However, the fact remains that he must take his chance with the caskets, and before doing so, he must go to the temple to swear that if he chooses wrongly, he will never again ask a lady to marry him. The Prince, Portia, and the others go off to the temple.

COMMENT: Oaths in the temple were expressly forbidden in Christian doctrine (Matthew 5:33-37), and Shylock's oath "by our holy Sabbath" is treated as a religious mockery. Yet Portia is party to Morocco's swearing.

SUMMARY: This brief scene is interesting and important for the following reasons:

1. The romantic plot of the caskets is advanced, and an interlude of high-comedy is provided as a gentle contrast to the iniquitous flesh-bond scene.

2. We are amused by the subtle and witty caricature of the Prince of Morocco which acts as a contrast to the grotesquely satirical portrait of Shylock the Jew.

3. We are given further evidence of Portia's wit, courtesy, and filial obedience as she equivocates with the Moor, obscures her distaste for him, yet admits she will marry him if he chooses the correct casket.

Act II: Scene ii

The scene is Venice once again, Launcelot Gobbo (the servant whom Shylock, in Act One, Scene Three, called an "unthrifty knave"), enters alone. He is debating with himself whether or not to run away from his master, whom he cannot abide. On the one hand the devil tempts him to leave Shylock, and on the other hand his conscience bids him remain. "Well, my conscience says, 'Launcelot, budge not.' 'Budge,' says the fiend. 'Budge not,' says my conscience." The irony of the situation, says Launcelot, is that conscience counsels him to remain with the Jew, who is a kind of devil, whereas the devil himself bids him run from the Jew. After thinking it over, he decides that "The fiend gives the more friendly counsel. I will run, fiend; my heels are at your commandment; I will run."

COMMENT: Launcelot Gobbo is the low-comedy clown in this scene, a type well-known in Italian *commedia*, where he was probably played as a hunchback or dwarf. (The name Gobbo is Italian for "crook't-backed," according to John Florio's Italian-English vocabulary of 1598). Renaissance audience found unnatural and misshapen creatures amusing in themselves, but the humor of physical appearance was only one of the kinds found in low-burlesque. Parody was another. Launcelot's opening speech is a mock debate of the kind frequently found in old morality plays in which a misguided Christian, through examination of his conscience, finds his way back to the straight and narrow path.

Launcelot's reasoning is confused and digressive, but it ultimately brings him to the realization that since the Jew is "a kind of devil" (the word "kind again, meaning "sort" and by nature"), he should not serve him, although conscience ordinarily requires a man to give loyal service to his master. Instead, he will give in to the fiend (who counsels servants to be disloyal to their masters) and leave the Jew's service. Launcelot thinks he is serving the fiend by leaving the "devil," a thought which confuses him and amuses us.

Among his digressions is the first of Launcelot's allusions to illegitimacy; he calls himself "an honest man's son," then ludicrously qualifies his remmark; he is not so sure. Another source of humor in Launcelot's character is his tendency to mispronounce and misuse words. He speaks of Shylock as the devil's "incarnation," meaning "incarnate." for example. He is also the simple-minded victim of superstition and is terrified of demons, for a camparison of which, see Marlowe's scene between the clown and Wagner in *Doctor Faustus*.

At this moment of resolution, Old Gobbo, Launcelot's father, enters, coming from far away to see his son after a long time. Because he is almost totally blind, Gobbo does not recognize his son, and asks him for directions to Shylock's house. The playful Launcelot decides to have some fun with the old man for a while and gives him confusing direction which will cause him to turn and turn and turn. When the old man asks if Launcelot lives there, his son asks if he means "Master Launcelot," but Gobbo says Launcelot is "No master, sir, but a poor man's son." The clown insists they are talking of "Master Launcelot," and the old man maintains it is plain and simple Launcelot. Finally his son says that Master Launcelot is dead. Gobbo is stunned by this piece of news; he says that the boy was the prop and staff of his old age, which causes Launcelot to query the audience, "Do I look like a cudgel?"

COMMENT: In this highly comic exchange between father and son, several kinds of humor are employed. The dialogue as a whole is a parody of the classical recognition scene, in which long lost relatives were reunited in the most improbable ways. Lancelot, who has already demonstrated reasoning prowess of a fool, decides to try "confusion," using a malapropism for "conclusions" (an exercise in logic), with his father, and repeatedly abuses the word "ergo" (Latin for "therefore"). Jokes about pedantry in logic were common stock in Renaissance comedy. Launcelot's confusing directions to his father include instructions to "turn" ("take the devious route to evil" especially, "to commit adultery") (I.iii.79-80; III.iv, 78-80) again and again, suggesting for the second time his father's promiscuous habits. The quibble over whether or not to call Launcelot "Master" is intended to expose the pig-headed literalness and pedantry of the simple old man, a country rustic (usually identified by a broad hat, cloak, and basket), and is a comic digression from Launcelot's jest, to make the old man cry, to "raise the waters" (with a probable pun on "urine").

At this point Lancelot decides to reveal his true identity. For a while he has a hard time convincing Gobbo, who cannot believe that this young man is really his son. However, Launcelot insists, "I am Launcelot—your boy that was, your son that is, and your child that shall be," and then he wins his point, for old Gobbo acknowledges him as his much-changed son with "what a beard thou got." He tells Launcelot that he has brought a present for Shylock, but the clown objects. "Give him a present?" he asks indignantly. Better "Give him a halter! I am famished in his service." Launcelot tells his father that he is determined to leave Shylock's service and to seek employment with Bassanio, who gives wonderful new liveries to his servants. He asks his father to give the present to Bassanio, whose service he wants to enter (for he is anxious to leave the Jew before he becomes one himself). Just at this moment, as luck would have it, along comes Bassanio in person.

COMMENT: After several further jests on the theme of illegitimacy Launcelot succeeds in convincing old Gobbo that he is his son. The old man fondles the youth's beard, remarking how greatly he has matured. Traditionally, the lines are accompanied by a farcical twist. Old Gobbo is made to stroke Launcelot's head as the youth kneels for his blessing.

Launcelot's description of his treatment by Shylock continues the stereotype of the Jew as an ungenerous and greedy miser who starves his servants. Launcelot's desire to leave Shylock before he becomes a Jew himself means that, as servants always imitate the manners of their masters, Launcelot will soon adopt the thrifty, ungenerous manners of the Jew. Servants' imitations of their masters were a popular comic theme in Shakespeare's plays (see Shallow and Davy in *2 Henry IV*) and are echoed in the behavior of Gratiano and Nerissa.

Bassanio enters, accompanied by servants. He asks one of them to make sure that supper will be ready by five o'clock, to do some other errands, and to fetch Gratiano, for Bassanio is preparing to sail for Belmont shortly. Launcelot urges his father to go up to Bassanio to request a position for his son. They approach Bassanio, but every time that old Gobbo starts to speak his son interrupts him to explain the situation in his own way. In this fashion and using a number of malapropisms, the two men talk and talk, but Bassanio can make nothing of their meaning. Old Gobbo gives him the present originally intended for Shylock (a dish of doves), and when Bassanio finally understands the nature of the request, he readily agrees to take Launcelot into his service, for Shylock (who had called Launcelot an "unthrifty knave") had unwittingly recommended his servant. Launcelot, for his part, states his preference for working with a Christian who had "the grace of God," rather than the Jew who simply has "enough" (in terms of worldly goods). Bassanio tells the clown to bid his old master farewell and orders that he be given a suit of livery more highly decorated than those of the other servants.

Launcelot is greatly pleased with his success. Looking at the palm of his hand, he pretends to read there a very satisfactory future for himself. Here's a small trifle of wives! Alas, fifteen wives is nothing; a 'leven widows and nine maids is a small coming-in for one man. And then to scape drowning thrice." In great glee he goes off with his father to take leave of Shylock.

COMMENT: The comedy again consists of the ridiculous mistakes in language and logic which Launcelot and his father make, and in the continued ridicule of Shylock as the stereotyped miserly Jew. Launcelot's complaints against his master prepare us for the dramatic presentation of the unbearable life led in the household of the close-fisted and puritanical usurer.

Bassanio's willingness to hire Launcelot on the basis of Shylock's displeasure with his servant is a key to Bassanio's attitude toward Jews. He does not believe anything Shylock says and considers it a mark of virtue for Launcelot to be in Shylock's disfavor.

After entering Bassanio's service, Launcelot, the rustic clown who misuses words, becomes a coarse duplication of his gentle and witty masters; he is then called a "wit-snapper," a sophisticated fool with "an army of good words" (III.v).

Bassanio gives some final orders to a servant named Leonardo concerning a feast that he will give tonight for his best friends. As Leonardo goes off, Gratiano appears and announces that he has a request. Without the least hesitation and without knowing what the request may be, Bassanio immediately replies, "You have obtained it." Gratiano then explains that he wants to go along to Belmont. Bassanio agrees, but asks his friend to moderate "with some cold drops of modesty" his "skipping spirit," lest his wild behavior give the wrong impression in Belmont of Bassanio's character. Gratiano readily agrees to put on a sober and pious expression and to act with utmost decorum. For this night, however, it is agreed that he will put on his "boldest suit of mirth," for there will be great merriment among the friends who will visit Bassanio at suppertime.

COMMENT: Although it is unstated, Gratiano would like to travel with Bassanio because he cannot bear to be parted from his esteemed friend, whose every move he wishes to imitate. Gratiano is a kind of gentleman fool, who parallels the servant-fool Launcelot in seeking Bassanio's company. When Bassanio marries Portia, Gratiano marries her maid, and when Bassanio gives his ring to the disguised judge, Gratiano gives his to the judge's clerk. Humor is provided by the imitative nature of fools and servants, and the Christian moral implicit in this comic theme is: a gentle master makes a gentle servant and an evil master makes devils of his followers. Gratiano, through Bassanio's gentle influence, curbs his loud ways to some extent. It is significant, however, that Gratiano can only emulate the surface of Bassanio's character; he cannot acquire its inner spirit (see Act IV).

As an ideal gentleman, Bassiano is unstintingly generous and obliging to his friends, and just as Antonio had granted his request for a loan, even before he had stated the nature of his request, so Bassanio grants Gratiano's suit without knowing what it is. This open-handed generosity and complete devotion to the ideal of friendship are designed as a sharp contrast to Shylock's mean spirit.

Gratiano's promised show of sobriety is really also an amusing caricature of the religous hyprocrite or puritan and implies that too many people—even those in Belmont—may judge a man by the appearance of his friend. In fact, Nerissa does just this later in the play, while the high-minded Portia wisely waits to see Gratiano's lord.

SUMMARY: This comic scene is amusing in itself, it also helps to move the plot along, and advances the themes of friendship and deceptive appearances.

1. Launcelot and Old Gobbo are introduced in this scene. The former will appear several times again.

2. Bassanio's suspicions about Shylock's generosity are confirmed by his hiring of Launcelot and his willingness to take Gratiano to Belmont.

3. The stereotype of Shylock as a miserly Jew is continued by Launcelot, and a caricature of a hypocritical or puritanical type is rendered by Gratiano.

4. The comic theme of servants who imitate their masters is introduced by Launcelot's defection to Bassanio and Gratiano's request to join Bassanio on his trip. It is underscored by the moral implication that servants and friends who are morally weak benefit from the guidance of noble Christian masters and friends.

Act II: Scene iii

Launcelot has come to Shylock's house to say goodbye to his former master. Jessica, the Jew's daughter, is there alone. She is very sorry that he is leaving, "Our house is hell," she declares, "and thou a merry devil / Didst rob it of some taste of tediousness," In parting she gives him a ducat and asks him to deliver a letter secretly to Lorenzo, who will be at Bassanio's house. Launcelot tearfully parts with her, calling her "most beautiful pagan, most sweet Jew!" He already suspects that a Christian (Lorenzo) has won her heart.

Launcelot leaves and Jessica, left alone, wonders what "heinous sin" it is that she is ashamed to be her father's child. Although she is his daughter by blood, she is completely alien to his way. She is secretly engaged to Lorenzo and, thinking of him, she swears aloud, "if thou keep promise, I shall end this strife, Become a Christian and thy loving wife!"

COMMENT: This brief scene introduces the beautiful and wistful Jessica. Her perfect spirit is displayed in her ability to recognize the "hell" of her Jewish household, to enjoy the jesting of Launcelot, whom she calls a "merry devil," and to love Lorenzo, a Christian.

She shares Launcelot's desire for mirth, but more than that, she shares his conflicting loyalties between conscience and the fiend, She is apparently torn by the desire to leave her father's house and go with Lorenzo and the desire to follow her conscience, which tells her that filial disloyalty is a "heinous sin." The same moral conflict which received comic treatment in Launcelot's opening scene is given pathos here when uttered by the disaffected "pagan" Jessica.

Filial loyalty, another moral theme in the play, has already been introduced by Portia, who has been made melancholy by her obligation to obey her father's will. The theme receives further examination in the plight of Jessica. The reasoning may seem obscure to the modern mind, but in Shakespeare's thought it was conceivable that Jessica could betray her Jewish father and still remain a pillar of virtue, while the Christian Portia, as a sign of her virtue, must remain firm in the performance of a daughter's duty. Symbolically, Jessica seeks release from the damnation of the Jews and looks for salvation in Christianity. From this theological point of view, Jessica's "betrayal" of Shylock is really an act of Christian virtue and faith; her obedience to a heavenly Father supercedes the necessity to obey her father in the flesh.

Act II: Scene iv

Lorenzo, Gratiano, Salarino, and Salanio are making plans for the evening's masque. Gratiano complains that they have not made good preparation, and Salanio declares that it is better not to have any masque at all unless it is "Quaintly ordered." Lorenzo assures his friends that two hours are sufficient time for them to find torchbearers.

Launcelot arrives with Jessica's letter for Lorenzo, who immediately recognizes the fair handwriting. The clown is on his way to "bid my old master the Jew to sup to-night with my new master the Christian." (We already know that Bassanio plans to feast all his best acquaintance this evening.) Lorenzo gives Launcelot some money and asks him to assure Jessica that he will come by on time, for she is to be his torchbearer in disguise this evening.

Salarino and Salanio exit with Launcelot. Lorenzo, left alone with Gratiano, reveals the plan for his elopement with Jessica that night. Jessica has a page's suit in which she will dress up, and she will take with her gold and jewels from her father's house when she leaves. "If e'er the Jew her father come to heaven, / It will be for his gentle daughter's sake."

COMMENT: This brief scene moves the action of the play along and engages an interest in the subplot, which concerns Jessica's elopement with Lorenzo.

The masque planned for the evening's entertainment was a semi-dramatic spectacle of ancient origin in which music was a major element. The participants donned disguises and rode or marched in procession to their destination and there performed dances, songs, or pantomines, usually of and allegorical nature. Masques "after the manner of Italy" became especially popular in the court of Henry VIII and remained in vogue until Milton's time. Besides suggesting the contemporary manners of Italy, the masque planned in *The Merchant* (but never carried out) has a special value for the sub-plot in that Jessica can conveniently disguise as a page in order to elope with Lorenzo.

A number of loose ends in *The Merchant* suggest that it was a revision of an earlier play. The masque incident may have appeared in an early version, and we may imagine the comic interlude that might have been developed with Jessica carrying a torch at the dinner that her father Shylock attended.

Lorenzo's character is expanded in this brief scene. Already presented as a quiet man, he is seen here as a devoted and courtly lover, who can turn a figure in praise of his lady in the conventional and accepted phrases of Renaissance romance poetry. Jessica's hand is whiter than the paper on which her note is written, and she is the "gentle" (with a pun on "gentile") daughter of the Jew, who may yet win a place for her father in heaven (from which all Jews are banned).

Act II, Scene v

Launcelot has found Shylock just about to enter his house. The Jew warns his former servant that in Bassanio's service "Thou shalt not gormandize / As thou hast done with me," nor sleep and snore all day long. While saying this he has been calling his daughter, but when Launcelot comically echoes Shylock's call for Jessica, Shylock reproves him. "Who bids thee call? I do not bid thee call." And Launcelot remembers that Shylock always told him not to do anything without bidding.

Jessica enters and Shylock gives her his keys, saying that he is going out for supper. He broods about going. "I am not bid for love — they flatter me —/ And yet I'll go in hate to feed upon / The prodigal Christian." He is vaguely uneasy and counsels his daughter to "Look to my house," for last night he dreamt of money-bags, which he superstitiously construes as a bad omen.

Launcelot urges Shylock to go to the dinner. "My young master doth expect your reproach," he says (mistaking the word "reproach" for "approach"). Shylock answers, "So do I his," (meaning "reproach" in its true sense. Parodying Shylock's omen, Launcelot prophesies that there will be a masque, which does not please Shylock at all. He bids Jessica to shut up all the casements of the house when she hears the drum and the "wry-necked fife," and not to look upon "Christian fools with varnished faces." He tells her, "Let not the sound of shallow fopp'ry enter / My sober house." Launcelot leaves, whispering cryptically to Jessica to be on the lookout for a Christian "worth a Jew's eye," that is, Lorenzo. Shylock doesn't catch what he says but asks his daughter, "What says that fool of Hagar's offspring" (that is, outcast), and she replies that he merely had said farewell. Her father declares that Launcelot is kind enough but that he eats too much and sleeps by day, which makes him an unprofitable sort of servant. Shylock is glad that the clown will now help to waste Bassanio's money. Before he departs, Shylock sends Jessica inside and bids her lock the doors: "Fast bind, fast find—/ A proverb never stale in thrifty mind."

COMMENT: Shylock shows that his hatred has confused his thinking. In his first speech he warns Launcelot that he will get little to eat in Bassanio's house. A few moments later, he calls Bassanio a "prodigal Christian," that is, a spendthrift and waster. Indeed, Launcelot need not expect to "gormandize" in the house of a Christian gentleman who would value moderation in all things (as Portia does); at the same time, he may expect generous treatment, which is not the same thing as "wasteful." Shylock cannot understand the behavior of Christian gentlemen at all.

Launcelot, characteristically, provides more comedy in this scene at the expense of the Jew. First he echoes Shylock's call for Jessica, although he knows that his former master does not like him to act unbidden. (The echo carries on the comic theme of imitative servants, and Shylock's chiding suggests that Launcelot cannot learn the Jew's ways.) Then, when Shylock forecasts trouble, superstitiously interpreting his dream of moneybags as an ill-omen, Launcelot parodies his former master in a nonsensical interpretation of a nosebleed (believed to be a bad omen) as a prediction of a masque. He seems to misuse words consciously in this scene, puns wittily on the worth of a Christian, and generally demonstrates a change of character since his transference to Bassanio's service. Whereas in former scenes he plays a rustic clown, in this scene he appears to be a knowing fool whose superficial nonsense is really a cover for astute observation.

Shylock's character is augmented along the usual lines of the stereotyped Jew. Now we learn that, symbolically, Shylock thinks of his daughter in terms of money, for the ill omen is of her elopement as well as her theft, while the prophetic dream is only of money. This idea will be developed further on in the play and is designed to suggest that Jews do not have natural family ties, that they breed money, not children. His loss of Jessica will not be tragic in this play, and the loss of his money will provide for a comic portrait of the Jew foiled.

Shakespeare had a tendency to portray his villains as puritanical types (see Prince John in 2 Henry IV and Iago in Othello). Possibly he was objecting to the Puritan movement then rising in England. Shylock is no exception. He hates masques and music and regards the disguised or costumed Christians who participate in such activities as "fools with varnished faces." His objection to music is significant, in this entirely derogatory portrait of Shylock, for it signifies that his soul is damned. Speaking from a Christian point of view (Act V), Lorenzo later says, "That man that hath no music in himself, / Nor is not moved with concord of sweet sound, / Is fit for treasons, stratagems, and spoils; / The motions of his spirit are as dull as night, / And his affections dark as Erebus. / Let no such man be trusted." Shylock is just such a man.

Elements of Shylock's character, introduced earlier in the play, are also continued in this scene. He swears "By Jacob's staff," which Jacob had used to breed speckled ewes and rams, and which is a symbol of usury or interest to Shylock. He decides to "go in hate, to feed upon / The prodigal Christian," using a phrase which literally means "to dine at the expense of" but which has unpleasant connotations of "devour." He seems compelled to go "feasting" even when he has no mind to. Both these remarks suggest Shylock's carnality and cannibalism again. His miserliness is given added emphasis in Shylock's ironic parting words: "Fast bind, fast find—."

Jessica is seen briefly once more, this time at home in her "hell," which consists of locked doors and closed casements, sober silence within, while the world outside rejoices. Her deception of her father, already suggested, is demonstrated dramatically when she lies about Launcelot's message from Lorenzo.

Act II: Scene vi

Gratiano and Salarino, disguised for the masque, are waiting for Lorenzo in front of Shylock's house. Gratiano marvels that Lorenzo is so late for a love rendezvous since lovers usually "run before the clock." But Salarino reflects that lovers hasten more when they make a promise than when they must keep it. Gratiano agrees, supporting his thought with the proverbial ideas that the man who sits down eagerly to a feast rises satiated; the horse that first races down a path returns wearily, and the ship that sets out gaily decked like a prodigal son returns again weather-beaten and "beggared by the strumpet wind." Cynically, Gratiano concludes, "All things that are / Are with more spirit chased than enjoyed."

At this moment, Lorenzo appears, apologizing for having been detained by business. He calls up to the window where Jessica appears, dressed in boy's clothing. She recognizes his voice but makes him identify himself anyway. He declares he is "Lorenzo and thy love," and she replies that he is her love, indeed, but is she his? Lorenzo reassures her. Jessica gives Lorenzo the casket she has stolen from her father and expresses embarrassment at being seen in boy's clothes. She objects to bearing Lorenzo's torch, for it will light her shames. Lorenzo assures her that no one will guess her true identity under her boy's disguise. When Jessica leaves the window to collect some more ducats, Gratiano praises her as "a gentile and no Jew," and Lorenzo swears he will love her in his "constant soul," for she is wise and fair and true. Jessica reappears on the street below, and they all exit.

COMMENT: The elopement of Jessica and Lorenzo is a typical device of romantic literature of the Renaissance. The nocturnal tryst, the presence of assisting friends, the wearing of disguises, are all or partly found in other Shakespearean plays (*Romeo and Juliet, Twelfth Night, Othello*). The nocturnal escape provides an appropriate romantic setting for the simple, lyrical, and beautiful love of Lorenzo and the lovely Jessica. Even Gratiano, who has just indulged in a string of cynical metaphors about lovers who are quick to surfeit, is so charmed by her aspect (appearances, again) that he refuses to accept her as a Jew and puns on her "gentile" nature.

Jessica's embarrassment at wearing boys' clothing was a comic twist in the Elizabethan production of the play where all female parts were played by male actors. It was a stage convention derived from Italian comedy that the disguised individual is never detected by other characters in the play. Lorenzo's reassurance that Jessica's identity will remain well-hidden is a means of informing her and the audience of the fact. Since the discussion is relevant to a masque which is never held, it too appears to be a hangover from some earlier version of the play.

The romance of Lorenzo and Jessica operates as a parallel to the main action of the play, the romance of Bassanio and Portia. Jessica, like Portia, brings wealth to Lorenzo. Both ladies disguise as males; both are associated with caskets (Jessica gives a casket of stolen riches to Lorenzo and later Portia is won by the choosing of a casket); both ladies are "wise, fair, and true" and win the eternal love of their husbands in the "constant soul."

One of Jessica's endearing qualities is her sense of shame, suggesting both modesty and humility. She is ashamed of her "exchange," an ambiguous term which refers to her unnatural disguise as a boy and also to her unnatural behavior as a disloyal daughter. She is reluctant to hold up a candle to her "shames," a word which occurs in the plural and suggests that there is something besides the disguise that is troubling her. She finds that these shames "in themselves . . . are too too light," which is to say that her elopement, theft, and transvestism are improper, that deception comes too easily to her. At the same time, she paradoxically suggests that her shames are really an illumination, and that her entire life, actual and spiritual, will be (en)lightened by this shameful escape. For a better understanding of her dilemma, reread Launcelot's moral debate in II.ii where the clown is torn between obedience to the devil (Shylock) and to the fiend. By choosing to follow the "evil" counsel of the fiend, Launcelot actually improves his lot; by acting as a "shameful" daughter, Jessica is equally improved.

Antonio finds Gratiano and tells him that the masque has been called off, for the wind has changed and the voyagers must board the ship tonight. Gratiano says he is delighted to be able to leave at once.

SUMMARY: The scene is important for the following reasons:

1. The brief exchange of love pledges between Jessica and Lorenzo is hurried but convincing. Jessica is as charming as ever, modest about appearing in boys' attire and ashamed of having betrayed her father. These characterizations and the romantic subplot will be continued.

2. Gratiano's character as a gentleman fool is continued in his cynical reflections on the fickleness of lovers, which was a stock theme in the jests and jokes of the sixteenth century.

3. Preparation is made for a change of scene and action when Antonio announces that the masque has been called off because the wind has changed.

Act II: Scene vii

Back in Belmont, the Prince of Morocco is about to choose among the three caskets in the presence of Portia and others. The Prince looks over the inscriptions on each casket to determine which one contains Portia's picture. The lead casket reads, "Who chooseth me must give and hazard all he hath." This blunt warning does not appeal to the Prince, who will "hazard" for "fair advantages," not for mere lead. The inscription on the silver casket reads, "Who chooseth me shall get as much as he deserves." The Prince ponders this carefully: "weigh thy value with an even hand," he warns himself. "Rated" by his own "estimation," he deserves the lady by reason of his birth, breeding, fortune, and most of all by reason of the great love he bears her. Turning to the gold casket, however, he reads: "Who chooseth me shall gain what many men desire," and suddenly the puzzle seems very clear to him. What many men desire is the lady, for suitors undeterred by arduous voyages through the desert or over the ocean have come from all over the world to seek her. It would be sacrilege to put her picture in a lead or silver casket instead of a gold one. He recalls that in England there is a golden "coin" with the figure of an angel engraved on it. Here is an angel (Portia) lying on a golden bed (the casket). "Here I choose, and thrive I as I may."

Deciding to unlock the gold casket, the Prince is horrified to discover a picture of Death with a message written in his hollow eye: "All that glisters is not gold; / Often have you heard that told. / Many a man his life hath sold / But my outside to behold. / Gilded tombs do worms enfold." With a grieving heart the Prince takes a hasty leave of Portia, who is quite content to see the last of him, saying, "A gentle riddance . . . / Let all of his complexion choose me so."

COMMENT: The commercial talk of Venice is echoed in the Prince's speech. Terms like "hazard," "advantages," "value," "rated," "coin," and "thrive" suggest that Morocco thinks only of the material value of the caskets' metals and the advantages his choice might have to him. In his final decision, he is deceived by appearances.

The death's head with the message in its hollow eye is uncovered in its golden casket as a *memento mori*, a reminder of death, a favorite theme and image in sixteenth century European art and literature. The play reaches a moral apex in the disclosure of the message carried within the eye of the skull: "All that glisters is not gold . . ." This tense dramatic moment is well contrived to emphasize the theme of deceptive appearance, that there is a life beyond the one visible to man. The symbol of the death's head conveys a spiritual message to mankind, that the flesh dies while the soul lives forever. It is an exhortation to Christians to heed the dictates of their eternal souls which are too often subordinated to the demands of the flesh.

Morocco's association of the gold casket with an English coin called an "angel" and with the angelic Portia is a ludicrous and far-fetched piece of logic, intended to make the Prince appear ridiculous. Moreover, the Prince's eloquent language couched in hyperbole borders on bombast. The Prince is a caricature and is portrayed as the Elizabethan stereotype of the Moor, a presumptuous and boastful warrior who is ignorant of European Christian values and of the distaste with which Europeans view his coloring.

Portia is relieved that Morocco has failed to chose correctly and bids "gentle riddance" (courteous and Christian riddance) to the Mohammedan Prince, punning on the word "gentile" as Antonio and Gratiano had done in connection with Shylock and Jessica, the main Jews in the play. Portia makes it abundantly clear that she personally does not favor a husband of dark "complexion" when she says, "Let all of his complexion choose me so." The ambiguous term "complexion" meant both "coloring" and "disposition," and the Moorish Prince is ill-favored in both.

SUMMARY: This scene is important for the following reasons:

1. The plot device of the caskets is implemented in this scene. We watch the Prince of Morocco as he deliberates over them, making himself ridiculous, and building tension as he ponders his choice.

2. We learn details of the legends on the caskets, and the content of the golden first choice—a death's head—is disclosed.

3. We learn that Portia is glad that the dark Prince chooses falsely and hopes that no other suitors of his color and disposition will try for her hand.

4. We are beginning to see the wisdom of the lottery, which was designed to weed out false lovers, whose faith in the appearance of things and blindness to inner values make two of them unacceptable as a husband to the worthy Portia.

Act II: Scene viii

In Venice once again, Salanio and Salarino are talking about recent events, particularly Shylock's reaction to the news that his daughter has run off with Lorenzo and has taken with her money and jewels of great value. Salarino explains that since Bassanio sailed for Belmont the same night that Lorenzo and Jessica eloped, Shylock suspected that the lovers were aboard the same ship. He brought the Duke of Venice down to the dock to search for them. But by the time they arrived it was too late, the ship was already gone. Furthermore, Antonio was there and swore that the lovers were not aboard, and the Duke learned from another source that Lorenzo and Jessica had been seen together in a gondola. Salarino is certain that Lorenzo is not on Bassanio's ship.

Salanio declares, "I never heard a passion so confused, / So strange, outrageous, and so variable / As the dog Jew did utter in the streets: / 'My daughter! O my ducats! O my daughter! / Fled with a Christian: . . . And jewels—two stones, two rich and precious stones, /

Stol'n by my daughter! Justice! find the girl! / She hath the stones upon her. . . ." Salarino adds with enjoyment that all the boys of Venice now follow Shylock, "crying his stones, his daughter, and his ducats."

COMMENT: Shylock is made to seem completely ridiculous. His reactions to Jessica's elopement and theft are described from the point of view of Salanio and Salarino, one of whom calls him "dog," and the other of whom paints the Jew as a grotesque and unnatural parent who cares more for his money than his daughter. They find him an appropriate object for Christian ridicule and enjoy the fact that the deceived usurer is bawdily mocked by the boys who cry "stones" (1. gems, 2. testicles) after him. Shylock's ominous dream of moneybags has come true, and the common prejudice that a Jew is only concerned with his money is given full expression in this scene.

In addition to the stereotype of the Jew, Shylock in this scene is said to behave like the "deceived father," a stock comic character in Renaissance comedy, whose protests against a daughter's elopement were often dramatized for the amusement of a conditioned audience. Shylock in this second-hand account is both deceived father and deceived Jew, another stock character of Italian street farce, rolled into one ridiculous creation designed to arouse the scornful laughter of the Elizabethan audience. What is remarkable about this caricature is that Shakespeare had it narrated and did not choose to dramatize it. This refusal to dramatize stock jokes may be taken as a sign of the extreme sensibility of the playwright to the human character he had created in Shylock.

Salanio recalls Antonio's debt next, and ominously remarks that Antonio will be made to pay for Shylock's loss if he does not meet his bond on time. To which Salarino adds that he had been thinking of Antonio's bond only yesterday, while listening to a report of a Venetian ship that had foundered in the English Channel; he had hoped it was not Antonio's ship.

COMMENT: This is another instance of foreshadowing, the anticipation of subsequent events in the play. Shylock's motive for revenge against Antonio later on is partly explained by the loss of his daughter and money at this point in the play. Such a motive is not just, but Shylock is in a "passion so confused," it should be remembered.

The two men agree to be gentle in breaking the news of the sunken Venetian vessel to Antonio, for "a kinder gentleman treads not the earth." As proof of Antonio's kindness and generosity, Salarino describes Antonio's parting from his friend Bassanio. Bassanio had promised to return as quickly as possible, but Antonio had urged him not to hurry for his sake and not

to worry about the Jew's bond, Bassanio was to take all the time he needed in Belmont for the courtship and "fair ostents of love." Antonio had bidden his friend goodbye with tears in his eyes, at which Salanio declares, "I think he only loves the world for him." The two gentlemen go off to seek Antonio to cheer him as best they can.

COMMENT: As contrast to Shylock's "outrageous" and despicable behavior, labelled and described in the first half of this brief scene, Antonio's gentle, generous, and loyal character is described in the latter half with an accompanying anecdote proving his loyal friendship, which is a major theme in this play.

The juxtaposition of these two character sketches prepares the way for the conftontation of Antonio and Shylock, men of opposing natures and beliefs, in the famous trial scene of the play. The personality traits revealed here in the descriptive narratives will be dramatized and should be remembered at that point. The scene provides a caricature of Shylock and a character sketch of Antonio, in which the hate of one is opposed to the love of the other. The scene acts as a transition between events and serves to move the plot from one point to another, by relating details of the plot which are not dramatized. Suspense is created by the suggestion that one of Antonio's ships may be lost.

Act II: Scene ix

In Belmont once again, the Prince of Aragon has taken the oath and is coming to choose among the caskets. Nerissa draws the curtains that conceal the three caskets and, with a flourish of horns, Portia enters with the Prince. He promises never to reveal to anyone which casket he chose and, if he fails, never to woo another maid in marriage, and to leave Belmont immediately. Portia explains that all who seek her "worthless self" take the same oath.

Arragon, like Morocco, quickly passes over the lead casket, saying, "You shall look fairer ere I give or hazard." Then, turning to the gold casket, he reads the inscription: "Who chooseth me shall gain what many men desire." Here, pausing to consider what this may mean, he decides that the "many are the fool multitude that choose by show, / Not learning more than the fond eye doth teach." He refers to the martlet, a bird that builds its nest on the outer walls of buildings and foolishly imagines itself safe from danger there. He, for his part, will not be deceived by outward appearances like the "barbarous multitudes."

Turning then to the silver casket, he reads: "Who chooseth me shall get as much as he deserves," which strikes him as just and proper, for no one should be granted privileges and titles of which he is unworthy. Pondering over the business at hand, the Prince muses that if all estates and offices were obtained purely on the basis of merit, there would be many reversals of fortune in the ranks of men. "How many then should cover [wear a hat] that stand bare, / How many be commanded that command."

Deciding to pick the silver casket on the basis of his own merit, the Prince unlocks the casket only to find inside the portrait of a blinking idiot. "Did I deserve no more than a fool's head?" he laments: "Is that my prize? Are my deserts no better?" Portia explains that his error was in presuming to judge his own worth, which is only for others to do. Along with the picture of the idiot in the casket is a scroll, which reads in part, "Take what wife you will to bed, / I will ever be your head. So be gone; you are sped." The Prince exits with his followers, and Portia remarks that these fools think they are so smart when they choose, but in fact have only wit enough to lose; and Nerissa adds that the fate of man is not in his own hands: "Hanging and wiving go by destiny."

COMMENT: The choosing of the caskets by Arragon parallels but does not precisely duplicate the scene in which Morocco chooses. A number of details are added to those already known about the rules of the lottery —the unsuccessful lover may not reveal his choice, for example, and he must leave Portia and Belmont immediately. Since there are three secret messages enclosed in each casket, each scene of choosing brings with it the pleasure of disclosure. Note that the first two suitors are each princes of foreign powers and that neither of them are sound of judgment or worthy of marriage with Portia. A satirical barb is intended, no doubt, at the careless values of contemporary princes. Only a perfect Christian gentleman like Bassanio may have Portia, who displays her humility here by referring to herself as "my worthless self."

Arragon is unconsciously ironic when he refers to the "fool multitude that choose by show," for he will do the same. The "martlet" referred to is a foolish bird who builds its nest on the outer walls of buildings which only seem to be safe. The image of the martlet is associated elsewhere in Shakespeare with the theme of deceptive appearances (see Caroline Spurgeon's *Shakespeare's Imagery*). Despite his awareness that appearances are often deceptive, Arragon is fooled by his own pride. He imagines himself more than a "common spirit" or the "barbarous multitudes" (with an unconscious allusion to Morocco). The proud Spanish Prince is unable to reason correctly because he is blinded by a false notion of his own desires into choosing the fool's casket. The moral comment on his choice is graphically

illustrated by the portrait of a blinking idiot, a thorough fool, which he finds inside. The fool's head, like the death's head, was a significant and popular image in medieval and Renaissance satirical art. It symbolizes the folly of man who too often submitted to pride, the first of the deadly sins, forgetting that faith, not reason, is the only true wisdom for man.

A servant (whom Portia addresses as "my lord") enters to announce the arrival of a young Venetian, who precedes his lord with courteous messages and rich gifts. The servant, greatly impressed with the new arrival, says that he has never seen "So likely an ambassador of love. / A day in April never came so sweet / To show how costly summer was at hand, / As this fore-spurrer comes before his lord." Portia pretends to take the news lightly and teases the servant that the Venetian must be a relative of his since he praises him so lavishly, but Nerissa prays that the Venetian will turn out to be Bassanio.

COMMENT: Portia is evidently feeling light-hearted, for she playfully calls her servant "my lord." This servant has undoubtedly seen all the suitors who have come so far, but none has made the favorable impression that the Venetian envoy makes. The advance arrival must be Gratiano in his assumed refinement. We may be sure that Bassanio is not far behind. Notice that the servant has judged the suitor by the appearance of his ambassador and that he associates the visitor with true romance by describing him in terms of a sweet day in April.

SUMMARY: The scene is important for the following reasons:

1. The casket plot is advanced as the proud Prince of Arragon chooses the silver box and wins a fool's head as his prize.

2. The theme of deceptive appearances is sustained and enriched by the theme of foolish wisdom.

3. The correct choosing of the casket is prepared for by Portia's clue that the man with judgment of heart, not of wit, will win the prize, and by the servant's announcement of the arrival of a fair envoy (Gratiano).

Act III: Scene i

Salanio and Salarino are discussing Antonio's affairs again. The news on the Rialto (the Venetian marketplace) is that Antonio has lost a rich ship on the Goodwin Sands in the English Channel. Salarino (comparing Report to an Elizabethan gossip who drinks ale and discusses her personal affairs among her cronies, pretending that she regrets the death of her third husband) hopes that Report is as much a liar as the tavern crone. Once more he praises "good Antonio," "honest Antonio," and wishes he had words more worthy of Antonio's name, but Salarino cuts short the eulogy and learns that Salanio is convinced that Antonio has lost a ship. Catching sight of Shylock at this moment, Salarino crosses himself to protect the prayer he has just made for Antonio, for he imagines that the devil incarnate comes "in the likeness of a Jew."

COMMENT: Salarino's reference to "gossip Report" is important enough to warrant Salanio's extended development of her figure as an Elizabethan tavern crone. This homely conceit serves to emphasize the capricious and untrustworthy nature of Report (a personification of news both true and false, also called Rumour and Fame), for it will turn out later that Antonio's ships have not come to permanent harm at all and that the crone is a liar. The conceit of the crone provides us with a microcosmic view of contemporary Tudor life and recalls the type of female immortalized in Chaucer's Wife of Bath and in Skelton's Elinor Rummynge.

Salarino's belief that the Jew was the devil incarnate was common-place enough and is expressed earlier in the play by Launcelot Gobbo. It is a piece of comedy injected at this point to prepare for the arrival of Shylock.

Shylock enters and, catching sight of the two young men, accuses them of being involved in his daughter's elopement. Salarino readily admits that he knew of the plans, and Salanio declares that Shylock himself must have known that Jessica was likely to leave her "dam" (parent). Shylock swears that she is damned for it, but Salarino replies that she will be damned only if the devil (that is, Shylock) is her judge. Outraged at the thought of her disobedience, Shylock exclaims with indignation, "My own flesh and blood to rebel" at which Salarino taunts him as if Shylock meant by this phrase that he had lustful wishes. Shylock explains that he means that his daughter is his own flesh and blood, but Salarino insists that there is an even greater difference between Shylock and Jessica than there is between jet and ivory or between red and white wine.

COMMENT: Shylock is enraged at the men whom he correctly suspects of having abetted his daughter's elopement, but the two Christian gentlemen parry Shylock's charges with witty word-play and anti-Semitic allusions, which were always reliable for securing laughs. Shylock turns "dam" into "damn," playing on these words without any hesitation, but he is too hateful and ill-tempered to win any admiration for his skill with words.

Whatever justifications are to found for Shylock's grievance over the elopement of Jessica, they are countered by Salanio's sensible explanation that it is the nature of children to leave their parents when they are old enough and ready to do so. Shylock must have known this, Salanio says. As for Jessica's fleshkinship to the usurer, Salanio claims that she is literally and figuratively vastly different in flesh from the old Jewish devil. She is a "white Jew," so to speak, and is associated with ivory and white (Rhenish) wine, while Shylock is associated with jet and red wine. (We may compare the white-and-black or red, (that is, the good-and-evil symbols, at this point, with similar ones used in connection with the Mohammedan Prince of Morocco, who was so proud of his dark complexion and red blood.) Christians or "gentle" people are characteristically associated with white; Jews, Mohammedans, and other villains and fools are associated with black and red.

Salarino asks Shylock for news of Antonio's ship, and the usurer replies that the merchant is surely bankrupt. He warns that Antonio had better "look to his bond," for Shylock intends to get even with him for the past. "He was wont to call me usurer," says Shylock; "He was wont to lend money for a Christian cursy" (courtesy), but now Shylock intends to get revenge for the past. Salarino declares he cannot believe that Shylock would take a pound of flesh, which is not good for anything, but the Jew insists that he has every intention of doing just that.

In a long and passionate speech, Shylock declares that he will use the flesh "to bait fish withal" if nothing else. In short, it will feed his revenge, for Antonio has disgraced him, hindered his business, laughed at his losses, mocked at his gains, scorned his nation, thwarted his bargains, cooled his friends, and heated his enemies. "And what's his reason? I am a Jew. Hath not a Jew eyes? Hath not a Jew hands, organs, dimensions, senses, affections, passions? —fed with the same food, hurt with the same weapons, subject to the same diseases, healed by the same means, warmed and cooled by the same winter and summer as a Christian is? If you prick us, do we not bleed? If you tickle us, do we not laugh? If you poison us, do we not die? And if you wrong us, shall we not revenge? If we are like you in the rest, we will resemble you in that."

COMMENT: This is one of the most interesting speeches in the play and one of the most problematical. Modern historical critics like E. E. Stoll and John Palmer support the view that Shakespeare's audience would have laughed at Shylock's assertion that the Jew is essentially no different from anyone else. Many Elizabethans believed as Launcelot and Salarino do, that the Jew was the devil incarnate. Everything that Shylock says in his famous explanation of his motives elicited the scorn of the Renaissance Christian, who believed that hatred and revenge were inherent Jewish traits.

The carnal or cannibalistic motif is introduced at the start when Shylock says he will feed fish with Antonio's flesh or "feed my revenge." And Shylock's entire description of Jewish-Christian similarities is based strictly on fleshly resemblances. Both Jew and Christian have "hands, organs, dimensions, senses, affections, passions." They eat the same food, another carnal habit; they bleed in the same way, another manifestation of bodily or physical likeness. And so on. But there the resemblance ends.

In the flesh, Jew and Christian may be very much alike. In the spirit, in their ways and manners, they are entirely different. This is the whole point which Shylock (and the Romantic reader) misses, which our Christian playwright thought a Jew would miss, and which the Christian audience believed constituted the essential and irrefutable difference. Shylock is totally lacking in gentle (and gentile) ways. He repays humiliation with revenge, not Christian "humility" (charity). He hates his enemy whom Christians are taught to love; he does not understand the "quality of mercy," we hear later, or any of the precepts in the Sermon on the Mount, which was interpreted by Christians as an overthrow, rather than an outgrowth, of Judaic law. Anti-Semitism which began with *New Testament* charges against the Pharisees was embedded in the Christian mind. The Pharisees' literal adherence to the fleshly laws of the *Old Testament* and their ignorance of the spirit of the law were major concerns of Jesus himself. Antonio *does* hate Shylock because he is a Jew, and Shylock accurately answers his own question on this matter: "What's his reason? I am a Jew."

Shakespeare's applause need not be based on the false notion of his futuristic tolerance of members of different races and religions, as Romantic critics once felt. Ridiculous black Moroccans and devilish Jews made good theater in Shakespeare's day, and they were designed within the prejudiced frame of reference of Elizabethan times. What is meritorious in the creation of Shylock, who could be seen in no other way by the Renaissance man, is that every aspect of this devilish incarnation is explored, and a serious attempt, which goes far beyond conventional vice comedy, is made to explain his malicious *raison d'etre*.

Comic characterization in Shakespeare's day meant the creation of a figure who embodied the vices as Renaissance Christians knew them. But Shakespeare went a step further than other writers of his time. He probed into the nature of villainy itself. He mixed the comedy of vice with the examination of evil, a much more awesome thing, and achieved strangely mixed comic creations that are neither completely ridiculous nor totally terrifying, but have in them the power to move the pity of modern audiences whose moral values are much more flexible than were the Elizabethans'. Shakespeare's comic characterizations often have an ambiguity that is difficult to comprehend and invites thoughtful probing.

One of Antonio's servants comes seeking Salanio and Salarino, who leave with him just after Tubal, another Jew and Shylock's friend, arrives, but not before Salanio has associated Tubal also with the devil. Shylock eagerly asks his friend, who has just come from Genoa, whether he found Jessica there. Tubal answers that he often heard of her but was unable to find her. Shylock moans, "Why there, there, there, there! A diamond gone cost me two thousand ducats in Frankford! The curse never fell upon our nation till now; I never felt it till now. Two thousand ducats in that, and other precious, precious jewels. I would my daughter were dead at my foot, and the jewels in her ear! Would she were hearsed at my foot and the ducats in her coffin!"

COMMENT: Shakespeare makes it appear that Shylock's chief concern is the recovery of the money and jewels that his daughter has stolen. This would prove, indeed, that Shylock was an unnatural and selfish man. Shylock's wish for Jessica's death may be a Christian interpretation of the Jewish tradition of preferring death to conversion, or to the custom of mourning as dead a Jewish man or woman who converts or marries a Christian, a custom which, in Elizabethan eyes would appear cruel or monstrous.

As if it were not enough to have Jessica steal his money, Shylock now bewails the loss of still more money spent in the search for her, "and no satisfaction, no revenge! Nor no ill luck stirring but what lights o' my shoulders, no sighs but o' my breathing, no tears but o' my shedding." Tubal reminds him that this is not really true. Antonio, for instance, has had a ship wrecked coming from Tripolis. Shylock pounces greedily on this news: "What, what, what? Ill luck, ill luck?", and then, "I thank God, I thank God! Is it true? Is it true?" Tubal assures him that he heard the news from one of the sailors in Genoa, and he adds that he also heard that Jessica spent eighty ducats in one night in Genoa. Miserable once again, Shylock exclaims: "Thou stick'st a dagger in me. I shall never see my gold again." Returning to the subject of Antonio. Tubal says that he met several of Antonio's creditors who are convinced that the merchant must be bankrupt. This information cheers Shylock again: "I am very glad of it. I'll plague him. I'll torture him. I am glad of it." Back to the subject of Jessica, Tubal remarks that he saw a ring that Jessica gave for a monkey, and Shylock, horrified, laments, "It was my turquoise; I had it of Leah when I was a bachelor. I would not have given it for a wilderness of monkeys." Tubal reminds him again that Antonio is certainly undone, and Shylock, determined to have vengeance, bids Tubal provide for an officer to arrest Antonio when the bond falls due. "I will have the heart of him if he forfeit, for were he out of Venice I can make what merchandise I will. Go, Tubal, and meet me at our synagogue; go, good Tubal; at our synagogue, Tubal."

COMMENT: Shylock is definitely a comic as well as sinister character in this scene. The theme of vengeance runs throughout his speeches, but he remains essentially comic because of his rapid shift in mood from despair to elation and back again, according to whether he thinks about his lost money or about Antonio's ill luck. As usual, Shylock repeats words and phrases over and over again, which adds to the comic effect.

SUMMARY: This scene is important for the following reasons:

1. We see the contemptuous way in which Salarino and Salanio treat Shylock, and we hear him tell them as well as Tubal of his absolute determination to have his bond from Antonio if his payment is late.

2. This scene contains the very famous speech by Shylock in which he insists that Jews are just as susceptible to physical suffering as Christians. Protesting Antonio's discrimination against him because of his religion, he says that Jews have learned from Christians how to seek revenge.

3. We learn that Antonio may have lost another ship. The plot thickens.

4. Tubal reports that Jessica is spending money freely in Genoa, and Shylock wishes his daughter dead with jewels and all upon her.

5. Once again Jessica's elopement is set beside Antonio's misfortunes, associating the two in Shylock's and our own minds. By association and not by direct statement, the motive for Shylock's cruelty toward Antonio is established as a desire to avenge the loss of his money and his daughter.

Act III: Scene ii

In Belmont again, Bassanio is ready to choose among the caskets. Portia urges him to wait a day or two, for she fears to lose his company if he chooses incorrectly. Too modest to confess her love directly, she remarks, "There's something tell me, but it is not love, / I would not lose you; and you know yourself / Hate counsels not in such a quality." She wishes he could stay a month or two so she could teach him how to choose correctly, but then she would be breaking faith, and this she will not do. She tells him that his eyes have divided her in two: one half is his and the other half is also his, for what is hers is also his. Talking on at length, she is trying to draw out the time before he must choose, but Bassanio begs to be allowed to try his fortune, for he cannot bear the rack on which he lives. Portia teases Bassanio for his

use of the word "rack," playfully accusing him of confessing love only in order to end his torture. Taking Portia's suggestion that he "confess and live," Bassanio answers that "confess and love" is all there is to admit. He is pleased that his torturer (Portia) "doth teach me answers for deliverance."

COMMENT: Portia and Bassanio are obviously attuned to each other, for Bassanio quickly learns how to use Portia's hint for his "deliverance." The harmonious lovers speak the courteous and witty language of love, which is saturated with religious connotation and demonstrates the correspondence in thought between the noble love of man and woman and the higher love which is eternal. "Promise me life, and I'll confess the truth," for example, is perfectly suited to a courtly love or religious context.

Portia finally bids him choose which casket contains her picture, saying, "If you do love me, you will find me out." She tells the others to stand all apart and orders music to be played while he chooses, so that if he fails he will make a swanlike end, fading in music. If he should win, however, then the music will be like the triumphant flourish when a new king is crowned or like the sweet sounds that a dreaming bridegroom hears at daybreak. She compares Bassanio to the young Alcides (Hercules) of mythology, who rescued the Trojan virgin from a sea monster, and herself to the sacrificed virgin, for her life and happiness depend on him.

COMMENT: Portia displays all the graces of the perfect lady. She prefers to use modest understatement rather than open declaration of her love, saying that her feelings are not the result of hate, and she is willing to instruct her suitor in the ways of courteous love. Her allusion to Alcides' rescue of the virgin shows the depth of her feeling for Bassanio and her fear of losing him.

The music called for at this point supplies the lyrical background for the romantically tense moment which ensues. It also works as a symbol of Portia's love, which like music is a manifestation of universal harmony.

While Bassanio comments on the caskets to himself, a song is heard, which begins: "Tell me where is fancy bred, / Or in the heart or in the head? How begot, how nourished? / Reply, reply."

Looking at the caskets, Bassanio first comments to himself that outward appearance is not to be trusted to reveal the inner truth of anything. He will not be duped by ornament, which so often deceives men in all affairs of life. In legal matters and in religion a gracious or learned voice often conceals evil and corruption. "There is no vice so simple but assumes / Some mark of virtue on his outward parts," Bassanio reflects. As if with his sixth sense, Bassanio unwittingly guesses at the contents of the boxes: "Upon supposed fairness, often known / To be the dowry of a second head, / The skull that bred them, in the sepulcher." Bassanio therefore will not put his trust in "gaudy gold" or silver, the "common drudge" used for business transaction. Instead, he chooses "meager lead," which threatens rather than promises anything.

COMMENT: During the choosing interlude, Bassanio gives no evidence that he heeds the words of the song or that he relies on hints that may be given in the song. He is too busy examining his own heart in order to make the crucial decision. Nevertheless, the song poses a three-line question, each of which ends in a word rhyming with "lead." A hint is definitely given to Bassanio, but the question that is more to the point is, does Bassanio need it? Bassanio's reasoning shows how wise he is; he is aware that "a second head" and "the skull" may lie behind "supposed fairness." Thus, he follows his heart and decides to hazard all for the lady he loves. There is a fairy tale quality in the conclusion of the casket subplot in that the man whom the lady truly loves is also the one who is deserving of her. This romantic notion is a clear reflection of the paradoxical Renaissance notion that all is not fair that seems so and that outer appearances reflect the inner nature of man.

Portia, overjoyed at seeing that Bassanio has chosen correctly, remarks in an aside, "O love be moderate, allay thy ecstacy / In measure rain thy joy, scant this excess. / I feel too much thy blessing. Make it less / For fear I surfeit."

COMMENT: We may recall that in Act One, Scene Two, Portia and Nerissa were talking about the virtue of moderation in all things and the evil of excess. Even at this moment of great joy, Portia has not forgotten the value of moderation, although her happiness is now complete.

Opening the leaden casket, Bassanio joyfully discovers Portia's picture inside. Amazed at the likeness of the portrait to the original, he wonders with a lover's amazement how the artist could have made the eyes so mobile, the lips so sweet, the hair so like a golden spider's web to trap the hearts of men, without himself falling in love with the sitter. Yet beautiful though the picture is, Bassanio declares it is but a poor shadow of the living Portia.

COMMENT: Bassanio shows that among his other virtues he is a good judge of painting. Using the conventional language and imagery of sixteenth century love poetry, he praises the virtues of the picture, using the popular conceit of shadow and substance (underscoring the theme of

appearance vs. reality), making a familiar analogy between the arts of painting and poetry, finding language insufficient to do justice to the portrait, and declaring both arts inferior to the living reality, Portia herself.

Together with the portrait is a congratulatory scroll that praises Bassanio for not choosing by external appearance, wishes him all good fortune, and bids him claim his lady with a loving kiss. Bassanio kisses Portia and remarks that he is still giddy with delight, unable quite to believe the reality of his good fortune.

Portia tells him that although for herself she would not be ambitious to be different, yet for his sake she wishes she were "A thousands time more fair, / Ten thousand times as rich," so that she might stand higher in his estimation and bring him greater delight. But, she confesses, the sum of herself "Is an unlessoned girl, unschooled, unpractised; / Happy in this, she is not yet so old / But she may learn; happier than this, / She is not bred so dull but she can learn; / Happiest of all, is that her gentle spirit / Commits itself to yours to be directed, / As from her lord, her governor, her king." She declares that everything she has is now his to command, in token of which she gives him a ring, bidding him guard it always as the symbol of their love. Bassanio swears that he will die rather than part with the ring.

COMMENT: Portia's acceptance speech to her lord Bassanio displays her in the full flower of perfect Renaissance womanhood. She is not ambitious, that is, she is quiet rather than restive. She is modest in her self-estimation. Her generous spirit makes her wish she had more virtue, wealth, and friends to give her husband than she already has. She humbly describes herself as an "unlessoned girl, unschooled, unpracticed," by which she means not that she is ill-educated but that she is ignorant of the ways of married love. However, she has a sufficient supply of animal spirits to make a good wife; she is "not bred so dull but she can learn." The religious quality of her love is suggested by the theological terminology she uses to express it; she is most happy to commit her "gentle [gentile] spirit" to the direction of "her lord," to whom she is now "converted."

Bassanio has already made a total commitment to Portia's love; Portia's speech now shows that her love is at least as great and as generous as his. An ideal marriage is about to take place, in which gentleness, courtesy, and love will reign. Castiglione could not have planned a better marriage in his *Book of the Courtier*. Portia's total submission to her husband is in keeping with the code of behavior developed for the gentlewoman of Queen Elizabeth's time; but the code did not expect her to curb her intelligence, wit, imagination, or initiative, and it was understood that great ladies were often equal to the tasks of men when the need for their greatness arose. Portia's defense of Antonio will constitute just such a need later in the play, and Portia will meet it.

The ring that Portia gives Bassanio in this scene is symbolic of the virginity which she also offers him. Later in the play, the ring will become the subject of several witty but bawdy jests on the chastity of wives. In the meantime, we may note how earnestly Bassanio promises to keep the ring until death.

Nerissa and Gratiano now announce that they too wish to be married, and they receive the congratulations of the future Lord and his Lady of Belmont. Just as Gratiano is making a ribald pun on a wager over which couple will have the first son, Lorenzo and Jessica unexpectedly appear, together with Salarino.

COMMENT: The blossoming of love between Nerissa and Gratiano parallels the love story of Portia and Bassanio, and of Lorenzo and Jessica, who suddenly appear at this point. Gratiano's brief explanation of the details of their courtship is sufficient unto the day, for his nature is apish as we have seen, and he imitates Bassanio's every move. Bassanio's influence is a good one in that he has led Gratiano to marry a wife who has studied and who imitates Portia's gentle and courteous ways. The compounding of felicity with felicity in the marriage of friends to friends was a conventional occurrence in the romantic comedy of the period.

Bassanio welcomes his friends, checking with Portia that he does not overstep his bound in thus exerting his newly won rights as a host. Lorenzo explains that although he and Jessica had not intended to come to Belmont, they had met Salarino traveling in this direction, and he had prevailed upon them to change their course. Salarino confirms Lorenzo's story, adding that he had a reason for bringing them along. He delivers Bassanio's greeting from Antonio and a letter, which Bassanio reads immediately. In the meantime, Gratiano urges Nerissa to make Jessica welcome. (Gratiano's engagement has already made him somewhat courteous, for he realizes that Jessica must be feeling shy and awkward and needs urging to feel welcome. Once again he imitates Bassanio, who has just welcomed Lorenzo.) The dismay that overcomes Bassanio as he reads the letter from Antonio prompts Portia to beg her husband to tell her what is the matter, for as his wife, she must share his sorrow as well as his joy.

COMMENT: We see for ourselves that Shylock's suspicion that Lorenzo and Jessica have escaped with Bassanio was totally unfounded, and that Antonio told the truth when he denied knowledge of their whereabouts. (A gentleman may equivocate, but he never lies.)

"Here are a few of the unpleasant'st words / That ever blotted paper," exclaims Bassanio. He explains to Portia that when he told her he was a gentleman with no money, / he was telling the truth, but he had omitted one very important fact, that a very dear friend of his bound himself to his keenest enemy to enable Bassanio to come to Belmont. Is it true, Bassanio asks Salarino, that all Antonio's ships have foundered at sea?

Salarino confirms the truth of the letter and adds that even if Antonio now had the money, Shylock would refuse it. Salarino declares that he never saw a creature so "greedy" to destroy his fellow man. Twenty merchants and the Duke have argued with him but no one can persuade him to relinquish his claim. Shylock threatens the Duke that if the bond is not held valid in court, foreigners will no longer trust in the justice of Venetian courts to uphold the legality of contracts. Jessica adds that when she was with him she had heard Shylock tell his friends "That he would rather have Antonio's flesh / Than twenty times the value of the sum / That he did owe him."

COMMENT: We learn that Bassanio had equivocated when he told Portia that "only my blood speaks to you in my veins," that his only wealth was the noble blood in his veins. Equivocation was an acceptable part of courtly behavior; it showed the linguistic skill of the gentleman who used it, and protected the gentleman from the necessity of being discourteous or of lying outright. Bassanio's grief is felt for Antonio, not for his omissions of truth during his courtship of Portia. His passionate self-recrimination is couched in the metaphorical language of flesh and blood (usually associated with Shylock), which Bassanio suddenly begins to use. He had used his friend to "feed my means"; the letter-paper is his friend's "body," and every word "a gaping wound / Issuing lifeblood." Through the use of this language, Bassanio reveals that he feels like an unnatural villain (like Shylock) because he has murdered his dearest friend.

The account Salarino gives of Shylock in connection with Antonio's forfeit continues the portrayal of the usurer as an unnatural and cannibalistic creature. Shylock bears the shape of man, which is to say, he appears to be a man, but the appearance is deceptive. He is "greedy" for Antonio's destruction. Jessica helps color the portrait by adding that Shylock had spoken in her hearing of his desire for "Antonio's flesh."

Bassanio explains to Portia that Antonio is not only his dear friend but also the kindest and best-natured man in Italy. When Portia learns that the sum of money in question is three thousand ducate, she exclaims: "What, no more? / Pay him six thousand, and deface the bond. / Double six thousand and then treble that, / Before a friend of this description / Shall lose a hair through Bassanio's fault." She bids him come to church to be married immediately, and then he can haste away to Venice, "For never shall you lie by Portia's side / With an unquiet soul." After he has paid the debt, twenty times over if necessary, she bids him bring Antonio back with him to Belmont. In the meantime she and Nerissa will live like maidens or widows, awaiting the return of their husbands.

Bassanio reads aloud the letter from his friend, in which Antonio explains that all his ships have been lost and that his bond is forfeit. Antonio is resigned to the fact that in paying his debt to the Jew he must lose his life, and he absolves Bassanio of anything he owes him. His only wish in life now is to see Bassanio once more, but he tells his friend that he must do just as he pleases about coming to Venice. "If your love do not persuade you to come, let not my letter," Portia, deeply moved by these words, urges great haste, and Bassanio promises to hurry to and from Venice as quickly as possible.

COMMENT: Portia's generosity is put to the test sooner than either she or Bassanio could have expected, and her word is no more than her deed. With splendid munificence she offers him twenty times the "petty debt" to rescue his dear friend. We will shortly see that Portia has wit as well as money to contribute to Antonio's cause.

The letter from Antonio is brief and very touching. He utters not a single word of complaint about his predicament and lays no blame on Bassanio. The melancholy disposition of noble Antonio will stand him in good stead, for it permits him to face death with courage and resignation.

SUMMARY: This scene is interesting and significant for the following reasons:

1. We see that Portia loves Bassanio as he loves her and fervently hopes that he will choose the right casket, which he does. The device of the caskets proves to have been a wise invention of her father, in determining the perfect husband for his daughter.

2. Portia and Bassanio are overcome with happiness, and Portia wishes only that she had more to give her husband in the way of material and spiritual advantages. Bassanio, however, can hardly wish for more than this gracious and delightful woman.

3. Portia gives Bassanio a ring, bidding him to guard it closely as a token of her love for him and his for her. We will see later in the play the erotic conversation that arises in connection with this ring.

4. Nerissa and Gratiano announce that they plan to marry also. This news compounds the happiness of the moment and shows how inferiors may benefit by the influence of noble friends.

5. Salarino, accompanied by Lorenzo and Jessica, bring Bassanio the evil news that Shylock intends to claim the pound of flesh from Antonio, whose ships have all failed to return. Bassanio is deeply distressed, and explains the situation to Portia, who promptly agrees to supply whatever sum of money is necessary to save her husband's friend. The couples go off to be married before Bassanio and Gratiano depart for Venice.

Act III: Scene iii

Antonio, guarded by the jailor and accompanied by Salanio, tries to speak to Shylock, but the usurer will not listen to his plea. Warning the jailer to keep a close watch on his charge, Shylock declares, "This is the fool that lent out money gratis." Antonio used to call him dog; well, now let him beware the fangs. "I'll not be made soft and dull-eyed fool, / To shake the head, relent, and sigh and yield / To Christian intercessors."

Antonio realizes there is no use in arguing or pleading any more with Shylock, who is bent on retaliating for all the times that Antonio saved other debtors from Shylock's extortions by lending them money free of interest. When Salanio tries to cheer the merchant by assuring him that the Duke will support him in court, Antonio does not respond. He believes that the Duke will be afraid of losing the confidence of the commercial community if he abrogates this one contract. Worn out by his griefs and losses, Antonio is resigned to his fate, and only hopes that Bassanio will arrive from Belmont in time to see him pay his debt," and then I care not."

COMMENT: This brief scene juxtaposes the protagonist and antagonist, Antonio and Shylock, still another time. Their characters as usual are set up as a contrast. The exacting and merciless Shylock insists he will have his bond, and we learn that the generous Antonio has often saved other debtors from falling into Shylock's clutches.

The scene is incremental rather than repetitive, for while it repeats old emphases, it adds new facts to the characterizations. Shylock's unflinching cruelty is established by his refusal to listen to Antonio's plea. The dog-epithet is repeated over and over again by Shylock himself, and Shylock comically admits the horrible fact that he intends to behave like a dog "since I am a dog." The humor of Shylock's self-characterization, however, escapes Salanio, who tags Shylock an "impenetrable cur," suggesting that his evil is dark and profound.

Antonio appears for the first time since his disaster in the role of suppliant to the usurer. We have already been prepared in the preceding scene to witness his grief and weariness. The present scene dramatizes Antonio as a melancholy man prepared to face death with courage and resignation.

Act III: Scene iv

In Belmont once again Lorenzo tells Portia how much he admires her noble conception of love and the dignity with which she bears the absence of Bassanio. He assures her that if she knew all the virtues of Antonio, what a true gentleman and friend he is, she would be even more glad of helping him than of her usual acts of kindness.

Portia replies, "I never did repent for doing good, / Nor shall not now." She declares that since close friends are generally similar in proportion, lineaments, manners, and spirit, Antonio must resemble Bassanio, who in turn is the reflection of her own soul. Therefore no effort can be too great to rescue such a man from "hellish cruelty." Suddenly embarrassed by this talk which, she says "comes too near the praising of myself," she changes the subject.

COMMENT: Lorenzo recognizes quite rightly that Portia is an extraordinary person. Few women could so magnanimously part with their husbands on their wedding day and bear with such equanimity the absence of a beloved. Portia's generosity is enhanced by her modesty, and we will soon see that these noble qualities are equalled only by her resourceful wit.

Portia tells Lorenzo that she and Nerissa have decided to remain in a neighboring monastery to live in prayer and contemplation while their husbands are away. She asks Lorenzo and Jessica to act as master and mistress of her estate during her absence, and Lorenzo readily agrees. Jessica wishes Portia "all heart's content," and Portia returns the wish.

When Lorenzo and Jessica exit, Portia asks her servant (named Balthasar) to take a message to her cousin, Doctor Bellario in Padua, from whom he will receive certain papers and clothing. She bids him bring these as quickly as possible to the ferry that goes to Venice, where she will be waiting for him. The servant hurries away and Portia tells Nerissa that they will shortly see their husbands without being recognized, for the women will be dressed up as young men. The lady gaily bets her maid that when they are disguised she will be "the prettier fellow of the two." In her

imagination she looks forward to wearing her dagger with a brave grace; to speaking in a high piping voice midway between that of man and boy; to walking with a manly stride; and to bragging of all the women who have died of love for him (her). "I have within my mind / A thousand raw tricks of these bragging jacks / Which I will practice." Nerissa asks if they "'will turn to men," and Portia chides her maid for putting a lewd cast on her intentions. The coach is waiting for them, and Portia promises to explain her plan to Nerissa on the way.

COMMENT: We witness an exchange of courtesies between Portia and Lorenzo which shows us just how gentle people behave. The gracious manners and language exchanged between Portia and Lorenzo should be noted and contrasted with the conversations Shylock holds with his servant, daughter, friend, or with Christians. The one is filled with compliments and good wishes, the other is filled with expletive and ugly metaphor. The gentle people of the play speak of love, friendship and generosity; the Jew of the play discusses money, revenge, hatred, and flesh.

Portia expresses one of the notions of Renaissance idealism when she says that there are similarities in size, shape, and physical characteristics, as well as in manners and spirit, among deeply devoted friends and lovers. She reasons that since Antonio and Bassanio are such close friends, and since she and Bassanio are such close lovers, then Antonio must be a "semblance of my soul." Although her explanation of her generosity comes very close to self-praise, Portia is actually explicating the New Testament commandment, "Thou shalt love thy neighbour as thyself" (Matthew 22:29, but also see Leviticus 19:18). In addition, Portia describes Antonio's situation as a "state of hellish cruelty," suggesting once more that Shylock is really a demonic creature.

We learn that Portia intends to go to Venice in disguise, accompanied by Nerissa. Unlike Jessica (II.vi), Portia is not embarrassed by wearing boy's clothing. On the contrary, she plans to get into the spirit of the disguise, and describes the silly foibles of bragging youths, which she plans to imitate, and shows once more what an observant caricaturist she is.

Despite the serious nature of the journey she is undertaking, Portia is filled with high spirits over the coming adventure. When Nerissa consciously or otherwise uses the ambiguous term "turn to" (1. become, 2. seek sexually), Portia understands it in its lewd sense. She displays the eroticism of a young bride, but her sexual conversation, as we shall see, is delicate and indirect. It is the less gentle Nerissa who appears to give the lewd cast to her words.

Act III: Scene v

Jessica and Launcelot are talking together in Belmont some time after Portia has departed from the house. The clown tells the girl that he fears she is damned, for the Bible says that the sins of the father are laid upon the children, and she is daughter to the faithless Jew. He says that he can only think of "a kind of bastard hope" that may save her, the hope that Shylock did not beget her. Jessica replies that then "the sins of my mother should be visited upon me." Launcelet hadn't thought of that; he declares that here can be no hope for her salvation, but Jessica reminds him that she will be saved by her husband, who has made her a Christian. Launcelot is not pleased with this solution, insisting that there are enough Christians already without adding more converts who will eat pork and raise the price of hogs.

COMMENT: Launcelot has come to Belmont with Bassanio and has been left behind when his master returns to Venice. As in his earlier scene, he is preoccupied with the subject of illegitimacy and salvation. His jests turn on the hope that Jessica may be her mother's bastard and thereby avoid damnation for the faithlessness of her father. The clown's comic treatment of bastardy and salvation is a thin and amusing disguise for the important theme of conversion which runs through this play. The conversion of Jews was a major concern among Christians, dating from the first century A. D. when the *New Testament* was written, and the conversion of Jessica is the crux of this scene.

At this moment Lorenzo appears and jestingly tells Launcelot that he will grow jealous of him if he gets Jessica into corners, but when his wife explains the nature of their conversation Lorenzo declares that he can answer the charge of raising the price of pork by converting Jessica to Christianity better than Launcelot can answer the charge of getting "the Moor" pregnant. Launcelot does not dispute this charge, merely playing on the words of his sentence: "It is *much* that the *Moor* should be more than reason; but if she be less than an honest woman, she is indeed *more* than I took her for."

COMMENT: Lorenzo's reference to "the Moor" it taken as evidence that Shakespeare, in writing *The Merchant*, had reworked an earlier play and had forgotten to tie up all the loose ends. However irrelevant this reference to the Moor may be, as the play stands, it teaches us that Moors and Negroes were regarded as the same, and that the "commonwealth" would look more harshly upon Launcelot's liaison with a Negro and the illegitimate child he had begotten upon her, than it would on Lorenzo's conversion of and marriage to a Jew. In the social hierarchy of the Renaissance Christian world we see, Jews were just a rung above Moors, and both were outcasts from the "commonweal."

Lorenzo throws up his hands at this nonsense, declaring that silence is better than such wit. He bids Launcelot tell the other servants to "prepare for dinner," and Launcelot replies, again with double meaning, that the servants are already prepared for dinner because they all have "stomachs" (sexual as well as eating appetites). He also refuses to "cover" (1. lay the tablecloth, 2. don a hat, 3. mount and impregnate the female), because he knows his duty. There is more punning by Launcelot on Lorenzo's order to "go to thy fellows, bid them cover the table, serve in the meat, and we will come in to dinner." Launcelot twists the words around so that they can be interpreted lewdly, and answers: "For the table, sir, it shall be served in; for the meat, sir, it shall be covered; for your coming in to dinner, sir, why let it be as humors and conceits shall govern."

Launcelot exits, and Lorenzo and Jessica remain on stage. Lorenzo comments that the clown's words show that he has a good memory, even if he makes utter nonsense of his wit. There are many fools "garnish'd like him" in higher social positions who, for the sake of "a tricky word," will obscure the sense of their matter.

COMMENT: The low-comedy of Launcelot is full of coarse sexual reference, calculated to amuse the "groundlings" (members of the lower class who paid a penny for standing room in the pit or orchestra), who probably came to see their favorite clown, Will Kemp, play the role. Launcelot's "wit-snapping" may be contrasted with the sexual allusions moderately sprinkled through the speeches of the romantic characters of the play. Launcelot's cruder double-entendres are intemperately heaped all in one place, exasperating Lorenzo, who is forced to ask, "Wilt thou show the whole wealth of thy wit in an instant?"

We have already seen that Lorenzo is a quiet man; now we learn that he is also a "plain man" who speaks with "plain meaning." Nevertheless, he tolerates the clown and appreciates his good memory and vocabulary inasmuch as fools in higher places willingly distort their meanings for the sake of an ambiguously clever word. Lorenzo is objecting to garnished speaking and false wit, which precious Elizabethans affected as a show of eloquence.

Lorenzo now asks his wife what she thinks of Portia, and Jessica replies that she cannot speak too highly of the lady of Belmont. She declares that Bassanio cannot help but live an upright life, "for, having such a blessing in his lady, / He finds the joys of heaven here on earth;" and if he does not deserve it here on earth, he is not likely to get it in heaven. As for Portia, "the poor rude world / Hath not her fellow."

COMMENT: In spite of her cloistered life in a Jewish household, Jessica is instinctively aware of Christian values. She describes Portia in the very terms used in the neo-Platonic schools of the Renaissance, without having been raised in their tradition. Portia is a perfect lady of virtue through whose love the gentleman learns to live the blessed and upright life, which will assure his mortal and eternal joy, Jessica says. It is to be understood that Jessica has come to this way of thinking "in reason," or that Lorenzo has already schooled her in these ideas.

Lorenzo happily remarks that he is just such a husband to Jessica as Portia is wife to Bassanio, but Jessica pertly replies that he must ask her opinion on that matter. When Lorenzo suggests that they go in to dinner, Jessica observes that she had better praise him "while I have a stomach" (the pun here is on her 1. appetite, 2. inclination.) Lorenzo answers this with another pun, saying she had better leave the subject for table talk, and then he will digest her words along with the food, no matter how bad. Finally, Jessica adds the last witty word, "Well, I'll set you forth" (1. lay out a feast, 2. praise you highly).

COMMENT: When Lorenzo compares himself to Portia, saying "even such a husband / Hast thou of me," he is being playful. But at the same time, he indicates that as a Christian, he too will provide Jessica with the blessed life on earth and in heaven.

The romantic couple are infected by Launcelot's wit and pun on the same words as did the clown. The cheerful banter of the newly-wed couple is designed to show how courteous and how happy they are and how well they deserve the rewards Antonio will soon win for them.

SUMMARY: This scene is a carefree interlude in the midst of the serious concern about Antonio's welfare, but under the guise of levity it resolves several important questions about courtesy and salvation.

1. Launcelot's crude concern over Jessica's salvation reflects questions in the audience's mind, which are answered by Lorenzo's assurance that Jessica's conversion will do the trick.

2. Jessica portrays Portia as a perfect Christian lady, revealing as she does so that she herself is one too.

3. Launcelot provides coarse jests on the Elizabethan stereotype of the Moor and on the sexual appetites of servants, while in contrast Lorenzo and Jessica exchange courteous banter on more pleasant subjects.

Act IV: Scene i

The scene is the court in Venice, where the Duke is presiding over the case of Shylock's claim to his pound of flesh. Antonio, Bassanio, Gratiano, and other Venetian noblemen are already present. The Duke expresses his pity for Antonio, whose adversary he declares is "an inhuman wretch, / Uncapable of pity, void and empty / From any dram of mercy." Antonio replies that he knows that the Duke has done his utmost to persuade Shylock to be merciful but to no avail. The merchant realizes that the law holds him responsible for the bond, and he is prepared to bear with patience and a quiet spirit the brunt of Shylock's fury.

COMMENT: In this famous courtroom scene, many threads of theme and character which run through the play are tied together. Antonio gives full expression to the characteristics of the melancholy Christian gentleman, which we have seen in part and of which we have been frequently told. The characters of Shylock and Antonio have been repeatedly set in opposition in earlier scenes, and once more are so placed by Antonio himself: "I do oppose / My patience to his fury." Antonio's Christian virtues are stated and displayed in his willingness "to suffer with a quiteness of spirit" the tyranny of the Jew.

Shylock enters the court and stands before the Duke, who tries once more to soften his heart by telling the creditor that all those present think that he is merely pretending to be cruel until the moment of execution when he will, in fact, show mercy to his victim. The Duke declares that even Turks and Tartars, people known for their savagery and never trained in "tender courtesy," would show greater humanity towards a man such as Antonio who has suffered so many losses all at once. He tells the usurer, "We all expect a gentle answer, Jew," (punning on "gentile" again), but Shylock is unmoved by this as by all other appeals to "human gentleness and love." He declares that he was sworn "by our holy Sabbath" to have his bond, and he warns the Duke of the consequence for Venice if the law is not impartially observed in this as in all cases.

COMMENT: The Duke's plea for "human gentleness and love" is symbolically a plea for the Jew's conversion. In the courtroom, the Duke expects Shylock to behave like a Christian, with "tender courtesy," and to give "gentle"

(gentle, gentile) answers. Shylock, however, is obdurate, and as the Jewish moneylender of the play, he is symbolic of all Jews. When the Duke points out that, while the act of demanding the bond is a legal one and the thought or motive behind Shylock's demand is "malicious," he is engaging in the age old controversy between *Old* and *New Testament* interpretations of the law of God. The Duke believes that Jews study and live by the letter of the old law, while Christians, he knows, live by the spirit of the old law, which is interpreted in the new. Metaphorically the old law was a "carnal commandment" (Hebrews 7:16), expressing "fleshly wisdom" rather than "the spirit of the living God" (2 Corinthians 3:3), and Shylock is its fleshly embodiment. Throughout the scene, Shylock's religious thought and practice are presented from the Christian point of view as literal, merciless, irrational, and heinously inhuman. Shylock's oath, "by our Holy Sabbath," is given as an example of how Jews desecrate the house of God by swearing in the temple (Matthew 5:33-37).

As for why Shylock prefers to have "the weight of carrion flesh" rather than his money, he announces quite simply that it is his "humor" (a physiological and mental disposition) to do so. He compares himself to man whose house is troubled by a rat and who is willing to pay ten thousand ducats to have it poisoned, which it is his priveledge to do. "Some men there are love not a gaping pig, / Some that are mad if they behold a cat, / And others, when the bagpipe sings i' the nose, / Cannot contain their urine for affection, / Master of passion, sways it to the mood / Of what it likes or loathes." And just as there is no rational explanation of why one man hates a pig, why another cannot abide a harmless cat, and why a third cannot contain his urine when listening to a bagpipe, so Shylock cannot and will not give a reason for his action other than the deep-seated hatred and loathing that he bears Antonio.

COMMENT: Shylock's reason for preferring the pound of flesh to money were confirmations of the stereotype so carefully built up in earlier scenes, and were a source of pleasure to the sanguine audience of Shakespeare's time. When Shylock says it is his "humor" to prefer flesh to money, he is proving a Christian point that Jews lived by "carnal commandments—" that they really were unnatural creatures. Shylock implies that his desire for Antonio's flesh is no more than an affection and is completely inexplicable; he can "give no reason," nor will he. Earlier in the play we have heard him justify his hatred of Antonio as the natural desire for revenge against a man who has injured his business prospects and his self-esteem in the past. We have heard Shylock say that if Antonio were gone from the community the usury business would improve, and we have heard him express hatred for the Christian Venetians

in general for making him an outcast from society and especially for stealing his daughter and much of his money away from him. But here in court, Shylock mentions none of these reasons. Instead, he makes himself ridiculous by comparing the unreasoning hatred he feels for Antonio with the irrational and inexplicable impulses found in all men. The examples that he gives of human nature mastered by strange and powerful passions are such as to excite disgust and contempt in his hearers. Yet Shylock seems to find them natural and unavoidable. The man who is over-come with loathing for a pig or cat, or a man who cannot contain his urine when he hears the bagpipe playing, are ridiculous types, and Shylock, by analogy, is ridiculous too. Shylock, however, is unaware of this and seems to embrace the ridiculous and the inexplicable in human nature as justification for his own passionate hatred of Antonio, which has now reached the point of murder.

From the Christian point of view, Shylock the Jew represents evil, the devil, anti-Christ, and all the forces of disorder, for he is unable to understand the Christian sense of right and wrong, which controls the behavior of the others in the courtroom.

Bassanio heatedly objects that Shylock has given no excuse for his cruelty, for all men do not kill that which they do not love, but the Jew replies that he is not bound to please Bassanio by his answers. He declares that no man truly hates that which he would not kill, and, having once been stung by a serpent (Antonio), he will not give it a chance to sting him again.

Antonio begs Bassanio not to argue with his credi-tor. "You may as well go stand upon the beach / And bid the main flood bate his usual heights; / You may as well use question with the wolf, / Why he hath made the ewe bleat for the lamb. / You may as well forbid the mountain pines / To wag their high tops and to make no noise / When they are fretten with the gusts of heaven," as to seek to soften that hardest of all things, Shylock's "Jewish heart." Accepting his plight, Anto-nio asks that the court proceed to render judgment, but Bassanio makes one last attempt, offering Shylock six thousand ducats instead of the original three thousand. Shylock, implacable, replies that if he were offered six times the original sum he would not take it but would insist upon his bond.

COMMENT: Of all present, Bassanio is by far the man most troubled by Antonio's plight, for he keenly feels his personal responsibility for the bond which his friend signed for his sake. Therefore, though Antonio is stoically resigned to his fate, Bassanio is not yet ready to give up the attempt to try to persuade Shylock to spare the merchant.

It is Antonio, however, and not Bassanio, who under-stands the nature of their adversary. Earlier in the scene, the

Duke called Shylock an "inhuman wretch," and that is exactly what Shylock shows he is, inhuman. What distinguishes a man from the animal world is the fact that man can be swayed by the voice of reason and of compassion. As Antonio remarks, however, Shylock's impulses to vengeance is as powerful and as elemental as any force of nature. Man can have as little hope to move him as to move the fierce wolf or the towering pine.

Intervening once more, the Duke asks Shylock how he can hope for mercy for himself when he shows none to others, but Shylock simply replies: "What judgment shall I dread, doing no wrong?" He tells his listeners that just as they have purchased slaves whom they treat like dogs or beasts of burden, so he is master of Antonio, whom he has bought with his money. And just as the Venetian nobles would never agree to free their slaves, so Shylock declares he will not set Antonio free, but will dispose of him as he pleases. He asks for justice and reminds the Duke that the prosperity of Venice will suffer if the law is not maintained in the city.

COMMENT: The Duke uses the Christian argument for mercy (Matthew 5:7), but Shylock refuses to admit that he is doing anything wrong, for according to his scrupulously legalistic and allegedly Jewish way of looking at the world, wrongdoing consists merely in breaking the letter of the law. Since by taking Antonio's flesh he will be fulfilling the terms of a legal contract, Shylock insists that his action is right, for it is lawful. He ignores, as it is the nature of the stereotyped Jew to do, the spirit of the law, which requires mercy to one's fellow man and even one's enemy.

From the modern's point of view, Shylock's comparison between his hold over Antonio and the power exercised by these self-righteous Venetian noblemen over their slaves, is the most effective justification he has offered for his conduct. What right do these slave-holders have to condemn him for disposing as he pleases with his human property as they do with theirs? No one present answers this challenge, and the silence on this subject raises a moot question about Shakespeare's attitude toward slaves.

It has been abundantly clear in the play, however, that servants in the homes of Christians were well treated and that they learned, by imitation of their masters, to behave in gentle ways. The Christian gentleman set a good example for his servant and thus guided the unwise and the untutored into the right way of life. Christians would not agree with Shylock that they abused their slaves, and Shylock has been wrong before about the treatment Launcelot would get in a gentile's service. Shylock himself does not believe in freeing slaves; he simply brings up the subject because they, like Antonio's flesh, are human possessions. The analogy was ridiculous to Renaissance Christians, who would never compare a Christian gentleman to an ignoble slave. The gentleman was born to command, the slave to follow. (Relevant to this issue is the historical fact that medieval Jews were forbidden to keep Christian slaves. Pagan slaves in the service of Jews were given their freedom upon conversion to Christianity.)

The Duke declares that he may dismiss the court unless Bellario, the learned jurist from Padua, arrives to determine the case. Salarino then announces that a messenger from Bellario is waiting outside. While this messenger is being sent for, Bassanio tries to cheer Antonio, swearing that he would rather die than permit Antonio to lose one drop of blood. Antonio, however, protests that he is more ready and more fit for death than his friend: "I am a tainted wether of the flock, / Meetest for death."

COMMENT: With characteristic melancholy, Antonio compares himself to a "wether" (a castrated male sheep) and to the "weakest kind of fruit," which are more fit to die than Bassanio, who, it is implied, is young, strong, virile, and high-spirited, who enjoys life and, therefore, should be allowed to live it. Antonio confirms what has already been implied, that he is an older man, no longer suited for the dance of love, that he has entered the contemplative stage of life and is ready for death.

Nerissa enters dressed as a lawyer's clerk, and while the Duke reads the letters that she brings from Bellario, Bassanio anxiously watches Shylock whetting his knife for the operation. Gratiano cannot contain himself at this sight. He declares that Shylock sharpens the knife on his very *soul* rather than on the *sole* of his foot, for no metal is as keen as the villain's sharp envy. Gratiano is almost ready to believe with Pythagoras that the souls of dead animals enter the bodies of men, since no other theory can explain Shylock's currish spirit, so "wolvish, bloody, starved, and ravenous." (Pythagoras was an ancient Greek philosopher who believed in the transmigration of souls after death.) Shylock, however, calmly replies to Gratiano that all his anger and harsh words cannot alter the seal upon the lawful bond. "I stand here for law," Shylock asserts.

Having read the letter, the Duke sends Nerissa to fetch Portia, and while she is gone he reads aloud the message from old Bellario, who explains that although he is too sick to come, he is sending in his stead a young and learned doctor of jurisprudence named Balthasar. He begs the Duke not to be apprehensive on account of the lawyer's extreme youth, promising that this Balthasar will bring to bear on the case both Bellario's considered opinion and his own learned judgment.

COMMENT: The interlude between Gratiano and Shylock augments the characterization of Shylock as an unnatural dog and of Gratiano as a loyal but coarse friend. Shylock's last statement, "I stand here for the law," not only is relevant in the context of the play, but signifies that Shylock represents the literal interpretation of *Old Testament* law. Portia's famous mercy-speech, which follows shortly, is set in direct opposition to Shylock's courtroom literalness.

Portia's disguise as a doctor is a dramatic necessity at this point in the play, for she could not plead in court as a woman, nor could a male doctor (say, Bassanio) have pleaded so convincingly for mercy, which was commonly regarded as a womanly virtue and one which men learned from women.

Portia enters, dressed as a Doctor of Law, and is welcomed by the Duke. Bidding the merchant and the Jew stand forth, she hears Antonio confess that he has signed the bond in question, and she declares, "Then must the Jew be merciful." When Shylock demands to know on what grounds he must be merciful, the young lawyer replies: "The quality of mercy is not strained; / It droppeth as the gentle rain from heaven / Upon the place beneath. It is twice blest; / It blesseth him that gives and him that takes." The sign of true grace in a king, she declares, is not a sceptre in the hand or a crown on the head, but mercy in the heart; for mercy is an attribute of God Himself, and earthly kings are most noble when they temper justice with mercy. "Therefore, Jew," Portia concludes, "consider this, / That in the course of justice, none of us should see salvation. We do pray for mercy / And that same prayer doth teach us all to render / The deeds of mercy." She hopes that he will be moved by these words to renounce his legal claim, but she concludes by saying that if he remains adamant, the Venetian court must pass sentence against Antonio.

COMMENT: This speech of Portia's is undoubtedly the most famous in the play and justly so, for in lyrical verse that is beautiful in itself it clearly states the moral and implies the doctrinal themes of the play: that courtesy teaches the heart to be gentle, that the gentle heart secures salvation, that the stern justice of the Old Law must give way to the mercy of the new, that the Jew must convert to Christianity, by persuasion if possible, by force if necessary.

Portia tells Shylock that what is most admirable in a king is not his power but the humanity with which he exercises this power, repeating the Christian precept also expressed in Shakespeare's Sonnet 94, which begins: "They that have power to do hurt and will do none ... They rightly do inherit heaven's graces." Until Antonio's bond fell overdue, Shylock was not a man with power to do hurt. Now that he has a

chance, however, Portia tries to persuade him to act in such a way as to merit "heaven's graces." She is, in effect, trying to persuade him to convert.

Shylock has emphasized the justice and the legality to his claim to Antonio's flesh. Now, Portia insists that mercy is a higher good than justice, for it ennobles the giver and the receiver. She asks Shylock to consider the thought that if God exacted justice from mankind, no one would get to heaven but in the same remark, she implies that if justice (symbolizing the Old Law) were followed by everyone (as it is by the Jews), then no one would be saved (that is, no one would be a Christian, the only kind of man who can be saved).

Portia has set before Shylock in clear and persuasive terms the moral imperative of Christianity by which he ought to act. Especially as one who has often been at the mercy of other people in the past, Shylock ought now to appreciate the grace-giving quality of mercy. This speech is highly significant in understanding Shakespeare's characterization of the stereotyped Jew. Shylock's heart cannot be moved by this truly effective pleader for the gospel of love and compassion. Now when Shylock proceeds in his cruel demand, Shakespeare shows, it is not for want of having heard such a pleader, but from his own warped nature. Shylock acts deliberately and in full knowledge of what he is doing.

Unmoved by Portia's appeal, Shylock still declares, "I crave the law." The lawyer then asks if Antonio is able to repay the bond, and Bassanio replies that he is ready to pay thrice or even ten times the original sum borrowed. Bassanio argues that if Shylock refuses this offer his only motive can be pure malice, and he begs the court to disregard the law just this once in order to save Antonio. Portia, however, denies this request. She refuses to set the dangerous precedent of ever tampering with the law.

COMMENT: Shakespeare, and his heroine Portia, realize that a strict regard to law is the necessary prerequisite for human society. To break the law once in a good cause is to set a bad example for the future, when the cause may not be so good. Then ends do not justify the means. When Portia finally saves Antonio she will do so within the framework of Venetian law.

Shylock gleefully cries out that the young lawyer is another Daniel come to judge: "O wise young judge, how I do honor thee!" He tells the court that he has sworn an oath to heaven that he will have his bond, and asks whether they think he would risk perjuring himself before God by changing his mind now.

COMMENT: The *Old Testament* name, Daniel, meaning "God is my judge," is associated here with righteous judgment. Daniel was the first judge to introduce cross-examination into trials when he saved Susanna from the false accusations of the Elders. Shylock alludes to the *Old Testament* as may be expected of him. Ironically, this "Daniel" will soon turn his righteous judgment against Shylock.

Portia scrutinizes the bond closely and, finding it all in order, declares that the Jew may have his pound of flesh to be cut off nearest the merchant's heart. Turning to Shylock once more, she asks him to accept the sum of three times his original loan and to bid her tear the bond. He refuses. Antonio, anxious to get his ordeal over with, urges the lawyer to proceed to judgment, and Portia tells the victim to prepare his bosom for the knife. "O noble judge! O excellent young man!" cries Shylock, reminding the court that the bond expressly stipulates that he may take the flesh "Nearest his heart." Portia bids him provide a doctor "for charity" to look after Antonio, but the usurer refuses, objecting that "'Tis not in the bond."

COMMENT: Our conception of Shylock's cruelty is sharpened when we learn that he had stipulated in the bond that he would claim the pound of flesh from the place nearest Antonio's heart. This gruesome provision reveals a new depth in Shylock's villainy and permits Antonio's grim jest on his debt of friendship in his next speech.

Bidding farewell to Bassanio, Antonio begs his friend not to grieve. He declares that he is well-prepared to endure his ordeal, taking comfort in the thought that he will be spared the misery of those men who outlive their wealth and are forced to end their days in cruel poverty. He bids Bassanio convey his greetings to Portia. "Tell her the process of Antonio's end,/ Say how I loved you, speak me fair in death / And when the tale is told, bid her be judge / Whether Bassanio had not once a love." In conclusion Antonio swears that as long as Bassanio is truly sorry to see him die, then he for his part does not repent paying his friend's debt "with all my heart."

Bassanio, overwhelmed with grief and frustration, declares that though he dearly loves his wife, he would willingly sacrifice her, or die himself in order to save Antonio. Without revealing her identity, Portia remarks that Bassanio's wife would not be very happy to hear him thus offer her life in sacrifice. Gratiano then declares that he also would gladly see his beloved wife in heaven if she might intercede there for Antonio, and Nerissa remarks that his wife would not take kindly to such an offer. Shylock, who has heard the protestations

of these Christian husbands and has taken them literally, declares that he would rather his daughter had married a thief ("any of the stock of Barabbas") rather than a gentile, if this is the kind of love that Christian husbands bear their wives.

COMMENT: Although Antonio has said little in this scene, Portia has spoken for him in her plea for gentle mercy. Now Antonio, in contrast to Shylock's extreme villainy in refusing to provide a surgeon, demonstrates the extreme of charity and friendship in his willingness to die for Bassanio.

There is dramatic irony, a subtle form of humor, in Antonio's desire that Portia "judges" his love for Bassanio, for Portia is presently playing judge and observes Antonio's display of love first hand. The idea of paying the friend's debt "with all my heart," a common metaphor both then and now, is a piece of verbal irony, for in the context of this scene, the statement has literal truth.

The grim humor of Antonio's jest becomes levity in the amusing interpolations by Portia and Nerissa in disguise. They do not interpret their husband's generous offers to sacrifice their wives as literally as does Shylock, who, over-hearing the conversation, expresses the belief that Christian husbands actually do sacrifice their wives. If put to the test, however, Christians like Antonio will do a great deal for a friend.

Proceeding to render judgment, Portia declares that the court awards Shylock a pound of flesh to be cut off from Antonio's breast. The Jew, greatly elated, praises this "Most rightful judge, Most learned judge." But his joy is short-lived. Portia then goes on to show that although he bond clearly gives him a pound of flesh, it makes no provision for blood. Therefore, if while claiming his pound of flesh Shylock sheds any Christian blood, he will lose all his possessions to the state in accordance with Venetian law. Now it is Gratiano's turn to gloat and to praise Portia "O upright judge! Mark Jew. O learned judge."

COMMENT: Shakespeare has skillfully built up the tension until it reaches its peak at this point in the play when Portia finally declares that the Venetian law must award Shylock the right to claim his pound of flesh. But just at the moment when all hope seems lost, the situation is saved by the loophole Portia has discovered in the contract.

Portia allows the court to believe that there is no hope for Antonio in order to test Shylock's resolution. It is her way of giving him every possible chance to change his mind, and, symbolically, to convert. She tries to appeal to Shylock's mercy, to his avarice, then to both. Next, she asks for a surgeon out of charity and is denied. Failing of these appeals, she invokes the letter of the law against Shylock. In other words, she first uses every means of persuasion open to her in Christian doctrine and human nature then she deals with Shylock on his own ground. Using literal interpretation of his bond, she thwarts his vengenance and turns the tables against him.

Surprised by this turn of events, Shylock declares his willingness to accept Bassanio's offer of three times the original value of the bond, but now Portia will not let the matter rest. She declares that since he asked for justice he shall get nothing but justice, that is, his pound of flesh, and warns him that if he takes either slightly more or less than just a pound he will lose all his property and will be condemned to death. Again Gratiano crows with delight, imitating Shylock's earlier praise of the lawyer: "A second Daniel! A Daniel, Jew!"

Hoping to salvage at least his original investment, Shylock declares himself willing to accept the original three thousand ducats, but again Portia insists that he shall get nothing but the forfeit. Shylock then decides to abandon his claim, and prepares to leave the court, when Portia tells him of the Venetian law that says if an alien is found guilty of attempting the life of any citizen, his property shall be divided evenly between the intended victim and the state. Furthermore, his life shall be at the mercy of the Duke to dispose of. Shylock is clearly guilty under this law and Portia advises him to bow before the Duke and humbly to seek mercy. Gratiano, delighted by this news, enjoys taunting Shylock in his humiliation.

COMMENT: Shylock had only considered the letter of the law in calling for justice, while Portia had implored him to obey its spirit. She knew, however, that if Shylock went ahead with his intention, he would be guilty of violating Venetian statutes. She herself was showing mercy by offering Shylock a way out before he proved unremittingly his guilt of attempting a citizen's murder. Gratiano's gleeful exclamations reflect the feelings of the Elizabethan audience, that delighted in seeing the villain foiled.

Before Shylock has a chance to say a word, the Duke pardons his life to show him "the difference of our spirit." He decrees that half the usurer's wealth must go to Antonio, but offers to reduce the debt to the state to a small fine. Shylock, however, is hardly grateful for this concession. "Nay, take my life," he tells the Duke, for without his wealth he cannot earn a living, and he feels he might just as well die now as starve in the course of time.

Portia then asks Antonio what mercy he can render Shylock. Gratiano mutters his hope that Antonio will offer nothing more than a free halter for the Jew to hang himself, but Antonio is a more generous spirit. He asks the Duke to let Shylock keep one half his possessions,

allowing Antonio the use of the other half until death, when it will go to Lorenzo and Jessica. The merchant also stipulates that Shylock must convert to Christianity and must make Lorenzo his legal heir. The Duke heartily approves these proposals and declares he will revoke his pardon if Shylock does not agree, whereupon Shylock consents. Portia bids the clerk draw up the deed of gift to his heirs for him to sign. Shylock, feeling ill by now, asks leave to go home and to have the deed sent after for him to sign. The Duke grants this request, and as Shylock leaves, Gratiano declares that if he had been judge he would have sent the Jew to the gallows rather than to the baptismal font.

COMMENT: The Duke and Antonio show Shylock "the difference of our spirit" by treating him with the Christian mercy that he refused to grant Antonio. They not only spare his life, but also spare him the poverty to which a strict adherence to the law would have reduced his estate. No "eye for an eye and a tooth for a tooth" justice for these truly Christian gentlemen. As in Portia's speech, "The quality of mercy is not strained" with them "it droppeth as the gentle rain from heaven," even before it is solicited.

Earlier, Shylock declared that he is no different from the Christians in seeking vengeance upon his enemies. "If a Jew wrong a Christian, what is his humility, Revenge. If a Christian wrong a Jew, what should his sufferance be by Christian example? Why, Revenge. The villainy you teach me I will execute, and it shall go hard but I will better the instruction." At the conclusion of this trial scene, however, we see that Shylock's picture of Christian vengeance does not apply to Antonio and the Duke, who are ideal gentlemen.

Gratiano, on the other hand, expresses the public's attitude toward Jews, which was far from ideal. Throughout the trial, he has acted toward Shylock as Shylock has acted toward Antonio, with hatred, contempt, and a total lack of charity. Like Shylock, Gratiano wants the full weight of the law to crush his enemy. He urges the Duke and Antonio to show the Jew no mercy, and as Shylock leaves the courtroom utterly defeated and feeling ill, Gratiano taunts him by wishing him the gallows rather than the baptismal font. The lowcomic impulse of the Shakespearean audience is thus satisfied by having the Jew as a butt and a convert at the same time.

The conditions that Antonio imposes on Shylock are kind and generous ones from the Christian point of view. Antonio would have Shylock behave naturally toward his daughter by having him leave her husband his wealth. We have already seen how deserving of good fortune the gentle Christian couple are.

The Duke and Antonio, in forcing Shylock to choose death or conversion, believe it is a kindness to provide for the Jew's salvation. As a convert, Shylock gets life and eternal life in exchange for the death and eternal damnation, which are his if he remains a Jew.

The Duke invites Portia to dinner, but the "lawyer" politely declines, explaining that "he" must return to Padua immediately. The Duke exists, and Bassanio offers the lawyer a fee of three thousand ducats, which Portia refuses, declaring: "He is well paid that is well satisfied / And I, delivering you, am satisfied." She wants no monetary reward and simply says "I pray you know me when we meet again," (the true meaning of which only she and Nerissa understand). Bassanio, however, insists upon her taking some remembrance, as a gift if not as a fee, and Portia agrees to accept his gloves. When her husband takes off his gloves, she notices his ring and says she will take that. Bassanio, greatly distressed, tries to dissuade her, arguing that the ring is worthless, and offers to find out the most precious ring in Venice instead. When Portia insists on having this one, he finally explains that it was given him by his wife, who made him vow neither to sell, nor to give, nor lose it. The lawyer then accuses Bassanio of selfishness and hypocrisy for refusing to part with the one insignificant trifle she requests. Knowingly, Portia declares that if Bassanio's wife were not insane and if she knew what the lawyer had done for Antonio, she would not begrudge her husband's parting with the ring. With these words Portia and Nerissa exit.

COMMENT: Portia naturally has no interest in monetary payment for her services, but she is playfully curious to test her husband's estimate of his wife. Will he obey her command literally? Does he think she is a madwoman who will not forgive him? She does her best to make him feel badly for refusing to surrender the ring. When Bassanio remains steadfast in spite of her arguments, Portia departs. She may be pleased with his loyalty but she is not pleased with his literal obedience to her command, for we must know by now that Portia values the spirit of the word far above literal fidelity to a promise.

Antonio, chagrined at Bassanio's refusal to give the ring to the lawyer, tells his friend to change his mind: "Let his deservings and my love withal, / Be valued 'gainst your wife's commandments." Bassanio, persuaded, sends Gratiano with the ring after the two young women to request them to come to Antonio's house, where the gentlemen intend to spend the night before setting out early in the morning for Belmont.

COMMENT: Although Bassanio has been proof against the doctor's urgings, he cannot hold out when Antonio tells him to break his wife's "commandments," a word which should remind us of the trial scene just past, with its issue

over literal and spiritual interpretation of law. The ring seems a small sacrifice to make compared with all that his friend has been willing to do for him, and the breaking of a "commandment" in the spirit of love will surely be forgiven mercifully.

SUMMARY: This scene, by far the longest in the play, is also the climax of the drama. The conflict between Antonio and Shylock, which represents the conflict between two religions and two ways of life, finally comes to a head and is resolved. The action of this courtroom scene can be divided into four parts: first, Shylock's inexorability before the Duke and Bassanio; second, Portia's ineffectual appeal to the Jew to show mercy to his intended victim; third, the resolution of the dispute in Antonio's favor by means of Portia's legal acumen, and the triumph of the *New Testament* and Good (the spirit of law) over the *Old Testament* and evil (the letter of the law); and finally, the problem of whether Bassanio should reward the lawyer with his precious ring. The crisis builds up in the first two parts of the scene as our concern for Antonio's safety increases. In the third part the tension is relieved, and in the fourth part the play returns to romantic comedy where it started and where it will end in the following act.

In this scene the two central characters of the play, the merciful Portia and the heartless Shylock, confront each other for the first and only time, and our attention is focused chiefly on them.

All appeals to Shylock's Christian charity fail, for he has none. Finally, Portia must resort to literalness herself. She turns Antonio over to Shylock's knife and then, surprisingly, turns on the usurer and has him charged with attempting the life of a Venetian citizen. Portia, disguised as a doctor of law, bears the entire responsibility for saving Antonio's life. She does her utmost to persuade Shylock to relent (symbolically, to convert), but when he fails to do so, she shows what a boomerang the law can be to those who insist on the letter and not the spirit of the law. Ultimately, Shylock is treated with Christian mercy, which includes a fine, the forefit of half his money, and his conversion to Christianity. The forced conversion is a logical consequence of Portia's eloquent and rational pleading, which proved to the Christian mind that persuasion was ineffectual and that force was the only means of dealing with a stubborn Jew.

The difference among the three Venetian friends, Antonio, Bassanio, and Gratiano, is nowhere clearer than in this scene. Antonio is calmly resigned to his fate, and his gentle melancholy and devoted friendship reflect the nobility of his soul. Bassanio is extremely concerned for Antonio, but although he loses his temper, he never loses his dignity as Gratiano does. Gratiano still behaves like a fool. Although motivated by noble feelings of friendship, his hissing of the villain fails to dignify his noble feelings, and his uncharitable outbursts and malicious sentiments toward Shylock show his kinship with the rabble.

The atmosphere of hatred is dispelled when Shylock leaves the stage and we return to the romantic affairs of Portia, who is trying to trick her husband out of a ring. Antonio's friendship prevails with Bassanio over his wife's command.

Act IV: Scene ii

The scene is another street in Venice, and Portia is bidding her "clerk" bring the deed of gift to Shylock for his signature. Gratiano comes upon them, bringing with him Bassanio's ring for "the lawyer" as well as an invitation to dinner. Portia declines the dinner but accepts the ring with thanks. She asks Gratiano to show her "youth" the way to Shylock's house, and when he agrees Nerissa whispers to Portia that she will try to get from her husband the ring she made him swear to keep forever. Portia replies, also in a whisper, that Gratiano will surely part with his ring too. She predicts that in Belmont their husbands will swear that they gave the rings to men, "but we'll outface them, and outswear them too." Nerissa and Gratiano exit one way, while Portia goes another, having planned to meet her maid shortly.

COMMENT: This very brief scene is important primarily in preparing us for the romantic comedy of the next and final act. For one thing, we see that Portia will bring back to Belmont with her the deed of gift for Lorenzo, which will gladden his heart. More significant, however, we see that Portia is sure that since Bassanio parted with his ring, Gratiano will follow suit. She is aware that servants and friends imitate the manners of their betters, and she approves of the gentle jest which Nerissa undertakes. Nerissa's desire for the ring, of course, is merely a desire to emulate her mistress.

Act V: Scene i

Back in Belmont, Lorenzo and Jessica are enjoying a beautiful moonlit night. "The moon shines bright. In such a night as this,/ When the sweet wind did gently kiss the trees / And they did make no noise, in such a night / Troilus methinks mounted the Troyan walls, / And sighed his soul toward the Grecian tents / Where Cressid lay that night," Lorenzo muses aloud, and Jessica, following his train of thought, fancies that on such a night Thisbe must have gone to her tryst with her lover Pyramus, when, frightened by a lion, she ran home again. Lorenzo thinks of Dido mourning after Aeneas, and Jessica imagines Medea gathering enchanted herbs to save her lover Jason. Finally Lorenzo says that on such a night, "Did Jessica steal from the wealthy Jew, / And with an unthrift love did run from Venice / As far as Belmont"; to which his wife teasingly replies that on such a night did young Lorenzo swear he loved her well, deceiving her with false vows of faith. Lorenzo replies that on such a night did Jessica slander her love but he forgave her.

COMMENT: The strident voice of Shylock has been silenced. Portia is on her way home, bringing promise of comedy over the ring. A lull settles over Belmont as two young lovers look at the moon. Beauty and happiness thrive in the enchanted world of Belmont where the play will end, as fairy tales do, with the promise that all will live happily ever after.

Up to this point, Lorenzo and Jessica have been kept in the background, but now they establish the mood of idyllic pearce and harmony in which the comedy will come to an end. The poetry is Shakespeare at his lyrical best. Through Lorenzo's words, we feel the balmy air, hear the faint wind stirring through the trees, and see the moonlight silvering over the entire scene. The young lovers, delighting in each other and in the beauty of the night, recall the ill-fated lovers of famous mixed couples of classical tradition, all of whom failed of achieving the ideal and constant love which Lorenzo and Jessica have. Troilus, prince of Troy, is seen mourning for Cressida, who has defected to the Greek camp and never will return. Thisbe, in love with Pyramus, the son of a hostile family, is depicted at the fearful moment when she flees the lion and drops her veil. (Supposing her dead when he finds the veil stained by blood of the lion's prey, Pyramus kills himself; later Thisbe comes upon his body and falls upon her lover's sword.) Dido, Queen of Carthage, is seen waving a willow (symbol of forsaken love) after Aneas has gone to meet his destiny in Rome. And Medea, the barbarian bride of the Greek prince Jason, is seen in a vignette, in which, out of love for her husband, she restores his father's youth, only to be cast aside later.

The misfortunes of these pagan lovers are recalled by way of contrast to Jessica and Lorenzo, who are emblems of "unthrift" (gentle, generous) love in the Christian tradition. This entire scene is notable for its numerous allusions to pagan mythology, which Renaissance philosophers interpreted allegorically in terms of neo-Platonic Christian values. These classical allusions enhance the atmosphere already created by the moonlight, music, and lyrical verse, and reinforce the theme of perfect Christian love which prevails in this last act.

The still of the night is interrupted by the arrival of Portia's servant Stephano, who brings words that his mistress and Nerissa are returning from the monastery and will be home before daybreak. Stephano is immediately followed by Launcelot who arrives crying, "Sola, sola! wo ha! ho sola, sola!" (imitating the sound of a post horn) and announces that a post (messenger) has just brought a "horn full of good news" (with a play on "cornucopia") that Bassanio will be home by morning. Lorenzo bids Stephano report these tidings indoors and send out the house musicians to play in the air.

Alone with Jessica again, Lorenzo re-establishes lyrical mood disrupted by the hurried arrival of the messengers, "How sweet the moonlight sleeps upon this bank!/ Here will we sit and let the sounds of music / Creep in our ears; soft stillness and the night / Become the touches of sweet harmony." He bids Jessica sit and look at the sky, which he calls the "floor of heaven" inlaid with "patterns of bright gold." He reminds her that "there's not the smallest orb which thou behold'st / But in his motion like an angel sings; / Still quiring to the young-eyed cherubins; / Such harmony is in immortal souls, / But whilst this muddy vesture of decay / Doth grossly close it in, we canot hear it."

The musicians enter and as they play Jessica remarks, "I am never merry when I hear sweet music." This her husband explains is because her soul is attentive. He reminds her that music affects even the wildest of animals, which is why legend tells that Orpheus (son of Apollo and consummate musician) could bend to his spell trees, stones and floods. Nothing in nature is insensible to "the sweet power of music." "The man that hath no music in himself, / Nor is not moved with concord of sweet sounds, / Is fit for treasons, stratagems, and spoils; / The motions of his spirit are dull as nioht, / And his affections dark as Erebus. / Let no such man be trusted. Mark the music."

COMMENT: Lorenzo's sensibility to beauty reveals the soul of a poet in what had seemed to be a quiet and plain young man. His reference to the music made by the heavenly bodies must be understood in the context of the Ptolemaic theory of astronomy that prevailed in Shakespeare's time. It was believed then that the stars moved around the earth, which was thought to be the center of the world, and as they moved they produced celestial music, audible only to the angels and to the souls of men in heaven. This divine music sounded the harmony of the universe and had its counterpart on earth in the voices and instruments sounded by men.

The musical harmony of the spheres, as a manifestation of universal order and unity, cosmic and earthly, in which God created heaven and earth, was a basic assumption among Elizabethans and was rarely explained, except in instructional literature, because it was such a familiar concept. Lorenzo, speaking to his Jewish wife, gives expression to the concept of the correspondence and unity of all things in nature and in heaven. He speaks as a poet in love and also as the instructor of Jessica in the gentle ways of life.

He explains to Jessica that the sadness she feels when listening to music is the hearkening of her soul to the celestial powers which quiet the passions and bring the soul peace and rest. This is what pagan writers meant when they showed that all things in nature, birds, beasts, even trees, became still at the sound of music. In this way, Lorenzo explains the Christian allegory of pagan myth to his untutored wife. He goes on to teach her that the man who does not love music signifies that his soul is not attuned to heavenly beauty, that it cannot rest, that it is on the road to hell (Erebus), and that it is, perhaps, incapable of salvation.

(Shylock, we may recall, hated the "vile squealing of the wrynecked fife," and the "sound of shallow foppery" [II.ii]. The savage beasts that prove tractable under the influence of Orpheus' harmony are more natural in this respect than Shylock.)

While the music is playing, Portia and Nerissa enter. Perceiving the light thrown by the small candle burning in her hall, Portia remarks, "So shines a good deed in a naughty world." When Nerissa observes that the candle was not visible as long as the moon was shining, her mistress answers, "So doth the greater glory dim the less. / A substitute shines brightly as a king / Until a king be by," and then his state seems paltry indeed as does a brook to the "main of waters." The music coming from her house now at night, sounds sweeter to her than it does by day, and she observes that nothing is absolutely good merely in itself, without reference to the circumstances. If the nightingale should sing by day, she would be considered no better a musician than a wren. "How many things by season seasoned are / To their right praise and true perfection!/ Peace! (music ceases) How the moon sleeps with Endymion,/ And would not be awakened."

COMMENT: Portia is no less sensitive than Lorenzo to the religious sentiment that "soft stillness and the night / Become the touches of sweet harmony."

She too believes there is a chain of correspondences among all things and that each thing has its proper place and its own perfection. The candle glowing in her hall reminds Portia that a good deed (the saving of Antonio) goes a long way, but not very far when considered in relation to celestial bodies, to the state, and to nature itself. The moon, at its end of the ladder of perfection, obscures the glow of its humble counterpart, the candle; the king outshines his substitute; the sea swallows up the brook. In Portia's mind, every creature in the entire design of nature reflects the perfect order of the universe, having its own place and function for making its contribution to the beauty of the world.

Portia's allusion to Endymion, the youth who sought perfect beauty and became the beloved of the moon goddess Selene, is in keeping with the romantic and religious mood established by Lorenzo and Jessica.

Recognizing Portia's voice, Lorenzo welcomes her home and she explains that she and Nerissa have been praying for their husbands' welfare which, they hope will be "the better for our words." (In fact, their husbands are very much the better for Portia's words spoken in the court of Venice, but Lorenzo thinks she is referring to the efficacy of prayer.) She has just time enough to ask that no one tell Bassanio that she has been away, when trumpets announce his arrival. By now the sky is growing light, and Bassanio greets his wife, saying that as long as she is present it is daylight for him even in the darkest night. To this Portia gayly replies. "Let me give light, but let me not be light / For a light wife doth make a heavy husband / And never be Bassanio so for me." (She is punning on the word "light," which meant "bright" and "unfaithful." She cordially welcomes the new arrivals, especially Antonio, declaring her intention of making him feel welcome more by deeds than by words.

COMMENT: Portia and Nerissa deliberately made all haste to return to Belmont before their husbands, for they do not want their joke to be marred by an suspicion of the truth on the part of the men. As we see, they have managed to arrive with not a moment to spare. Portia's entry dispels the lyrical atmosphere of the scene and introduces through her wit, the sophisticated and spirited comedy of the ring which follows.

Nerissa and Gratiano have been talking apart when suddenly a quarrel develops, for Nerissa has noticed that her husband's ring is missing. He swears that he gave it to the judge's clerk, and wishes the young man were "gelt" (castrated) rather than that his wife should be so disturbed. Justifying himself to Portia, Gratiano explains that it was just a "paltry ring" engraved with commonplace poetry—"Love me and leave me not." Nerissa, angry that he should speak so slightingly of the value of the ring and of the quality of the poetry, reminds him of his oath to wear it to his grave. She pretends to believe that he gave it to some other woman, but Gratiano swears he gave it to a youth, "A kind of boy, a little scrubbed boy / No higher than thyself."

Portia reproves Gratiano for parting with his wife's first gift and tells him she is positive that not for all the wealth in the world would Bassanio give away the ring she gave him.

At this, Basanio remarks in an aside that had better cut off his left hand to conceal the truth from her, but too late, Gratiano tells all. Bassanio ruefully admits that he too gave away his ring when no other payment would be accepted by the judge. Pretending she is outraged, Portia swears, "By heaven, I will ne'er come in your bed / Until I see the ring," and Nerissa echoes this vow. Poor Bassanio entreats his wife to be reasonable: "If you did know to whom I gave the ring, / If you did know for whom I gave the ring, / And would conceive for what I gave the ring, / And how unwillingly I left the ring / When naught would be accepted but the ring, / You would abate the strength of your displeasure." But Portia will not be so easily reconciled. "If you had known the virtue of the ring / Or half her worthiness that gave the ring, / Or your own honor to contain the ring, / You would not then have parted with the ring." She refuses to believe that any reasonable man would have insisted on being paid with a ring whose chief value was sentimental, and she declares, like Nerissa, that some woman must have gotten the ring. When Bassanio explains that his sense of honor required him to part with the ring for the judge who had saved Antonio's life, Portia warns her husband that she will be just as generous with her favors to the judge as he was. "I'll not deny him anything I have, / No not my body nor my husband's bed"; and Narissa declares she will do likewise. Gratiano, indignant warns that if his wife plays loose her lover had better watch out, for "I'll mar the young clerk's pen."

COMMENT: There are strong echoes here of the pseudo-legalistic debates held in the twelfth-century courts of love under the auspices of Eleanor of Aquitaine. For their amusement, the ladies of these ancient French courts would hear complaints made by lovers concerning discourtesies, broken vows, or infidelities. The issues would be disputed at some length and the judges would decide the fault as Portia playfully does here.

The imitative behavior of Gratiano and Nerissa augments the comedy of the rings, in which the witty ladies utterly confound their husbands. The ladies make the most of sexual ironies which the Elizabethan audience understood very well. The body and the bed Portia shared with the learned doctor are her own, of course. The ring, which meant "female genitalia" as well as "a circlet worn for ornament," is especially significant in this reunion of lovers whose marriages have not yet been consummated.

Antonio is miserable at being the cause of this quarrel, but Portia reassures him that he is not at all to blame and is most welcome. Ever the loyal friend, Antonio now offers Portia his soul as bond for Bassanio's future fidelity, just as formerly he offered his body as bond to Shylock. This suggestion satisfies Portia, who gives Bassanio the ring he gave away to the judge, asking him to keep it more faithfully than before. Her husband recognizes the ring, and in a last bit of teasing Portia tells him that she got it from the judge who lay with her last night, and Nerissa says the same of the clerk. The men are dumbfounded, but before they have time to become very angry, Portia reveals the truth: that she was the doctor and Nerissa the clerk. Relieved and amazed, Bassanio declares, "Sweet doctor, you shall be my bedfellow. / When I am absent, then lie with my wife."

There are other wonders in store. Portia gives Antonio a letter explaining that three of his ships have unexpectedly come to port and that he is once again a wealthy man. Next she gives Lorenzo and Jessica the deed of gift from Shylock, promising that they will be his heirs. Lorenzo with wonder and admiration declares, "Fair ladies, you drop manna in the way / Of starved people."

COMMENT: Report (the gossipy crone of the Elizabethan tavern) has been a liar after all. See III.i.

It is almost morning. Portia suggests that they all go inside where she will answer their questions. As they all exit Gratiano says that his first question will be whether Nerissa would rather remain with the company or go to bed now that it is two hours to day. "But were the day come, I should wish it dark / Till I were couching with the doctor's clerk. / Well, while I live I'll fear no other thing / So sore as keeping safe Nerissa's ring."

COMMENT: After the trial scene in the Fourth Act we may well have wondered how Shakespeare will manage to write an interesting final act that will not be anti-climatic or just dull. The answer is the sophisticated sexual comedy of the rings, which solves the dramatic problem of ending the play. It introduces a note of pretended or apparent discord among the married couples, which increases the surprised delight that accompanies the revelation of the truth and the restoration of perfect harmony in Belmont.

We have already remarked that Portia is a many-sided personality. In the trial scene we saw her maturer qualities: intelligence, eloquence, wit, poise, and deep ethical understanding. Here we see the sophisticated and witty side of the Portia who told her husband (III.ii) that she was "an

unlessoned girl, unschooled, unpractised,' who (III.iv) relished the prospect of dressing up as a youth. Portia has a sense of fun; she can be a bit of a tease, yet she does not lose her sense of proportion; and when she realizes that the joke has gone far enough (that is, when Antonio begins to feel uncomfortable), then she knows it is time to stop. She has never really been angry at Bassanio for giving away the ring; he, for his part, only now learns the truly remarkable character of his new wife, who brings good fortune and good news to every person on stage.

The traditional ending for a comedy is marriage, but in this comedy the wedding took place in the Third Act. What has not yet taken place, however, is the consummation of the marriage, since the husbands had to leave for Venice immediately after the wedding service. The latter part of this scene is full of sexual innuendos and double-entendres (for example, Gratiano's "I'll mar the young clerk's pen"), as well as explicit sexual references (for example, Portia's accusation that Bassanio was unfaithful and her ironic warning that she would deceive him in return). This raciness is definitely in the comic mood that dominates this last act of the play, which now ends with the promise of fidelity in marriage as Portia promises to "answer all things faithfully" and Gratiano suggestively to keep "safe Nerrisa's ring."

SUMMARY: This final scene is important for the following reasons:

1. The essentially comic spirit of the play is restored back in Belmont after the darkly somber implications of the trial scene. We end on a joyous note of universal happiness and well-being, now that Antonio's ships have come safely home, and Lorenzo and Jessica will be heirs to Shylock, and the young husbands and wives are together once more.

2. The first part of the scene contains some beautiful lines of poetry spoken by Lorenzo, whose words evoke the moonlit night of Belmont, and hymn the power of music to bring heavenly peace to the human and the animal breast. Up till now Lorenzo's character has only been suggested, but he now assumes full shape as a highly poetic, gentle, and spiritual young man in whose imminent good fortune we rejoice.

3. Portia and Nerissa engage in highly witty sexual play as they reproach their husbands for giving away their rings. The ladies pretend they will be as liberal with their favors (their bodies) as their husbands were with their rings, but when the joke has gone far enough, Portia explains that she and Nerissa were the doctor and the clerk, to the amazement and delight of her hearers. The scene then ends on a merrily salacious note, as all the characters trip off to hear the details of Portia's marvelous disguise.

Character Analyses

ANTONIO   the merchant of the title, is a rich and highly respected citizen in Venice, possessed of many friends. Yet, by nature, Antonio is a melancholy man, a silent and reflective gentleman who values friendship more than anything in the world. His is gentle and melancholy which persists equally when fortune smiles or frowns upon him. He believes that life is a stage on which each man plays his part; reality itself begins in heaven. Nevertheless, Antonio never seeks to dampen the spirits of his gay Venetian friends to suit his own mood, for as an older and more experienced man, he realizes that youth must have its fling. His love for Bassanio is one of the noblest friendships in literature. "My person, my purse, my extremest means," he gladly offers to Bassanio with an unstinting generosity that does not flag when he is finally threatened with death. Antonio never blames Bassanio nor repents his own decision to sign the bond for his friend's sake. Once redeemed, Antonio shows perfect Christian charity, returning good for ill, and showing mercy to Shylock after the latter's inhuman attempt on his life. His call for Shylock's conversion is an act of grace, for the greatest charity a Christian gentleman can do is to help save a man's soul.

The Antonio whom we see on the stage is unfailingly kind and gentle towards his friends and ultimately merciful towards his enemy, but he is also the Antonio whom Shylock describes as spitting upon him and kicking him in public. This is acceptable behavior for a Christian toward a Jew, who, in Elizabethan eyes, was no better than a dog. Who would not spit on a man who makes a profit out of other men's needs (for this is the way Antonio sees Shylock)? Still, it is a measure of Shakespeare's sensibility that he never lets us see Antonio act in this way. Antonio exemplifies the noblest virtues of the perfect Christian gentleman in Renaissance society throughout the play.

BASSANIO   friend to Antonio and later husband to Portia, is also a noble, generous, and honorable young man. He captivates the hearts of two of the most high-minded characters in the play, Antonio and Portia. We learn as soon as we meet him that he has not only already spent his fortune, but is also in debt, principally to Antonio. He is seeking a way to mend his ways, pay his debts, and retrieve his fortune by marrying Portia, whom he loves. His profligacy is to be regarded kindly, for it is a sign of high spirits and noble birth. The young Renaissance gentleman was expected to philander in his youth so that he could learn the evil ways of the world and come to reject them. His choice of Portia as

his wife is to be admired, for she is also of noble birth, mind, and beauty. Through her, he will be able to mend his ways, live a blessed life and win eternal salvation.

Bassanio moves in a Christian world where, among gentlemen, generosity is the rule, and where wealth is freely given and accepted among friends. There is nothing miserly about Bassanio. When Gratiano asks for a favor, Bassanio grants it even before knowing what the favor is (II.ii). As soon as he learns of the peril in which his friend Antonio stands, he hurries to his side. Bassanio's grief and remorse are no less than what we expect of the impassioned friend. He has the goodness of soul which enables him to choose correctly among the three caskets, but he lacks the resourcefulness and wit to find a way out of the bond. In imagination and ethical seriousness, Bassanio is less remarkable than his wife, yet he is the man whom she loves and in whom Belmont will find a noble and honorable lord.

GRATIANO   another Venetian friend, is by nature garrulous, gregarious, and often rather crude. As he himself says, "Let me play the fool, / With mirth and laughter let old wrinkles come / And let my liver rather heat with wine / Than my heart cool with mortifying groans" (I.i). This is the Gratiano who speaks "an infinite deal of nothing." There is a cynically reflective side to him as well, when he muses in a moment of tranquility on the fleeting nature of desire(II.vi); and he shows generosity later when he appreciates the fact that Jessica must feel strange in Belmont and therefore bids Nerissa make the girl feel at home (III.ii).

Gratiano is to Bassanio what Nerissa is to Portia, a sort of weak echo to the principal romantic lover. Thus Gratiano woos the maid when Bassanio woos the mistress, and when Bassanio gives his ring to the judge, Gratiano gives his to the clerk. Bassanio teaches his friend courtesy, but Gratiano is clearly a less generous man than Bassanio, for he is the only Christian in the trial scene who taunts Shylock and who urges that no mercy be shown him, Although his counsel does not prevail, his spiteful words reflect the popular attitude toward Jews. His is the voice of common humanity, seeking revenge. Finally, Gratiano's racy turn of mind keeps up an undercurrent of sexual innuendo which contributes to the comic spirit of the play.

SALANIO AND SALARINO   friends of Antonio and Bassanio, serve to create the atmosphere of Venice and to advance the plot, but we know almost nothing at all about their personal lives or what sort of men they really are. It is the language of these two men that in the first scene tells us of high masts and proud sails on the merchant ships, of rich and exotic cargoes, of danger on the seas, all of which helps to create a sense of the magnificence and the romance of Venice. It is also from the mouths of these two men that we hear of Shylock's reaction to Jessica's elopement, of his intention to claim his pound of flesh if Antonio fails the payment, and of the various Venetian ships reported lost and very likely including Antonio's. The dialogues between Salanio and Salarino thus take the place of narrative and bridge the gaps in time, which the dramatist does not want to depict on stage. Such friends as these would surely have raised the money to repay Antonio's debt on time if they had had it. We can only assume that, like Bassanio and Lorenzo, they were "unthrifty young gentlemen."

LORENZO another young Venetian, is a quiet young man who is contrasted by the voluble and loquacious Gratiano early in the play. He has the initiative to plan and execute an elopement with Jessica and offers her constant love. As he tells Launcelot, he is a plain man given to plain speech, by which he means he is not a foolish word-twister. Lorenzo really comes into his own as a romantic and gentle Christian in the last act, when, musing on a moonlit night in Belmont, he reveals his profoundly poetic and religious sensibility to beauty of all kinds, especially to music. He teaches Jessica the ways of earthly and heavenly love, and his good fortune at the end of the play accords with the nobility of his nature.

THE DUKE OF VENICE as the ruler of his city-state, knows that his first duty is the enforcement of law and the maintenance of order. We hear about him first when Salanio and Salarino describe how Shylock brought him down to the docks to search for Jessica. He appears only once, in the trial scene, where the Duke admits that as head of state he must protect the commercial interests of Venice by upholding the contract for the pound of flesh and tries to persuade Shylock to be merciful. He shows mercy himself by pardoning Shylock his life, reducing his fine, and offering him a chance to convert.

THE PRINCE OF MOROCCO is a comically exotic figure in Belmont, with his dark skin and white robes and his flowery language. At once proud and shy, confident and nervous, the Prince speaks boastfully in the sententious, almost pompous tones of a man who does not quite feel himself accepted in Christian surroundings, as in fact he is not, on account of his religion and color. Failing to perceive the difference between outer show and inner reality, he chooses the gold casket, whose inscription promises what many men

desire. The Prince is a ridiculous figure who is politely but coolly dismissed by Portia.

THE PRINCE OF ARRAGON like the Prince of Morrocco, fails to make the essential distinction required by the ordeal of the caskets: that is, to distinguish between external illusion and internal reality. Arragon is keen enough to discount the fair promise of the gold casket, which he realizes appeals to the "fool multitude." He is an aristocrat who disdains associating with the common herd, but his pride is his undoing, and he is taken in by the inscription on the silver casket, which promises that he will get what he deserves. Because Arragon is sure that he deserves Portia he does not deserve her and does not win her.

SHYLOCK the Jewish moneylender, is one of the most interesting and one of the most controversial of Shakespeare's characters. Discussion of *The Merchant of Venice* generally centers around Shylock, and yet the play was not called *The Jew of Venice* (a title given to it in 1701), Shylock is not onstage most of the time, and does not appear at all in the final act. Why then do we feel that he is the center of the play? The answer is that Shylock is given the most passionate, most memorable speeches and actions in the play, and his character is etched in bold strokes across its entire surface, leaving an indelible mark on the words and actions of all the other players. He is a believable human being as well as an outrageous villain and comic butt, and has become all things to all men.

Some readers view Shylock as a proud and a passionate man who has long stored up in his heart the humiliation suffered at the hands of the hostile Christian world and is now ready for revenge. But the historical fact is that anti-Semitism was a perfectly acceptable feeling in the sixteenth century, and Shakespeare developed Shylock as the stereotyped comic figure of the villainous Jewish moneylender. Shakespeare was capable, however, of seeing the universal principles of human nature embodied in all men, so that he made Shylock believable as the revengeful Jew. Shylock is the villain of the piece; there is no doubt about that. He hates Antonio for hindering his business and for treating him with terrible contempt in public, and we must not doubt that from the very beginning Shylock had hoped to get his revenge on Antonio by arranging the flesh-bond.

Jessica's elopement and theft of his money and jewels increase Shylock's resentment against the Christian world, so that, although he might have had second thoughts about executing his revenge, he is no longer troubled by them after Jessica's elopement. Having found himself victimized by Antonio, Shylock wants as good as he gets. Symbolizing the stern justice of *Old Testament* law, Shylock is a passionate man thirsting for revenge and the ridiculous figure of stereotyped Jewish obstinacy, hatred, and literalness. Usually comic, he is at times grotesque, and at times even touching ("Hath not a Jew eyes . . ."). He is a villain of perserverence and restless energy, who is, nevertheless, foiled by good Christians in the end.

TUBAL   a Jew and a friend of Shylock, appears only once (III.i), to report the result of his search for the absconded Jessica, but we have already heard of him (I.iii) as the man who will supply Shylock with the funds for Antonio. This Tubal is clearly a serviceable friend, undertaking a trip to Genoa on Shylock's behalf and running to secure the arresting officer for the day that Antonio's bond will fall due. Of the nature of the man himself we know nothing and need to know nothing for the purposes of the drama. In his one appearance, he alternately throws Shylock into despair over Jessica's squandering of the stolen wealth, and then again raises Shylock's hopes that Antonio will be bankrupt. In so doing Tubal helps to emphasize the grotesquely comic aspect of the moneylender.

LAUNCELOT GOBBO   servant to Shylock and then servant to Bassanio, is, as Jessica calls him, "a merry devil." In Shylock's service, he is a rustic who misuses words and plays crude jests. He teases his old father and Jessica in the spirit of fun, but he mocks Shylock with more spite. The fact that Launcelot finds life in Shylock's house so distasteful is a telling factor against the Jew, for in stage tradition such servants were expected to admire and emulate their masters. When Launcelot transfers to Bassanio's service, his crude humor turns to wise foolery and his vocabulary, puns, jests, and ironies become sophisticated. When Launcelot describes the struggle between his conscience and the devil, he reflects the problem Jessica must face: whether to remain with Shylock or to seek a better life with a Christian. Although we never hear Jessica debating this question, we are, in effect, persuaded of the virtue of her decision because we understand the rightness of Launcelot's. Both characters are presumably much better treated and better educated in the households of Christians.

OLD GOBBO   Launcelot's father, appears only once, when he comes bringing a present to Shylock, whom he at first does not recognize because of his almost total blindness. Like his son, Old Gobbo is a comic rustic figure, constantly mispronouncing or misusing words. Launcelot is under the impression that Old Gobbo was a philanderer in his youth.

PORTIA   the lady of Belmont, is one of Shakespeare's great heroines, whose physical beauty, lively intelligence, quick wit, and high moral seriousness have been nurtured in an atmosphere of wealth and freedom. Like a princess in a fairy tale, she is famed throughout the world for her beauty and her virtue, and her suitors are put to a standard test (the caskets) in order to win her hand. But Portia is no ordinary fairy tale princess. Although she dutifully abides by her father's restrictions concerning her marriage, she is made weary by the necessity to obey. Her satirical comments about her suitors reveal a sharp wit and a keen insight into human nature and suggest that she could choose a husband for herself very well.

It is in the trial scene, however that we see the full extent of her wit, her intellect, and her charity. Her adventurousness, sureness of purpose, and intelligence save her husband's friend. But Portia is not interested only in saving Antonio; she would like, if possible, also to save Shylock from himself, and to this end she appeals eloquently first to his moral sensibility and than to his avarice. The money that she urges Shylock to accept in lieu of Antonio's flesh is her own money, freely given to Bassanio. For Portia, money cannot be weighed in the balance with a human soul, and when she finally must resort to legal argument in order to rescue Antonio, she still stands for mercy. It is to the ethical preaching of Portia that Shylock owes his life in the end.

While Portia can rise to heights of dignity and eloquence, she remains, after all, a playful and tender wife. Although she dominates the trial scene, we need have no fear that she will overpower her husband at home, for underneath her teasing is a womanly gentleness, an "unschooled" innocence, that promises Bassanio all felicity in his marriage.

NERISSA   Portia's maid, is not so much a servant as a companion who possesses much the same kind of wit and gaiety as her mistress, although she does not demonstrate the ethical concern which ennobles Portia. As Portia's maid, she emulates her mistress' manners, but she cannot be expected to perceive the inner nature of the gentle heart. Nerissa is to Portia what Gratiano is to Bassanio, a similar but less impressive, less noble edition.

JESSICA   Shylock's daughter, has her father's blood but not his manners. She is a gentle girl who finds life in her father's home unbearably tedious and irksome. It is presumed that she has struggled with her conscience before eloping with Lorenzo, taking with her those jewels and ducats about which Shylock complains. Unlike her father, Jessica does not hesitate to spend money in order to enjoy life. She converts to

Christianity under the instruction of Lorenzo and has an eye for the beauty and the harmony which comprises the Christian world view. She is more modest than Portia, who is not embarrassed to wear men's clothing, and she has the perception to notice that Portia is an extraordinary woman, whom she will probably try to emulate.

OTHER MINOR CHARACTERS include **LEONARDO**, servant to Bassanio, and **BALTHASAR** and **STEPHANO**, servants to Portia, as well as various attendants in the court.

Othello

Scene-by-Scene Summary and Comment

Act I: Scene i

The scene opens on a street in Venice. It is night. Roderigo and Iago are engaged in a heated discussion over the latter's failure to perform the services he has been paid for, that is, to keep Roderigo informed of Desdemona's affections. Her elopement with Othello the Moor has just come to Roderigo's attention.

COMMENT: In his list of actors, Shakespeare describes Roderigo as "a gull'd gentleman." A "gull" is the Elizabethan slang for "dupe," equivalent to the American "sucker." Roderigo is Iago's "gull" because he has paid Iago to win Desdemona's love for him, presumably after he has failed to win it himself, while Iago has no intentions of fulfilling his part of the bargain.

Roderigo implies that Iago has abetted the elopement and does not really hate the Moor as he had said. Iago protests. His hatred for the Moor is a very real one, especially since the general has refused to appoint him lieutenant, despite the humble suits made in his behalf by three great men of the city. Iago complains of Othello's pride and "bombast circumstance" and is angered by the appointment, in his stead, of Michael Cassio, an educated military theoretician of Florence, who has had no practical experience in war. Iago himself has shown his courage fighting with the Moor at Rhodes, at Cyprus, against Christians and heathens, but the ungrateful Moor has made Cassio lieutenant, while Iago remains "his Moorship's ancient."

COMMENT: Roughly, the hierarchy of the Venetian army ran as follows: Othello, full general and supreme commander; Cassio, lieutenant-general and Othello's designated successor; Iago, third in the chain of command, roughly chief-of-staff.

It may be supposed that Iago's hatred of the Moor is a real one. Clearly, he has had a great deal of military experience and is qualified for the post, for later when Cassio is disgraced, Iago is made lieutenant. His quarrel with Cassio's education or "bookishness" reflects the age-old conflict between thinkers and doers. The fact that Cassio is a Florentine probably adds to Iago's anger.

Iago has received payment from Roderigo to press his lovesuit with Desdemona. Presumably, the money was then spent to pay the "three great ones of the city" who lobbied for Iago's appointment as lieutenant. These petitioners seem to have explained their failure to accomplish their mission by attributing to Othello evasive tactics, that is, "bombast circumstance" (roundabout or ceremonious talk). Othello is a proud man, indeed, but he has an open and trusting nature and is not given to evasions in the beginning of the play. This disparagement of his character, therefore, may be attributed to the failure of the "great ones" or to Iago's hatred.

Notice that Iago and Roderigo find themselves in similar circumstances. Iago has been rejected by the Moor; Roderigo by the Moor's wife, Desdemona. The similarity of situation can be traced to the original story of the Moor and "Desdemona" told by Cinthio in the *Hecatommithi*, where the roles of rejected lover and ensign to the Moor were played by a single character.

At Iago's outburst of grievances, Roderigo expresses surprise that the ancient continues to follow the general whom he hates so much. Iago assures his companion: "I follow him to serve my turn upon him." In following the Moor, Iago follows himself and serves neither for love nor duty, he asserts. "Whip me such honest knaves," he says of those who after long and faithful service are cashiered when they are old and useless. He expresses his admiration for the man who appears to perform his duties, but actually attends unflinchingly to his own interests, using his masters only for his own gains. The self-interested man has "soul," Iago declares, and such a man of "soul" is he.

COMMENT: Iago reveals his true nature to Roderigo, who is incapable of understanding the implications of Iago's self-interested "soul." Logically, Roderigo should conclude that as Iago serves the Moor for his own gains, so must he be serving Roderigo.

The speech shows Iago's contempt for conventional Christian conceptions of the ideal servant. Iago reveals himself as a rebel, an enemy to social order; he has junked the long-standing feudal idea that there is a special beauty and dignity in service to one's master. The idea of service was a Christian principle, devoutly followed throughout the Middle Ages and Renaissance. Based on the biblical paradox of the first being last and the last first, this principle was reflected in one of the papal titles, "the servant of the servant of God." The antithesis of Iago's contemptuous view of service is expressed elsewhere in Shakespeare. Adam, the faithful servant of Oliver in *As You Like It*, reflects "the constant service of the antique world / When service sweat for duty, not for need [reward]."

Roderigo seems inclined to brood over the good fortune of Othello (whom he calls "thick-lips") in winning Desdemona, but Iago calls for action. Rouse Brabantio, Desdemona's father, Iago advises. Let her enraged kinsmen poison Othello's joy and spread plague on his delight. Roderigo agrees.

Immediately, the unseemly pair arrive at Brabantio's house. Iago urges Roderigo to raise a horrible cry as if the whole town were on fire, and he joins him by shouting, "Thieves!" A sleepy and confused Brabantio appears at the window. Roderigo and Iago ask him the condition of his house, knowing that he will be unable to answer their questions. Vulgarly, Iago informs him that his "white ewe" has gone off with a "black ram," meaning, of course, that his daughter has eloped with a dark-skinned Moor or a Negro. (Elizabethans made no distinctions between the two.) More respectfully, Roderigo identifies himself, but he is prevented from speaking further by Brabantio's charges of drunkenness and his reminders that Roderigo is unwelcome both to his house and to his daughter.

Patiently, Roderigo attempts to convey his information, but Iago breaks in and, alluding to Othello's race, warns Brabantio that his daughter is being covered by a "Barbary horse" (named from "Barbary" on the coast of North Africa) and that his grandchildren will be "gennets" (black horses).

COMMENT: Brabantio is a powerful and cultivated citizen, a member of the governing Venetian oligarchy. He has found Roderigo unworthy of his daughter's hand in marriage. Apparently, Roderigo refused to take no for an answer and continued his suit until Brabantio was forced to charge him "not to haunt about my doors." This charge is an appropriate reason for Roderigo's hiring Iago as a go-between.

Shakespeare deliberately contrasts the speech of Roderigo and Iago. Roderigo addresses Brabantio courteously, while Iago uses the bawdy language of the barracks and ale-house.

Brabantio, shocked at this report, asks the "profane" (foul-mouthed) wretch to identify himself. Receiving another virulent report about his daughter and the

Moor, Brabantio himself identifies the speaker as a "villain."

COMMENT: Brabantio's tag for Iago is precisely the one Shakespeare used to describe the character in his "list of actors." The "villain" was a traditional character in native English miracle and morality plays and was frequently called the "Vice" or the "Herod." His function was always to incite mischief or inspire evil, but he was essentially a comic character, for those who rejected the divine goodness inherent in human nature were conventionally regarded as fools. The villain or vice was the greatest fool of all. Those in the old morality plays, like Iago in this scene, used foul language, to the amusement of medieval audiences, and gave the most malicious interpretations possible to the behavior of others.

Iago starts to retaliate the name-calling, but as if out of respect to Brabantio, he cuts himself off and replies, "You are—a senator." Infuriated, Brabantio promises to make Roderigo answer for the insults of the unidentified villain. Still patient and respectful, Roderigo at last gets the opportunity to deliver his message. In a speech ornamented with rhetorical flourishes, Roderigo informs the senator that his fair daughter has been transported by a common knave, and that, if he knows of this elopement and has consented to it, his informants are guilty of "bold and saucy wrongs." If he does not know of the elopement, then he has wrongly rebuked the informants. With much civility, Roderigo assures Brabantio that he would not trifle over so serious a matter and advises the father to confirm the report of his daughter's revolt.

Addressed in the only language to which he is capable of responding, Brabantio becomes alarmed. He calls for lights, arouses his retainers, and admits that he has had a dream not unlike Roderigo's report. Then he repeats his cry, "Light, I say! light!"

COMMENT: Brabantio's cry for light is not only a demand for illumination, but part of the texture of light-dark imagery that runs through the first scene. The entire action takes place at night, it should be remembered, but several illuminations occur during the scene. As her father sleeps in darkness and in ignorance, Desdemona, the "white ewe," steals off in the night with Othello, the "black ram." Brabantio soon learns that his "fair" (light) daughter has eloped with the Moor; his call for light appropriately accompanies this enlightenment and the simultaneous illumination or explanation of his dream. Iago too has made substantial revelations on this dark night. He reveals his black hatred for the Moor, his jealousy of Cassio, and his intention to serve his own evil ends.

As Brabantio departs to rouse his household, Iago takes his leave of Roderigo. It is unwholesome, he explains, to be discovered in an action against the Moor, his general. Besides, he tells Roderigo, Brabantio's action against Othello will only "gall him with some check," for Venice needs the Moor to protect its interests in Cyprus. Othello's equal as a military leader cannot be found, Iago maintains, and although he hates the Moor, he must follow and pretend to love him "for necessity of present life." He tells Roderigo to lead Brabantio and his party to the Sagittary (apparently an inn) where Othello can be found.

COMMENT: Iago says he must follow Othello "for necessity of present life," an ambiguous motive, which may mean "because Othello is needed in the Cyprus wars" or (because Iago has expressed his self-interest so strongly) "because I still need Othello for my own purposes." Either Iago regards Othello as indispensable to the military defense of the Venetian republic, or he wishes Roderigo to think he does. It is not Iago's intention at this time to work the complete destruction of the Moor in order to help Roderigo win Desdemona. He expects only to "gall" (irritate) the Moor, to "poison his delight," or "plague him with flies," and vex his joy.

In his relationship to Roderigo, Iago is like the debtor Shakespeare often describes. When payment is demanded, he satisfies his creditor with a small sum, promising a great deal more than he gives or intends to give. Since Iago cannot turn Desdemona over to Roderigo at the moment, he arranges to "gall" Othello "with some check." Later on, Iago promises, Roderigo may win the lady herself.

As Iago departs, Brabantio returns still wearing his dressing gown; he is attended by servants whose torches light the night. He has checked Desdemona's room, and, indeed, she is gone. Between outbursts of grief for the fate of father, Brabantio questions Roderigo for details. Where did you see her? Was she with the Moor? What did she say? Are they married? When Roderigo expresses the belief that they are married, Brabantio's grief is augmented considerably. How did she get out! he wails. Without waiting for an answer, he accuses his daughter of betraying her blood. Clutching at straws, he seeks an explanation for her betrayal in stories he has read of young girls who have been deceived by charms. Roderigo agrees that he has read stories of such enchantments. Now Brabantio sends for his brother, and in the next breath bemoans the fact that he had refused her to Roderigo.

COMMENT: Half-mad with grief, Brabantio utters phrases which are difficult to interpret. "Some one way, some another" appears to mean "Some [men are knaves in] one way, some [are knaves in] another." He has saved his daughter from the knave Roderigo only to lose her to a worse husband, Othello. Since the sentence is incomplete, it is possible to fill out the thought in a variety of ways but it is clear that Brabantio's opinion of Roderigo as a son-in-law is only slightly higher than his opinion of the Moor.

At last Brabantio asks where he can find the Moor, and Roderigo agrees to show him the way. Calling for officers and promising to reward Roderigo, Brabantio goes off to find Othello.

SUMMARY: The opening scene establishes the following points:

1. It introduces the main characters of the play, directly through the appearance of Roderigo and Iago, indirectly through conversation concerning Othello, Desdemona, and Cassio.

2. It establishes the time, place, and action of the play. The first scene takes place in Venice at a time when the Turks were attacking the island of Cyprus, a colony of Venice in 1570; it is suggested that subsequent scenes will take place on Cyprus where Othello must lead his military forces. The action of the play, Iago's plot against Othello, is set in motion by Roderigo's employment of Iago as substitute in his courtship of Desdemona and by Iago's own failure to be appointed as lieutenant.

3. It provides valuable information about Othello before he appears on stage. Othello has eloped with Desdemona, whom Roderigo wants; he is not easily influenced and has appointed Cassio to a post Iago wants; he is the best general available to the Venetian Republic, and he is about to lead an expedition against the Turks.

4. It shows Iago in action as a "self-interested" man, an accomplished instigator, or an "agent provocateur." He has made a gull of Roderigo, bilking him of money without fulfilling the services promised, and he has converted Brabantio into a gadfly who, serving Iago's purposes as well as his own, will pursue and irritate Othello in his hour of joy.

5. It introduces Brabantio, an influential senator in the Venetian oligarchy and the father of Desdemona, in order to supply background for Desdemona's character. She is a lady of noble lineage, ordinarily shy and obedient, who, for the sake of the Moor, has abandoned her family and position.

Act I: Scene ii

On another street in Venice, Othello, Iago, and several attendants bearing torches appear. Iago is in the middle of a description of his encounter with Brabantio. He tells Othello that Brabantio's remarks so angered him that he felt like killing him but was restrained by the fact that, apart from war, he has never "contriv'd murther," that is, he has never murdered in the heat of passion or for personal reasons. Othello approves of Iago's restraint, but Iago continues to insist on the enormity of the provocation. Brabantio spoke so disparagingly of the Moor's honor that it took all the "godliness" within Iago to refrain from harming the man. He warns Othello that Brabantio is extremely powerful in the government of Venice and, like the Duke, has two votes in the senate. (Historically, this would be impossible.) Brabantio will certainly try to divorce the couple and seek every legal means of redress against Othello.

COMMENT: Having enraged the unwilling father-in law against his daughter's new husband, Iago now attempts to goad Othello into anger against Brabantio. Othello does not take the bait, although Iago persists, stressing Brabantio's vilifications of the Moor, his power in the senate, and his ability to take strong legal action against Othello.

Othello replies that Brabantio may do his worst; he is assured that his military services to the government will outweigh Brabantio's complaints. Furthermore, Othello asserts, although he does not like boasting, he will make known the fact that he is descended from a royal line. In all due humility, Othello states, his family is equal in honor and rank to the house of Brabantio. He informs Iago that he would not have given up his "unhoused free condition," his bachelor freedom, for anything in the world, except the deepest love.

COMMENT: Othello's reaction to the potential threat of Brabantio is one of calm and dignity; he has the self-assurance suitable to the commander of men. He has no apologies to make to anyone, and he is not easily angered.

Lights are seen in the darkness as Cassio and several officers with torches arrive. Iago, who is expecting Brabantio, warns Othello to retreat and hide. Othello proudly refuses. Standing his ground, he states confidently, "My parts, my title, and my perfect soul/ Shall manifest me rightly."

COMMENT: Othello is not only self-assured, but trusts that other men, when presented with the facts, will decide for the truth. Othello's refusal to hide is a mark of his open nature, which will deteriorate later.

Othello now recognizes his lieutenant Cassio and his officers, whom he calls "servants of the Duke" and "friends." Cassio delivers the Duke's summons to Othello. Messengers have been arriving one after the other from the Venetian galleys, and many of the Duke's consuls are already assembled to discuss the emergency. They have sent three times for Othello, who could not be found at his usual lodgings. Othello replies, "'Tis well I am found by you," and promises to join Cassio after he has spent a moment in the house.

COMMENT: Although he is a fearless man of war, Othello does not like personal conflict. He seems relieved to be found by Cassio rather than Brabantio, for he prefers to be engaged in national rather than domestic strife.

Perplexed at Othello's delay, Cassio asks Iago what is going on. In a vulgar periphrasis, Iago explains that Othello is married. He is interrupted by Othello's return before he can tell Cassio the name of the bride.

At this point, Brabantio, Roderigo, and armed officers with more torches arrive on the scene. Again, Iago warns Othello of Brabantio's malice. Denouncing Othello as a "thief," Brabantio signals his retainers to draw their swords. An incurable fighter, Iago singles out Roderigo as his special opponent.

COMMENT: Iago offers to fight Roderigo in order to protect him from harm so that he can continue to make use of his purse, or he wants to kill Roderigo, for whom he has no further use, to avoid paying his debt or fulfilling the promised service. At this point, Iago has not clearly fitted Roderigo into his revenge scheme.

Contemptuously, Othello refuses to respond to Brabantio's violence. "Keep up your bright swords, for the dew will rust them," he advises. Diplomatically, he informs Brabantio, "Good Signior, you shall more command with years / Than with your weapons."

The outraged father looses a stream of invective against Othello. He damns him, calls him an enchanter, insists that the "tender, fair, and happy" Desdemona was so shy of marriage that she shunned the "curled darlings of our nation," that is, the foppish and elegant suitors of the Venetian courts. He insists that Desdemona has been intimidated; why else would he lay her fair head on his "sooty bosom?" The answer must lie in Othello's use of poisonous drugs or black magic, offenses under the law. Brabantio demands Othello's arrest and orders the officers to subdue him if he resists.

Patiently, and with great dignity, Othello assures Brabantio that he has no intention of resisting and agrees to go wherever Brabantio chooses in order to answer his charges. Brabantio chooses prison, where he plans to keep Othello until court convenes to hear the case. Othello then informs Brabantio that he has been summoned by the Duke on business of state and asks how he shall obey both men at the same time. An officer confirms Othello's assertions, and for the first time during this troubled night, Brabantio learns that the Duke is in council. Although he surmises that the state is in danger if the council is assembled at this late hour of the night, Brabantio asserts, "Mine's not an idle cause." He decides to bring his complaint against Othello before the Duke immediately.

COMMENT: Othello's cool command of the situation in which Iago instigates and Brabantio rages is visible throughout this scene. Notice how tactfully he allows Brabantio to decide that Othello is to be brought to the Duke rather than to prison. The air of self-assurance never leaves Othello during this scene. He is confident that his heroic service, his noble lineage, and his general merits make him deserving of Desdemona and will win him the approval of the senate.

SUMMARY: The scene serves the following purposes:

1. It presents Othello personally for the first time in the play. It helps establish an authentic image of Othello as an alert and poised leader, considerate and diplomatic, but capable of drastic and decisive action. He is a proud man, but not vainglorious; he knows that boasting is no honor. He is thoroughly convinced of his own integrity ("my perfect soul"), and trusts unquestioningly in the integrity of other men.

2. It shows that the exotic marriage has aroused opposition among conventional but decent people like Brabantio who easily become the tool of malicious men like Iago.

3. It establishes Othello's position as leading military figure in the Venetian state, a position he is careful not to abuse. Unlike Iago, Othello shows his dedication to service and duty.

Act I: Scene iii

It is still the same night. The scene now shifts to the Duke's council chamber where the Duke and senators discuss and assess various conflicting reports of the size of the Turkish fleet and its whereabouts. Although they do not fix the enemy's number, the dispatches confirm that the enemy fleet is bearing up to Cyprus. The Duke too becomes convinced that Cyprus is in danger, just as a sailor arrives with a message that the Turks are really heading for Rhodes. One senator argues that this is a Turkish trick. Cyprus is more important to the Turks than Rhodes, and it should not be presumed that they would attempt to conquer Rhodes when Cyprus is both easier to win and more profitable to possess. The Duke confirms this belief that Cyprus is the real target.

Another messenger arrives hard upon this decision to report that Turkish ships do, indeed, head for Rhodes, but that a second fleet follows behind and steers for Cyprus. The Duke is certain, then, that Cyprus is in danger.

COMMENT: The council is here discussing various conflicting reports received from the navy, which have already been mentioned by Cassio. Shakespeare frequently relies on the device of the conflicting messages (as in *Part 2 Henry IV*) to establish an atmosphere of danger, uncertainty, and disorder of the sort usually occasioned by war.

At this point, both parties, Othello's and Brabantio's, enter the chamber. Breaking protocol, the Duke first greets Othello with the news that he must be employed at once against the "Ottomans." Then, noticing Brabantio, the Duke apologizes for not seeing him at first. He welcomes Brabantio to court, expressing regret that he had lacked the senator's help this night.

COMMENT: This small piece of apparently insignificant action, the Duke's welcoming Othello before Brabantio, is laden with meaning. The Duke's breach of protocol (the conventional etiquette of court and state, requiring that the highest ranking man be attended first) reflects the uncertain and disordered atmosphere of the situation; it suggests that social hierarchies and amenities are artificial ones since they are so easily ignored in times of emergency. The Duke's favoring Othello with the first greeting forecasts his subsequent judgment in favor of Othello and against Brabantio. As Brabantio is not seen first here, so will his cause be "overlooked" later.

Barely returning the Duke's greeting, Brabantio proceeds to outline his daughter has been "abused, stol'n . . . and corrupted." He is so anxious to stress the illegal means by which she was taken, that is, the "spells and medicines" of witchcraft by which she was deceived, that he neglects to name the defendant at first. The Duke promises that Brabantio himself will be allowed to pass judgment on the miscreant, that is, Brabantio will read "the bloody book of law" against his daughter's deceiver "though our proper son / Stood in your action."

COMMENT: This is neither the first nor last instance in which Shakespeare uses dramatic irony and has the character express sentiments which the author knows he will later regret. The Duke's own son does not stand in Brabantio's action, of course, but someone equally important to the Venetian cause, Othello, does.

Much to the regret of the Duke and all the senators, Brabantio points to Othello, the man whom state affairs have brought to court. Although the Duke has believed the charges made by the noble and trusted senator, he now turns to Othello and asks him what he has to say in his own defense. Impatiently, Brabantio insists that Othello has nothing to say but to agree. Nevertheless, Othello speaks. Showing the same tact he had employed with Brabantio before, he does, indeed, begin by agreeing that he has taken Brabantio's daughter. So much is true and no more. Humbly (and eloquently), he asserts his rudeness of speech and his inability to defend himself with the polished smoothness of the civilian. His skill is in "broil and battle," he cleverly reminds the court, and he must rely on the "gracious patience" of the Duke to listen to the "unvarnished tale" of his courtship and by what magic he won Brabantio's daughter.

COMMENT: Once more Othello's self-possession and directness is explored, this time in his address to the Duke and his court. Despite his claim of "rudeness," he is a most eloquent speaker and is distinctly gifted as a diplomat. He flatters his adversaries, states his own case directly, and does not bother to refute the charges. Rather than deny the crime attributed to him, he wisely stresses his virtues, his skill in combat, which the senators themselves are able to confirm. (An advocate whose plea begins with a truth recognized by all has taken the first step in winning the favor of the jurors.) Paradoxically, Othello offers to explain by what magic he won Desdemona; this is also a diplomatic approach. He chooses not to contradict or deny that he has used "magic," but when the true nature of this "magic" is known, that is, when the paradox is explained, Othello will be vindicated. (Open contradiction is sure to arouse someone's hostility; agreement never fails to win some sympathy.)

Brabantio, however, mistakes Othello's reference to "magic," and passionately interrupts again, repeating the reasoning by which he has concluded that fair, gentle Desdemona must have been drugged. She was a quiet maiden, never bold, and so bashful that she blushed at her own emotions. It is unthinkable that such a timid young lady should oppose her own nature, the modesty befitting her youth, the manners of her country, the honor of her name, and everything else, and fall in love with a man whose very aspect she feared to look at.

COMMENT: The purpose of the interruption is to describe Desdemona in greater detail just before her appearance. She is, indeed, a maiden of modesty, honor, and all the rest. Yet she has opposed her "nature." Brabantio's

reference to nature is a reference to the humanist code of behavior (of the sort drawn up by Baldassare Castiglione in *The Book of the Courtier*), in which persons of a given rank, appearance, education, and sex were expected to conduct themselves with decorum, in accordance with the rules drawn up for that class. Thus, it was "natural" for fair Desdemona, the young daughter of a noble Venetian family, to be shy and retiring, to be obedient to her father, and to marry a man whose race, rank, wealth, and beauty were similar to her own. On the other hand, Castiglione's "perfect lady" always married for love and had the courage to command armies. Desdemona is always the "perfect lady," despite her father's charges.

The Duke responds to Brabantio's outburst by informing him that assertions are not proofs. (He is beginning to suspect that Brabantio's case is unfounded. Notice the parallel situation later when Othello demands proof from Iago of Desdemona's infidelity.) One of the senators asks a direct question. Did he or did he not use drugs? Still, Othello avoids a negative answer and suggests that Desdemona be called to speak before her father. While she is being fetched, Othello offers to recount their courtship.

COMMENT: When Othello avoids a direct answer to a direct question, he is not being evasive. He seems to feel that the negative answer is the evasive one and prefers to state positive facts, assuming that the listeners will make the right deductions. This is the way he treated the "great ones" of the city who sued for Iago's appointment. Rather than say "no," he advised them that Cassio has been chosen. Here, Othello seems to feel that Brabantio would only be aroused to new violence if Othello denies the charges. Thus, he asks that Desdemona answer her father directly. In this way, Othello hopes to eliminate unnecessary altercation. The matter will be settled finally when Desdemona speaks. In the meantime, he will describe the events which led to their marriage, that is, he will speak truthfully and openly, thereby giving the senators an opportunity to answer their own question. (The audience, moreover, will have the opportunity of learning the events which occurred prior to the opening of the play.)

In a long autobiographical account, Othello then reveals his romantic and adventurous life. He had been a frequent guest in Brabantio's house where he had told his adventures in Desdemona's hearing. For many years, he has been a soldier and has engaged in "battles, sieges, fortunes." He has repeatedly risked his life without question. He had once been captured and made a slave, but had managed to escape. He had been in all sorts of dangerous and mysterious places, vast caves, vacant deserts, high mountains. He has known

Cannibals, the "Anthropophagi," and "men whose heads / Do grow beneath their shoulders."

COMMENT: "Anthropophagi" is another name for cannibals, referring to a particular race of man-eaters. Cannibals are mentioned in Philemon Holland's translation of Pliny's *Natural History* (1601), which may have been Shakespeare's geographical source book. The race of men with misplaced heads is mentioned in Raleigh's *Guiana* and in other old travelers' books. They are sometimes thought to be Russians who in winter wore huge fur hats which gave travelers the impression that their heads grew in the center of their bodies.

Othello's adventures, the sieges, capture and enslavement, and mysterious travels were of the sort frequently found in the Greek romances, which were in vogue in Shakespeare's time. Because of his strange experiences, Othello is sometimes described as a heroic barbarian who has become civilized, that he is, in fact, a "noble savage." Shakespeare was acquainted with the concept of the "noble savage," which had been described by the French essayist and philosopher, Michel de Montaigne, whom Shakespeare read (and quoted verbatim in *The Tempest*).

Continuing his narrative, Othello tells how Desdemona was attracted by fragments of his tales, which she had overheard as she came and went about the house. Privately, she requested that he repeat them to her in full. As she listened, she wept over his trials and hardships. Finally, she stated that she would welcome such a man as her suitor. Thus encouraged, Othello proposed marriage. "She loved me for the dangers I had pass'd / And I lov'd her that she did pity them." This was Othello's only witchcraft, he concludes; "Let Desdemona witness it."

COMMENT: Othello's tale of courtship is not unfamiliar in the history of western literature. Dante's Paolo won Francesca by reading with her the romantic tales of Lancelot and Guinevere. Early puritan tradition, in fact, deplored tales of romance for this very reason, because it was believed that stories of love had the power to subdue and mislead young innocents. There is, indeed, an air of magic and enchantment about the adventures Othello relates, and it is this kind of enchantment, not drugs, that worked the seduction of Desdemona.

Desdemona's pity may be regarded by the modern reader as insufficient reason for falling in love. In medieval and Renaissance tradition, however, the lady's pity was the first requisite for the suitor's cause. It was thought then, and even today, that "pity is akin to love." The traditional lover of romance literature became pale and wan and threatened to die if the lady did not show mercy (pity). Thus, moved to pity, the lady would surrender some token of favor, a kerchief or ring which he would wear on his person. The lover was next ready to deepen her affections by engaging in battle or in tournaments. His success in such ventures would finally win her total esteem and her hand in marriage (or, if she were already married, adultery might follow). After the marriage, the lady became the complete subject of the husband.

Although some steps in the courtship procedure of conventional romances have been eliminated in this play, Desdemona and Othello are lovers in this romantic tradition. Desdemona's courageous and determined manner in the elopement and in the action immediately following, and her subsequent passive submission to Othello's jealousy, are not contradictions of character but are duplication of the dual role (before and after marriage) played by the traditional heroine of romance literature.

At the conclusion of Othello's narrative, Desdemona appears, attended by Iago and several others. The Duke declares that Othello's story would win his daughter too. Before hearing Desdemona's testimony, the Duke asks Brabantio to reconcile himself as best he can to "this mangled matter," to this irregular marriage. Brabantio, however, insists that Desdemona be heard before a decision is made. Gently, he asks his daughter if she knows where her obedience lies. He is clearly unprepared for the answer she gives him. Desdemona replies that her duty is divided. She owes obedience and respect to her father because he gave her life and education, but even for this reason does she now owe obedience to her husband, for her mother had showed her that a woman, once married, must prefer her husband to her father.

Desdemona makes it abundantly clear that she married Othello through her free choice, and, with this declaration, Brabantio's case collapses. Brabantio makes the best of what he considers a bad situation and gives Othello Desdemona apparently with all his heart. But he admits that if Othello did not already possess her, he would do everything in his power to keep her from him.

COMMENT: Desdemona's first brief statement in the play demonstrates that she is the obedient maiden her father had described. Her brevity speaks for her modesty; at the same time, she demonstrates the independence of mind that characterizes a lady of noble blood with Desdemona's education. She is courageous enough to act on her feelings and has the determination and wit needed to justify her actions.

In a conciliatory speech, the Duke asks Brabantio to smile at his loss, for, in smiling, he prevents the thief from enjoying his discomfort. Wryly, Brabantio suggests that Venice, if it loses Cyprus, may also smile and thus deprive the Turks of their victory. He accepts the Duke's decision reluctantly and finds no ease to his grief in the Duke's words. "I never yet did hear / That the bruised heart was pierced through the ear." Thus, still unreconciled to his daughter's marriage, he asks the Duke to move on the business of the state.

The Duke appoints Othello Commander-in-Chief for the military defense of Cyprus. In no way embarrassed or upset by what has happened, Othello courteously but firmly requests that the state make living arrangements for his wife in accordance with her rank and education. Brabantio refuses to quarter his disobedient daughter, although the Duke has suggested it. Desdemona interposes in her quiet and unaffected way to ask that she may accompany Othello to Cyprus. In doing so, she makes an important declaration about the kind of love she has for this man:

> That I did love the Moor to live with him,
> My downright violence and storm of fortunes,
> May trumpet to the world. My heart's subdu'd
> Even to the very quality of my lord.
> I saw Othello's visage in his mind,
> And to his honours and his valiant parts
> Did I my soul and fortunes consecrate.
> So that, dear lords, if I be left behind,
> A moth of peace, and he go to the war,
> The rights for which I love him are bereft me,
> And I a heavy interim shall support
> By his dear absence. Let me go with him.

Othello adds his own request to Desdemona's. He does not ask that Desdemona be with him simply to satisfy his rights as a husband, "but to be free and bounteous to her mind." Love will not interfere with Othello's responsibilities for the conduct of the war.

COMMENT: Othello's request that Desdemona accompany him for her sake rather than his own has been interpreted to mean that Othello is sexually impotent. Othello speaks of "the young affects / In me defunct" in regard to "heat" or sexual desire. Later in the play (II. iii. 354), Iago refers to Othello's "weak function" with which Desdemona "may play the god." One critic, horrified by miscegenation, insists that the marriage must be platonic. The common sense position is that this is a real marriage, that Desdemona, in referring to "the rites for which I love him," frankly speaks of the marriage rites, the consummation of the marriage. Othello is not a young man by Elizabethan standards, where the average age of death was forty-five. His sexual drive has been modified by his advanced years but not curtailed. Shakespeare stresses in Desdemona's and Othello's speeches both the spiritual affinity which exists between the lovers and the physical

attachment they have made to one another. Desdemona "did love the Moor to live [physically] with him," but her heart was completely vanquished "even to the very [spiritual] quality of my lord." Othello, of course, wishes to assure the senate that he will not stint in his military efforts merely because his wife is with him.

The request of the newly wedded couple is granted by the Venetian senate, and the Duke affirms to Brabantio that "Your son-in-law is far more fair than black."

As the senate adjourns, Othello is given meaningful advice by the first senator and by Brabantio. The senator urges Othello to use Desdemona well, while Brabantio warns: "She has deceived her father, and may thee." Othello answers, "My life upon her faith!"

COMMENT: Each of these remarks is an example of Shakespeare's "foreshadowing" technique. Othello will not use Desdemona well, we will learn shortly. Brabantio's warning, which Othello belies at this point, will be remembered and believed later, and Othello will give up his life as a result of Desdemona's fidelity. It is the discovery of her loyalty which makes Othello kill himself.

When the Duke and senators leave, Othello entrusts Iago with Desdemona's safe voyage and asks him to have Emilia, his wife, wait on her. Then, with only an hour left to attend to love and business, Othello departs with his bride.

COMMENT: Desdemona, whom we have met for the first time in this scene, reveals herself as an aristocratic girl, who observes all the conventions but who, at the same time, has a determined mind of her own. She had handled Brabantio with tact and firmness. She is a little shy in making her request to go to Cyprus with Othello ("let me find a charter in your voice / T'assist my simpleness"), but she makes it gracefully and forcibly. Her subsequent passivity in regard to Othello is explained by the traditional submissiveness of wives to their husbands which Desdemona has learned from her mother. It may be that her heart was "subdued" too completely, that she lacked a certain needed realism in order to cope with his suspicions. One of the most potent effects of this tragedy is Desdemona's suffering under Othello's later tyranny. At this point in the play, however, he gives her freedom; he is "free and bounteous to her mind."

Roderigo has witnessed the entire action and when the council chamber is cleared, he turns to Iago and announces that he is going to drown himself. To live without Desdemona would be torment, and although he is ashamed of his foolishness, he admits that he has not the "virtue" (an inherent power of character) to amend the foolishness.

Anxious to save his dupe, Iago responds heatedly. In all twenty-eight years, he has never met a man who knew how to love himself. Personally, Iago argues, he would rather be an ape (a creature without reason) than kill himself for a woman. As for "virtue" (the naturally endowed powers Roderigo says he lacks), we are what we will ourselves to be, Iago asserts. If we had not this will, we'd be nothing more than beasts, subject to "carnal stings" and "unbitted lusts." Fortunately however, man has reason to cool his lusts. Love is only a form of lust, Iago tells the incredulous Roderigo; it is a condition that exists only with the permission of the will.

COMMENT: In a curious perversion of puritan logic, Iago reveals that he is a man of will (mind rather than feeling). Unfortunately, he confuses love with lust and negates both forces. Lust is to be overcome in order to achieve noble deeds (as Othello does), but love is universal and absolute. The love of woman is the bottom of the ladder to heaven, for only through human love experienced in youth can man learn to know the divine love of God; so thought some of the humanists of the high Renaissance.

Iago is a self-interested man who loves himself rather than woman. (He will never get to heaven.) We learn, in addition, that he is twenty-eight, that he has found all men to be fools, that he believes in the essential corruption of human nature and in the supremacy of will. Iago is not subject to the demands of the flesh, and he does not believe in the absolute existence of love.

Iago's cold philosophy makes little impression on Roderigo, but when Iago tells the foolish lover again and again to put money in his purse to follow the wars, and to wait for Desdemona to tire of the Moor, Roderigo's hopes begin to rise. Iago assures him that love which begins violently ends in the same way, and that Desdemona, finished with the old Moor, will begin to look for a young lover. He promises that Roderigo will enjoy Desdemona yet, if Iago's wits and "all the tribe of hell" (which apparently serves as inspiration to his wit) are any match for the barbarous Moor and the "supersubtle" (sophisticated) Venetian, Desdemona. Once more resolved to live, Roderigo agrees to follow Iago's advice and sets off at once to sell his land.

COMMENT: Iago associates himself with the traditional Vice of morality literature in at least two ways. First, he asserts that he does not believe in love; he sees it only as the permission of the will to the lusts of the body. This is truly a satanic notion, for love between man and woman was regarded by Christians of Shakespeare's world as the human version and manifestation of divine love, a love which had absolute existence and could not be "willed" by man. Secondly, Iago suggests that "all the tribe of hell" may assist his wit (intellect), implying thereby that he himself is an instrument of hell.

Left alone, Iago utters the first soliloquy of the play. He states that he has only saved Roderigo for the sake of his purse and for the fun that the foolish man gives him. Otherwise, he would not waste his time expending his hard-earned knowledge of human nature on such a "snipe" as Roderigo. Reaffirming his hatred for Othello, Iago then says rather strangely that he suspects the Moor of having relations with his own wife (Emilia), yet he doesn't know or seem to care whether or not his suspicion has any foundation.

COMMENT: A soliloquy is a convention of the Shakespearean theater in which the character speaks his thoughts aloud. Since there is no dramatic interaction taking place during a soliloquy, it is generally presumed that the character is speaking the truth. The soliloquy tends to explain the paradoxical behavior of a character. Thus, Iago, who does not mean what he says, whose feelings are often contrary to his actions in the play, is given the largest number of soliloquies in the play; while open-natured Othello, who means what he says, for the most part, does not have to explain himself in the soliloquy convention.

Regarding Emilia and Othello's adultery, Shakespeare seems to be suggesting that malice precedes cause in a character like Iago and that his malice can feed on false as well as true reports. We learn later that suspicion is begotten and feeds upon itself. This seems to be precisely what Iago is demonstrating here.

Next, Iago works out a plot against Othello, which he formulates as he speaks. Since the Moor has faith in his ancient (Iago), he will be inclined to believe Iago when he suggests that Cassio is too familiar with Desdemona. According to Iago, Othello is an "ass" because he has a "free and open nature." Othello thinks others are as honest as he "that but seem to be so." Delighted by the plan he has just devised, Iago exclaims, "Hell and night / Must bring this monstrous birth to the world's light."

COMMENT: Iago's malicious plot is purposefully associated with hell and with unnatural "monstrous" deeds engendered there, which are too heinous for the light of day and may be enacted only in the dark of night. Iago's final lines produce the most horrific of the dark images that blight the first act and forecast doom to the heroic, idealistic lovers, Othello and Desdemona.

SUMMARY: In this scene we have passed beyond ordinary dramatic exposition to what is technically called "the growth of the action." Conflict has been foreshadowed in relation to the marriage by the arguments of Brabantio, who has left us with an ominous portent: "Look to her, Moor, if thou hast eyes to see. / She has deceiv'd her father, and may thee." (Iago is to repeat this idea in a later context: "She did deceive her father, marrying you," in III, iii, 207.) Dramatically, the scene establishes the following points:

1. It makes clear the stature of Othello as a leader, a man of dignity and widespread respect.

2. It explains Othello's romantic and adventurous background and how very plausible was the love that developed between Othello and Desdemona.

3. It shows us the beauty and charm of Desdemona, and her capacity for independent action.

4. It stresses the marriage as basically one of intellectual and spiritual compatibility.

5. It brings into sharp contrasting focus the idealistic and inspiring qualities of the wedded couple with the malice and cynicism of Iago.

6. It shows the "monstrous birth" of Iago's plot to destroy the unsuspecting couple.

Act II: Scene i

Some weeks have passed. The action moves on to Cyprus. Montano, a leading citizen of Cyprus, discusses the war with two gentlemen. Montano is satisfied that the Turkish fleet has either sought refuge somewhere or has been destroyed in the course of a terrific storm that has been raging. A third gentleman brings news that the Turkish fleet has, indeed, suffered serious losses and that Cassio has arrived in Cyprus. Othello, who has been given the full powers of governor of the island, is still at sea. The gentleman reports that Cassio is worried about Othello's safety. Montano expresses his hope for Othello's safe return, for he once served under the Moor and found him to be a perfect commander.

Cassio now joins the group. Having heard Montano speak of Othello, he thanks him for his praise. He assures Montano that Othello's ship is a strong one and his pilot well-skilled; he has good hopes for the governor's safety. A second ship is sighted, and, as Montano and Cassio await a report on its passengers, Cassio tells his companion that the Moor is married to "a maid / That paragons description and wild fame; / One that excels the quirks of blazoning pens."

COMMENT: Cassio has already been described as "bookish" by his rival, Iago. Now he demonstrates this bookishness in elaborate praise of Desdemona. His diction is elegant

and his manner courtly; neither Iago nor Othello, both practical men of war, will appreciate or understand his courtly ways with Desdemona.

Desdemona's ship has arrived. She is accompanied by Iago, Roderigo, and Emilia. Desdemona thanks Cassio for his effusive welcome and expresses her fear over Othello's delayed arrival. A bantering conversation ensues when Cassio kisses Emilia's hand in greeting and renders her speechless. But she finds her tongue when Iago describes her as a chiding wife and she warrants that he shall never write her praise. Iago goes on to defame the female sex in general. Encouraged by the company, he recites several proverbial jests about the frailty of women. Everyone takes them in good humor, including Desdemona, who calls Iago a "profane and liberal counsellor." Cassio is forced to admit that Iago speaks truthfully and to the point, and suggests that Desdemona will find greater merit in Iago as a soldier than as a scholar. Cassio next extends the courtesy of aristocratic hand-kissing to Desdemona, as Iago looks on. In an "aside" (a stage whisper, another convention of the Elizabethan theater, in which the speech is intended only for the audience's hearing), Iago comments: "He takes her by the palm. Ay, well said, whisper! With as little a web as this will I ensnare as great a fly as Cassio."

COMMENT: As a polished Florentine gentleman following the new fashion of Renaissance courtesy, Cassio kisses hands. Iago's "limericks" or anti-female verses express his true view of women but Cassio and Desdemona interpret his behavior as that of a typical rough-hewn soldier, somewhat extrovert and vulgar, but with a heart of gold. Iago's stage whisper indicates his truly sinister (and quasi-puritanical) nature; he is never at rest, never relaxed. Even during this exchange of social pleasantries, he is planning to make an evil situation out of a gentle courtesy.

At last Othello arrives. He embraces Desdemona and expresses his supreme happiness at this moment of reunion. She is his "soul's joy." "If after every tempest come such calms / May the winds blow till they have waken'd death!" Othello then expresses the fear that such great contentment as he feels just now cannot come twice in a single lifetime.

COMMENT: Othello's expression of fear is an example of "tragic foreshadowing," a technique used sparingly but effectively by Shakespeare. We have had a previous example when Brabantio has warned about the possibility of Desdemona deceiving Othello (I.iii.294). Critics often speak of such statements as "ironic." The irony here lies in the fact that Othello has spoken much more prophetically than he had any reason to suspect in fearing that such contentment will not come again.

Desdemona replies with a hopeful picture of a future full of tenderness and love. Othello responds by putting his hand upon his heart which has almost stopped beating through the weight of emotion. Kissing her, he says that kisses ought to be the greatest "discords" they may ever be forced to experience. Iago, looking on, reveals his satanic thoughts in another "aside." Grimly jesting on his undeserved sobriquet, "honest Iago," he picks up Othello's musical metaphor: "O, you are well tun'd now! / But I'll set down the pegs that make this music / As honest as I am." Prattling happily about the victory, the good people of Cyprus, and his joyous reunion with his bride, Othello leads Desdemona off to his castle.

We now have a long chorus-like dialogue between Iago and Roderigo, in which Iago assures his dupe that Desdemona loves Cassio. Iago pours out his envy, spleen, and disdain for the marriage of Othello and Desdemona. He again reveals his contempt for sex, and he reduces all human relationships to the lowest common denominator. Iago pictures Desdemona as an animal of aggressive sexuality. Dulled by the "act of sport," and obviously promiscuous as all women are, she will seek a handsome man to renew her interest in love. Othello, according to Iago, is not physically attractive, and Desdemona, who already showed her imbecility in choosing such a braggart, will soon be bored with him. Here is where Cassio will come in, for he has what women of "folly and green minds look after." In fact, Iago declares, "the woman hath found him already." Roderigo objects; he cannot believe any such thing; Desdemona is "full of most blessed condition." "Blessed fig's end!" Iago shouts; "the wine she drinks is made of grapes." (She is only human.) Besides, she indulges in courtesies, which are prologue to lust.

COMMENT: Shakespeare has here made an important contribution to the characterization of villainy, of the evil man. The villain here is not a man of vicious habits. Neither a drunkard nor a philanderer, but a man of iron self-control, with a very low emotional temperature. As long as they have warm hearts, Shakespeare sympathizes with sinful individuals who succumb to the vices of the flesh (e.g. Falstaff). But Shakespeare's evil man is totally unsympathetic. Iago is egocentric and without fellow-feeling; he is cool and self-disciplined; he has no use for women.

Next, Iago broaches his plan to get Cassio out of the way by having Roderigo provoke an incident which will put Cassio in a bad light as an undisciplined officer. With Cassio ruined, Roderigo will be better able to effect his purposes (Iago's actually).

When Roderigo departs, Iago, in a second soliloquy, reviews his accomplishments of the day and his plans for the future. He reveals his belief that Cassio actually loves Desdemona. He decides that her love for Cassio will make a likely and credible story (but it will only be a story). Whatever else Iago feels about the Moor, he does admit that Othello will make a good husband, for he "is of a constant, loving, noble nature." Iago then restates his self-induced idea that Othello may have committed adultery with Emilia and decides to seduce Desdemona himself in order to be "even'd with him, wife for wife." Considering the possible failure of his plan to seduce Desdemona, Iago devises an alternate plan. If the seduction fails, he will make Othello incurably jealous of Cassio. Of course, the fool Roderigo must play his part properly if Cassio is to fall into Iago's power, an idea which appeals to Iago. Next Iago expresses his belief that Cassio (if he tried) could seduce Emilia. Finally, Iago gloats over the thanks he will receive from Othello "for making him egregiously an ass," that is, he envisions how Othello will thank him for falsely informing on Desdemona and Cassio.

These are the evil conceptions formulating in Iago's mind. Iago realizes that his plan for revenge is only roughly outlined, but he states his intention of working out the details as the events occur: "'Tis here [in his head], but yet confus'd." Knavery is unpredictable, Iago says; its course becomes clearer only after it is put into effect.

COMMENT: Although this second soliloquy has caused critics to charge Shakespeare with inconsistency in the characterization of Iago, it is possible to reach a satisfactory explanation of Iago's remarks. In this soliloquy, Iago is engaged in the act of thinking; he is making tentative and alternative plans; he is testing and checking his ideas for their probability and workability. His thoughts are still unorganized, and they are presented in the manner in which they occur to him, a manner resembling the "internal monologue" technique used by modern novelists. If we place these thoughts into logical order and fill in some ideas which are understood but not spoken, we get the following results: Iago begins with a single overall aim, to revenge himself against Othello. Next, he examines certain given factors. These are his real beliefs: that Cassio loves Desdemona, that all women are fickle and adulterous, that Desdemona, being a woman, is potentially adulterous, that Othello will be a satisfactory husband (consequently, Desdemona may not become adulterous), and that Roderigo is a willing but not necessarily an able accomplice. Now the question for Iago is how to work his revenge within this given framework. The soliloquy explores possible answers to this question. Not all the statements in it are statements of fact.

Some are possibilities, such as "For I fear Cassio with my nightcap too." This means that Cassio is so young, attractive, well-educated ("bookish"), eloquent, and courteous, that Iago himself, recalling no doubt that Emilia was speechless when Cassio kissed her hand only moments ago, fears his potential powers over Emilia. The Moor, therefore, may very well believe Iago's trumped-up charges against Cassio and Desdemona.

SUMMARY: This scene has succeeded in showing the following developments as part of the "growth of action":

1. A transition is effected between Acts I and II, moving the scene of action from Venice to Cyprus and bridging several weeks of time from the eve of the Turkish war to the day of victory.

2. Emilia and several minor characters are introduced in this scene. Emilia, a sharp-tongued wife according to Iago's report, is a spirited wench. Cassio, who made a brief appearance prior to this scene, is developed here as a courteous and eloquent gentleman whose manners suggest his own downfall to Iago.

3. Othello and Desdemona, reunited on Cyprus, have every reason to look forward to a fruitful and happy future. Their reunion is a moment of sheer and complete happiness. Whatever may happen in the future, they have at least known this.

4. With poisonous compulsiveness shown in his cynical contempt for mankind, Iago is seen formulating his plans for revenge, using Roderigo as a tool in his device.

Act II: Scene ii

This is scarcely a scene at all. On a street in Cyprus, an official messenger or "herald" reads a proclamation that there is to be a public festival, with free food and drink for all, to celebrate the utter destruction of the Turkish fleet. Moreover, Othello's marriage is to be honored with dancing, bonfires, and other sport.

COMMENT: Such celebrations were customarily held after victories. Dramatically, this scene of less than fifteen lines prepares us for festivities (most of which will not be shown) during which military discipline will be relaxed. Obviously, there will be drinking and disorder in the camp on this night, making it possible for Iago to work his plot against Cassio more effectively.

The call for bonfires and revels between five and eleven at night reminds us of Iago's first soliloquy when his plot was first "engendered" and Iago proclaimed, "Hell and night / Must bring this monstrous birth to the world's light." We may easily imagine the ensuing festival as a kind of Walpurgisnacht (a drinking feast held on the eve of May 1 in honor of St. Walpurgis, during which, it was believed, witches rode the night to some appointed evil rendezvous). The proclamation of the feast serves as an omen of and contrast to the stark tragedy which follows it.

Act II: Scene iii

Othello, Desdemona, Cassio, and attendants are present as the scene opens in a hall of Othello's castle. Othello admonishes Cassio in "honourable step" (moderation). The festival should not outrun discretion, Othello cautions, and guard duty is to be observed as usual. Cassio promises to instruct Iago accordingly and to supervise the frolics personally. Othello concludes the interview, observing that "Iago is most honest," a good man for the job.

COMMENT: Despite his brief appearance at this point, Othello exhibits his special wisdom as commander of the army. He himself does not partake of the more riotous aspects of the festivities; he has his charge as governor constantly in mind, believes in moderation and in caution, and in delegating authority to men he trusts.

Unfortunately, it is this trusting nature which brings about the misfortunes of the night. Othello's words and Cassio's answers are laden with tragic irony. At Iago's instigation, Cassio will forget moderation and discretion, and will imbibe too much. His personal supervision of the watch will be the most undesirable thing this night, and Iago, of course, is not honest at all.

Iago reports to Cassio just after Othello leaves with his wife and attendants. At Cassio's suggestion that they begin their watch, Iago protests it is too early to renew their duties; it is only ten o'clock. Othello's departure should not be a sign that the feast is over, Iago states; the general has left early because he is anxious to enjoy his wife. "He hath not yet made wanton the night with her," Iago explains, "and she is sport for Jove."

COMMENT: Iago's explanation for Othello's early retirement on the night of the feast is an ambiguous one. It has been interpreted to mean that Othello has not yet consummated his marriage to Desdemona because of his hasty embarkation from Venice on the eve of the Turkish attack. It may also mean that Othello has not yet enjoyed his wife since his arrival on Cyprus earlier that day. In either case, Iago is alluding to the connubial rites, which he feels Othello is anxious to perform.

Cassio responds to Iago's vulgar description of Desdemona with several courtly phrases of his own. She is "exquisite"; she is "a most fresh and delicate creature"; she is "perfection." Iago, on the other hand, finds her "full of game," "a parley to provocation," "an alarum to love."

COMMENT: The blunt military language of Iago serves as a contrast to the polite speech of the educated Florentine, Cassio. Cassio seems to disapprove of Iago's metaphors, but he sees them as characteristic expressions of the practical soldier and does not take them as insults to Desdemona. Iago may be trying, without much success, to suggest her availability to Cassio, who Iago believes is in love with her.

Pleading with Cassio not to hurry to the military watch, Iago invites him to a "stope of wine" with "a brace of Cyprus gallants." Cassio declines, saying he has already had one watered glass of wine tonight and that it has not agreed with him. Iago insists; it is a "night of revels," and besides, the gallants are waiting outside for his company. With characteristic politesse, Cassio goes at once to greet the gallants, leaving Iago alone momentarily.

In a brief soliloquy, Iago expresses his belief that if he can succeed in getting Cassio to take one more drink, the lieutenant will become as quarrelsome as a young lady's dog. Now Roderigo (who cannot always be counted on to play his part properly) is already drunk (and thus, oddly enough more reliable) and has been appointed to guard duty that night. In addition, Iago has plied with wine three Cypriots, mettlesome young men, sensitive to "honor," who are also to keep watch. Amid this "flock of drunkards," it would seem easy to provoke Cassio to some offensive action, which would arouse all of Cyprus against him (and make his dismissal mandatory). As Cassio returns with Montano, several gentlemen, and a servant with wine, Iago's reflections break off with the lines:

> *If consequence do but approve my dream,*
> *My boat sails freely, both with wind and stream*

COMMENT: In addition to Cassio's inability to drink and Roderigo's unreliability unless he is drunk, the touchy relationship between the proud Cypriots and their Venetian governors is another factor in Iago's plot. Iago has an uncanny skill for detecting everyone's foibles and for incorporating them into his malicious designs.

It should be noted that Iago calls his thoughts "my dream" and that he is not certain that his "dream" or plot will work as he hopes. The statements in Iago's soliloquies, therefore, are not statements of "fact" but of hope and of probability. When some of Iago's ideas are not subsequently enacted in the play, this should be taken to mean

that Iago's revenge plot is working out according to one set of plans and that alternate schemes have not been necessary. So, for example, although Iago says he will try to seduce Desdemona, he never actually makes such an attempt because it would not suit the particular "knavery" that is set in motion during the feast night.

Montano now insists that Cassio should have a drink, and Cassio, caught up by the spirit of the feast, accepts. Iago swings into action, singing two boisterous songs, which he has learned in England, a country of expert drinkers. Iago has skillfully turned the social occasion into a drinking party.

COMMENT: The drinking party, Iago's ditties, and his jokes about England operate as a comic interlude between the more serious scenes of the play. The Elizabethan audience was a heterogeneous one, and Shakespeare devised his plays to suit the tastes of all. Thus, many of his plays have comic sub-plots underscoring the serious events of the main plot. Perhaps, in no other play was Shakespeare more successful in uniting comedy with tragedy as in *Othello*. Here there is no sub-plot to interrupt the progress of the main events (unless Roderigo's suit may be regarded as one); instead, there are relevant interludes which have direct bearing on the main section. Iago's anti-female verses, recited during the first interview between Cassio and Desdemona, have a similar function in the play. They provide comic entertainment in themselves and, at the same time, work as ironic commentaries on the plot. The hackneyed (and Iago's personal) belief that all women are fickle and adulterous is the basis of Iago's revenge scheme; the drinking party with Cassio is the first stage of the scheme.

Cassio begins to show the effects of wine and is very self-conscious about it. He begins to talk about religious salvation. Inadvertently, he throws a barb at Iago (who has suffered by Cassio's promotion) when he says "the lieutenant is to be saved before the ancient." (This is, ironically, also true.) "Do not think, gentlemen, I am drunk. This is my ancient; this is my right hand, and this is my left," Cassio raves, as he staggers away from the party.

Montano (who holds his liquor well) suggests that the party return to duty and mount the watch. Assuming a pitying air, Iago tells Montano that Cassio, "this fellow that is gone before," is really a fine military man. Unfortunately, his drinking vice is as great as his virtue as a soldier. Othello puts too much trust in him, Iago fears. Some day, Cassio's drunkenness will cause the whole isle of Cyprus to shake.

Alarmed over the safety of his island, the Cypriot gentleman Montano asks, "But is he often thus?" With mock reluctance, Iago replies that Cassio frequently drinks himself to sleep, for if he is sober, he will stay awake all day and night. Montano, now more concerned, suggests that Othello be informed of Cassio's habits; perhaps the general takes his lieutenant too much on appearances and does not penetrate his real deficiency.

COMMENT: Montano makes another ironic pronouncement. Othello does, indeed, believe the appearance or outward behavior of men, but it is Iago who should be mistrusted, of course, not Cassio.

Roderigo appears briefly, and Iago secretly orders him to follow Cassio. He departs at once. Meanwhile, Montano continues his ironic commentary on the Moor's favored officer. It is dangerous for Cassio to be in command; the Moor ought to be informed, Montano decides. With his usual duplicity, Iago asserts that he loves Cassio and would not inform on him for all "this fair island."

COMMENT: Cleverly, Iago shifts the burden of playing informer to Montano, who for the sake of Cyprus, "this fair island," presumably could do what Iago, a Venetian, would not. Iago pretends to value the interests of his friend Cassio above the interests of Cyprus. It will not be necessary for Montano to speak to Othello, however, for in a moment Cassio will seal his own doom.

It is sometimes supposed that Iago, acting as a kind of chorus or commentator on the events in the play, knows of Cassio's imminent disgrace and dismissal and is preparing Montano (for the sake of Cyprus) to protest his reappointment, should Othello decide to reinstate the dishonored lieutenant. But if Iago is a prophetic chorus, he should know that the reappointment will never take place, just as he knows about the forthcoming disgrace. It is more reasonable to suppose that Iago is merely assuring himself of a new dupe should Roderigo fail to incite Cassio to work his own disgrace. In addition, his suggestion of the danger to Cyprus from Cassio's drunkenness serves as dramatic foreshadowing. The author knows what is coming next, but Iago does not.

Noise suddenly erupts from "within" (offstage), and Cassio appears, driving Roderigo before him. Angrily, Cassio tells Montano that this rogue, this rascal (Roderigo), has tried to teach him his duty. Roderigo and Cassio come to blows. Montano intervenes and Cassio threatens him roughly. As Montano and Cassio tussle, Iago slyly directs Roderigo to run off and rouse the town. Iago next turns to the combatants and makes a feeble effort to break up the fight. Hearing bells in the distance, Iago pretends to wonder who rang them.

Belatedly, Iago warns Cassio to desist or he will awaken the town and be disgraced forever.

Having heard the bells, Othello arrives at once. Montano exclaims that he has been wounded. (Some editions of the play indicate that Montano faints at this point, but in view of Othello's subsequent line, "Hold for your lives," it is apparent that Montano, although wounded, is still on his feet and doing battle. "Faint" may be a misreading for "feint"—(a movement with a sword).

His sense of military propriety shocked, Othello cries, "Hold"; Iago echoes his command. Are we like the Turks, to kill ourselves when heaven has prevented our enemies from killing us? Othello demands. He reminds the combatants that they are Christians, not barbarians, and warns, "He that stirs next. . . / . . . dies upon his motion." Acting swiftly and decisively, Othello orders that the bells be silenced, for it will frighten the inhabitants of Cyprus out of their senses. Next, he turns to "honest Iago," whose face he finds "dead with grieving." He charges Iago "on his love" for his general to identify the troublemaker.

COMMENT: Although attention has been focused on Othello since his arrival on the scene, Iago's presence should not be overlooked for a moment. He parrots Othello's command that the fighters hold, even though they are likely to obey the general's first word. During Othello's speech, Iago has apparently donned an expression of grief, parodying the general's reproach with appropriate grimaces. In short, he has behaved like a comic "yes-man."

Iago replies that he cannot identify the miscreant. Only moments ago, he reports, Montano, Cassio, and all were as friendly as bride and groom undressing for bed. (Iago slyly alludes to what he supposes Othello and Desdemona were doing before the bells sounded, hoping to infuriate the Moor all the more because he has been disturbed at such a moment.)

With feigned innocence, Iago disclaims any knowledge of the cause of this "opposition bloody." Turning to the others, Othello pursues his inquiry. Cassio asks pardon; he cannot speak. Next, Othello asks Montano, reputed in his youth for his serious and peaceful nature, why he has suddenly turned "night-brawler." But Montano, who has been seriously wounded in the fight, finds it difficult to speak. He refers Othello to Iago for the explanation and intimates that he has fought only in self-defense.

Othello is annoyed with everyone's reticence and warns them not to anger him further. Echoing the Duke's promise to Brabantio to punish his own son if it is required by justice, Othello promises to punish the offender though he turned out to be his own twin brother. The crime of disturbing the peace is a serious one, for Cyprus is still a "town of war," and its people are still anxious and fearful over the dangers they have just escaped. To hold a private quarrel "in night, and on the court and guard of safety? 'Tis monstrous," Othello declares. "Iago, who began 't?" the Moor demands.

COMMENT: Othello uses the same words to describe the nocturnal disturbances raised in the "town of war" as Iago had used to describe the revenge plot he had devised at the end of the first act. Both are monstrous acts that take place in the night. Thus, the "private quarrel" and Iago's revenge-plot are linked metaphorically, emphasizing the fact that they are literally one and the same thing. When Othello turns to Iago to repeat his questions about who began the fight, an ironic touch is added to the scene, for clearly the answer is Iago himself.

Montano, too, urges that Iago tell the truth, reminding him that if he shows partiality to Cassio because of personal friendship or official ties, he is no soldier. Iago admits that Montano has hit home. He would rather lose his tongue than use it against Cassio. However, he is convinced that speaking truth could not injure the lieutenant. He describes how he and Montano were engaged in conversation when Cassio came running in with sword drawn, pursuing some fellow (Roderigo, whom Iago pretends he does not know). Montano interposed, attempting to restrain Cassio, while Iago pursued the other fellow to prevent his cries from terrifying the town. The fellow eluded him, but hearing sword-play and Cassio's swearing (as he had never heard him do before), Iago returned to find Montano and Cassio at blows. This is all he knows, Iago states. Damning Cassio finally in a pretended defense, Iago suggests that surely Cassio must have endured from his victim some "strange indignity, / Which patience could not pass." Othello acknowledges Iago's desire to ameliorate Cassio's guilt. Turning to Cassio, Othello informs him that though he loves him, he relieves him of his duties as an officer forever.

Desdemona (who has heard the disturbance) arrives to inquire about the matter, but Othello puts her off and sends her back to her room. Advising Montano that he personally will attend to his wounds, he has him taken away. Next he orders Iago to placate any Cypriots who have been disturbed by the commotion. Such is the soldier's life, he tells Desdemona.

COMMENT: Othello is especially concerned about restoring and maintaining order in Cyprus now that the war with the Turks is over. He shows the same concern any general would have with the discipline of his men and with the opinion of the inhabitants of occupied territory. Iago is

aware of Othello's responsibilities and interpolates his own concern for the town during his testimony, thereby confirming Othello's faith in him. Since the hearing is held in a public place, in a town under martial law, Othello has no other choice than to dismiss Cassio even though he loves him.

Iago and Cassio are now left alone. Apparently Cassio has begun to groan, for Iago now asks him if he is hurt. Cassio replies that he is hurt past all surgery and begins to confide in him at once. Cassio is distraught by the public loss of his reputation. What's reputation, asks Iago, but nothing at all? (He is going to tell Othello in a later scene that reputation is practically everything.) Cassio is being punished as a matter of military policy; there is no hard feeling behind it. To his satisfaction, Iago learns that Cassio cannot identify Roderigo. The drinking had blurred his mind, and he can remember the events of the night only as "a mass of things." Iago tells Cassio to stop worrying about his drunkenness: "You or any man living may be drunk at a time." He advises him to try to get his post back through Desdemona's influence, "for she holds it a vice in her goodness not to do more than is requested." Cassio is very grateful to "honest" Iago for his constructive advice and leaves Iago, who must attend to his guard duty.

Once alone, Iago expresses his thought in another soliloquy. Alluding to his conversation with Cassio, he gloats, "And what's he then that says I play the villain?" Doesn't he give Cassio the most probable advice, freely and honestly showing him the way to win Othello's approval again? Desdemona can easily be made to support a cause, for she is as bounteous as the four elements (fire, air, earth, and water), which are free to all. In turn, Desdemona can win over Othello, for his "soul is so enfetter'd to her love," that he will grant her every wish. "How am I then a villain?" Iago asks again with melodramatic heaviness and malicious delight. He addresses himself to the "Divinity of hell" and compares his methods to those of devils, who, when they wish to entice a soul to "blackest sins," first put on "heavenly shows" of virtue.

Planning his next move, Iago decides that, while Desdemona appeals to Othello to recall Cassio to his post, Iago will pour the libel into Othello's ear that she is motivated to aid Cassio by adulterous lust. Iago's eventual triumph will be the destruction of all his enemies through Desdemona's virtue: "And out of her own goodness make the net / That shall enmesh them all."

COMMENT: No one has called Iago villain, but the Elizabethan audience most assuredly thought it. In fact, the audience may have very well hissed and shouted names at

Iago's more reprehensible deeds. Traditionally, the villain was regarded as a comic figure, and Iago is an especially good comedian. In addition to his bawdy, antifemale jests, his robust drinking songs, his mockeries and grimaces, Iago expresses the habitual astonishment of deadpan innocence that must have been very funny to Shakespeare's audience. For example, when Cassio says he doesn't remember what happened when he was drunk, Iago exclaims, "Isn't possible?" (III.iii.286.) Later, when Othello says farewell to tranquility and war, Iago responds with the same feigned innocence, "Isn't possible, my lord?" (III.iii.358). This sardonic humor in the face of others' sufferings underscores Iago's demonic cruelty, while at the same time his humor relieves momentarily the ugliness of the cruelty.

Once more Iago displays his ability to identify the weaknesses of others: Othello's compliance to Desdemona's wishes is his "weak function." Iago is equally good at identifying virtue (which he regards as another form of weakness). Desdemona's bounteous nature is the goodness, which will make the net to ensnare Iago's enemies.

The prospect of destroying goodness through *goodness* affords Iago particular satanic satisfaction. His invocation to the "Divinity of Hell," his diabolically perverse logic, and his equation of his own methods with those of the devils, serve as additional reminders that Iago is fiend-like himself.

Roderigo enters, interrupting Iago's reflections, and declares his impatience to win Desdemona. He has been sorely beaten tonight, Roderigo complains, but he fears that all he will get from his pain is the experience of it, a depleted purse, and not much more wisdom than he had before. Iago scolds the impatient suitor: everything takes time; wounds, for example, must heal by degrees. He reminds Roderigo that he works by wit, not witchcraft, and that wit must await the proper moment. He reviews the plan to Roderigo, pointing out that things are going as scheduled. Even though Roderigo has been slightly hurt in the action, Cassio has been dismissed. The rest will follow in good time, just as fruits must blossom before they can ripen. Be patient a little longer, Iago advises. Then, observing that the sun is rising, Iago remarks, "Pleasure and action make the hours seem short."

Dismissing Roderigo, Iago continues his cogitations. Two things must be done next, he decides: his wife, Emilia, must arrange a meeting between Cassio and Desdemona, and the Moor must be brought to witness their encounter.

COMMENT: Although the revenge-motive has initiated Iago's plot and continues as the basis of his action, Iago no longer contemplates the reasons for his malevolence. He is now totally immersed in the action of evil itself and observes how quickly time passes when one is engaged in "pleasure and action." (Contrast Iago's failure to mull over the cause

for the revenge and his pleasure in evil action with Othello's concern for "the cause, the cause" even as he is about to slay Desdemona.) Iago's moves continue to be associated with diabolism. When he disclaims "villainy" or denies the use of witchcraft, he is suggesting his affiliation with both forms of evil.

SUMMARY: This scene accomplishes the following purposes:

1. The plot is advanced as Iago has a brilliant success in "sabotaging" Cassio, while keeping himself completely in the clear. In fact, he gains greater favor for his own claim to the lieutenancy and still manages to remain on friendly terms with Cassio, so that he can continue to abuse him.

2. Othello's character is amplified. His ability to punish a culprit even though he loves him deeply is revealed in Othello's summary dismissal of Cassio and prepares us for his subsequent mistreatment of Desdemona. He continues to display his trust in the appearances of men when he accepts Iago's grief-ridden face as a true show of grief and Iago's testimony as the whole truth of Cassio's disgraceful behavior.

3. Cassio's noble and trusting nature is demonstrated by his innocent faith in Iago and aligns him with Othello, a man of similar nature, who will also become a victim of Iago.

4. Iago's characterization becomes more and more dehumanized in this scene as Shakespeare probes into the nature of evil and associates Iago with "knavery," "villainy," the "Divinity of hell," "devils," and "witchcraft." Iago expresses his "pleasure" at the action of the night and displays the malicious glee at turning goodness to evil, which is commonly associated with demonic forces.

5. Roderigo continues his function as Iago's dupe and the impatient suitor of Desdemona. In this role, he urges Iago to new depths of deviltry and so assists in the movement of the plot.

Act III: Scene i

It is morning now. Cassio is seen in the court before the castle in the company of musicians whom he has engaged to play for Othello. He bids them play briefly, and when the General appears, they are to wish him "Good morrow."

As the musicians begin to blow their tune, a Clown emerges from the castle and asks them if their instruments have been to Naples.

COMMENT: This is apparently an allusion to the nasal drawl of Neopolitan speech, or to the nasality caused by venereal disease for which Naples was notorious.

The musicians identify their noisemakers as "wind instruments," which incites the Clown to several ribald puns on "wind," "tale," and "tail." The Clown delivers a gratuity from the General and tells them that he only admires music that cannot be heard. Unable to comply with this request, the musicians depart.

COMMENT: This comic interval, which opens the third act of the play, is devised to relieve and relax audience tensions which have been built up in the previous scene. It is also an attempt to favor the "groundlings" (vulgar members of the audience) with some ribald burlesque. The monstrous deeds of the night have been developed as far as they can go for the time being. Now in the light of day the musicians' pipes and the Clown's puns blow away the evils of the night. Since a minimum of scenery was used on the Elizabethan stage, intervals such as this one also set the time and place of the new action.

Cassio next addresses the Clown, and curbing his "quillets" (word-play) with a piece of gold, he asks him to entreat Emilia to have a word with him.

Iago arrives and is surprised to see Cassio stirring so early. Cassio informs the ancient that he has taken the liberty to send for Emilia in order to ask her to arrange an interview with Desdemona. Iago promises to send her down immediately and offers to assist further by drawing the Moor out of the way so that the interview can be held privately. As Iago leaves on his errand, Cassio remarks, "I never knew / A Florentine more kind and honest."

COMMENT: References to Iago's "honesty" run like a refrain throughout the play. Tragically ironic, these references serve as continual reminders, even in relatively innocent scenes such as this one, that all is not what it seems to be, that Iago is not "honest."

Emilia arrives promptly, greets the "good lieutenant," and expresses her sympathy for his misfortune. She informs Cassio that the General and his wife are discussing his misadventure at this very moment. Desdemona is already defending his cause, but the Moor has replied that Cassio's victim, Montano, is a very prominent man in Cyprus and has important connections. It would be bad policy to reinstate Cassio, Othello feels, even though he loves his former lieutenant dearly. In fact, Othello "needs no other suitor but his likings," and were it not for political prudence, he would reappoint Cassio at the first opportunity. Despite Emilia's report, Cassio importunes an interview with Desdemona, and Emilia agrees to arrange one.

COMMENT: Desdemona, we learn, is already inclined to assist Cassio. She has not seen him since her debarkation on the previous day, though perhaps momentarily during the night, but she has known him in Venice, as we learn later on. She believes he has given her husband loyal service. Othello's reasons for dismissing Cassio have been suggested before; they are now given emphasis through Emilia's restatement of them. Othello is, above all, a good governor, diplomatic and politic, and does not wish to arouse the hostility of the Cypriots.

SUMMARY: This scene accomplishes the following:

1. It effects a transition between Acts II and III, sets the time and place of the new action, and accomplishes comic relief from the tensions of the previous scene.

2. Cassio's impatience is displayed and advances the action of the plot. Although he learns from Emilia that the Moor has forgiven him, he is not content until he is completely restored. His impatience makes him arrange a meeting with Desdemona and provides Iago with the means of furthering his schemes.

Act III: Scene ii

This scene of less than ten lines takes place in a room in the Castle where Othello is conducting business with Iago and several gentlemen. Concluding his affairs, Othello hands over some letters to Iago which are to be given to one of the pilots of the fleet and delivered to Venice. He tells Iago he will be inspecting the "works" (fortifications) and asks the ancient to report to him there on his return. The gentlemen accompany Othello as he departs to make the inspection.

SUMMARY: This scene shows that Othello is engaged in business, thereby leaving Desdemona free to conduct her interview with Cassio. Iago has promised to keep him out of the way, but we shall soon see that he has no intention of doing so.

Act III: Scene iii

COMMENT: This scene of great length, almost 480 lines, is one of the greatest and most astounding in English literature. Dramatically, it is a technical achievement that has no match, for it aptly deals with psychological action rather than physical action, yet it does not allow audience interest to flag for a moment. Drama is basically an imitation of experience through action. It is easier to stage a physical conflict (and psychological changes directly resulting from such conflict) than to dramatize psychological persuasion and the process by which a character yields to this persuasion. Some terrible events occur during this scene, but they happen in the mind, in the psychological changes wrought in Othello by Iago's skillful manipulation of words and ideas. With the exception of strategic entrances and exits, there is relatively little physical movement in the scene. Nevertheless, it is full of inner action and is breathtaking in its intensity.

The third scene of Act III shifts to a garden in the castle where Desdemona, Cassio, and Emilia conduct the interview, which was originally suggested by Iago. Cassio implores Desdemona to take swift action in his behalf, for he fears that long delays and postponements may cause Othello to forget him. Desdemona promises to act at once. She will watch Othello and "tame" and "talk him out of patience." She assures Cassio that she will plead his cause as if it were her own, "for thy solicitor shall rather die / Than give thy cause away."

COMMENT: Desdemona will, indeed, die in Cassio's cause; this is another instance of Shakespeare's dramatic irony. During the interview, a number of polite exchanges occur in which Desdemona behaves just as Iago had predicted she would. She is bounteous in nature and certainly is easily subdued "in any honest suit."

Toward the end of the conversation, Othello and Iago are seen approaching. The forthright and uninhibited Desdemona bids him stay to hear her speak in his defense, but Cassio is too embarrassed to face the General he has offended and abruptly takes his leave of the ladies.

COMMENT: Accidental behavior on the part of the principals aids Iago's machinations from the start. Shakespeare makes it abundantly clear that Iago can improvise shrewdly, and Cassio's hasty departure gives Iago his next opportunity to implement his scheme for revenge.

When he sees Cassio leave Desdemona, Iago mutters, as if to himself, "Ha! I like not that." Believing Iago has addressed him, Othello inquires, "What doest thou say?" Assuming reluctance to speak, Iago replied, "Nothing, my lord; or if—I know not what." Casually, Othello turns to another subject, "Was not that Cassio parted from my wife?" Affecting surprise, Iago answers evasively, "Cassio, my lord? No sure, I cannot think it, / That he would steal away so guilty-like, / Seeing you coming."

COMMENT: Iago has injected his first shot of poison into Othello's bloodstream and exhibits his full technical skill in creating suspicion. Clearly, Cassio is leaving the company of Desdemona, but Iago's pretended denial and his description of the "guilty-like" figure causes Othello to interpret the scene from Iago's malevolent point of view. It is not suspicion yet but curiosity.

Now Desdemona greets Othello and her first words are about Cassio, who "languishes in your displeasure." She pleads for "present reconciliation" between Othello and Cassio, for the latter has "erred in ignorance and not in cunning." But Othello, still curious to identify the "guilty-like" figure, wants to know if Cassio has just departed. He has, Desdemona replies, adding that Cassio has been humbled by grief and urging that Othello call him back at once.

Othello wants to postpone his forgiveness. (He is probably hoping that Cassio's misconduct will be forgotten presently, and the reinstatement can then be made without raising the objections of the entire town.) Desdemona, however, becomes insistent. In fact, she nags. She wonders what Othello would ask her to do that she would deny "or stand so mammering on." She reminds him how Cassio came wooing with him and defended him when Desdemona had disdained him. Finally, Othello yields, saying that he will deny her nothing. He beseeches her, in return, to leave him alone. Whereupon, Desdemona grants his wish immediately, calling upon Emilia to witness what an obedient wife she is. Upon her departure, Othello remarks: "Perdition catch my soul / But I do love thee! and when I love thee not, / Chaos is come again."

COMMENT: Another note of tragic irony and dramatic foreshadowing is present in Othello's last lines. When he finally does turn against his beloved wife, chaos does have a bloody reign.

Desdemona, in her ardent petition for Michael Cassio's cause, has reminded Othello about their close friendship. Cassio had helped him woo her, acting as a go-between for the lovers, in accordance with Renaissance romance tradition. Ever on the alert, Iago next takes up this point.

Iago asks Othello whether Cassio knew of his love when he first wooed Desdemona. Told that he did, Iago affects surprise at learning this. "Indeed," he exclaims and refuses to explain his surprise. He claims the question was asked only "for a satisfaction of my thought," and when probed for further explanation, he evasively parrots Othello's words:

> *Iago: I did not think he had been acquainted with her.*
> *Othello: O, yes, and went between us very oft.*
> *Iago: Indeed?*

Othello: Indeed? Ay, indeed! Discernst thou aught in that? Is he not honest?
Iago: Honest, my lord?
Othello: Honest? Ay, honest.
Iago: My lord, for aught I know.
Othello: What dost thou think?
Iago: Think, my lord?
Othello: Think, my lord?
> *By heaven, he echoes me. . . .*

COMMENT: Shakespeare creates a marvelous dramatic dialogue to show how suspicion can be created by insinuation and be left to feed and grow upon itself. The secret lies in avoiding explicit accusation. If a man says, "John stole five dollars," the accusation is both definite and limited. But if he says, "I didn't think you knew John," he immediately raises the question, "Why, what's the matter with John?" In the latter case, the insinuation is unlimited. The inquirer is encouraged to supply his own answers, and he is free to think the worst if he wishes to. This is Iago's technique: he fosters suspicion by using undefined insinuation.

Othello declares that Iago is playing echo "as if there were some monster in his thought / Too hideous to be shown."

COMMENT: Unconscious irony, such as Othello's allusion to "monstrous thoughts," permeates the play. It combines a touch of humor with tragic reminders and adds the element of horror to the events by associating them with "monstrousness" and at time with hell.

His curiosity excited, Othello appeals to Iago's love for him to reveal his thoughts. Iago answers this appeal indirectly. He asks if Othello is assured in his love for him; to which Othello replies he is convinced that Iago loves him. He adds that the delaying tactics Iago is using are tricks commonly employed by false, disloyal knaves. In "honest" Iago, however, these evasions indicate that Iago is a man who weighs his words carefully before speaking.

Thus assured, Iago states that he thinks Cassio is honest, and Othello agrees. Slyly, Iago next suggests that he has no basis for his belief in Cassio's honesty except the fact that "men should be what they seem." Infected by the suspicions Iago has successfully planted so quickly, Othello demands that Iago speak what he thinks no matter how horrible his thoughts may be. With a sense of timing and pace, Iago refuses to utter his thoughts at first. He pretends to be uncertain about his ideas. Suppose they are "vile and false"; after all, the best of men is subject to an occasional unclean thought. In a long, carefully measured preamble which says nothing definite, Iago points out his own tendency "to spy into abuses"; often his "jealousy" (suspicion) "shapes faults that are not." He cautions Othello against prying into his thoughts, for they are "not for your quiet nor your good." (This is the truth, of course, but Othello has no way of knowing that Iago is speaking with conscious irony.) Then, in his famous speech on reputation in which he reverses the position he took when discussing the subject with Cassio (in II.iii), Iago asserts:

> *Who steals my purse steals trash; 'tis something, nothing;*
> *'Twas mine, 'tis his, and has been slave to thousands;*
> *But he that filches from me my good name*
> *Robs me of that which not enriches him*
> *And makes me poor indeed.*

COMMENT: When Iago asserts that "men should be what they seem," he makes another insinuation about Cassio and introduces the theme of appearance versus reality, which is reiterated throughout the play. The theme is brought into focus at this point for particular ironic purposes, but it also serves to create an atmosphere of universal doubt.

When Iago alludes to his own "jealousy," to his tendency to be "vicious in my guess," he increases Othello's suspense, while he creates, at the same time, an avenue of escape for himself, should Othello reject his suspicions.

Finally, Othello demands, "By heaven, I'll know thy thoughts." But Iago, adopting an air of rugged independence and injured integrity, replies firmly, "You cannot . . . / Nor shall not." "Ha!" cries Othello. This "Ha!" is open to two interpretations. One is that the image of Desdemona's infidelity has sprung into the mind of Othello. Iago has been able, by subtle insinuation, to bring it to a monstrous birth. The other interpretation is that the "Ha!" merely expresses Othello's impatience with Iago's reluctance to be straightforward. In any case, Iago now assumes that suspicion has taken hold of Othello and warns, "O, beware, my lord, of jealousy! / It is the green ey'd monster." Othello still fails to catch the drift of Iago's meaning. Is Iago trying to advise his master against a jealousy which he does not feel? Does Iago think that "blown surmises" and "inference" will make him jealous? Othello asks. Desdemona's behavior cannot be misinterpreted; though she is fair, enjoys feasts, loves company, has all the graces of speech, song, play, and dance, yet she is virtuous. Confidently, Othello states, "She had eyes, and chose me. No, Iago; / I'll see before I doubt." Furthermore, if he were ever furnished with proof, still he would not be jealous, for he would discard love and jealousy simultaneously.

COMMENT: As Desdemona tells Emilia in a later scene, Othello is not the jealous type. Othello believes this to be true himself. He is a confident man, assured in his own virtue and in his wife's, but he is curious. We have seen how his gorge began to rise when witnesses had refused to testify about Cassio's fight with Montano; we have seen him again cajoling, demanding, insisting on knowing the meaning of Iago's insinuations. It is this curiosity, not an inherently jealous or suspicious nature, which will cause Othello to follow Iago's next piece of advice and seek out the truth of Iago's innuendoes.

Iago expresses pleasure at learning that Othello is not a jealous man, for this will give him leave to prove his loyalty with "franker spirit." At the moment he has no proof, but he suggests that Othello keep his eye on Desdemona and Cassio. He informs Othello that he knows the ways of Venetian women very well. Their conscience on matters of adultery "is not to leave it undone, but keep't unknown." He reminds Othello of Desdemona's former duplicities: she deceived her father by marrying the Moor, and when she pretended to fear Othello's looks, she loved them most.

COMMENT: It should be remembered that Iago and Desdemona are Venetian, while Othello is a Moor, who has spent most of his life at war and in strange, uncivilized lands. He does not know the ways of Venice, nor of its women, and Iago's information is curious and interesting to him. He is completely unaware of the fact that Desdemona's pretended disdain was part of the pattern of courtship in Venice.

Having gone as far as the situation will permit, Iago now apologizes for imparting his suspicions to the General. Othello protests that he is deeply indebted to Iago for unburdening his thoughts. He insists they have not troubled him, as Iago continues to apologize for expressing such unsettling thoughts and as he cautions the Moor not to misunderstand him. Iago has only expressed his suspicions, nothing more. This is understood, Othello claims, "And yet, how nature erring from itself—"

COMMENT: Iago has indeed struck home. At the very same time that the Moor insists that he is not moved to jealousy, his mind begins to inquire, "And yet. . . ." The seed of suspicion has been sown.

Seizing on the idea of "erring nature" in Othello's moment of doubt, Iago pounces, "Ay, there's the point!" He submits that "her" (Desdemona's) unwillingness to accept the numerous matches her father proposed to her with men of similar "clime, complex-

ion, and degree" (which it was natural for her to do) marks her as a woman with "a will most rank," in which "foul disproportion, thoughts unnatural" are harbored. With all due apologies to Othello, Iago adds, he is not speaking of Desdemona in particular. Even so, Iago fears, "her" will, on reconsideration, may cause her to compare Othello with her own countrymen and to repent her original choice of husband. Othello has heard enough. He bids Iago farewell, asking him to report if he perceives anything more and to set his wife Emilia to observe Desdemona.

As soon as Iago leaves, Othello gives vent to the grief that has been building up. "Why did I marry," he groans. He is certain that Iago knows more than he is willing to tell.

COMMENT: We have now reached the climax—the highest point of tension, the decisive turning point—of the play. And what a climax it is! Exclusively mental, the scene is written with superb dramatic artistry. A thought is born in Othello's mind; the monstrous image of Desdemona's infidelity is conjured up. Dramatically, this hideous, most painful thought is indicated by a single cry of painful awareness, by the pathos of the simple ejaculation, "Why did I marry?"

Iago's consummate skill in innuendo has sired the "green-ey'd monster"; Othello's imagination will nurture it. Iago has said nothing definite; he has, in fact, warned Othello against Iago's own suspicious nature, his tendency to think the worst, his possible inaccuracy; and Othello has fallen heedlessly into the trap.

Suspicion, as well as jealousy itself, is an important theme in Othello's tragedy. Shakespeare shows how suspicion is sown and how easily it feeds upon itself. Frank communication is the only cure for it, but suspicion makes communication difficult from the start. Perhaps, Othello's love for Desdemona is imperfect, is tainted with egoism or insecurity, for he seems to fall into the trap too readily. Yet, he has every reason to believe "honest and loyal" Iago even though Iago has only voiced suspicions without proof.

Iago returns with an afterthought. Making another plea for moderation, he suggests that Cassio should not have his place back yet, so that Othello can be watchful and note whether or not Desdemona goes out of her way to support him. With that Iago takes his leave once more.

A soliloquy of Othello's fellows; it is indignant and pathetic at the same time. Iago, he thinks, is "exceeding honest" and really knows what life is about. He himself is a black man, on the older side ("declin'd / Into the vale of years") and has not the gift of making sweet love-talk as "chamberers" (wanton gallants) do.

COMMENT: The fact that Othello is "declin'd into . . . years" may have special significance in his characterization. The critic Granville-Barker explains that in all Othello's years he has never been in love. Late in his life, he meets Desdemona, whose love for him creates a new "self" in Othello. "It is a self created by her love for him," Granville-Barker states, "and will be the more dependent, therefore, upon his faith in that. It will be besides, a dangerously defenceless self, since he is no longer a young man . . . and between it and the rest of this character, fully formed and set in far other molds, there can be no easy interplay. The division between old and new in him—between seasoned soldier and enraptured bride-groom—presages the terrible cleavage to come."

Some unpleasant images of life with an unfaithful wife pass ominously through Othello's mind. Then, as he sees her coming, the nightmare lifts and gives way to the heavenly image of Desdemona: "If she be false, O, then heaven mocks itself! / I'll not believe it."

But the psychological stress to which Iago has submitted him now has its physical effects. Faintly, he accuses himself of harboring evil thoughts. Then Othello attributes his mutterings to a severe headache. Desdemona offers him a handkerchief (later we find that it is a special heirloom) with which to bind his forehead. In his agitation, Othello drops it, and it is retrieved by Emilia, who recalls that Iago has tried to persuade her to steal it for quite some time. Now that she has the opportunity, she decides to have the "work" (embroidered design) copied and given to Iago, though she has no idea what he wants it for. But then Iago enters and forcibly takes it from her, refusing to return it, although Emilia complains that Desdemona, "Poor lady, she'll run mad / When she shall lack it." Iago summarily orders Emilia away.

Left alone, Iago works on his plot again. He will plant the handkerchief in Cassio's lodging. Something may come of it. The Moor is already inclined toward suspicion, and Iago is sure it will soon grow into a belief.

COMMENT: There has been much adverse criticism of the plot machinery of "the dropped handkerchief," dating as far back as Thomas Rymer, who in *Short View of Tragedy* (1693) dismissed *Othello* as the "bloody tragical farce of the dropped handkerchief." Even the modern critic E. E. Stoll is disturbed by the handkerchief device: "The numerous coincidences (like Othello's and Desdemona's not noticing that the precious handkerchief is the one that she had dropped, and Bianca's arrival, in Act IV,i, precisely when wanted) may, by rapidity of action, be obscured but not justified—unless they are in melodrama."

In several sad, melodious lines, uttered like an incantation, Iago observes the approaching figure of Othello:

> . . . . *Not poppy, nor madragora,*
> *Nor all the drowsy syrups of the world,*
> *Shall ever medicine thee to that sweet sleep*
> *Which thou ow'dst yesterday.*

Othello greets Iago with the violent accusation: "Ha! Ha! false to me?"

COMMENT: For a moment, it may be believed that Othello has come to his senses, has uncovered Iago's deception, and is about to tear him limb from limb as he soon threatens to do. Through the use of ambiguous lines, Shakespeare creates momentary suspense, but the anticipation of Iago's discovery is shortly reversed.

George Lyman Kittredge, the famous Shakespearean scholar, interpreted this line as a reflective one. Othello does not see Iago, and he is talking of Desdemona, whom he addresses in his mind as false. In view of what follows this need not be the case.

Othello finds Iago false because he has set Othello "on the rack" by giving him "to know't a little," that is, by causing him to suspect his wife without proving the case finally, one way or the other. We have seen the rage which curiosity awakens in Othello on several other occasions. He cannot abide ignorance of a situation or doubt about the nature of events; he himself recognizes what agony it is to him to know only a little. Not long before (Ll. 241-2 of the same scene), Othello voices his suspicion of Iago's concealments: "This honest creature doubtless / Sees and knows more, much more, than he unfolds." Now he calls Iago "false" for setting him in doubt and for continuing to withhold information from him.

When Iago inquires the reason for Othello's wrath, Othello replies that before Iago had given him reason to suspect Desdemona, Othello had enjoyed her company freely. Now his pleasures are tainted by doubt. Hitherto, Othello says, "I found not Cassio's kisses on her lips." If only he knew nothing at all, Othello complains. Othello is deeply depressed. Empassioned by despair, Othello bids farewell to "Pride, pomp, and circumstance of glorious war." Finally, he turns against Iago again: "Villain, be sure thou prove my love a whore!" (For once, Othello has correctly identified the character of "honest" Iago, but, ironically, he does not know it.) He demands that Iago bring him "ocular proof" of Desdemona's treachery. If Iago has lied, he will wish he had been born a dog rather than answer to Othello's "wak'd wrath."

Owing to his lack of self-control, the result of his tortured state of mind, Othello is here no match for the calculated hypocrisy of Iago. Iago answers Othello's demands with a complaint to the world at large. After all, what has he done but be "honest" and demonstrate his love for Othello? "Take note, take note, O world," Iago cried, "To be direct and honest is not safe."

(There is grim humor in Iago's complaint, for we know that he means exactly what he is saying. Since Othello does not, this is another instance of dramatic irony.) Othello recants his threat; Iago must continue to be honest. By way of apology, Othello explains his agonizing conflict: "I think my wife be honest, and think she is not." He describes his new hateful image of Desdemona; her face is "now begrim'd and black as my own face." Othello now changes his threat to a humble request for satisfaction; then, his determination returning, he asserts that he will be satisfied. (Othello has played right into Iago's hands; the villain has a handkerchief, we may recall.) "But how? how satisfied, my lord?" Iago asks. Do you want to see the actual act of adultery being committed? This would be hard to bring about, but "imputation and strong circumstances" are easily produced. Othello bites. "Give a living reason she's disloyal," he asks Iago. Now Iago tells how he has recently slept in the same bed with Cassio and has heard him mutter various compromising things about Desdemona in his sleep. Othello reacts violently to this tale: "O monstrous! monstrous!"

COMMENT: Shakespeare makes it clear that Othello's capacity for judgment has deteriorated; Othello is prepared to accept less in the way of solid evidence than he was initially. Reason is less able to guide him as his passion takes over, and he has increasing difficulty in distinguishing between reality and appearance. This scene has already marked Othello's willingness to believe the suspicions Iago has been feeding him. Now, with his cry of "monstrous," Othello shows that he is utterly convinced. The "monstrous birth" that Iago had planned at the end of Act I has been labored forth. The climax of the play having been reached, the resolution—the working out of the plot which has been developed up to this point—begins.

Affecting moderation, Iago says, "Nay, this was but a dream." (He has something more tangible to offer.) Iago now introduces the matter of the handkerchief "spotted with strawberries," which, luckily, he has acquired only a few moments ago. Cleverly improvising, Iago claims that he has seen Cassio wipe his beard with it. (Apparently, Othello has not noticed that it was this same handkerchief which Desdemona had offered him for binding his forehead.) Iago declares that "it speaks against her with other proofs." Utterly con-

vinced for this moment Othello completely loses control: "All my fond love thus do I blow to heaven . . . / Arise, black vengeance, from the hollow hell! Agitated by his terrible passion, he is reduced to calling for "blood, blood, blood," as Iago prods him to further depths by urging patience, and by suggesting that he may change his mind.

In the heat of anger, Othello swears never to change his mind and, like the icy currents of the Pontic sea, never to change his course, never to look back, never to cease till he has had his revenge. Kneeling, he takes a sacred vow on these words. Iago kneels beside the crazed Moor and adds his own oath, swearing to serve the wronged Othello in "what bloody business ever."

COMMENT: The diabolical oath which Othello and Iago make in terms of "blood, blood, blood," "bloody thought," and "what bloody business ever," has frequently been compared with a devil's compact, sealed (as Doctor Faustus' was) by the sign of blood.

Othello accepts Iago's fellowship in revenge and consigns Cassio to Iago's sword. Iago now agrees to exchange Cassio's friendship for the Moor's, but he sustains his role as "honest" Iago by asking that Desdemona be spared. Passionately, Othello denies this request, damning Desdemona as a "lewd minx." He retires to devise a means of killing her, but not before appointing Iago his new lieutenant.

SUMMARY: It is not easy to summarize this lengthy but fast-moving scene. Every word and gesture has had special meaning in drawing the play to its climax. Iago is like a deadly insect gradually stalking, then stinging its victim to death; each of his moves, whether calculated or improvised, is perfectly timed.

1. The scene is designed to convince us through dramatic representation that a man like Iago can deceive a man like Othello and lead him to a dangerous and destructive resolution. Therefore, from start to finish, the scene demonstrates Iago's powers of psychological and verbal manipulation. Shakespeare achieves his design superbly.

2. Iago manipulates Othello so that the poisoned thought of Desdemona's adultery springs directly from the mind of Othello, although the venom has been injected by Iago. Iago has given this scene its potent atmosphere, but the fact that Othello seems to have thought of the idea himself gives it a more corrosive effect.

3. The scene shows Othello in a state of mental flux. The state of his mind changes in response to each of Iago's proddings. Othello becomes curious, then insistent, then enraged. His doubt subsides temporarily when he sees the heavenly Desdemona again. But doubt, once planted, burgeons rapidly. Othello is completely consumed by it and is prepared to take Iago's allegations concerning Cassio's dream and Desdemona's handkerchief as evidence itself.

4. This is the climactic scene of the play, beginning with the insinuations about the "guilty-like" Cassio and ending with Othello's oath of revenge.

5. The beginning of Othello's moral decline is portrayed in this scene. From the moment he allows Iago's insinuations to take hold of his mind, the fiber of his character begins to disintegrate.

Act III: Scene iv

The scene takes place in front of the castle. Accompanied by Emilia, Desdemona asks the Clown where Cassio "lies" (1. lodges, dwells; 2. speaks falsely, "stabs"). The Clown replies equivocally with puns on "lie," "stab," and "lodge." He fails to produce the information, for he really does not know. In periphrastic terms of a comic nature, the Clown agrees, however, to search out Cassio.

COMMENT: The Clown, a stock character in Shakespearean drama, appears infrequently and briefly in *Othello*. Both here and in III.i, the Clown is used to provide comic relief, following a terrific scene of dark passion. As one critic describes him, Othello "in commotion reminds us rather of the fury of the elements than of the tumult of common human passion." After the emotional hurricane of the preceding scene, the Clown's puns are as welcome as the calm following a storm.

Desdemona tells Emilia that she is disturbed by the loss of her handkerchief; she would rather lose a purse full of money. But she consoles herself (with the dramatically ironic), "And but my noble Moor / Is true of mind and made of no such baseness / As jealous creatures are, it were enough / To put him to ill thinking." (Attention is called here to the importance of the handkerchief in the plot and to Othello's usually unsuspecting nature. Desdemona will be unable to recognize Othello's jealousy when she sees it, for she has a decidely different view of his character.) Surprised that a wife can so describe her husband, Emilia inquires, "Is Othello not jealous?" Emphatically, Desdemona replies, "I think the sun where he was born / Drew all such humours from him."

COMMENT: Emilia's experience as Iago's wife makes her think on principle that all men are jealous. She does not know about Othello's suspicions or for what purpose the handkerchief has been used.

Othello enters and takes Desdemona's hand. Dissembling affection, he says her hand is moist. Desdemona interprets "moist" to mean that she has not been dried by age and sorrow, but Othello says that it is a sign of "fruitfulness and a liberal heart" (wantonness is suggested). In pretended jest, he prescribes loss of liberty, fasting, and prayer as a remedy for the "sweating devil" (spirit of sexual desire), which he finds in her hand. It is a noble hand, Othello continues, and a "frank" one. Desdemona replies that her hand is indeed a "frank" one (meaning "generous," magnanimous"), for it was this hand that gave her heart to Othello.

COMMENT: In medieval physiology, the body contained four major fluids or "humours": blood, yellow bile, phlegm, and spleen (black bile or black choler). The preponderance of a particular fluid in a person marked him as sanguine, choleric, phlegmatic, or splenetic (melancholic). It was believed that the mental disposition of a person corresponded to his physiological attributes. The heat and moisture, which Othello mentions, were characteristics of the sanguine temperament, which was a cheerful, generous, amorous one. Othello stresses the amorous (lecherous) aspect of Desdemona's nature, while Desdemona emphasized her love and generosity.

Following this mingled conversation in which Desdemona playfully reverses Othello's insinuating diagnosis, Desdemona informs her husband that she has sent for Cassio to speak to Othello. Othello ignores this piece of information and, claiming a cold in the head, asks for her handkerchief. Desdemona expresses regret that she does not have it with her. Othello reproves her for not having it and then gives an account of why the handkerchief is so important. Since the handkerchief plays so important a part in the plot machinery of the play, the description is repeated here.

> *That handkerchief*
> *Did an Egyptian to my mother give.*
> *She was a charmer, and could almost read*
> *The thoughts of people. She told her, while she*
> *kept it,*
> *'Twould make her amiable and subdue my father*
> *Entirely to her love; but if she lost it*
> *Or made a gift of it, my father's eye*
> *Should hold her loathly, and his spirits should hunt*
> *After new fancies. She, dying, gave it me,*
> *And bid me, when my fate would have me wive,*
> *To give it her. I did so; and take heed ont';*
> *Make it a darling like your precious eye.*
> *To lose't or give't away were such perdition*
> *As nothing else could match.*

"There's magic in the web of it," Othello assures the distressed wife. It was sewn by a two-hundred year old Sybil in "prophetic fury" and "dy'd in mummy which the skilful / Conserv'd of maiden's hearts."

COMMENT: The handkerchief was the Moor's first gift to Desdemona. Emilia refers to it as "that the Moor first gave to Desdemona" (III.iii.309), and Othello tells Iago "'twas my first gift" (III.iii.436). If this gift was given during the courtship and is truly a magic handkerchief, then Othello did use magic to win Desdemona, and he lied to the Duke's court. If the courtship was conducted without magic as Othello told the court, he may be lying now; the handkerchief may not have these properties. Othello may be inventing the tale to test or frighten Desdemona. On the other hand, the handkerchief may have been the first gift after marriage, none having been given before; Othello's present story then may be taken as a true one. The problem is a complex one, for Othello had an open nature when he testified in the Venetian court; now, under Iago's influence, he is capable of duplicity. The commentaries which follow are based on the assumptions that the handkerchief was a marriage gift and contained magic properties.

Desdemona's surprise and distress mount as she listens to this tale. She cannot produce the handkerchief, but she denies that it is lost. (This is Desdemona's first deception, and, as we shall see, it will contribute to her ultimate destruction.) Artfully, she refuses to fetch the handkerchief, claiming that Othello has used the story as a trick to dissuade her from discussing Cassio.

COMMENT: By providing it with a history, Shakespeare emphasizes the significance of the handkerchief and prevents it from becoming a trivial prop. The magic origins of the handkerchief make it symbolic of Othello's mysterious and romantic past, which originally had won Desdemona's love. It is also symbolic of constancy in love, one of the important themes of the play. By losing the handkerchief, Desdemona symbolically loses Othello's love. Thus, the handkerchief becomes more than a cog in the machinery of melodrama; the tale of its magic properties makes it an organic element in the texture of the play.

Repeatedly, Othello insists on seeing the handkerchief, while Desdemona answers each of his demands with a plea for Cassio. Othello leaves in a rage.

COMMENT: Once more Othello becomes enraged when his demands are refused. This time his anger is far more ominous, for he utters no threats. During his earlier inquiries into Cassio's misconduct and Iago's suspicions, he relied on Iago's word. His dependence for information on his newly appointed lieutenant increases. He will turn to Iago again

and believe what he is told, for Othello must have prompt answers to his question.

As Othello departs, Emilia repeats the question she had asked prior to this angry interview, "Is not this man jealous?" (This time, however, the question is rhetorical.) Desdemona confesses, "I ne'er saw this before." (His wife is the first to note that Othello has changed.) She repeats her concern for the lost handkerchief, but Emilia, still wondering over Othello's strange behavior, merely reflects on the fickleness of men, "They eat us hungrily, and when they are full, / They belch us."

COMMENT: The plot thickens. Emilia does not say what has happened to the handkerchief, though she knows perfectly well (III.iii). Like her cynical husband, she believes in the worst generalities that can be made of man. To her way of thinking, the handkerchief is irrelevant; she is convinced that Othello has tired of his wife and is using the lost handkerchief as an excuse to berate her.

Iago and Cassio now join the ladies. Iago has been insisting that Cassio importune Desdemona once more. Cassio asks Desdemona for a final decision; he does not want to keep pleading. If his reinstatement is denied, he will seek some other fortune. Regretfully, Desdemona explains her situation. She has been pressing his suit, but Othello is not in a good mood, his "humour" has altered. In reply to Iago's question, Emilia says that Othello has just gone away "in strange unquietness." Iago pretends to be surprised at the news. He has seen Othello maintain his calm in the fiercest heat of battle, even when his brother's life was destroyed. "Something of moment" must be disturbing the Moor. Desdemona urges Iago to see Othello.

COMMENT: By suggesting that "something of moment" is afoot, Iago hopes to keep Desdemona from guessing that Othello is jealous. By maintaining her ignorance, he can continue to use her innocent association with Cassio to his own advantage.

Meanwhile, Iago's facts about Othello's life and character heighten the contrast between Othello's "strange" new humor and his previous one. Desdemona's statement that Othello is "in humour alter'd," suggests that Othello is now suffering from too much spleen (melancholy), whereas previously he had been phlegmatic (cool, self-possessed, slow to anger), as Iago describes the Moor on the battlefield.

Shakespeare's art is a subtle one. Othello is central to the play, and even when he does not appear, his characterization is continued. The single reference to his "alter'd humour" and Iago's subsequent description of Othello in battle achieve two purposes: in terms of the plot, Desdemona is misled to believe that Othello suffers under cares of state; in terms of the character, Othello's change is observed and emphasized.

Latching on to Iago's suggestions that something important is disturbing her husband, the humble Desdemona decides it is some business with Venice or some matter of state. Apologizing for her husband, Desdemona explains to Emilia that men frequently mistreat their wives when they have great worries on their minds. "We must not think men are gods," she cautions Emilia, blaming herself for thinking unkindly of Othello before Iago's suggestion clarified his outrageous behavior. Emilia, more realistic, prays to heaven that state-matters are truly the cause of Othello's conduct, and not some jealousy of Desdemona. Thinking of her own husband, Emilia asserts that wives need not give their husbands cause for jealousy, for "'tis a monster / Begot upon itself, born on itself."

COMMENT: In her description of jealousy, Emilia echoes Iago, who called jealousy "a green-ey'd monster which doth mock / The meat it feeds on." Emilia's knowledge of jealous men has been learned at Iago's school, which Othello has been attending too. Her interpretation of Othello's behavior is the correct one, of course.

Despite her awareness of Othello's ill-humor, Desdemona decides to find him and once more advance Cassio's cause, this time "to my uttermost." Cassio is asked to await her return.

As Desdemona and Emilia leave, Cassio is left alone onstage. Bianca arrives and is greeted with much familiarity by Cassio, who states that he was planning to pay her a visit very shortly. Bianca too was just on her way to Cassio's lodgings, for, she complains, he has not been to see her for an entire week. This is a long time for lovers. Cassio explains that his absence was owing to the pressure of "leaden thoughts," but he promises to make up for his absence when he can do so without interruption. As if to turn the conversation, Cassio gives Bianca a handkerchief and asks her to copy its pattern. Bianca is immediately suspicious that the handkerchief has come from some new mistress. Cassio explains that he found it in his chamber and does not know its owner. Before he must return it, he would like to have a copy of the design, which he finds most attractive.

COMMENT: The embroidered design of the handkerchief spotted with strawberries was sewn by a Sybil in "prophetic fury." Apparently, it has the magic power of winning the admiration of those who see it. Desdemona had a special affinity for this token from her husband even before she heard its history. Iago too had liked the design

and had often urged Emilia to steal the handkerchief for him. Perhaps, he intended even then to use it in some plot; perhaps, he was drawn to it by its magic powers.

The chain of accidents connected with the handkerchief strains credibility if the magic cloth is viewed as an ordinary accessory. The Elizabethan audience was a susceptible one, and many of its members believed in magic. (Witches were burned in Salem long after Shakespeare's day.) It would be better to suspend one's disbelief in magic than to allow modern reason to spoil Shakespeare's play.

Cassio asks Bianca to leave him, for he is awaiting the General and does not want to be found with a woman. Bianca is reluctant to go; she asks Cassio to walk her a bit of the way and presses him to dine with her that night. Anxious to get rid of her, Cassio promises to see her soon, and Bianca takes her leave as the scene ends.

SUMMARY: This scene is important in several respects.

1. It establishes the fact that Othello's character is undergoing change. Hitherto self-possessed and slow to anger, he is rapidly becoming irritable, strangely unquiet, and melancholic. He is clearly struggling with his jealousy and attempts to check Iago's allegations in regard to the handkerchief. For the first time in the play, "open-natured" Othello practices duplicity by confronting his wife indirectly and making evil insinuations about her character under the guise of good fellowship.

2. The plot progresses slowly as the implications of the dropped handkerchief are examined in detail from various points of view. Its strange history is unfolded, giving it symbolic value in the development of the theme of constancy; Othello makes the handkerchief vital to his love for Desdemona; Desdemona's distress over the loss of it increases; Emilia is unimpressed with the importance of the handkerchief; Cassio's innocent admiration of its design arouses Bianca's jealousy, and his own interest in it portends doom for its owner, Desdemona.

3. The scene reveals that minor moral weaknesses are widespread (and implies that minor vices lead to major catastrophes). Desdemona lies directly (about the loss of the handkerchief); Emilia lies indirectly (by withholding information about it); and Cassio arranges an assignation with a woman of loose morals. All these acts play their parts in the final catastrophe.

Act IV: Scene i

The scene is again the yard before the Castle. Iago and Othello are in the midst of an earnest conversation. (Their opening remarks are somewhat ambiguous, but they may be interpreted in terms of the lines which follow.) Iago asks Othello if he will think a kiss in private an "unauthoriz'd" (unwarrantable) thing, and Othello insists that he does not think but knows it to be so. Next, Iago asks if it is possible for Desdemona to spend an hour in bed with a lover and mean no harm. Othello, of course, asserts that this is impossible. Iago contends that as long as they do nothing, they are merely committing a minor sin, "But if I give my wife a handkerchief —"

COMMENT: Iago is engaged in the game of insinuation again. He states that lying in bed naked so long as one does nothing is only a minor sin, but if one gives his wife a handkerchief—The unfinished sentence implies the following ending: if she gives it to another man, then the sin is major, a mortal one, an unpardonable one.

Reminded of the handkerchief, Othello compares it to a "raven o'er the infected house." Iago pretends to make light of the handkerchief (implying that he has more incriminating evidence to report). Cassio has admitted his intimacies with Desdemona. Othello is thoroughly shaken. His mind gives way, and he utters a series of disjointed and confused thoughts (all highly relevant to the situation, but without syntax) before falling into a trance. Chanting diabolically, Iago gloats, "Work on / My medicine, work! Thus credulous fools are caught."

Cassio enters at this point. In reply to his question, Iago states that the Moor has "fall'n into an epilepsy." Refusing his assistance, Iago asks Cassio to withdraw, promising to speak to him after the General recovers. Cassio leaves.

As soon as Othello recovers, Iago asks about his head. Othello imagines he is being mocked (that an allusion has been made to the horns on his head, traditionally ascribed to cuckolded husbands). Iago denies having made such an allusion. He wishes Othello would behave like a man, or, if he feels like a beast (with cuckold's horns), then he should be comforted in the knowledge that the city is full of such beasts. In fact, Othello is better off than millions of men who do not know they are being deceived. No, Iago asserts, he personally would rather know the truth about his wife, and knowing his own nature (vengeful), he knows what she would be (punished). Othello is impressed by Iago's wisdom.

Next, Iago informs Othello that Cassio had been there and that he will come back. Othello is to conceal himself, and he will overhear the truth from Cassio's own lips. Othello hides.

COMMENT: Once before Iago had suggested that Othello hide, but Othello, then direct and open-natured, had refused to do so. Brabantio was on his way to have the Moor arrested, and the Moor insisted on being found. Othello's willingness to hide at Iago's urging bears witness to the deterioration of his character.

Cassio returns, and Iago begins to question him not about Desdemona, as Othello has been led to believe, but about Bianca, the local prostitute.

Iago starts a stream of rough banter, alleging, among other things, that Bianca has spread the rumor that Cassio intends to marry her. Cassio thinks this is a hilarious joke. Meanwhile, Othello in his hiding place interprets the laughter as Cassio's exultation over his conquest. Bianca returns at this point and angrily shakes Desdemona's handkerchief in Cassio's face. On second thought, she has decided that Cassio has been unfaithful to her, that the handkerchief is "some minx's token," and that she would be a fool to "take out" (copy) its work. When Bianca leaves in a huff, Iago sends Cassio after her to quiet her down, learning first that Cassio will dine at Bianca's that night. Othello comes out of hiding prepared to murder his former officer.

COMMENT: This scene indicates that Othello is attempting a real investigation, but he is too much blinded by jealousy to understand what he sees and to realize that he cannot really hear the conversation between Iago and Cassio.

Othello claims his heart has turned to stone, yet when he thinks of Desdemona's sweetness, her skill in embroidery, in music, her plenteous wit and invention, he is deeply moved, "But yet the pity of it, Iago! O Iago, the pity of it, Iago!"

COMMENT: Although Desdemona's virtues have been extolled before, Othello's description suggests that she is a "perfect lady" of the sort outlined in Castiglione's *Book of the Courtier*. Being unbookish and untutored in the ways of Venetian society, Othello does not realize that Desdemona cannot be the adulteress he thinks. This is indeed a pity.

Othello is now totally convinced of Desdemona's guilt. Determined to kill her, he asks Iago to get him poison. But Iago suggests a more symbolic revenge: "Strangle her in . . .the bed she hath contaminated." Othello is pleased with the justice of this method. Iago undertakes to dispose of Cassio.

A trumpet sounds. Desdemona enters in the company of her cousin Lodovico, the Venetian ambassador, and other attendants. As Othello reads the letter he has received from Venice, Desdemona explains to Lodovico that there has been a misunderstanding between Othello and Cassio, which she hopes her cousin will clear up. Othello listens to her conversation, interjecting ominous remarks, which he pretends are commentaries on the letter. Angered by Desdemona's reference to "the love I bear to Cassio," Othello asks her if she is wise (that is, to admit her love publicly). When she expresses her pleasure at Cassio's appointment as Othello's deputy-governor, he becomes violently angry and publicly strikes her. Everyone in the distinguished assembly is shocked. Othello's private torture is now public property. He deepens the effect of his barbarous conduct by hinting at her promiscuity: "Sir, she can turn, and turn, and yet go on / And turn again." Lodovico can make no sense of the behavior of the "noble Moor," the man of undaunted courage and monumental dignity, whom he had hitherto known.

After Othello storms out, Iago insinuates that Othello is often brutal and could get worse. But after arousing Lodovico's curiosity, he puritanically asserts: "It is not honesty in me to speak / What I have seen and known." The innuendo strikes home at once. Urged to observe the Moor himself, Lodovico departs, convinced that he has been "deceived in him [Othello]."

SUMMARY: This scene continues to portray the debasement of Othello, deepening our sense of pity for the utter disintegration of the noble character. The audience's hatred for Iago is intensified as pity for Othello increases. The scene shows the following things:

1. Othello has made some effort to investigate Iago's allegations, but he is unable to judge what he sees and falls under Iago's greater psychological dominance.

2. Iago has his usual luck in that everyone does the wrong thing at the right moment for Iago.

3. The private tragedy has become public knowledge; evil spreads rapidly; it is infectious.

Act IV: Scene ii

In a room within the castle, Othello questions Emilia about Desdemona's activities. She assures him that Desdemona is honest. Cassio has been with her, of course, but never alone. Emilia was never sent to fetch a fan, gloves, mask, or anything else. In short, Emilia insists, she is ready to wager her soul on Desdemona's virtue. "That's strange," Othello reflects, as he sends Emilia to call Desdemona. But as soon as Emilia leaves, Othello decides that, although Emilia has made an adequate defense of her mistress, it is no more than any bawd would do. Besides, Emilia is a subtle whore, who

keeps a private room full of villainous secrets on the one hand, and on the other, she will kneel and pray with the most virtuous. Othello says he has seen her do it (that is, pray). And with that, he dismisses her testimony.

Emilia returns, escorting Desdemona. Gently, Othello invites Desdemona to "... come hither." Then, dangerously, he tells her to look into his eyes, to show her face. Turning to Emilia, he bids her get to work, close the door, attend to her "mystery" (duty, the function of a madam of a brothel).

COMMENT: Othello tortures himself in this scene by pretending his wife is a prostitute, Emilia the madam, and he the stranger visiting her.

He urges Desdemona to damn herself by swearing (falsely, he presumes) that she is his wife, and to be "double-damned" by swearing she is honest.

COMMENT: Here Othello displays his tragic dilemma: Now that suspicion has been engendered, there is no way to get rid of it. If Desdemona says she is faithful, his suspicion will make him doubt her; if she says she is not, she will only confirm his suspicion. He can only believe her if he already trusts her, in which case he would not be suspicious at all.

At last Desdemona realizes that the Moor is jealous. She swears she is faithful but to no avail. Othello is a pathetic sight. He shoos her away and bursts into tears. (Desdemona is thoroughly perplexed; she cannot believe he means his accusations and still thinks "something of moment" is the cause of his suffering. But what connections has that with her?) She asks if he suspects her father, Brabantio, to have been behind his recall to Venice. If so, she implores, he must not blame her, for she too has lost Brabantio's favor. Moved by self-pity, Othello says he could have endured the most painful afflictions, but to be discarded by the woman he has loved or to keep her "as a cistern for foul toads / To knot and gender in"—this is beyond endurance. (The image of adultery as a cistern full of toads is particularly foul and conveys precisely the horror Othello felt for this act. Other horrific images and outrageous epithets follow.) He compares Desdemona's chastity to "summer flies in the shambles"; she is a "fair paper" inscribed with "whore," a "public commoner," an "impudent strumpet," and "heaven stops the nose" at her rank smell. Desdemona asserts her innocence time and again, but she can do nothing with this madman. Sarcastically, Othello apologizes for mistaking her for the "cunning whore of Venice, / That married with Othello," and he calls for Emilia with several equally unsavory epithets. Concluding his fantastic conception (the pretense that he is visiting a brothel), he pays Emilia the madam's fee and asks her to unlock the door and keep secret his visit.

COMMENT: Othello is clearly maddened with grief and has devised a fantastic playlet (like modern psychodrama), in which he acts out his fears that Desdemona is a whore, that Emilia is her bawd, and that men pay to visit his wife. The scene is all the more horrific in that Othello is the only player and ladies are defenseless against his loathsome epithets and lewd insinuations. The maggots of filth have taken over Othello's disintegrating mind.

Othello leaves Desdemona totally dazed; she describes her condition to Emilia as "half-asleep." (She has been through a nightmare and has not yet fully awakened.) In a grotesque bit of word-play on "my lord" and "thy lord," Desdemona pathetically argues with Emilia that since "my lord" is the same man to both of them, Emilia's lord, Iago, is Desdemona's lord too. She orders that her wedding sheets be put upon her bed and that Iago be called.

COMMENT: Desdemona's grim jest is most appropriate at this point. It shows that she has reached the very bottom of despair from which there is nowhere else to go but up. Her feelings are beyond tears. The jest, like Othello's fantasy, hinges on the theme of adultery. Her chastity, having been denied so violently, becomes an appropriate subject, Desdemona feels, for her own game of "adulteress." Her request for an interview with Iago appears aptly in the context of her pathetic jest, but it is also a real request, for she hopes that Iago can help her.

Emilia returns promptly with Iago. Desdemona is too full of self-pity at this point to state her wishes clearly. Emilia tells Iago that Othello has abused and "bewhored" Desdemona. Desdemona asks, "Am I that name, Iago?" (Delicately, she refuses to use the word "whore.") Covering his malicious delight, Iago innocently asks, "What name, fair lady?" But Desdemona is evasive, "Such as she says my lord did say I was." Emilia, suffering from fewer inhibitions, bluntly states. "He call'd her whore." A fine thing, indeed, Emilia broods, to call a woman whore who has refused fashionable marriages, and has left her father and her country to be with her husband. With sarcastic virulence, Emilia repeats all the inquiries Othello had made of her. Finally, Emilia states her suspicion that some slanderer has been at work. She tells Iago that it was some such "base notorious knave" that caused him to suspect her with the Moor.

COMMENT: Desdemona seems to be too dazed to notice this remark, for if she had heard it she would have been embarrassed by it at the least. Emilia, who genuinely loves her mistress, is outraged at Othello's treatment of her. She does not yet suspect Iago. We may be learning here that Emilia's and Desdemona's alleged adulteries were invented by the same villain.

In another piece of dramatic irony, Desdemona asks Iago for advice. How can she win her lord again, she asks the villain. Iago tells her not to worry; it is some business of state that has caused him to act this way. Trumpets sound, announcing dinner which the Venetian envoys are to attend. Desdemona and Emilia leave for it.

The scene concludes with a conversation between Roderigo and Iago. Roderigo has begun to suspect Iago. He tells him that "your words and performances are not kin together"; Iago's words and deeds do not correspond. Roderigo has given Iago enough jewels for Desdemona to corrupt a nun. (Obviously, the jewels have been pocketed by Iago.) Roderigo threatens to demand them of Desdemona. If they are forthcoming, he will repent his "unlawful solicitation" if not, he will demand satisfaction of Iago. Iago devises another impromptu scheme. Othello will be leaving with Desdemona, unless some accident causes him to stay. Now, if Cassio were removed, if he were incapable of taking Othello's place, the Moor and his wife would have to stay on Cyprus. If Roderigo, will undertake to knock out Cassio's brains, Iago will be there to second him. It is high supper time as the scene ends.

SUMMARY: This scene accomplishes the following dramatic purposes:

1. It illustrates the progress of Othello's degradation (the brothel scene) and prepares us for his nadir, when he becomes a murderer.

2. It serves to accentuate the nobility, innocence, and tenderness of Desdemona both in the terrible confrontation with her husband and in her conversation with Iago.

3. The machinery of the plot is running down. Othello is prepared for murder; Desdemona is prepared to be cast off; Iago is arranging to have Roderigo and Cassio finish each other off (but the villain will be foiled); Emilia is prepared to expose her mistress' slanderer (and will pay for her loyalty with her life).

4. Preparation is made for Iago's downfall in the next and last act. The height of irony is reached when Desdemona appeals to Iago for help. After this, Iago's powers can only decline. Emilia's rage will turn against her husband when she finally uncovers his villainy, and Roderigo's incipient rebellion against Iago augurs the downfall of the villain.

Act IV: Scene iii

Othello, Lodovico, Desdemona, Emilia, and attendants are assembled in another room in the castle. As the scene opens the supper has ended and Lodovico is taking his leave. Othello offers to walk with his guest part of his way. He orders Desdemona to go to bed for the night, to dismiss Emilia, and await his return.

COMMENT: Shakespeare, having reduced the maddened Othello to a most pitiable spectacle, next imparts pathos to Desdemona.

When the ladies are left alone, Emilia remarks that Othello looks gentler than he did before. (This is the calm before the next storm.) Desdemona asks for her nightclothes and hurriedly prepares for bed, for fear of displeasing her husband. As she undresses, she expresses her love for the Moor even though he is stubborn, scolding, and angry. Emilia reports that she has laid the bed with the wedding sheets as Desdemona had ordered. As if presaging doom, Desdemona's thoughts fly to death. She asks Emilia to shroud her in her wedding sheets should she die before her attendant. Then she tells Emilia about a song she once learned from her mother's maid—a girl called Barbary—whose lover went insane and forsook her. The song is called "Willow." It is an old song, Desdemona recalls, "but it express'd her fortune, / And she died singing it." That song has been in her mind all night. She has all she can do to keep from singing it, Desdemona says, and she tries to forget her troubles with idle chatter about Lodovico. But the diversion doesn't work, and Desdemona sings poignantly: "The poor soul sat sighing by a sycamore tree, / Sing all a green willow."

COMMENT: Desdemona is in a state of morbid trepidation. She speaks of death, arranges for her shroud, and recalls the story of the young maid Barbary (possibly because she was black) whose situation obviously parallels her own. Desdemona cannot get Barbary's death-song out of her mind. Psychologically, Desdemona is displaying apprehension dramatically; she is foreshadowing her death.

Desdemona asks Emilia whether there actually are women who commit adultery; she would not do such a thing for all the world. Emilia replies, "The world's a huge thing. It is a great price for a small vice." She would not do such a thing for a trifle, but "who would

not make her husband a cuckold to make him a monarch?" In a more serious vein, Emilia argues that it is the indifference and misbehavior of husbands that lead women to sin. Emilia's thesis is that women have the right to live by the same moral standard as men.

COMMENT: Emilia, though basically a decent person, is more realistic than Desdemona and has a coarser sense of humor. Her earthy values serve as a contrast to the idealism of Desdemona.

SUMMARY: This scene serves the following dramatic objectives:

1. The scene provides a psychological pause after the tensions built up during the preceding action. Desdemona's poignantly beautiful lyric serves as a lull before the next storm.

2. It emphasizes the noble innocence of Desdemona by contrasting it with the earthy realism of Emilia.

3. It makes Desdemona the object of our pity and deepens the tragedy of her impending death.

4. It creates suspense by effecting a delay between Othello's decision to kill Desdemona and the actual killing.

5. It heightens the enormity of Othello's crime by providing time for his premeditation and eliminating the possibility that Othello murders in the heat of passion.

Act V: Scene i

The scene shifts to a street in Cyprus near Bianca's house. Iago and Roderigo are preparing to ambush Cassio. Roderigo has misgivings about murdering Cassio, but he reasons that death is merely the departure of a man, and this murder may bring him satisfying results. Iago is also uncertain about the outcome, but he sees enormous gains no matter what happens. Roderigo is to do the actual killing; if Roderigo survives, Iago will have to restore the jewels intended for Desdemona and which Iago has misappropriated. It is to Iago's advantage that Roderigo dies in the encounter with Cassio. Cassio's death is also desirable, for "he hath a daily beauty in his life / That makes me ugly." Besides, Cassio would expose Iago's lies to Othello if he ever learned of them. No, Iago must have them both out of the way.

COMMENT: Among his other villanies, Iago emerges here as an uninhibited killer. This is also the first time Iago shows concern for his own safety and expresses fear of exposure. This my be taken as another forecast of Iago's imminent downfall.

Cassio arrives; Roderigo attacks. As he feared, Roderigo's onslaught is unsuccessful. In fact, Cassio is protected by a coat of mail and succeeds in wounding Roderigo. Iago now emerges from concealment, wounds Cassio in the leg, and flees. Othello, hearing Cassio's cries, is delighted with Iago's work ("O brave Iago, honest and just / That hast such a noble sense of thy friend's wrong"). He leaves without examining Cassio's supposed corpse.

Both wounded men lie on different parts of the stage, calling for help. At a distance, Lodovico and Gratiano hear their shouts. Iago returns with a light and finds Cassio. "What villains have done this?" he asks. Iago calls Lodovico and Gratiano to help Cassio and goes off in "search for the bloody thieves." Finding Roderigo, Iago stabs him to death. Lodovico commends Iago on his timely action, and all turn to assist Cassio. Roderigo's last words have been, "O damned Iago! O inhuman dog!"

COMMENT: Roderigo has been the first to suspect Iago of double-dealing; now he is the first to realize his betrayal and condemn the traitor. Other recognitions will follow.

Bianca rushes out of her lodging and is terribly distraught. On the spur of the moment, Iago decides to implicate Bianca in the ambush of Cassio. He tells the gentlemen that he suspects "this trash / To a part in this injury." Next, he feigns the discovery of Roderigo, whom the Venetians, Lodovico and Gratiano, know. Through artfully phrased question, Iago continues to cast suspicion on Bianca for engineering the death of Roderigo. Cassio is put in a chair, and the General's surgeon is called.

Emilia arrives and learns from Iago that Cassio's misfortunes are "the fruits of whoring." There is a brief exchange between the two women in which Bianca claims (perhaps with justice) to be as honest as Emilia. Bianca freely admits that Cassio "supp'd" at her house, and Iago uses this statement to charge her with the crime. Emilia is sent to inform Othello and Desdemona of the disaster, and Iago (once more foreshadowing his own fall) privately expresses doubt: "This is the night / That either makes me or fordoes me quite."

SUMMARY: This brief scene is filled with action; it completes the resolution of the play and prepares us for the conclusion.

1. Iago has succeeded in a minor objective—ridding himself of Roderigo and saving himself the embarrassment of accounting for the jewels.

2. He has not succeeded in a major objective—ridding himself of Cassio. Iago's fortune is beginning to change. Hitherto, accident and coincidence have always worked in

his favor. This time, Lodovico's and Gratiano's untimely arrival has prevented Iago from finishing off Cassio.

3. Iago is as quick-witted as ever in turning opportunity to his advantage. Bianca, because of her reputation as a prostitute, easily falls into his net. (Shakespeare has too many things to consider in the crowded canvas of his last act to bother with Bianca again. Presumably, she is exonerated. She is implicated in the crime here in order to stress Iago's restless capacity for intrigue and evil.)

Act V: Scene ii

The final scene of the play shifts to a chamber in Othello's castle. Desdemona is in bed. Carrying a candle, Othello enters. He sees Desdemona asleep and beings to speak: "It is the cause, it is the cause, my soul."

COMMENT: This fatal scene opens with a poignant and magnificent speech by Othello. He has recovered some of his composure, which he had originally possessed when "the full senate found [him] all in all sufficient."

Othello uses the word "cause" (guilt, reason for punishment) in its legal sense. The word suggests that Othello has made a judicial decision, reached after a careful examination and evaluation of the evidence. Othello does not want to commit a "crime of passion" or an act of revenge (a kind of "wild justice" as Francis Bacon defined it.) He has always taken pride in his own restraint, his cool command, and his sense of justice. Now he brings these qualities to bear in his calculated decision to execute Desdemona, "else she'll betray more men."

Othello declares that he will not name the "cause" to the "chaste" stars. Looking down on fair Desdemona, he declines to shed her blood or scar "that whiter skin of hers than snow / And smooth as monumental alabaster." (He plans suffocation, which leaves no marks.)

COMMENT: A good deal of the play takes place in the night where monstrous thoughts are engendered and brought to light (cf. I.iii.409-10). Images of light are woven into the dark fabric of this final scene to heighten by contrast the blackness of tragic events.

Murder must be done, and darkness is needed for the crime. "Put out the light, and then put out the light," Othello says, addressing the candle. Playing on two meanings of the word "light," (1. candlelight; 2. light of life), Othello says, "If I quench thee / the taper / . . . / I can again thy former light restore." But the light of Desdemona, once extinguished, is out forever. He addresses Desdemona as a "pattern of excelling nature" and compares her to a rose, which, once plucked, must wither. Moved by his reflections, he kisses his sleeping wife. So affecting is that kiss that Othello is tempted to break his sword of "justice." He is even brought to tears, cruel tears, but he soon regains his former resolve.

Desdemona wakens and timidly asks, "Will you come to bed, my lord?" (Stern in his sense of justice, Othello does not want to damn Desdemona's soul.) "Have you pray'd?" he asks. He urges her to confess her sins before being killed. "Talk you of killing?" Desdemona asks, apprised for the first time in the play of Othello's full intentions. "Heaven have mercy on me," Desdemona cries. She expresses her hope that he does not mean this, but she sees the rolling of his eyes and is reduced to terror. At last Othello tells her the cause of his anger: "That handkerchief which I so lov'd and gave thee / Thou gav'st to Cassio." Sensibly, she tells him to send for the man and ask him. She pleads with Othello, telling him that she never did offense to him in her life, never loved Cassio "but with such general warranty of heaven / As I might love." Angrily, Othello responds that he himself saw Cassio with the handkerchief in his hand. His fury increasing, he blames Desdemona for turning his sacrifice into a murder, that is, for making him angry so that he will kill in passion and not in cool justice. (He regards the calculated killing as a "sacrifice" to the God of justice.) As for Cassio, he is dead. Ambiguously, Desdemona cries, "Alas! he is betray'd and I undone." She burst into tears, which Othello interprets as grief for Cassio: "Out, strumpet! Weep'st thou for him to my face?" Smothering her pleas for mercy, he kills her before she has prayed.

Suddenly, there is a knocking at the door. It is Emilia coming to report Roderigo's death and the attack on Cassio. The knocking continues as Othello tries to make sure that Desdemona does not linger in pain. "By-and-by," Othello calls, assuring himself that Desdemona is dead. He surmises correctly that Emilia has come to report on Cassio: "If she come in, she'll sure speak to my wife." Suddenly, the awful realization occurs. "My wife! my wife! I have no wife." (These words recall Desdemona's grim jest on the loss of "my lord" and echo hollowly in the death chamber.)

Emilia continues to call. In a moment, Othello answers, drawing the curtains around Desdemona's corpse. Emilia enters with the news, that foul murder has been done. Before she can finish her message, Othello sums up the deeds of the night:

> . . . *It is the very error of the moon;*
> *She come more nearer earth than she was wont,*
> *And makes men mad.*

COMMENT: Emilia's knocking at the door to bring news in the midst of the murder is the same technique Shakespeare used in the knocking at the gate scene in *Macbeth*.

A death cry comes from Desdemona, "O, falsely, falsely murther'd." Emilia discovers her dying mistress; "O who hath done this deed?" she cries. "Nobody, I myself," Desdemona gasps before she dies. Othello feigns innocence momentarily, then passionately charges, "She's, like a liar, gone to burning Hell! / 'Twas I that kill'd her." Then her lie makes her more than the angel and Othello the blacker devil for killing such a one, Emilia retorts. They exchange their judgments of Desdemona's virtues and remain deadlocked on either side of the question until Othello says, "Thy husband knew it all." Emilia is stunned. "My husband?" she repeats over and over again. "I say thy husband. Dost understand the word?" Emilia curses Iago's soul and turns her fury against Othello, whom she now calls Desdemona's "filthy bargain."

Emilia yells for help and, at the same time, spits abuses at the Moor: "O gull! O dolt! / As ignorant as dirt!" Montano, Gratiano, Iago, and others respond to her cry. At once Emilia demands that Iago explain and clear himself. Iago equivocates at first, but he is forced to admit that he accused Desdemona. Emilia discloses the murder to the shocked assembly. Gratiano, Desdemona's uncle, finds some consolation in knowing that Brabantio has died before this calamity. Othello explains the cause of the murder and mentions the handkerchief. Now Emilia understands the whole plot. Stricken with shame and remorse, Emilia insists on speaking. Iago draws his sword, threatening to quiet her forever, but Emilia shows the episode of the dropped handkerchief in its true light.

Othello runs at Iago when he hears the truth, but he is restrained by Montano and disarmed. Iago stabs Emilia and flees. Now dying, Emilia asks to be buried by the side of her mistress. Montano takes off after the villain, and Gratiano goes to guard the door, leaving Othello and Emilia alone.

COMMENT: Othello's terrible certainty of his wife's betrayal is revealed as a fantasy. He must now accept the excruciating knowledge that Desdemona was true.

Othello castigates himself for losing his sword to Montano. He feels there is no point in living now that Desdemona is dead. Meanwhile, Emilia has become delirious and addresses her dead mistress. Singing snatches of the "Willow" song, Emilia defends her mistress to the "cruel Moor" with her dying breath.

Recalling that he has another sword in his chamber, Othello finds it and calls for Gratiano, whom he addresses as "Uncle." When Gratiano enters, Othello shows him the weapon, boasts of his skill in using it, and in a torrent of self-recrimination, mourns for his dead wife.

COMMENT: Othello wants the sword to prevent anyone from coming to him. He has no desire to fight.

He delivers a long, heart-rending speech. He knows that he has come to the "very sea-mark of my utmost sail"; it is his "journey's end." "Where should Othello go?" he asks. He looks upon the corpse of Desdemona—"O ill-starred wench! / Pale as thy smock!" On judgment day the look that she bears in death will send his soul to hell. His surge of wild rhetoric ends in a moan; "O Desdemona! Desdemona! dead! O! O! O!"

Iago is brought back, a prisoner who has in part confessed to his "villainy." Othello succeeds in wounding him on his next try. Then, Othello asks forgiveness of Cassio, who has been brought in on his chair. He wants to know why "that demi-devil," Iago, has ensnared his body and soul. Intractable to the end, Iago replies, "Demand me nothing; what you know, you know / From this time forth I never will speak word." What is not confirmed about Iago's plot by various witnesses is supplied by letters found on the person of Roderigo. The details of the story are clarified but the tragedy cannot be undone.

Othello is to be relieved of his command; he will be returned to Venice as a prisoner until his case is disposed of. But Othello has other plans. In his final speech, he says Venice is aware of the service he has rendered her. Lodovico and the others are to report to him as he truly is, exaggerating nothing, casting malice on nothing: "then must you speak / Of one that lov'd not wisely but too well." Othello punctuates the end of his speech by stabbing himself to death: "Set you down this; . . . / I took by th' throat the circumcised dog / And smote him —thus."

Before dying, Othello addresses the body of Desdemona: "I kiss'd thee ere I killed thee. No way but this— / Killing myself, to die upon a kiss." He falls upon her bed. In the briefest of eulogies, Cassio says, ". . . He was great of heart." Lodovico expresses the feelings of all when he calls Iago, "O Spartan dog / More fell than anguish, hunger, or the sea!" and consigns the "censure of this hellish villain" to Cassio.

COMMENT: While Othello's final kiss points to some sort of reconciliation with man and suggests the possibility of his religious redemption, the critic Paul Siegel, author of *Shakespearean Tragedy and the Elizabethan Compromise*, takes another approach. "In committing self-murder at the conclusion he [Othello] is continuing to follow Judas' example. His behavior in his last moments, therefore, would have confirmed Elizabethans in the impression that his soul is lost, which they observed from the dramatic irony of his offering Desdemona an opportunity, as he supposes, for salvation and then withdrawing it in a rage, not realizing that his own salvation is at issue and forgetting that those who do not forgive will not be forgiven."

SUMMARY: The last scene of the play ties up all the loose threads of plot, theme, and characterization.

1. Othello intends the killing of Desdemona to be a calculated "sacrifice" to justice, not a murder and a butchery, but he fails in his intention and is forced to kill Desdemona in the heat of anger. Shakespeare shows that Othello does not really regain the self-control which distinguishes him in the early acts of the play.

2. When it is too late, Othello learns the truth from Emilia, that his suspicions are unfounded. During his last moments of life, he knows the anguishing truth. Othello dies, a self-murderer, declaring that he was "one not easily jealous," but "perplex'd in the extreme."

3. Iago is unmasked by his own wife whom he kills. He refuses to speak further. His powers of destruction finally turn against his own person, and he is destined for torture and execution.

A fitting conclusion to this summary of the tragedy of Othello is Dr. Samuel Johnson's evaluation of the play as a whole. No one can say more in a few words: "The beauties of this play impress themselves so strongly upon the attention of the reader, that they can draw no aid from critical illustration. The fiery openness of Othello, magnanimous, artless, ardent in his affection, inflexible in his resolution, and obdurate in his revenge; the cool malignity of Iago, silent in his resentment, subtle in his designs, and studious at once of his interest and his vengeance; the soft simplicity of Desdemona, confident of merit, and conscious of innocence, her artless perseverance in her suit, and her slowness to suspect that she can be suspected, are such proofs of Shakespeare's skill in human nature, as, I suppose, it is vain to seek in any modern writer. The gradual progress which Iago makes in the Moor's conviction, and the circumstances which he employs to inflame him, are so artfully natural, that, though it will not be said of him as he says of himself, that he is *a man not easily jealous*, yet we cannot but pity him when at last we find him *perplexed in the extreme*."

CHARACTER ANALYSES

OTHELLO   Shakespeare, in his major work, has a special gift of creating characters about whom no last, definite, and final word can be expressed. There always exists some area of "ambiguity"—the possibility of two meanings, even of multiple meanings. The sensitive reader is left to "ponder"; he experiences the same reaction to a Shakespearean character as he does to people in real life; certain things he definitely knows about them; other aspects of the person are left mysterious, shadowed, about which he can only surmise. Characters in a Shakespeare play, like real people, may not completely *know* themselves; they may have subconscious urges, unexamined attitudes, improvised reactions to new situations. Shakespeare is able to catch this aspect of real experience. His characters have a great degree of "fluidity"; and this is true just as much of a comparatively straightforward character such as Othello as that of a complex, introverted character such as Hamlet.

First, then, let us consider what we obviously know about Othello.

(1) He has been a successful professional soldier, a *condottiere* of the type well known to Italian Renaissance history. The small, but often powerful, Italian city states frequently engaged free-lance generals, with their own private armies, to do their fighting for them on a contractual basis. Their own citizens preferred to pursue trade and the arts. Venice, in the historical period of Othello, was one of the richest states in Europe, its power out of all measure to its geographical size. It had gained its preeminence by roughly corresponding to a great "free port" for the Mediterranean. Traders had confidence that their contracts would be legally enforceable there; that Venetian law, in these respects, was tolerant and international in viewpoint. Shylock, the *Merchant of Venice*; suffered in certain respects, but there was no impediment to pursuing his business and having recourse to law for the enforcing of his contracts. Nor does the Venetian republic hesitate to place Othello, whom we assure to be a Negro, though some maintain he is an Arab (in any event, a man of quite different racial background from that of the Venetians), in supreme command of its armies. What is a little unusual about Othello's appointment is that he is placed in command of Venetians, with Cassio, a Venetian general, second-in-command. There is no mention anywhere in the play of contracted mercenaries. Othello tells us himself that his entire experience has been military. He has lived in camps, engaging in the arts of war, since he was a boy of seven. The only part of the great world that he knows is that which pertains to broils and battles. He has traveled extensively in distant and mysterious regions, including those of the "Cannibals" and the "Anthropophago." He had once been taken prisoner and sold into slavery, but had managed to escape. He has loved the "pride, pomp, and circumstance of glorious war!" He loves its color and glitter—the plumed troops, the neighing steed, the spirit-stirring drum.

Othello takes his part in a definite historical setting. The *Aldus Shakespeare* states: "The island of Cyprus became subject to the republic of Venice in 1471. After this time, the only attempt ever made upon the island by the Turks was under Selim the Second, in 1570. It was then invaded by a powerful force, and conquered in 1571. We learn from the play that there was a junction of the Turkish fleet at Rhodes for the invasion of Cyprus; that it first sailed towards Cyprus, then went to Rhodes, there met another squadron, and then resumed its course to Cyprus. These are historical facts, and took place when Mustapha, Selim's general, attacked Cyprus, in May, 1570; which is therefore the true period of the action."

(2) The second important fact we know about Othello is that he possesses a "public image" of great dignity (regardless of whether, as some critics maintain, he is inwardly insecure). The Venetian senate unanimously approved of him ("all in all sufficient"). Even Brabantio, who is later to have a bitter quarrel with him, invited him often to his own home. When Brabantio cannot effectively prevent Othello's marriage, he still shows respect and appreciation for Othello ("I here do give thee that with all my heart . . ."). Far from bragging and telling "fantastical lies," as Iago alleges to Roderigo, Othello tells the simple truth without being apologetic or conceited. When Brabantio begins to proceed against him, Othello is unimpressed. He knows that his own services to the "signiory" will "out-tongue his complaints." He is a man of royal ancestry as well as a man who has proved himself by his own achievements. He married Desdemona because he loved her, and refuses to be evasive in regard to Brabantio. "My parts, my title, and my perfect soul / Shall manifest me rightly." When his followers and those of Brabantio are about to get into a bloody conflict, Othello, with a word of command that is also courteous, quiets both sides: "Good signior, you shall more command with years / Than with your weapons." Before the senate, he recounts the details of his life factually, yet eloquently. His arguments are indisputable, and no one holds what he has done against him. Even the Duke who is presiding, says, "I think this tale would win my daughter, too." He is placed in charge of the war against the Turks. In no way excited or embarrassed by what has occurred, Othello,

firmly though ceremoniously, demands that the State arrange suitable accommodation for his wife and proper servants. Obviously, Othello is a person conscious of his own worth. He does not have to be aggressive, "push himself" because of any inferiority complex. He has the maturity required to recognize the legitimate rights and feelings of others. Under normal circumstances, he never degrades anyone. Though he may be a man with a "round, unvarnish'd tale," he has the qualities of a good diplomat, in the higher and more sincere sense of that word.

(3) Another obvious fact about Othello is that he is a "Moor." The full title of the play reads: *The Tragedy of Othello, The Moor of Venice.* The term "Moor" has been in dispute. Coleridge asks, can we imagine Shakespeare "so utterly ignorant as to make a barbarous Negro plead royal birth?" Schlegel, on the other hand, pursuing the "noble savage" interpretation of Othello, observes "what a fortunate mistake that the Moor, under which name a baptized Saracen of the northern coast of Africa was unquestionably meant in the novel, has been made by Shakespeare, in every respect, a Negro!" A. C. Bradley argues with reference to Coleridge, who had maintained that it would show a lack of balance on the part of Desdemona to fall in love with a Negro, that this *was just what* Brabantio was alleging! Bradley will not go so far as to say that Shakespeare imagined him as a Negro and not as a Moor, "for that might imply that he distinguished Negroes and Moors precisely as we do but what appears to me nearly certain is that he imagined Othello as a black man, and not as as light-brown one." Marvin Rosenberg observes in *The Masks of Othello*: "Probably Burbage played Othello black, rather than tawny, for this was the theater tradition that survived unbroken— as Shakespearean traditions usually did, unless an important social or theatrical development intervened— until widespread Negro slavery. Othello changed to "tawny" in the 1800s to free the role from the unfortunate connotations borne by that growing social evil, and to preserve the vision of a gallant, high-hearted man whose lineage, though strange, is in no way inferior to that of his hosts, nor is thought so by them. His apartness is a badge, not a shame." Othello's color was meant to have romantic associations. Shakespeare was still close to the medieval tradition where in most delineations of "The Adoration of the Magi" a black man is presented as one of the Kings. He is quite removed from the impact of Puritan Christianity which tended to put certain nationalities and races "outside the pale."

(4) Another obvious fact about Othello is that he is, and was meant to be, a *romantic* figure. Iago may regard him as a "wheeling and extravagant stranger of here and everywhere," but his adventurous and traveled background stirred the Venetian senate. He brings sugges-

tions of a mysterious non-European world, of the Egyptian sibyl who had given his mother the strange handkerchief: "there's magic in the web of it." Two hundred years of the Sibyl's life went into the making of it, "dyed in mummy which the skilful / Conserv'd of maiden's hearts." Othello's public image of discipline an self-control has, in contrast to his adventurous and mysterious background, a special romantic appeal of its own; it is something quite outside ordinary experience. Iago himself is shocked by Othello's anger, because it is so unexpected. "Can he be angry?" he asks. He has seen the cannon "puff" Othello's brother from his very arm, and he has remained absolutely cool. Adventure, excitement, racial uniqueness, cool head, and cool decision combine to make this romantic image.

(5) It is also clear that Othello's romantic background and his difference in race create certain disadvantages which become important in the action of the play. Shakespeare is not writing a "problem" play about the marriage of a Negro and a "white" woman. In fact, the play is so universally human that for long intervals we completely forget about the difference in race. But Iago scores a decisive point by insinuating that Othello really knows very little about Venice and Venetian women. Othello overtly refers to the fact that he is not a "chamberer" intimate with the niceties and intrigues of social life: "for I am black / And have not those soft parts of conversation / That chamberers have . . ."

We now come to examine those major points, relative to the character of Othello, about which knowledge must be "ambiguous" and "fluid."

(1) What is the nature of Othello's love for Desdemona? Robert B. Heilman in *Magic in the Webs Action and Language in Othello* sees in the play a contest between Othello's vow of love and Iago's "wits" (intellect). "Thou know'st," Iago says, "we work by wit, and not by witchcraft. . . ." Dr. Heilman comments: "*Wit and witchcraft*: in this antithesis is the symbolic structure, or the thematic form, of *Othello*. By witchcraft, of course, Iago means conjuring and spells to induce desired actions and states of being. But as a whole the play dramatically develops another meaning of *witchcraft* and forces upon us an awareness of that meaning: *witchcraft* is a metaphor for love. The 'magic in the web' of the handkerchief, as Othello calls it, extends into the fiber of the whole drama. Love is a magic bringer of harmony between those who are widely different (Othello and Desdemona), and it can be a magic transformer of personality; its ultimate power is fittingly marked by the miracles of Desdemona's voice speaking from beyond life, pronouncing forgiveness to the Othello who has murdered her. Such events lie outside the realm of 'wit'—of the reason, cunning, and wisdom on which Iago rests—and this wit must be

hostile to them." Thus is an articulately sensitive expression of a point of view common in modern criticism: that Othello falls from a great intuitive faith into a complicated rationalizing in which he becomes the easy victim of Iago's "wits."

Why should such a fall take place, unless there was some preexisting weakness in the quality of his love? Such critics as G. R. Elliott and F. R. Leavis have emphasized a strain of egoism in Othello (which may constitute his "tragic flaw," as we shall discuss later). He certainly fails to trust his own intuition in an acute moment of crisis, though it was the same intuition that had led to his unconventional and romantic marriage, "to be free and bounteous to her mind." When Iago has started to poison his mind, Othello catches a glimpse of Desdemona, and exclaims, "if she be false, O, then heaven mocks itself! / I'll not believe 't." That was the right intuition which Othello failed to maintain because, these critics argue, his love was far from being perfected. Of course, viewing the other side of the picture, we have to admit that Othello pays a disproportionate, even a monstrous, price for his lack of perfection. After all, in normal life, a man, as husband and father, grows and deepens in the knowledge of love. If absolute selflessness were a prerequisite to marriage, would anyone qualify? The play indicates pretty clearly that Othello's marriage would have been happy and successful if Othello had not fallen into the hands of so skilled a manipulator as Iago.

(2) We now come specifically to the question of the "tragic flaw" in Othello. According to the tradition of tragedy as stated by Aristotle in his *Poetics* (a tradition followed by the Renaissance), the tragic hero must not be an entirely good man, or one who is completely evil, but, rather, a man who on the whole is good but contributes to his own destruction by some moral weakness (the "fatal flaw"). The reason for this, as Aristotle sees it, lies in the emotions that tragedy is meant to excite in the audience. They are "pity" and "fear." If an entirely good man is destroyed, we do not feel pity but indignation with the universe. If an evil man comes to an evil end, we have no feelings in the matter whatever. We think that he got his "just deserts." But we pity the man who, having contributed in some way to his disaster, meets with a punishment out of all proportion to what he has done. "Fear" arises from our anxiety for the character as the play unfolds. We hope against hope that he will succeed in getting out of his difficulty. And, after the disaster is final, we fear for *ourselves*. For if an Othello, with all his great qualities and achievements, receives such a blow, what might the rest of us expect from life? One critic, Hazelton Spencer, actually cannot locate a tragic flaw in Othello. "Critics have searched for a tragic flaw in Othello, something to justify his miserable end, on the theory that to present the fall of an innocent man is, as Aristotle holds, incapable of arousing and purifying the emotions of pity and fear. Pity is uppermost in this tragedy, all the more because, humanly speaking, Othello is blameless. He is set before us, in his first appearances, as noble and calm. In his dying speech he describes himself as 'one not easily jealous,' and that is clearly the expression that Shakespeare wishes to leave. Othello is a normal man, and the play is not a study of the passion of jealousy. Why, then, does the magnanimous hero fail so wretchedly?" This critic takes the view that it is Othello's business in this play to be deceived, and leaves it more or less at that. Consequently, he finds the play more *pathetic* than tragic. Rosenberg in *The Masks of Othello* extends the concept of tragic flaw much more widely than does Aristotle. In effect, he says, to be human is to have a tragic flaw. True, Othello is one of the finest, one of the noblest of men. "But to be the best of men is still to be frail, to be subject to vanity, pride, insecurity, credulity, and the other marks of mortality. So Othello is no sugar hero of romance. He errs terribly. But the artistic design does not require from him an early "sin to bring on retribution; his tragic flaw is that he is human."

IAGO Everyone is agreed that Iago is an outstanding study in whatever the word "evil" connotes. Some would argue that it is a more effective study than that of Satan in Milton's *Paradise Lost*. Both Iago and Satan are skilled deceivers, accomplished liars, experts in applied psychology, in the manipulation of the innocent. While theologically it might be maintained that Satan creates more havoc, waste, and suffering than Iago, it is long range rather than immediate, generalized rather than specifically personal. Shakespeare's situation creates much more horror. Milton also could have created much more horror, if he had violated Scripture, and showed Adam killing Eve in jealous rage! Behind Satan's action is a clear motive, however unwarranted. To cause Adam to sin is part of a master plan of the war on heaven, the course of which the devils had debated in detail. Behind Iago's actions are only the workings of his own dark mind. Several schools of thought have developed to account for them. One finds Iago humanly explicable—at least in part. This school accepts at least several claims that Iago makes at their face value. For example, Iago had a just grievance in being passed over for promotion in favor of Cassio, that Othello had had actual relations with Iago's wife, and so on. Another school more plausibly brings the apparatus of modern psychiatry and psychoanalysis to bear on the probings of Iago's mind. Some, like A. C. Bradley, find Iago's behavior explicable enough without taking Iago at face value or bringing modern psychological studies to bear. Some follow the "motiveless malignity" tradition of

Coleridge. Others resort to identifying Iago with "Satanism" or just regarding him as a dramatic prop, an impetus to action. In the case of Iago, the list of what we know without question about him is comparatively brief. Besides these things, and the over-all conviction that he is evil as anyone can be, nearly everything else that is said about him must fall within the label of "ambiguous."

As in the case of Othello, we shall start with the facts we know. First, we must realize that it is difficult to distinguish fact from fiction in what Iago says. As A. C. Bradley puts it, "One must constantly remember not to believe a syllable that Iago utters on any subject, including himself, until one has tested his statement by comparing it with known facts and with other statements of his own or other people, and by considering whether he had in the particular circumstances any reason for telling a lie or telling the truth." We know that Iago is "his Moorship's Ancient." We can rely on his statement that he applied for the higher position of lieutenant-General, but not for his account of the qualifications of Cassio, or the reasons for the rejections of Iago's application. We can reasonably infer, from Shakespeare's sources (though not from any explicit statement in the play), that he is handsome, superficially attractive ("a man of the most handsome person . . . very dear to the Moor . . . he cloaked with proud and valorous speech . . . the villainy of his soul with such art that he was to all outward show another Hector or Achilles"), a man of about twenty-eight years of age. In the play itself, he expresses, in exchange with others, sharp and bantering wit. He has successfully and deliberately created an image of his own straightforwardness and trustworthiness. "Honest" is practically his first name. He is married to Emilia, who is the "lady-in-waiting" to Desdemona. A. C. Bradley suspects that Iago did not have an aristocratic background, and that his wife is "almost in the relation of a servant to Desdemona." The play really makes nothing clear on this point. Desdemona is sufficiently important socially to have an "aristocratic" lady-in-waiting in her train, which we can reasonably suppose is limited in number because of the military conditions under which Desdemona was permitted to go to the front in Cyprus with Othello. In any event, Iago's public image is geared to that of the "soldier" rather than to that of the "gentleman." We can take as his true views Iago's contemptuous comments on others—Roderigo is a "snipe" only to be used for "sport and profit"; the Moor is to be led by the nose like a jackass; and so on. More difficult to assess are Iago's expressions of genuine admiration ("The Moor . . . is of a constant, loving, noble nature"; Desdemona is "fram'd as fruitful / As the free elements"). We can subscribe to the theory that

Iago actually recognizes goodness, truth, beauty in an objective way, and then consciously rejects them:

> So will I turn her virtue into pitch,
> And out of her own goodness make the net
> That shall enmesh them all.

But it is also possible that Iago performs "chorus" functions. Some of his comments are detached and universal, not necessarily in his proper dramatic person as Iago. Neither, of course, of these interpretations is necessarily inconsistent with the other. We also know that Iago is a killer, that he hates Othello, but his motivations are "ambiguous." We have now come to the end of the list of what we know for certain.

We come to consider the wide area of ambiguity of more uncertainty connected with Iago.

(1) One school of critics is prepared to accept Iago's allegation that Othello has committed adultery with Iago's wife, Emilia. Actually, Iago says "I know not if't be true; / But I, for mere suspicion in that kind, / Will do as for a surety." Later in the play he voices a similar suspicion about Cassio: "For I fear Cassio with my night-cap too . . ." Yet at no point in the play does Iago express any indignation about his wife. He kills her in the last act, but for quite different reasons—she is confirming the evidence against him. Might not Shakespeare's point be that malice comes first, a shaky rationalization afterwards? Once Iago hates Othello, is he prepared to believe any hatred-bearing fantasy against him? To the acceptance of Othello's adultery is sometimes added the assumption that Cassio was preferred over Iago for the appointment to the lieutenancy because Cassio had been the "go-between" in Othello's wooing of Desdemona (there is certainly no statement to this effect in the play). As one critic puts it, "once outer motivations for Iago are accepted, he can be seen as a relatively decent man plunging for the first time into wickedness. . . ." But both the text and the test of the theater itself are against this point of view.

(2) Interpretations of Iago in the light of modern psychological analysis are more fruitful. He is "sick," "disturbed," a "vindictive neurotic." Believing in the supremacy of the will and of the intelligence, with scarcely any ability really to "relate" to people, he sees them merely as objects he must compulsively exploit. He is not neurotic in the way it might be argued that Milton's Satan is. He is not seeking for public and cosmic glory. But like Satan, he is seeking absolute mastery. The words of Clara Thompson in *An Outline of Psychoanalysis* apply well to Iago: "The neurotic loses in the process [i.e., that of seeking absolute mastery] his interest in truth, a loss that among others accounts for his difficulty in distinguishing between genuine feelings, beliefs, striving, and their artificial equivalents

(unconscious pretenses). The emphasis shifts from being to appearing." The neurotic "must develop a system of private values which determines what to like and accept in himself, what to be proud of. But this system of values must by necessity also determine what to reject, to abhor, to be ashamed of, to despise, to hate. Pride and self-hate belong inseparably together; they are two expressions of the same process." Rosenberg in *The Masks of Othello* quotes Karen Horney's *Neurosis and Human Growth* much to the same effect: "Love, compassion, considerateness—all human ties—are felt as restraints on the path to sinister glory . . . he must prove his own worth to himself." Such analysis supports, rather than opposes, William Hazlitt's remark that "Iago is an amateur of tragedy in real life" and the argument of A. C. Bradley that Iago's sense of superiority wanted satisfaction.

(3) A. C. Bradley has undertaken in *Shakespearean Tragedy* to show that Iago's character is quite explicable. While Bradley does not go in for psychological terminology, his analysis is in itself basically psychological though always in reference to actual events in the text. Bradley emphasizes Iago's enormous self-control allied to his belief that absolute egoism is the only rational and proper attitude, and that conscience or honor of any kind of regard for others is an absurdity. Bradley does not consider Iago ambitious; he is not envious in the sense that competitors outrun him. He is only highly competitive (and dangerous without scruples) when his sense of superiority is wounded. He does not care for Emilia, but, on the other hand, he becomes furious at the thought of another man "getting the better of him." Bradley argues that Iago does not love evil for evil's sake, but he does regard goodness as stupid. Goodness weakens his satisfaction with himself, "and disturbs his faith that egoism is the right and proper thing." Bradley cannot find any *passion* in Iago, neither of ambition nor of hatred. As good a summary as any of Bradley's detailed position lies in these words: "Iago stands supreme among Shakespeare's evil characters because the greatest intensity and subtlety of imagination have gone to his making, and because he illustrates in the most perfect combination the two facts concerning evil which seem to have impressed Shakespeare most. The first of these is the fact that perfectly sane people exist in whom fellow-feeling of any kind is so weak that an almost absolute egoism becomes possible to them, and with it those hard vices—such as ingratitude and cruelty—which to Shakespeare were far the worst. The second is that such evil is compatible, and even appears to ally itself easily, with exceptional powers of will and intellect."

A more recent critic, Marvin Rosenberg, who believes that Iago is perfectly understandable in terms of neurosis, elaborates an insight in quite an opposite direction to that of Bradley. He makes an important distinction between the Iago in dialogue with other people and the Iago of the soliloquies. The latter, he says, reveals a "raging torment." "Far from being passionless, this inner Iago is one of great fury of passion, the more furious because so much feeling has been smothered when he is with people."

(4) Coleridge actually leans to the "Satanism" view of Iago, for, in his opinion, Iago is "next to devil, and only not quite devil." But he is one of the first major critics to suggest that it is rather pointless to seek human reasons for Iago's behavior. Elmer Edgar Stoll thinks that we should regard Iago as a necessary "impetus" to the dramatic action, and not try to prod him rationalistically. He is the villain by dramatic necessity, and would have been so accepted by the Elizabethan playgoer. Hazelton Spencer has argued that Iago has to be accepted in terms of centuries of English stage-villainy. He belongs to the tradition of the devil of medieval history plays, of Judas, of the bad angels, of the Vice of the morality plays. These did not receive or require "any accounting for." The trouble about this point of view is that most readers of Shakespeare find Iago far too absorbing to leave him on this level. He seems to cry out for explanations!

(5) We come, lastly, to various religious or quasi-religious interpretations of Iago. Most religiously-minded people have been brought up in a Socratic interpretation of evil. If a man has the proper knowledge, he will seek the good. No man can deliberately seek evil, though he may actually pursue evil under the mistaken impression that it is the good. Though man by his nature seeks the good, he may be misled into seeking a "mistaken" good. "Evil, be thou my good" is considered a Satanic principle rather than a human possibility. Of course, the possibility has to be recognized (certainly in medieval and Renaissance literature) that sin and intellectual degeneration to some extent correlate. This is the situation present in Christopher Marlowe's Dr. Faustus and in Milton's Satan. The more they fall into evil, the less capable are they of making realistic judgments, though, ironically, they become more cocksure of themselves. A man may not start out by choosing evil for its own sake, but, by degrees and increasing involvement in sin, his judgment becomes impaired so that he fails to distinguish between good and evil. Goodness may challenge, disturb, embarrass, and be overtly rejected. Iago goes pretty far along the Satanic route when he thinks of using Desdemona's goodness as the "net that shall enmesh them all." This would seem to be a statement that could not be relegated to his "chorus" function. Of course, we get into a difficult problem of words if we maintain that a man who hates goodness is really insane. It is hard to set up a firm definition of insanity; such definitions depend upon social conven-

tion to a great degree. On the surface, Iago seems sane enough. But one aspect of mental illness permits unimpeded use of the intellect while a man's *emotional* life is in ruins. This is pretty much Iago's position.

An important school of Shakespearean critics finds religious symbolism in all Shakespeare's great works. Paul Siegel in *Shakespearean Tragedy and the Elizabethan Compromise* has interpreted *Othello* against a background of Christian theology. Iago has something of the function of Judas. Robert Heilman also sees Iago functioning as the enemy of salvation. "His most far-reaching method is to seduce others philosophically—to woo them from assumptions in which their salvation might lie (faith in the spiritual quality of others), to baser assumptions that will destroy them (their freedom to act in the light of the accepted unregeneracy of all about them). Iago the moral agent is akin to Iago the philosopher: there is a common element in stealing purses, stealing good names, and stealing ideas needed for survival."

DESDEMONA   Though Desdemona is by no means a "simple" character, she is the least involved in ambiguity of any in the play. We know, from Othello's words, that she is the "gentle" Desdemona. As the daughter of a distinguished member of the Venetian oligarchy, she had her choice of suitors among the "wealthy, curled darlings of our nation." Emilia, in that terrible scene in which Othello shouts "whore" at Desdemona, reminds us that she has "forsook so many noble matches, / Her father and her country and her friends." Brabantio describes his daughter as "a maiden never bold; / Of spirit so still and quiet, that her motion / Blushed at herself." He just cannot understand how such an apparently quiet and dutiful girl could do anything so audacious as to elope with Othello. How could she err "against all rules of nature"?

In the investigation of Brabantio's charges against Othello before the Senate, Desdemona speaks softly but with determined authority:

> . . . My noble father,
> I do perceive here a divided duty:
> To you I am bound for life and education.
> My life and education both do learn me
> How to respect you; you are the lord of duty;
> I am hitherto your daughter: but here's my husband,
> And so much duty as my mother show'd
> To you, preferring you before her father,
> So much I challenge that I may profess
> Due to the Moor my lord.

This is a lucid explanation of the duties of children to parents and of married people to one another—firm, and only offensive in the degree that real facts are offensive. Brabantio has nothing further to say on the subject: "on to state affairs." If there be some suspicion as the play develops that Desdemona lacked judgment and enterprise in her handling of Othello, she certainly exhibits perfect poise and confidence in the beginning. She acts with tact and originality in asking the Duke to assist her in making a request, while at the same she makes clear, without apology, the nature of her love for Othello. "That I did love the Moor to live with him / My downright violence and storm of fortunes / May trumpet to the world." She wants permission to go with Othello to Cyprus, otherwise "the rites for which I love him are bereft me." She is frank, unaffected, economical, and to the point. Brabantio's remarks towards the end of the scene are not strictly in keeping with his previous generosity in acceding to a state of facts about the elopement ("I here do give thee that with all my heart"):

> Look to her, Moor, if thou hast eyes to see:
> She has deceiv'd her father, and may thee.

This is a dramatic foreshadowing or premonition (illusory in fact) that in no way compromises Desdemona's absolute honesty. Iago is later to makes use of the allegation that Desdemona deceived her father.

When we next see her, she has arrived in Cyprus before Othello. Having been welcomed by Cassio and Montano, she engages in some relaxing banter with Iago. This is carried on with perfect propriety, but it shows that Desdemona is not timid and retiring, a shy violet. She greets the disembarked Othello with a mature sense of what marriage and being a wife mean. "The heavens forbid / But that our loves and comforts should increase, / Even as our days do grow!"

When we see Desdemona on stage again, she has been listening to Cassio's plea for reinstatement into Othello's good graces. Our first impression that Desdemona is a determined girl, having known her own mind in her elopement with Othello, is here confirmed again:

> I give thee warrants of thy place: assure thee,
> If I do vow a friendship, I'll perform it
> To the last article . . .

Desdemona appears briefly during the course of the temptation scene (III, iii) just long enough for the handkerchief to be dropped—the episode that becomes so important a part of the machinery of the plot. When Othello sees her again, she has no reason to suspect the chain of events that have been set in motion against her, With typical single-mindedness she pursues the subject of Cassio's reinstatement while Othello, now poisoned by Iago, is concerned with one thing only, the whereabouts of the handkerchief. She lies in saying that the handkerchief is not lost, paying little heed to its importance. She is amazed when Othello storms off in anger. In a rather typical way of wives dealing with the tantrums of husbands, she assumes that business of some kind must have upset him.

The fact has to be realized that Desdemona is trapped in a very fast movement of events. Iago's plot has worked with lightning speed in less than one "dramatic" day. Desdemona has had only brief and casual moments with her husband; she has had no reason to anticipate such an outburst as that of Othello storming into her apartment and calling her "a public commoner" (IV, ii). She already knows that something is seriously wrong, for Othello had already publicly struck her, but she continues to think of the cause as some temporary nervous derangement based upon frustration in the running of his affairs. "If haply you my father do suspect / An instrument of this your calling back, / Lay not your blame on me: if you have lost him, / Why, I have lost him too." In answer to Othello's angry charge, what else can she do but to express a firm, straightforward denial?

> If to preserve this vessel for my lord
> From any other foul unlawful touch
> Be not to be a strumpet, I am none.

A modern reader would be unhistorical if he expected a Desdemona to say something like "what in the deuce is the matter with you, Othello? You had better see your psychiatrist at once." An almost ritualistic courtesy is part of the Shakespearean world. This creates a sense of dignity, but also too much distance at times for the kind of "in-fighting" that human life requires. Desdemona always refers to Othello as her "lord": "I hope my noble lord esteems me honest." Her immediate reaction to Othello's behavior is one of numb shock.

In a following sequence, she ironically confides in Iago, asking him, "What shall I do to win my lord again?" Shakespeare emphasizes two facts about Desdemona in this exchange. With all her straightforwardness and courage, Desdemona is extremely sensitive; she cannot use the word "whore." But with that keen moral sensitivity is combined a love of that deep kind which Shakespeare has described elsewhere in one of his sonnets:

> . . . Love is not love
> Which alters when it alteration finds
> Or bends with the remover to remove
> (Sonnet CXVI)

Even if Othello shakes her off to "beggarly divorcement," even if "unkindness may do much," nothing will "taint" her love.

Desdemona orders her wedding sheets to be placed upon her bed. Shakespeare emphasizes this gesture as a symbol of peace and reconciliation, though ironically Desdemona is to lie murdered upon them. Singing the "willow" song, still unaware of any more immediate menace than the wind knocking upon the door, she thinks, in a rather detached way, of the meaning of adultery. She would not do such a wrong "for the whole world." Shakespeare contrasts Desdemona's exalted standards with those of the practical and down-to-earth Emilia: "Why, the wrong is but a wrong i' the world; and having the world for your labor, 'tis a wrong in your own world, and you might quickly make it right."

Some critics have felt that Desdemona says the "wrong things" on her deathbed. Actually, Desdemona seems very much in "character." Shakespeare skillfully indicates how entirely subjective, how entirely belonging to the world of Iago-induced fantasy, is Othello's reaction to her words. Realistically, and with complete poise, she tells Othello to send for Cassio and to ask whether she ever gave him the handkerchief. She does not know that Othello believes him to be dead. Her statement, "Alas! he is betray'd and I undone," indicates a perfectly natural and sudden realization of a plot against her. She bursts into tears—the first time this is indicated in the play. After the mounting tension, this would be in keeping with a personality as determined and as poised as hers. Shakespeare underlines Othello's complete subjectivity by causing him to refer the tears immediately to the presumed death of Cassio: "Out, strumpet! weep'st thou for him to my face?" Othello, beside himself, smothers her without allowing her time for prayer. Emilia knocks at the door; Othello finds Desdemona not quite dead; he returns to his work. In the presence of Emilia, Desdemona has breath enough to say, "a guiltless death I die."

A. C. Bradley states that the suffering of Desdemona is, "unless I mistake, the most intolerable spectacle that Shakespeare offers us. For one thing, it is *mere* suffering; and . . . that is much worse to witness than suffering that issues in action. Desdemona is helplessly passive. . . . She is helpless because her nature is infinitely sweet and her love absolute." We feel that Bradley exaggerates Desdemona's passiveness. The speed with which development takes place, and with which Desdemona is not directly connected, is an important element to consider. A. C. Bradley himself points out that Othello murdered his wife within a few days, probably a day and a half, of his arrival in Cyprus and the consummation of his marriage. Shakespeare is not technically accurate about time, and actually the audience has an impression of longer time lapses. But the point is that events are meant to move with an almost incredible swiftness. Insofar as Desdemona is passive, she had little time to orientate herself to what everything was about. But her character, as the facts indicated above show, was not normally passive. Marvin Rosenberg does not believe in pressing the image of a "heavenly" Desdemona in contrast to Iago's "diabolism." He puts what seems to be the facts rather eloquently: "It seems to me as dangerous to rob Desdemona of her human frailty as it is to steal her essential goodness from her. Fortunately for the long life of Shakespeare's play, she no more personifies divinity than deceit. . . . But we care intensely for this young, passionate woman who ran away secretly from her father's house to the arms of her lover, who has a healthy desire to be with her husband on her wedding night, who cries when she is struck, and who fears death terribly. Divinity is beyond our pity; but we weep for the mortal woman who was Desdemona."

EMILIA   A. C. Bradley, in his analysis of Emilia, has one observation of particular relevance: "She is the only person who utters for us the violent common emotions which we feel . . ." "Terror and pity are here too much to bear; we long to be allowed to utter indignation, if not rage; and Emilia lets us feel them and give them words." Emilia is an "army" wife, used to the hard and concrete facts of her husband's profession, without possessing much in the way of imagination, but having firm convictions and common sense. She cares little for social veneers, and speaks her mind without hesitation if the situation demands it. She is the "honest" wife who is the counterpart to the "honest" Iago (except, of course, that she is genuinely "honest")—rough-hewn, frank. Iago had had evidently similar suspicions about her marital loyalty as Othello had in regard to Desdemona, but she must have had the skill to handle this tough specimen of humanity. In Act IV, ii, she turns to her husband, after voicing her conviction that "some base notorious knave" had incited Othello against his wife, declaring:

> . . .Some such squire he was
> That turn'd your wit the seamy side without,
> And made you to suspect me with the Moor.

She does not become important in the play until the fourth and fifth acts. She has, however, been instrumental in finding the handkerchief and passing it on to Othello (III, iii). She neglected to reveal that she knew its whereabouts when Othello demanded it (III, iv). From her own experience in marriage she seems to have acquired a generally hostile attitude towards men:

> 'Tis not a year or two shows us a man:
> They are all but stomachs, and we all but food;
> They eat us hungerly, and when they are full,
> They belch us.

She becomes intensely indignant at Othello's treatment of Desdemona (IV, ii). In the "willow" scene (IV, iii) she does her best to comfort and console Desdemona. She also protests against the "double" sexual standard of men. Women also have "affections, / Desires for sport, and frailty." If men do not observe standards, women are not likely to, either.

Emilia is the first to arrive at the bedchamber of the murdered Desdemona, where Othello is still standing. Othello proclaims his deed, even when the dying Desdemona has exculpated him by saying that she did it herself. In fact he refers to her statement as further proof of what a liar she is! Othello refers to her husband, Iago, as the source of his knowledge. Emilia, in an utter trauma, keeps repeating "my husband!" Emilia, unlike Othello, has no doubts about her own powers of intuition:

> If he say so, may his pernicious soul
> Rot half a grain a day! he lies to the heart:
> She was too fond of her most filthy bargain.

She remorselessly lashes into Othello: "O gull! O dolt! / As ignorant as dirt!" Emilia "smells" it, and her suspicions are confirmed after Othello gives an account of the handkerchief. She incriminates her husband, who publicly kills her by stabbing her in the back. Dying, she wishes to be laid by the side of her mistress, for whom obviously her affection was much greater than for her husband. She dies in excruciating pathos, singing Desdemona's song of "Willow, willow, willow": "I will play the swan, / And die in music."

BRABANTIO   We meet Brabantio in the opening scene of the play. He and his household have been aroused by Roderigo and Iago. The latter pushes the panic button, shouting, "thieves, thieves." He describes the elopement of Brabantio's daughter in the lowest possible physical terms. We learn that Brabantio has definitely refused Roderigo for a son-in-law and does not want him to haunt his doors. Roderigo gives a fairly restrained account of what has happened. Brabantio calls for light and arouses his people. He is profoundly shocked: "O, she deceives me / Past thought!" He immediately thinks of the use of "charms," or love-philtres in which the Elizabethans believed. By these "the property of youth and maidhood / May be abus'd." He sets out to arrest Othello on charges of being a "practiser / Of arts inhibited and out of warrant." Othello cannot be arrested, because he has just been called to the Venetian senate on state business. Brabantio decides to press his charges before the senate.

Brabantio's major assumption is that the elopement errs "against all rules of nature." His case explodes, first because of the obvious sincerity and dignity of Othello, secondly because of the irrefutable evidence of Desdemona herself. The Duke advises Othello to "take up this mangled matter at the best." Brabantio, while a man of strong prejudices, is open to reason, and has a great respect for law. He generously gives his daughter to Othello, at the same time frankly saying: "Which, but thou hast already, with all my heart / I would keep from thee." Brabantio's last lines in the scene (I, iii) seem to contradict his previous general impulse:

> Look to her, Moor, if thou hast eyes to see:
> She has deceiv'd her father, and may thee.

The obvious explanation here is that Brabantio is doubling as "chorus" for the purpose of dramatic foreshadowing. It seems utterly out of place for him to doubt his own daughter's capacity for marital fidelity—*if thou hast eyes to see.*

We have two further references to Brabantio in the play. In Act IV, ii, the scene in which Othello treats Desdemona as if she was an inmate of a house of ill fame, Desdemona does not see the grave import of Othello's behavior. She feels that Othello is behaving in this way because of some worry over public business. Lodovico, the Venetian ambassador, had brought news that Othello had been recalled to Venice and that Cassio was to replace him. With this in mind, Desdemona says: "If haply you my father do suspect / An instrument of this your calling back, / Lay not your blame on me." There is no actual evidence in the play that Brabantio had anything to do with Othello's recall. The second reference is in a statement of Gratiano (V, ii). He says that he is glad that Desdemona's father is dead. The implication is that Brabantio has been spared the horrible news of Desdemona's death. Gratiano alleges that he had died from grief over Desdemona's marriage: "They match was mortal to him, and pure grief / Shore his old thread in twain . . ."

CASSIO Cassio features importantly in the plot mechanism of the play, but he is comparatively unemphatic as a personality and as a dramatic character. He is more acted upon than acting. Basically he is a Venetian gentleman of the officer class, with a dedicated, though not fanatical, interest in his own career and advancement.

At the beginning of the play, Iago alleges that he is an untried officer, a mere theorist: "mere prattle, without practice, / Is all his soldiership." In the play he does not act very competently as an important officer. In his own words, he had "very poor and unhappy brains for drinking." Knowing that, he, however, allows himself to take that extra drop too much. He becomes intoxicated while on duty in a city under martial law. Iago, who has prearranged all the circumstances that are to lead to Cassio's disgrace, refers in this

scene (II, iii) to Cassio as a soldier "fit to stand by Caesar / And give direction." He adds, of course, that his incapacity for drinking will some day lead to disaster. Othello had little choice but to dismiss Cassio on the spot from his command, for Cassio had been publicly drunk on duty.

Irony is piled on top of irony, for Cassio goes to Iago for consolation and advice. Iago tells him not to worry about his reputation—it's nothing! It is characteristic of the mediocre strain in Cassio that he is chiefly concerned with his reputation, not the danger to the city, or the embarrassment to the army. Iago argues that there are ways of regaining the general's good graces, that Cassio's punishment is more a matter of policy than of malice. He advises Cassio to plead through Desdemona: "Our general's wife is now the general…" "She is of so free, so kind, so apt, so blessed a disposition, she holds it a vice in her goodness not to do more than she is requested . . ."

Cassio, as a careerist, is punctilious about surface social forms. On the quay side in Cyprus he has exhibited the new fashionable etiquette by kissing Desdemona's hand. Iago resented this symbol of a higher social world: "With as little a web as this will I ensnare as great a fly as Cassio." Cassio has a "smooth dispose (appearance) . . . fram'd to make women false." "The knave is handsome, young . . ." We learn that Cassio was the go-between in Othello's wooing of Desdemona (III, iii), according to the special conventions of Renaissance courtship. Obviously Cassio had been selected for this service (before his appointment as second-in-command of the army) because of his special social training. Cassio is what the British would call "a nice chap." But he has no deep convictions, and his moral code is strictly limited to what men of his class did. He would not think of violating sexual morality in regard to a "lady" (Desdemona), but with regard to a woman of much inferior social status, the army courtesan, Bianca, his principles are of quite a different kind. His immediate implementation of Iago's advice ("the general's wife is now the general") is social to employ a band of musicians to play before the general's apartment on the morning after the consummation of the marriage. Othello is annoyed and pays them money to go away!

In his relationship to Desdemona it is assumed that, as soon as circumstances permit, Cassio will be reinstated in his army position. Desdemona says that Othello shall in "strangeness stand no further off / Than in politic distance." Cassio has a realistic view about his career. "Politic distance" may last far too long! Someone else may be temporarily appointed ("I being absent and my place supplied"), and such appointment might become permanent ("My general will forget my love and service"). We need not go into the details of how

Desdemona, in her determined forthrightness and innocence, argues on behalf of Cassio. She has a distinctly feminine view, a deeply human view, and cannot understand the rational rigors of army discipline. Friends are friends, and what *if* wars must makes "examples" of people?

Desdemona insists on bringing the matter of Cassio to Othello's notice at the very time that he is so agitated by the disappearance of the handkerchief (III, iv). He leaves in a fury. Cassio appears on the scene immediately afterwards. Ironically, he is still pursuing his quiet careerist aims, totally unaware of the impending cyclone of the tragedy. In effect he wants to know where he stands. If Othello's answer is definitely no, he will seek some other career ("And shut myself up in some other course, / To fortune's alms").

It is not necessary to elaborate Cassio's relationship to Bianca in detail. We have discussed elsewhere the machinery whereby Iago is able to convey the impression to Othello (IV, i) that the dialogue between Iago and Cassio about Bianca is really about Desdemona. It is dramatically ironic, of course, that Cassio's immoral relationship with Bianca becomes an unconscious instrument for the destruction of Desdemona. It is this relationship to Bianca also that provides the opportunity for the attempt on Cassio's life in Act V, Scene i.

At the end of the play, when the chain events set in motion by Iago are unravelled, Othello asks pardon of Cassio. After Othello's suicide, Cassio is left to rule in Cyprus.

RODERIGO Roderigo has to be understood in terms of the tradition of "Courtly Love"—something quite outside normal American experience. We have commented on this in Act I, Scene i. We know that Roderigo had attempted to court Desdemona before she came to know Othello. Brabantio, Desdemona's father, would have none of it. Roderigo is so infatuated with Desdemona that he sincerely believes that he can come to some underhand arrangement with her. Even within the terms of Courtly Love we are meant to consider him a good deal of a fool. He is described in the *Dramatis Personae* as a "gulled" gentleman—"gull" is the rough Elizabethan slang equivalent of our term "sucker." And Iago, indeed, never "gives this sucker an even break."

While technically a "gentleman" (a man of "aristocratic" birth—"gentle" in this sense), Roderigo exhibits the lowest form of Venetian decadence. Iago takes money shamelessly from him ("Thus do I ever make my fool my purse") on the illusory promise of making the "arrangement." We learn in Act IV, Scene ii, that Roderigo has placed valuable jewels in the hands of Iago to be transferred to Desdemona for the purposes of seduction. Iago, of course, misappropriates the property.

From the point of view of dramatic structure, Roderigo serves the purpose of completely filling in the portrait of Iago. The long conversations between them bring into sharp focus Iago's underlying values and his skill in the manipulation of others. Roderigo wants to drown himself on learning of Desdemona's marriage, but Iago assures him, in his cynical way, that the marriage cannot last. It would be a "sport" to make a "cuckold" (i.e., deceived husband) out of Othello. Let Roderigo disguise his appearance and follow the couple to Cyprus.

In Cyprus, Iago persuades Roderigo to become the agent for Iago's plot to disgrace Cassio: He's rash and very sudden in choler, and haply may strike at you: provoke him, that he may; for even out of that will I cause these of Cyprus to mutiny . . ." Roderigo does just that, with complete success.

Roderigo has quite a "disturbed" and inconsistent personality. When Iago had attempted to persuade him of a possible, even a probable, adultery between Cassio and Desdemona, Roderigo could not believe it: "I cannot believe that in her; she's full of most blessed condition." Yet, in spite of his high regard for Desdemona, he is aiming at a similar arrangement himself! We learn in Act V, ii, that the jewels he has entrusted to Iago to give to Desdemona "would half have corrupted a votarist." Roderigo is about to show some signs of manhood; he is no longer going to tolerate what he has "foolishly suffered" at the hands of Iago. But Iago winds him around his finger. Othello may leave for Mauretania, taking Desdemona with him. The only way to delay his departure is by the killing of Cassio. Roderigo is not immediately pliable to the proposition ("I will hear further reason for this"), but we have no doubt that Iago will "manipulate" him. Roderigo attempts to kill Cassio from ambush but bungles the assignment, and is himself wounded. He is then killed by Iago under the pretense of having stumbled on Cassio's "robbers." Iago wants to be sure that there will be no claim on the jewels that he has himself stolen, and he welcomes the removal of a potential witness. Roderigo had undertaken the projected murder in a completely detached way: "'Tis but a man gone." Robert Heilman comments on this line: "It does away with every value of imperative or speculation that 'man' or the death of man traditionally evokes, and it makes 'a man' simply a neutral instance of a category, a statistical item, an object that can be acted on without moral responsibility." If Cassio's mediocrity is concealed under a smooth social veneer, Roderigo is a "gentleman" decadent to the point of being a would-be adulterer, an ineffective practitioner of murder, and a complete fool. Even Iago has some admirable qualities compared to those of Roderigo's. The dramatic reason that we do not react to him with more contempt is that his role in the play is a very minor one, basically serving as a means of bringing Iago into focus.

BIANCA While Bianca is a woman of loose morality, she seems, on her part, to be genuinely in love with Cassio. While she is listed as a "courtesan," her behavior is more like that of a "mistress." In Act III, iv, she has felt Cassio's absence deeply. His relationship to her is much more casual. He is somewhat embarrassed by it; he does not want Othello to see him in her company. Iago always gives the lowest possible estimate of people, and we have to make allowance for his perverse exaggeration. He describes Bianca (IV,1) as "a housewife that by selling her desires / Buys herself bread and clothes . . ." He claims that when Cassio hears of her, he cannot restrain from "excess of laughter." Actually when Iago suggests that Cassio might marry her, Cassio does burst into laughter (the concealed Othello is led to believe that the reference is to Desdemona). Her "unconscious" role in the matter of the handkerchief has been previously dealt with. Cassio is attacked coming from an assignation at her lodgings. Iago, assuming that Cassio is dead, tries to implicate her in the presumed murder (V, i).

OFFICIAL FIGURES: DUKE OF VENICE, MONTANO, LODOVICO, GRATIANO All these characters are in the background of the action. The Duke is a dignified and impartial judge, advising Brabantio to make the best of an established state of facts. Montano is the young governor of Cyprus, distinguished, as Othello says (II, iii), by "gravity" and "stillness"; his name is great "in mouths of wisest censure." He is wounded in the drunken brawl that disgraces Cassio. Lodovico is a kinsman of Brabantio, and Gratiano is Brabantio's brother. Lodovico acts as the Venetian ambassador in the recall of Othello to Venice (though later Iago says that Othello is going to Mauretania). He witnesses Othello's public striking of his wife. Along with Montano and Gratiano, he is present on stage in the last moments of Othello's life. He produces the letters proving the intrigues of Iago and Roderigo. Gratiano tells us that Brabantio died through grief over Desdemona's marriage.

Romeo and Juliet

Scene-by-Scene Summary and Comment

Prologue

The play opens with a sonnet spoken by a chorus. (Actually, the prologue was probably spoken by a single actor, the same actor who will speak the sonnet at the beginning of Act II.) These fourteen lines outline the action of the play and its effect on the lives of the characters. In Verona, a pleasant Italian town, two equally important families who have long harbored grudges against each other break out into open feud. Romeo, son of the Montague family, and Juliet, daughter of the Capulet family, fall fatally in love, and it is only through their love and their death together that the long strife between the two families can also die. This "death-mark'd" love is the subject of the play.

COMMENT: The device of an introductory chorus was used by Shakespeare in more than one play. It was an excellent way to set the scene and to capture the attention of the audience. The fact that in this case the prologue is a sonnet illustrates the formal, graceful rhetoric characteristic of Shakespeare at this time and of this play in particular. The chorus makes clear what will happen in the play, but not how it will happen. To find that out, you are asked to have the patience to listen to the actors present their play. That it will end in tragedy is sure, because of such words as "star-cross'd" and "death-mark'd". This is one of the relatively few premonitions in the play.

Act I: Scene i

Sampson and Gregory, two of Capulet's servants, armed because of the long-standing feud, are joking with each other as they walk in Verona. Sampson declares that he will "not carry coals," that being the work of laborers. He means that he will not submit to being humiliated by the servants of Montague. Gregory retorts that if they did carry coals, they would be colliers, and colliers had the reputation of being dirty and of cheating. Sampson returns the pun so as to clarify his meaning: if "we be in choler [anger], we'll draw

[swords]." Gregory continues to banter, deliberately misunderstanding Sampson, and implying that Sampson is a coward who is slow to draw his sword and quick to run when faced with danger. Sampson enjoys being teased and finally gets the upper hand by announcing that he will either cut off the heads of the maidens of Montague, "or their maidenheads, take it in what sense thou wilt." Gregory quibbles and the two exchange a few more bawdy jokes, until they find themselves actually drawing swords because Abraham and Balthasar, servants of the Montague family, appear.

COMMENT: Here are two typical clowns, whose ribald wit and humor is intended to catch your interest and make you laugh. Shakespeare often enjoyed puns, or plays on words, such as those Sampson and Gregory make, and these are typical of him at this time.

There are two other points that warrant attention here. First, the feeling of emergency is felt immediately. The servants are armed, and their conversation, for all its joking, is concerned directly with the feud and with the need for courage on their part. Perhaps they are whistling in the dark or making jokes because they really do feel something ominous. Sampson's threats sound like empty boasting. Secondly, the sexual content of the jokes and boasts establishes one of the themes, later to be taken up by Mercutio and by Juliet's Nurse, and by the whole play. The important aspect here is that love is treated as simply lowlife sex, although with real warmth and gusto.

Facing the Montague family servants with drawn swords, Sampson and Gregory continue to joke with each other, but more furtively. Sampson again makes a phallic reference by saying "My naked weapon is out," and Gregory still implies that Sampson will run away with fright. Yet it is Sampson who takes up the challenge and shows his bravado first by provoking a fight. At this moment Gregory, who has been urging the fight, sees Tybalt, a Capulet, coming, and tells Sampson to assert that his master is better. What Gregory has not seen is Benvolio, a Montague, coming from the opposite direction. The four servants draw swords and begin to fight.

COMMENT: The tension mounts during this short scene, and it becomes clear that the feud is real, that both sides are looking for a fight, and that all assume a bravado that will lead inevitably to a renewed feud.

Coming quickly upon the fighting men, Benvolio tries to stop them, saying, "Put up your swords; you know not what you do." But Tybalt, seeing Benvolio with his sword unsheathed, derides him for fighting among cowardly menials. Although Benvolio wants only to stop the fight and "keep the peace," Tybalt is furious, and declares that he hates peace as much as he hates hell and the Montagues. Benvolio and Tybalt fall to fighting and are joined by more Capulets and Montagues. The sound of clashing swords is joined by the clubs of Officers of the Peace, who call out for the downfall of both the feuding houses that disturb Verona's peace.

COMMENT: The difference between the characters of Tybalt and Benvolio is very clear. To Benvolio, fighting is caused by ignorance, and those who fight do not know what they are doing and are not aware of the consequences. He wants only to have peace between the two families and is dismayed at this senseless renewal of the feud. Tybalt is far more impetuous. He uses the word "hate" twice, and "death" once. He wants to kill, and to him this cold war between the families can only end in drawn swords. Ironically, through the joking of the servants the feud has begun again.

Lord Capulet and Lord Montague now come on the scene. Both are anxious to join the fight but are restrained by their wives. It is only when Escalus, Prince of Verona, arrives with his followers that fighting ceases. Prince Escalus scolds both families bitterly, calling them "enemies to peace" and therefore "beasts" instead of men, who have three times broken the peace of their town and its people, making even old men take sides. He declares that the penalty for another fight shall be death.

COMMENT: The uppermost feeling in the minds of the townspeople, the audience, and even the wives of Capulet and Montague, is that peace, not war, is desirable. Throughout the play peace is desired by the two major characters, but peace is only finally won through death. Prince Escalus speaks not only for the town but for the whole play when he suggests that if nothing else stops the feud, it will be ended by making death the punishment for it.

Only Lord and Lady Montague and Benvolio remain as the others depart. Benvolio explains how the feud began again. But Lady Montague is more concerned about her son, Romeo, whom she has not seen that day. Benvolio did see him, walking at dawn without company and clearly preferring to be left alone. Montague comments that Romeo has been in such a mood for quite awhile, weeping and mooning, staying out all night but going in as soon as the sun rises, locking himself in his room with the curtains drawn as if to make "himself an artificial night." Montague tells Benvolio that he does not know the cause, but "would as willingly give cure as know." At this point they see Romeo coming, and Benvolio tells the Lord and Lady to "step aside" while he attempts to find out what is bothering Romeo.

COMMENT: This description of Romeo is a stereotype of the romantic lover of Shakespeare's time. He keeps to the darkness and the night; he writes poetry; and he revels in sorrow, tears, secrecy, and being alone. The audience would probably recognize Romeo's "affections" or attitudes instantly.

Yes, Romeo is in love, but the lady does not "favour" him, so he mourns, and the hours seem long. Romeo would like to change the subject away from Benvolio's questions, but when Benvolio presses him, he pours out his heart in a series of paradoxes: "O brawling love! O loving hate! . . . O heavy lightness! O serious vanity!/ Misshapen chaos of well-seeming forms!/ Feather of lead, bright smoke, cold fire, sick health!" Romeo is miserable, forlorn, and hang-dog because he is in love; and he tells Benvolio that he accepts this change in himself as part of love: "This is not Romeo, he's some other where." He loves a woman who does not love him, and who insists on remaining chaste. Romeo refuses to say who she is. Benvolio suggests that Romeo try to forget her and begin looking at other pretty girls, but the young lover insists that he cannot, that such a thing is impossible. They leave, and Benvolio goes to report to Lord Montague.

COMMENT: Romeo's description of his feeling is important. It confirms the idea of an Elizabethan stereotype. Romeo uses all the conceits or artificial conceptions about the feeling of love that were current in Elizabethan England. He has replaced life with literature, and he has assumed the artificial poses of love in a book. His speech is in rhymed couplets, or pairs of lines, which are not commonly found in Shakespeare's blank verse. The use of such couplets indicates that Shakespeare intends Romeo's language to be considered flowery and ornamental and that we can take Romeo's protestations a little less than seriously. Romeo describes love with all the conventionally contradictory words, such as "bright smoke, cold fire," which were used in love sonnets at that time. His beloved is beautiful, but remote and cruel, refusing to show her feelings or give up her chastity.

This is significant because, although we do not know it yet, Romeo has not met Juliet, and thinks he loves Rosaline, who is also a Capulet. His artificial feelings will later be contrasted with real ones. The true emotions may be expressed by contradictories, but they will be genuinely felt, and will be involved with the meaning and imagery of the play. They will not be these distant, literary ones. Romeo says he is not himself, and indeed he only becomes his true self when he finds Juliet.

SUMMARY: The action of the play has begun, and three main themes can be seen:

1. The feud between the Capulets and the Montagues has started again because of servants spoiling for a fight. The fact that such seemingly insignificant people could start the feud again gives us a feeling that the feud is fated to take place and can only lead to disaster and death before it runs its course. Even Benvolio's efforts are lost because of the rashness of Tybalt. The impetuosity and speed of the action strengthen our feeling that fate will become important in our understanding of the play.

2. There is an omen of death heavy in the air. Tybalt has spoken of hate, and Prince Escalus has made death the penalty for fighting. We begin to think that, despite everything, the feud can only end through death.

3. At the same time, there has been much talk of love. The servants speak of bawdy sexual love. Romeo has illustrated an elevated, artificial, literary love. Clearly, love in all its aspects will be a major theme.

We have met Lords Capulet and Montague, heads of the two feuding households. Also introduced was Prince Escalus, governor of Verona. These are the three leaders, but not the main characters. Formality is a keynote here and can be seen again later in the occupation with such social customs as invitations to a party and formal proposals of marriage. There is formality of structure apparent in the language and in the very idea of a feud, which divides the play and characters into two parties. We have sampled various important styles of language, such as the coarse humor of servants (who do not speak in blank verse) and the flowery rhetoric of Romeo. All this will be developed further.

Act I: Scene ii

Having met the Montagues, we now meet Lord Capulet, walking through Verona's streets with Paris, a relative of Prince Escalus. They are returning from visiting the Prince, and as they walk they discuss the recently imposed penalty for further feuding. Capulet feels that men of their age should be able to keep peace. Paris agrees, but soon turns the conversation to a matter closer to his heart: his wish to marry Capulet's fourteen-year-old daughter, Juliet. They have discussed the suit of marriage before, and Capulet maintains that she is yet too young. He urges Paris to wait two years, when she will be "ripe to be a bride." Capulet hesitates. His words reveal that he loves his daughter deeply, and has placed all his remaining hope on earth in her. Still, he favors the marriage, and if Paris can win Juliet's consent, Capulet will not oppose it. He invites Paris to a party to be held at his house that evening. At the party will be many pretty young girls, "Earth-treading stars that make dark heaven light," and Lord Capulet would have Paris see them all in comparison with Juliet before he makes up his mind.

COMMENT: This is the first we hear of Juliet, and it is not surprising that we hear of her in the context of love and peace. Capulet and Paris, an old man and a young one, both come from the freshly renewed feud. But they hope that age with its wisdom will further the cause of peace. Paris is in love with Juliet. That Capulet also loves her is clear, for he dotes on her, and will even let her have the final word about whether to marry. (Traditionally, marriages between members of aristocratic families were arranged by the parents.) Just as Capulet, in his old age, hopes for peace, he puts his hope for life in his daughter. He is shown to be a dignified old man and an indulgent father.

Besides the theme of love and peace, we have here clearly described the contrast between youth and age. That contrast is illustrated by the conversation between the old father and the young lover and later becomes thematic.

Capulet has given to one of his servants a list of people whom the servant is to see are invited to Capulet's party. The servant cannot read the list, however, and after puzzling over it a bit, he stops two strangers in the street and asks them to read it to him. The strangers are none other than Romeo and Benvolio, still discussing Romeo's love-sick state and what to do about it. Benvolio again tells his friend, in a series of images, that a new love affair alone will cure old lovesickness. Again Romeo tries to turn the conversation and, in the next breath, bewails his state. The servant then interrupts and Romeo, after jesting with him, reads the list of guests to be invited, as the servant reveals, to Capulet's party that evening. The servant adds, before departing, that if they are not Montagues, they will surely be welcome. One of the guests whose name Romeo read out was the fair Rosaline.

COMMENT: This adds a new twist to the plot. It is not strange that the servant cannot read, as few of that class were literate. It would be natural for him to stop two aristocratic men on the street, ask them to read the list, and then hospitably extend the invitation to them. But it is chance, and seems like fate, that these two men are both Montagues, and one is Romeo. Again, as in the renewal of the feud, the intervention of what appears to be accident has forced the action in the direction designated by the prologue. Along with the importance of being literary, and of such formalities of life as invitations and hospitality, we are struck by a larger, more fateful force on the action.

Romeo and Benvolio promptly decide to "crash" the party. It suits the purposes of both. Kindly Benvolio sees it as a chance for Romeo to compare Rosaline with other young ladies. He hopes she will not withstand the comparison, and that this romance will be cured by a new one. Of course, Romeo protests fervently, again claiming that this could never be. His language is loaded with contraries and comparisons of his love to religion. But he would be happy to go, just to see her. They depart.

COMMENT: Romeo is still in love with love, speaking of it as a religion, a comparison derived from courtly love traditions (see Introduction). Benvolio is still gentle, considerate, and sincerely intent on helping Romeo with good advice. The characters have not changed, but chance, or fate, and the impulsiveness of youth, are taking them to a party at the house of their enemy, on the very evening of the renewed feud.

SUMMARY: This scene has done much to further the exposition of the play; that is, it has furthered the action by introducing another set of possibilities. Paris is officially courting Juliet, and is to make his decision tonight at Capulet's party. Romeo is to go to his enemy's traditional celebration, to see Rosaline or to begin to forget her. Although neither the audience nor the characters know it, the party will be of vital importance, for there Romeo will meet Juliet. The exposition also serves to introduce more characters: in this case, not only Lord Capulet and Paris, but by reference, Juliet herself. We have seen more of Romeo's posturing, of Benvolio's steadfastness, and of the formalism and the power of fate which characterize the play.

Act I: Scene iii

The scene changes now from Verona's streets to the house of the Capulets, where Lady Capulet is telling the old Nurse to call Juliet. The Nurse swears by the purity she had when she was a twelve-year-old that she has called Juliet, and calls again. Juliet comes, obediently. Lady Capulet has something to tell her daughter, and at first tells the Nurse to go, then lets her stay as she has known Juliet since birth. The mere reference to how long she has known Juliet starts the Nurse onto a string of repetitive memories that both mother and daughter are hard put to bring to a halt. The Nurse knows Juliet's age to the day (two weeks younger than fourteen years), because her own daughter, Susan, was born on the same day and died soon after. Because of these circumstances she had become Juliet's wet nurse, which she remained for three years, until the earthquake. Rambling through her memories, the Nurse remembers the very day when Juliet was weaned from her milk. (This was accomplished, as was the custom in Elizabethan times, by rubbing wormwood, a bitter herb, on the breast. From this the child recoiled.) Even the day before the weaning, the Nurse remembers Juliet had been able to walk by herself, had fallen, and bumped her head. The Nurse's husband had picked up the crying child and jokingly said, "Dost thou fall upon thy face?/ Thou wilt fall backward when thou has more wit." At this colorful reference to her own yet far-distant puberty, the baby had stopped crying as though she had understood and agreed. The Nurse, delighted at the old joke, especially as Juliet is now of age, repeats it twice with vigor and laughter. She relishes all the details and the appropriateness of the sexual reference. She is enjoying herself so much, that not until Juliet has reminded her does she begin to run down, and only adds that she wants to see Juliet married once.

COMMENT: While we have met Juliet, we as yet know no more of her than that she is a docile young girl. Our chief interest in this passage is commanded by the Nurse. She is a wonderfully talkative old woman, whose language is abundant, colorful, and fully realized. Only she could speak these lines, and we become concretely aware of her character as much from her manner of speaking as from what she says. She is funny, gross, and delights in both humor and sex. The content of her speech here stands in direct contrast with the demure attitude of Juliet to follow, and her interest in seeing Juliet married is so that Juliet, too, may enjoy sex as the Nurse has.

Marriage is indeed the subject that Lady Capulet has called Juliet to discuss, and she promptly asks her daughter how she feels about marrying. Juliet replies, "It is an honour that I dream not of." The nurse, from her own point of view, praises Juliet for that answer, saying marriage is definitely an honor. Lady Capulet takes Juliet's reply as it was meant, with the emphasis on the word "dream," and encourages her to think about marriage, as Paris wishes to marry her. Both the Lady and the Nurse consider Paris a flower of manhood, and Lady Capulet launches into a long rhymed speech, comparing Paris to a book that is beautiful to see and to read, and which only lacks a binding: that is, a wife. She wants Juliet to see him at their party this very evening, and she urges Juliet to consider marrying him. Juliet answers, "I'll look to like, if looking liking move." A servant comes to announce that the party is about to begin without them, and the scene ends.

COMMENT: Lady Capulet, as a distinct contrast to the Nurse whose whole view of love is natural, presents Paris as a possible husband in a wholly artificial way. She uses elaborate and ingenious conceits expanding on the metaphor, "Read o'er the volume of young Paris' face." Our picture of her is of a literate lady of society who stresses manners and expresses herself in a correspondingly formal and artificial way. It almost seems as if she takes marriage lightly, although she clearly wants this one to take place. Juliet speaks only in response, and her responses indicate a shy, sweet, innocent girl, young and docile, yet more humbled at the thought of love than she is to her mother's will. (See the above quotations.)

SUMMARY: The theme of this entire scene is love and marriage, and three distinct viewpoints have been presented:

1. The humility and wonder of Juliet, an untried young girl, is the simplest.

2. Lady Capulet approaches marriage as a worldly transaction, "So shall you share all that he doth possess,/ By having him making yourself no less." This is not cold of her; it was often the attitude among parents who arranged marriages for their children. A sense of the need of a moral core in a husband shows in her words, "'Tis much pride/ For fair without the fair within to hide." Still, her sense of love itself seems to be somewhat superficial, a matter for pretty speeches.

3. As opposed to the more artificial view of Juliet's mother, her Nurse's view is natural. Love can be almost equated with lust, and both are matters for pleasure and fun. To Lady Capulet's remark that Juliet will be no less for marrying Paris, she retorts, "No less! nay, bigger; women grow by men." Marriage means sex, and sex means pregnancy, when women grow bigger. For the Nurse it is all as simple, natural, and enjoyable as that.

The introduction of Juliet has been made, and if she is only a slip of a girl as yet, our idea of her is rounded out

and humanized by the Nurse's speeches which—run full circle from birth through weaning, puberty, and marriage, to pregnancy. The contrasted Nurse and mother were probably the formative influences on Juliet.

Act I: Scene iv

Romeo and Benvolio, along with a retinue of masked entertainers and torchbearers, are on their way through Verona's streets to Lord Capulet's party. With them is Mercutio, who is objective, as he is not a member of either of the feuding families, but is a relative of the Prince. He is also Romeo's close friend and confidant. It was traditional that masked gatecrashers should deliver a humorous "apology" for their intrusion, but to Romeo's question about what their apology shall be, Benvolio replies that there should be none. "Let them measure us by what they will,/ We'll measure them a measure [dance out a formal dance pattern], and be gone." Benvolio prefers to overlook such usual frivolities, perhaps because they are going among enemies. Romeo, still keeping his love-sick attitude, declares that he does not even want to dance, and would rather carry a torch, as torchbearers do not dance. Mercutio chides him and Romeo replies with wit, though still on the same theme, that the "soles" of others' shoes are light for dancing, but his "soul" is too heavy. Mercutio again prods him, and, extending his wit with words still further, Romeo continues to protest that he is so "bound" by love that he cannot "bound," that is, jump and dance about, or rise above the boundaries of ordinary conduct. When Mercutio "cracks" that at this rate, Romeo will be such a burden on love that it will be crushed, Romeo retorts that love is not tender, but rough, and "it pricks like a thorn." Mercutio crowns the wordplay with his words to the effect that if Romeo would treat love as it treats him, he'd have the better of it.

COMMENT: Despite Romeo's posturing as a sad lover, we see him here in a playful exchange of sophisticated witticisms with his friend, Mercutio. This is their accustomed manner together: light-hearted, worldly men-about-town who delight in testing their skill with words against each other. Although Romeo still claims that he is suffering, he enjoys the jesting, and the other side of his nature shows through. Mercutio is totally at home in this gay bachelor atmosphere, and while he is concerned for his friend's being down at the mouth, he is skeptical about what strikes him as sentimental, and wishes Romeo would come out of it.

Mercutio, for one, is exhilarated at the prospect of the party, and although he has been invited—as we know from hearing his name read off the servant's list (see scene 2 of this act)—he calls for a mask, then decides his face is ugly enough to serve as a mask, and puts the real one aside. Romeo still wants a torch so that he won't have to dance, and can give over the game and be a spectator. "Dun's the mouse" ("Keep still|") replies Mercutio, and again takes up the game by teasing Romeo for being a stick-in-the-mud. But the raillery slows, for Romeo has had a foreboding dream.

COMMENT: That Mercutio truly cares for Romeo is made still clearer here by his efforts to rouse his friend and draw him fully into the festival feeling. He jokes, not without some deliberate meaning, about his own ugly face. He urges Romeo to take the "good meaning," that is, the encouragement from his words, and he does not really, as we shall see in the next speech, brush off Romeo's mention of a bad dream.

At Romeo's mention of a dream, Mercutio launches into an extended (forty-two lines) speech of great fantasy and virtuosity, beginning with, "O, then I see Queen Mab hath been with you." It is a real flight of the imagination, and is well known as the "Queen Mab speech." He calls Queen Mab "the fairies' midwife," and describes her as being as small as a figure carved in the stone of a ring. She comes in a cart made of an empty hazel nut, fitted with parts made of grasshopper wings, spider webs, and moonbeams, and drawn by tiny creatures across the bridges of sleeping men's noses. When she rides through the brains of a lover, he dreams of love. She visits all sorts of people, and whomsoever she visits dreams that night of his greatest desires, or of the chief occupation of his life. Nor are they all good dreams. She is mischievous, Queen Mab, and sometimes she puts knots in horses' manes, a bad omen. She does much, and all that she does is fabulous. Mercutio is cut short by Romeo, who says "Thou talk'st of nothing." Mercutio assents, "True, I talk of dreams,/ Which are the children of an idle brain,/ Begot of nothing but vain fantasy,/ Which is as thin a substance as the air,/ And more inconstant than the wind." Benvolio reminds them that they are making themselves late to the party, and before they leave, Romeo adds that for him, they will not be too late, but too early, for he is still filled with premonitions of something about to happen that can only end in his death.

COMMENT: Mercutio's wonderful speech, while it is perhaps irrelevant to the play in subject matter, is very important.

1. It is a totally high-spirited, absurd product of imagination. A rare, fragile fantasy, full of delicacy and speed, beautiful sounds and images. Just this lightness and extravagance would be enough to win Mercutio to our hearts. The strength of our feeling for him will later play an important part when the tragic action of the play begins with his death.

2. On another level, the Queen Mab speech is not so light. It modulates from a sheer conjuring trick into far more real images of soldiers starting awake as if fresh from battle and of women taught to bear the weight of men and children. Mercutio wholly delivers himself to the speech, and the changing tone illustrates both his desire to free his friend Romeo's mind of the omens of a bad dream, and his deep perception of, and sympathy with, the effect of such a dream. It reveals Mercutio as a man who knows much of men, their waking and sleeping troubles, and who is a true friend to Romeo. The depth of this friendship is also focal in the tragedy to follow.

3. Still keeping his light tone, Mercutio brushes off his Queen Mab speech in the last quotation above. But there is some bitterness at himself here. He says he speaks of dreams, and by that he means that Queen Mab herself is but a dream, emerged from his own "idle brain." He says that what we know to be the product of his genius is born out of nothing, is "vain fantasy" and "inconstant." He is not only skeptical, but disillusioned at what he feels is hollowness within himself. This self-deprecation and examination, this bitterness in such a seemingly lighthearted good fellow, allows us to understand his cynicism, and cements our feeling about him utterly.

The Queen Mab speech has been used to speed up the mood, but Romeo's foreboding continues too strongly, and he says, before he leaves, "My mind misgives/ Some consequence, yet hanging in the stars,/ Shall bitterly begin his fearful date/ With this night's revels, and expire the term/ Of a despised life closed in my breast/ By some vile forfeit of untimely death." This is a crucial speech. It is not spoken in the conceits we have come to associate with Romeo's attitude of love. Indeed, it is a real premonition, for at this festival he meets Juliet, and their love leads directly to their deaths. It is "hanging in the stars," as foretold in the prologue's reference to "star-crossed lovers." (See the discussion of the influence of stars in the Introduction.) Stars are also significant later in the love imagery which Romeo and Juliet will share. The very quality of Romeo and Juliet's love contains its own destruction, and in that sense is fated to end in untimely death.

SUMMARY: Established in this scene were the following:

1. Romeo is a brilliantly amusing young man, when he is not musing over his love. His friends enjoy him for his vivacity and worldly wit.

2. Mercutio, a still more brilliant wit, and a more skeptical one than Romeo, is a deep friend of his, one of true feeling as well as wonderful fancy.

3. Romeo's introspection has led to a very real feeling of some evil occurrence to come, and we share it with him.

4. The theme of sleep, which becomes an important one to the lovers, is introduced as the cause for Romeo's feeling of ill-omen and fate, and as the subject for Mercutio's wild fantasy. Sleep has many aspects, and Shakespeare recognized it as a source for many of man's feelings and desire. Later, sleep becomes the object of desire, as the only time when parted lovers can find happiness.

Act I: Scene v

After two scenes of preparation, we have come to the party at Lord Capulet's. We must remember that Romeo is here to see Rosaline, and Juliet to consider Paris as a future husband. The scene opens with bustling servants, cheerily fetching and carrying, calling to each other and cursing each other good-naturedly as they complete preparations for the party. As the servants go off, Lord Capulet with Juliet and his household comes to meet the entering guests and the maskers, Romeo among them. Capulet is in a jovial mood as host, a role he clearly enjoys. He threatens to accuse any lady who does not dance of having corns, and he remembers with the men the last time when he came masked to parties and courted ladies. He calls for music, which is struck up, and merrily calls orders to the servants. Again, he comments on the unexpected fun of maskers, and wonders with a cousin at the years passed since they played at such a role. This talk of maskers brings our attention to Romeo, who, amidst the gaiety, has called a servant apart from the crowd, and now asks, in a hushed voice "What lady is that." The lady is Juliet, whom he sees across the hall, and although the servant cannot answer his question and the room between them is alive with activity, it is as though no one else were in the room besides the two of them. He stands apart, and rapturously praises her: O, she doth teach the torches to burn bright . . . . Beauty too rich for use, for earth too dear." His speech is simple, but full of graceful images, and in one word, he foreswears any love he has ever felt before.

COMMENT: This scene, when correctly staged, makes the audience feel that already Romeo and Juliet are alone in a crowd, and this will be essentially true throughout the rest of the play. Romeo's rhymed speech has now dropped all conceits and is true to feeling. His images of her, as a jewel in the ear of an Enthiopian (a Negro) and as a dove among crows, are strong. They place her in the context of whiteness, purity, and light amidst darkness. These images will remain central to our understanding of their love. Instantly, he forgets all courtly-love and feels the real thing.

Tybalt overhears Romeo speaking, becomes immediately furious at hearing a Montague's voice, calls for his sword, and inventing the excuse that Romeo has come to scorn the traditional Capulet feast, prepares to fight. He is restrained by Capulet himself, who was chastized by the Prince just this morning for feuding, and who now prefers peace. Besides, Capulet is the host, and he does not want his hospitality marred. Forcefully stating, "It is my will," and "He shall be endured," Capulet flies into a small temper himself, and even calls Tybalt "a saucy boy," only to be distracted away by his duties to his guests. Tybalt, fuming at having to be patient, and promising that Romeo's intrusion will end bitterly, retreats.

COMMENT: Tybalt has shown his colors again as a rash, ill-tempered, antagonistic man. He relents only when Capulet becomes angered, orders and threatens him, saying, "I'll make you quiet." Tybalt has not given up, and he promises to harbor a grudge that will play no small part in the action. Capulet, host at his own party, is feeling beneficent and generous. His response to the presence of a Montague is indulgent, and he voices praises he has heard on Romeo's behalf. He is in such a genial mood that only a disruption of his party can put him out of temper, and that not for long. But the flare-up of both men indicates how close emotions are to the surface, even at a pleasant party.

In the commotion, Romeo has stolen across the room to where Juliet stands, and the two are alone together at one side of the hubbub. There is a precious silence around and between them. Romeo removes his mask, steps toward her, and their first words to each other form a sonnet. In his previous speech about her, Romeo hoped to touch Juliet's hand, and so bless his own hand. Now his first words are, "If I profane with my unworthiest hand/ This holy shrine." His lips, "two blushing pilgrims," he offers, as a gentler sin than the touch of his rough hand, but Juliet replies, "Good pilgrim, you do wrong your hand too much," and with natural sweetness tells Romeo that saints and pilgrims kiss by clasping hands. (It is stage tradition that Romeo's masking costume is that of a pilgrim.) If hands kiss, then Romeo's lips will pray, and he prays for a kiss to purge his sin. They kiss, and the feeling between them is so strong that Juliet's only defense against her own heart is to remark, lightly and playfully, "You kiss by the book." The Nurse interrupts them to tell Juliet she is wanted by her mother.

COMMENT: Shakespeare often intensifies emotional effect by changes of pace and contrasts of setting. Here he has done both admirably. Action has been fast since the Queen Mab speech, and now the two lovers meet in the middle of hilarious gaiety and activity. Also, anger and the presence of the feud have made themselves felt just preceeding this first expression of love. To further set apart the two lovers, they speak a sonnet. Their meeting is a meeting of two very young people, shy, sweet, and serious. The images of their first exchange of words are those of religion: Romeo calls Juliet a "holy shrine"; they speak of devotion, pilgrims, saints, prayer and sin. It is no ordinary case of love at first sight, but a holy sacrament, hushed and sacred.

Juliet having gone to her mother, Romeo takes the opportunity to ask the Nurse who her mother is. The reply—that she is Lady Capulet—so astounds Romeo that he cannot answer before the Nurse adds her humorously pedestrian comment that whoever marries Juliet will be a rich man. Romeo responds "My life is my foe's debt." It is a stark reply. Already Romeo feels he would die without Juliet, and so he is in debt for his life to a family enemy. Benvolio, probably noticing his friend's agitation, urges that they leave, but, as he is herding Romeo out they are stopped by the hospitable Capulet, offering them food. This they refuse. As they depart, the party ends, and Capulet, satisfied, heads for bed.

COMMENT: Romeo has had to face the hardest blow that could possibly be dealt him, and he has met it squarely, accepting in one bare sentence all the difficulties it places on him. His sudden love is so real that, in moments, he has matured enough to say what would never have been expected of him before. He speaks in a paradox, but this one is charged with bitter meaning and acceptance of a burden beyond his previous experience.

Juliet, returning as the guests depart, is more subtle about finding out who Romeo is. She asks her Nurse the names of several departing guests before she asks Romeo's. As her Nurse goes to find out who he is, she comments to herself, "If he be Married,/ My grave is like to be my wedding bed." She, too, feels that

separation from this new-found lover would be her death. Her Nurse returns with far worse news, that he is a Montague, to which Juliet responds, as bravely and as stricken as Romeo, "My only love sprung from my only hate!" When her Nurse asks her what she is telling herself, she covers it up, saying it is only a rhyme she has just learned. The guests have all gone, and Juliet and the Nurse retire.

COMMENT: Already, as in Romeo's case, Juliet is gaining in maturity. She has fallen in love as deeply as he, and, as with Romeo, separation seems like death. She, too, sees a paradox in the ironic fate of loving an enemy. Her growing sophistication shows also in the means by which she twice, by slight deceptions, hides from the Nurse her true feelings. The emotion of love is bringing out the womanliness within the young girl.

For those who know the play, Juliet's words to the effect that her grave may be her wedding bed have added power. During the tragic course of the play, her wedding bed actually does become her grave. This twisting of the audience's emotions when they know a meaning for words of which the speaker is not aware, is frequently used by Shakespeare. It is a device known as Dramatic Irony.

SUMMARY: In the tumult of a party, and reminded, by Tybalt's outburst, of the feud between the houses, the two lovers have met.

1. Their meeting is alone in a crowd, and is sanctified by an air of holiness. The treatment of love as a religion was an integral part of the courtly love tradition (see the Introduction) but Shakespeare uses it in no ordinary way. Love is holy here, and not even Friar Laurence, the man of God, will put this love in tension against the love of God, as was part of the courtly love custom. Shakespeare wishes to unify earthly and celestial love, and to give this love affair the attributes of both. The sacredness of Romeo and Juliet's passion will be emphasized throughout the play.

2. The doom the lovers face is impressed on the audience by Tybalt's fury, and by two separate realizations. Both Romeo and Juliet face fully the desperate reality of their situation without trying to hide or disguise it from themselves. In this, love has acted as a maturing force, changing them from childhood abruptly. The fore-doomed atmosphere is enhanced by the nature and degree of their love, and by the impetuous rapidity of their falling into love.

Act II: Chorus

The chorus, like the prologue, is a sonnet. The two poems were probably both spoken by the same actor.

Here, the important events of the first act are reiterated. Rosaline did not stand as beautiful in comparison with Juliet, and a new affection has replaced the old desire in Romeo's heart. But now, when both Romeo and Juliet are in love, they are prevented from natural courtship by the feud between their families. Only because their passion is so strong will they find the strength and means to carry on their secret courting.

COMMENT: This chorus is straightforward. It both reviews the past and envisions the future, and so provides a transition for Romeo's abrupt change of heart. What is to come will be none too easy, but there is still a promise of joy for the lovers.

Act II: Scene i

Romeo, fresh from meeting Juliet at Capulet's party, has ducked away from his comrades in search of solitude in which to contemplate this new state of events. Passing Capulet's orchard, he cannot find heart to take final leave of Juliet's house quite yet. It is as though he were made of the same earth as the orchard, and that earth were recalling him. He jumps over the wall, and fast on his heels come Mercutio and Benvolio, in search of him. Instead of continuing to call Romeo, Mercutio tries to conjure him up like a ghost from the grave. First he invokes Romeo by the image of his love-sickness: sighs, rhymes, and Cupid. When this brings no response, he tries by conjuring an image of Rosaline, whom he supposes, naturally enough, that Romeo still loves. Even playfully sensual images bring no angry stirring in the bushes. Benvolio relents, remarking that since Romeo is blind with love, dark fits him best, and they had best leave him alone. Mercuito now seems half angry, as he laughingly deals his last blows, a few coarse sexual remarks, and then he, too, gives up. They go away, Benvolio commenting that there is no use in looking for someone who does not want to be found. As they leave, Romeo, who has overheard it all and must be thankful for Benvolio's characteristic tact, mutters to himself a retort to Mercutio's derision: "He jests at scars that never felt a wound." This completes the rhyme scheme of the sequence, and puts a poignant end to the jocose indecencies.

COMMENT: Romeo is as passionately love-sick as Mercutio teases him for being, but in a new and different way, and with a wholly different woman. The humor and pathos of the scene are caused by the fact that Mercutio is not aware of this new twist, and all his pointed, ribald remarks fly far

a field without his knowing it. At the same time, they come dangerously close to hitting home. Throughout the scene we can see Romeo, crouching close to the other side of the fence, listening with mixed emotions to comments that have lost their sting and yet offend his new-found young passion. It is this that elicits his own whispered retort to Mercutio, as if to say "you joke about old, healed scars of love, but you have never even felt a wound such as I now have to suffer with."

Act II: Scene ii

No sooner have Mercutio's raucous laughter and jokes echoed down the street for the last time, than Romeo sees a window illuminated in Capulet's house, and a girlish figure standing there. "But soft! what light through yonder window breaks?/ It is the east, and Juliet is the sun." These words break from him, and begin his famous soliloquy (a speech spoken by one person to himself alone). The conceits of romantic love return, but with new life and vigor. The moon, he thinks, is sick and pale with jealousy at Juliet's brilliance. As she steps full into view on the balcony, Romeo can at first do little but exclaim "O, it is my love!" and wish to tell her so. He feels that she is speaking, and he wants to answer, but falls back shyly. Instead he becomes enraptured with her eyes, calling them stars, and her cheeks, which would make real stars dim in comparison, and again her eyes, which, if they were set in heaven, would make birds think it was daylight by their brightness.

COMMENT: This speech, and the entire scene to come, is conventional, almost formal. At the same time, this speech begins a sustained flow of pure lyricism that lasts throughout the scene. Romeo is enthralled. Juliet is the light of day in darkness to him, and his speech moves among images expressing this light: the sun, the moon, the stars. She appears like a revelation of some high truth in the middle of dark chaos. Romeo's speech is even slightly confused, as indeed he is himself, caught between being struck dumb and finding poetry welling out naturally from his mouth.

The scene on the stage would clearly embody Romeo's impassioned imagery. Juliet would be on one of the balconies that were part of the construction of an Elizabethan theater. Standing high above her lover, she would seem to be all that he named her. There would be some distance between Romeo below and Juliet above, and the tension of this distance would be used to enhance and carry along this long ardor that they share.

Juliet, high on her balcony, is so filled with emotion at their recent meeting that all she says is "Ay, me!" She does not know her lover is in the garden below, and she is lost in remembering. Romeo, delighted to hear her voice, breathes out praises. To him, she is a "bright angel," a messenger from heaven before whom mortals fall thunderstruck. She lights up the whole sky. But when Juliet speaks again, she is mournful: "O, Romeo, Romeo!" Why must her love be Romeo, a Montague and an enemy? She wishes she could deny her name, and offers, if he loves her, to give up her own name, presumably by marrying him. For only the name is an enemy, not anything that is an inseparable part of Romeo, the man. She vows that if he will give up his name, he shall have all of her in exchange. Romeo, stepping from the shadows, takes her at her word, and declares aloud that he will be Romeo no longer.

COMMENT: Romeo's continuing comparison of Juliet to divinity, and to all sources of light, is cut off by her spoken thoughts. In speaking her wishes into the night, Juliet has unknowingly declared her love to her lover. She is very innocent and shy, and would not have spoken so openly on purpose. In puzzling over the menace that lies in his name, she has introduced a more somber note to the rhapsody. But the newness and wonder felt by the lovers in this shining religion of love shortly overcome even this.

Hearing Romeo speak up to renounce his name, Juliet is startled, and demands to know what man has overheard her. But he cannot tell her his name, as he has just given it up for love of her. She knows his voice, and when she asks if he is Romeo, a Montague, he replies that he is not, if she dislikes the name. In reality, this giving up the names is a token of love, and the pair know that they cannot renounce what they have been born to. Juliet first fears for Romeo's safety, but he brushes this aside, declaring that no walls or danger could daunt his love. He fears more from one hostile glance of her eyes than from the swords of her relatives. Eased by Romeo's assurances, Juliet softens to shy, gentle coquetry: If it were not for the "mask of night," he would see her blush at having been overheard. "Fain would I dwell on form," she says, and withdraw what was spoken, so that they might pursue a formal courtship. But it is too late for that. In the profusion of her love, she asks first that he swears he loves her, and then, if he thinks she is too quickly won, she promises she will deny her love, so that he may court her. Otherwise, she would never deny it.

COMMENT: The lover's speeches run over into each other, so excited and joyful are they. Juliet, who is so truly untried, is overcome at the strength of her own feeling, and

her thoughts bound and rebound between expressing her love and keeping her proper distance, so that Romeo will not love her less for being forward. The themes of formality and convention find direct expression here. Both are a little shy at the inevitable speed of things, and would like to linger through the courtship, savoring the sweetness of the flirtations and declarations of love. But their situation, which is one of emergency and which they must face, does not allow it. They will proceed most unconventionally to marry speedily and to flout all parental demands. Their love makes them individuals and rebels, contrasting them with the rest of the conventional world. Still, they court and flirt now, while they can.

Romeo wants only to swear his love, and he swears by the moon. Juliet does not want that, as the moon is not constant, but has its phases. If he must swear he must swear by himself, but when he starts to do so, she again cuts him short. She wants no swearing. Their love making has been so beautiful to her that she is afraid it will end as suddenly as it began, like a fateful flash of lightning. Juliet would prefer that the bud of their love have time to blossom. To allow for that, she would say good night now, but Romeo detains her. He wants to exchange vows, but Juliet has given hers, and more would just be extra. Still, when she hears her Nurse calling her, she finds she can't bear to leave Romeo, and tells him to wait until she can come back. While she is gone, Romeo speaks to the night: "O blessed night! I am afeared,/ Being in night, all this is but a dream,/ Too flattering-sweet to be substantial."

COMMENT: Both lovers fear the fleeting, momentary quality of their love. Juliet compares the love to a brief flash of lightning in the darkness, a short brilliance in the night. Romeo blesses the night, for it has brought him joy, and at the same time, he fears that the joy may be no more than a dream coming during a night's sleep. The lovers love the night, which lets their love shine out, but they sense a menace in it, the same menace of the impermanent and vulnerable as was spoken of by Mercutio as "vain fantasy," in Act I, Scene iv.

Juliet returns to her window, and whispering hastily to her lover while her Nurse calls to her from the room behind, she says that if he wishes to marry her, Romeo should send word the next day by her messenger. If not, she pleads that he leave her alone. Again she vanishes within, while Romeo finds the night impossible without her light. Yet one last time she reappears, just as he is going, and calls him. She wants only to ask what time she should send her messenger tomorrow. She has forgotten her real purpose in calling him back. Perhaps it was just to linger a bit longer with him. The two do not want to say good night yet, and Juliet embroiders their lingering with her playfulness: She would like him to go, but no farther than a pet bird on a string who can be tugged back when its mistress wants, "So loving-jealous of its liberty." Only she knows that if he were her bird, she might kill him with too much loving. At last, calling "Good night, good night! parting is such sweet sorrow/ That I shall say good night till it be morrow," Juliet goes in for the last time, and Romeo stands a moment in the darkness, then departs himself for a visit to his priest and confessor.

COMMENT: Using the ancient device of lovers who do not wish to part from each other, Shakespeare strung out his duet just a bit longer, and finally released the audience gently back to earth with Romeo's last words.

SUMMARY: This scene has been an interlude in the action, a long, lyrical love duet in which Juliet leads. The love between the two innocents has been presented as a light in the darkness, brilliant, but threatened always by the possibility of being put out. (This causes them to plunge in head first, and accounts for the swift progress of their love.) The stars, previously used as images of fate, are here described by Romeo as being eclipsed by the light of Juliet. This switch has meaning: The tragic fate of their love seems dull and unimportant, is eclipsed, when put beside the brightness of the love itself. These images of light and night will be repeated and expanded, until they are no longer images but symbols of the love shared by Romeo and Juliet, and of its unavoidable end.

Act II: Scene iii

It is early morning, and Friar Laurence, the monk who is Romeo's confessor, is up and about already. He is educated in the lore of herbs and their powers, and since herbs, if they are to keep their full potency, must be gathered before the sun has dried the dew from their leaves, he goes out at dawn to fill his "osier cage," or basket, "With baleful weeds and precious-juiced flowers./ The earth that's nature's mother is her tomb;/ What is her burying grave, that is her womb." The good Friar comments on the cycle of life, on plants growing from the earth and decaying back into it. All things in nature, even the most vile, have a special function and good use on earth. At the same time, the Friar knows that even the best things on earth can be misused for the purpose of evil. Both properties can exist in the same plant; for example, an herb can be beneficial to the health if smelled, but poisonous if eaten. Everything lies in how we use what nature gives

us, and this is true even of men, who can use or misuse their own inherent qualities, so causing themselves to be good or evil.

COMMENT: After the necessary yet deliriously lyrical interlude during which Romeo and Juliet have established their special love, we return to the demands of the action. Although the previous scene seems swift when we remember that in it an entire courtship took place, it had the nature of a beautiful pause. The pace must now pick up. Friar Laurence's long speech begins with a description of grey dawn coming with smiles to chase away night, and with it comes the time when the day's work must be resumed. The speech allows for the modulation from night to day, from ease to activity.

The Friar's speech shows him to be a good man, with a philosophical turn of mind. He is aware of the powers of his knowledge of herbs, and his intention will always be to use these powers for the furthering of good, not evil. This well-intentioned quality in the Friar, coupled with his knowledge of drugs, plays an important part in the development of the plot, when the lovers find it necessary to try and extricate themselves from dangerous complications.

Romeo, who has been up all night wooing Juliet, now comes to see the Friar. The Friar is surprised to see him, feeling that a youth, with no cares to make him sleepless, should still be sleeping at this hour, or else must be disturbed in mind or body. He feels this is not so in Romeo's case, and guesses that he had not been to bed at all. Romeo acknowledges the truth of the guess, while quickly assuring the Friar that "the sweeter rest" he had was not with Rosaline, for he has forgotten her and the sadness she brought him. Romeo riddles the Friar a bit, saying he has been with his enemy, who has wounded him and been wounded by him, but that the cure for both their wounds is within the monk's "holy physic," or sacred healing power. He quickly clarifies things, however, telling the Friar that he and Juliet have pledged their love for each other, and that it only remains for the Friar to join them forever in marriage this very day.

COMMENT: Romeo not only respects the Friar, but shares a camaraderie with him, as is made evident by the Friar's pleased questioning about why Romeo is not asleep—and by Romeo's light-hearted punning about the wounds of love and their remedy, marriage. This love of Romeo for Juliet has not left him mournful, as he was over Rosaline, but full of high-spirited joy, even in the face of grave obstacles. Nothing can be quick enough for him; he loves without restraint and with all the impetuosity of the young, and he must make their love sanctified and eternal by immediate marriage.

Friar Laurence is bowled over by this abrupt change, and comments on the changefulness of youth. Only yesterday Romeo cried salt tears for a love that did not even last long enough to be seasoned by that salt. The Friar's ears still ring with Romeo's groans, and while he had encouraged Romeo to bury that love, he didn't intend that another love should spring up instantly. Still, he admits that he felt that Romeo was loving according to a book he could scarcely even read yet. Apparently, the Friar senses from Romeo's elation that this is not love by the book, but the real thing. Also, he hopes that the love and marriage of a Montague to a Capulet might force an alliance between the two feuding houses, and change the hate between them to love. On hearing this approval, Romeo cries, "O, let us hence; I stand on sudden haste." To this impetuousness the monk replies, "Wisely and slow; they stumble that run fast."

COMMENT: For all his forbearance, the Friar is here contrasted with Romeo. Although he ends by approving the marriage, he cautions Romeo against hurting himself by being hasty. The Friar is sympathetic, but even he cannot understand the urgency that is inherent in this love, and that propels it and the lovers forward. He remains rational and wise, and wishes Romeo would be so too, because he does not grasp that the very nature of the feeling rules out all caution and rationality. Romeo and Juliet have a sympathizer, but their love remains beyond his understanding. Because of the chasm between their emotions and all rationality, they stand essentially alone.

SUMMARY: The following have been treated in this scene:

1. Herbs and potions, which can do both good and evil, depending on how they are used.

2. The possibility of the love between Romeo and Juliet serving to bridge the gap between their families.

3. The irrevocable, involuntary, and irrational speed of Romeo and Juliet's romantic fervor. It leads them to immediate action, without reflection, and accounts for the amazing velocity of the play. This love is on a pinnacle, beyond the understanding of those not moved by it. It promises not only to be speedy, but to be very much alone, shared only by the lovers. Even the kindly Friar cannot keep the two lovers company in their flight of love.

Act II: Scene iv

Mercutio and Benvolio, abroad in Verona this morning, wonder where Romeo is. They know he has not been home, and fear Rosaline will drive him mad. Tybalt, angered by Romeo's uninvited appearance at the Capulet festival, has sent him a challenge to duel. Benvolio feels sure Romeo will answer not just the letter, but the man and the dare; but Mercutio says Romeo is already dead, slain by a woman's eye, a love song, and Cupid's arrow, and not in the manly state necessary to fight Tybalt. "Why, what is Tybalt?" asks Benvolio. In lore, Tybalt is the name for the prince of cats. Mercutio punningly states that this Tybalt is more than prince of cats, but a master of the laws of ceremony, one who fights with a sense of timing as natural to him as keeping time to music is to those who sing. Yet Mercutio clearly despises Tybalt, despite his skill with a sword, and goes on to make fun of him as a silly dandy who is at least as concerned with having fashionable manners and clothes as he is with fighting like a true gentleman.

COMMENT: Mercutio's witty sally on Tybalt makes clear to us that he detests the man, finds him despicable, shallow, ridiculous, and lacking in true manliness. But it also makes a point of Tybalt's being an adept fighter, no small adversary to Romeo. Tybalt's challenge to Romeo is indeed serious, as we find out later. Mercutio's extreme dislike of Tybalt is equally serious and important.

Just now, Romeo comes into view, and the two men begin a chanting tease. Mercutio calls him a dried herring, without its roe. He means that without Rosaline, Romeo is like a herring without its mate: he dries up and becomes "fishified." Running through all the heroines of literature, Mercutio states the faults Romeo must find in them in comparison with Rosaline. But he is glad to see Romeo, and ribs him about having slipped away the previous evening. Romeo, just come from the Friar, is in a fine, delighted frame of mind, and he warms up to the fast-flying witticisms immediately. He scores many good returns over Mercutio as their conversation skips from courtesys and courtesy to dancing pumps, the singularity of jests, and finally runs a "wild goose chase" around itself. Periodically Mercutio, who is delighted at Romeo's return to free-spirited word play, protests that Romeo is in excellent form: "Thy wit is very bitter sweeting; it is a most sharp sauce." Romeo retorts that Mercutio is a "broad goose," using "broad" to mean obvious, indecent, and unrestrained all at once. Mercutio is pleased beyond answering, and bursts out: "Now art thou sociable, now art thou Romeo; now art thou what thou art, by art as well as by nature," and adds the sexual pun that love had made Romeo "hide his bauble (the stick carried by a fool or jester) in a hole." Benvolio stops Mercutio there, to prevent his tale from becoming "large" (meaning both long and licentious).

COMMENT: This scene has been like a fast set of tennis, the verbal ball bouncing merrily back and forth. Romeo is truly in love, we know that well. Gone are his attitudes of despondancy. He is joyful, and his spirited sense of humor has returned full force, allowing him to exceed even his old self in light-hearted repartee. Mercutio, who loves him, is overjoyed not only at Romeo's clever words, but at his return to his full self. In saying "Now art thou what thou art, by art as well as by nature," Mercutio is not only playing happily with words. He has stated his basic belief: A man must be himself, no matter what; he must be true to his own nature and strengthen it by the use of his mind. He must be self-sufficient, must stand alone on the hard ground of reality, without the romance of such ideals as love or dreams. And yet, as we shall see with respect to Mercutio, a man must stand for and respond to what he believes and feels. These few short words to Romeo are the key to Mercutio's life and death.

As the men conclude their jest, the Nurse and her servant Peter arrive. The Nurse is the messenger Juliet promised to send to Romeo. She is on an errand of courtship and is about to speak with highly-bred gentlemen. It is a role she enjoys, and to play it to the full, she affects the airs of a lady of breeding, holding a fan before her face in modesty as she approaches. After one quip to the effect that her fan is prettier than her face, Mercutio falls in with the play-acting and greets her as a gentlewoman, only to instantly affront her assumed gentility by saying, "The bawdy hand of the dial is now upon the prick of noon." Romeo, and even gentle Benvolio, fall in with this spirit of raillery for and at the Nurse. Mercutio even breaks into song, intimating that the Nurse is a prostitute now gone stale with age. He and Benvolio depart, leaving Romeo to share the confidence the Nurse has requested.

COMMENT: The Nurse reveals herself beautifully in her attempt at discreet, lady-like demeanor with the young bachelors. She is conscious of and enjoys her own affectation. She is not really offended at their making fun of her, but enjoys that and the bawdy jokes also without ever letting her airs drop. For all his lightness, Romeo must know immediately that she comes from Juliet, and be anxious to talk with her.

The Nurse asks who that rogue was, referring to Mercutio. True to the role she has chosen, her sense of dignity is offended by him. She must express this to Romeo, and in the vigor with which she does so she lets her demure facade drop, breaking out into, "Scurvy knave! I am none of his flirt-gills"; that is, not one of Mercutio's loose, flirtacious wenches. Resuming the role, she chides Peter for not defending her, then turns

to Romeo and gets down to business. First, she gets in her warning that Romeo had better not be playing double with her young mistress. Romeo protests, and tells the Nurse of his hopes to marry Juliet that very afternoon in Friar Laurence's cell. He urges that Juliet find a means to be there. He also promises to send a ladder, which shall be his means for reaching Juliet tonight so that they may consummate their marriage. All this the Nurse promises to relay to her mistress. True to herself, she must prattle away a bit about Paris, his suit for Juliet's hand, and how Juliet turns pale when the Nurse teasingly says that Paris is the more handsome. She tells him that Juliet has some small verse about Romeo and rosemary. (Rosemary is the flower of remembrance, used at weddings and, what is ironical in this case, also at funerals.) Romeo breaks this off, and leaves.

COMMENT: This is the Nurse's scene. She is herself in the role of the lady she has chosen to play, and equally herself in her lapses from that role. We feel concerned that her meandering old memory will fail to transmit Romeo's messages correctly. At the same time, we are amused at her changes of attitude, and at her description of "sometimes" teasing Juliet, as if the love affair between her mistress and Romeo had been going on for some weeks now, instead of a bare twelve hours. In the minds of both the lovers and the audience the love is at once as young as twelve hours and as ancient as all love. In the midst of her chattering, the Nurse's reference to the proposed marriage of Juliet to Paris, which will have its effect on the line of action, strikes an ominous undertone, as does her mention of the rosemary. We may also notice here that there is no indication of Romeo's feeling jealous at the mention of Paris. The lovers have clasped hands, a sign of giving trust, and neither one ever doubts the other.

SUMMARY: Much has happened in this scene.

1. Romeo has blossomed, and shown his full self, in the witticisms that boom from his inner happiness. His old attitudes are gone forever, and we see that the value of his stereotyped love for Rosaline is to contrast with, and so help define, this new, completely untypical and individual love.

2. Mercutio, Romeo's closest companion, has been presented still more clearly, and has voiced his keynote of being true to oneself. His jolly sensuality and his realism are contrasted with and used to help define Romeo, who endorses the idealisms of love and dreams, and whose wit emerges from these rather than from realism.

3. The Nurse, Juliet's closest companion, is to Juliet what Mercutio is to Romeo: that is, a balancing, contrasting force of the more realistic and baser instincts of life. She, like

Mercutio, is true to herself, even when she plays a role. The sensuality of both these companions to the hero and heroine is always out in the open, never obscene.

4. The arrangements for the immediate marriage and the wedding night have been settled upon. This impels the plot forward and the progress of the love affair. Everything is moving swiftly now. This scene, which is a long one, has gone rapidly. Beneath the impetuous speed we are reminded of the ever-present threats to the lovers' happiness.

Act II: Scene v

Juliet is alone in her father's orchard, waiting impatiently for her Nurse to return with Romeo's message. The Nurse promised she would be back in half an hour, but for three long hours Juliet has waited. It is now noon, and the young girl is in a small frenzy. She wishes her messengers to Romeo could be thoughts, which would fly like doves or the wings of the wind, driving back the shadows of the hills as they fly. It seems a long journey that the sun has traveled from morning to midday. If the Nurse were as young and full of passion as Juliet, she would move between the two lovers like a tossed ball, carrying their messages. Though Juliet knows the Nurse is old and slow, this much delay seems to her to result from someone pretending to be dead.

COMMENT: Juliet's impatience as she waits to hear if she is to be married equals Romeo's. She loves and thinks of him with all the powers of her imagination, and her reckless, loving thoughts rival Romeo's for their beauty of imagery. No speed is enough for her, she is so caught in the flood of their love. She cannot feel complete unless the passion they share is advancing full speed ahead.

The Nurse and Peter now come, and Juliet greets the Nurse with high excitement. Peter is sent out, and she questions the Nurse urgently. But the Nurse, as if in answer to Juliet's previous remark on old people, only complains about her weary joints. Juliet has no sympathy at present; she wishes the Nurse had her young bones, and she had the Nurse's news. The Nurse only retorts that her mistress can wait till she has caught her breath. Juliet is getting irritated. The Nurse has spent more breath complaining than the answer to the question, "Is thy news good or bad?" would take. In answer, the Nurse takes a tone of derision, and uses it to praise highly Juliet's choice of a husband. Juliet knows Romeo's value, all she wants to hear is whether or not they will be married. Again the Nurse returns to patter about her aches and pains. Driven to distraction, Juliet has been unsympathetic to the ailments of old age,

and the Nurse, partly out of perversity and partly from desire to be pitied and given attention, will play this game until her young mistress shows some response to her complaints. Seeing this at last, and regreting her own unresponsiveness, Juliet softens, and caresses her Nurse. But when the Nurse teasingly starts to relinquish her news, only to interrupt herself with a question about the whereabouts of Lady Capulet, it is the last straw. Juliet speaks crossly and abruptly, with real irritation. Then only does the Nurse answer, in a short, concise, and surprisingly accurate speech, describing the plans for the marriage this afternoon at the Friar's, and for the ladder which will let Romeo come to his bride and consummate their marriage that evening. Juliet joyfully departs for Friar Laurence's cell.

COMMENT: The Nurse pettishly teases Juliet now, even as we have seen Mercutio taunt Romeo. She wants her share of attention and thanks. Her concern, partly real and partly pretended, over her own physical condition is indicative of her natural, defensible egotism. Juliet shows a slight degree of the same quality in her single-minded efforts to extract the news, but she has passion on her side. The Nurse is actually being quite cruel. Yet when she relents and tells her the news, she does so with a genuine acknowledgment of how Juliet must be feeling. She gently chides her mistress's blushes, and calls Romeo's coming by ladder at night his ascent to "a bird's nest." The delays before the telling are used dramatically to contrast with the previous and coming scenes, and to make the audience share the urgency of Juliet's emotion. The device also enhances the contrast between the slow, unemotional state of age and the blinding speed of youth in love. Notice that Romeo, the Nurse, Juliet, and even the Friar, all think of the marriage and its consummation as being one, a whole in which both parts are equally holy.

Act II: Scene vi

It is the time and place of the wedding. Romeo and Friar Laurence speak quietly to each other as they wait for Juliet. The Friar asks for heaven's smile on the marriage, so that it may not be followed by sorrow. Romeo adds his "Amen," but for him, no amount of sorrow can weigh more strongly than the joy of a moment with his bride. If the Friar only joins their hands in holy marriage, he will dare "love-devouring death" to do whatever it might. He will have named her for his own, and that is enough. The Friar answers with his moderation and wisdom: "These violent delights have violent ends,/ And in their triumph die, like fire and powder,/ Which as they kiss consume." He enjoins Romeo to love moderately, so that he may love long.

COMMENT: Romantic love of this total, all-embracing, rapid kind has full sway over both lovers. They accept it, revel in it, and by doing so unwittingly taunt death. The Friar's words are a true prophesy. The kind of love that these two people have chosen and surrendered to cannot, by its very nature, be moderate or longlasting. We cannot picture Romeo and Juliet continuing through the normal cycle of prospering and waning love, of children, of middle and old age. They only have their being now, as intense lovers. Their love can only do that against which the Friar warns: meet, light up in a brief, brilliant flame, consume itself, and end in an unlooked-for death. This is what will happen, and it is what Romeo and Juliet have chosen without realizing.

The Friar's moderation would be impossible for them, and they do not want it. They have placed their bets on the highest form of love, where the spiritual and the earthly unite. Others cannot understand this, and the lovers are alone.

Juliet comes, and her step is so light that Romeo fancies it would not break the gossamer of summer air. She greets the "ghostly," meaning spiritual, Friar. The imaginations of both Romeo and Juliet are on fire. If her joy leaps up as high as his, Romeo bids her to sweeten the air with the music of her imaginings about the love they will share. Her answer is that she must speak of substance, not ornament, but that the substance of her love is so great that she cannot add up half the wealth of it. The Friar then takes them to his inner chamber, where he will by "Holy church incorporate two in one."

COMMENT: This is the wedding, where Romeo and Juliet will "die" as two separate individuals in order to become one unified whole. Their love for each other is not voiced in terms of the sensual or corporeal, but expressed as the delight of freed imaginations, and of more feeling than can be expressed. Their speeches form a short, but highly charged antiphony, as they go to their union.

SUMMARY: The whole act, which began with the courtship in the orchard, has progressed quickly but with changing pace, to this quiet climax in marriage. For the audience, the true fatal nature of the love becomes more vivid as the lovers are united forever. The threat of the feud, and the ominous prophesy of the Friar, have subtly built up the sense of underlying danger and prepared us for the act to come. This marriage is a calm before a storm.

Act III: Scene i

The afternoon has drawn on after the wedding, and has become hot. Benvolio, who is with Mercutio, observes that hot weather makes hot tempers, and since the Capulets are about, he pleads that they go home and escape more fighting. Mercutio, who feels mischievous, jestingly accuses Benvolio of really wanting a fight, and of being quick to pick one over slight excuses, such as a man cracking nuts when Benvolio has hazel eyes. Benvolio maintains that if he were as soon moved to quarrel as is Mercutio, his life would not be worth a "fee-simple." At this juncture the Capulets do appear, with Tybalt leading them. Mercutio cares not, and at Tybalt's request for a word with them, tauntingly suggests that he ask for a word and a blow. He dares Tybalt to find a reason for fighting him. He pretends that Tybalt has called himself and Benvolio "minstrels," a faintly derogatory word implying vagabonds, and he draws his sword as a fiddler draws his bow, to make Tybalt dance. He is deliberately provoking the antagonistic Capulet. When Benvolio suggests that the two of them should either keep their quarrel rational or go some place private, Mercutio retorts that men can stare, but he is not going to budge.

COMMENT: The contrast with the preceding scene is vivid. Mercutio, his high spirits subjected to the sluggish heat, is in fact feeling quarrelsome. From his speech earlier this morning, we know that he has profound distaste for Tybalt. He disregards peace-loving Benvolio's pleas, and tries to antagonize this man he dislikes.

Romeo, newly married an hour since, appears just at the crucial point. It is Romeo that Tybalt wants to fight and for whom he has been waiting, despite Mercutio's jabs: "Here come my man." But Mercutio is angered at Tybalt's resistance to his gibes, and he takes this remark of Tybalt's in its lowest sense, that of calling Romeo a servant. Tybalt deliberately insults Romeo, trying to entice him to a duel. But Romeo's state of mind has transcended the sarcastic irony of such name-calling as "The love I bear thee can afford/ No better term than this—thou art a villian." No one knows of the marriage but Romeo and the audience, and Romeo's suspenseful pause, and the riddling response he gives is perplexing to everyone on the stage. Tybalt refuses to be forgiven for slandering, and has no intention of missing his chance to revenge the grudge he holds. But Romeo continues his mysterious talk of loving the Capulet name as well as his own. His comrades are astonished.

COMMENT: We must examine Romeo's responses. Perhaps he is so uplifted by being now one with Juliet that he views this petty picking of fights from a supreme distance, and can only react with all-embracing love to the insults of his new cousin. Perhaps his immediate reaction is to seek vengeance, but he has effectively squelched the impulse and holds it under control in the light of his new relationship to Tybalt. Tybalt has seen Romeo intruding at a family party, and has perhaps observed Romeo's attention to Juliet, which would only add insult to injury. To Benvolio and Mercutio, Romeo must still appear as Rosaline's love-sick pup, too weak to put his manhood to the test of a duel. And to Mercutio, such weakening love bears all the earmarks of self-indulgent idealism. This action of Romeo's infuriates him, even though the feud is not his.

Mercutio, livid, cries out, "O calm, dishonorable, vile submission!" and draws on Tybalt, saying that he means to have one of the nine lives of the king of cats. Tybalt answers by drawing and, ignoring Romeo's cry to Mercutio to stop, they fight. Romeo then draws himself, calling to Benvolio to help him, and rushes to break up the fight. As he tries to separate his cousin and his friend, he blocks one of Mercutio's parries. Tybalt and his followers withdraw, and as they do, Mercutio clutches his side, saying, "I am hurt,/ A plague o' both your houses. I am sped," a cry which he repeats more than once while the scene lasts, "Ay, ay, a scratch, a scratch; marry, 'tis enough." Romeo is stricken, and to his inquiries Mercutio replies that the cut is "not so deep as a well, nor so wide as a church door," but that it is enough to make him a "grave" man by tomorrow. An abusive torrent bursts from Mercutio, vilifying Tybalt, "a dog, a rat, a mouse, a cat, to scratch a man to death! a braggart, a rogue, a villian, that fights by the book of arithmetic!" Why did Romeo try to come between them? It was this, says Mercutio, that caused the fatal wound. Romeo did what he thought would be best, but Mercutio again curses both houses, and turns to Benvolio to be carried out. Romeo stands stunned, muttering painfully to himself at the indignity he feels over what has happened, and confirming Mercutio's thoughts in a simpler and stronger speech than he has yet used: "O sweet Juliet,/ Thy beauty hath made me effeminate,/ And in my temper soften'd valour's steel." Almost immediately Benvolio returns. Mercutio, the "gallant spirit" that scorned the earth, is dead. Romeo can see nothing but the blackness of this day, and many more to come. He bows his head to this new fate.

COMMENT: This scene, long prepared for by the hovering feud, by the presentation of Mercutio's vibrant character, and by our understanding of Tybalt as well, now marks the turning of the play from high romance to tragedy. Mercutio, whose creed is to be true to himself, could not but be enraged and deeply offended by what seems to him the lily-livered conduct of the friend he loves. If Romeo lacks the pride in himself necessary to retaliate to Tybalt's despicable taunts, Mercutio will do it. To him, Tybalt is a low animal that crawls on his belly, lives by a lifeless set of rules, and scratches its prey to death. The realistic, ironic, life-loving man finds that his only choice is to defend manhood and selfhood against such infamies, and so, despite himself, he dies for an ideal. Dying, he does not give up his fight, but puns wryly and cynically, and curses violently, until he has no more breath. The lyricism of Queen Mab has guttered out with a growl. The audience has heard much of Mercutio, and we feel his was a precious spirit.

Suddenly, furious Tybalt shows himself again. This is too much for Romeo. Abruptly he casts away the "respective lenity" that had resulted from his marriage. He calls to Tybalt that Mercutio's soul is waiting, and one or both of their's must accompany it. Tybalt's answer rings: it will have to be Romeo's soul. The two fall to furious, earnest fencing, and Romeo kills his new cousin. As Tybalt falls, Mercutio is avenged, and Romeo has at last stood for his own honor. Benvolio cries to him, "Away, away" for the citizens are aroused and the newly established penalty for such fighting is death. Romeo groans, "O, I am fortune's fool!" and forces himself to run off.

COMMENT: Romeo has been hurled from his position of ecstasy to one of pitiful misery, and in this turnabout he shows himself to be built of stern fiber. Without the smallest indulgence in superfluous grief, he has trumpeted out his challenge to Tybalt. The loss of Mercutio must be repaid in kind. On having killed the man, Romeo is yet more deeply stunned. With his fate a ringing menace in his ears, he gathers his strength, accepts his fate, and leaves.

Citizens come running and close on their heels come both the feuding households and Verona's Prince. Amidst cries for vengeance, Benvolio explains to Prince Escalus what has occurred. He perhaps exaggerates Romeo's humility, and in the exaggeration lie the tones not only of desire to protect Romeo, but of annoyance at Romeo's conduct. The tale is otherwise vivid and true to the facts. Lady Capulet accuses him of natural prejudice in favor of the Montagues, and asks for Romeo's death. Lord Montague's answer is that Romeo only gave Tybalt the punishment coming to him. The Prince ponders, weighing both sides. His conclusion is that Romeo shall be exiled, and that for the pointless loss of Mercutio, one of his own family, he shall exact heavy fines from both the feuding households. Romeo must leave Verona immediately. If he is caught first, he will be put to death. The Prince can have no more mercy, for his past leniency has seemed only to give license to more murdering.

COMMENT: Here, in the very core of the play, justice is once more meted out by the Prince. His first appearance was at the play's beginning when the fatal feud revived. He comes now at the play's turning, when the chain of what seem to be accidents has culminated in loss. The peace he requested has resulted in the grievous death of one of his own relatives. He serves here as a figure of justice and of a sterner, more forcefully demanded peace. His presence ends the chaos and the loss that have ensued since the scene began. Some order is restored. But imposed on the lovers is a fate of what would seem to be eternal separation. That is the punishment hardest to bear, and the justice that seems least just. The Prince, who marks always the structural points in the plot when fate and chance clash with cataclysmic effect, will only come again at the play's end.

SUMMARY: The gathering speed and ill-omen of the play have found a climax in the tragic loss of Mercutio, a man we treasured, and in the exile of Romeo from Verona. Accident has again reared its head as a determinant of action, and we now realize that it is fate.

1. The death of Mercutio proves to be the play's turning point, and from here the love of Romeo and Juliet will hurtle them down to doom.

2. Youth and Romeo, which stand for love, have again clashed against the hate of the elders who initiated this feud, and in doing so have only furthered the cause of hate and war, while trying to do the opposite.

3. Romeo has again broadened and deepened in character; first by refusing to fight with his new cousin Tybalt; next, by accepting the burden of vengeance for his friend Mercutio, recognizing it as his honor and duty, and killing Tybalt, despite his relationship; and finally by accepting the fate that all this has brought upon him.

Act III: Scene ii

Juliet, unaware of what has just happened, waits out the passing of the day in her father's orchard. She is more impatient than ever, for tonight Romeo is to come to her as her husband. At the opening of the scene, she delivers an impassioned soliloquy, well known as "Juliet's invocation to the night." Beginning with the words,

"Gallop apace, you fiery-footed steeds," she urges the sun on to its setting in the west, so that night may arrive sooner. "Spread thy close curtains, love-performing night." She longs for the shelter of darkness, when Romeo can come to her unseen. The dark suits lovers, for love is blind and the beauty of lovers is enough light for them. Juliet compares night to a "sober-suited matron, all in black," who will teach her how to lose the game of love to her lover. Only by losing can she win. Changing the image to one of falconry, this tender girl compares herself to a falcon: a hawk or bird of prey used by hunters for catching pheasants and quail. Until released for the kill, a falcon is kept quiet by having its head enclosed in a small black hood. When nervous or anxious for the kill, a falcon will "bate," or beat its wings rapidly. So Juliet hopes that night will "Hood my unmann'd blood, bating in my cheeks." With the word "unmann'd" she had used the language of falconry to refer to her own virginity. She invokes night, and she invokes Romeo, the lover who is "day in night," and who will glide on the wings of night like "new snow on a raven's back." All she asks is that this night bring Romeo to her. After that, if he dies (which Juliet does not imagine), the night may take him back, may set him in the heaven with stars. Then "All the world will be in love with night, and pay no worship to the garish sun." For love belongs to Juliet now that she is married, but she does not own it, and she can't own love until Romeo posesses her. Because of that she is waiting now, as impatiently as a child waits for a festival.

COMMENT: The soliloquy is a magnificent one. From the vigor of its opening lines, on through all the changes of tone and pace, the speech shows Juliet in a new light. Her voice has more resonance, her images more strength, and her passionate imagination has gained in maturity. Despite the fact that there is a profusion of images, all coming hard and fast, the soliloquy is based on the unifying images of night and light. Juliet courts this night, which by its darkness will allow Romeo's safe journey to her, and will teach her how to perform the act of love, how to play the game she must lose in order to win. The only light she needs is Romeo himself, who is "day in night." The light of day and the "garish sun" offer nothing to her; they are only "tedious." It is night that is "loving," for it blesses her love with its darkness and silence, and lets that love shine out. Even the stars, emblems of the fate she does not recognize, seem to be good: Romeo will be made eternal by the stars. And here, remembering what has happened in the preceding scene, we are struck by the tragic irony of Juliet's whole rapturous speech. It is like singing in the face of death. So does Juliet hasten the coming of her wedding night.

Now the Nurse comes, carrying with her the very cords Romeo has prepared to let him come to his wife tonight. They are to be thrown over the balcony so that he may climb up. To Juliet these ropes, as well as any word connected with Romeo, are harbingers of joy. But the Nurse flings the ropes to the ground and with shocking sorrow, begins to mourn, saying "He's gone, he's killed, he's dead." Juliet, assuming the nurse means Romeo, can only say, "Can heaven be so envious?" By envious she means not only jealous of their happiness, but malicious. The nurse takes the latter meaning and retorts that Romeo can be envious. This is more than Juliet can bear, and she bursts out, "What devil art thou that dost torment me thus? This torture should be roar'd in dismal hell." She demands to know if Romeo has killed himself, and playing on the various meanings of "I," "aye," and "eye," she makes it clear that her misery hangs on the Nurse's answer. The Nurse, who is never straightforward enough to give a simple answer, does not answer yes or no, but launches into a gory description of how she saw the wound with her own eyes. Juliet, beside herself with dismay, cries "O break, my heart!" and "Vile earth, to earth resign, end motion here." The only interpretation that she can give to the Nurse's words is that Romeo is dead, and that is Juliet's own death sentence.

COMMENT: The sudden news of tragedy has abruptly descended on Juliet, and her fortunes reversed, her rapture changes to misery. She does not know the truth of what has happened, but suspecting the worst, she is swallowed up by grief. The Nurse, who is always one to relish any occasion where her own sentimentality can be indulged, has gone about delivering the news to her young mistress with complete disregard for the girl's feelings. This unnecessary cruelty on the Nurse's part prompts Juliet's anger, and it is an anger with which we sympathize. Age, which is represented by the feuding families, and the lack of true feeling, can afford to dawdle and play meanly with the impetuous emotions of youth. Not only is the Nurse shown in her true character as a self-centered old woman who grabs at any chance to indulge her emotions to the fullest. The Nurse is old, and as such, she is contrasted with Juliet. The Nurse must squeeze whatever feeling she can from the present tragedy, while Juliet's feelings run riot before she even knows exactly what has happened.

At last, the Nurse begins to clarify her news. She reveals that it is Tybalt for whom she mourns. Juliet, convinced of Romeo's death, now thinks that both are dead: "Then, dreadful trumpets, sound the general doom!/ For who is living if these two are gone?" But the Nurse finally lets the full blow fall, and reveals that Tybalt was killed by Romeo, and that Romeo himself

is banished. Juliet, by now utterly confused by one reversal after another and worked up to an extreme emotional pitch by the Nurse's playful devices, lets loose a torrent of words reviling the Romeo she loves: "O serpent heart, hid with a flowering face!" and "Despised substance of divinest show!" Using all the opposites of evil and good at her command, she curses her lover as a fiend who hides evil in sweet and even holy trappings. The Nurse picks up this cry, and, claiming that all this sorrow is making her old, she says, "Shame come to Romeo!" But hearing her curses in the mouth of another brings Juliet to her senses. She retorts with all her spirit, "Blister'd be thy tongue/ For such a wish! he was not born to shame:/ Upon his brow shame is ashamed to sit." Realizing what she herself has just done, Juliet adds, "O, what a beast was I to chide at him."

COMMENT: The Nurse has played on Juliet's emotions, and so milked the girl's feelings that she is no longer herself. When she finally understands the truth, her fury at Romeo is expressed in conceits and contraries such as we have heard Romeo use about Rosaline. But here the confusion and excess of Juliet's emotional state give the opposites true meaning. We have come full circle, to the point where expressive feeling can find no other means of expression. But the jolt of hearing the Nurse add her two cents worth makes Juliet realize what she has said. She turns from cursing her lover to cursing her Nurse, who deserves it, and the dignity with which she declares that Romeo was not born for shame convinces us that this is the true Juliet.

When the Nurse asks Juliet how she can praise a man who killed her cousin, Juliet retorts that she cannot speak badly of her own husband, and is overcome with remorse that she, a newly wedded wife, could mangle her own husband's name. She realizes that had Romeo not killed Tybalt, Tybalt would surely have killed him. She should shed tears of joy that her husband still lives, not of sadness at her cousin's death. But she still finds herself crying uncontrollably, no matter what comfort she tries to offer herself. Why? Gradually she begins to remember the word she would rather forget, a word that was worse than news of Tybalt's death: "Banished!" If Tybalt's death wants another grief to keep it company, Juliet would rather it were anything than this. To her, the news of Romeo's exile is worse than news that everyone, including herself, is dead. "There is no end, no limit, measure, bound, In that word's death." The Nurse tells Juliet that her parents are mourning Tybalt, but the girl's tears are all for her lover's banishment. Seeing the cords which Romeo had sent as a "highway" to her bed, and with which the Nurse began this long telling of sad news, Juliet picks them up. She will take them to her wedding bed, "And death, not Romeo, take my maidenhead!" The Nurse finally sees what true depth of misery she has caused Juliet. She is remorseful. Feeling that her mistress might really kill herself, she offers what comfort she can. She will go find Romeo, who is hiding in the Friar's cell, and make sure that he will come tonight. Juliet brightens at this, and hands the Nurse a ring to give to Romeo, so that he will know that she is still true to him and wants him to come.

COMMENT: The word "banished" has echoed and re-echoed through these speeches like a refrain of doom. Juliet has recovered herself, only to discover the heaviest grief of all. The cords, which should have been a reminder that tonight the two lovers would joyfully seal their marriage, have instead become a symbol of grief, of marriage not consummated, and even of threatening death. By these artistic devices, Shakespeare impresses on us the great misery of Juliet. Even the Nurse emerges from her self-involvement and weary old age enough to realize what a cruel blow has been dealt to her mistress in the very heat and anticipation of the coming fulfillment of young love. The last note struck before the scene ends is one of hope in the middle of despair, of a light in the midst of gathering darkness.

SUMMARY: The scene has moved from the gathering brilliance and joy of Juliet's invocation and anticipation of her wedding night to the gathering gloom of tragic banishment and threatened death. Fate seems to be closing in, even while the night, so greatly desired by the lovers, descends. Everything that promised joy now seems an evil omen, (even the cords by which Romeo will ascend to his wife's window) and because of this Juliet's speech in opposites is not out of place. The cruelty of the Nurse, who by slowly relishing the moments of grief has driven Juliet to distraction, emphasizes again the separation of the lovers in their youth and swift passion, from the world of old age, rationality, and cruelty. In this scene Juliet, like Romeo in the previous scene, has realized fully what a threat there is to their love, and has even participated in it by allowing herself to be tricked into cursing her own husband. She has accepted this threat offered by the rest of the world, and at the same time she has given herself over completely to her love, and sent her ring to Romeo as a token.

Act III: Scene iii

Romeo, fearful because he has killed Tybalt, has fled to the safety of Friar Laurence's cell. The Friar, coming from a quick stroll around Verona where he has found news of Romeo's punishment, calls Romeo out from the inner room where he is hiding. The Friar speaks of Romeo as "wedded to calamity," and Romeo asks him what doom the Prince has pronounced. The young lover only hopes it is less than "dooms-day." Confident that his news will be of some comfort, the Friar tells Romeo that he is not sentenced to death, but is instead banished from Verona. At this, Romeo cries out abruptly "Ha, banishment! be merciful, say 'death.'" To him, as to Juliet, banishment is worse than death. The world beyond Verona seems to offer nothing but hell, and to be exiled to hell is surely not less than being dead. To say that banishment is less than death is, for Romeo, as cruel as smiling while delivering the death sentence. But to the Friar's way of thinking, Romeo is being rudely unthankful in refusing to see the mercy with which the Prince has ignored the rule that death shall be the punishment for killing.

COMMENT: The similarity between the reactions of Romeo and Juliet to the sentence of exile is very clear. Both lovers consider banishment no better than death. The similarity between this scene and the previous one will become more and more evident. The two scenes balance each other at the center of the play. Contrasted, however, are the two confidants of the lovers: that is, the Friar and the Nurse. Instead of prolonging and falsifying the telling of bad news, the Friar speaks directly, and optimistically, delivering his news in one sentence.

Romeo is not to be so quickly dissuaded from his grief. He has said that any place but Verona is hell. He feels this, just as he feels that wherever Juliet strays is heaven. Dogs, cats, mice, even the flies that feed on decaying flesh will have the honor and "courtship" (that is, the chance at courtliness and the courting) of gazing at Juliet's hands and at her blushing virgin lips. But he, Romeo is banished. He would rather be killed by poison or knives, for the very word kills him. "Banished" is a word for the damned who howl in hell. Romeo wonders how his spiritual confessor, the Friar, can have the heart to use it. The Friar does not want to use the word; he wants to give Romeo the armor to ward off the stings of banishment: the armor he offers is philosophy. "Hang up philosophy" says Romeo, unless it can reverse these misfortunes. The Friar wants to discuss Romeo's state philosophically, but Romeo stops him by saying, "Thou cans't not speak of that thou dost not feel." If the Friar were young, in love, just married, had just killed a man and been banished, then Romeo feels he might have a right to talk. But, Romeo also feels sure the Friar would not talk; instead he would tear his hair and fall to the ground. So saying, Romeo does throw himself to the ground in a frenzy of despair, "Taking the measure of an unmade grave."

COMMENT: Romeo's grief, in its wildness and despera-tion, is much like Juliet's. His speech, like hers, echoes with doom hanging in the often repeated word "banished." Like her, he is so beside himself with misery that he feels exile is death, and he even starts invoking death. Since the holy Friar is the opposite of the earthy, licentious Nurse, he tries to suppress the overwhelming emotions of Romeo by being direct, optimistic, and philosophical—instead of indulging in emotional display by deceitfulness, pessimism, and sen-timent. His effect on Romeo is similar to the Nurse's effect on Juliet: both are goaded to an even more frantic distraction of grief. Romeo finally collapses on the floor.

The parallelism of this scene and the previous one is deliberate. It shows how similar are the passions of the lovers for each other. By contrasting the Nurse and the Friar, Shakespeare has made it clear that adults of the most widely differing temperaments and characteristics cannot under-stand this passion of young love. Whether self-indulgent or philosophical, old age is incapable of comprehension or even proper sympathy in this case. Romeo goes so far as to tell the Friar this. Again, the passion of love is kept aloft—isolated from age, from being temperate, and in fact, from the play itself.

The aloneness of the lovers is crystal clear. It is love alone that can direct their actions.

As Romeo throws himself to the floor in despair, there is a knocking at the Friar's door. The Friar is concerned at the idea of the young exile being discov-ered. He tells Romeo to get hold of himself and hide before he is found. Romeo refuses, saying that if his love hides him then he will be hidden. When the Friar finally gives up and asks who is there, we hear with relief the voice of the Nurse, saying that she comes on an errand for Juliet. The Friar is as relieved as the audience, and lets the Nurse enter. When she sees Romeo, for whom she is searching, lying on the ground in a fit of distracted grief, she declares that her mistress is in the same pitiful state, "weeping and blubbering." She tells Romeo that for Juliet's sake he must stand up like a man. To this persuasion Romeo responds and recovers himself. His first words are of Juliet. Does she think he is a murderer now that he has killed her cousin? Where is she? How is she? What is she thinking? The Nurse answers that Juliet only cries, falls on her bed, and calls out first Tybalt's name, then Romeo's. Romeo is afraid that his name can only mean death to his young wife. He draws his sword, and is ready to plunge it into whatever part of his body houses his own name.

COMMENT: Romeo is still distraught, and he responds to the Nurse's indirect answer just as Juliet did: with a fervor of unhappiness and even an effort to kill himself. The Nurse is again savoring every drop of emotion that can be wrung from the scene, and again she is unintentionally cruel.

Seeing Romeo draw his sword is too much for the kind Friar. He jumps to prevent the act, and in doing so lets loose a torrent of invective at such impetuosity, and, as it seems to him, lack of maturity in Romeo. "Art thou a man?" he asks. Romeo's form is a man's but his tears have been those of a woman and his acts those of a wild beast. The Friar is amazed; he had thought Romeo's disposition was "better temper'd," that is, more moderate. So Romeo has killed Tybalt; does he now want to kill himself, and by doing so, kill Juliet too? The Friar declares that Romeo is shaming his own shape, love, and wit. When the Friar's speech reaches this point, his anger begins to subside and the philoso-phy he has been wanting to encourage replaces it. The Friar's language and the structure of his speech become more formal. Using the three aspects of shape, love, and wit, he cautions Romeo. The misuse of these three things in a man changes his shape into mere wax, lacking in manliness; his love into a lie that can only kill itself; and his wit into a blaze of ignorance. Romeo has been doing this to himself. But the Friar encourages his young friend also, reminding him to be happy: for Juliet is alive; Romeo himself, instead of being dead by Tybalt's sword has killed his would-be killer; and the law that would have had him executed has softened and only exiled him. The Friar sees all this as a "pack of blessings," which Romeo mistakenly ignores. He warmly advises the young lover to go to his new wife, to comfort her, and only to be cautious and leave for the town of Mantua early enough to escape detection. Turning to the Nurse, the Friar sends her back to Juliet with the news that "Romeo is coming." The Nurse praises the Friar's good advice, and the Friar tells Romeo that he will find a time when he can joyfully call him back to a reconciled family, his marriage with Juliet, and a pardon from the Prince. The Nurse promises to deliver her message. Romeo, completely restored at the prospect of seeing Juliet, tells the Nurse that Juliet should prepare to "chide" him. He accepts the ring his beloved has sent, and as the Nurse bustles out, Romeo's "comfort is revived" by it. The Friar, feeling his old genial self again, says goodbye to Romeo, and adds his warning that Romeo take care when leaving Verona. The Friar will keep him posted as to what is happening in his absence. Romeo, who values the Friar highly, leaves to go to his bride, saying, "But that a joy past joy calls out on me, / It were a grief so brief to part with thee."

COMMENT: The disparity between youth and age is again emphasized by the Friar's long philosophical speech in which he advises Romeo to be careful and moderate. It is cautiously worded and formal. Even the Friar's initial anger is expressed in clear parallels and comparisons, and all his wisdom comes from temperance. He scolds Romeo for not being himself temperate, for the good Friar does not understand that being temperate is incompatible with Romeo's whole state of being at present. But it is not these balanced phrases about shape, love, and wit that cause the rise in Romeo's spirits. Instead it is the Friar's urging that he go to Juliet immediately that prompts Romeo to regain himself. The threat of the feud and the sentence of exile are a heavy reminder in the Friar's warnings. The audience hears them, even if Romeo, in his joy, seems oblivious. When Romeo receives the ring, the scene comes full circle with its companion scene, in which Juliet sends the ring, and we look forward to the joyful, but secret consummation of the marriage.

SUMMARY: This scene has directly paralleled the preceding one, has completed the preparations for the marriage night, and has heightened the foreboding tragedy by showing us Romeo's response to it. The Nurse and the Friar have been contrasted, and together they illustrate the incompatibility and lack of understanding between old age and youth. The impossibility of any meetings of the mind between the lovers and their confidants is clear, and the plot rushes forward as impetuously as the lovers themselves.

Act III: Scene iv

Abruptly we find ourselves at the Capulet house, where Lord and Lady Capulet are talking to Paris about his proposal of marriage to Juliet. Capulet explains that, due to the misfortune of Tybalt's death, they have had no time to pursue the matter of Juliet's marriage. She and her parents loved Tybalt, and Capulet sighs philosophically, saying "Well, we were born to die." Juliet will not be down tonight, and Lord and Lady Capulet themselves would have been in bed by now, if it were not for their visit with Paris. Paris is sympathetic to these things, and prepares to take his leave. Lady Capulet promises to speak to her daughter about this marriage tomorrow, but her husband is even more anxious to seal the match. He breaks in, saying that he feels he is on firm ground in promising Juliet's assent to the proposal: "I think she will be ruled/ In all respects by me." He is sure

that Juliet will do as he tells her. "Turning to his wife, he tells Lady Capulet to go to Juliet tonight, immediately, after Paris leaves, and tell her that Paris loves her and that she is to marry him.

COMMENT: Lord Capulet speaks in his usual relaxed way, but his attitude toward the proposed marriage has changed greatly. Whereas before he emphasized Juliet's youth and suggested that Paris wait a few years, but left the final word to his prized daughter, he now feels just the opposite. He wants this marriage to take place as soon as possible. He will tell Juliet she is getting married, not ask her opinion of the matter. He even calls Paris "my son," being so sure that his daughter will oblige him. This is not incompatible with his former characterization. Throughout the scenes in which he appears, and especially at his own party where he bosses the servants and scolds Tybalt for his outburst, he has shown himself to be conscious and proud of his role as lord of the household. He likes to think of himself as genial, liberal, and kindly, and he truly loves his daughter, for he first says that she alone can make the decision. But actually he allows no opposition to his will, and since he feels sure he knows what is best for his daughter, he now promises for her. There is some psychological justification, also, for his change of heart. More feuding has added to the old disfavor of his family among the people of Verona, and his own Tybalt has killed a relative of the Prince. This is the apt and politic time for Capulet to restore his good name by marrying his only daughter to another of the Prince's kinsmen. Paris is a good match besides, being both noble and rich.

Lord Capulet is anxious to have the marriage as soon as the proper time for grief has elapsed. He settles on Thursday, three days from now, and hopes that Paris will approve of this haste. In view of Tybalt's recent death, and so that no one will think his own family didn't love him, the wedding will be kept small and sober, with only a few guests. Paris agrees to all this readily; for him, tomorrow would not be too soon. Everything settled, Capulet calls for a servant to light his way to bed and tells his wife to give Juliet the news and prepare her for the marriage. With a comment that it is so late it might even be called early morning, he bids "Goodnight."

COMMENT: Our impression of Lord Capulet's haste is reinforced, and this, added to the shortness of the scene, strengthens our own feeling of the speed of the plot. There is added irony in the fact that we know Juliet is married already. She is not mourning for Tybalt, as her parents suppose, nor is she expecting such news as this. She is with her new husband now. Capulet's last remark about whether to call the time late night or early morning leads directly and ironically to the next scene, where the parting couple do call it early, and feel it to be too early to part.

SUMMARY: This short, quick scene, falling as it does between the preparations for the lovers' wedding night and their leave-taking after their night together, has more than one effect:

1. It enhances the speed of the action, and more importantly, our feeling of the necessity for speed, by setting a wedding date only three days off.

2. It strikes us with the bitter irony of preparing for a marriage when we know that a particularly beautiful one has already taken place, and is now being consummated. Romeo's banishment is tragic news, but it is an irony of fate that the threat of this other marriage is partially caused by the same incident.

3. We are impressed more strongly than ever with the doom that overhangs the love of Romeo and Juliet.

Act III: Scene v

It is Capulet's orchard at night. Again we find Juliet high aloft on her balcony, with the light from the room behind her setting her off. But this time, Romeo is not below her; he stands with her on the balcony. They have spent one glorious night together, but the time has come for them to part, and for Romeo to go into exile. As the scene opens, Romeo has apparently begun to take his leave, and the first words we hear are Juliet's "Wilt thou be gone? It is not yet near day." The lovers have heard a bird singing. Juliet says it is the nightingale, a bird known for serenading in the night. She denies that it is the lark, a bird which sings at the break of day, and insists sweetly on the fact that there is a nightingale in her garden who sings each night from a certain tree, saying it was his call they heard. She wants Romeo to believe her so he will not leave yet. But Romeo knows "It was the lark, the herald of the morn," and he points to the malicious light that is beginning to cut through the clouds in the east, where the sun will rise. "Night's candles are burnt out," he says, "and jocund [jolly] day/ stands tiptoe on the misty mountain tops:/ I must be gone and live, or stay and die." Despite his consciousness of the anguish of departure and the sure death that will find him if he stays, Romeo's images are permeated with the joy of the night he has just spent. Juliet refuses to recognize what she knows to be true. She hopefully insists that the light is a meteor sent as a torch to guide Romeo to Mantua, and that he can linger still a while longer.

COMMENT: We have waited for this scene with high anticipation, through the past three scenes; to have it begin with the parting of the lovers, however ecstatic, increases the sense of joy as being fleeting, and of the need for haste. The orchard we connect vividly with the first sweet wooing and parting of the lovers, only one night previous, and it is the perfect place for this scene. Perfect, also, is the vision of Romeo and Juliet, now married in soul and in body, standing together on the lighted balcony, where before they were separate. The images of night and darkness as being welcome and joyful, and of the light of day as bringing threats of separation, of making dim the light of love that glows brightly at night, are more fully presented than ever. The bird they love sings at night, the light of dawn is malicious, and the meteor, mentioned by Juliet, is like an image of their love: a miraculous and sudden brilliance in the dark heavens that dies out too soon.

Romeo is vulnerable to the persuasions of his beloved. He will stay and be put to death if she wishes. He will say that the grey of dawn is only a reflection of the moon (Cynthia), and that the calling of that bird in the sky is not that of the lark. "I have more care to stay than will to go" he says, and he welcomes death because Juliet seems to prefer it to parting. But Juliet does not want him to die, and she immediately changes her tune, says that it is day, and that he must leave quickly. That bird is the lark, but instead of making "sweet division"— that is, singing a series of short lyric notes instead of one long one—its song seems to her to be "harsh discords," because it pronounces the "division" of herself from Romeo. As the lark "hunts up" the day, that is, arouses it, so it hunts Romeo out of town and away from her. The light of dawn increases as she speaks, and she wails, "O now be gone; more light and light it grows." Romeo answers, "More light and light, more dark and dark our woes!" The Nurse entering Juliet's room (from which they are curtained off as they stand on the balcony), interrupts gruffly with "Madam." She warns that Juliet's mother is coming to her room, and adds, "The day is broke; be wary, look about." Juliet can only answer in dismay, "Then window, let day in, and let life out." Romeo kisses her, and climbs down from the balcony.

COMMENT: That Romeo would stay and die if Juliet preferred, we must believe. He has just spent a night of the highest joy he has ever known, and even death seems slight beside it, especially if Juliet prefers it. But she hopes for more such joy, and wants to live. Only daylight brings with it cruel revealing lights that force unpleasant realities of these lovers, who are infused with the darkness of their night together, and the brightness of their love. The most unpleasant reality is their parting. As the light increases, the blackness of the pain of parting to which they must submit also increases. They feel this strongly, and so hate the light, as is clear in Juliet's outpourings against the lark, and in Romeo's cry of their darkening woe. The cruel reality of day and the necessity for caution is finally brought home to them by the Nurse. She represents to the lovers the lack of understanding of the outside world, the reality of the baser side of life, and old age which forever advises caution. Her voice and words grate across their duet unpleasantly, but seal the facts they must face in the hated daylight. She begins the lovers' leavetaking.

The benevolence of night and the menace of light is carried still further in both the images of speech and the actions of the lovers. Daylight not only means darkening woe, but, as we see in Juliet's last words, death. The lovers live in darkness; the day and the parting seem to make the life of their love impossible, seem to threaten to replace their love in darkness with the eternal darkness of death. The imagery of light and dark, so played upon in their courting, has begun to take shape and affect the action. Evil, fate, the realities and cautions of old age, and the outside world are all becoming connected with the daytime. Love is possible only at night and stands opposed to all other elements in the play.

The lovers part. Juliet, calling to her "love-lord" and "husband-friend" begs that she hear often from him, for in the space of a minute of their separation, days will seem to pass. Romeo assures her that he will let no chance of sending her news escape him. He is sure they will be together again, to talk over joyfully the pains of their separation. But even as he says this, Juliet is startled by what seems an evil vision. As she looks down at him in the grey light below, he seems to resemble a corpse, and she cries: "O God! I have an ill-divining soul:/ Methinks I see thee, now thou art below,/ As one dead at the bottom of a tomb." Romeo, seeing her pallor, has the same sensation, but comforts her by saying, "Dry sorrow drinks our blood," meaning that their sadness at parting has drawn the blood from their faces. Calling "Adieu," he leaves quickly.

COMMENT: This final parting is full of ill-omen. The lovers' promises to send messages back and forth are, we know if we have read the play before, somewhat ironic. It is the failure of a message to reach its destination that precipitates their tragedy. The mutual vision of the lovers, seeing each other dead and cold in a tomb, is starkly prophetic. That is exactly how and when they will meet again.

As Romeo disappears into the growing morning, Juliet speaks of fortune, and hopes it will be as fickle as men say it is, for then it will turn the misfortune of this parting back to good fortune, and the lovers will be together again. Just then, Lady Capulet enters, and Juliet, wondering what unusual happening causes her mother to be up this late or to have arisen this early, goes in to her. Seeing her daughter's tear stained face, Lady Capulet expresses surprise. Juliet says she is not feeling well, but the Lady, assuming the tears have been shed over Tybalt's death, chides her daughter. Even if she washed her cousin's grave with tears, she could not make him alive, and while much grief indicates great love, too much grieving is a sign of stupidity. Juliet takes up this cue as a way to keep her secret from her mother and still not have to restrain her own excessive feeling of grief at parting from Romeo. She speaks on two levels, and referring within herself to Romeo, she says, "Yet let me weep for such a feeling loss." Trying to console her daughter, Lady Capulet says she should try to feel her friendship for Tybalt, not her loss. If Juliet must cry, it should be over the fact that the man who killed Tybalt is alive. Juliet senses fully the irony of this conversation, and whispers to herself that she pardons that man, and yet no man gives her more grief. Overhearing the last of this, the Lady says that of course Juliet grieves that the murderer lives, to which Juliet replies ironically that her grief is that he lives too far from her hands. Then, fearing that she will be discovered in her word-tricks, she adds what her mother assumed she meant, that she wants vengeance. To soothe the girl, Lady Capulet promises to send someone to Mantua to poison Romeo. At this Juliet is frightened, but replies with great presence of mind, that if this is to be done, she must "temper" the poison. She means, of course, not to make it stronger, but to make it completely ineffectual. She goes so far as to say that she can't bear to hear Romeo named, when she cannot even go to him and "Wreak the love I bore my cousin Tybalt/ Upon his body." She truly means "love" but again her mother assumes she means revenge. But the Lady's visit has another purpose; she changes the subject, saying she brings "joyful tidings," and Juliet only answers that she needs some joyous news.

COMMENT: Juliet's wondering as to why her mother comes so early or late hearkens back to Capulet's last words at the end of the scene in which he promised Juliet in marriage to Paris, and made plans for a quick wedding. So we are reminded of Lady Capulet's errand, and the irony of it hangs like a sword over the already ironic scene. Juliet is still in great sorrow for Romeo. The cleverness with which she covers over the tears she cannot hold back, attributing them to Tybalt's death and convincing her own mother, makes us again aware of how rapidly she is becoming an adult and a woman. The double meaning of all her words about Romeo keeps our interest, and both Juliet and the audience take a certain pleasure in this bitter audacity. The scene is a study in dramatic irony. Even the reference to poison is, as we will discover, ironic and foreboding.

Lady Capulet tells Juliet that her father, out of concern for her grief, has arranged for her an especially happy day in the near future. On Thursday she is to marry the gallant young nobleman, Paris. Juliet retorts abruptly that Paris will not make her into a joyful bride, then covers this over by protesting at this haste in the midst of Tybalt's loss, and at being married without even being courted. She swears she will not marry, and to make her mother feel the finality of this as well as to give vent to her feelings, she swears she'll first marry Romeo (whom they know she hates). At this point, Lord Capulet comes himself, with the Nurse, to see how his daughter responds. He is in high spirits, and makes jokes about the dew, the rain, the shower of tears his daughter has cried out. He compares Juliet to a ship in the midst of a storm, shaking her own body with winds of sighing and tides of crying. He turns to ask his wife if she has delivered "our decree," and Lady Capulet tells him Juliet refuses, adding "I would the fool were married to her grave." Capulet can't believe his ears, and asks if Juliet is not thankful, proud, and blessed to be given such a husband. Juliet answers that she is not proud of what she hates, but she is thankful to her parents even for this hateful thing they have done out of love for her. Capulet is extremely irritated. He calls his daughter's answer "chop-logic," that is, a mere bargaining with twisted logic. He imitates her manner offensively. Growing more infuriated as he speaks, the Lord says "Thank me no thankings, nor proud me no prouds," meaning he will have none of either. Ranting, he declares in vivid language that Juliet will dress and get herself to Paris at the church on Thursday, or he will drag her there. By this time he is beside himself with rage at being opposed by Juliet, and referring to her great pallor, he calls her a waxy-faced "baggage," another word for a slut. At this, both Juliet and her mother call out in protest, but Capulet is going full blast. He repeats his demand that Juliet marry on Thursday, making it an ultimatum by adding that if she doesn't, he'll never look at her again. He wants no answers; in his rage his fingers itch to slap his daughter, and he calls her a curse on his life.

COMMENT: Lady Capulet sincerely believes she is bringing happy news. Indeed, we of the audience have every reason to believe that Paris would, under other circumstances, have made an excellent, loving husband for Juliet. But we share with Juliet the irony of this "happiness" she is offered. She is shocked, and her abrupt refusal is understandable, but with an adult instinct for self-preservation she covers her feelings quickly, using more words of double meaning. Her mother's remark in response to this refusal that she'd rather have Juliet "married to her grave" rings not only an ironic, but a fateful tone. Part of the irony of this

scene has been its comparative calmness, and all these layers of irony are finally broken by Lord Capulet's utter fury. This aspect of his temperament has been established in a milder way by his outburst when Tybalt began to start a fight at the Capulet feast. We now see Capulet in full. He is old, testy, and not to be crossed. Capulet is lenient only when it suits him. We have seen that he has his reasons for wanting this marriage immediately, and it does not suit him to be lenient now. His anger, expressed as always in his loose, colorful, and direct language, has been prepared for throughout the scenes in which he has appeared.

Lady Capulet and Juliet can offer no retort to the Lord's stream of invective. It is the Nurse who breaks in and tells him he must blame himself for so losing his temper. He snaps back sarcastically, suggesting that "my lady wisdom" save her tongue for gossiping. The Nurse persists, and when Capulet calls her a "mumbling fool," Lady Capulet at last finds words. "You are too hot," she says. His anger subsiding only a bit, the Lord finds he must defend his rashness. He says he has thought much about whom he will match with his only daughter, and now he has found the perfect match, a man against whom no objections can be made. After all this, he cannot abide his daughter, "wretched, puling fool," having the nerve and stupidity to say no. With menace, but comparative calm, he delivers his last word: Juliet may think it over, and if by Thursday she still refuses to marry, he will turn her out of house and home forever, and let her "Hang, beg, starve, die in the streets." This is his final warning, and he leaves.

COMMENT: It is significant that only the realistic and plain spoken old Nurse, who is surely the gossip Capulet calls her, can interrupt his ranting, and does so to accuse the Lord straight-out of being unfair. Even though he is annoyed at this, Capulet senses her justice (the Nurse is older than he) and calms down enough to explain his anger, and to deliver with more deliberation his ultimatum. His speech retains its vigor and slanginess, but it is not so vulgar. By the time he exits, we firmly believe that he has set his aging mind on this, and will not be swayed. How his already secretly married daughter will manage, we cannot think.

Juliet begs for pity first from the clouds, then from her mother. If the marriage cannot be delayed for a month or a week, Juliet asks that they "make the bridal bed in that dim monument where Tybalt lies." But Lady Capulet refuses even to discuss the matter, and leaves as abruptly as her husband did. Clearly, the marriage must be prevented. Juliet is caught; her husband is alive on earth, and her religious faith forbids her to have two husbands. She cannot break such a stern law of the Church, but the only way she can see of preventing such a sin is for Romeo himself to die, leave earth, and go to heaven. The misery of such a prospect, and indeed of all that lies before Juliet, makes her turn and beg for comfort from her Nurse. The Nurse can only offer one solution. Since Romeo is banished, it is unlikely that he would return to challenge Juliet's marriage to Paris, and even if he dared, he could not do it openly. Considering this, the Nurse gently advises her mistress to marry Paris. Hoping to win Juliet to this, she begins to extol Paris's virtues, calling him an eagle; he is so quick and handsome. She says Romeo is a "dishclout," meaning he can't compare with Paris, and that this second marriage will be better than the first. Even if Juliet doesn't agree to this comparison of the two, the Nurse thinks Romeo is as good as dead, being permanently absent, and therefore he is of no use to Juliet. Juliet, astounded, asks the Nurse if she means this. The Nurse curses herself if she doesn't. Juliet's answer, "Amen," indicates that she too curses the Nurse for these thoughts. But she only says mildly that she is comforted, and that she will now go alone to Friar Laurence, where she will make her confession to having displeased her father. The Nurse goes to tell Lady Capulet this encouraging news. The moment she is out of sight, Juliet bursts forth, "Ancient damnation! O most wicked fiend." She curses the Nurse furiously, and cannot even decide whether the Nurse sins more in suggesting that she have two husbands, or in hypocritically degrading the Romeo she has so often highly praised. She severs herself forever from the Nurse: "Go counsellor;/ Thou and my bosom henceforth shall be twain." She resolves to go to the Friar for advice, and if he can give none, to find the strength to die.

COMMENT: Juliet is truly caught between heaven and earth. All her choices offer only evil and misery. She even goes so far as to ask to be put in the tomb with Tybalt rather than marry on Thursday. She does not know how close this request comes to what actually will occur. When she goes to her old Nurse for comfort, that Nurse, who truly cares for her mistress, does her best. But she sees the problem in a different light, and makes a very base, unpleasantly realistic response. To her, hypocrisy and bigamy are not sins, but part of everyday life. She sincerely and openly recommends what seems to her the only natural course, the only path to a happy life. This is not only old age speaking; the Nurse's opinion on the problem affirms life as she sees it, and as we know it in her by her vigor: long, pleasurable, and without conscience. To Juliet, such an attitude is horrid and repugnant beyond comprehension. She is young, fervently in love, and of a religious and idealistic mind. She would no sooner be unfaithful to her husband than she would break the decrees of heaven. The Nurse's way seems to offer not a pleasant and easy life, but misery, self-hatred, and torture. So she curses her old confidante and cuts her off, although

her canny and adult instinct for self-preservation allows her to mask her response with hypocrisy. She is now alienated from all the world but her love, Romeo, and her religion, represented by the Friar. This alienation, coupled with her predicament and the passion of a young girl in love with all the depth of her self and her imagination, ends the scene on a fierce, ominous note. We believe she will find the strength to die, if the Friar cannot help her.

SUMMARY: The scene is a long and complex one, but through it are established the following:

1. The images of love-provoking night and love-dispelling day have gathered potency and have begun even to effect the action. Day has come to mean all the harsh reality, old age, and outside world which threaten the lovers. Day looms almost as large as the fate which propels the action. Even love, although it prospers only at night, gives, by its impetuosity, greater speed to the fateful direction of the plot.

2. Accident and circumstance, in the form of the double killing of Mercutio and Tybalt, have already put great opposition in the lovers' way by resulting in the banishment of Romeo. They now add another stumbling-block: Lord Capulet's unrelenting insistence on Juliet's immediate marriage to Paris. This insistence not only puts another obstacle before the lovers, but adds a sense of the necessity of still greater speed. In these many repercussions, we see clearly that the duels at the beginning of the act were fateful.

3. The characters of Lord Capulet and the Nurse are rounded out, and are now totally alien to Juliet. She herself shows new strength and growth in her ironic handling of her own grief when faced with her mother and in the subtle retraction by which she pretends to agree with the Nurse. There is a female capacity for necessary deception here, but it leaves her completely alone. She has no one with whom to share secrets, and she must stand on her own two feet.

4. Irony plays a larger part than ever, as the plot becomes more complicated and the strands of action interweave.

The Act itself has reached its culmination. The play's initial turn to tragedy, with the deaths of Mercutio and Tybalt, took place in the first scene. The result for the two lovers was Romeo's exile and a repetition of the threat of the feud. Romeo and Juliet's grief at this banishment and their anticipation of the night together have been fully realized in their loving leave-taking. The feud asserts itself again as the reason for Capulet's insistence on Juliet's marrying Paris. The act closes with Romeo off alone in Mantua, Juliet an alien in her own house, and the additional obstacle of another marriage threatening the lovers.

Act IV: Scene i

The act opens, as we might have expected, in Friar Laurence's cell. But it is Paris, not Juliet, who is visiting the good Friar. Apparently, Paris has asked him to perform the coming marriage between himself and Juliet. The Friar realizes as fully as we do the dangerous implications of such a union. His first words are full of perplexity and hesitation: "On Thursday, sir? the time is very short." Paris answers that this speed is Capulet's wish, and that he, too, is anxious to marry soon. The Friar then raises the objection that Juliet has not yet given her consent, but Paris can explain that also. He did not wish to speak of love in a house full of grief, and Lord Capulet urges the speedy marriage specifically so that his daughter will not mourn herself into oblivion over Tybalt. The Friar mutters to himself that he wishes he could think of a reason that he was free to tell, which would explain why this marriage should be put off.

COMMENT: The Friar, who has all along objected to hastiness as immoderate, now finds himself objecting again. This time, however, he has a reason: the completed marriage of Romeo and Juliet, about which he is not at liberty to speak. So he hesitates, and defers decision. In this hesitation, we begin to see the Friar's fault. Perhaps he should go directly to Capulet and tell him outright of the marriage. Once again, the speed of the action appears as inevitable and fateful.

At this point, Juliet arrives at the cell. Paris greets her as "my lady and my wife," and although Juliet must be taken aback to see him, she answers demurely, "That may be, sir, when I may be wife." Paris says she shall be his wife, as of Thursday, to which Juliet makes a noncommittal, but assenting, reply. Their conversation proceeds in single-line remarks and replies. Paris presses her to declare her love for him, but she sidesteps his efforts with coy modesty. Paris comments that her face is abused with tears, and she answers that her face was bad enough before the tears. When he admonishes her not to slander her face, for it is now his, she only replies cryptically that perhaps it is his; at any rate, it is not hers. What she means is that it belongs to Romeo. To escape further conversation, she turns to the Friar and asks if she may see him now or should she come later? The Friar asks Paris to leave them alone and he does so, but not before promising to come for Juliet early Thursday and taking a parting kiss as he goes. When she is alone with the Friar at last, Juliet's composure leaves her, and she breaks into cries of grief. The Friar tries to comfort her, saying that he knows what has happened, and that it strains his wits to fully grasp the awfulness of it. Juliet wants only to know how to prevent the marriage. If the Friar has no answer, she only asks his blessing on her suicide. Her hand and heart have been joined to Romeo's in holy wedlock, as the Friar knows. Before her hand could clasp another's or her heart perform such treachery as another marriage, she would use her dagger to end the life in both hand and heart. Can the Friar restore her to true honor? She urges him to answer, for if he cannot, she will kill herself.

COMMENT: The reserve and caution with which Juliet responds to Paris is commendable. She does not let him think her unwilling, lest he go to question her father; nor is she ever in the smallest gesture or word untrue to Romeo. Paris exerts some degree of pressure on her, calling her his love, and kissing her. It is not surprising that she loses all control as soon as she is alone with the Friar. Her speech deals with the hands and heart by which she pledged herself to Romeo, but there are no pretty images here. Her language is plain, for she is in deadly earnest, and would willingly kill herself with a dagger if there were no help for this situation. She is impassioned with grief now, and is even more impetuous than before. Nor is it the last time we will see her ominous dagger.

The Friar quiets her, for he sees some hope. It is a desperate hope, but in the face of the threat of another marriage, better than none. If Juliet is desperate enough to kill herself, perhaps she will be willing to undergo something very close to death, but not death itself, which could free her from her shame. Juliet is all eagerness, declaring she would jump off a battlement, go among thieves and serpents, be chained among bears, and even allow herself to be shut into a sepulchre of the dead (a "charnel-house"). On this last her headstrong imagination catches, for it holds the greatest horror. She says she would let herself be covered with stinking, rattling, yellow bones, or even hide in the shroud of a newly dead man. She has trembled at hearing her own descriptions, but she would do any of these, "Without fear or doubt, To live an unstain'd wife" to Romeo.

COMMENT: The Friar's yet unspoken plan, which offers some hope for Juliet to live and be true to her lover, involves undergoing something similar to death. Juliet, who loves Romeo with the full force of her being, seizes on even the faintest hope. Her charged imagination runs riot among all the horrors she can conceive that she would endure for the sake of this hope. She dwells longest on going into a house of the dead, and associating with the corpses there. What she does not know is that something of exactly this nature will be required of her. She will have to seem to die, and be buried, in order to live.

The Friar, convinced by Juliet's desperation that she has the strength to do this, begins slowly to outline his plan. She is to go home, act cheerful, and pretend to agree to the marriage. Tomorrow night, Wednesday, the night before the wedding, she is to get into bed, and drink the liquid from a small vial or container which the Friar will give her. She will feel her veins grow cold, and her pulse slow to a standstill. She will sleep—cold, pale, and without breath—and it will be a sleep "Like death, when he shuts up the day of life," stiff and corpse-like. This will last forty-two hours, and then she will awaken pleasantly. The bridegroom, in the meantime, will find her and think her dead; and as is customary, she will be placed in full dress on an open bier or platform, and taken to the Capulet family tomb. While this happens, the Friar will send letters to Romeo explaining it all. Romeo will come to Verona and meet the Friar; and at the time that Juliet awakens they will be standing watching her in the tomb. Then Romeo will take Juliet with him to Mantua, and she will be free from shame. The Friar only hopes she will not lose her valor and be afraid to take the drug. Juliet's response is, "Give me, give me!" The Friar gives her the little flask and wishes her well, saying he will send to Romeo immediately. "Love give me strength! and strength shall help afford," are Juliet's words as she leaves the Friar's cell.

COMMENT: We know the Friar is a man educated in the lore of herbs and potions. We scarcely doubt that this liquid of his will perform as he says it will. As always, the Friar's tone is rational and cautious. He is doing his best to help the young girl he has secretly married. And yet the prospect of this temporary death is chilling, like a wind foreboding evil. It is too much like real death, of which there has been sufficient warning, and we wonder if all this connivance and deceit are necessary. The audience, along with Juliet, accepts the good man's plan, but not without a premonition of dread and a shudder.

SUMMARY: The necessity for some quick action is apparent, as the marriage of Juliet to Paris has already reached the stage of concrete preparations for the ceremony. Juliet threatens to kill herself, and later imagines vividly all the horrors of a tomb, full of rotting bodies. Finally, the only hope lies in a kind of temporary death, induced by the Friar's drug. The theme of death, which has been ominously hinted at in earlier scenes, is now presented fully and occupies an entire scene. The lovers' only hope lies in death of a temporary nature. This brings to mind how, throughout the play, night and darkness, which are parallel to death, have been the lovers' only source of joy.

Act IV: Scene ii

The scene is the Capulet house, and the mood is merry, in contrast to the previous one. Capulet sends out one servant with a list of guests to be invited to the wedding feast. Another servant he sends to fetch twenty cooks, and the servant promises to bring back only cooks who enjoy licking their own food from their fingers. The Nurse tells Capulet that Juliet is with the Friar, and he comments that he hopes the visit will do his peevish, self-willed daughter some good. Juliet appears at that moment, and the Nurse notices that she looks merry. "How now, my headstrong! where have you been gadding?" calls her father in jolly tones. Juliet answers that she has repented her opposition to him and has been told by the Friar to beg her father's pardon. She does so now with a nice gesture. At this Lord Capulet is delighted, sends out a servant to tell Paris, and decides to hold the wedding tomorrow, Wednesday, instead of Thursday, as was planned.

COMMENT: The scene does seem bustling and gay, but our knowledge of the situation, the desperate plan under way, and Juliet's deception, dim the atmosphere. Capulet, who loves his daughter, is genuinely and heartily glad to see her, and even teases her at being willful before he knows for sure that she has changed her mind to suit his will. When she apologizes, he is so pleased that he makes plans to have the wedding a day earlier. At this, we feel a certain dread, knowing the exactness of the Friar's timing.

Juliet tells her father how she met Paris at the Friar's and gave him as much love as her modesty would allow. Capulet is even more pleased. Now he wants Paris brought to him, and praises the Friar for having so well directed his daughter. Juliet goes off with the Nurse to prepare clothing for the wedding. When Lady Capulet protests that they cannot be ready by tomorrow, Capulet says he'll handle things. His wife may go help Juliet; he intends to stay up all night and even play housewife. He calls for a servant, then realizing that they are all running errands he decides to go himself to see Paris and prepare him for the wedding. His heart is "wondrous light," now that his wayward Juliet has come back to him.

COMMENT: The light mood continues to be ironical. This happiness which Lord Capulet feels at his daughter's giving in to him is pitiable, in view of what we know is to happen. Moving the marriage up one day is done by the Lord in happy haste. Ironically, this will only hasten Capulet's own grief, and it may have deadly consequences. The speed of the plot has been increased by this whim of old Capulet, and as the action hurries forward, the feeling of fatefulness and evil doom grows with it. Under the surface of this gay interlude, another threat has materialized. Perhaps Juliet, in her great desire to be convincing and so preserve herself for Romeo, has played her part too well.

Act IV: Scene iii

In her bedroom, Juliet and her Nurse have finished preparing the dress she will wear tomorrow. Juliet asks that the Nurse leave her alone tonight; she pleads that she has many prayers ("orisons") to make, so that heaven will forgive the sinfulness she is about to begin. Lady Capulet comes to offer help, but Juliet has nothing more to do. She asks her mother to take the Nurse, who could help the Lady with her own preparations, as Juliet wishes to be alone. Telling the young girl to rest well, the Nurse and Lady Capulet leave.

COMMENT: Juliet has carefully contrived to be alone, as she plans to take the Friar's drug. She will rest more deeply and longer than the Nurse and Lady Capulet suspect.

"God knows when she shall meet again" Juliet says to herself as her Nurse and Mother depart. She faces a great trial, and although she feels alien to them, she is not sure when she will again see any humans at all. Already, fear makes her blood run cold, and she cannot feel the heat of her own life. She is tempted, and starts to call the Nurse back for comfort. But there is nothing the Nurse can do to help: "My dismal scene I needs must act alone." She considers the flask of liquid, "Come vial," and wonders what will happen if the drug does not work. She will not marry, and to assure herself of that she puts her dagger within easy reach. Again she questions, fearfully, whether perhaps the Friar has not given her real poison, to avoid the dishonor that would fall on him if it became known that he had performed her marriage to Romeo. She fears this, but she knows better, for the Friar has always proved himself a holy man.

COMMENT: Juliet has now come face to face with the taking of the potion. She is very much alone. She fears it, for she is about to submit herself to the unknown. Her fear is first, that the liquid will not work, then, that it will work too well. But she masters both these feelings, explaining them away as most unlikely.

Yet another fear occurs to the young girl, the fear that she will wake in the tomb too early, before Romeo comes to "redeem" her. This she accepts as a justified fear, and she begins to imagine herself stifling and suffocating in the foul air of the vault, and dying of slow strangulation before Romeo arrives. And if she doesn't die for lack of air? If she lives, she will find herself in the midst of night, death, and the terror of "an ancient receptacle," containing the bones of ancestors hundreds of years old, "Where bloody Tybalt, yet but green in earth,/ Lies festering in his shroud." This image of decaying flesh brings to her mind a worse terror, that of the undead spirits whom she has heard frequent tombs of the dead. Juliet's imagination races and riots with these dreadful visions, and she sees herself, waking early to hideous odors and "shrieks like mandrakes torn out of the earth." (Mandrakes were roots grown from the bodies of criminals who had been executed and buried; when torn up, they were supposed to omit wild shrieks that would drive insane whoever uprooted them.) Picturing this, she sees herself driven distraught with fear, playing madly with the bones of her ancestors; pulling Tybalt's mangled body from beneath his shroud; and finally, in crazed desperation, knocking out her own brains with some old bone. Wrought to a pitch of terror by her own frightened imaginings, Juliet now thinks she sees Tybalt's ghost vengefully attacking Romeo, his killer. She tries to stop the ghost, she seems to fail, and in her frenzy, she believes Romeo to have been killed. Without another thought, she swallows all the potion and tries to join her Romeo in death, crying, "Romeo, I come! this do I drink to thee." Juliet now falls, senseless, on her bed.

COMMENT: Juliet, overcome with the horrors of waking alone in a death-filled tomb, has finally succeeded in drinking the liquid in which both her hope and her fear lie. Her speech is a series of images increasing steadily in frenzy and horror; finally she envisions the thing she fears most, Romeo's death, and finds in her desire to be with him the strength to drink. That she is able to drink at all is a tribute to her character. Being alive among the dead was the thought that prevented her. Death itself holds no such fears, if in death she joins her love. In drinking the liquid, Juliet believes momentarily that she is joining Romeo in eternity, an idea which is to develop into a major theme. She celebrates this by drinking a toast to her lover. Romeo later makes the same gesture of a toast when, drinking poison, he joins her in death. In a sense, Juliet's taking of the potion is a symbolic suicide. The scene itself abounds with evil omens of death to come. But death is not so bad as living among the dead or as living without love.

Act IV: Scene iv

It is early morning now, and the Capulet household is alive with the bustle of wedding preparations. The Nurse is sent to get spices. Dates and quinces are needed. Capulet is going about, arousing all those not-yet busy, and making sure no cost is spared on the baked meats. The Nurse scolds him playfully, calling him "cot-queen," a derogatory term for a man who is acting as a housewife, and telling him to get some rest. Lord Capulet refuses to sleep, saying he has been up all night before with less reason. Even Lady Capulet is in good spirits, and says his previous all-night vigils were mouse-hunts; that is, chases after women. Capulet only ribs her in turn for being jealous.

COMMENT: The household is yet unaware of what awaits them in Juliet's room. Their gaiety holds much irony for us, especially after the desperate scene just witnessed. The low-life, bawdy jocularity of all three major figures only serves to enhance the difference between them and the lovers, and to rub salt in the wound they have not yet discovered.

Servants go to and fro, one with something the cook needs, one in search of dry logs. Lord Capulet hurries them, and they make jokes for his benefit. He awaits Paris, who will come with the musicians. Presently music is heard, and Capulet calls the Nurse. She must go wake Juliet and dress her up properly, while the Lord chats with the bridegroom. Capulet calls, "Make haste, I say."

COMMENT: Like the previous scene of bustle, this interlude is ironic in its mood. But it serves to mark time, and to create an atmosphere of haste and anticipation. It modulates the pace of the action while increasing our impression of unavoidable and necessary speed. With music, glad cries, and haste, the next scene is ushered in.

Act IV: Scene v

We come, with the Nurse, to Juliet's chamber. Juliet lies hidden from sight on the curtained bed. Calling and scolding cheerfully, the Nurse bustles about, perhaps drawing the curtains from the windows. She believes her mistress is fast asleep in bed, and as the Nurse hurries around she tries to rouse Juliet with cries of, "lamb," "lady," "slug-a-bed," and "bride." She admits that Juliet has need of a bit of sleep now, for surely Paris plans to keep her sleepless these coming nights. Still, she is

surprised that Juliet sleeps so deeply, and finally the Nurse is moved to pull the curtains of the bed apart. There lies Juliet, fully dressed, which seems strange. The Nurse starts to shake her, but the body beneath her hands feels stiff and chill. Horrified, the Nurse wails, "Lady! Lady! Lady!" and "Help, help! my lady's dead," in a crescendo of despair. Lady Capulet, hearing this commotion, comes in quickly to see what is the matter. The Nurse can only point and cry, "O lamentable day!" and "O heavy day!" Seeing for herself how her daughter lies, Lady Capulet moans, "My child, my only life,/ Revive, look up, or I will die with thee," and calls for help. Now comes Lord Capulet. Paris is waiting, and the Lord, annoyed at this delay, has come to see that his daughter come quickly. He is greeted by both his wife and the Nurse, crying the word "dead" over and over. His first reaction is close to anger: "Ha! let me see her. Out, alas!" He feels how cold and stiff she is, and sees how pale, and it seems to him that death has come "like an untimely frost" to this sweet flower. The Lady and the Nurse can say little; they mourn the sadness of this day and time. And for the first time, Capulet himself can find no words, not even a wail, for death "Ties up my tongue."

COMMENT: Juliet is not dead; she sleeps like death. The sleep is totally convincing, and Nurse, mother and father are all stricken. The only words they can find to express their grief are "Dead," "day," and "time" or "untimely." They blame the day and the time, as the lovers have done, for their misfortune. It is not only her death that strikes them, it is the untimeliness of it. It comes too soon, she was too young, too many things awaited her in life, for this to have happened now. In fact, it is the speed of this that shocks them all speechless. The fateful speed that has compelled the action now strikes a blow.

Hurrying in come the Friar and Paris with the bridal musicians. The Friar asks, "Is the bride ready to go to church?" This prompts Capulet to regain his words, She is ready, he says, to go to church and never return. On the eve of the wedding, Death has slept with Paris's bride, and she, the flower, lies deflowered (robbed of her virginity) by death. It is Death who has married Juliet and is now Capulet's son-in-law and heir. Capulet can only die and leave all he has, including life, to Death. Paris, for whom this day promised much, stands bewildered. Lady Capulet now curses the day, this miserable hour in the pilgrimage of time, for having taken her one poor cause for joy out of life. The talkative Nurse finds no coherent thought and can only curse repeatedly the black day, the hateful day. Now Paris finds words: He has been divorced by death and now can only love in death. And again Lord Capulet cries out. His child was his soul; his soul lies martyred, and all joy is dead for him.

COMMENT: There is little differentiation, if any, among the expressions of grief by these very different characters. Their mourning makes one long, repetitive incantation of sorrow. It is more like a chorus than like individual voices, and the chorus comes in response to Lord Capulet's single, distinctive speech on Juliet's marriage to Death. It is as if this speech has summed-up and given expression to all the bitterness and bereavement they feel. They join in chorus to give witness and affirmation to that speech. The chorus emphasizes once again how each person blames the day, the time, the untimeliness, and the speed with which death has come.

This scene and these indistinct, unindividualized expressions of grief will stand in sharp contrast to Romeo's reaction to the same news. The grief of the parents and fiancé is no less real, but its amorphous quality differs greatly from the strength and poetic defiance we will find in the grief of Juliet's husband and lover. The meeting of death and marriage will also grow in meaning as we near the end of the play.

The Friar knows the true state of things, and he only has retained his composure. He interrupts them now, and tries to calm their grief with chiding philosophy, saying, "Peace, ho! for shame! confusion's cure lives not/ In these confusions." He explains that these friends and relatives shared Juliet with heaven, and now heaven has all of her, and keeps her from death by giving her eternal life. This is an honor and a joy far greater than any of them could have offered her, and they are selfish not to be happy for her sake. He adds, "She's not well married that lives married long,/ But she's best married that dies married young." Juliet had once kept rosemary for Romeo (Act II, Scene iv line 225), and we noted then that this evergreen herb, symbolizing eternal life and remembrance, was used at both weddings and funerals. Appropriately, the Friar mentions the herb now, bidding the mourners to put their bridal rosemary around the corpse, dress her in the robes in which her wedding was to be celebrated, and carry her to the church. Juliet indeed seems to have married Death. Capulet adds his directions: everything that was to be used for the wedding festival will now be used for the funeral. The wedding dinner will be a burial feast, the hymns will be dirges, "And all things change them to the contrary." The Friar tells them all to prepare to accompany Juliet's body to the grave and adds his warning: heaven has punished them for something, and they must now stop all disobedience to heaven's will. All leave, except the Nurse, to do the Friar's bidding.

COMMENT: The calm manner of the Friar as he breaks in on the chorus of grief, reminds us of the ironic fact that Juliet is not dead, and that these people grieve for nothing. His consoling words of religious philosophy depict death as a blessing that frees the soul to eternal life. The Friar's comment that the best marriage is that of a girl who dies young is surely descriptive of the marriage of Romeo and Juliet. Their love is such that we cannot picture them having children and growing old together. It is too ecstatic and swift a passion for that, and moves by its own power toward some earlier end. The image of Juliet as married to Death, begun earlier in the scene by Lord Capulet, is picked up by the Friar. The tone is changed from bitterness to celebration—of Juliet's gaining a place in heaven by being Death's bride. As if to emphasize this, she will be mourned and buried in her bridal clothes. We remember how she took the potion in an effort to join her husband and complete her marriage in death. Capulet still feels this reversal, this "contrary" as being cruel, but he concedes. All contraries—death and marriage, love and hate—seem to be growing together.

As the mourners go to church, the musicians remain behind, preparing to leave also. Most likely they are the same musicians who played at Capulet's party, when Paris was to consider his proposed bride, and when Romeo and Juliet fell in love. The Nurse tells them to pack up their instruments, commenting how pitiful is the state of things, and goes herself to mourn. Peter, one of Capulet's servants, comes in. He asks for the song "Heart's ease" to ease his heart, for, he says, his heart itself is playing the tune, "My heart is full of woe." Peter is sad, but it is the musicians who feel that music would be inappropriate. Yet gaiety gets the best of them, and instead of making music, they exchange witticisms about music and the money they hope to earn by it. Finally, they go off, planning to wait until the mourners return, so that they may have a free dinner.

COMMENT: This scene is short and light-hearted, giving comic relief, that is, a chance to rest from sorrow and laugh a bit, to the audience. We do not feel that the scoffers are profane, for we know Juliet is not really dead. The real gaiety here mocks the Friar's philosophic happiness and mocks also the previous scenes when merriment was tinged with irony. We have been given a breather before the long, tragic ascent of the next act.

SUMMARY: This is one of the few scenes in the play devoted to outsiders rather than to the lovers. From one point of view, it shows how the adult world reacts to grief: not individually, nor with any particular distinction of will and imagination, but in a collective chorus of sorrow. At the same time, the theme of love in death and marriage to death, which relates directly to the lovers, is explored. In this way the lovers, their predicament, and their images are kept uppermost in our minds.

This act has been a short one, and full of interludes. It has served to increase our sense of impending doom by concentrating on the proposed marriage of Paris to Juliet, and by the ruse to avoid this marriage, which involves a temporary death on Juliet's part. The deathsleep gives full play to imaginings of the horror of the grave and to the grief of the family. The speed of the action has been increased by the ironic interludes, by moving up the day of the wedding, and by strengthening our own feeling that all speed is necessary to escape the threat that hangs over the lovers. By now, the play is moving at a reckless pace.

Act V: Scene i

The scene is Mantua, where Romeo is in exile. Surprisingly, he is in a light-hearted, elevated frame of mind. If he may trust the flattery of dreams, joyful news must be coming to him. He relates his dream: "I dreamt my lady came and found me dead." Juliet came to him and revived him by breathing kisses of life on his lips, and when he regained life, he found he was an emperor. Romeo sighs happily, reflecting that love is so sweet that even its shadows and sorrows, such as this separation from Juliet, are "rich in joy."

COMMENT: To Romeo, the important part of the dream is that he saw Juliet. She came to him and kissed him, bringing life with her. Perhaps he does feel dead without her, but at any rate, he is so in love that the mere appearance of his bride seems a good omen, and he is not struck by the part of the dream that immediately catches our attention. For what the audience notices is that Romeo is dead in his dream. Forebodings of some misfortune have piled up gradually as the play progressed, and after the last scene, we are alert to references to death. The entire last act has dealt with Juliet since Romeo's absence. Vivid in our minds is the scene when she takes the potion and goes, as she imagines, to join Romeo in death. That Romeo should respond to such a dark dream with such joy seems like the last possible irony.

At this point, the messenger, whom Romeo's dream has led him to expect with happiness, appears. It is Balthasar, a servant of the Montague household, come fresh from Verona. Romeo welcomes him heartily, showering him with questions: is there a letter from the Friar? How is Juliet? And his parents? Before Balthasar can answer any of these, Romeo asks again about Juliet,

"For nothing can be ill if she be well." In that case, nothing goes ill, answers Balthasar, but he speaks more slowly, and with a marked difference of tone. Juliet is well, for her body is in the tomb and her soul is with the angels. The servant watched her being placed in the Capulet vault, and then hurried to Mantua to tell Romeo. At this point, Balthasar breaks his somber tone and begs Romeo's pardon for bringing him such news. Romeo's first words come slowly. He is stricken and almost unbelieving as he says, "Is it even so?" And then, in a burst, in one short, ringing phrase, he expresses his reaction: "Then I defy you, stars!"

COMMENT: Balthasar brings the news as he knows it, and he is very sorry that he must tell his master this. He delivers the information without beating around the bush, but at the same time philosophically, for he is trying to offer Romeo the same kind of religious consolation that the Friar offered Juliet's parents: that is, that Juliet is well off because she is in heaven. It is Romeo's response to which we pay attention. We hear none of the grief-stricken wailing, no berating of the untimeliness of death, none of the chorus of woe that we heard when Juliet was discovered in death-like sleep on her bed. Romeo's mourning is one line long, for from here on his life and actions will be his mourning. It is not only distinctly individual, this line of his; it is marked with a range of emotion, poetry, and strength that cannot be found in all the many lines with which Juliet has been mourned in the preceding scene. Romeo is bewildered and hurt beyond belief by the immensity of this loss; his mind cannot encompass the misery that has struck so swiftly, and he questions that it can be true. Then, summoning himself, he defies the stars in heaven. The stars, shining in the dark of night, have watched over the love he shared with Juliet. When he first saw her on the balcony, her eyes seemed like the stars. As night, when the stars shine, has been the only time their love was blessed, the stars have always seemed beneficent. Yet, there is a second meaning for stars. They are the directors of fate and fortune, and they influence the actions of men. From the Prologue on, the lovers have been "star-crossed," or ill-fated. Romeo, in defying the stars, expresses his feeling of having been betrayed. The stars seemed to bless him in love and now show themselves treacherous. Fortune and fate have turned against him, and have done their worst in killing the one thing he treasured. He will defy fate now, not be governed by it. He will act in spite of it and take his life in his own hands.

Immediately, with headlong speed, Romeo begins to act. He asks Balthasar to go to the place where Romeo has been staying, get a pen and paper, and hire horses; for Romeo intends to leave tonight. The good servant, seeing his master looking "pale and wild," fears that Romeo is about to do something rash and cautions him to have patience. Romeo protests that Balthasar is mistaken and should hurry away on these errands. Almost as an afterthought, he asks whether there are no letters for him from the Friar. When the servant assures him that there are none, Romeo shrugs and hastens him on, saying he will join Balthasar soon.

COMMENT: We do not know Romeo's intention, but we are as sure as Balthasar that it is an impetuous one. That Balthasar suggests caution makes clear once again how far removed from the world's understanding Romeo has become. He lives alone in a world of love, distant from all things mundane and moderate, and now that Juliet is gone he is truly isolated. The strength of character he has gained through loving shows in the simplicity with which Romeo grieves, in his defiance and his immediate action. He feels he has no time, but must rush to Verona and Juliet. The scene is imbued with a sense of overwhelming haste, with only a single pause: Romeo's question about a letter from Friar Laurence. We wonder, ourselves, remembering that such a letter was to have been sent, and that had it arrived, Romeo would now know that his Juliet is alive.

Romeo's intention is promptly clarified. His first words after Balthasar's departure are, "Well, Juliet, I will lie with thee to-night." Without wasting a second, he begins to consider how he will carry out his intention. The thoughts of desperate men quickly find a way to do whatever mischief they set their wills to. Romeo remembers an apothecary (a druggist) situated not far from where he is now. The man was obviously poor: dressed in rags, thin, miserable, and worried. His shop had looked shabby, its shelves bare except for what trifles he had managed to put on them for the sake of appearances. As Romeo had passed by, the pathetic poverty had caught his eye, and the thought had come to him that only from such a person could one buy poison. (The penalty for selling poison in Mantua was death, and only a man desperately in need of money would take the risk.) Romeo finds the shop, and calls the apothecary to him.

COMMENT: Romeo's first line deserves attention. His intent in all these hurried actions becomes frighteningly clear. He will go to Juliet's tomb, enter it, and there he will take his own life. He will die at the side of his dead beloved, and in death he will join her. The word "lie" brings in a symbolic meaning as well. To lie with someone is to have sexual intercourse. The sexual act is often referred to in literature as "dying." Here, the sexual act, which consummates the marriage of two bodies, has come to mean the same as death, which completes the marriage of two souls in eternal life. Death and marriage are one, and Romeo is going to his death and eternal marriage with Juliet. It is appropriate that Romeo's mind lights on poison as the

means to this eternal end. Poison has figured in the play since the Friar mentioned his knowledge of such lore in his first speech. Juliet has taken a similar drug, which has brought her so close to death that everyone, Romeo included, believes her dead. Before taking the potion, the horrors of death loomed large in her mind. Indeed, she reacted to it as though it were poison. In taking it at last, her mind was so confused with death that she thought Romeo was dead, and she was going to join him in death, the eternal marriage, just as he now proposes to join her. The entire scene of her mourning parents equated death and marriage and prepared us for this one. That equation is now fully realized, and the theme of death as the consummation of love becomes the motivating force of the action.

Romeo now talks to the apothecary, offering him forty ducats (a large sum of money, as ducats were made of gold) in exchange for a dram of the quickest-acting, most fatal poison the man can provide. Romeo describes graphically the effects he wishes this poison to have. The apothecary admits that he has "such mortal drugs," but adds that the penalty for selling them is death. "Art thou so bare, and full of wretchness,/ And fear'est to die?" Romeo points out that starvation, oppression, and contempt are clearly shown in the apothecary's appearance. Clearly, no one in such an extreme of misery can think that the world and its laws are his friends, or that such laws will make him rich. Break the law, Romeo urges, and by breaking it, get rid of this poverty. The apothecary consents, because of his poverty but against his will, to sell the poison, and Romeo says he pays the man's poverty, not his will. The apothecary gives him enough poison to kill twenty men instantly. Romeo pays him, and as he does so he comments that the gold is a worse poison and kills more men than this liquid. He says goodbye, adding kindly to this man that he should buy food and get some flesh on him. The poison is, for Romeo, a cordial or sweet liquor to be used at Juliet's grave.

COMMENT: Romeo's character has greatly broadened. Even in the midst of his distress, he has much sympathy for this poor man and helps the apothecary keep his pride by his manner of persuasion, his realization that a man's will means more than his poverty, and his recognition that gold can be an evil drug, although the world and its laws do not recognize this. He seems to sense a kinship with the man, in that they both suffer so much and are so alienated from the world as to risk death. (Indeed, Romeo is as alone now as Juliet was when she took her potion. The theme of the lovers' separateness has been thoroughly realized.) Romeo, who feels so close to death himself, is only surprised that the apothecary hesitates for an instant at the thought of the death penalty.

SUMMARY: Much worth noting has happened in this short scene.

1. Romeo, hearing of Juliet's death, has chosen to join her. The marriage of death is fast becoming the controlling image of the play.

2. Romeo has shown the greatness of his character and imagination in his short but profound reaction to the tragic news.

3. The impetuous speed that has been characteristic of the love now becomes part of Romeo's conscious will, as he hurries to his death.

4. The fatefulness—the stars, which have ominously threatened the lovers throughout the play, now seem to hold full sway. At the same time, Romeo defies fate, and takes control of his actions. This double aspect of fate and the defiance of fate seems contradictory. To understand it, one must realize that love has transformed Romeo and Juliet. They have gained their stature as characters through it, and we know them primarily as lovers rather than as people. Each has chosen this love and, in such an impetuously quick, passionate love, a quick and early end is inherent. True romantic love can have no other alternative. It is like a meteor, a streak of light that fills the sky for a moment and then disappears in darkness forever. As the Friar has said, "These violent delights have violent ends," and it was he who compared such passion to the kiss of fire and powder, the very meeting of which causes the destruction of both. The Friar has also made the statement that, "She's best married that dies married young," meaning that such love is the highest. In choosing this kind of love, the lovers choose their own end. In that sense, they have a hand in their own fate, just as the seemingly involuntary speed of the play is a result of the love they have chosen, and the lovers they have chosen to be. The critics' maxim that character is fate echoes in our minds here, as Romeo bends his will toward accomplishing the death that fate has decreed, and becomes both the master of and mastered by that fate.

Act V: Scene ii

Once again we find ourselves in Verona, and at the cell of Friar Laurence. Someone is knocking and calling at his door, and the Friar answers eagerly. Upon conceiving the desperate plan to help Juliet and giving her the potion, he had sent, as promised, a message to Romeo in Mantua explaining the plan. Two days have passed, and he expects that his messenger, a monk named Friar John, will be returning now with Romeo's reply. It is indeed Friar John at the door, and Friar Laurence welcomes him, pressing him for Romeo's answer. But Friar John has another story to tell, and one that bodes no good. He had gone to find yet another monk to accompany him to Mantua. This third friar had been visiting the sick, and as Friar John spoke to him of the journey, searchers came. The job of searchers was to roam through Verona and seal up houses where people with infectious diseases lived, thus preventing such sickness from spreading. These searchers sealed up the house where Friar John and his companion were talking, suspecting it to be some such house of disease. Friar John could not get out and never got to Mantua. Fearfully, Friar Laurence asks who did take the letter to Romeo. The sad answer is that no one did. People were so afraid of catching the disease that Friar John could persuade no one to take the letter to Mantua, nor even to return it to Friar Laurence.

COMMENT: This answers our question, and Romeo's, as to why he has not heard from Friar Laurence. Chance and accident have once again joined with fate, and the result is another grave, unforeseeable misfortune for the lovers. We know that if Romeo had only received the Friar's letter, he would not now be in his present desperate and final state of mind.

Friar Laurence is shocked, and cries out, "Unhappy fortune." He explains that the letter was not trivial, but concerned directions of great importance. He asks Friar John to help him now by finding an iron crowbar and bringing it to the cell quickly. Friar John, seeing he has inadvertently had part in causing some calamity, is all too willing to be of help, and leaves immediately. Friar Laurence then expresses his own intention to go to Juliet's vault alone. She will be awakening within three hours, and he is sure that she will blame him severely for not having notified Romeo. The Friar's plan is to take the young girl from her tomb and hide her in his cell while he sends yet another message to Romeo, telling him to come for his wife. Feeling very sorry for Juliet, who is "closed in a dead man's tomb," the Friar leaves.

COMMENT: What the Friar does not realize is that Romeo has heard of Juliet's supposed death, and is coming to join her in death. The failure of his message to reach Romeo is far more fatefully serious than the Friar imagines. We know the good Friar will do his best, but the blunders of accident and the swiftness of fate seem to be more than he will be able to handle. Still, there is some hope that he will reach the vault in time, meet Romeo there, and be able to prevent the course the action has taken. This scene makes vivid in our minds how it is the speed of what is happening that forms the greatest threat, and that only perfect timing will prevent tragedy. Speed and timing, which grew out of the impetuous love, have become movers of action.

Act V: Scene iii

We come now, at night, to the place on which all the action converges. It is a graveyard and the vault of the Capulet household. We expect various people, but the man we see there now was not expected. It is Paris, come with flowers to the tomb of the girl he loved and intended to marry. He has a young boy with him, a page who carries his torch. Paris tells the boy to put out the torch, so that they will not be discovered. The boy is to lie down under the nearby yew trees, and put his ear to the ground. As the earth of the churchyard is loose from the constant digging of graves, the boy will be able to hear the approach of any footsteps, and can whistle a warning to Paris. The page is a bit afraid, all alone in a graveyard, but he goes off to obey his master. Turning to face the closed vault where Juliet lies, Paris mourns, "Sweet flower, with flowers thy bridal bed I strew."

The bridal bed is made of dusty stone, for it is a tomb, and Paris intends to come each night to water it with his tears and strew it with flowers, as he does now. The page's whistle pierces the air, and Paris wonders "what cursed foot" has come to interrupt this ritual of love's grief. Seeing a torch, he begs the night to hide him from view, and goes off a way.

COMMENT: Paris grieves sincerely. He has never done anything to make us dislike him, and that he loved Juliet truly we do not doubt. His images in grief are those with which she was first mourned, as a girl in the flower of life who's to be his bride, and has become death's bride instead. Paris is not original, but he is genuine. The yew trees mentioned are symbols of sorrow. The night, always so welcomed by the lovers, is feared by Paris's page. Indeed, we are struck by the fact that if Paris's grief and love were equal in force to Romeo's, he would not be content to mourn. The contrast between the two is made clear.

It is Romeo who approaches. He is just arrived from Mantua, and with him is his servant, Balthasar, carrying the torch, and a hammer and crowbar. Romeo, unaware that he is being watched, takes the tools and torch from Balthasar and gives him a letter. The letter is to Romeo's father, and Balthasar is to deliver it early next morning. Romeo instructs the faithful servant not to try and restrain him. He explains that he is going to "descend into this bed of death," that is, enter the tomb, partly to see his lady's face, but mostly in order to take from her finger a precious and important ring. Balthasar must leave immediately, and if he is suspicious and returns, Romeo threatens to tear him limb from limb and cast his remains all over the churchyard. "The time and my intents are savage-wild,/ More fierce and more inexorable far/ Than empty tigers or the roaring sea."

Balthasar promises to leave his master alone, and Romeo assures him that only by doing so can Balthasar show his friendship. Romeo gives the servant money and wishes him well in life. Despite all this, Balthasar mutters to himself as he leaves that he fears his master's looks and doubts his intentions. He will hide nearby.

COMMENT: That Romeo is highly wrought up is clear from his manner of speaking. His phrases are short and jerky, abrupt and to the point. His tone to the servant is harshly commanding. His threat to Balthasar is not a pretty one; he seems to compare himself to a savage beast. We know very well what desperate plan he has in mind, and that he is not going into Juliet's tomb for any ring. It can be easily surmised that the letter to his father will explain his suicide and the reasons for it. Balthasar himself senses from his master's wildness of manner that something is afoot, and despite the threats, the servant feels his presence may be of some value.

Romeo picks up once more the imagery of death and marriage by calling Juliet's tomb a "bed of death." Visually, the sight of the impassioned young man holding the torch aloft in the darkness would recall to the audience the imagery of his love as a light at night, a brilliance in the darkness. His intention is clear, but he says that the time, as well as the intent, is fierce and inexorable. He has already taken hold of his destiny. By now his love and the very speed of this action he has determined on have him in grip. There is no going back; his death-marriage he has chosen, and it is not to be avoided now, for the time is at hand and has control. It is a complex relation between his own free choice and unavoidable fate that Romeo expresses in this one sentence.

Romeo approaches the tomb he is about to open, and addresses it, calling it a "Womb of death," and an awful mouth which has filled itself with Juliet, "the dearest morsel of the earth." With his tools, he pries open the "rotten jaws," that is, the door of the vault, declaring that to spite this mouth of death for taking Juliet, he will cram it with more food, meaning his own dead body.

COMMENT: Romeo is involved in a fierce action, and his language is vivid with the hate he feels at death for taking Juliet and with the abandon in which he will get his revenge on death by killing himself, thus reaching Juliet anyway. The speech is a single rich, developed metaphor, and again the theme of the sexual consummation of marriage in death is struck by the words, "Womb of death," addressed by Romeo to his beloved's tomb. To enter such a "womb" is to begin the final sexual act which will climax in dying. The mouth which has swallowed Juliet is the mouth of the womb of death.

Paris has been watching all this, infuriated by what he sees. As he understands it, Romeo has murdered Juliet's cousin, and, since it is believed that Juliet died of her grief over Tybalt's death, Romeo is indirectly her murderer. Now the banished man has the nerve to come and threaten to shame the bodies he has killed. Paris emerges from his hiding and shouts at Romeo, commanding him to stop this unholy action. Does Romeo really think he need carry revenge further than death? Paris wants to arrest Romeo, and take him to his death sentence for breaking his exile. "Thou must die," cries Paris, to which Romeo replies, "I must indeed; and therefore came I hither." Romeo does not know who cries at him from the darkness. He pleads to this young man not to tempt him, for he is desperate, and easily urged to a fury that would bring the sin of another killing on his head. Romeo begs Paris to leave, saying, "By heaven, I love thee better than myself,/ For I come hither armed against myself." Romeo does not wish to fight, and his madman's advice to this unknown challenger is to flee. But Paris refuses, and continues to try to arrest Romeo. It is almost with a sigh that Romeo, seeing no other alternative, begins to fight. The page sees them, and runs to call the guards. Romeo kills Paris, whose dying request is to be laid beside Juliet in the tomb. Hearing the request, Romeo looks at the face of this young man he has killed and sees it to be Paris, cousin of his friend Mercutio. Vaguely he remembers that, on the swift ride from Mantua, Balthasar told him Paris was to have married Juliet. Romeo's mind was so distracted during that ride that he is not sure whether he heard this, dreamed it, or just madly assumes it because of Paris's last request. But he will fulfill the request, and he carries dead Paris to "a triumphant grave" in Juliet's tomb.

COMMENT: Paris, of course, knows nothing of what there has been between Romeo and Juliet, and he has every reason to suspect the most vile motives on Romeo's part in coming here. Though Paris is not a violent man, he cannot watch to see what will happen, but must attempt an arrest. Romeo's state of mind does not permit any interruption. Their fight is inevitable.

We are very sad at Paris's death. The young man has done no wrong. Throughout the play, he has appeared to be honorable and of fine sensibility. His only fault was to love Juliet, and he could not have prevented this. The love was not returned, the marriage never realized; now, in an effort to protect his love, he has been killed, without even knowing the true state of things. We feel he has suffered unduly at the hands of fate.

Romeo speaks from the heart in trying to persuade Paris to leave. He knows too well that the only other alternative is a fight to the death, and he wishes only to kill himself, not

this young man. On hearing Paris's last request to be placed near Juliet, Romeo feels immediate kinship for him. It would have been Romeo's own request had the result of the fight been different. When he realizes that here is another who has loved Juliet and died for her, he can only sympathize and do his best for the dead man. There is no jealousy here; Romeo's character has widened beyond that.

As he carries Paris into the tomb, Romeo hears himself calling it a grave. It is not a grave, he says, but a lantern, for Juliet's beauty transforms it to a "feasting place full of light." He lays Paris down, commenting that this dead man has now been buried by another dead man, and how, before death, men are known to make merry. Such merriment is called the "lightning before death," and he wonders if that is his present state. He sees Juliet fully now, and exclaims, "O my love! my wife." Death has not lessened her beauty, and Romeo, seeing how the color still remains in her face, says, "Thou art not conquer'd; beauty's ensign yet/ Is crimson in thy lips and in thy cheeks,/ And death's pale flag is not advanced there." Seeing Tybalt's sheet-covered corpse, Romeo thinks that by killing himself, he will be killing Tybalt's enemy and murderer, and avenging his death. "Forgive me, cousin!" he says, and turns back to Juliet, puzzling that she has remained so beautiful. To his distracted mind, it seems that "unsubstantial Death" is in love with Juliet, and keeps her here in the dark to be its beloved. Romeo can't allow that: he will stay in this "palace of dim night" with Juliet forever, taking his eternal rest, and will "Shake the yoke of inauspicious stars/ From this world-wearied flesh." He takes his last look at his beloved, his last embrace, and with his kiss he seals finally "A dateless bargain with engrossing Death." Drawing the vial of poison from his pocket, he invokes it as the bitter and desperate pilot which will guide the boat of his body, sick and tired of this sea of life, onto the rocks of death. With the gesture of a toast, "Here's to my love!" Romeo drinks down the poison he calls a cordial. The drug is quick. His lips move from the kiss of the poison to Juliet's lips, and "With a kiss I die."

COMMENT: Romeo says that a dead man brings dead Paris to a tomb. He means himself. With his decision to die, he parted from life. He accepted his fate with such determination to force it to a conclusion that he feels himself to be dead. He has grown to maturity so fast that he even calls his own contemporary, Paris, "young." Now Romeo waits only so that he may join Juliet. When he sees her, his breath is taken by her beauty. He remarks more than once that she seems alive, untouched by the pallor of death. Indeed, the ironically tragic reason for this is that Juliet is alive, and on the verge of waking. It is all a matter of timing, but Romeo rushes to his own death. He has bargained with death for Juliet, and all he needs to implement his own death and to join her is a guide. That guide is the poison. He dies, as he wished, beside Juliet, and goes, as he hoped, to join her. His final gesture is a toast, much like Juliet's previous toast to him when she took the potion, and with it, symbolic death.

Romeo's entire speech brings a final resolution to the imagery of light and dark. The lovers have always loved at night, and their love was the source of all light for them. Now, amidst the darkness of death in a tomb, love sheds enough light to transform the vault into a festival of brilliance. At the same time, the vault is a "palace of dim night." These two contraries are possible now, for marriage has become one with death, so that light and darkness mean the same thing. For the sake of love, Romeo has chosen to submit to darkness, to die, in order to live eternally in the light of love with Juliet. Love is light, death is darkness, and as love and death are inseparable, so are their corresponding images. Their love has been a meteor, a brilliant flash in the night that fades quickly. But as the darkness of death takes over, eternal light is promised. So Romeo shakes off at last the "yoke" that fate has placed on him.

By accepting willfully the death that can't be avoided, that was destined by the very quality of love he shared with Juliet, Romeo in one gesture accepts his fate and transcends it. That gesture is his own murder. We grieve, but we sense his triumph. And we are conscious that the images of light and dark, love and death, the stars and fate, have reached their resolution and climatic conclusion. But Juliet is alive. The failure of timing, which accounts for the Friar's failure to be here by now and Juliet's not waking just moments earlier, will be enough to ensure an equally tragic and triumphant death for her.

At this point the Friar, who has hurried so much that he has managed to stumble over every grave in his path, appears. He carries tools for opening the vault, but sees, to his surprise, that the Capulet tomb is open and lit from within by a torch. Meeting Balthasar, he asks whose torch it is in the tomb. The servant replies it is Romeo's and that he has been there a full half an hour. Balthasar has sworn at the threat of death not to stay, so he fears to accompany the Friar and show himself to Romeo. But he does tell the holy man that he has had a dream that Romeo fought and killed another man before entering the tomb. The Friar is filled with fear that something has gone badly amiss. He advances to the tomb, calling Romeo's name, and soon finds blood stains and swords to witness the truth of Balthasar's dream. In a moment the Friar sees Romeo, all pale, and with him a bloody Paris. No sooner has he taken this in than he sees Juliet stir and waken. She sees the Friar, but she is yet oblivious to the head that lies heavily on her

breast. Remembering everything in a flood, she asks, "Where is my Romeo?" Approaching noises are heard, and the Friar urges Juliet to quickly leave this "nest/ Of death, contagion, and unnatural sleep:/ A greater power than we can contradict/ Hath thwarted our intents." He tells her that on her bosom lies her dead husband, that Paris is dead too, and he promises to find a place for her in a convent of nuns. Only she must come now, without questions, for the watchmen are coming and the Friar does not dare stay. As Juliet refuses to move, he flees.

COMMENT: The Friar's actions have lately struck us as of dubious wisdom, though we know they are full of good intentions. This scene confirms for us what we sensed in him: a certain lack of moral strength. He is grieved and shocked to the extent that he loses his moderation and fails to comprehend how Juliet must feel. And he is too frightened at the enormity of the tragedy to be able to face his responsibility for Juliet's life now. What frightens him is the thought of the blame that society will put on him if his involvement becomes known. He feels guilty, and he runs. Juliet's answer to the Friar when he begs her to leave is scornful. The child-turned-woman has wakened from death, found her lover incomprehensibly dead and her comforter, the Friar, ready to flee in fear of discovery. It is too much.

Juliet is left alone, to do what she must. Her mind is clear about her love for Romeo, so much so that she scarcely has time to express it or her overpowering grief at his death before she goes to join him. She sees a cup in his hand, and knows that he has poisoned himself only moments too soon. She chides him, in her gentle way, at having left no poison for her. She feels so close to him and to death that she can scold sweetly for a moment before she kisses his lips to see if any poison is left there. Having kissed Romeo she murmurs, "Thy lips are warm," and the pathos of that cry brings down on us like a bludgeon how this accelerated action has doomed the love, how the lovers' happiness hung on a few fateful minutes. It was lost because Juliet had not quite awakened and Romeo had not been able to waste a moment in joining her. Juliet now hears the voices of the watchmen; she, too, senses the need for speed. She takes Romeo's dagger and stabs herself, saying, "This is thy sheath; there rust, and let me die."

COMMENT: Juliet, like Romeo, loves faithfully beyond death, and goes willingly to join her lover in death and eternity, the final marriage. There is almost nothing to say at this point in the play. Romeo and Juliet have died tragically. The ironies of fate and timing have run their course and can do no more. We are stricken with a sense of the beauty of this love, and the tragic inevitability with which it led the lovers to an early end. Yet we know that such love had to end soon and sadly, and we realize that the beauty of it has justified the grief we feel now. The death-marriage is a triumph.

The watchmen, led by Paris's page-boy, enter abruptly. Seeing blood, some leave to search the grounds. It is clear that Juliet is newly dead. Messengers are sent to Prince Escalus, the Capulets, and the Montagues, and the watchmen are puzzled. They cannot comprehend from this slaughter what has happened. Balthasar and the Friar have been found and are brought in and held for questioning. Now the Prince enters, with Lord and Lady Capulet close behind him. All have heard cries of fear in the streets, and gravely the watchman tells them of the three deaths. Balthasar and the Friar are being brought forward for questioning, but this is interrupted by the Capulets, both of them overcome with horror at the sight of Juliet's fresh blood and the Montague dagger "mis-sheathed" in her breast. Lord Montague enters on this cue. His wife has died, during the night, of grief at her son's exile. What other grief awaits him? With something akin to resignation, Montague sees his son and heir, dead before his time. The Prince now calls a halt to all mourning, in order that the ambiguities and complications of this triple death may be clarified. He calls the suspects, and the Friar steps forward, "both to impeach and purge" himself of all this murder. He tells, as quickly and simply as he can, the story of the love and marriage of Romeo and Juliet, Tybalt's death, Romeo's exile, the bethrothal of Juliet to Paris, his own plan to save her from dishonor, the accident of the letter failing to reach its destination, and the inevitable end. The Nurse will bear witness of the marriage, says the Friar, and adds that, if it is judged that any of this is his fault, he will accept the death penalty. Prince Escalus pardons him. Balthasar now speaks, and gives to the Prince the letter Romeo had meant for his father. The letter supports the Friar's statement, and the story has been put back together.

COMMENT: The scene is long and stern. It shows the grief of the Prince and the two households and gives the Friar a chance to stand for himself. His tale emphasizes the faults of fate, of haste, and of the feuding families as well as his own, and we see that he deserves our pardon as well as the Prince's. It prepares us for the final judgment.

Calling the two feuding families to him, the Prince admonishes, "See what a scourge is laid upon your hate,/ That heaven finds means to kill your joys with love." The Prince himself has lost two relatives by not punishing the feuders harshly enough to make them stop. Capulet and Montague, each pledging gold statues of the other's child, shake hands and vow to feud no more. The play ends on a note of "glooming peace," "The sun for sorrow will not raise his head." The Prince challenges everyone to think this over and closes the play with the words, "Never was a story of more woe,/ Than this of Juliet and her Romeo."

COMMENT: The play has come full circle, and completed itself as was foretold in the Prologue. All true poetry has fled with the lives of the lovers, and the ending seems grey. The stars have led here, and the final irony of fate lies in the sacrifice of the joys of the parents in order to cure their mutual hate, and in the fact that the sacrifice was made through love. From the outside point of view, perhaps fate's view, this reconciliation of the feud was the point of the play. To us, the play has been about Romeo, Juliet, and the beauty of their tragic love.

The play started with a street fight between the houses, at which the Prince appeared and which he censured heavily. The tragic turning was Mercutio's death, and Prince Escalus was present then, to punish and warn further. Now, this figure of justice, judgment, and peace presides over the final scene, clinches the reconciliation, mourns the lovers, and gives us our sense of the completed structure of the play as it ends.

SUMMARY: Every theme of the play has reached its climax and resolved itself. The tragedy has found its mark, and with it, the play's meaning has reached its culmination. To summarize the final scene is to summarize the play, for here flower the seeds planted throughout. Some are:

1. The coming-together of the contrasting imagery of light and dark and simultaneously, the culmination of the parallel themes of love and death. Light and dark become love and death, and all contraries become inextricably one.

2. In opposition to these image-clusters has been the outside world: the moderation of age and the hate of the feud. These forces alienated the lovers and their love, and now by their death the same forces are reconciled to peace.

3. The speed of the fate that has had control throughout is a speed born in the love of Romeo and Juliet. As it grew from the love, so it takes over and leads to death.

The play abounds in the lyricism of love, despite its desperate ending in death. It is world-famous for its portrayal of idealistic young love, faithful till death. As such, many critics consider the play to be not a tragedy of love, but a hymn of praise to this transforming, romantic love which triumphs even over death. The name "Romeo" means "lover" all over the world, for the lovers and their passion have become prototypes. Tragedy has been made beautiful by Shakespeare, and through his art, the theater has become a vehicle for poetry as much as for drama. He achieves this by a formal, almost musical series of contrasts between youth and age, fate and free will, joy and hatred, love and death. During the course of the action, these seemingly incompatible elements grow together like themes in music until they fuse into a single melody.

Character Analyses

ROMEO   During the course of the play, Romeo grows to manhood. When we first meet him, he is a stereotype of the lover: cherishing solitude and night, pensive, pale and sad. He assumes all the attitudes of a rejected suitor; he writes poetry; his speech is a series of contradictory exclamations. At this juncture, Romeo knows no more about love than what he has read in the books he emulates, and he is actually in love with love. His posturing makes him the brunt of much joking on the part of his friends, Mercutio and Benvolio. These two worldly, witty men have loved Romeo for his own devil-may-care brilliance, and they sense that his present hang-dog attitudes are not true to him. Their judgment is correct, for all Romeo's mooning about ceases when he meets Juliet, and in loving her he discovers that joy, not sadness, is part of love. After arranging for his marriage to Juliet, Romeo meets Mercutio and Benvolio. His wit is all air and fire, and he parries each of Mercutio's verbal thrusts so brightly that Mercutio is wholly charmed, and welcomes back the true Romeo.

But the true Romeo has not yet fully emerged. He is not only a courtly, carefree young man. He is capable of the deepest passions of love. In his initial courtship of Juliet, at her father's party and in the orchard, Romeo's entrancement is still, though feelingly, expressed in somewhat typical gestures of holy adoration. His comparison of Juliet to the source of all light is not wholly new either. For Romeo is not an original lover; he is the epitome of all romantic lovers, the consummate lover. In the love duets, the heights of his imagination and expression are equalled by Juliet. It is the thoroughness of his loving, his complete lack of conflict or hesitation in any matter that concerns Juliet, the utter commitment with which he abandons himself to the intense, swift passion, that distinguishes him as a lover. Romeo is not practical or realistic, but his preoccupation is not necessarily indicative of dreamy absent-mindedness. When Tybalt is insulting him and goading him to enter combat, neither lack of courage nor love-sickness constrains Romeo. Rather he is elevated by love for Juliet to an encompassing love which does not permit of fighting, and he is all too conscious of his new status as a relative of the man who challenges him. This complex and moral awareness puts dueling out of the question, but the secrecy of the marriage makes an explanation equally impossible. Romeo's ambiguous retorts are mistaken for softness by his comrades. What really precipitates the fight, then, is the fact that love has completely alienated Romeo from the world. When real honor demands that the youth fight he does so and revenges Mercutio's death to his own severe detriment. Later, this alienation and consequent lack of practicality emerges more clearly, when Romeo falls to the floor of the Friar's cell in a faint of despair. This does, at first, seem like weakness. Yet the desperate fight, Romeo's exile, his overwhelming love for Juliet, and the total lack of understanding displayed by even the Friar for the all-consuming nature of Romeo's passion, provide sufficient explanation for the lapse.

Romeo's ability to die for love comes as no surprise. We are prepared for it by his falling in the Friar's cell, and by his willingness, after the wedding night, to risk his life to stay in Verona if Juliet so wishes. It is the manner of Romeo's choosing to die that comes as a revelation. Gone are all traces of the standard responses of a lover. Gone, also, is the momentary inability to act that we noticed in his behavior at the Friar's. With the words, "I defy you, stars," Romeo takes fate firmly in his hands and determines the time and manner of his own death. In the very brevity of his words and speed of his actions lies Romeo's stature as a character. He does not pause, either for self-indulgent emotion or in lack of conviction, but with unwavering courage he goes to search out his love in death. Love has become life for him, and without Juliet there can be nothing but death in living. Romeo has come to manhood, but his whole indentity as a human being lies in loving. He is not only alienated from the world; he now cares nothing for it or its trappings. He is purely and voluntarily a lover.

Romeo's battle with Paris only demonstrates how much he has forsaken the world. By the time he reaches the tomb he is so given over to death and love, so separate from life and the world, that he can call himself a dead man. His passion now absorbs itself in dying, as it did before in loving. His farewells to life are scarcely farewells. They seem more like greetings to death and Juliet. His imagination and passion have reached their ultimate peak when he dies. In that sense, Romeo has truly triumphed.

JULIET In the four day space of the play, Juliet grows from a charming fourteen-year-old child to womanhood. Her first appearance with her Nurse and mother as they prepare for the party catches the sweet affirmative aspect of her nature, but she seems merely a docile, untried girl. The Nurse's warm, rambling speech about Juliet's babyhood, with its savoring of the bawdy, gives us a hint of the atmosphere in which this girl grew. Lady Capulet's more cool, sophisticated, and premeditated point of view gives us another. But neither proves to have had much influence, and Juliet seems quite blank until she loves Romeo. The holy aura that surrounds their first meeting is apt, and emphasizes the girl's innocence. Yet it is she who breaks the mood and shows her true responses when, half blushing at the passion she has aroused, half teasing to cover her emotion, she remarks, "You kiss by the book." Later, in the orchard, it is again Juliet who puts their love on frank and open ground by unwittingly professing her feelings aloud before the hidden lover. These traits of innocent coyness, teasing, and yet openness, remain with Juliet throughout. Her gentle images at this meeting are quite her own, for example, her wish that Romeo were her pet bird, whom she would allow to hop away, but who could never escape altogether because of the string she would hold. Juliet enjoys the strain of loving completely, wishes for a longer courtship, and is aware that the sadness of parting is a sweet one. Her perception is expanding rapidly, and she is the practical one who proposes the immediate marriage.

In fact, Juliet is always the practical one, the one who implements action. At the same time her impatience contributes largely to the speed of the love affair. Waiting for her Nurse to come with news of the marriage plans, waiting for the wedding night to fall, Juliet's passion is clear, and so is the vulnerability of the passion. It is at these instances that her imagination becomes extravagant and reaches peaks of exhilaration that result in such poetry as her invocation to the night. She gradually emerges as a girl of much fire as well as charm. But the vulnerability is still there, and the Nurse takes advantage of it in the scene where she tells Juliet of Tybalt's death and Romeo's banishment.

As Juliet gains in womanliness, she acquires facility with such feminine tricks as necessary deceptions. She successfully deceives both her Nurse and her parents concerning her change of heart about marrying Paris. In fact, with her characteristic fervor she succeeds too well, with the result that the marriage is moved forward another day, and the whole pace of the action is quickened. But Juliet's fervor extends as well into her desperation to preserve her honor, and by that she acquires a sternness of will that allows her to affirm the Friar's plan. Her deepening womanhood is proved in this and in her ultimate suicide. At the Friar's before determining on the plan, and again alone in her room when she is about to take the potion, Juliet's fertile imagination runs rampant with visions of the horrors of the grave. But the all-pervasive, all-enveloping nature of this blossoming woman's passion lifts her finally beyond this. When Juliet takes the potion, she does so for the sake of love. She believes she is marrying death in order to join Romeo, whom she envisions dead, and she toasts him triumphantly with the liquid, just as he later toasts her with the poison. To her, as to Romeo, life is where love is. She, like him, is completely alienated from the world. She finds comfort nowhere, and must rely wholly on herself. Even her scorn for the Friar's fearful flight from the tomb is but a faint emotion. She can scold Romeo in the old, loving way for leaving her no poison. It is with joy that she gives Romeo's dagger its final sheath in her bosom and goes to find love in death, since there is none in this world.

MERCUTIO The worldly, witty, man-about-town who is Romeo's best friend attracts much attention from the critics. In a sense, Mercutio is one of Shakespeare's dramatic devices. The character wins our liking and is then sacrificed, thus becoming the pivot on which romance turns to tragedy. It is the Queen Mab speech, so often called an irrelevant tangent, that secures our affections for Mercutio. Before that, we are merely charmed by his sophisticated, irreverent, and often bawdy jesting, by his worldly flippancy and cynicism. But the Queen Mab speech transforms him before our eyes. The depth of Mercutio's love for Romeo is evident in this attempt to cheer him. The rare, extravagant fantasy of his vision confronts us, and we truly admire this light-tongued man. That Mercutio has plumbed deeply the troubles of men becomes evident in the change of his tone to encompass such images as that of a soldier starting awake from dreams of a bloody battle. Our feelings are truly clinched when Mercutio proceeds to brush off the genius of this speech as a "vain fantasy" that has no real substance. We realize then that Mercutio's scorn emerges from his disillusion with himself, his sense that his life and being are based on emptiness.

This is not to say that Mercutio dislikes life. He lives with gusto, and he has a strong creed about how to live. The creed is never stated, but it becomes clear to us through negatives, such as Mercutio's intense dislike of Tybalt, whom he refers to derogatorily as the prince of cats. Although Tybalt is an able fighter, he is also, in Mercutio's eyes, a shallow dandy with ridiculous affectations, lacking in any true manliness. For this, Mercutio detests him. When Tybalt begins his sally at Romeo, and Romeo does not respond, Mercutio must. Not only is he ashamed at Romeo's weakness and lack of sense of honor, he is enraged by Tybalt's sassiness. When Tybalt strikes home because of Romeo's attempt to keep peace, it is too much. Mercutio is dying, but he utters a stream of invective against the senseless feud, and against Tybalt, the creature who lives by narrow rules and scratches the life out of others. Mercutio has always taken pride in his own realism. Now he has taken up his sword to fend off infamy from his true ideals of manhood and selfhood. For those ideals he dies, but not easily. He goes down vehemently, giving vent to bitterness and cynicism with all the wry wit for which we know him.

THE NURSE

Here we have one of the simplest, yet most fully alive, characters in the play. The Nurse delights and dismays us often, at times even simultaneously. She is an old woman nearing senility. Her thoughts are permeated with a genuine relish for all things concerning sex, especially the simplest and lowest forms of bawdry. Her vivid, colloquial speech follows the ramblings of her mind, resulting in repetitions and irrelevancies, such as we see in her funny, ribald account of Juliet as a child. She enjoys anything glamorous, and is pleased to take the airs of a lady when bearing messages between her mistress and Romeo. She assumes this role with aplomb, and is as much herself in such a ridiculous posture as when she drops the role for a round of curses at the disappearing Mercutio who has made fun of her.

The Nurse has many privileges at the Capulet's, can talk back to the Lord when he is in ill temper, and can tease him when he feels cheerful. She takes her liberties too far with Juliet, however. For the Nurse indulges herself fully in whatever twinges of emotion she can, and such self indulgence can become cruelty. Taking advantage of her age, and seriously wishing for a little sympathy from Juliet, she treats the fervent, impatient girl to an agonizingly long digression before she will tell her the wedding plans. More cruel and offensive still is the Nurse's presentation of the news that Tybalt is dead and Romeo sentenced to exile. The Nurse's rambling and exclaiming is, in this case, deliberately contrived to squeeze the last drop of emotion from the situation. She is indulging her taste for excesses of passion, if vicariously, and Juliet suffers greatly by it.

Thus, the Nurse's predilection for the lower passions makes it impossible for her to understand Juliet. One could have expected their final alienation. The Nurse's suggestion that Juliet abandon Romeo and marry Paris is, for Juliet, the final blow. But this response to the situation is exactly what we look for from the Nurse. It is hardy, callous realism, based on the old woman's intrinsic belief that life is to be enjoyed, no matter how. Nothing less than the death of Juliet, whom she really did love, can reduce this garrulous Nurse to a creature pained beyond her powers of expression. For that is how we see her last.

FRIAR LAURENCE

The gentle Friar plays a linking role in the play, for he is the only true connection between the lovers, with their isolated passion, and the harsh outside world. He is a sympathetic person, and he uses all the means at his disposal to make the love possible and at the same time to reconcile it with the exigencies of reality. He first condones the love as a means for bringing an end to the bitter feud. To this end, and simultaneously to promote the happiness of the two young people, he performs the marriage. When the complications of Romeo's exile and Juliet's proposed marriage to Paris ensue, he uses his knowledge of herbs to effect the best solution he can and does his best to inform Romeo. That the message never reaches its destination is not the Friar's fault.

This linking role, coupled with the philosophy he expounds, shows the Friar as a man of reason. Often he counsels Romeo to be more temperate, and he does this with the young man's happiness at heart. He hopes to save the lovers from the violent end to which such violent passions often lead. But precisely because of this belief in moderation and reason, the Friar fails to understand the lovers. To such a man as he, the degree to which their love is absolute, and the beauty and speed which is consequently engendered, are all inconceivable.

But this failure of understanding is not his alone. It is true of all the characters in the play, with the difference that only the Friar tries to understand. What we do consider a fault is his failure in moral strength. The Friar lectured Romeo severely for losing control of himself when faced with exile. Again, it was he that brought the wailing grief over Juliet to an end, directing the participants to take hold of themselves, find solace in religion, and begin the necessary preparations for the funeral. The Friar has stood for moral strength, but when, in the tomb, he is faced with the freshly dead bodies of Paris and Romeo, and the intractability of Juliet, the Friar cannot face the responsibility of his own role in all this. In the end, it is society he sides with, for it is the censure of society he fears when he runs guiltily away. In presenting his defense, he seems forgivable, but his stature has diminished in our eyes. We see him at last as a well-intentioned pawn in a game played between fate and the passion of love. It is merely regrettable that this gentle, reasonable man has not the height or breadth of feeling to comprehend either one of the two.

LORD CAPULET The touchy, talkative man has but one position in life: that of master of his household. To lose his command of this would be to lessen his own imposing stature. When it suits him, Capulet is expansive, generous, hearty. He can leave the decision about her marriage to his daughter, and can warmly welcome masked intruders at his party, even if they come from the enemy household. But where it concerns the public image of his own house, Lord Capulet's will is inviolate. He forbids Tybalt to disrupt his party with a fight, and for all his genial mood, his temper bristles at Tybalt's slightest indication of going against his wishes. When further fighting clouds the Capulet name, the Lord becomes politic. He would not lose favor with Verona's Prince, and to prevent any such eventuality, he makes final the arrangements for his daughter to marry Paris, a relative of the Prince. He retracts his more generous offer to let Juliet decide for herself and decides for her. He actually cannot conceive that she would oppose his wishes, and it comes as a shock when she does. To be balked like this, to have his will crossed, seems to him like outright denial of his position as lord of the house.

Capulet becomes enraged. His language throughout is colorful, but in this state of infuriation, it becomes scathing. He streams forth a series of vilifying rebukes at his daughter, calling her to task for her impudence and threatening to turn her out on the street if she does not suit her will to his.

But Capulet, for all his willfulness and ill temper, is a man of feeling. He genuinely loves his daughter, and over-indulges himself in his extreme rage. He is gentle with her again before she even apologizes, and his delight with her pretended change of heart is pathetic, in view of the circumstances. Nothing will do for her then but a great festivity, and he happily gives up a night's sleep to arrange it. All his genial, free speech flows back, and he jests merrily. When Juliet is discovered dead, this man of abundant, rich language is at first struck silent. When he does speak, the tenderness with which he images his grief sets the tone for the chorus of mourning. His role in the play is as a partisan of hatred, but Shakespeare has made him into a solid character, comparable to the old Nurse in the simple completeness of his being.

Sample Essay Questions and Answers

1. ANTONY AND CLEOPATRA

Question: Does Cleopatra love Antony or merely use him?

Answer: Shakespeare leaves some doubt about the relationship between Antony and Cleopatra. Plutarch says that Cleopatra first went to meet Antony intending to seduce him. She made him fall in love with her to avoid his wrath. Enobarbus implies this when he describes the meeting to Agrippa and Maecenas, and Cleopatra admits as much when, adorning herself for death, she says, "I am again for Cydmus, to meet Mark Antony." She boasts also of her conquests of former Roman conquerors, Julius Caesar and Pompey the Great. After her treachery at Actium, Antony accuses her of a triple infidelity: She left Julius Caesar for Pompey; she left Pompey when Antony conquered her; and now she will leave him for the next winner, Octavius Caesar. And he dies, forgiving her certainly, but perhaps still doubtful of her loyalty, unless Diomedes' brief "Which never shall be found" is enough to reassure him. For he takes for granted that she will seek her safety with Caesar. Shakespeare never says clearly whether she played a part in the mass surrender of Antony's troops in their final defeat. And her last hours in the monument are a patchwork of inconsistency. She says in Act 4, Scene 15, right after Antony's death, that she too is resolved to die by her own hand. But then we find her trying to make some arrangements with Caesar. It cannot be for her children, because in killing herself she abandons them to the "destruction" which Caesar threatens. It is never completely clear whether she commits suicide because she cannot live without Antony, or because she cannot live with Caesar. The reason may be that Shakespeare did not know himself, because the story he is dramatizing from Plutarch does not tell him. So rather than add anything untrue or change the original he incorporates the inconsistency into Cleopatra's character, where it enhances her cunning and her "infinite variety."

2. HAMLET

Question: Does Hamlet procrastinate in prosecuting his revenge?

Answer: Despite recent arguments, particularly by Grebanier, to the effect that Hamlet does not procrastinate because he has moral scruples about the validity of the ghost's evidence until after Claudius' guilty response to the performance of the play within the play and then only has a single opportunity before his exile which he does not utilize because he finds Claudius praying and prefers to wait until he can catch him in an act which has "no relish of salvation in't," the answer would seem to be an emphatic yes, in accordance with a long tradition of criticism. Though the dramatic action of the play does not reveal more than the single opportunity when Claudius is alone in prayer, this dramatised opportunity occurs two months after the meeting with the ghost when Hamlet had said that he would be "swift" and "sweep to my revenge." In the "rogue and peasant slave" soliloquy, which occurs shortly before the so-called "single opportunity," Hamlet admits that he has been "unpregnant of my cause" and wonders whether he is a "coward." It is only after he is filled with disgust with himself for his long delay that he rationalizes his delay with an admittedly sound scruple about the evidence of the ghost and decides to test it by performing a dramatized repetition of Claudius' crime before his eyes. When he has his opportunity shortly after confirming Claudius' guilt, he rationalizes it away with the damnable argument that Claudius' soul might escape eternal damnation. But that this was not his single opportunity is shown shortly after, when, *en route* to his exile in England, Hamlet refers to his "dull revenge" in the important soliloquy in which he admits: "I do not know / Why yet I live to say 'This thing's to do'; / Sith I have cause and will and strength and means / To do't." And he now vows, in opposition to his attitude of the past two months: "O! from this time forth, / My thoughts be bloody, or be nothing worth!"

3. JULIUS CAESAR

Question: What is the relationship between Brutus and Cassius?

Answer: Brutus and Cassius are friends of long standing who, as opposite types, have apparently fallen out with each other many times. When they are first seen in conversation, Cassius expresses the fear that Brutus no longer loves him; he suggests that he is the more dependent member of the friendship when he is happy to learn that Brutus' "ungentle" eyes are not directed at him. Apparently inconsequential, this subtle exchange between the two men sets up the relationship they continue to have with each other for the remainder of the play. Cassius is an intelligent man, a keen observer of human nature; he makes practical decisions of questionable morality, but he admires and honors the virtue and reputation of his friend Brutus and is too dependent on his love to oppose his friend for very long.

Although their conflicting natures are never forgotten, there are two major scenes in which the differences between the men are brought into sharpest focus. The first is the meeting of the conspirators in Brutus' garden, where Brutus rejects without compromise three of Cassius' proposals. He refuses to kill Antony, refuses to swear an oath, and refuses to invite Cicero to join the conspiracy. In each case, Cassius' suggestions are based on sound practical reasons. In each case Brutus' rejections are based on his constancy to moral principles. In every case, Cassius submits to Brutus' decisions, not without some argument.

The second scene in which the idealistic and practical natures of the two men are contrasted is the famous Quarrel Scene, which takes place in Sardis. Here Cassius' emotional dependence on Brutus' love is most visible, and Brutus' coldly rational appraisal of his friend's behavior is given its most extreme expression. The argument concerns practical corruption vs. absolute morality in the conduct of war. Despite his conviction that a general must overlook petty corruption and sometimes use unjust means for obtaining funds, Cassius finds his own position untenable in the face of the higher morality of Brutus, whom he reveres. Brutus is immovable to his friends' frailties of judgment and nature. He provokes Cassius' choleric disposition to greater shows of rashness and cruelly taunts him with a promise to mock (reject) him, which he knows Cassius cannot endure. Cassius is brutally pushed to the point where he asks Brutus to kill him. Having reached its nadir, the argument can go no farther, and a reconciliation takes place in which Cassius makes most of the apologies. At the close of the scene, Cassius' opposition is completely enfeebled. He protests only once more to

Brutus' decision to attack the enemy on level ground rather than take the defensive from the vantage point in Sardis. At the close of the scene, Cassius addresses Brutus as "my lord." His submission is so total that he never argues with Brutus again. In the final moments before battle, he asks Brutus how he plans to face defeat if it should come. When he cannot make Brutus realize that his choice may be capture or suicide, he simply bids him a fond farewell.

Thus, the relationship between Brutus and Cassius is that of friendly antagonists. Allies in the conspiracy, they differ in every other respect. Their humors, philosophies, morals, and ideals are at odds at every point. There can be little doubt that Cassius and Brutus are intended as foils for each other, through which the characters can be examined in all their complex ramifications.

4. KING LEAR

Question: Discuss the various aspects of madness in the play *King Lear*.

Answer: When Lear first realizes the extent of Goneril's ingratitude, he cries out, "O, let me not be mad, not mad, sweet heaven! / Keep me in temper: I would not be mad!" This prayer is repeated many times in the play, but nevertheless madness inexorably descends on the King. It takes many forms: the "trial" of Goneril and Regan in the hovel during the storm, the ineffectual curses on his daughters, the almost hysterical speech about sexual license in Act IV, Scene 6, and the wearing of flowers and weeds toward the end of the play. Lear's madness is more than the senility of the very old. It includes madness in the sense of bitter anger at the injustices of the world, and much of what Lear says when he is mad is very true and sane indeed. The anger of his madness reaches its peak during the storm; afterwards Lear is generally more subdued, and almost childlike. It is almost as if Shakespeare were saying that in order to achieve a sane and balanced vision of a mad world one must go mad oneself. Lear's madness is compared and contrasted in the storm scenes with the madness of the Fool and the pretended madness of Edgar. As the Fool says, "This cold night will turn us all to fools and madmen." The Fool is gibbering with terror and must be comforted by Kent. Edgar has taken the disguise of a harmlessly mad beggar with a religious persecution mania—he keeps seeing demons everywhere. Edgar's idea, of course, is that no one will suspect, or even take notice of Tom of Bedlam, the poor mad beggar, and so he will be safe from Edmund's plotting for the time being. In the storm scenes, King, Fool and beggar-noble are all reduced to the level of madness, but of varying degrees of intensity and purpose. Lear is brought to a calmer vision of his plight toward the end of the play by means of Cordelia's unvarying love, and the common-sense treatment of the physician, who realizes that the only "cure" for the King's condition is rest and loving care. The forces that drove him mad in the first place cannot be undone.

5. MACBETH

Question: What is the theme of *Macbeth*?

Answer: By "the theme" of *Macbeth* one means the principal idea of the play, an idea that is seen in dramatic clothing probably in every act of the play. Abstracting a theme from a play is not identical to establishing a point as fact: an abstracter is working from the data of the play to an idea; therefore, he is working toward an opinion—others may form other opinions of a play's theme, and authors do not, as a rule, inform readers or audiences of their themes.

In *Macbeth*, as in other Shakespearean plays, we find that *appearances are one thing, reality is another.* This abstraction is too general to apply only to *Macbeth*. A more specific configuration of the main theme (there are also minor themes) of *Macbeth* is that *a man is deluded who thinks that he can play with evil and remain unchanged: mankind, yielding to evil, which of course appears to be good, is led to destruction.*

In Act I, this idea is embodied in Macbeth's and Lady Macbeth's response to the salutations of the Witches. Macbeth and his lady regard the greetings as Thane of Cawdor and future king as prophecies, and, further, with respect to the kingship, they contemplate murder of the incumbent, Duncan, although Macbeth is not told by the Witches to kill Duncan for his crown. In Act II, the Macbeths are deceived by the apparent ease and subsequent guiltlessness with which they can compass Duncan's death. They proceed in regicide, but Macbeth goes further than contemplated, because of his now-disturbed mind, to kill the two grooms. In Act III, Macbeth arranges the murder of Banquo and Fleance; but Fleance, who chiefly means the prospect of continuing Banquo's line, escapes. The murders of Banquo and Fleance had seemed to be assured, but the reality is otherwise. In Act IV and Act V, Macbeth wrongly reads the sayings of the Second and the Third Apparitions—the prophecies that "none of woman born / Shall harm Macbeth" and he is safe "until / Great Birnam Wood to high Dunsinane Hill / Shall come against him." Significantly he takes no particular notice of the saying of the First Apparition to "Beware Macduff." In Act V, these three oracular utterances come true as Macbeth learns to his horror when Malcolm's army, disguised by

branches from Birnam Wood, comes against his castle and when Macduff, confronting Macbeth, informs him that he "was from his mother's womb / Untimely ripp'd" in Caesarian birth. Macbeth learns in death that appearances pointed one way, but reality, rock-hard, lay in the opposite direction. Against this rock he is crushed.

6. THE MERCHANT OF VENICE

Question: What is the dramatic function served by Salanio and Salarino in *The Merchant of Venice*?

Answer: In the very first scene, Salanio and Salarino help to create our sense of the atmosphere of Venice by their elaborate descriptions of the ships that ply the seas loaded with exotic cargoes. Their imagery conjures up for us a resplendent Venice thriving on a glamorous commerce with the romantic Orient. In the later scenes of the play Salanio and Salarino take the place of a narrator or chorus, for it is in the course of their conversations that certain aspects of the plot are advanced without being dramatized . It is through Salanio and Salarino that we learn of Shylock's reaction to Jessica's elopement: his wild outcries for his daughter and his ducats, and his suspicion that Bassanio and Antonio conspired with Lorenzo in the escape. It is also through Salanio and Salarino that we hear the first rumor of a Venetian ship lost at sea and later hear of others. Finally, Salanio and Salarino are used to provide narrative descriptions of Antonio and Shylock and the judgments with which we are expected to evaluate these characters.

7. OTHELLO

Question: How is *Othello* dramatically constructed?

Answer: The traditional divisions of a drama are exposition, rising action, climax, falling action, and the conclusion or dénouement.

Exposition: The exposition has to identify the characters and sketch at least their general relationships to one another. Wherever possible, the characters should be shown performing acts significant of their personalities; they should be shown in action rather than be described. Shakespeare generally moves swiftly. In the opening scene, Shakespeare establishes the dissatisfaction of Iago and the fact of Othello's elopement, and then we are placed in the midst of action—Iago and Roderigo awakening the Brabantio household. In I, ii, a fight is imminent between the Brabantio and Othello forces, which Othello is able to prevent from going further by his dignity and diplomacy. We also witness the double-dealing of Iago; no one has to inform us about his capacity for dangerous deception. We *see* it! In I, iii, we have the great senate scene which establishes the relationship of Othello and Desdemona to one another and which enables Othello to recite his romantic autobiography at length—but still within the terms of the dramatic action. At the end of the scene in the long prose conversation between Iago and Roderigo, the conditions of the main conflict to come are established. Roderigo hopes to form an immoral relationship with Desdemona through the agency of Iago. Iago assures him that the marriage cannot last. In a soliloquy, Iago tells us that he plans to ruin Cassio, by leading Othello to think that Cassio is "too familiar with his wife." Cassio, the man who got the appointment that Iago was seeking, appeared briefly in I, ii, largely for the purpose of expositor identification.

The Rising Action. The rising action implies complication and growing conflict. The characters, who have been identified in the exposition and who, at least in this play, have already been engaged in conflicts but not in *the* conflict, now become involved with one another and lay the groundwork of the major conflict. In II, i, we witness two separate arrivals in Cyprus from Venice: first, that of Desdemona, Iago, Roderigo, and Emilia; second, that of Othello himself. Iago is preparing to make something of Cassio's exercising the new Venetian courtesy of hand-kissing. Desdemona and Othello greet one another for one moment of supreme happiness, but Iago stands to one side declaring: "O, you are well tun'd now! / But I'll set down the pegs that make this music, / As honest as I am." Iago, in a long passage with Roderigo, confides his plan of removing Roderigo's supposed rival corrupter, Cassio, by provoking some action that will put Cassio in a bad light. In II, iii, this plan is carried out. Cassio is induced to drink too much; Roderigo provokes him to a fight. Othello dismisses Cassio on the spot from his command. After Cassio's disgrace, Iago advises him to plead to Othello through Desdemona. In a soliloquy, Iago reveals his major design—to convince the Moor that Desdemona's intercession for Cassio is due to an adulterous relationship with him. The rising action is now drawing near to the climax. Iago is excited by his destructive ideas: "Pleasure and action make the hours seem short."

The Climax. The climax always occurs in the third act of a Shakespearean play. Aristotle in the *Poetics* used a Greek word for the climax meaning "the tying of the knot." He thinks of the exposition as consisting in laying out the various threads of the story; the rising action presents the criss-crossing of these various threads;

the climax shows the point where these threads are most *tightly* tied together. The climax is the point of highest tension where the conflict is totally joined, and where the suspense of the audience is greatest. "Whatever is going to happen in this situation, whatever is going to result from it?" the audience asks itself. The climax might be said to contain a series of climaxes within itself—like a series of Chinese boxes, each one being removed soars to reach the innermost one. The first two scenes of Act III are merely informative. The climax of the play lies in III, iii. This is a very long scene of nearly 480 lines. This has been analyzed in detail elsewhere. Iago is able to "psychologize" Othello into suspicion without overtly saying anything. The birth of suspicion within Othello's own mind might well be considered the climax within the climax. Iago marks it with his incantation: "O beware, my lord, of jealousy; / It is the green-eyed monster which doth mock / The meat is feeds on. . . ." Othello is torn by his love of Desdemona and his long standing trust in Iago. He sees Desdemona for a brief moment, and we feel for an instant that Othello may escape Iago's temptation. But Iago begins to present alleged evidence about the handkerchief, which Emilia had just given to him, and about things Cassio was alleged to have said in his sleep. Othello seems convinced for the time, and he and Iago kneel together to swear revenge.

The Falling Action. The falling action presents the consequences already implicit in the climax. Every dramatist has a difficult problem artistically after the climax. The climax is the point of highest tension, and the dramatist is subsequently in danger of weakening and diluting too much the tension he has created. He had to avoid "anti-climax" by introducing new sources of interest into the drama. Shakespeare's traditional method in tragedy is to raise the possibility that the hero or "protagonist" may find means of escaping the fate that is overtaking him. While Shakespeare does not say so in so many words, he shows us *dramatically* that Othello has had some second thoughts after the crisis in III, iii. He is looking into the "exsufflicate and blown surmises" matching Iago's "inference." He may not be doing this very effectively, because Iago is already exercising a very effective psychological domination over him. But at least he tries and this gives the audience some hope that the protagonist may yet pull out of his troubles. In III, iv, he asks Desdemona for the handkerchief. If she could have produced it, Othello's suspicions might well have ceased. From then on, the curve of Othello's fortunes turns downwards, but obviously he is still seeking what seems to him to be sure evidence. Iago arranges, in IV, 1, a sequence which seems to amount to Cassio's confession of guilt. At the end, Othello publicly slaps Desdemona in the face. In Act

IV, ii, Othello directly confronts Desdemona with the accusation of adultery. He refuses to accept her denial, but, from the audience's point of view (the audience, that is, which has not already seen or read the play) the possibility exists up to that moment that Desdemona might convince Othello to the contrary. From this point on, there is no real possibility of Othello's turning back, though even in the death scene of Act V, ii, the audience still hopes that Desdemona may be able to say something that will clear her. In V, i, the attempt is made on Cassio's life, to which Othello was a prior party.

The Conclusion or Denouement. The falling action flows almost imperceptibly into the denouement, and it is almost arbitrary to say where one ends and the other begins. The killing of Desdemona is, in one sense, a final act of the tragedy, but the play is so constructed that a good deal of explanation is called for, particularly in regard to the unmasking of Iago. Emilia stumbles on the facts of Iago's intrigue. Othello, overcome with shock and remorse, kills himself.

8. ROMEO AND JULIET

Questions: To what degree are Mercutio, the Nurse, and the Friar responsible for the tragedy of *Romeo and Juliet*?

Answer: Mercutio reacts strongly to Romeo's refusal to respond to Tybalt's provoking insults. Such a reaction is to be expected of such a character, for Mercutio's code of manhood requires that provocations of that despicable nature be answered as honor demands. The occasion calls for a fight, and since Romeo shows no signs of giving battle, Mercutio does.

His death, however, is virtually accidental, and it is the accidental death that triggers the action leading to Romeo's banishment and the subsequent tragedy. There is nothing in Mercutio's character that can be blamed or held responsible, unless it is that lack of understanding toward the lovers' passion that he shares with almost all the other characters in the play.

The Nurse can be blamed somewhat more. Her relation to Juliet as confidante is comparable to Mercutio's relation to Romeo. But Romeo does not turn to Mercutio for help. Juliet does turn to the Nurse, and the Nurse, whose nature is basely realistic, gives the only response that could be expected of her. She advises infidelity, a suggestion despicable to the pure-spirited girl. In advising this, the Nurse lets Juliet down, and leaves her no one to turn to but the Friar. Had it been in the Nurse's nature to propose a simpler solution, such as telling Juliet's parents the truth, the tragedy might have been avoided. But such speculations are useless, and it can only be said that the Nurse is responsible by default, because of her innate nature.

The Friar is confidant to both Romeo and Juliet, and plays a more integral and deliberate part in the action leading to tragedy. It is he that condones and performs the secret marriage. It is he that gives Juliet the crucial sleeping poison and accepts the responsibility for informing Romeo of this state of events. Both actions might be objectively judged foolish, but they were done with the best intentions to reconcile the feud and help the lovers. He causes the deaths far more directly than either Mercutio or the Nurse, but he cannot be held ultimately responsible. It is a fateful accident that the message does not get through. In the final analysis, it is only fate and the fated quality of the love that can be blamed.

Also from the publishers of ARCO Books—

ℳ MONARCH NOTES
Available at Fine Bookstores Everywhere

ACHEBE - Things Fall Apart
AESCHYLUS - The Plays
ALBEE - Who's Afraid of Virginia Woolf
AQUINAS, ST. THOMAS - The Philosophy
ARISTOPHANES - The Plays
ARISTOTLE - The Philosophy
AUGUSTINE, ST. - The Works
AUSTEN - Emma/Mansfield Park
AUSTEN - Pride and Prejudice
BECKETT - Waiting for Godot
Beowulf
BRADBURY- The Martian Chronicles
BRECHT - The Plays
BRONTE - Jane Eyre
BRONTE - Wuthering Heights
BUCK - The Good Earth
CAMUS - The Stranger
CATHER - My Antonia
CERVANTES - Don Quixote
CHAUCER - Canterbury Tales
CHEKHOV - The Plays
CHOPIN - The Awakening
COLERIDGE - Rime of the Ancient Mariner
CONRAD - Heart of Darkness/Secret Sharer
CONRAD - Lord Jim
COOPER - Last of the Mohicans
CRANE - Red Badge of Courage
DANTE - The Divine Comedy
DE BEAUVOIR- The Second Sex
DEFOE - Robinson Crusoe
DESCARTES - The Philosophy
DICKENS - Bleak House
DICKENS - David Copperfield
DICKENS - Great Expectations
DICKENS - Hard Times
DICKENS - Oliver Twist
DICKENS - A Tale of Two Cities
DICKINSON - The Poetry
DINESEN - Out of Africa
DOCTOROW- Ragtime
DONNE - The Poetry & The Metaphysical Poets
DOSTOYEVSKY - Brothers Karamazov
ELIOT - Middlemarch
ELIOT - Silas Marner
ELIOT - Murder in the Cathedral & Poems
ELIOT - The Waste Land
ELLISON - Invisible Man
EMERSON - Writings
EURIPIDES, AESCHYLUS, ARISTOPHANES -
The Plays
EURIPIDES - The Plays
FAULKNER - Absalom, Absalom!

FAULKNER - As I Lay Dying
FAULKNER - Light in August
FAULKNER - The Sound and the Fury
FIELDING - Joseph Andrews
FIELDING - Tom Jones
FITZGERALD - The Great Gatsby
FITZGERALD - Tender is the Night
FLAUBERT - Madame Bovary/Three Tales
FORSTER - Passage to India/Howard's End
FRANK - Diary of a Young Girl
FREUD - Interpretation of Dreams
FROST - The Poetry
GARCIA-MARQUEZ - One Hundred Years of Solitude
GOETHE - Faust
GOLDING - Lord of the Flies
Greek and Roman Classics
GREENE - Major Works
HAMMETT - The Maltese Falcon/Thin Man
HARDY - Far from the Madding Crowd
HARDY - The Mayor of Casterbridge
HARDY - The Return of the Native
HARDY - Tess of the D'Urbervilles
HAWTHORNE - House of the Seven Gables/ Marble Faun
HAWTHORNE - The Scarlet Letter
HELLER - Catch-22
HEMINGWAY- A Farewell to Arms
HEMINGWAY - For Whom the Bell Tolls
HEMINGWAY - Major Works
HEMINGWAY - The Old Man and the Sea
HEMINGWAY - The Snows of Kilimanjaro
HEMINGWAY - The Sun Also Rises
HESSE - Siddhartha
HOMER - The Iliad
HOMER - The Odyssey
HUGO - Les Miserables
HUXLEY - Major Works
IBSEN - The Plays
JAMES - Portrait of a Lady
JAMES - The Turn of the Screw
JAMES - Washington Square
JOYCE - A Portrait of the Artist as a Young Man
KAFKA - Major Works
KEATS - The Poetry
KESEY - One Flew Over the Cuckoo's Nest
KNOWLES - A Separate Peace
LAWRENCE - Sons & Lovers
LEE - To Kill a Mockingbird
LEGUIN - The Left Hand of Darkness
LEWIS - Babbitt
LOCKE & HOBBES - The Philosophies
LONDON - Call of the Wild

(Continued)

(Continued)

MACHIAVELLI - The Prince
MARLOWE - Dr. Faustus
Marxist & Utopian Socialists
MELVILLE - Billy Budd
MELVILLE - Moby Dick
MILLER - The Crucible/A View from the Bridge
MILLER - Death of a Salesman
MILTON - Paradise Lost
MORE - Utopia
MORRISON - Beloved
Mythology
The New Testament
NIETZSCHE - The Philosophy
The Old Testament as Living Literature
O'NEILL - Long Day's Journey into Night
O'NEILL - The Plays
ORWELL - Animal Farm
ORWELL - 1984
PATON - Cry the Beloved Country
PLATO - The Republic and Selected Dialogues
POE - Tales and Poems
POPE - Rape of the Lock & Poems
RAWLINGS - The Yearling
REMARQUE - All Quiet on the Western Front
Rousseau & the 18th Century Philosophers
SALINGER - Catcher in the Rye
SALINGER - Franny & Zooey
SARTRE - No Exit/The Flies
SCOTT - Ivanhoe

SHAKESPEARE - Antony and Cleopatra
SHAKESPEARE - As You Like It
SHAKESPEARE - Hamlet
SHAKESPEARE - Henry IV, Part 1
SHAKESPEARE - Henry IV, Part 2
SHAKESPEARE - Henry V
SHAKESPEARE - Julius Caesar
SHAKESPEARE - King Lear
SHAKESPEARE - Macbeth
SHAKESPEARE - The Merchant of Venice
SHAKESPEARE - A Midsummer Night's Dream
SHAKESPEARE - Othello
SHAKESPEARE - Richard II
SHAKESPEARE - Richard III
SHAKESPEARE - Romeo and Juliet
SHAKESPEARE - Selected Comedies

SHAKESPEARE - Sonnets
SHAKESPEARE - The Taming of the Shrew
SHAKESPEARE - The Tempest
SHAKESPEARE - A Winter's Tale
SHAKESPEARE - Twelfth Night

SHAW - Major Plays
SHAW - Pygmalion
SHAW- Saint Joan
SINCLAIR - The Jungle
Sir Gawain and the Green Knight
SKINNER - Walden Two
SOLZHENITSYN - One Day in the Life of Ivan Denisovich
SOPHOCLES - The Plays
SPENSER - The Faerie Queene
STEINBECK - The Grapes of Wrath
STEINBECK - Major Works
STEINBECK - Of Mice and Men
STEINBECK - The Pearl/Red Pony
SWIFT - Gulliver's Travels
THACKERAY - Vanity Fair/Henry Esmond
THOREAU - Walden
TOLKEIN - Fellowship of the Ring
TOLSTOY - War and Peace
TURGENEV - Fathers and Sons
TWAIN - Huckleberry Finn
TWAIN - Tom Sawyer
UPDIKE - Rabbit Run/Rabbit Redux
VIRGIL - The Aeneid
VOLTAIRE - Candide/The Philosophies
VONNEGUT - Slaughterhouse Five
WALKER - The Color Purple
WAUGH - Major Works
WELLS - Invisible Man/War of the Worlds
WHARTON - Ethan Frome
WHITMAN - Leaves of Grass
WILDE - The Plays
WILDER - Our Town/Bridge of San Luis Rey
WILLIAMS - The Glass Menagerie
WILLIAMS - Major Plays
WILLIAMS - A Streetcar Named Desire
WOLFE - Look Homeward, Angel/Of Time and the River
WOOLF - Mrs. Dalloway/To the Lighthouse
WORDSWORTH - The Poetry
WRIGHT - Native Son
YEATS - The Poetry
ZOLA - Germinal

MACMILLAN • USA